# *BRAVE NEW WORDS*

The Oxford Dictionary of Science Fiction

# Brave New Words

The Oxford Dictionary of Science Fiction

*Edited by* JEFF PRUCHER
*Introduction by* GENE WOLFE

OXFORD
UNIVERSITY PRESS

# OXFORD
UNIVERSITY PRESS

Oxford University Press, Inc., publishes works that further Oxford University's
objective of excellence in research, scholarship, and education.

Oxford  New York Auckland  Cape Town  Dar es Salaam
Hong Kong  Karachi  Kuala Lumpur  Madrid  Melbourne
Mexico City  Nairobi  New Delhi  Shanghai  Taipei  Toronto

*With offices in*
Argentina  Austria  Brazil  Chile  Czech Republic  France  Greece
Guatemala  Hungary  Italy  Japan  Poland  Portugal  Singapore
South Korea  Switzerland  Thailand  Turkey  Ukraine  Vietnam

Published by Oxford University Press, Inc.
198 Madison Avenue, New York, NY 10016
www.oup.com/us
www.askoxford.com

Oxford is a registered trademark of Oxford University Press

Library of Congress Cataloging-in-Publication Data
Prucher, Jeff.
  Brave new words : the Oxford dictionary of science fiction / Jeff Prucher.
    p. cm.
  Includes bibliographical references.
  ISBN-13: 978-0-19-530567-8 (alk. paper)
  1. Science fiction—Dictionaries.   I. Title.   II. Title: Oxford dictionary of science
fiction.
  PN3433.4.P78 2007
  809.3'876203—dc22        2007037280

ISBN-13: 978-0-19-530567-8

9 8 7 6 5 4 3 2

Printed in the United States of America on acid-free paper

*for* REBECCA

# Acknowledgments

A great many people helped and encouraged me in writing this dictionary. I am grateful to my editorial board, Mark L. Olson and Anthony R. Lewis, who gamely read everything I wrote, for their many suggestions and gentle corrections. They saved me many times from errors large and small; any errors or infelicities to be found in the text are my own.

I feel extremely lucky to have had Erin McKean as my editor. This dictionary was her idea to begin with, and I am thankful to her for giving me the opportunity to write it. Her continued advice and understanding throughout the process have been extraordinary.

I am grateful to the *Oxford English Dictionary* and its Science Fiction Citations Project (see next page) and to Jonathan Lighter, Jane O'Connor, and Grant Barrett of the *Historical Dictionary of American Slang* for generously allowing me to use their citations.

Many others have contributed citations, information, suggestions, technical assistance, and advice at various stages of the dictionary: Liz Duffy Adams, John Aegard, Grant Barrett, Ian Brookes, Charles N. Brown and *Locus*, Peter Coogan, Leonardo De Sá, Malcolm Farmer, Victoria Elizabeth Garcia, Joseph Gerharz, Damien Hall, Michelle Hlubinka, Sean Kleefeld, Steve Lieber, Richard Lupoff, Jeff Michael, Orion Montoya, Jason Mosser, Bill Mullins, Will Murray, Sara Ryan, Peter Sattler, Nick Seidler, Nisi Shawl, Jesse Sheidlower, Ivo Thomas, and the good folks on the American Dialect Society mailing list. The paging staff and interlibrary loan department of the San Francisco Public Library were extremely helpful in fielding all manner of increasingly arcane requests, as were the special collections departments of the Temple University and University of California, Riverside libraries. Special thanks are due to Alistair Durie and Fred Galvin for the sheer volume of citations they found or verified for me, and to Mike Christie both for his citations and for his thoughtful editorial suggestions.

Finally, Rebecca Novick has been a constant source of encouragement. Her enthusiasm for, and unflagging belief in, both me and the dictionary have made this book possible.

# The *Oxford English Dictionary* Science Fiction Citations Project

The majority of the citations in this dictionary came from the *Oxford English Dictionary* Science Fiction Citations Project, which has been collecting citations for science fiction terminology since 2001 (online at www.jessesword.com/sf). I am indebted to *The Oxford English Dictionary*, John Simpson, Chief Editor, and Jesse Sheidlower, Editor-at-large, for making this information available to me, and to Sue Surova, Mike Christie, and Malcolm Farmer for their roles in creating and overseeing the project. I am additionally indebted to everyone who has taken the time to submit citations, comments, and suggestions to the project; their names are listed below. This dictionary would not exist without their efforts. I have made every attempt to make the list complete, and I offer my apologies to anyone I may have omitted.

Cyril Alberga
Eric Albert
Brian Aldiss
Brian Ameringen
Karen Anderson
Ted Anderson
Robert Andrews
Fred Bacon
Daniel Bambeck
Tom Becker
Gregory Benford
Ruth Berman
James Birdsall
Eric Boehm
Edward Bornstein
Alan Bostick
Mark Bourne
Tim Boyer
David Bratman
Patrick Broadhurst
Jennifer Broekman
Ralf Brown
Evelyn Ellen Browne
John C. Bunnell
Mary Aileen Buss
Katrina Campbell

Adam Canning
Robert Carnegie
Eric Casteleijn
Ted Chiang
Greg Childers
Joe Christopher
Sam Clark
Dan Clore
John Clute
Steve Coltrin
Alan Cox
Apollo Crum
Jonathan Dale
Andrew Dalke
Robert Dana
Ray Dassen
Christopher Davis
Stephen Dedman
Brian Denehy
Richard Dodson
Michael Dolbear
John Doyle
Gardner Dozois
Alistair Durie
Patrick Dusoulier
Jason Dyer

David Dyer-Bennet
Tom Easton
Dan Efran
John Eggeling
Mark English
David Eppstein
Conrad Feinson
David Ferguson
Sheila Finch
Rachel Flynn
Courtenay Footman
Enoch Forrester
Susan Francis
Daniel Frankham
Jonathan Franks
Matt Freestone
Mitchell J. Friedman
Sarah Canfield Fuller
Stuart Gale
Fred Galvin
Meg Garrett
Imran Ghory
Suzanne Gibson
Robert Godwin
Lee Gold
Guy Gordon
J. Greely
David Greenebaum
John Groth
Irene Grumman
Hal Hall
Alex Harman
Andrew Hatchell
Rick Hauptmann
Cameron Hayne
Derek Hepburn
Paul Hoffman
Randy Hoffman
Karen Holland
Brian Hopper
Richard Horton
William Howe
Matthew Hoyt
Jeffrey Glen Jackson
Steve Jackson

Eddie Janusz
Mikael Johansson
Alexx Kay
Edward Keyes
Fruma Klass
Roberto Labanti
James A. Landau
Dave Langford
Jeff Lassahn
Faith Lawrence
Russell Letson
Robert Lichtman
John Locke
M. Lohr
Gavin Long
Svante Lovén
Simon Lyall
Frederic Marchal
Andrew May
Elizabeth McCoy
Murry McEntire
Gary McGath
Ethan Merritt
Kathleen Miller
Jamie Morris
Bill Mullins
Chris Murrian
Graham Nelson
Bryn Neuenschwander
Scott Neugroschl
Larry Niven
Larry Nussbaumer
Maureen O'Brien
Mark Olson
Ben Ostrowsky
Cory Panshin
Bill Patterson
Susan Payne
Lawrence Person
Charlie Petit
Carol Phillips
Christopher Pound
Michael A. Pusateri
Michael Quinion
Varun Rao

Brandon Ray
Eric Raymond
Colette Reap
Elisabeth Riba
Bob Rickard
Frank Robinson
Roger Robinson
Paul Rubin
Jay Rudin
Doug Rynda
Suzanne Saunders
Andy Sawyer
Robert Schmunk
Nic Schraudolph
Richard P. Scott
Bill Seabrook
Kay Shapero
Mark Shawan
Anton Sherwood
David Siegel
David Silberstein
David Silver
Steven Silver
Rex Smith
Bill Snyder
Eva Snyder
Rachel Sommer
Lucius Sorrento
David Starner
Keith Stokes

Mike Stone
Joshua Stratton
Christopher Stuart
Geri Sullivan
David Summers
Michael Swanwick
Talin
David Tate
Katrin Thier
Dan Tilque
Treesong
Leslie Turek
Joan Marie Verba
Kevin Wald
Tall Walt
Janet Walz
Greer Watson
Lawrence Watt-Evans
Simon West
Gary Westfahl
Tom Whitmore
Roger Wilcox
Douglas Winston
Jeff Wolfe
Garrett Wollman
Robert Woodward
Stuart Young
Cheryl Yuhas
Leah Zeldes

# Contents

# Preface: The Stars My Definition

When I tell people that I'm writing a dictionary of science fiction, their responses tend to be one of two types: either to ask something along the lines of "so, do you read a lot of science fiction?" or to try to guess what words will be in the dictionary. The former response is probably familiar to most of you who are reading this. The latter responses are always quite interesting, and generally follow a pattern. Serious SF readers, for some reason, almost always mention **ansible.** More casual readers (or viewers) usually suggest **cyberspace, grok,** or **tardis.** Then there are those who seem to have had little exposure to SF, and are surprised to find out that **robot** was coined by a science fiction writer.

There is a third possible response, however: "Why write a science fiction dictionary in the first place?" Few people have ever asked this, which is no doubt polite of them, but it is to my mind the most interesting question. There are, of course, many possible answers, all true to some extent. One is that many of the terms defined herein have never appeared in a dictionary before, or not in the senses that are used in science fiction, despite the fact that many have been in wide use in the science fiction community for most of a century. Another is that a specialist dictionary can often provide more nuanced definitions or sense breakdowns than will be found in a general dictionary. See, for example, the entry for **alien** (adj.), which shows a more complex history than you will see in most dictionaries. (This is not necessarily to fault general dictionaries, but merely to recognize different priorities.) But the reason that is most compelling to me takes us back to the people who did not know the provenance of **robot**. The fact is, the language of science fiction (and of science fiction fans) permeates mainstream (that is to say, non–science-fiction-related) language and culture—from obvious computer and aerospace terms such as **cyberspace** and **spaceship** to drug slang, underground comix, and environmentalism (**beam me up, ghod,** and **doomwatch,** respectively)—but this linguistic influence has gone largely unrecognized. This dictionary, then, in part at least, is an attempt to redress that.

As befits a dictionary of science fiction, the bulk of the words included are those that were coined in, or with reference to, science fiction. These are primarily from the twentieth century, but sometimes go back to earlier scientific romances and proto–science fiction. (My use of "science fiction" here excludes, for the most part, the genre of fantasy, while recognizing that the boundary between the two is indistinct at best; words that are used in both genres are represented, as are those found in such hybrid genres as science fantasy.) However, to construct a dictionary that includes the name of every device or concept that ever appeared in a science fiction story would verge on madness, since most stories contain at least one neologism or new usage of a word. There are a great many terms, however, that are used by many authors in similar ways, and these are what will be found in this book. I have also limited the field to terms used in multiple fictional universes. A word like "dilithium," therefore, which is familiar to many people from *Star Trek*, does not appear here, since it has little or no currency outside of that setting. An exception to this rule are words that have entered mainstream English. Thus **newspeak** is included, since it went directly from *Nineteen Eighty-Four* into widespread use.

Sometimes, too, a word is coined in a work of science fiction that becomes adopted into mainstream English with an entirely different meaning than the one used in science fiction, and I have included these meanings as well. This may simply be a matter of noting a figurative usage in the main definition (such as **mind link**, which is used figuratively to indicate a close mental accord in addition to its literal meaning of "a telepathic connection"), but in many cases a term has become established in its non–science fiction sense, and these are given full definitions (for example, **space cadet** meaning "someone who appears to be out of touch with reality"). A related category of words are those that make direct reference to a work of science fiction, typically to the title, as in **doomwatch** and **Stepford**.

A handful of words that were not coined in science fiction also appear. Some of these are included because, like **cyborg**, they are so closely associated with science fiction that not having them would leave a noticeable gap. Others, like **air-car**, are necessary for fully understanding the history or use of a related term, in this case both **aero-car** and **groundcar**. Additionally, I have included names for the inhabitants of all nine planets (at the time of this writing) of the Earth's solar system plus the Earth's moon, even though many of these first appeared in works of non-fiction, thinking it preferable to include the complete set.

The language of science fiction involves more than just books, television shows, and films, however. There is a also a vocabulary that has developed in order to discuss or criticize science fiction works. Many of these words, including **science fiction** itself, designate genres and subgenres, but others such as **world-building** and **infodump** refer to aspects of writing science fiction, and others still, like **novum**, arose out of academic criticism. In addition to the various names for the genre of science fiction and its subgenres, I have included entries for genres that either include science fiction (such as **genre fiction**) or which often overlap science fiction (such as **horror**).

The final major category of words are those created by science fiction fans themselves. Like most subcultures, science fiction fandom has is own slang or jargon, often called **fanspeak**, which helps bind the community together and distinguish it from mundane society. While most terms used in fandom have largely remained there, many have filtered out—some into related fandoms such as comics and wargaming, others to communities in which many fans also participate, such as paganism and computers, and some, like **fanzine**, have spread into the world at large. Fannish words of all varieties are included in the dictionary.

Words whose first appearance is later than 1999 have been excluded from this dictionary. This is essentially an arbitrary date, but words need time to penetrate a culture, and it is too early to tell, for example, how far the revivified television series *Battlestar Galactica* will spread its euphemistic expletive "frak" (or "frack") or whether the "new weird" will persist as a label for the loose movement/subgenre it currently describes.

Coming back to the question, "why a science fiction dictionary," there is at least one more besides those given above: it's a lot of fun. Certainly, any excuse to read piles of science fiction is a good one, and I have discovered (and rediscovered) many authors and stories along the way. But my greatest pleasure has been from discovering that words I had previously thought were rare, or which were wholly new to me, in fact have a long history; or finding unfamiliar meanings of familiar words; or discovering that a seemingly mundane word had a science-fictional origin. It is my hope that readers of this dictionary will be able to find similar pleasures as they browse through its pages.

# Introduction: Speak Science Fiction Like an Earthling

You will be spared all references to Samuel Johnson, who wrote the first English dictionary, and James Murray, who spent his life writing the first Oxford English Dictionary. I urge you to learn about both, even so; dictionaries and the "ink-stained wretches" who compile them can be wonderfully interesting things.

This dictionary is twice as interesting as most because it is a dictionary of science fiction. If you don't find science fiction interesting, you should, for half a dozen reasons.

First because it is a—no THE—popular literature sprung from the technical branch of the human tree. Science fiction readers, and writers, are almost entirely those interested in science and technology. The reader may be a physicist and the writer a bird watcher. Stranger matchups occur every day, and physicists and bird watchers have more in common than may be apparent to either. They meet in science fiction, about which this book will teach you a great deal.

Second, because science fiction is of Anglo-American growth. There were precursors in other tongues, perhaps most notably *True History*, by Lucian of Samosata; the precursors, however, were just that—runners before. One woman and one man have been seriously proposed as the first real science fiction writers. They are Mary Wollstonecraft Shelley, the author of *Frankenstein*, and Herbert George Wells, the author of *The Time Machine*. The first was, of course, the wife of Percy Bysshe Shelley, the man who wrote "Hymn to Intellectual Beauty" and one of England's greatest poets. The second was a London science teacher who wrote a masterpiece when a lengthy illness left him too weak to teach. They showed the way, both of them, and this book makes that clear.

Robert A. Heinlein, Isaac Asimov, Ray Bradbury, and Arthur C. Clarke are customarily named as the greatest science fiction writers of the century now past, the successors of Wells and Mary Shelley. The first three are Americans and the last English. Continental European science fiction writers complain bitterly (I have heard them) that their countrymen will read nothing that has not been translated from English—that readers in places like Germany and Scandinavia consider only anglophone science fiction the real thing. Yves Meynard, whose mother tongue is French, writes in English. (He offers to translate his own books for French publishers.) A Spaniard I know (P. R. Gomez) is doing the same thing. All this is in sharp contrast to other literatures. Those who study Shakespeare know how deeply indebted he was to the Italians.

Third, because science fiction permeates our culture. The car you drive was made in part by industrial robots; so were the plastic toys of the kid down the street. Space travel has become a reality, and we say routinely that it is in its infancy—this though we have sent men to Luna and robots (yes, more robots) to Mars. Demonstrators march against genetically altered vegetables, blithely unaware that human selection has been altering the genetic makeup of vegetables for untold thousands of years.

At lunch yesterday, two elderly women were chatting in the booth next to mine. One said, "What amazed me was how many of them had gotten both knees and both hips replaced." The second replied, "Oh, yes! Bionic people." This book will help you understand the world in which you live, and the one in which you may be living a few years from now.

Fourth, because science fiction offers a world of new friends and activities. The closely related genres of science fiction, fantasy, and horror occasion hundreds of **cons** (look it up!) all over the United States, with more in Britain and Australia— plus a few more scattered across Continental Europe. Some people like to dress up like characters from the novels of Anne McCaffrey and Andre Norton. Some like to watch movies and TV shows from years past. Many more, like me, like to talk over books and stories. Three or four cons are held somewhere just about every weekend; if you live in a major city, five or six should take place within easy driving distance each year. Finding them will be no problem if you have internet access. If you don't, *Isaac Asimov's Science Fiction Magazine* prints a list in each issue, as do others.

If you go to a few cons, you'll meet some weird people and a few exceedingly weird people; but most of the people you meet will be a lot like you. You choose your friends, as elsewhere. It will help if you can talk the talk, and that's where this book comes in again. What is **corflu**? **Contraterrene matter**? When is a fan **croggled**? What's a **crudzine**? What is **cyberpunk**? **Steampunk**?

You're holding the answers.

Fifth, because you're interested in writing and getting paid for it. Any literate person can write; a ballpoint pen and a tablet are all it takes. You write whatever you like and drop it in a drawer; years and years from now, when you are long gone, "they" will discover your writings and acclaim you a genius.

Right.

But if you want to be published and paid, it takes a bit more. Science fiction and fantasy are large hungry markets, fields that welcome a dozen newcomers every year. Just reading the quotations in this book will teach you a lot and point you toward authors you ought to read while you write. Going to cons (see above) will let you meet established writers, agents, and editors, all people you should know. Even publishers like the amazing Tom Doherty, my own publisher at Tor Books, come to cons. The late great Jim Baen of Baen Books, Tom's friend and partner, came to cons, too. At Trinoc*con a few weeks ago, I spoke with Jim's successor, Toni Weisskopf.

Sixth, last, and most important, science fiction is interesting because science fiction is fun. It has to be. It receives no subsidies, which means that unless people like it and are willing to pay for it, it cannot exist. It will widen your horizons like nothing else. It will thrill and terrify you, and make you laugh and cry. It boasts stories as original and funny as Neil Gaiman's "Forbidden Brides of the Faceless Slaves in the Nameless House of the Night of Dread Desire" and stories as quietly chilling as that same Neil Gaiman's "The Price." There are stories about cats (like that one), stories about dogs, and stories about living planets. There are stories about children, stories about women (read almost anything by James Tiptree, Jr.), stories about men, stories about machines, and even stories about creatures who speak by emitting odors. There are stories that neither you nor I could imagine.

Along the way you will encounter **cyborgs**, **daleks**, **droids**, **Earthers** (like me), **eetees**, **empaths**, **espers**, and many more. Don't worry, this book will introduce you to all of them.

Just as long as you don't stop reading it at the end of the Introduction.

*Gene Wolfe*

# Guide to the Dictionary

## Form and Order of Headwords

An entry always begins with the headword in boldface type. The headword is given in the most common form, followed by variant spellings, also in boldface. Because the majority of compound words found in science fiction can be written as a single word, as two hyphenated words, or as two separate words, only the most common form is given for these; variations can be found in the citations.

Entries are listed in strict alphabetical order. Headwords with the same spelling but different parts of speech are ordered as follows:

*abbr.*
*n. or pl. n.*
*adj.*
*adv.*
*v.*
*interj.*
*pref.*
*infix*
*suff.*

## Part of Speech

Words are classified in this dictionary into the parts of speech listed above. The part of speech is given immediately after the headword or after a pronunciation. Words that occasionally function as other parts of speech without any significant changes in meaning have this noted after the definition.

*Noun* is used to classify all words with nominal function, including single words, compound or phrasal nouns, proper nouns, verbal nouns (when not treated under the verb), and nominalizations of verbs or verb phrases. Attributive use of a noun is not usually noted, but can be seen in the illustrative citations; if it is especially prevalent or if the meaning is notably different, however, this usage may be presented separately as an adjectival entry.

*Verbs* are not generally labeled for transitivity; in most cases, the definition and the illustrative citations make clear whether or not the verb takes an object.

## Etymology

The etymology appears in square brackets, following the part of speech. The majority of science fiction words are formed from Standard English words: by semantic shifts, by making compounds, or by adding standard affixes (such as *non-* or *-ish*). Etymologies are not generally supplied for these words, since the etymologies can be found in standard dictionaries. However, if the source term is rare or obsolete, or has a substantially different meaning than the derived word, an etymological note is often included. Neologisms with no obvious etymology are indicated by the phrase "coined by" in the etymology.

If there are several headwords that have the same root, or that are variants of each other, an etymology is only given at the headword with the earliest citation.

## Definition

Definition numbers and letters are given in boldface type. Individual senses of a word are labeled with Arabic numerals. Definitions for terms with multiple senses are ordered by the date of the earliest citations.

The degree of precision possible in sense division depends greatly on the amount of available evidence. If the evidence for one sense is slight, this definition may be run into an existing one, typically separated by a semicolon, or by the words "hence" or "also." In other cases, it has been possible to divide and define much more closely related senses simply because the evidence is more abundant.

If a word is a synonym of another word, the definition will usually be cross-referenced to that word (see "Cross References," below). The word that is cross-referenced is the oldest word that has that meaning, unless one term (such as *science fiction* or *spacesuit*) is clearly the more common term.

Because of the nature of science fiction, it is not usually safe to assume that an entity referred to in a definition is human, or shares such modern human characteristics as male and female sexes; the pilot of a spaceship, for example, could just as easily be a robot, AI, alien, energy being, genetically altered posthuman, or member of a group mind as it could a modern human being. For this reason, the words "they" and "their" are used when a third-person pronoun, singular or plural, is called for. While the use of "they" as a singular pronoun is sometimes controversial, it is, in this context, preferable to substituting a cumbersome and inadequate phrase such as "he, she, it, or they" or to making a convoluted rewording to avoid using a pronoun altogether. Similarly, words such as "someone" or "being" in definitions of science-fictional words should be interpreted in the broadest, least human-centric terms. Definitions of words relating to science fiction fans and writers, however, can be assumed to have human referents.

The reader should note that the extended context, in addition to that provided in a citation, has often facilitated the accurate placement of a citation, even though such placement may seem problematical at first glance. Users of this dictionary seeking full contexts of the citations are referred to the original works cited.

## Usage and Status Labels

Certain definitions in this dictionary bear additional comments. These may consist of information about frequency, currency, and other aspects of usage.

A label of "Now *hist.*" indicates that as far as can be determined, a word is only used in historical contexts. This typically means that the word itself, while still remembered, is no longer in active use.

The label "*Joc.*" indicates that a word is likely considered humorous by the person using the word.

"*Derog.*" is used to indicate that a word is typically used in a negative manner. Many words that refer to a being of some kind can be derogatory in some contexts, some words that are derogatory in some fictional universes might be unremarkable in others, and words that are often derogatory can sometimes be used in a neutral or positive matter. Because of this, the "derog." label is used only when the derogatory use is especially common or noteworthy.

Words labeled "*Obs.*" have not been in use after 1970, to the extent that the available evidence shows.

## Variant and Derived Forms

Variant forms—except for those given directly after the headword—and derived forms are listed in boldface, and follow the usage or status label. If there is significant evidence for a derived form or variant part of speech, it will appear as a separate headword.

Variant forms are preceded by the word "also." If there are many variations, the phrase "also *vars.*" may be used, and these variants will be found in the illustrative citations. For variant parts of speech, see the discussion at "Parts of Speech," above. The form is "also as *adj.*" or the like. Derivative forms are preceded by the word "hence," followed by the part of speech.

## Cross-References

Words that are treated elsewhere in this dictionary are given in small capital type, followed by the part of speech or sense number when necessary. Cross-references that follow the word "Compare" in a definition point to synonyms, antonyms, and words with related or overlapping meanings.

## Discursive Notes

The discursive note, in square brackets, is usually the last element preceding the body of citations. It may cover a variety of subjects depending on the needs of an entry, including etymological material.

## Citations

Citations are ordered strictly chronologically based on the date of the citation's first publication. A citation is placed in square brackets if it does not actually exemplify the use under discussion but can contribute to the understanding of the history or meaning of a term, or if the allusion is clearly to the term but does not explicitly use it or uses a related form of the term.

## Dating and Bibliographic Style

The overriding concern has been to supply a date that most accurately reflects the time the word was used. The citations in the dictionary only give the date of the specific citation and enough information about the edition used to allow the work to be tracked down. The *Bibliography of Books Quoted* contains more complete publication information.

When a citation is known to have originated earlier than the work in which it is found (e.g., for a story reprinted in an anthology or collection), or if the citation is not from the first publication of a work, the first date given is the copyright date or date of first publication. The date of the edition from which the citation was taken is given in parentheses before the page number. In some instances, a reprint of a book or story will be cited without indication of an earlier publication. If the citation is the first use of a word, this is usually because the work was rewritten and the term being defined was not used in earlier publications. With subsequent citations, little effort has been made to verify the original sources of fix-up novels, book versions of serialized novels, revised editions, etc. when the earliest version was published later than the first citation for a given term.

The abbreviation *ca*, for Latin *circa* "about," is used immediately before a date to indicate that the date is approximate. It is used most commonly with the composition date of posthumously published works.

The abbreviation *a*, for Latin *ante* "before," is used immediately before a date to indicate that the citation was written before the date given, but it is not possible to be any more accurate. In all cases citations are dated no earlier than is defensible on the basis of evidence.

Authors are identified by their initials and last name, as they appear in the publication being cited; thus many early stories by Robert A. Heinlein and fan writing by Robert Silverberg are attributed to "R. Heinlein" and "B. Silverberg," respectively.

Authors are usually given for all citations from science fiction or science fiction fan-related publications. However, because the citations come from multiple sources, each with slightly different standards, authors cannot always be determined, and are sometimes missing from such citations. Unattributed citations, usually editorial matter in periodicals, are also given without an author. Authors of citations taken from mainstream periodicals are not listed unless they are well known in their own right or have some relationship to science fiction, and authors of citations from Usenet and email lists are never given. Authors writing under a pseudonym are enclosed in square brackets. A complete key to the pseudonyms quoted in the citations is included at the end of the dictionary.

If an author is being quoted in another work that he or she did not write, or if the citation is from an untitled work in a periodical, the author's name will be followed by "in." If the citation is from a titled work in a periodical or in a book that contains multiple works (such as an anthology or omnibus), "in" is used to separate the author and title of the quoted work from the bibliographic information for the work it appears in. If the author of the citation is also the author or editor of the book the citation came from, the author's name is only given once.

The articles *a*, *an*, and *the* have been removed from all titles in the citations. The full titles of books appear in the *Bibliography of Books Quoted*.

Page and column references indicate the page and column in which the word under discussion appears, not where the extract begins. If the term is broken over two pages or columns, both are given. "Unpag." is used when a citation is drawn from a source with no page numbers.

When quoting from documents found in digital resources which do not include pagination, even for items which originally appeared in printed form, no page numbers have been given; however, in all cases there should be sufficient information to find the term in the digital resource, if not in the original printed form.

Citations are recorded exactly as they appear in the source, with several minor exceptions. Each citation begins with a capital letter and ends with closing punctuation. Citations have been conformed trivially to the modern American standards of punctuation. For example, single quotation marks are used inside double quotation marks, and commas and periods are placed inside a closing quotation mark. Words that originally appeared underlined or in boldface have been changed to italics; however, characters that are used to suggest font style or emphasis in citations from sources such as Usenet and email lists have been preserved. Spellings, use of italics (except as noted above), capitalization, etc., have not been changed.

Since the main concern has been to represent the meaning of the word, a source has often been quoted selectively, as by starting or finishing a quote in the middle of a sentence or by use of ellipses contained in square brackets ("[...]") in order to save space and emphasize the use; ellipses which do not appear in brackets are part of the citation. Line-break hyphens are indicated by "[-]" in places where is it not clear whether the author intended a word to be hyphenated or not. Although the citation itself has never been altered (except as noted above), some of these abridgements may change the style or rarely the meaning of an author's words. In no case should a citation be taken to represent the viewpoint of the quoted author.

## Selection

The sources for the citations in this dictionary are primarily print sources, especially books and periodicals. I have tried, however, to include examples from as many different types of writing and media as possible, since the genre of science fiction encompasses not only prose fiction, film, and television, but also comic books, newspaper comics, video games, role-playing games, theater, poetry, songs, and more. I have also made extensive use of online sources, including services such as ProQuest and Lexis Nexis that store print media in searchable databases, Usenet newsgroups, blogs, and some webpages. Because of the need to date citations, however, I have limited online citations to those that can be dated with some degree of accuracy.

The number of citations given does not necessarily correspond to an entry's actual frequency of usage. However, unusually common expressions are often accompanied by multiple citations, and definitions supported by only three citations tend to be less common. Headwords that are used in science fiction as well as other areas of discourse include citations from representative works of these areas. Additional citations are included for several reasons: to indicate continuity through a word's history; to illustrate nuances that cannot succinctly be placed in the definition; and to illustrate the minor variations in form that a word takes.

In every case, the earliest citation in each sense is the earliest that can be documented from the available evidence. However, due to the scarcity of many early science fiction publications and the ephemeral nature of most fan publications, many terms in this dictionary were likely in use prior to the earliest evidence herein. An attempt has also been made to provide reasonably current citations for words still in use, but a lack of recent citations does not necessarily indicate that a word is falling out of use.

## Sidebars

Throughout the dictionary are a number of sidebars, containing lengthier discussions on various topics than are possible in the definitions and discursive notes. Headwords mentioned in the sidebars appear in boldface; example words used in the sidebars that do not appear in the dictionary as headwords are in italics.

# Abbreviations Used in this Dictionary

| | | | |
|---|---|---|---|
| < | is derived from | mag. | magazine |
| a | ante (before) | Mar. | March |
| abbr. | abbreviation | Mass. | Massachusetts |
| adj. | adjective | Md. | Maryland |
| adv. | adverb | Mich. | Michigan |
| Apr. | April | Minn. | Minnesota |
| Ariz. | Arizona | n. | noun |
| attrib. | attributive(ly) | Neb. | Nebraska |
| Aug. | August | Nev. | Nevada |
| Austl. | Australia | Nov. | November |
| ca | circa (about) | N.Y. | New York |
| Calif. | California | obs. | obsolete |
| cap. | capitalized | Oct. | October |
| coll. | collection | Oh. | Ohio |
| Dec. | December | orig. | originally |
| derog. | derogatory | Pa. | Pennsylvania |
| ed. | edition, editor | perh. | perhaps |
| e.g. | exempli gratia (for example) | pl. | plural |
| ency. | encyclopedia | pref. | prefix |
| et al. | et alii, et alia (and others) | rev. | review |
| Fr. | French | R.I. | Rhode Island |
| Feb. | February | sci. | science |
| fig. | figuratively | S.E. | Standard English |
| Fri. | Friday | Sept. | September |
| Ger. | German | SF | science fiction |
| Gk. | Greek | S-F | science-fiction |
| hist. | historical | Sk. | Sanskrit |
| Ia. | Iowa | suff. | suffix |
| i.e. | id est (that is) | Tex. | Texas |
| ibid. | ibidem | trans. | translator, translated |
| Ill. | Illinois | U.K. | United Kingdom |
| infl. | influenced | unpag. | unpaginated |
| interj. | interjection | v. | verb |
| intro. | introduction | Va. | Virginia |
| Jam. | Jamaica | vars. | variants |
| Jan. | January | vol. | volume |
| joc. | jocular(ly) | Wash. | Washington |
| Kan. | Kansas | Wis. | Wisconsin |
| L. | Latin | | |

# Pronunciation Key

## Vowels

| | | | | | |
|---|---|---|---|---|---|
| ɑ | farm | ɛə | fair | oʊ | rope |
| æ | cat | ɪ | ship | ʊ | good |
| ai | nice | i | keep | u | rude |
| au | shout | ɪə | hear | ʊə | poor |
| ɛ | set | ɔ | pause | ə | about |
| ei | claim | ɔɪ | boil | ʌ | tub |

## Consonants

The following have their usual English pronunciations: b, d, f, h, k, l, m, n, p, r, s, t, v, w, and z.

| | | | | | |
|---|---|---|---|---|---|
| ð | **then** | ŋ | **ring** | θ | **think** |
| dʒ | **jump** | ʃ | **shore** | ʒ | **azure** |
| g | **get** | tʃ | **chip** | | |

## Stress

ˈ   primary stress
ˌ   secondary stress

These are vertical stress marks that precede the stressed syllable.

# Instructions for Antedating Citations

While I have made every effort to locate the earliest citations for every word in this dictionary, earlier uses can undoubtedly be found for a great many of them. In many cases, I was unable to locate the first appearance of a book or story, and had to cite the first usage of a term from a reprint. It is also possible that words labeled as obsolete may have been used more recently than the last citation given. If you know of, or discover, any such evidence, please send the citation to the appropriate contact listed on the "how to cite" page on the Oxford English Dictionary Science Fiction Citations Project's website: **www.jessesword.com/sf/**. Complete instructions for submitting citations can also be found there. Please do not send comments about *Brave New Words* to the OED project's editors, however; any faults to be found herein are mine alone.

# a

**actifan** *n.* (pl. **-fans, -fen**) [*active* + *fan*] a person who participates in fan activities, such as publishing a fanzine, working on conventions, writing letters to magazines, etc. Compare PASSIFAN.

**1944** J. B. Speer *Fancyclopedia* 6/1: With the increase in the number of prozines, [...] a flood of new fans came into fandom, usually thru the Triumvirs' activities, and many remained and became actifans.
**1947** *Startling Stories* (Jan.) 107/1: If there are any fans in North Carolina, would you please get in touch with me [...]. If you even read StF you'll do. You don't have to be an actifan, just so you read StF.
**1950** A. Rapp *Spacewarp* (Jan.) 2: Palmer announced at Cincy that OW would eventually be liked not only by the herd of non-actifan readers, but also by the fans.
**1958** R. M. Holland *Ghu's Lexicon* 3: ACTIFAN—Active fan. One who proves that misery really does love company by attempting to spread and intensify the disease as much as possible. He organizes and officers fan clubs, publishes or writes for fan or pro zines, writes innumerable letters, etc., etc., etc., ad infinitum.
**1995** *Dragoncon: NASFiC? or ComicCon?* (Usenet: rec.arts.sf.fandom) (July 15): Worldcon site selection as administered is generally only voted on by a minority, I do believe, of Worldcon attendees. Most of those who vote are very probably actifen.

**aerocar** *n.* an AIRCAR.

**1900** F. C. Smale *Abduction of Alexandra Seine* in *Harmsworth Mag.* (Nov.) 291/1: The aerocar which had brought him was still outside the large bay window swinging gently to and fro at its moorings in the summer breeze.
**1929** A. G. Stangland *Ancient Brain* in *Sci. Wonder Stories* (Oct.) 403/1: Aerocars floated about in the air above the thoroughfares. Jak explained that invisible repulsion rays suspended them in space.
**1941** N. Schachner *Beyond All Weapons* in *Astounding S-F* (Nov.) 136/1: He slid back into the aërocar, two badly frightened Circle Guards with him; the seals were set and he soared away.
**1995** W. J. Williams *Metropolitan* 102: A pair of small helicopters, emergency orange, wait with blades drooping, and a pair of aerocars stand on their pads.
**2005** *Onion* (June 23) 1/4: We're stacking hover-cars on top of solar-powered aerocars, and they just keep on coming.

**AI** *abbr.* ARTIFICIAL INTELLIGENCE.

**1973**: see quote in ARTIFICIAL INTELLIGENCE.
**1984** W. Gibson *Neuromancer* (1989) 73: Wintermute is the recognition code for an AI.
**1992** A. Steele *Labyrinth of Night* 133: The AI's will be minding the ship while it's parked in orbit, so we can stretch our legs a bit on the ground.
**1993** K. S. Robinson *Red Mars* 13: But Frank had gotten the day's emergency code out of the fire department AI that morning.

**2004** M. Jarpe & J. A. Sheen *Bad Hamburger Mag. of Fantasy & SF* (Dec.) 63: You're speaking to an AI located in Hong Kong called 6C21-75869S4.

**air-car** *n.* a personal flying vehicle; a flying car. Compare AEROCAR.

**1829** *Mechanics' Mag.* (Vol. XI) 181: The air-liner has time, in all cases (assuming that the air-car is air-worthy) to concert proper measures for his safe descent.

**1871** *New-York Times* (Aug. 7) 4/4: A like ignominious end befell that pretentious air[-]car which so long excited the curiosity of our citizens.

**1934** H. Bates *Matter of Size* in *Astounding Stories* (Apr.) 52/1: In several scattered places were other roof doors like the one he had emerged from, and straight ahead stood a row of transparent objects that had to be the air-cars.

**1957** L. Brackett *All Colors of Rainbow* in *Halfling & Other Stories* (1973) 150: He found driving a strain and yearned for the fleet little air-cars that darted so easily and safely through the peaceful skies of the Federation worlds.

**1969** R. Silverberg *Across Billion Years* 214: Up we went, into the aircars, and away, flying at a height of perhaps a hundred meters.

**1989** D. Simmons *Hyperion* (1990) 301: Their lifters could fail but, even so, the residual charge in the EM generators would allow the aircar to descend safely from any altitude.

**alien** *n.* an (intelligent) being from a location in the universe other than one's own, especially one not from the earth. Also used *fig.* Compare SPACE PERSON 1, STARMAN 1, STAR-PERSON.

[**1820** T. Carlyle *Collected Letters of Thomas Carlyle & Jane Welsh Carlyle Vol. 1* 286: I am like a being thrown from another planet on this dark terrestrial ball, an alien, a pilgrim among its possessors.]

**1934** P. Barshofsky *One Prehistoric Night* in *Wonder Stories* (Nov.) 697/1: Nearby, a group of intelligent aliens were cutting small growth and testing them with many forms of apparatus.

**1939** [E. Binder] *Impossible World* (1967) 59: The thought of a human being, one of their own kind, a captive of the aliens, sent fire through their veins.

**1947** A. E. van Vogt *Cataaaaa* in *Fantasy Book* (Vol. I No. 1) 41/2: When an alien arrives on an inhabited planet, there is usually only one way he can pass among the intelligent beings on that planet without being recognized for what he is.

**1957** L. Brackett *All Colors of Rainbow* in *Halfling & Other Stories* (1973) 144: Even in the big urban centers an alien like himself could hardly walk down the street yet without attracting an unwelcome amount of attention.

**1971** W. F. Nolan *Biographical Intro. Edge of Forever* (1971) 25: In the novel Chad's hero runs into humanoid aliens during his fishing jaunt in Colorado, and agrees to help them find a way back to their home planet.

**1977** I. Watson *Alien Embassy* (1978) 87: Significantly, none of the aliens were mammals of any sort.

**1981** *Times (London)* (Oct. 5) 28: Of course it could turn out that [...] most of them are aliens from Planet Quango or other taxpayer-finance unheavenly bodies.

**1991** M. Weiss *King's Test* 8: The media ate this stuff up—vids of ghastly aliens flaming across the screens of billions of terrified galactic viewers.

## In phrase:

**space alien** an alien specifically not from the earth. [This phrase is often associated with reports of or stories about UFOs and abduction by aliens.]

**1954** *Fantastic Universe* (May) 134: Cinema-makers are now trying to avoid further boycotts by using space aliens for villains.

**1977** J. Williamson *Youth against Space Algol* (Spring) 10/3: The space aliens are already becoming a vital feature of the series.

**1992** D. Adams *Mostly Harmless* 28: "Probably them space aliens," he said, bending over and prodding at the edges of the small indentations with his stick.

**2002** J. Evanovich *Visions of Sugar Plums* 7: Suppose he was from outer space, and he conducted an anal probe while I was unconscious? [...] "What are we looking at here?" I asked him. "Ghost? Vampire? Space alien?"

**alien** *adj.* **1.** other than one's homeworld; of another planet or place in the universe.

**1919** A. Merritt *Moon Pool* (1994) 355: Flashing out, and this only when the—face—bore its most human resemblance, into twin stars large almost as the crown of little moons; and with that same baffling suggestion of peep-holes into a world untrodden, alien, perilous to man!

**1926** I. Edman *Adam, Baby, & Man from Mars Journal of Philosophy* (Aug. 19) 449: Adam, the Baby, and the Man from Mars have always been invoked in the history of thought as the only three unprejudiced observers of the human scene—Adam, fresh from the hand of his Maker, the Baby new to earth and sky, and the Man from Mars on his first visit to an alien planet.

**1939** [E. Binder] *Impossible World* (1967) 13: At times, the breath of adventure wafted from the spaceways—tales of hidden lands on alien worlds, fabulous creatures and heroic deeds.

**1939** F. B. Long, Jr. *Dweller in Outer Darkness in Thrilling Wonder Stories* (Aug.) 62/2: A crystal-encrusted burrow leading deep into alien earth.

**1958** R. Silverberg *Invaders from Earth* (1987) 17: Kennedy found himself staring at an alien landscape, oddly quiet, oddly disturbing.

**2.** unlike anything that could have originated on the Earth.

**1929** J. Williamson *Sci. Wonder Stories* (Aug.) 243/1: I felt far more of it than I saw—a will, a cold and alien intellect, a being, malefic, inhuman, inscrutable. It was a thing that belonged, not in the present earth, but in the tomb of the unthinkable past, or beyond the wastes of interstellar space, amid the inconceivably [sic] horrors of unknown spheres.

**1936** H. P. Lovecraft *Astounding Stories* (June) 132/2: According to these scraps of information, the basis of the fear was a horrible elder race of half polypous, utterly alien entities which had come through space from immeasurably distant universes.

**1975** C. L. Moore *Bright Illusion Best of C. L. Moore* (1978) 79: They were more numerous than mankind's two, and their functions were entirely different. Reproduction here was based on an utterly alien principle.

**3.** of an alien or aliens.

**1934** P. Barshofsky *One Prehistoric Night Wonder Stories* (Nov.) 697/1: Tirelessly, the alien horde labored on, struggled to make this planet, yet in its infancy, theirs.

**1942** A. E. van Vogt *Astounding SF* (July) 26/1: That will be the result of my earlier presence, and will not recur now that so many alien presences have affected its—sanity!

**1970** A. McCaffrey *Ship Who Sang* (1991) 3: Helva scooted around in her shell [...] studying her lessons in trajectory, propulsion techniques, computation, logistics, mental hygiene, basic alien psychology, philology.

**1977** F. Herbert *Dosadi Experiment* 100: Aritch stared with distaste at the displayed hand. *There were no webs between the alien fingers!*

**1991** *SF Chronicle* (May) 24/1: A woman, carrying an alien child, is due to give birth.

**4.** that originated on another planet or place in the universe or that was made by the inhabitants thereof.

[**1913** A. Meynell *Christ in Universe Poems* 115: But in the eternities, Doubtless we shall compare together, hear A million alien Gospels, in what guise He trod the Pleiades, the Lyre, the Bear.]

**1944** F. Brown *Arena Astounding SF* (June) 72/1: And an alien ship, all right.

**1960** *Gleaner (Kingston, Jam.)* (Feb. 7) 23/1: Scientists there were deeply disturbed by the prospect, not that Earth would be invaded by alien bacteria, but that we might "export" germs to the Moon.

**1979** M. Z. Bradley *Bloody Sun* 26: But this much concession had been made to custom of the alien Terrans, that some of the goods for sale were on racks and tables.

**1987** M. Crichton *Sphere* 15: Let's soften that to say "contact": alien contact.

**1993** K. S. Robinson *Red Mars* 89: They had stumbled upon a long-abandoned alien spaceport.

## In phrase:

**alien life form** a creature from another planet or place in the universe.

[**1931** E. E. Smith *Amazing Stories* (Sept.) 557/1: I have thought of it at length. It is disgusting. Compelled to traffic with an alien form of life!]

**1946** A. B. Chandler *Astounding SF* (Mar.) 127/1: A most definite alien life form.

**1970** A. Norton *Dread Companion* (1984) 44: A poohka was an alien life-form from off-world.

**1985** S. Sucharitkul *Alien Swordmaster* 5: We stopped to couple with every alien life form we conquered.

**alternate future** *n.* an ALTERNATIVE FUTURE.

**1941** A. Bester *Probable Man* in *Astounding S-F* (July) 89/2: He will always land in another of the infinite number of alternate futures coexisting.

**1950** C. D. Simak *Time Quarry* in *Galaxy SF* (Nov.) 146/1: That meant that Asher Sutton could not, would not be allowed to die before the book was written. However it were written, the book must be written or the future was a lie. [...] Alternate futures?

**1979** I. Asimov I. Asimov & M. H. Greenberg *Isaac Asimov Presents Golden Years of SF* (1983) 194: "Greater Than Gods" is a non-series story about an alternate future.

**1985** N. Spinrad *Isaac Asimov's SF Mag.* (July) 181/1: But science fiction may be [...] set in any time, past, present, and future. Indeed, it may be and has been set even in *alternate* pasts and presents, and the same work may encompass several alternate futures.

**alternate history** *n.* **1.** a timeline that is different from that of our own world, usually extrapolated from the change of a single event; the genre of fiction set in such a time.

**1954** *Mag. of Fantasy & SF* (Feb.) 40: Here is yet another adroit variant ... with a startling footnote to the alternate history of our own Old West.

**1967** A. Norton *Operation Time Search* 6: You have heard of the alternate history theory—that from each major historical decision two alternate worlds come into being.

**1992** M. Resnick *Intro.* in *Alternate Presidents* ix: A growing sub-genre of the field is the Alternate History story: what if Jesus had never lived, what if the Spanish Armada had destroyed the British fleet, what if the South had won the Civil War?

**2002** *SFRA Rev.* (Jan.–Feb.) 7/1: I have watched SFRA grow and develop for most of its history, and I have heard and read the ideas and dreams of its members [...]. In some "alternate history" of SFRA, perhaps these dreams have already been fulfilled.

**2.** a work in this genre. Compare ALTERNATIVE HISTORY 2, UCHRONIA.

**1992** *Locus* (Aug.) 4/1: Alternate histories fit into the science fiction field because their history connects back to some moment of our past.

**1993** P. Nicholls J. Clute & P. Nicholls *Ency. of SF* 1293/1: Only HW [Howard Waldrop] would have written [...] an alternate history (featuring 4 alternate worlds) with time travel from a dystopic future, Amerindian Mound Builders, Aztec Invaders, ancient Greek merchants in power-driven boats and much more.

**2002** P. Heck *Asimov's SF* (Sept.) 137/1: Here's an alternate history based on the assumption that a series of comet impacts in the mid-nineteenth century forced the British empire to relocate the center of its government to India.

**alternate reality** *n.* an ALTERNATIVE WORLD.

**1950** J. D. MacDonald *Shadow on Sand* in *Thrilling Wonder Stories* (Oct.) 27/1: We have made the basic and very important discovery of a twin planetary system corresponding to our own, separated from us only by a symbolic logician's definition of reality. [...] The twin world exists because any definitive explanation of reality presupposes alternate realities.

**1968** K. Laumer *Assignment in Nowhere* 51: They created a field in which the energy of normal temporal flow was deflected at what we may consider right angles to the normal direction. Objects and individuals enclosed in the field then moved, not forward in time as in nature, but across the lines of alternate reality.

**1989** L. Frankowski *Flying Warlord* 195: "What? No. I'm not all right, you idiot! I'm dead! Don't you realize that we just saw me die?" "But you know that this is some kind of alternate reality. It's not exactly real."

**1989** G. A. Effinger *Everything But Honor Isaac Asimov's SF Mag.* (Feb.) 120: When they returned to T0, Placide and Fein discovered [...] that their excursion in time had not changed the past, but rather created a new alternate reality.

**1992** *Locus* (Aug.) 31/3: Anyone reasonably well-read in sf will pick up on the possibility of alternate realities here, but things get stranger.

**alternate universe** *n.* an ALTERNATIVE WORLD.

**1950** [A. Boucher] & J. F. McComas *Fantasy & SF* (Dec.) 104: At last the superlative magazine series [...] recounting Harold Shea's experiences with the mathematics of magic in alternate universes, is all in print.

**1977** R. Scholes & E. S. Rabkin *SF: History, Sci., Vision* 178: The term "alternate universe" may refer simply to the universe in which history follows an alternate time stream, but more strictly speaking, it refers to a universe somehow complete and yet coexistent with ours.

**1990** *Thrust* (Winter) 30/3: Sci fi was applied to the most miserable sort of juvenile fiction, [...] even to sword & sorcery fiction and alternate universe novels.

**1994** *Interzone* (Mar.) 27/1: I remember hearing that a long time ago Salman Rushdie entered, but didn't win, an sf novel contest. Perhaps in some nearby alternate universe he did win.

**2004** *San Francisco Chronicle* (Sept. 15) F4/3: But for pastry chefs like Falkner, Luchetti and Weil, working with Splenda was like a trip to an alternate universe where nothing went as it should.

**alternate world** *n.* an ALTERNATIVE WORLD.

**1944** F. Leiber *Business of Killing* in *Astounding SF* (Sept.) 61/1: I am visiting the alternate worlds in search of one that has learned how to do away with the horrid scourge of war.

**1968** K. Laumer *Assignment in Nowhere* 51: From that beginning grew the Imperium—the government claiming sovereignty over the entire Net of alternate worlds. Your world [...] is but one of the uncountable parallel universes, each differing only infinitesimally from its neighbor.

**1975** J. Gunn *Alternate Worlds* 213: Science fiction writers [...] have considered the possibility that there may exist, side by side with our Earth, separated from it by time or dimension, alternate worlds split off by moments of great (or small) historic actions or decisions.

**1983** D. Duane *So You Want to Be Wizard?* 112: Is this an alternate world, maybe? The next universe over?

**1987** N. Spinrad *Isaac Asimov's SF Mag.* (July) 181/2: And that strange hybrid of science fiction and fantasy, the alternate world story, in

which one aspect of history or the environment is arbitrarily altered and the consequences worked out with science fiction's characteristic extrapolative rigor.

**2002**: see quote in ALTERNATIVE HISTORY 2.

**alternative future** *n.* one of many possible futures; a future that may come about by actions taken while traveling back in time.

**1939** C. L. Moore *Greater Than Gods* in *Astounding S-F* (July) 144/2: There was an alternative future. [...] Somehow, that other future had come to him, too.

**1941** A. Bester *Probable Man* in *Astounding S-F* (July) 88/2: His choice decided which of those futures he shall enter and make real for himself, although in theory each alternative future may coexist and be real unto itself.

**1974** T. N. Scortia in R. Bretnor *SF, Today & Tomorrow* 142: The science fiction writer, as we remarked before, is somewhat less successful in his extrapolations of social and political trends. Here he is dealing with alternative futures and must restrict the premises of his extrapolation to a relatively few factors or to even one.

**2004** J. Fforde *Something Rotten* 128: My father had told me that Cindy would fail to kill me three times before she died herself, but there was a chance the future didn't have to turn out that way—after all, I had once been shot dead by a SpecOps marksman in an alternative future, and was still very much alive.

**alternative history** *n.* **1.** ALTERNATE HISTORY 1.

**1977** B. Aldiss *Future & Alternative Histories* in B. Ash *Visual Ency. of SF* 123/1: Silverberg's "Trips" [...] depicts tourist trips to such alternative histories as those where the Industrial Revolution never happened.

**1979** A. C. Clarke *Fountains of Paradise* 87: Almost all the Alternative History computer simulations suggest that the Battle of Tours (AD 732) was one of the crucial disasters of mankind.

**1989** I. Watson *World Renews Itself* in M. Bishop *Nebula Awards 23* 8: This time, however, the distancing devices are the fantasy elements of hexes and effective magic and the SF paraphernalia of alternative history.

**1996** D. Pringle, et al. *Ultimate Ency. of SF* 28/2: The alternative history template involves setting a story in a world which might have developed had some crucial event in history happened differently.

**2.** ALTERNATE HISTORY 2. Hence alternative historian, *n.* Compare UCHRONIA.

**1976** B. Ash *Who's Who in SF* 12: *Alternative histories*, tales of Earth with usually one historical detail changed in the past, and chronicling the resulting effects today.

**1990** *Thrust* (Winter) 9/3: In this excellent alternative history, vampires rule the world of the 17th century.

**1996** D. Pringle, et al. *Ultimate Ency. of SF* 29/1: It was World War II that became the favourite topic of alternative historians. Stories set in worlds where Hitler was victorious are numerous.

**2002** K. S. Robinson *Locus* (Jan.) 7/1: There are all kinds of double binds in writing an alternative history. Do you make the alternate world better or worse?

**alternative reality** *n.* an ALTERNATIVE WORLD.

[ **1941** A. Bester *Probable Man in Astounding S-F* (July) 88/1: In 2941 when you started your journey through Time, you were a reality. In 1941 you were a reality. But now, back in 2941, you're an alternative reality existing in the wrong alternate.]

**1990** *Thrust* (Winter) 7/3: Bishop [...] dares to introduce sick unicorns from an alternative reality into our contemporary world of AIDS.

**1994** P. Anderson *Stars Are Also Fire* 97: The end of separatist Luna was in sight, however long a delaying campaign Niolente and her cohorts might wage. Yet, in some hypothetical quantum-mechanical alternative reality—

**alternative universe** *n.* an ALTERNATIVE WORLD.

**1944** P. S. Miller *As Never Was* in *Astounding S-F* (Jan.) 34/1: As any schoolchild learns, the time shuttler who goes into the past introduces an alien variable into the spacio-temporal matrix at the instant when he emerges. The time stream forks, an alternative universe is born.

**1952** M. Reynolds *Alternate Universe* in *Other Worlds* (Nov.) 75/2: "Explain this alternative universes deal again." "I was about to. There are, he proved, an infinite number of universes coexisting, an infinite number of space-time continuums."

**1993** *Dragon Mag.* (Mar.) 86/2: "Return of the King," featuring an alternative universe where an Elvis Presley revival threatens the existence of rap music.

**alternative world** *n.* one of many possible space-time continua, having a different history or physical laws than our own space-time continuum.

**1943** A. E. van Vogt *Search* in *Astounding S-F* (Jan.) 56/2: That was today in the alternative world to this one.

**1956** A. Cogan *In Cards* in *Galaxy SF* (June) 128/2: Maybe it was some sort of alternative world we saw, showing us what could happen if we didn't work hard at our marriage.

**1977** *Nation* (Sept. 10) 216/3: His virtually ignored recent novel might have received the attention it deserves, for his imagination of present and alternative worlds is comparable to theirs.

**2000** R. K. J. Killheffer *Mag. of Fantasy & SF* (Aug.) 26: Perceiving the world [...] as "contingent," a product of historical accident, merely one of millions or billions of possibilities: that's sf at its heart, imagining alternative worlds future, past, or parallel.

**2003** M. Berry *San Francisco Chronicle* (June 1) M3/3: The plot twists, turns and swoops in unpredictable ways, the rules of the alternative worlds are revealed more by implication than by exposition.

**android** *n.* [< modern L. *androides* < Gk. *andr-*, "man"] an artificial being that resembles a human in form, especially one made from flesh-like material (as opposed to metal or plastic). [Early cites refer to an alchemical creation and to purely mechanical automata.]

[ **1727–51** E. Chambers *Cyclopædia:* Albertus Magnus is recorded as having made a famous *androides.*]

[ **1883** J. Ogilvie *Imperial Dictionary of English Language* 102/1: *Android* [...] A machine in the human form, which, by certain springs, imitates some of the natural motions of a living man.]

**1936** J. Williamson *Cometeers* in *Astounding S-F* (Aug.) 146/2: "The traffic that brought him such enormous wealth was the production and sale of androids. [...] Eldo Arrynu," amplified Jay Kalam, "had come upon the secret of synthetic life. He generated artificial cells, and propagated them in nutrient media, controlling development by radiological and biochemical means."

**1940** E. Hamilton *Captain Future & Space Emperor* in *Captain Future* (Winter) 17/2: It was a manlike figure, but one whose body was rubbery, boneless-looking, blank-white in color. [...] Following this rubbery android, or synthetic man, came another figure, equally as strange—a great metal robot.

**1950** L. Brackett *Dancing Girl of Ganymede* in *Halfling & Other Stories* (1973) 42: He stepped back and said, "You're not human." "No," she answered softly. "I am android."

**1954** A. Bester *Fondly Fahrenheit* in [A. Boucher] *Best from Fantasy & SF (Fourth Series)* (1955) 13: The robot is a machine. The android is a chemical creation of synthetic tissue.

**1968** J. Russ *Picnic on Paradise* 151: She realized that he had no face, or none to speak of, really, a rather amusing travesty or approximation, that he was, in fact, a machine [...]. Someone had told her then "They're androids. Don't nod."

**1983** R. Sheckley *Dramocles* (1984) 12: The squeaky voice that androids have despite great advances in voicebox technology.

**1989** W. Shatner *Tekwar* (1990) 29: A very handsome android butler [...] was walking a platinum-haired poodle along a hedge-lined path. He looked human, except for his eyes.

**1994** B. Hambly *Crossroad* 256: She had finally found him, or the android he had built to house his mind and personality.

**2002** D. Danvers *Watch* 293: But he's no android. Anchee is a post-human.

**2005** J. Johnson-Smith *American SF TV* 88: The android Data, a purely mechanical being with a highly complex "positronic" brain who spends his time longing to experience and understand emotions.

**Anglic** *n.* [perh. < *Anglic, adj.,* referring to the Angles or the English peoples] a future language descended from Modern English.

**1957** P. Anderson *Among Thieves* in H. Turtledove *Best Military SF of Twentieth Century* (2001) 7: As he accepted the folio, Unduma noticed the book beside it, the one Rusch had been reading: a local edition of Schakspier, [...] in the original Old Anglic.

**1969** R. Silverberg *Across Billion Years* 10: But he's intelligent, sophisticated, speaks Anglic with no accent at all, can name the American presidents or the Sumerian kings or anybody else out of Earthside history.

**1974** L. Niven & J. Pournelle *Mote in God's Eye* (1993) 189: The Moties do not understand our language now, but they can make recordings; and later they will understand Anglic.

**1999** R. Fawkes *Face of Enemy* (2001) 475: She had spoken in Anglic, and so he had ignored her. She tried again in the H'kimm dialect.

**annish** *n.* ['ænɪʃ] [*ann*iversary + ISH] the issue of a fanzine published on an anniversary of its first appearance.

**1950** A. Rapp *Spacewarp* (Jan.) 2: March brings us SPACEWARP's Third Ann[-]Ish.

**1952** J. Wellons *Thrilling Wonder Stories (letter)* (Dec.) 140/1: But for those who *do* like the Cap, may I second Joe Kinnon's motion for an Annish for Futurians.

**1960** J. Speer *Novus Ordo Fandorum* in *Fancestral Voices* (2004) 190: Begin, neo, to plan thy little subzine, though it never see an annish.

**1966** L. Carter *Handy Phrase-Book in Fannish* in *If* (Oct.) 66/2: If your fanzine lasts a year (many don't) you put out a particularly large Anniversary Issue called "the Annish."

**ansible** *n.* [coined by Ursula K. Le Guin] a device that enables instantaneous communication over any distance. Compare ULTRAPHONE, ULTRAWAVE.

**1966** U. K. Le Guin *Rocannon's World* 113: Noting the coordinates at which the ansible sender was set, he changed them to the coordinates of the League HILF Survey Base for Galactic Area 8, at Kerguelen, on the planet New South Georgia.

**1977** O. S. Card *Ender's Game* in *Analog SF-Sci. Fact* (Aug.) 118/1: The ansible sent words as they were spoken, orders as they were made. Battleplans as they were fought. Light was a pedestrian.

**1988** V. Vinge *Blabber* in *Threats… & Other Promises* 254: "It's an ansible." "Surely they don't call it that!" "No. But that's what it is."

**1995** E. Moon *Winning Colors* 89: When I was commissioned, we didn't have FTL communications except from planetary platforms. I was on *Boarhound* when they mounted the first shipboard ansible.

**2004** I. Stewart & J. Cohen *Heaven* 21: Although an ansible link conveyed messages instantaneously, the link could not be set up any faster than a ship could carry an encryption disk.

**anti-agathic** *n.* [< Gk. *agathos,* "good," presumably mistaken for *thanatos,* "death"] something (such as a drug) that prolongs life. Also as *adj.*

**1954** J. Blish *At Death's End* in *Astounding SF* (May) 36/1: So what you're looking for now is not an antibiotic—an anti-life drug—but an anti-agathic, an anti-death drug.

**1954** J. Blish, *At Death's End* 41/1: You see, Joint knows about the anti-agathic drug, even though Appropriations and the Pentagon don't.

**1958** H. Ellison *Nothing for My Noon Meal* in *Ellison Wonderland* (1962) 169: With the new anti-agathic drugs, people just aren't dying.

**1967** J. Blish *Okie* in D. Knight *Cities of Wonder* 119: The Utopians lacked the spindizzy and anti-agathics—but they had something called molar valence.

**1999** S. S. Tepper *Singer from Sea* (2000) 363: Our people on the ark ship were provided with a carefully engineered DNA antiagathic to slow down their aging after they landed on the new planet.

**2004** K. Traviss *City of Pearl* 376: Do you seriously think that, given a whole sample, some biotech firm would [ … ] throw the anti-agathic uses away?

**antigrav** *n.* a device that produces ANTI-GRAVITY.

**1945** *Startling Stories* (Summer) 6/1: Well, cut off my antigravs and call me flighty—it really is here.

**1954** D. R. Hughes *Breathing Space* in *Vargo Statten SF Mag.* (Jan.) 61/2: "They *have* got antigravs" screeched Largoth, frantically.

**1974** J. Blish *Star Trek 10* 83: Quiet and undisconcerted, Spock went to the box, affixing antigravs to it.

**1995** D. Carey & J. I. Kirkland *First Frontier* 343: Organize all hands and have them pick up the scattered pieces of the platform and those antigravs over there.

**antigrav** *adj.* ANTI-GRAVITATIONAL.

**1941** T. Sturgeon *Artnan Process* in *Astounding S-F* 56/2 (June): The ship settled down gently, her antigrav plates moaning.

**1955** M. Clifton *Sense from Thought Divide* in J. Merril *SF: Best of Best* (1967) 227: He had given me the assignment of putting antigrav units into production.

**1977** S. Marshak & M. Culbreath *Price of Phoenix* (1985) 2: The two *Enterprise* security men materialized, took a firmer grip on the anti-grav lifts, and stepped carefully off the platform.

**1989** J. M. Dillard *Lost Years* 264: She'd never gotten spacesick in her whole life, not even after antigrav maneuvers.

**1998** W. Shatner *Spectre* 33: Both oblivious now to the gala party that swirled around them on the immense antigrav platform that floated through the night.

**anti-gravitational** *adj.* that opposes or nullifies the force of gravity.

**1900** G. Griffith *Visit to Moon* in *Pearson's Mag.* (Feb.) 141: By means of the "R. Force," or Anti-Gravitational Force, of the secret of which Lord Redgrave is the sole possessor, they are able to navigate with precision and safety the limitless ocean of space.

**1911–12** H. Gernsback *Ralph 124C 41+* (1952) 120: Our anti-gravitational screen still let through some of the gravitational waves, or fifty per cent of the energy, which we could not seem to counteract.

**1931** C. A. Smith *Adventure in Futurity* in *Wonder Stories* (Apr.) 1236/2: I finished my descent of the cliff by the use of an anti-gravitational device.

**1956** A. C. Clarke *What Goes Up* in *Mag. of Fantasy & SF* 31/1 (Jan.): The final clue to the antigravitational nature of the field came when they shot a rifle bullet into it and observed the trajectory with a high-speed camera.

**anti-gravity** *n.* a force that is opposite in effect to gravity; the technology required to produce such a force. Also as *adj.*

**1896** *Massillon (Oh.) Independent* (Dec. 24) 8/1: Telegraph communication with Mars had become as easy as that between New York and Chicago, while a trip to the planet was made comfortable in an anti[-]gravity machine.

**1909** *Daily Press* (May 5) 4: I create a vacuum and fill it with anti-gravity ozone and everything inside the space covered by that vacuum goes whizzing into the air, never to come back.

**1932** M. Walsh *Vanguard to Neptune* in *Wonder Stories Quarterly* (Spring) 311/1: But the antigravity apparatus will have to be capable of generating a greater repulsive force than is required for ordinary interplanetary conditions.

**1950** A. C. Clarke *History Lesson* in *Sci. Fantasy* (Winter) 71: In the time that man had taken to progress from the Pyramids to the rocket-propelled spaceship, the Venusians had passed from the discovery of agriculture to anti-gravity itself—the ultimate secret that man had never learned.

**1979** A. C. Clarke *Fountains of Paradise* 44: At first I thought you had some anti-gravity device—but even I know that's impossible.

**1984** D. Brin *Practice Effect* 36: The idea of antigravity excited Dennis.

**1992** D. Knight *Why Do Birds* (1994) 165: You think they had antigravity or something?

**antispinward** *adv.* in or toward the opposite direction that something (a space station, galaxy, etc.) is rotating. Compare SPINWARD.

**1970** L. Niven *Ringworld* 152: To antispinward was the largest mountain men had ever seen.

**1977** J. Varley *Ophiuchi Hotline* (2003) 21: She faced the sun, which was a small but very bright disc just to antispinward of Saturn.

**1985** G. Bear *Eon* (1998) 363: They backtracked anti-spinward to the zero compound.

**1992** V. Vinge *Fire upon Deep* 143: Probably a single system in Middle Beyond, 5700 light-years antispinward of Sjandra Kei.

**2000** D. Gerrold *Jumping off Planet* (2001) 207: Alexei looked anti-spinward expectantly, so I followed his gaze.

**anywhen** *adv.* in or to any point in time.

**1941** [C. Saunders] *Elsewhen* in *Astounding S-F* 100/1 (Sept.): "Where are the others?" "Where? Anywhere," replied Frost with a shrug, "and any *when*."

**1955** I. Asimov *End of Eternity* (1990) 20: I am certain you don't smoke. Smoking is approved of hardly anywhen in history.

**1971** R. Silverberg *In Entropy's Jaws* in R. Hoskins *Infinity 2* 224: Anything. Anywhere. Anywhen. You're free to move along the time-line as you please.

**1988** I. McDonald *Desolation Road* (2001) 331: One second later a time quake ripped away the mayoral office into anywhen and replaced it with a quarter hectare of green pasture, white picket-fence, and three and a half black and white cows.

**2001** J. Fforde *Eyre Affair* (2002) 2: I wasn't a member of the ChronoGuard [...] although the pay is good and the service boasts a retirement plan second to none: a one-way ticket to anywhere and anywhen you want.

**APA, apa** *abbr.* [*A*mateur *P*ress *A*ssociation] an organization that produces a publication consisting of fanzines or other works created by its members, which are sent to an editor who collates them and distributes the bundle of combined works back to the members.

**1944** J. B. Speer *Fancyclopedia* 3/1: Several former fans have disappeared into the mundane APA's, and several other well-known scientifictionists, notably H. P. Lovecraft, have been active ajays at the same time.

**1977** B. Ash *Visual Ency. of SF* (1978) 274/3: The first, FAPA (Fantasy APA), was founded in 1937 by Donald A. Wollheim on the lines of more mundane (non-fandom) apas.

**1981** *Dragon Mag.* (June) 23/2: An APA is like a collection of letters which writers address to one another and to the public.

**1998** *Speculations* (Aug.) 10/1: David Weber came to me because his brother and I are in the same APA.

**apazine** *n.* [APA + -ZINE] a fanzine contributed to an APA mailing.
[**ca1944** F. J. Ackerman *Fantasy Flanguage in* [Anon.] *What Is Science Fiction Fandom* 29: These mags are of two classes: *Subzines* or subscription mags, and *FAPAzines* or mags published in FAPA [i.e., the Fantasy Amateur Press Association].]
**1953** B. Silverberg *Spaceship* (Jan.) 6: Plus apazines of all descriptions.
**1959** *Savoyard* 2 (Dec.): For official apazines, the perpetrator ought to be able to wait until the next mailing to have his included.
**1979** D. Schweitzer *Occasionally Mentioning SF* in *SF Rev.* (Jan.) 33/3: A fanzine for general circulation in fandom is called a genzine (general interest fanzine) as opposed to one for an amateur press association (apa) which is called an apazine.
**1993** D. Fratz *Twenty-Year Spree* in *Quantum* (Spring–Summer) 53/3: My APAzines had names like *Poppycock, Horse Feathers, Crap,* and *Bull.*

**artificial gravity** *n.* any force created by technological means that mimics the effects of gravity. Compare PSEUDO-GRAV, PSEUDO-GRAVITY.
**1930** W. O. Stapledon *Last & First Men* (1931) 274: An "artificial gravity" system, based on the properties of the electro-magnetic field, could be turned on and regulated at will, so as to maintain a more or less normal environment for the human organism.
**1932** E. K. Sloat *Beyond Planetoids* in *Amazing Stories* (Aug.) 422/1: The mate's heavy, clumsy boot, with its artificial gravity plate, sunk deep in his side.
**1954** *New York Times* (Apr. 3) 1/7: Mr. Shternfeld presented the picture of a vast tubular artificial space platform that would revolve at a rapid rate while circling the earth. The revolutions would give it artificial gravity, he said.
**1968** *Vital Speeches of Day* (Aug. 1) 624/1: Will man eventually need artificial gravity to permit him to go beyond certain limits of orbital stay?
**1986** D. Carey *Dreadnought* 69: The ship whined, straining against its own artificial gravity, creating a gyro effect.

**2002** M. J. Harrison *Light* (2004) 69: They fucked her, slept, and later asked Seria Mau if she could turn the artificial gravity off.

**artificial intelligence** *n.* [orig. the name for the science of creating "intelligent" computer programs] a sentient, self-aware computer or computer program.
**1973** G. R. Dozois *Chains of Sea* in R. Silverberg *Chains of Sea* 83: While the humans scurried in confusion, the Artificial Intelligence (AI) created by MIT/Bell Labs linked itself into the network of high-speed, twentieth generation computers placed at its disposal.
**1991** *Locus* (Nov.) 21/1: Its science-fictional content is certainly cyber enough: artificial intelligences reaching for true sentience.
**2003** G. Westfahl *Space Opera* in E. James & F. Mendlesohn *Cambridge Companion to SF* 206: John Clute's *Appleseed* (2001) offers a densely written portrait of a universe where a travelling merchant encounters artificial intelligences.

**astrogate** *v.* to navigate in space.
**1941** R. Heinlein *Common Sense* in *Astounding S-F* (Feb.) 138/2: My Chief Engineer assures me that the Main Converter could be started, but we have no one fitted to astrogate.
**1948** R. A. Heinlein *Space Cadet* 70: And you laddies expect to learn to astrogate! Better by far you should have gone to cow colleges.
**1958** T. Sturgeon *Comedian's Children* in *Man Who Lost Sea* (2005) 118: Can you astrogate?
**1980** J. D. Vinge *Snow Queen* (2001) 139: I meant that you can't go home until Cress is strong enough to astrogate again.
**1994** G. Wolfe *Lake of Long Sun* 222: He'd try to take over Mainframe, the superbrain that astrogates and runs the ship.

**astrogation** *n.* [Gk. *astro-*, "star" + navi*gation*] the practice or science of astrogating.
**1931** D. Lasser *Conquest of Space* 207: In interplanetary travel we must develop an exact science of three-dimensional astrogation through the heavens.

**1950** R. A. Heinlein *Farmer in Sky* (1975) 47: Please, sir, we're in astrogation.

**1978** B. Shaw *Ship of Strangers* (1979) 133: Part of Aesop's memory, in a section of the astrogation data bank, had unaccountably decayed and needed to be replaced.

**1994** B. Hambly *Crossroad* 161: We're an independent research and communications corporation contracted to assist with astrogation.

**astrogational** *adj.* used for astrogation.

**1941** M. Jameson *Blockade Runner* in *Astounding S-F* (Mar.) 47/1: He thumbed through the log, squinted at the makers' nameplates on each bit of astragational [sic] gear, [...] and sniffed the air appraisingly.

**1950** T. Sturgeon *Stars Are Styx* in *Galaxy* (Oct.) 80/1: I [...] gave him a preliminary look at the astrogational and manual maneuvering equipment and controls.

**1957** R. A. Heinlein *Citizen of Galaxy* in *Astounding SF* (Oct.) 119/1: Data poured into the ship's astrogational analogue of space and the questions were: Where is this other ship? What is its course?

**1994** [L. A. Graf] *Firestorm* 31: The landing party has been denied access to the Elasians' astrogational charts.

**astrogator** *n.* one who astrogates. Compare SPACE NAVIGATOR.

**1935** S. G. Weinbaum *Planet of Doubt* in *Astounding Stories* (Oct.) 108/1: Harbord was a good astrogator.

**1953** R. A. Heinlein *Starman Jones* (1980) 186: I'll astrogate—shucks, I suppose it's all right to call me the astrogator, under the circumstances.

**1970** R. F. Young *Starscape with Frieze of Dreams* in D. Knight *Orbit 8* (1971) 109: He pictures [...] an obese astrogator poring over charts in its chartroom.

**1995** J. Barnes *Kaleidoscope Century* (1996) 250: Don't try to hack the control systems—you could screw up life support. Besides, you're not an astrogator.

**astronavigation** *n.* ASTROGATION.

**1935** A. M. Phillips *Martian Gesture* in *Wonder Stories* (Oct.) 572/2: It would retard the development of astronavigation indefinitely, a hopeless, indecisive, futile effort.

**1941** E. F. Russell *Astounding S-F* (May) 100/1: To qualify for membership, you had to perform a feat of astro-navigation tantamount to a miracle.

**1989** [G. Naylor] *Red Dwarf* 61: Rimmer was sitting at his slanting architect's desk, [...] making out a revision timetable in preparation for his astronavigation exam.

**1995** P. David *Captain's Daughter* 175: Making astronavigation interesting was not an easy task.

**astronavigator** *n.* an ASTROGATOR.

**1941** E. F. Russell *Jay Score* in *Astounding S-F* (May) 95/1: The stunt was a theoretical one frequently debated by mathematicians and astronavigators, and often used by writers in stories.

**1960** M. Clifton *Eight Keys to Eden* (1965) 22: Sure, it was only a three-man crew—himself, a flight engineer, an astro-navigator.

**1979** L. Iribarne *trans.* S. Lem *Tales of Pirx Pilot* (1990) 198: Unable to sleep, he opened a volume of Irving's memoirs—of astronavigator fame—and read until his eyes began to burn.

**2001** D. Abnett *Xenos* 259: The admiral's astronavigators have finished plotting the course of the heretic fleet.

**atomics** *n.* **1.** any device powered by nuclear fission.

**1932** J. W. Campbell, Jr. *Electronic Siege* in *Wonder Stories* (Apr.) 1247/2: The slim, graceful ship rose smoothly into the atmosphere, [...] as the gentle hum of mighty Farrel Atomics poured their millions of horsepower into the McKinley space-drive discs.

**1944** C. D. Simak *Huddling Place* in R. Silverberg *SF Hall of Fame, Vol. I* (1970) 265: Webster smiled at the fireplace with its blazing wood. [...] Useless because atomic heating was better—but more pleasant. One couldn't sit and watch atomics and dream and build castles in the flames.

**1952** C. Oliver *Blood's Rover* in D. G. Hartwell *SF Century* (1997) 968: The two men fell silent then, looking at the neat brown rows of sacks, feeling the star ship tremble slightly under them with the thunder of her great atomics.

**1972** M. Z. Bradley *Darkover Landfall* (1987) 10: There evidently wasn't a leak in the atomics after all—that girl from Comm checked out with no radiation burns.

**2.** atomic weapons.

**1948** E. E. Smith *Triplanetary* 96: Six of those targets that did such fancy dodging were atomics, aimed at the Lines.

**1964** F. Herbert *Dune World* in *Astounding SF* (Jan.) 72: Outside of atomics, I know of no explosive powerful enough to destroy an entire worm. They're incredibly tough.

**1975** B. Lumley *Transition of Titus Crow* in *Titus Crow, Vol. 1* (1997) 184: We're no longer allowed to toss atomics around willy-nilly, Henri.

**1988** J. M. Ford *Preflash* in *Heat of Fusion & Other Stories* (2004) 114: And we'll have guns guns guns 'Til atomics blow the Commies away-y-y!

**2001** P. Reeve *Mortal Engines* (2004) 6: The Ancients destroyed themselves in that terrible flurry of orbit-to-earth atomics and tailor-virus bombs called the Sixty Minute War.

**avian** *n.* a bird-like alien.

**1937** O. Stapledon *Star Maker* in *To End of Time* (1953) 303: We supposed at first that the mental unity of these little avians was telepathic, but in fact it was not.

**1948** [W. Tenn] *Ionian Cycle* in *Thrilling Wonder Stories* (Aug.) 116/2: The saffron sky was obscured by multitudes of black winged avians dipping in short angry circles.

**1961** P. Anderson *Day After Doomsday* in *Galaxy* (Dec.) 15/2: He went over and took the avian in his arms. The beaked, crested head rested on the man's breast and the body shuddered.

**1977** A. D. Foster *End of Matter* 21: He found he could easily see over the heads of even the tall avians in the crowd.

**1990** A. McCaffrey & J. L. Nye *Death of Sleep* (1992) 283: They were jealous of their position as the only sentient avians in the FSP.

**2002** A. Reynolds *Redemption Ark* 358: It knew of the previous cleansing, the wiping out of the avians who had last inhabited this local sector of space.

**avian** *adj.* bird-like; of an avian or avians.

**1930** W. O. Stapledon *Last & First Men* (1931) 302: The flightless yet still half avian race that now possessed the planet settled down to construct a society based on industry and science.

**1948** [W. Tenn] *Ionian Cycle* in *Thrilling Wonder Stories* (Aug.) 112/1: Imagine! [ ... ] Another civilization in embryo—avian this time. An avian culture would hardly build cities.

**1965** P. Anderson *Analog SF-Sci. Fact* (July) 38/1: Torches guttering in sconces threw an uneasy light [ ... ] on sleazy garments, avian faces, unwinking eyes.

**1979** D. Drake *Hammer's Slammers* (1985) 59: Their sharp-edged faces, scale-dusted but more avian than reptile, stared enraptured at one of their number who hung in the air.

**1999** D. Duane *Storm at Eldala* 15: Besides the colonists, there's a considerable presence of scientists studying the riglia, those avian sentients they found.

# b

**bacover** *n.* [bæˈkʌvər] [*back* + *cover*] the back cover of a magazine or book.

**1951** L. Hoffman *Ether Jiggles* in *S-F Five-Yearly* (Nov.) 3: Gleefully we perused those two copies, noting such achievements as a five-color bacover (counting black).

**1964** J. Speer *Ramac in Sky* in *Fancestral Voices* (2004) 135: On a *SusPro* bacover I had it being done by a roomful of typists at the Fantasy Foundation.

**1975** E. Weinstein *Fillostrated Fan Dictionary* 42: From Hyphen#4, it is a sort of bacover quote.

**2005** *Thoughts before diving in...* (Urth Mailing List) (Jan. 3): As indicated by the (rather gushing) quote from my NYRSF review of "The Knight" on the bacover.

**BDO** *abbr.* a BIG DUMB OBJECT.

**1993** P. Nicholls in J. Clute & P. Nicholls *Ency. of SF* 119/1: Sf's much vaunted sense of wonder is seldom more potently evoked than in a good BDO story.

**1999** C. J. Cherryh – second time's charm (Usenet: rec.arts.sf.written) (Sept. 21): There *are* Cool Things, but they don't tend to be Toys For The Boys or BDO.

**2001** *Interzone* (Oct.) 28/2: *Ananda*, the mooted final chunk of the Chaga Saga [ ... ] has back-burnered, but suffice to say that [ ... ] there'll be a resolution with Shepard, who'll make it back from the BDO.

**2005** J. D. Owen *Infinity Plus* (Internet) (Mar. 12): Terry Pratchett's BDO is somewhat more whimsical in nature, as befits a world that is built for fantasy, rather than SF, adventures. Discworld, after all, is based on old cosmology, being a disc of material resting on the backs of four huge elephants, who in turn are standing on a giant turtle swimming through space.

**beam** *v.* to travel or to transport (something) by means of a matter transmitter.

**1951** S. A. Peeples, D. A. Kyle & M. Greenberg *Dictionary of SF* in M. Greenberg *Travelers of Space* 24: The transported matter is usually broken into its component atoms, keyed, "beamed" and reconstructed by a specially keyed receiver.

**1964** G. Roddenberry *Cage* in S. E. Whitfield & G. Roddenberry *Making of "Star Trek"* (1968) 48: We get our first look at this procedure, too, as it beams them to materialize on the planet surface far below.

**1992** N. Stephenson *Snow Crash* 34: You can't just materialize anywhere in the Metaverse, like Captain Kirk beaming down from on high.

**1993** *SF Age* (Jan.) 5 (*ad*): A collector's delight filled with insider info and memorable moments, including behind-the-scenes footage and bloopers from both the series and the movies. Beam Aboard!

**2004** J. Fforde *Something Rotten* 161: I waved good-bye as he and his two guards were beamed out of my world and back into theirs.

In phrases:

**beam me up (Scotty)** used figuratively to express disbelief or a desire to depart quickly.

[ **1966** B. Sobelman _Return of Archons ("Star Trek" script)_ (Nov. 10) 2: Captain, beam us up. Quick! Emergency! ]

**1984** _American Banker_ (July 31) 52/1: "Beam me up Scotty, there's no prospect of finance down here." Undoubtedly, that's what _Star Trek's_ Captain Kirk [ ... ] would say if he came here in search of bank loans to fund extraterrestrial activities.

**1990** _Syracuse (New York) Herald-Journal_ (June 4) B5/1: "You're waiting for someone. I've heard that one twice already tonight." (Oh no. Caught. Beam me up, Scotty—yuppie Klingon approaching.)

**1999** J. Traficant _Congressional Record_ (Jan. 19) H249/3: This furby cyberpet [ ... ] has just been designated as the next great threat to our freedom. Beam me up, Mr. Speaker. Beam me up.

**beam (me) up (to Scotty)** to get high on or take crack cocaine.

**1986** _Gettysburg (Pa.) Times_ (Oct. 1) 5/3: Jumps means crack. Look at him all jumped up. He's telling us, "beam me up."

**1990** _New York_ (May 28) 27: Drug-related expressions are well documented. "Beaming up" means a crack high.

**1992** M. Gelman _Crime Scene_ 104: Being despiteful meant beaming up to Scotty with a sweet drag on a glass pipe.

**beam-me-up (Scotty)** _adj._ science-fictional. Compare BUCK ROGERS. [Not generally used within the science fiction community.]

**1988** _Daily Herald (Arlington Heights, Ill.) TV Mag._ (Mar. 5–12) 25/4: In demonstrating his new invention—the ultimate beam-me-up Scotty device—a scientist's DNA accidentally gets spliced with that of a housefly.

**1989** _Daily Gleaner (Kingston, Jam.)_ (Aug. 8) 16/6: The main achievement of this beam-me-up kitsch is that it doesn't show boredom with the series.

**1997** _Syracuse (New York) Herald-Journal_ (Dec. 11) A19/1: It looks like the "Beam-me-up-Scotty" magic of "Star Trek." But a startling laboratory result might help scientists build more powerful computers.

**beanstalk** _n._ a SPACE ELEVATOR.

**1979** C. Sheffield _How to Build Beanstalk_ in _Destinies_ (Aug.–Sept.) 46: We now have the major feature of our "basic Beanstalk." It will be a long, strong cable, extending from the surface of the Earth on the equator, out to beyond the geostationary orbit. [ ... ] We will use it as the load-bearing cable of a giant elevator, to send materials up to orbit and back.

**1979** C. Sheffield _Web between Worlds_ 36: If we don't build a Beanstalk, somebody else will— and once one is working, the number of rocket launches will drop to zero.

**1982** R. A. Heinlein _Friday_ 1: I have never liked riding the Beanstalk. [ ... ] A cable that goes up into the sky with nothing to hold it up smells too much of magic.

**1999** L. Niven _Rainbow Mars_ (2000) 41: Mr. Secretary, I think that tree is an orbital tower, a Beanstalk.

**2002** J. C. Wright _Golden Age_ (2003) 347: We only had twenty beanstalks reaching down to the K-layer in the Jupiter atmosphere.

**becroggle** _v._ see CROGGLE.

**belter** _n._ one who lives in an asteroid belt, especially an asteroid miner.

**1966** L. Niven _Warriors_ in _If_ (Feb.) 152/2: You noticed a habit of mine once. I never make gestures. All Belters have that trait. It's because on a small mining ship you could hit something waving your arms around.

**1969** W. Richmond & L. Richmond _Phoenix Ship_ 34: _The Belt_, he thought. _I'm going to be a Belter now._

**1974** J. Pournelle _Galaxy SF_ (May) 105/2: Belters are asteroid miners—they flit from asteroid to asteroid, slicing them up for the mineral wealth they presumably contain.

**1987** R. Reed _Hormone Jungle_ (1989) 7: And there is the multitude of Belter worlds, each unique.

**1993** G. Bear _Moving Mars_ 386: Cameron gave me an eager, anxious look, backed away, spun around with the expert grace of a belter, and took a tunnel leading to the surface.

**BEM, bem** _n._ [bug-eyed monster] a BUG-EYED MONSTER; an ALIEN.

[ **1939**: see quote in BUG-EYED MONSTER. ]

**1940** P. Farrell _Thrilling Wonder Stories (letter)_ (Nov.) 120/2: Incidentally, Mr. Bergey, the

BEM's on your latest smear have extremely jovial expressions on their pans to be as tough a bunch of eggs as Friend made them out.

**1949** F. Brown *All Good Bems* in *Thrilling Wonder Stories* (Apr.) 128/2: They were really Bems, by the way. Two heads apiece, five limbs—and they could use all five as either arms or legs—six eyes apiece, three to a head, on long stems.

**1950** P. S. Miller *Astounding SF* (Feb.) 124/2: There have been times, before and since, when science fiction seemed to be largely made up of screwy animals—call them BEM's, if you like—but from the moment we met Weinbaum's ostrichlike little Martian, Tweel, we knew that this was different.

**1952** J. Merril *Preface* in *Beyond Human Ken* xi: All, that is, except the standard-brand, English-speaking, tentacle-waving monster from Mars, the BEM, or Bug-Eyed Monster.

**1961** P. Lupoff *Absolute Xero* in P. Lupoff & D. Lupoff *Best of Xero* (2005) 86: A peaceful pastoral scene of a spaceman surrounded by some graceful grey bems rather resembling sorely overstuffed bats.

**1965** L. Niven *Worlds of Tomorrow* 71/2 (Mar.): I've been ordered not to move by a BEM that doesn't take No for an answer.

**bheer** *n.* [bɪər] [*beer* + -H-] beer.

**1959** R. H. Eney *Fancyclopedia II* 15: No less important to fannish than mundane drinking, this useful beverage is even given divine honors by the sect of Beeros, and worshipped either as Beer or Bheer.

**1966** D. A. Grennell *Pilgrim in Never-Never Country* in *S-F Five-Yearly* (Nov.) 20: I miss tomato juice in glass bottles and I miss Heilemann's Special Export bheer.

**1975** E. Weinstein *Fillostrated Fan Dictionary* 51: Thou shalt not drink up the bheer before I get there.

**2003** *Is Bheer really one of 4 fannish food groups* (Usenet: rec.arts.sf.fandom) (Apr. 2): I think the 4 fannish food groups are sugar, chocolate, grease and caffiene [sic]. Bheer doesn't fit in here unless you put chocolate in with sugar.

**Big Brother** *n.* [after Big Brother, the head of state in George Orwell's novel *Nineteen Eighty-Four*] an all-powerful, all-seeing, authoritarian ruler or government.

**1949** [G. Orwell] *Nineteen Eighty-Four* 209: One could infer [...] the general structure of Oceanic society. At the apex of the pyramid comes Big Brother. Big Brother is infallible and all-powerful [...]. Nobody has ever seen Big Brother. He is a face on the hoardings, a voice on the telescreen.

**1957** *Economist* (Oct.) 208/2: The reporting to the Privy Council of any evidence discovered by this court of "misconduct in the administration of security organisations" would usefully discourage the Big Brother mentality.

**1968** B. Bettelheim *Saturday Evening Post* (July 27) 9/2: Neither a medieval absence of privacy nor a Big Brother's spying that leaves nothing unpublic will do.

**2005** *Times of India, Pune* (June 24) 5/5: Mumbai University is taking up the role of big brother and will soon tell students what to wear and what not to wear to college.

**big dumb object** *n.* a very large, mysterious artifact of unknown or alien origin encountered in space or on another world. Compare B D O.

**1981** R. Kaveny *SF in 1970s* in *Foundation* (June) 25: Early in his career he brought back into fashion—naively but effectively—the resonances and charms of Big Dumb Objects like the Ringworld: as painted stages go, his Meccano universe was sort of loveable.

**1993** P. Nicholls J. Clute & P. Nicholls *Ency. of SF* 119/1: BIG DUMB OBJECTS An unfailingly popular theme in sf is the discovery, usually by humans, of vast enigmatic objects in space or on other planets.

**1998** G. Zebrowski *Afterword* in C. Pellegrino & G. Zebrowski *Dyson Sphere* (1999) 200: The history of science fiction is filled with large structures; but it is a mistake to consider them as mere genre conceits, "big dumb objects," as some have called them, growing out of the desire to have purely fictional dramatic extravagances.

**2003** M. J. Harrison *Locus* 69/1 (Dec.): There's nothing like big dumb objects and going very fast in space.

**2005** J. D. Owen *Infinity Plus* (Internet) (Mar. 12): Both feature rather interesting Big

Dumb Objects as their main setting. In Larry Niven's case, it's the ubiquitous *Ringworld*, a great, sun-encircling artifact with the land area of a million Earths.

**biopunk** *n.* [*biology* + cyber*punk*] a subgenre of science fiction which explores the societal effects of biotechnology and genetic engineering.
**1992** *GURPS: Problems (was What's wrong with...)* (Usenet: rec.games.frp) (May 17): I wrote my own biopunk game, because none of the others fitted.
**1997** *Interzone* 54/1 (Aug.): In the 1990s, sf reflects the increasing dominance of the New Biology, from Paul Di Filippo's biopunk fictions (cyberpunk described ways of positively enhancing the body by mechanical or silicon chip implants; biopunk examines a more fundamental consumerist option, change not just of our bodies but of our cells) to radical reappraisals of the extremes of ecological and evolutionary theory.
**1999** P. J. McAuley *Frankenstein's Daughters* in J. L. Casti & A. Karlqvist *Mission to Abisko* 147: Sterling has also written a very perceptive short story [...] introducing the idea of gene hackers, the biopunk equivalent of cyberpunk's computer hackers.
**2002** C. Lalumière *Locus Online (Internet)* (May 21): If anatomical SF were a commercialized subgenre (biopunk?), then Michael Blumlein would be its William Gibson.

**blaster** *n.* a weapon that fires a blast of destructive energy.
**1925** N. Dyalhis *When Green Star Wanes* in *Weird Tales* (Apr.) 6/2: Instinctively I slid forward the catch on the tiny Blastor, [sic] and the foul thing vanished—save for a few fragments of its edges—smitten into nothingness by the vibration hurled forth from that powerful little disintegrator.
**1938** H. Kuttner *Hollywood on Moon* in *Thrilling Wonder Stories* (Apr.) 26/2: Blast out the lakes and canals—whittle down the peaks and mounds with atomic blasters—file them into the shape of gigantic buildings.
**1945** [M. Leinster] *Ethical Equations* in *Astounding SF* (May) 11/1: The blasters are

those beams of ravening destruction which take care of recalcitrant meteorites in a spaceship's course when the deflectors can't handle them.
**1954** F. Brown *Sentence* in *Angels & Spaceships* 170: "I sentence you to death," said the solemn Antarian judge. "Death by blaster fire at dawn tomorrow."
**1958** A. Norton *Star Gate* 189: The hold people were at bay, held so by the weapon the false lord fingered—the blaster with which he had once threatened Kincar.
**1961**: see quote in SUB-ETHER.
**1983** I. Asimov *Robbie* in *Complete Robot* (1995) 167: Pirates were giving chase and the ship's blasters were coming into play.
**2001** *SF Chronicle* (July) 23/2: A collection for thoughtful readers who want more than blazing blasters in their SF.

**blast-off** *n.* the act of blasting off.
**1944** [G. Vance] *Double-Cross on Mars* in *Amazing Stories* (Sept.) 151/1: Visible [...] was a long, gleaming line of fighter-ships, in blast-off formation, on the Martian space field.
**1956** M. Z. Bradley *Fantastic Universe* (Mar.) 72/2: Spaced at random on the inside of the sphere were three skyhooks [...] into which the passenger was snugged during blastoff in shock-absorbing foam.
**1958** *New York Times Mag.* (Jan. 26) 61/1: The camera [...] will record the blast-off in color from far closer than any human eye.
**2004** L. Wagener *One Giant Leap* 146: Armstrong and Scott were completing their final checklist for blastoff.

**blast off** *v.* (of a person or being) to take off in a spaceship, especially one propelled by rockets; (of a spaceship) to take off.
**1937** E. E. Smith *Galactic Patrol* in *Astounding Stories* (Sept.) 31/2: How long do you figure it'll be before it's safe for us to blast off?
**1943** L. Brackett *Halfling* in *Halfling & Other Stories* (1973) 9: I'm blasting off next Monday for Venus, and then Mars, and maybe the Asteroids.
**1962** *New York Times* (Sept. 13) 16/1: Under this method, a lunar rocket would be formed by a rendezvous of parts orbiting the earth. It would blast off from that parking orbit and land on the moon.

**1970** A. McCaffrey *Ship Who Sang* (1991) 207: She could hardly blast off now. She'd fry the quartet of notables.

**1986** S. Ride & S. Okie *To Space & Back* 7: The words and pictures in this book will help you imagine what it's like to blast off in a rocket and float effortlessly in midair while circling hundreds of miles above the Earth.

**blowup** *n.* a war that destroys a culture or the vast majority of a population. *Obs.* Often *cap.*

**1945** [L. Padgett] *Beggars in Velvet* in *Astounding S-F* (Dec.) 14/2: After the Blowup, the fringes of the radioactive areas had caused the mutations of which the telepaths were the only survivors, aside from the occasional monsters—reptiles and harmless beasts—that still lived near the blasted areas.

**1946** [L. Padgett] *Time Enough* in *Astounding SF* 127/2 (Dec.): Had the Blowup been due only to the atomic blast, man might have rebuilt more easily, granting that the planet remained habitable.

**1947** J. Speer *It's Up to Us* in *Fancestral Voices* (2004) 188: Little leisure can be seen in the post-Blowup world.

**1949** F. Brown *Letter to Phoenix* in *Angels & Spaceships* (1954) 104: It's not like a blow-up war, when nine-tenths or more of the population of Earth—or of Earth and the other planets—is killed.

**BNF** *abbr.* [Big Name Fan] someone who is well-known or influential in science fiction fandom.

**1950** L. Hoffman *Chaos* in *Quandry* (Oct.) 5: COMING NEXT ISH: A department devoted to the BNF of tomorrow. 'Twill be the neofan of today who is the Tucker or Laney of tomorrow.

**1953** L. B. Stewart *Thrilling Wonder Stories* (*letter*) (Aug.) 133/2: Fandom [ . . . ] has a rigid social structure, too—a pyramid of subtle gradations that culminates in that awesome capstone, the mighty BNF (Big Name Fan, to you igerunt uninitiates).

**1961** J. Koning *Withdrawal* in *S-F Five-Yearly* (Nov.) 24: By this time, Craig was a BNF, both within the FOCUS circle and without, but he still had all his enthusiasm and determination.

**1987** T. Easton *Analog SF/Sci. Fact* (Sept.) 163/2: But he was also an SF fan—a BNF, in fact.

**1997** M. Resnick in M. Resnick & P. Nielsen Hayden *Alternate Skiffy* 109: Jack Haldeman is not only a top-notch skiffy author of long standing, but also a BNF (Big Name Fan).

**boat** *n.* a SPACESHIP. Compare CRAFT, CRUISER, SHIP, SPACE CAN, SPACE CAR, SPACE-CRAFT, SPACE CRUISER, SPACE FLYER, SPACER 2, SPACE VEHICLE, SPACE VESSEL, TIN CAN, VESSEL.

**1928** E. E. Smith & L. H. Garby *Skylark of Space* in *Amazing Stories* (Sept.) 549/1: "We can kill him as soon as he gets far enough away from the boat," said Seaton as, with Dorothy clinging to him, he dropped behind one of the ledges.

**1940** [L. Gregor] *Flight to Galileo* in *Astonishing Stories* (Oct.) 106/1: A comet zoomed from the other side of the asteroid. Reeves, in his little boat, groaned against his chair straps.

**1952** J. Blish *Bridge* in *Astounding SF* (Feb.) 75/1: In shape it was not distinguishable from any of the long-range cruisers which ran the legs of the Moon-Mars-Belt-Ganymede trip. But it grounded its huge bulk with less visible expenditures of power than one of the little intersatellary boats.

**1967** K. Laumer *Thunderhead* in *Day Before Forever & Thunderhead* (1968) 163: The heavy Fleet boat descended swiftly under the expert guidance of the battle officer. At fifty feet, it leveled off, orbited the station.

**1989** P. Anderson *Boat of Million Years* (2004) 433: Boats entered atmosphere. After several sorties had provided knowledge of surface conditions, they landed.

**2005** J. Whedon *Serenity, Shooting Script* in *Serenity, Official Visual Companion* 60: Zoe, is Wash gonna straighten this boat out before we get flattened?

**body-waldo** *n.* a waldo that consists of an entire movable body (as opposed to just an appendage); the device used to operate such a waldo. Compare WALDO.

**1963** P. Anderson *After Doomsday* (1968) 98: They're remote-control mechanisms [ . . . ]. Yes, they're just body-waldos.

**1973** [J. Tiptree, Jr.] *Girl Who Was Plugged In* in *Screwtop/Girl Who Was Plugged In* (1989) 26: Three thousand miles north and five hundred feet down a forgotten hulk in a body-waldo glows. **1999** [H. Clement] *Half Life* (2000) 16: The exceptions were Goodall, whose own senses were drowned in pain too much of the time to let him use a body waldo safely.

**bot, 'bot** *n.* [abbr. of *robot*] a ROBOT.
**1969** R. Meredith *We All Died at Breakaway Station* in *Amazing Stories* (Jan.) 130/2: When they got my ship the only part of me that the 'bots were able to get into cold-sleep was my head, shoulders and a part of my spine.
**1977** G. Benford *Snatching Bot* in *Cosmos SF & Fantasy Mag.* (May) 25/1: "What's your name, little bot?" The robot squats mutely.
**1984** D. Brin *Practice Effect* 23: Compared with some of the sophisticated machines Dennis had worked with, the exploration 'bot wasn't very bright.
**1991** M. Weiss *King's Test* 8: Yanking it off, he tossed it over his shoulder to the 'bot.
**2001** *Time* (Nov. 19) 87: This Pentium-powered bot uses sonar sensors to keep her from bumping into walls [...] as she rolls along.

**braintape** *n.* a recording of the entire contents of a person's mind. Also as *v.*
**1979** O. S. Card *What Will We Do Tomorrow?* in *Worthing Saga* (1990) 401: Mother's Little Boys took the body out and disposed of it, and Mother's braintape was put into safekeeping by those who would never harm it.
**1982** R. Rucker *Software* (1997) 129: Mr. Frostee still used Phil's brain-tape when he needed repairs.
**1999** S. Dedman *Foreign Bodies* (2000) 225: It seemed unlikely that Skye would have the time to braintape every volunteer who came forward, but maybe these men had given themselves away somehow.
**1999** Dedman, *Foreign Bodies* 230: The laws upwhen prohibit the use of braintapes to create multiple versions of the same person, and there are no exceptions made, even for swap-hopping.

**brave new world** *n.* [after Aldous Huxley's dystopian novel *Brave New World*, itself a

reference to Shakespeare's *The Tempest*] a dystopian society resulting from the failures of technological or social advancements; a situation resembling such a state of affairs.
**1933** *Annual Register 1932* 35: The driving force that sweeps Mr. Huxley on to presenting every nook and cranny of his Brave New World to the fiercest light of inquiry is the heart-corroding disgust he feels for human society as it will become according to his vision.
**1972** *Manitowoc (Wis.) Herald-Times* (Nov. 21) 4/7: Quite a brave new world this United Nations has become.
**1999** P. Majer & C. Porter *Intro.* in K. Čapek *Four Plays* xi: The play is a gloriously dystopic science-fiction fantasy about them and the brave new world of the men who mass-produce them.
**2005** L. Menand *New Yorker* (Mar. 28) 78/2: Conditions in this brave-new-world Britain [...] are all spooky editorial surprises.

**Buck Rogers** *adj.* science-fictional; characteristic of dated or hackneyed science fiction. Compare BEAM-ME-UP (SCOTTY), *adj.*
**1946** G. Conklin *Intro. Best of SF* xxvi: Thus, I have avoided such stories as are usually to be found between lurid magazine covers showing luxuriantly-fleshed females scantily clad in either a leopard's skin or a two-piece Buck Rogers outfit with a bare twelve inches of midriff.
**1950** V. L. McCain *Other Worlds Sci. Stories (letter)* (May) 160/1: I feel you would have really done a more impressive job retaining the *Astounding* part of the cover and leaving the Buck Rogers devices to the funny papers.
**1964** *Western Kansas Press (Great Bend, Kan.)* (June 23) 10/2: A "space snoop"—a flying television camera with a Buck Rogers jet pack that could sniff out objects in space—has been developed by an aerospace firm here for the Air Force.
**1975** *Lincoln (Neb.) Star* (Mar. 24) 4/4: Back of all this Buck Rogers and scientific fiction stuff about broken Soviet submarines, dead sailors, and the efforts of the CIA to recover the Soviet missiles and codes, there is the much larger strategic question.

**bug-eyed monster** *n.* an alien, especially one portrayed stereotypically. Also used *fig.*

**1939** M. Alger *Thrilling Wonder Stories (letter)* (Aug.) 121/2: Speaking of The SPWSSTFM, the cover inspired me to organize the SFTPOBEMOTCOSFP. (Society For The Prevention Of Bug-Eyed Monsters On The Covers Of Science-Fiction Publications.)

**1949** F. Brown *All Good Bems* in *Thrilling Wonder Stories* (Apr.) 125/2: B-bems?... You mean you are b-bug-eyed monsters? That's what Elmo means by Bems, but you aren't.

**1951** *New York Times Book Rev.* (Dec. 15) 16/3: A series of short science fiction interludes inserted between chapters [...] are not only irrelevant, but read as though the printer accidentally dropped some bug-eyed monster copy into the wrong book.

**1957** M. Lesser *Name Your Tiger* in [Anon.] *Weird Ones* (1962) 54: But I tell you, I *saw* this here thing. Bug-eyed monster, with tentacles.

**1961** *Oakland (Cal.) Tribune* (July 17) 12/7: You might think that all this exposure would turn a 13-term Congressman into some sort of bug-eyed monster, but Mr. Brooks comes through without the slightest variation from Main Street normality.

**1979** D. Adams *Hitchhiker's Guide to Galaxy* (1981) 50: Are you trying to tell me that [...] some green bug-eyed monster stuck his head out and said "Hi fellas, hop right in, I can take you as far as the Basingstoke roundabout?"

**1993** *SF Age* (Jan.) 6/1: When I was younger, and I was challenged about my liking of science fiction by others who wanted to put it down as mindless fluff about rockets and bug-eyed monsters.

# Communications & Entertainment

Science fiction writers have spent a lot of time imagining how technology will change our lives. Much of this has had to do with living or traveling in outer space, or creating artificial intelligences. But a great deal of inventive thought has also gone into the future of communication and entertainment.

The *viewer* is one of the most common entertainment and media/communications devices in SF. Essentially SFnal television screens, viewers can be divided into two rough groups: devices that typically only display images (**vidscreen, vision screen,** and **visiplate**), and devices that both send and receive images (**videophone, vidphone, viewphone,** and **visiphone**). Additionally, there are a number of viewers that are regularly used in either category, such as **telescreen, viewscreen, vision plate,** and **visiscreen**.

Since modern-day devices are typically only capable of two-dimensional reproduction, it is a natural step to imagine three-dimensional images. Devices that can produce or display them have gone by a dizzying array of names, including **three-D** (or **3-D**), **three-v** (or **3V**), **tri-D, trideo, tri-dim, tri-v,** and **tri-vid.** The *hologram* has also suggested several terms, including **holo, holoscreen, holotank,** and **holovision**. Photographs are often replaced with **solidographs,** or simply **solidos.** And if adding an extra dimension isn't enough, the **feely** allows a viewer to experience the emotions of the characters being observed.

Non-visual communication devices also abound. For relatively short distances, as from an orbiting spaceship to the planet's surface or between spaceships, **comlinks, commsets, suit radios,** and **tight-beams** can do the trick. For much greater distances, as between stars, something such as an **ansible, ultraphone,** or **ultrawave** is generally necessary.

SF writers were also quick to explore the possibilities of the personal computer and the Internet. William Gibson is well known for coining the word **cyberspace,** the notional location where communication between computers takes place, but many other computer terms also arose in SF. The first **webcast** occurred in Daniel Keyes Moran's novel *The Armageddon Blues,* for example. And it should not be surprising that SF writers were the first to describe malicious software as a **virus** or **worm,** since, in order to portray a convincing future, they must not only imagine advanced technologies, but also the ways in which they may be misused.

# C

**chrononaut** *n.* a TIME TRAVELER.

**1963** G. Fox *Highwayman & Mighty Mite* in *Atom* (Apr./May) 20: I've been training since my last trip in the *time pool!* [ ... ] I'm becoming a regular "chrononaut"!

**1974** P. K. Dick *Little Something for Us Tempunauts* in E. L. Ferman & B. N. Malzberg *Final Stage* 287: Addison addressed the Soviet chrononaut. "Officer N. Gauki [ ... ] what in your mind is the greatest terror facing a time traveler?"

**1982** M. Bishop *No Enemy but Time* 78: One of the older females had a vessel so expertly woven that I wondered if some unsung chrononaut had dropped back in time to give it to her.

**2001** A. Steele *Chronospace* 61: Although no one knew what they were, several theories had been advanced to explain the sightings, the most popular being that they themselves were chrononauts, yet from farther up the timestream.

**2002** D. M. Hassler *New York Rev. of SF* (Apr.) 22/1: Two plausible chrononauts from a research institution based on the moon three centuries in the future journey back to 1937 in order to study the *Hindenberg* explosion.

**chronoscope** *n.* a device which displays events that happened in the past or that will happen in the future. Hence **chronoscopy.** Compare TIME-VIEWER.

**ca 1938** C. S. Lewis *Dark Tower* (1977) 19: "What one wants, in fact, is not a sort of time flying-machine but something which does to time what the telescope does to space." "A *chronoscope* in fact," suggested Ransom.

**1940**: see quote in TIME VIEWER.

**1947** R. Dragonette *Eye to Future* in *Astounding SF* (Feb.) 62/2: It seems that something happened to one of their Chronoscopes—those little devices they scattered back in the time stream which would radiate visually, everything that happened within their range.

**1956** I. Asimov *Dead Past* in S. Schmidt *Fifty Years of Best SF from Analog* (1980) 211: No chronoscope can possibly see back in time further than 1920 under any conditions.

**1956** Asimov, *Dead Past* 187: For two years I have been trying to obtain permission to do some time viewing—chronoscopy, that is—in connection with my researches on ancient Carthage.

**1987** D. S. Garnett *Only One* in J. Clute, D. Pringle & S. Ounsley *Interzone: 3rd Anthology* (1988) 58: If the chronoscope (as I named it) fell into the wrong hands, the consequences did not bear contemplation.

**Clarke orbit** *n.* [after Arthur C. *Clarke*, who first proposed the concept] an orbit around a planet in which a satellite or other object remains over the same point on the planet's surface.

[**1945** A. C. Clarke *Wireless World* (Feb.) 58/2: An "artificial satellite" at the correct distance from the earth would [ ... ] remain stationary over the same spot and would be within optical range of nearly half the earth's surface.]

**1976** K. Laumer *Analog SF-Sci. Fact* (Dec.) 175/1: Both Arthur Clarke and Norman Spinrad made use of a term which I have long considered unnecessarily clumsy, to wit "synchronous," as "geo-synchronous orbit." For some time in my work I have employed the term "Clarke orbit," which is simple and gives Arthur the credit due to him.

**1984** K. S. Robinson *Icehenge* 208: Well, Connie, we're in a Clarke orbit, so we don't have to worry about orbital velocity.

**1998** *Network Computing* (EBSCOhost) (Mar. 15): The Clarke orbit [...] makes it appear that the satellite is stationary in its relationship to earth.

**Clarke's First Law** the statement that if a distinguished but elderly scientist states that something is possible, he is probably right, but that if he states that something is impossible, he is probably wrong. Also **Clarke's Law.**

[**1962** A. C. Clarke *Profiles of Future* 25: I have tried to embody this fact of observation in Clarke's Law, which may be formulated as follows: "When a distinguished but elderly scientist states that something is possible, he is almost certainly right. When he states that something is impossible, he is very probably wrong."]

[**1964** *Profil du futur* front free endpaper: Quand un savant distingué mais vieillissant estime que quelque chose est possible, il a presque certainement raison. Mais lorsqu'il déclare que quelque chose est impossible il a très probablement tort. 1re Loi de CLARKE]

**1972** A. C. Clarke *Report on Planet Three* 129: Clarke's First Law: When a distinguished but elderly scientist states that something is possible, he is almost certainly right. When he states that something is impossible, he is very probably wrong.

**1997** G. Flandro in D. W. Swift *Voyager Tales* 74: One of the things I learned was that you have to be very careful not to be discouraged by experts. [...] This important principle was expressed most elegantly by the science fiction writer Arthur Clarke in the form of Clarke's Law: "If a highly respected and well-established authority tells you something is possible, then he is probably right; if he tells you something is impossible, he is probably wrong."

**2004** L. Niven *Intro. Scatterbrain* 5: Old men aren't always right. Clarke's law applies here.

**Clarke's Second Law** the statement that the only way of discovering the limits of the possible is to venture a little way past them into the impossible.

[**1962** A. C. Clarke *Profiles of Future* 31: But the only way of discovering the limits of the possible is to venture a little way past them into the impossible.]

[**1964** *Profil du futur* front free endpaper: La seule façon de découvrir les limites du possible est de s'aventurer un peu au-delà d'elles, dans l'impossible. 2e Loi de CLARKE]

**1977** A. C. Clarke *Profiles of Future* 39: But the only way of discovering the limits of the possible is to venture a little way past them into the impossible. [Footnote begins] The French edition of this book rather surprised me by calling this Clarke's Second Law.

**Clarke's Third Law** the statement that any sufficiently advanced technology is indistinguishable from magic. Also **Clarke's Law.**

**1968** A. C. Clarke *Sci.* (letter) (Jan. 19) 255/2: Clarke's *Third* Law is even more appropriate to the UFO discussion: "Any sufficiently advanced technology is indistinguishable from magic."

**1992** S. Perry *Brother Death* 183: Clarke's Law said that a highly advanced technology might well appear to be magic to a less advanced society viewing it.

**1998** R. Dawkins *Unweaving Rainbow* (2000) 132: Does Clarke's Third Law then entitle us to believe any and every yarn that folk may spin about apparent miracles?

**2001** M. Pesce *True Magic* in J. Frenkel *True Names & Opening of Cyberspace Frontier* 225: Although Bacon espoused the virtues of reason, he wasn't above Clarke's Law; all sufficiently advanced technologies are—even in the early seventeenth century—indistinguishable from magic.

**2003** W. McCarthy *Point & Click Promise Hacking Matter* 114: This is a Clarke's Law type of technology, bordering on the magical.

**cloaking device** *n.* a device which renders something invisible or undetectable.

**1968** D. C. Fontana *Enterprise Incident* ("Star Trek" script) (June 13) IV-61: The cloaking device is operating most effectively, sir. And the Commander informed me even their own sensors cannot track a vessel so equipped.

**1980** D. F. Glut *Empire Strikes Back* 133: Could a ship that small have a cloaking device?

**1986** J. M. Dillard *Mindshadow* 11: Cloaking devices, Captain [...]. It would explain why we detected no vessels in the immediate area.

**1989** N. Pollotta & P. Foglio *Illegal Aliens* 270: Disguised how? Camouflage? A jamming field? Or is it some sort of cloaking device that bends our scanner beams 180 degrees around the target?

**1998** *Interzone* (Feb.) 44/1: At some point, [...] a rookie pilot would accidentally turn off the cloaking device, momentarily revealing an alien dreadnought in the Earth's upper atmosphere.

**clubzine** *n.* a fanzine published by a science fiction fan club.

**1969** H. Warner, Jr. *All Our Yesterdays* 283: Quicky the mimeograph became supreme even in circumstances where fewer than fifty copies of a fanzine were needed, like local clubzines and FAPA in its early years.

**1975** E. Weinstein *Fillostrated Fan Dictionary* 82: the Mallorn [...]: Clubzine of the Tolkein Society.

**1980** [L. del Rey] *World of SF* 141: Some fan clubs published magazines—clubzines.

**2004** J. Stinson *E-National Fantasy Fan* (Mar.) 5: I owe much thanks to Susan Van Schuyver and Ruth Davidson, among others, for allowing me to continue editing the clubzine.

**COA** *abbr.* change of address.

**1961** *Fanac* (May 6) 1: The first contributor of an accepted news item (not a COA) is entitled to a free issue, as are all other Good People who send in locs, cartoons, etc.

**1962** D. Lupoff *Cry (letter)* 32 (June): CoA notices in Axe and Fanac (and Xero), we figured, [...] should inform everybody of the move sooner or later.

**1991** R. Rogow *Futurespeak* 57: COA lists help keep track of people.

**2000** N. Brooks *It Goes on Shelf (Internet)* (Jan.): Roger Reus, who says in an e-mail that he has gotten computerized and notes a COA to [...] Richmond VA.

**2006** D. Langford *Ansible (Internet)* (Mar.): *C.o.A.* If anyone moved house last month, they failed to tell *Ansible*.

**cognitive estrangement** *n.* [in part < Ger. *Verfremdung*, "estrangement" or "alienation," after dramatist Bertolt Brecht's concept of *Verfremdungseffekt*] the effect brought on by the reader's realization that the setting of a text (film, etc.) differs from that of the reader's reality, especially where the difference is based on scientific extrapolation, as opposed to supernatural or fantastic phenomena.

**1972** D. Suvin *On Poetics of SF Genre* in *College English* (Dec.) 372/2: In the following paper I shall argue for a definition of SF as the *literature of cognitive estrangement*.

**1979** G. Graff *Literature against Itself* 99: The "radical disorientation" of perception and the "cognitive estrangement" discovered by recent critics in the conventions of science fiction may result in a dulling of the audience's sense of reality.

**1987** P. K. Alkon *Origins of Futuristic Fiction* 230: By placing an account of the French Revolution after a series of fantastic episodes [...] *Les Posthumes* is well designed to achieve the effects now described as cognitive estrangement.

**1996** P. Alkon *Cannibalism in SF* in G. Westfahl, G. Slusser & E. Rabkin *Foods of Gods* 150: This story offers rich possibilities for symbolic interpretation but little invitation to that cognitive estrangement by which readers are invited to reconsider their own situation from the radically alien perspective of a depicted or implied alien environment.

**2003** F. Mendlesohn *Intro.* in E. James & F. Mendlesohn *Cambridge Companion to SF* 5: Cognitive estrangement is the sense that something in the fictive world is dissonant with the reader's experienced world.

**cold sleep** *n.* the suspension of physiological activity by lowering a person or creature's body temperature in such a way that they may be revived many years later without suffering from the effects of aging; the act of undergoing such a process. Compare CRYOSTASIS.

**1941** R. Heinlein *Methuselah's Children* in *Astounding S-F* (Aug.) 96: By converting some of the recreation space to storerooms and adapting the storerooms thus cleared to the purpose of cold-sleep, the ship was roomy enough.

**1954** A. Norton *Stars Are Ours!* (1955) 44: The formula for the "cold sleep." [ ... ] We go to sleep, hibernate, during that trip—or else the ship comes to its port manned by dust!

**1966** R. Zelazny *This Moment of Storm* in *Mag. of Fantasy & SF* (June) 22/1: After several turns at ship's guard, interspersed with periods of cold sleep, you tend to grow claustrophobic and somewhat depressed.

**1984** W. Gibson *Neuromancer* (1986) 192: The reason Straylight's not exactly hoppin' with Tessier-Ashpools is that they're mostly in cold sleep. There's a law firm in London keeps track of their powers of attorney. Has to know who's awake and exactly when.

**ca 1985** [J. Tiptree, Jr.] *Trey of Hearts* in *Meet Me at Infinity* (2001) 97: Might as well get used to Deneb time—although of course she will travel in cold-sleep, which will reset all her physiological cycles.

**1990** A. McCaffrey & E. Moon *Sassinak* (1991) 88: To be stuck on one planet, or shipped from one to another by coldsleep cabinet? Horrible.

**2000** K. MacLeod *Cosmonaut Keep* (2001) 47: He could have *lived* with a universe whose interstellar gulfs could be crossed only with generation ships, cold-sleep or ramscoops.

**cold-sleep** *v.* to undergo the process of cold sleep; to put someone into a state of cold sleep.

**1956** R. A. Heinlein *Door into Summer* in *Mag. of Fantasy & SF* (Oct.) 14/2: Damnation, he was quite capable of refusing to let me cold-sleep.

**1973** R. C. Meredith *At Narrow Passage* (1975) 107: Trebum is standing by [ ... ] in case he doesn't make it. Sol-Jodala will then coldsleep him and try to revive him in Altheon.

**1992** A. McCaffrey & M. Lackey *Ship Who Searched* (2002) 127: You don't have the facilities to cold-sleep fifty people.

**1997** *Interzone* 55/2 (Oct.): The Aristos, extropians who want to coldsleep into a future where immortality is available, are only sketchily portrayed and quickly dismissed.

**cold sleeper** *n.* one who is in a state of cold sleep.

**1969** R. Meredith *We All Died at Breakaway Station* in *Amazing Stories* (Jan.) 127/1: The cold sleepers will stay where they are.

**1992** V. Vinge *Fire upon Deep* (1993) 125: She had seen the coldsleepers burning on the ground below the ship, but those *inside* might have survived.

**1994** M. O. Martin & G. Benford *Trojan Cat* in L. Niven, et al. *Man-Kzin Wars VI* 288: Crew of three to five, carrying well over three hundred coldsleepers, with a sizable cargo bay.

**collapsium** *n.* any of a variety of extremely high-density substances.

**1963** H. B. Piper *Space Viking* (1975) 33: Living quarters and workshops went in next, all armored in collapsium-plated steel.

**1980** [L. del Rey] *World of SF* 323: *Neutronium:* supposedly, matter collapsed to high density or composed mostly of neutrons, used as a shield on spaceships against radiation. Sometimes called collapsium.

**2000** W. McCarthy *Collapsium* 6 (2002): But instead of moons and planets, one could also make black holes of these things, black holes held rigidly into stable lattices, a phase of matter known as "collapsium."

**2005** B. Baldwin *Defiance* 269: Tongues of radiation fire escaped immediately from the Gorn-Hoff's hull as its collapsium hullmetal un-collapsed in the torrent of energy from our disruptors.

**comlink, commlink** *n.* [*com*munication + *link*] a COMSET. Compare SUIT RADIO.

**1976** G. Lucas *Adventures of Luke Starkiller* (Apr. 19) 70: A stormtrooper comes down the ramp of the pirate starship and waves to the gantry officer and points to his ear indicating his comlink is not working.

**1983** D. Brin *Startide Rising* 403: Gillian reached for the comm link, but the carrier wave cut off before she could say another word.

**1987** G. Bear *Forge of God* (1988) 47: You'll have commlink.

**1988** W. T. Quick *Dreams of Flesh & Sand* (1989) 95: Barely thirty seconds passed before her commlink monitor lit up with the smiling face of Frederick Oranson.

**1991** M. Weiss *King's Test* 139: The voice of the captain of the shuttlecraft came over the comm-link.

**1994** B. Hambly *Crossroad* 11: Kirk was already on his feet, speaking down into the comm link to Transporter.

**2001** E. Colfer *Artemis Fowl* 53: Root himself was on the other end of the comlink.

**2005** M. Rosenblum *Green Shift* in *Asimov's SF* 109 (Mar.): His com link, an earring that looked like a natural diamond, had just informed him that security wanted to talk to him.

**commset** *n.* see COMSET.

**completism** *n.* the desire to possess a complete set of something, such as every book written by an author or every issue of a specific magazine or comic.

**1944** J. B. Speer *Fancyclopedia* 13/1: A novel type of completism is Rothman's record and determination of attending every major convention held in this country.

**1986** T. Nielsen Hayden *Over Rough Terrain* in *Making Book* (1994) 82: Completism is a form of lunacy not without honor.

**1994** *3 lyrics questions* (Usenet: rec.music.beatles) (Jan. 6): I have to make a confession: I never understood why anybody would want to buy those 3" CDs (other than obsessive completism).

**2003** *Balkanisation of Who [was Thoughts on New Group]* (Usenet: rec.arts.drwho.moderated) (Jan. 4): Selling to the avid fan, who often buys for the sake of "completism," doesn't seem as likely to encourage experimentalism or even quality.

**completist** *n.* one who desires to collect a complete set of something.

**1944** J. B. Speer *Fancyclopedia* 13/1: *Completist*, a dope who tries to have a complete collection in some line. The line may be as broad as having all the prozines ever published, or as narrow as collecting all the Golden Atom tales or all official correspondence during ones incumbency in some office.

**1946** S. Moskowitz *Immortal Storm* in *Fantasy Commentator* 333 (Fall): The only subscribers who went along with Dollens were such "completists" in the field as Miller, Wollheim, McPhail and the like.

**1954** [A. Boucher] *Mag. of Fantasy & SF* 91 (Dec.): Robert Shafer's THE CONQUERED PLACE [...] fails equally as fiction and as extrapolation; for completists only.

**1967** *New Yorker* 38/1 (Sept. 16): Gerry de la Ree [...] identified himself as a forty-three-year-old "completist." "That means I buy everything that comes out in the field, and never throw anything away."

**1994–1995** J. VanderMeer *Infernal Desire Machines of Angela Carter* in *Why Should I Cut Your Throat?* (2004) 289: The Carter completist may wish to compare the United States and British versions of this story.

**2002** P. Kincaid *New York Rev. of SF* 1/2 (Dec.): The early volumes in particular were crowded with stories that had never been published before, most of them deservedly so, and that could have been of interest only to the obsessive completist.

**comset, commset** *n.* [*com*munication + *set*] a two-way communications device, especially one small enough to be easily carried, worn, or integrated into the helmet of a spacesuit. Compare COMLINK, SUIT-RADIO.

**1966** C. Anvil *Strangers to Paradise* in *Analog SF-Sci. Fact* (Oct.) 36/1: Some of the components the technicians left look to me like they'll work the 3-V on the comset here.

**1987** S. H. Elgin *Judas Rose* (2002) 14: Bellena shrugged, trim and handsome and larger than life on the comset screen of the desk.

**1992** G. D. Nordley *Poles Apart* in G. Dozois *Good New Stuff* (1999) 234: Mary left her comset on her belt, where it could see and record everything.

**1995** K. MacLeod *Star Fraction* (2001) 15: The gun was picking up electronic spillover from the bomb's circuitry [...] and bouncing it via the security guard's commset to British Telecom's on-line bomb-disposal expert system.

**2004** S. J. Van Scyoc *Virgin Wings* in *Mag. of Fantasy & SF* (Dec.) 50: An elderly man wearing a comm-set and a scarlet sash approached.

**con** *n.* [shortening of *convention*] a convention, especially one held by or for fans of science fiction, fantasy or related subjects such as comics, role-playing games, filk, etc.

**1942** L. Shaw *Planet Stories (letter)* (Spring) 128/2: Three more cheers for the 4 WS-F Con.

**1946** B. Tucker *Bloomington News-letter* (Apr) 1: Sixteen characters attended the First Post-Radar-Contact-With-the-Moon Con.

**1961** J. Koning *Withdrawal* in *S-F Five-Yearly* (Nov.) 25: Even before the con, the outgroup fanac of the circle had been dying, but after the con, and that party, the FOCUS group's interest seemed to turn entirely inward.

**1983** T. Nielsen Hayden *Hell, 12 Feet* in *Making Book* (1994) 72: I went to the Worldcon and the fannishness was thick and heady indeed, but what got me through the con was massive and systematic abuse of my medications.

**1990** *Con attendance (was Re: Can Comics Industry grow up?)* (Usenet: rec.arts.comics) (Oct. 6): I used to go SF and other types of cons. The only ones I go to nowadays are gaming cons.

**2005** *I-Con at Stony Brook?* (Usenet: rec.arts.sf.fandom) (Dec. 20): From my experience, it might be best to think of I-Con as five small cons in one, a literary con, a "media" con, an anime con, a comic con, and a gaming con.

**-con** *suff.* **1.** used in names of conventions, frequently in combination with a prefix referencing the location of the convention.

**1940** B. Tucker *Le Zombie* (Feb. 10) 4: CHICON CHAT DEPT

**1942** B. Tucker *Le Zombie* (May–June) 8: Two entirely different groups of writers produced the report [...] with Moskowitz, Van Houten and Taurasi writing on the Nycon itself.

**1951** M. Reynolds *Case of Little Green Men* 52: The tenth anniversary of the first World Science Fiction Convention is to be held here in this city in a few days, Lieutenant. We call it the AnnCon as an abbreviation of Anniversary Convention. The Eighth Convention, held in the Northwest, we called the NorWesCon; the one in New Orleans, Louisiana, was the NolaCon.

**1979** D. Schweitzer *Occasionally Mentioning SF SF Rev.* (Jan.) 33/3: You won't find very much of this at a worldcon or a large regional because only a fraction of the attendees are hardcore fans.

**1984** T. Nielsen Hayden *Over Rough Terrain* in *Making Book* (1994) 89: After Iguanacon my constructive fanac was almost entirely on paper.

**2004** D. Langford *Another Convention Diary: Torcon 3 Argentus* 12/2: In general, although the conrunning purists were bitterly critical, tradition and goodwill kept Torcon reasonably on course.

**2.** used generically in the names of conventions, with a prefix indicating the subject or focus of the convention. Compare RELAXACON.

**1944** J. B. Speer *Fancyclopedia* 30/2: Fancon—Name given a gathering in Bloomington around the end of 1943; possibly not intended as a distinctive proper name.

**1952** A. Budrys *Planet Stories (letter)* (Nov.) 111/1: If the mat for the liver pill ad comes in, out goes the stfcon publicity.

**1991** R. Rogow *Futurespeak* 330: The fans of STAR WARS battle the fans of STAR TREK in the pages of letterzines and through the panels of media-cons.

**1996** R. C. Harvey *Art of Comic Book* 47/2: In the summer of 1964 another convention for comics fans was conducted in New York by a fellow named Bernie Bubnis, who also coined the term "comicon."

**2005** *Conventions* (Usenet: rec.arts.sf.fandom) (Oct. 17): I don't much approve of non-fannish musicians showing up at a filkcon just to perform.

**congoer** *n.* a person who attends a con or cons.

**1960** *Profanity* (Feb.) 33: Were fen to know their work on behalf of the con-goer was appreciated, there might not be so much in evidence the reluctance to take on the duties of a committee.

**1969** H. Warner, Jr. *All Our Yesterdays* 275: Regular con-goers could be excused for the feeling that this was where they came in.

**1993** *Locus* (Oct.) 5/3: Downtown San Francisco proved to be a very atmospheric location, with the street people and the all-night activity providing an interesting setting for costumed con-goers.

**1996** J. Quick *Dragon Mag.* (Nov.) 68/2: Running the gamut of the role-playing community, we serve the young, the old, the hardened con-goers [...] and everyone who cares about role-playing games.

**conreport** *n.* a written description of an individual's experiences at a con.

**1953** R. Bloch *And now, from his own typer...* in *Quandry* (May–June) 18: That boy Willis has done it again! His is the Conreport to end all con reports, and for the life of me I don't know how he does it.

**1959** R. H. Eney *Fancyclopedia II* 172: A conreport of impressive bulk, *The Harp Stateside*, recorded Walt's adventures here and the campaign had much to do with development of the present *entente cordiale* between American and English fandom.

**1965** D. Hoylman *Twilight Zine* (Apr. 13) 29: Contents page notwithstanding, my article on Pacificon II was not intended to be a "conreport" in the usual sense.

**1992** H. Warner, Jr. *Wealth of Fable* 338: He criticized fanzine con reports in which "a detailing of the number of hamburgers consumed en route often consumes more wordage than a description of program events, and mention of a first meeting with a new fan from Squeegee, Wyoming is deemed more spaceworthy than an appraisal of the guest of honor."

**continuum** *n.* [shortening of *space-time continuum*] a universe.

**1946** G. O. Smith *Pattern for Conquest* in *Astounding SF* (May) 148/1: I doubt that the separation between different space continuums is infinitesimally small. [...] I predict that we are in the space next door to our own.

**1949** H. Kuttner *Hollywood on Moon* in *Startling Stories* (July) 122/1: It marks the orbit of a body in another continuum—a fourth dimensional continuum. It's a hole in space, a hole created by a planet in another Universe.

**1952** L. S. de Camp *Blunderer* in *Treasury of Great SF Stories No. 1* (1964) 74/2: Actually Antichthon is in the same continuum as Earth but at the other end, where the universe curves back on itself.

**1966** A. B. Chandler *Edge of Night* in *If* (Oct.) 127/1: And that was when this alternative universe, this continuum in which Grimes and his people were invaders, had run off the historical rails.

**1978** B. Shaw *Ship of Strangers* (1979) 188: It appears that we have an entire continuum to ourselves.

**1998** I. MacDonald *Days of Solomon Gursky* in G. Dozois *Mammoth Book of Best New SF, 12th Coll.* (1999) 253: PanLife, that amorphous, multi-faceted cosmic infection [...] had filled the universe long before the continuum reached its elastic limit and began to contract.

**2005** P. Di Filippo *Asimov's SF* (Mar.) 133/1: This deft, thrilling, steampunk excursion into an alternate continuum where Martian Heat-Ray technology and the perfection of Doctor Frankenstein's researches have resulted in a world-dominating twenty-first-century British Empire is one of the grandest counterfactual rides going.

**contraterrene** *adj. Obs.* made of anti-matter. Compare SEETEE, TERRENE.

**1941** R. S. Richardson *Inside Out Matter* in *Astounding S-F* (Dec.) 112/1: Contraterrene means just that—a type of matter exactly the opposite of ordinary or terrene matter. Instead of atoms composed of a positive nucleus surrounded by electrons, it consists of a negative nucleus surrounded by positrons.

**1943** [W. Stewart] *Opposites—React!* in *Astounding S-F* (Jan.) 11/2: That needle would seem to be an artifact—think of it—of contraterrene life!

**1946** [J. J. Coupling] *Astounding SF* (May) 105: We've known about atoms with protons and electrons for a long time; there have been suggestions of atoms with inverted structure—contraterrene atoms.

**1958** *Journal of British Interplanetary Society* (Vol. XVI) 540: Some of the larger meteor craters found on the Earth's surface [...] may have been due, not so much to meteors of earthlike matter and great size, but rather to the impact of anti-matter or contraterrene material.

**corflu** *n.* [correction *flu*id] a fluid which permits typographical errors to be corrected on, e.g., a mimeograph stencil or typewritten page.

**1960** J. Speer *Novus Ordo Fandorum* in *Fancestral Voices* (2004) 190: Of them who have not breathed corflu, never was one knighted to St. Fanthony.

**1972** R. Nelson *Intro. to Time Travel for Pedestrians* in H. Ellison *Again, Dangerous Visions* 139: Dreams of the Hugo while high on corflu (which you actually have gotten, at last, old superfan).

**1975** E. Weinstein *Fillostrated Fan Dictionary* 29: A brand name for Corflu used on bond paper is Liquid Paper.

**1996** F. M. Busby *Progress is Where You Find It* in *SF Five-Yearly* (Nov.) 5: Composing on stencil requires alert concentration; a fan in a hurry can't afford too many pauses for the application of Corflu.

**corpsesicle, corpsicle** *n.* [*corps(e)*, + *ic*icle or pop*sicle*] a person in cold sleep.

**1966** R. C. W. Ettinger *Worlds of Tomorrow* (Nov.) 71/2: His wife, Mildred, has made many contributions, including a new name for the frozen, brittle people: Homo Snapiens. (This is certainly more dignified than Fred Pohl's "corpsesicles.")

**1969** F. Pohl *Age of Pussyfoot* 210: It is true, however, that no corpsicle has yet been thawed and returned to life.

**1986** L. M. Bujold *Shards of Honor* in *Cordelia's Honor* (1999) 245: I guess you would get—pretty hardened, after a while. Is it true you guys call them corpse-sicles?

**1997** G. Bear *Slant* (1998) 5: The frozen near-dead are another matter. [...] The corpsicles racked in their special refrigerated cells in Omphalos, Giffey believes, might be worth several hundred million dollars apiece.

**cosy catastrophe** *n.* a disaster or post-apocalypse story which focuses on a character or characters who take advantage of the situation to pursue self-indulgent pleasures and attempt to rebuild society according to their (usually white and middle-class) values.

**1973** B. W. Aldiss *Billion Year Spree* 293: It was then that he embarked on the course that was to make him master of the cosy catastrophe. *The Day of the Triffids*, by John Wyndham, was serialised in *Colliers*, and appeared in hardcover in England in 1951.

**1995** D. Broderick *Reading by Starlight* 26: Our attention is directed to the soothing benefits of a reasserted background order. [...]

Interestingly, this is precisely the dynamic which governs the narrative choices of [...] the John Wyndham "cosy catastrophe" formula.

**1999** A. Sawyer in I. Q. Hunter *British SF Cinema* 76: These ideas are not completely incompatible with the concept of the "cosy catastrophe"—it can be argued that competent bourgeois Mandarins who triumph over catastrophe to reinsert the values of England and the Empire are as "bleakly Darwinian" as any other example of bleak Darwinians.

**2003** *Mainstream Writers who dabbled in SF* (Usenet: rec.arts.sf.written) (Sept. 25): It's one of the first "cosy catastrophes" in that everyone else is dead but the narrator can still find food and Burgundy when he wants to.

**counter-gravity** *n.* anti-gravity.

**1951** N. Bond *Vital Factor* in *No Time Like Future* (1954) 10: I've solved their secret. My idea is based on the principle that lets them fly. Electromagnetism. Utilization of the force of gravity. Or its opposite: counter[-]gravity.

**1952** I. Asimov *Currents of Space* in *Astounding SF* (Oct.) 11/2: They would skim along, a foot above the road, gliding on the cushioned smoothness of the counter-gravity field.

**1978** B. Shaw *Ship of Strangers* (1979) 146: She paused and electrostatically cleansed herself of the dust, pebbles and spacefield litter that were swirling within her counter-gravity field.

**2006** *Stimulating gravity with idealized thrust—what are the complications?* (Usenet: rec.arts.sf.science) (Mar. 20): Anybody remember that station-on-the-Sun story from long ago in which the counter-gravity was provided by such a cyclotron in the ceiling?

**craft** *n.* a SPACESHIP. Compare BOAT, CRUISER, SHIP, SPACE CAN, SPACE CAR, SPACECRAFT, SPACE CRUISER, SPACE FLYER, SPACER 2, SPACE VEHICLE, SPACE VESSEL, TIN CAN, VESSEL.

**1934** E. E. Smith *Triplanetary* in *Amazing Stories* (Jan.) 28/1: Finally they were out in open space, shooting toward distant Tellus at the maximum acceleration of which their small craft was capable.

**1946** M. W. Wellman *Solar Invasion* in *Startling Stories* (Fall) 18/1: Quickly Joan set the beam-mechanism which would serve as a tow-rope between her own craft and the *Comet*, and within five minutes they had cleared Asteroid No. 697 on the Earthward trail.

**1979** P. Anderson *Ways of Love* in *Destinies* (Jan.–Feb.) 12: This craft had chanced to pass near enough a burnt-out black dwarf that they changed her program and put her in orbit around it for scientific study.

**1985** R. Rucker & B. Sterling *Storming Cosmos* in B. Sterling *Globalhead* (1994) 26: In an accidental crash, a socially advanced alien pilot would naturally guide his stricken craft to one of the planet's "poles of uninhabitedness."

**1993** *SF Age* (Jan.) 65/2: When you see all these craft coming out of hyperspace, the effect is staggering.

**credit** *n.* a unit of currency, often the basic unit of currency of a future culture.

**1934** J. W. Campbell, Jr. *Mightiest Machine* in *Astounding Stories* (Dec.) 23/1: Right enough, and tell me why I have to build that five-million-credit flying laboratory.

**1941** I. Asimov *Nightfall* in R. Silverberg *SF Hall of Fame, Vol. I* (1970) 161: It cost two thousand credits.

**1957** R. Silverberg *Neutral Planet* in *World of Thousand Colors* (1984) 200: The twin planets had become visible—uninhabited Fasolt a violet ball the size of a quarter-credit piece dead ahead.

**1972** A. D. Foster *Tar-Aiym Krang* 23: If I give no answer I will refund your credits.

**1982** A. McCaffrey *Crystal Singer* 227: Those black crystals brought you a total of twenty-three thousand credits.

**1993** J. Pournelle & S. M. Stirling *Prince of Sparta* 183: We be needing CS credits and Friedlander marks someday too.

**croggle** *v.* [*crush* + *goggle* or perh. b*oggle*] to astound, shock, or bewilder. Hence **croggled,** *adj.* Also **becroggle.**

**1959** R. H. Eney *Fancyclopedia II* (1979) 38: *Croggle* (Grennell), roughly meaning shocked into momentary physical or mental paralysis; a portmanteau-word, apparently, combining "crushed" and "goggled," and usually passive or reflexive in application.

**1962** B. Kujawa *Cry (letter)* (June) 24: Ella said he brought her a lil box of panties (yes...panties!) with appropriate lil sayings on them...am properly croggled and would like to know what those "sayings" were.

**1967** A. Budrys *Benchmarks* (1985) 133: But the best editors have always had a reasonably well defined group of writers clustered around them; what croggles me here is that they're somebody else's group.

**1980** M. Z. Bradley *Darkover Retrospective* in *Planet Savers/Sword of Aldones* (1982) 347: When I finally figured out that she was asking if I was sad at not winning a Nebula, I was becroggled. I finally found my voice and told her that in twenty-five years of reading and writing science fiction, I had heard a hell of a lot of gauche questions, but that really took the cake.

**1997** *Fish, chips & Pam Wells.* (Usenet: rec.arts.sf.fandom) (May 20): I croggled a bit at this; I mean, I can't think of a shop here other than delis that would have as many as 12 different olives.

**2002** *Unbelievable.* (Usenet: rec.arts.sf.fandom) (June 17): We croggled the attendants and the folks standing in line by getting in the cars, three rows of us, and singing (with hand motions).

**crudzine** *n.* a fanzine of poor quality.

**1975** E. Weinstein *Fillostrated Fan Dictionary* 32: Crudzine[...]: An entire fanzine of CRUD.

**1977** S. Wood *Propellor Beanie* in *Algol* Summer–Fall (23/1): It's really easy to start a genzine. All you need are a couple of neos with lots of time and enthusiasm [...] and a certain amount of mood-enhancers and sheer lunacy to get you to the point at which the thing stops being a great idea for Real Soon Now, and starts being a reality. A lot of crudzines are born that way.

**1991** T. Nielsen Hayden *Pastafazool Cycle* in *Making Book* (1994) 157: It is regrettable that Bowling Green's publications can sometimes make crudzines look good.

**1999** M. J. Pustz *Comic Book Culture* 182: Called "crudzines" by critics, many of these particularly amateurish magazines lasted only a few issues as fans quickly began to focus their energies on the more successful, well-respected publications.

**cruiser** *n.* a SPACESHIP. COMPARE BOAT, CRAFT, SHIP, SPACE CAN, SPACE CAR, SPACE-CRAFT, SPACE CRUISER, SPACE FLYER, SPACER, SPACE VEHICLE, SPACE VESSEL, TIN CAN, VESSEL.

**1912** E. R. Burroughs *Princess of Mars* (1917) 277: I rose steadily and at terrific speed raced through the Martian sky followed by [ . . . ] a swift cruiser carrying a hundred men and a battery of rapid-fire guns.

**1934** J. Williamson *Legion of Space* in *Astounding Stories* (June) 114/2: "Another legion cruiser," observed Jay Kalam. "Scouring space for the *Purple Dream!*"

**1954** T. Godwin *Cold Equations* in R. Silverberg *SF Hall of Fame, Vol. I* (1970) 480: When a call for aid was received the nearest cruiser would drop into normal space long enough to launch an EDS with the needed supplies or personnel.

**1974** J. Haldeman *Forever War* (1976) 204: They wheeled around to intercept the second cruiser, by then a few light-hours away, still being harassed by fifteen enemy drones.

**1985** M. Larson *Pawns & Symbols* 173: As a matter of fact, cruiser time is out of sync with planet time.

**2004** G. Wolfe *Prize Crew* in *Postscripts* (Spring) 45/1: We found that Miscreet ship abandoned three days after the battle—a light cruiser from the look of her, just drifting way out between suns.

**cryostasis** *n.* COLD SLEEP.

**1975** [J. Tiptree, Jr.] *Momentary Taste of Being* in *Her Smoke Rose up Forever* (2004) 286: Ninety-percent viability after ten-year cryostasis.

**1993** J. Brunner *Muddle Earth* 11–12: I told you: he faked his death and cryostasis!

**1998** W. Shatner *Spectre* 84: Seven are in cryostasis awaiting burial.

**2001** *Interzone* (July) 41/2: We found decayed bodies in thick frozen brine and thought it was cryostasis gone wrong.

**cyberpunk** *n.* **1. a.** [*cyber*netics + *punk*] a subgenre of science fiction that focuses on the effects on society and individuals of advanced computer technology, artificial intelligence, and bionic implants in an increasingly global culture, especially as seen in the struggles of streetwise, disaffected characters.

[ **1983** B. Bethke (title) *Amazing Stories* (Nov.) 94: Cyberpunk ]

**1984** G. Dozois *SF in Eighties* in *Washington Post Book World* (Dec. 30) 9/3: But surely the wild and woolly "outlaw fantasy" Waldrop began producing in the '70s played some part in shaping the esthetics and literary style of the "cyberpunk" movement.

**1988** *Times Literary Supplement* (Oct. 21) 1180/3: The subgenre of science fiction now widely known as Cyberpunk, in which life in the computerized jungle of the near future can only be survived by young street-wise masters of software interfaces and the arts of combat.

**1992** *SF Age* (Nov.) 70/2: Many of us no longer conceive of [ . . . ] a world where computers and electronic networks and free exchange of information enhance our lives rather than creating the grisly world of cyberpunk.

**1996** B. Sterling *Workshop Lexicon* in R. Wilson *Paragons* 352: In proper ideologically-correct cyberpunk fashion, the Turkey City Lexicon was distributed uncopyrighted and free of charge.

**2000** *Interzone* (Feb.) 52/1: If cyberpunk has an enduring characteristic, it is not so much the fusing of information technology and Chandleresque *noir*, but the rejection of the monolithic futures of traditional science fiction in favour of fragmentation, plurality and a gleeful inversion of the accepted power-structures.

**b.** a writer of such stories; occasionally, a character in such stories.

**1984** G. Dozois *SF in Eighties* in *Washington Post Book World* (Dec. 30) 9/1: About the closest thing here to a self-willed esthetic "school" would be the purveyors of bizarre hard-edged, high-tech stuff, who have on occasion been referred to as "cyberpunks"—Sterling, Gibson, Shiner, Cadigan, Bear.

**1991** *Fantasy* (Spring) 37/1: What do you think of the experimental, and often deliberately controversial, fiction of the New Wave, Cyberpunks, etc.?

**1996** D. Pringle, et al. *Ultimate Ency. of SF* 56/2: There are many young people in the world who ardently desire to *be* cyberpunks; they regard the rapidly-expanding and fundamentally anarchic Internet as their natural environment.
**2006** P. Di Filippo *Washingtonpost.com (Internet)* (Jan. 15): There have been at least two subsequent generations of cyberpunks since that school of science fiction broke big in 1984.

**2.** someone who illegally accesses computer networks, often with malicious intent.

**1989** C. Stoll *Cuckoo's Egg* 245: This was a sensitive medical device, not a plaything for some cyberpunk. Some poor computer geek, indeed.
**1992** B. Sterling *Hacker Crackdown* 56: I exempt the word "cyberpunk," which a few hackers and law enforcement people actually do use. The term is drawn from literary criticism and has some odd and unlikely resonances, but, like hacker, cyberpunk too has become a criminal pejorative today.
**1993** *Wired* (Sept./Oct.) 90/2: Cyberpunks are setting the stage for a coming digital counterculture that will turn the '90s zeitgeist utterly on its head.

**cyberpunkish** *adj.* resembling or reminiscent of cyberpunk. Hence **uncyberpunkish,** *adj.*

**1989** I. Watson *World Renews Itself* in M. Bishop *Nebula Awards 23* 9: Pat Cadigan's first novel, *Mindplayers*, explores the fast track of the brain-wired consciousness industry in hardbitten, wisecracking, cyberpunkish style.
**1990** K. Rolston *Dragon Mag.* (Feb.) 56/2: The SHADOWRUN campaign setting is a cyberpunkish 21st century minus the spaceflight and plus a major, uncyberpunkish twist—the Awakening of Magic.
**1992** *Locus* (Aug.) 13/1: "Death of Reason" is a very good near-future cyberpunkish detective thriller, featuring lots of interesting gizmos like biostatic technology.
**1996** *SFX* (May) 24/3: The final piece of the definition I favour is clan-identity. This is seen in many "cyberpunk-ish" stories, in terms of both the street gangs and the corporate structure.

**cyberspace** *n.* the entirety of the data stored in, and the communication that takes place within, a computer network, conceived of as having the properties of a physical realm; the environment of virtual reality. Compare MATRIX.

**1982** W. Gibson *Burning Chrome* in *Omni* (July) 72/2: I knew every chip in Bobby's simulator by heart; it looked like your workaday Ono-Sendai VII, the "Cyberspace Seven."
**1984** W. Gibson *Neuromancer* (1989) 51: Cyberspace. A consensual hallucination experienced daily by billions of legitimate operators, in every nation, by children being taught mathematical concepts [...]. A graphic representation of data abstracted from the banks of every computer in the human system.
**1991** H. Rheingold *Virtual Reality* (1992) 17: Although I stayed in cyberspace for just a few minutes, that first brief flight through a computer-created universe launched me on my own odyssey to the outposts of a new scientific frontier.
**1993** *S-F Studies* (Nov.) 451: In a hypertext digressions of any length can be hidden in the cyberspace "behind" any word or image on the screen.
**1996** *SFX* (May) 38/3: I also wanted some sense of the "rush" of travelling through cyberspace, the sense a hacker has of the different computer networks all being linked together, like a modern city with all of its fibre-optic connections.

**cyborg** *n.* [*cyb*ernetic + *org*anism] a creature whose body has been modified to extend its abilities beyond its normal limitations; a creature whose body consists of both biological and mechanical elements. Compare POSTHUMAN, TRANSHUMAN.

**1960** *New York Times* (May 22) 31/1: A cyborg is essentially a man-machine system in which the control mechanisms of the human portion are modified externally by drugs or regulatory devices so that the being can live in an environment different from the normal one.
**1966** F. Herbert *Eyes of Heisenberg* in *Galaxy Mag.* (Aug.) 143/1: From the shoulders down, where Glisson's arms had been, now dangled only the empty linkages for Cyborg prosthetic attachments.
**1971** [J. Tiptree, Jr.] *Mother in Sky with Diamonds* in *Galaxy Mag.* (Mar.) 148/1: The old cyborg op couldn't care less. He had

electrode jacks all over his skull and his knuckles sprouting wires.

**1985** G.R.R. Martin *Manna from Heaven* in *Analog SF/Sci. Fact* (mid-Dec.) 32/1: Roggandor's cyborg ambassador was as broad as he was tall, made in equal parts of stainless duralloy, dark plasteel, and mottled red-black flesh.

**2003** A. M. Steele *Madwoman of Shuttlefield* in *Asimov's SF* (May) 70: A Savant: a posthuman who had once been flesh and blood until he'd relinquished his humanity to have his mind downloaded into cyborg form, becoming an immortal intellect.

**cyborg** *v.* to make someone into a CYBORG.

**1976** J. Varley *Bagatelle* in *Galaxy, Incorporating Worlds of If* (Oct.) 16/2: Something always distracted me. So when I heard of this place where they would cyborg me and get rid of all that, I jumped at the chance.

**1987** N. Spinrad *Little Heroes* (1989) 20: You just do the best you can and our wizards will cyborg you into a superstar.

**1988** *Locus* (Apr.) 27/2: Richard Paul Russo's "Listen to My Heartbeat" involves a woman who has cyborged herself for spaceflight, and her boyfriend who couldn't bring himself to do the same.

**1995** *Interzone* (Jan.) 57/2: It is set forty years after Roger Torraway was unwillingly cyborged to enable him to explore Mars without needing external life support systems.

**cyborged** *adj.* made into a CYBORG.

**1976** J. Varley *Bagatelle* in *Galaxy, Incorporating Worlds of If* (Oct.) 11/2: It's a cyborged human connected to a bomb, probably a uranium device.

**1983** N. Spinrad *Void Captain's Tale* (1984) 104: Did I seek to experience the subjective eternity of the Great and Lonely through which my machineries had propelled my cyborged demon lover through feedback with the Circuit?

**1993** J. J. Pierce *Intro.* in [C. Smith] *Rediscovery of Man* ix: "Scanners" [...] the bizarre tale of the cyborged space pilots who are dead though they live, and would rather kill than live with a new discovery that has made their sacrifice and its attendant rituals obsolete.

**cyborging** *n.* the process or act of making someone into a CYBORG.

**1978** R. Lupoff *Algol* (Nov.) 51/1: It deals with the modification of a human being, through surgery, biological conditioning and cyborging techniques, to "become" a "Martian."

**1989** O. S. Card *Mag. of Fantasy & SF* (Aug.) 32/2: Do you want to read a serious extrapolative novel, [...] in which cyborging, brain transplants, and genetically-altered chimeras bring new wonders and new horrors to humanity?

**1997** D. Weber & S. White *In Death Ground* (2000) 57: His Orglons represented the obscene end-product of the unrestricted cyborging on which humankind had turned its back after some bad experiences in the twenty-first century.

**cyborgisation, cyborgization** *n.* CYBORGING.

**1994** B. Stableford *Les Fleurs du Mal in Asimov's SF* (Oct.) 125: He was playing about with brainfeed equipment [...]. Not just memory boxes or neural stimulators, but mental cyborgization.

**1996** D. Pringle, et al. *Ultimate Ency. of SF* 41/2: Stories dealing with the cyborgization of humans for the purpose of exploring other worlds include Arthur C. Clarke's "A Meeting With Medusa."

**2001** A. Reynolds *Chasm City* 48: The Chimerics in general had taken cyborgisation to new extremes, blending themselves and their animals with machines.

**cyborgised, cyborgized** *adj.* CYBORGED.

**1989** O. S. Card *Mag. of Fantasy & SF* (Aug.) 32/2: Watch these people in flux—cyborgized, rejuvenated, crippled, genetically altered; dehumanized as refugees, samurais, mercenaries, machines.

**1996** D. Pringle, et al. *Ultimate Ency. of SF* 41/2: Various Doctor Who adventures [...] featured the cyborgized alien Daleks.

**2000** B. Stableford *Fountains of Youth* 304: There were not quite so many who felt that the work of galactic exploration ought to be the province of cyborgized humans rather than silver-piloted probes.

# d

**dalek** *n.* ['dælɛk] [coined by Terry Nation for the BBC television series *Doctor Who*. Nation originally claimed that he got the word from the spine of an encyclopedia volume "dal–lek," but later retracted that claim.] in the *Doctor Who* universe, one of a race of evil mutant cyborgs; in general use, a monster, robot, or automaton.

**1963** *Radio Times* (Dec. 26) 11/1: Dalek voices: Peter Hawkins, David Graham.
**1979** *Nation* 181/2 (Sept. 8): Derek Jenkins [...] feels dehumanized by what he does. Even punching a time clock at the start of the day "is an act of surrender." The strange work clothes— goggles, masks and the other protective paraphernalia—make a man march like "a Dalek to your machine."
**1989** *Ottawa Citizen* (ProQuest) (Apr. 18): You are met by a dalek on wheels that lumbers to the main terminal. Why can't planes pull up at the main terminal?
**1993** *Guardian (London)* (ProQuest) (Aug. 28): The playwright Dennis Potter yesterday likened the heads of the BBC to a "pair of croak-voiced Daleks" who had led the organisation into a near-fatal crisis.

**dark side** *n.* **1.** the side of an object in space (such as a spaceship or planet) that faces away from the closest star. Compare FARSIDE.

**1939** N. S. Bond *Mercurian Menace* in *Dynamic Science Stories* (Feb.) 62/1: The things that destroyed Galactic's darkside station in two weeks without even leaving a trace behind.
**1956** A. Bester *Stars My Destination* (1996) 17: Great rents in the hull were blazes of light on the sunside and frosty blotches of stars on the darkside.
**1972** *Oakland (Cal.) Tribune* (Apr. 19) 2F/3: Young, Duke and Thomas K. Mattingly II climaxed a three-day, 240,000-mile outward journey from earth by sweeping behind the moon's darkside at 12:09 p.m. PST today.
**1998** M. Flynn *Rogue Star* (1999) 270: Night lived on Darkside. The sun had not touched it for tens of thousands of years, perhaps eons.

**2.** (often *cap.*) the force of evil.

**1976** G. Lucas *Adventures of Luke Starkiller* (Mar. 15) 42: He used the power of the force for evil [...]. Vader was seduced by the dark side of the force and it consumed him.
**1995** S. Adams *Dilbert* in *Syracuse (New York) Herald-Journal* (Jan. 18) D13: I can't decide if I should stay with engineering or pursue a career in management. In my heart I'm an engineer but I hear a voice calling me to the dark side.
**1997** [J. K. Rowling] *Harry Potter & Sorcerer's Stone* (1999) 110: He says Malfoy's father didn't need an excuse to go over to the Dark Side.
**2005** K. Reed *Paranoia & What Follows* in *New York Rev. of SF* (Oct.) 6/1: The darkside abides, but it doesn't always prevail.

**dayside** *n.* the side of an object in space (such as a spaceship or planet) that faces the closest star.

**1914** J. R. Kippax *Call of Stars* 334: The day side of the Moon is exposed to the Sun's intense heat for a fortnight at a stretch.

**1942** C. L. Moore *There Shall Be Darkness* in *Astounding S-F* (Feb.) 20/2: Artificial lighting is rare on Venus, which never knows true darkness on Dayside.

**1961** *Gettysburg (Pa.) Times* (Apr. 14) 1/7: Gagarin told how the night and dayside of the earth looked from space.

**1988** A. C. Clarke *2061: Odyssey Three* 109: The only safe way to study places like dayside Mercury.

**1994** [L. A. Graf] *Firestorm* 2: Kirk shook his head in wonderment, turning back toward where the roiling black mass was quickly obscuring a large swath of the planet's dayside.

**death ray** *n.* a weapon that fires a beam which kills anyone struck by it; the beam produced by such a weapon.

**1915** A. B. Reeve *Exploits of Elaine* in *Lima (Oh.) News* (Mar. 21) 26/1: CHAPTER IX.—THE DEATH RAY.

**1924** *New York Times* (May 25) 1/2: Dr. T. F. Wall, lecturer in electrical research in Sheffield University, claims to have discovered a "death ray."

**1943** J. W. Campbell, Jr. *Astounding S-F* (Jan.) 6/1: A death ray might conceivably be a sort of catalyst—a peculiar form of energy, very little of which could upset the delicate chemistry of life.

**1961** J. B. Priestley *Saturn over Water* 85: You may have some ridiculous ideas [ . . . ] that we are [ . . . ] discovering fantastic gases or death rays out of science fiction.

**1998** C. Pellegrino *Afterword* in C. Pellegrino & G. Zebrowski *Dyson Sphere* (1999) 219: Riding an antimatter rocket is like riding a giant death ray bomb: you want to put as much distance as possible between yourself and the engine.

**deep space** *n.* **1.** the region of space between stars or far from the home star.

**1934** E. E. Smith *Triplanetary* in *Amazing Stories* (Apr.) 54/1: Bradley swore a mighty deep-space oath and braced himself against certain annihilation.

**1939** E. E. Smith *Grey Lensman* in *Astounding S-F* (Oct.) 26/2: Like most of the girls here, I suppose, I have never been out in deep space at all. Besides a few hops to the moon, I have taken only two flits, and they were both only interplanetary.

**1945**: see quote in HOMEWORLD.

**1959** J. J. McGuire *To Catch Alien* in F. Pohl *Star SF No. 6* 112: Look how bad things were for a while when we went out into deep space, how many planets were colonized by mutinous crews.

**1972** M. Z. Bradley *Darkover Landfall* (1989) 126: This morning I've got to tell a deep-space communications expert with absolutely no other skills, that his job is completely obsolete for at least ten generations.

**1976** C. Holland *Floating Worlds* (1977) 89: I've never been in a deepspace ship before.

**1991** M. Weiss *King's Test* 5: The guard [ . . . ] looked as if he wished the ship's hull would crack open, suck him into deepspace.

**2.** the region of space outside the Earth's atmosphere.

**1954** *Journal of British Interplanetary Society* 16 (Vol. XIII): These specialized "deep-space" rocket vehicles would, of course, be re-fuelled and serviced from satellite ships.

**1969** *Daily Telegraph (London)* (Jan. 11) 1/4: They will also send back to Earth information about deep space during the 155 million-mile journey [ to Venus ].

**2002** G. Dyson *Project Orion* 205: By deploying them in individual orbits in deep space, maximum security and warning can be obtained. At these altitudes, an enemy attack would require a day or more from launch to engagement.

**deflector** *n.* a force field that protects something (such as a spaceship or city) from potentially harmful objects or energy. Also **deflector field, shield,** etc.

**1945**: See quote in BLASTER.

**1949** A. Coppel *Runaway* in *Planet Stories* (Spring) 33/2: In those days no one had ever heard of deflectors, and a free passage through the Belt was a one in a thousand chance.

**1968** G. Coon *Arena ("Star Trek" script)* (Nov. 3) 9: We've returned fire with all phaser banks. Negative against his deflector screen.

**1970** R. Silverberg *Tower of Glass* in *Galaxy Mag.* (June) 83/2: In flight, an automatic deflector field surrounds the ship to ward off all oncoming free-floating particles, which of course could be enormously destructive at such velocities.

**1980** D. F. Glut *Empire Strikes Back* 207: "The deflector shields are going," he reported to Leia and Chewbacca.

**1985** M. W. Bonanno *Dwellers in Crucible* 44: Vulcan cities were deflector screened against the worst weather.

**different story** *n.* a science fiction or fantasy story. Now *hist.*

**1928** *Amazing Stories* (Sept.) 513: Here again we have the perfect "different" story. Dr. Keller has picked a subject which, to the best of our knowledge, has never been used in Scientifiction before, and it makes a most interesting exposure of heredity in general.

**1932** *Amazing Stories* (Aug.) 386/1: Mr. Jones, noted for his Professor Jameson series, has some very interesting theories on this subject, which he propounds in very vivid manner in this entirely "different" story.

**1945** S. Moskowitz *Immortal Storm* in *Fantasy Commentator* 171 (Fall): He was, moreover, the leading advocate of science fiction with the accent on science. Not scientific romances, fantasies, or "different" stories, but *science*-fiction.

**1988** L. S. de Camp & C. C. de Camp *Business of SF* in J. Gunn *New Ency. of SF* 76/2: In America in the early 1900s, the Munsey Company published in its magazines what it called "different stories," many of which would later be called SF.

**dimension** *n.* a universe coexistent with our own, but which cannot be perceived or accessed by ordinary means and which often possesses different physical laws; an ALTERNATE REALITY or PARALLEL UNIVERSE. Also *fig.* Compare PLANE.

[**1896** H. G. Wells *Plattner Story* in *New Review* (Apr.) 352: The curious inversion of Plattner's right and left sides is proof that he has moved out of our space into what is called the Fourth Dimension, and that he has returned again to our world.]

**1922** H. G. Wells *Men like Gods* (1923) 22: And now he imagines himself in some sort of scientific romance and out of our world altogether. In another dimension.

**1931** *Wonder Stories (letter)* (Mar.) 1193/1: I was told that there were many more such races in the universe, though in other dimensions.

**1931** C. Hamilton *Garden of Delight* in *Fitchburgh (Mass.) Sentinel* (Aug. 1) 7/4: Their places were taken by a blaze of love, passion and desire which seemed to shake the stand. Her hand trembled under his touch and he and she stood for a moment in another world, another dimension.

**1933** H. P. Lovecraft *Dreams in Witch-House* in *Weird Tales* (July) 102/2: One might, for example, pass into a timeless dimension and emerge at some remote period of the earth's history as young as before.

**1952** L. Falk & P. Davis *Mandrake Magician* in *Humboldt Standard (Eureka, Cal.)* (Aug. 16) 1A: This isn't an ordinary door frame. It's a "doorway" to another dimension, another world!

**1977** C. Kapp *Chaos Weapon* 49: "Why does he flicker like that?" "Because he travels in several dimensions, of which this is only one. He visits the others constantly, thus at no time is he fully here."

**1979** P. Anderson *Gate of Flying Knives* in I. Asimov, et al. *Mammoth Book of Short Fantasy Novels* (1986) 20: Philosophers of a later, more rationalistic era elaborated this into a theory of parallel universes. [...] You will understand that my condition has made me especially interested in the theory of dimensions.

**2001** *Cult Times* (Feb.) 67/4: A girl is kidnapped on her wedding day by a telepathic criminal who has travelled from a parallel dimension to find her, because she is identical to his lost love in his own world.

**dimensional** *adj.* between dimensions.

[**1928** K. Meadowcroft *Invisible Bubble* in *Amazing Stories* (Sept.) 510/2: They are apparently harmless to life but they seem to be closely associated with the dimensional relations of matter.]

**1933** H. P. Lovecraft *Dreams in Witch-House* in *Weird Tales* (July) 102/1: It was by no means impossible that Keziah had actually mastered the art of passing through dimensional gates.

**1944** L. Brackett *Veil of Astellar* in *Thrilling Wonder Stories* (Spring) 59/2: Dimensional walls are no barrier to thought.

**1959** F. C. Gale *Galaxy Mag.* (June) 141/2: Spaceships long gone, they resort to dimensional travel via the "Star Gate," winding up on an alternate Gorth where their counterparts have made an even greater mess of the planet.
**1986** *Appendix* in G.R.R. Martin *Wild Cards* 409: A salient feature of the so-called "gadgets"—anti-gravity belts, dimensional portals, armored suits—is the fact that none of them can be replicated.

**dirtside** *adv.* on or to the surface of a planet or moon (as opposed to in space).
**1953** R. A. Heinlein *Starman Jones* 64: If you mess it up, I'll leave you dirtside and raise without you.
**1955** [A. North] *Sargasso of Space* (1957) 30: We can fuel this ship for one trip—one trip. If we make it to Limbo and there's no return cargo—well, [...] you know what that will mean—dirt-side for us!
**1987** C. Claremont *FirstFlight* 33: That same week, the Mission Specialists began loading and stowing their gear, the crew spending as much time aboard the spacecraft as dirtside at DaVinci.
**1994** L. M. Bujold *Mirror Dance* 19: The third crate, smaller than the second, proved to contain a set of half-armor, lacking built-in weapons and not meant for space, but rather for dirtside combat.
**2003** H. Phillips *Gate between Hope & Glory* in S. Lee & S. Miller *Low Port* 47: You're afraid that if the bosses [...] find him with unauthorized personnel they maybe won't bother with a shuttle when they send him dirtside, yeah?

**dirtsider** *n.* a person who lives on a planet.
**1992** A. McCaffrey & M. Lackey *Ship Who Searched* (2002) 2: He decided to get married, raise a brood of his own, and settle down as a dirtsider.
**2001** D. Gerrold *Bouncing off Moon* 26: I do not think anyone will go to Earth for a long time. I certainly will not. I have Luna muscles, Luna bones. I have no desire to be toothpick-man on planet of crazy dirtsiders.
**2003** K. Lowachee *Burndrive* 10: He couldn't imagine never setting foot on a station, especially with Pax Terra so near Earth. Dirtsiders were an odd bunch sometimes.

**disaster novel** *n.* a work that portrays a global catastrophe (of natural, man-made, or extraterrestrial origin) and its aftermath. Also **disaster story.** [Often used in the film industry to refer to disasters on a much smaller scale.]
[**1959** *Lima (Oh.) News* (May 1) 11/6: She has been rented by producer Andy Stone for his new picture, a disaster story based on a sinking ship.]
**1975** *New York Times Book Rev.* (Nov. 23) 53/1: From the team that brought you the screenplay of *The Glass Inferno* comes a disaster novel [*The Prometheus Crisis*] that makes their earlier effort seem pale as a cookout.
**1979** D. Pringle in P. Nicholls *Ency. of SF* 173/1: American disaster novels are fewer in number. Oddly enough, where British writers reveal an obsession with the weather, American writers show a strong concern for disease.
**1985** M. Drabble *Oxford Companion to English Literature (Fifth Ed.)* (1991) 34/1: The term "apocalyptic literature" is used in a broader sense to describe prophetic writings generally, of a range which includes many of the works of Blake, [...] the "disaster" novels of J. G. Ballard, and other Science Fiction writers, etc.
**1987** J. J. Pierce *Great Themes of SF* 143: John Christopher (1922–) is a specialist in the realistic, Earthbound disaster novel, and his "No Blade of Grass" [...] is typical of the school: A mutant virus infects the world's grain crops, leaving billions to face starvation.
**2004** R. K. J. Killheffer *Mag. of Fantasy & SF* (Oct./Nov.) 44/2: It's frightening, as any consideration of impending catastrophe must be, but in a quieter, more theoretical way than a conventional disaster story.

**disintegrator** *n.* a weapon that reduces its target to its component parts. Also **disintegrator ray.**
**1925**: See quote in BLASTER.
**1939** C. D. Simak *Cosmic Engineers* in *Astounding S-F* (Apr.) 138/1: The disintegrators, crystallizing a much vaster field of energy, might accomplish the destruction of a universe.
**1951** S. A. Peeples, D. A. Kyle & M. Greenberg *Dictionary of SF* in M. Greenberg

*Travelers of Space* 19: A disintegrator totally destroys matter by molecular dissemination.

**1993** D. Beason & K. J. Anderson *Assemblers of Infinity* 42: Is there a disintegrator ray out there, zapping anything that happens to trespass on the construction site?

**2005** T. Oliveira *Beyond Rift* 40/2: This incredibly durable disintegrator is capable of putting out heavy point damage under the right conditions.

**disruptor** *n.* a variety of energy weapon. Also **disrupter.**

**1931** N. Schachner & A. L. Zagat *Emperor of Stars* in *Wonder Stories* (Apr.) 1216/2: The disruptor rays had absolutely no effect upon these creatures. Matter was differently constituted here—earth forces were unable to break up these atoms.

**1953** A. Norton *Star Rangers* 52: Rolth used a palm disrupter as lightly as a color brush to etch into its side the name, homeworld, and the rank of that thin wasted body they had laid to rest there.

**1957** T. Sturgeon *It Opens Sky* in *Man Who Lost Sea* (2005) 68: In his hand, steady as an I-beam, rested a sonic disrupter aimed at Deeming's midsection.

**1968** G. Coon *Arena ("Star Trek" script)* (Nov. 3) 7: We're hopelessly outnumbered. Our hand phasers against those disruptors...

**1986** L. M. Bujold *Shards of Honor* (1991) 9: The officer's belt hung heavy with equipment, but the disruptor holster on his right hip was empty, as was the plasma arc holster on his left.

**1997** L. Shepard *Vermillion* (Mar.) 10: Apart from a ringing in my ears, there were only the whining of disruptor fire.

**doomwatch** *n.* [the name of a BBC television series which aired from 1970–72] observation with the intent to avert or mitigate environmental disasters, especially those caused by human activities.

[**1970** *New Scientist* (Apr. 2) 3/2: BBC-TV's new scientific soap-opera, *Doomwatch*, has been fortunate in its first selection of topics to warn us about.]

**1970** *Guardian (London)* (Dec. 23) 1/1: The Government Chemist [...] tested 50 tins of tuna bought throughout the country [...]. Mr Prior

said: [...] "We shall be getting on with this—this Doomwatch, if you like to call it that."

**1977** *Geographical Journal* (July) 295: Bruce Campbell, in a refreshingly non-doomwatch analysis of the prospects for wild life, emphasizes the wide and intelligent interest now devoted to conservation.

**2003** A. Wild *Soils, Land & Food* 91: There is a doomwatch scenario that attributes the spread of deserts primarily to the activities of man.

**doomwatcher** *n.* one who predicts or looks for signs of ecological disasters.

**1971** *New Scientist* (title) (Mar. 18) 622: Doomwatcher incarnate.

**1971** *Brainerd (Minn.) Daily Dispatch* (Aug. 31) 4/7: It scorns one particular doomwatcher for proposing towns in which only horses and horse-drawn vehicles would be admitted.

**1978** *Nature* (Oct. 19) 577/2: As WMO sees it, hard evidence does little to support many of the disaster hypotheses of the doom-watchers.

**1997** *Gleaner (Kingston, Jam.)* (Aug. 26) B8/2: The dryland area studied in this project is just the kind used by the so-called "doomwatchers" to argue their case.

**doubleplusungood** *adj.* extremely bad; the worst. Often *joc.*

**1949** [G. Orwell] *Nineteen Eighty-Four* (1949) 45: times 3.12.83 reporting bb dayorder doubleplusungood refs unpersons rewrite fullwise upsub antefiling. In Oldspeak (or standard English) this might be rendered: The reporting of Big Brother's Order for the Day in the *Times* of December 3rd 1983 is extremely unsatisfactory and makes references to nonexistent persons. Rewrite it in full and submit your draft to higher authority before filing.

**1984** *sri-arpa.189 re: read(fd,&y,sizeof(y))* (Usenet: net.lang.c) (Mar. 25): Saying that the standard is "doubleplusungood" doesn't give much consolation to whoever has to rewrite almost every program in existence when porting C to a problem machine.

**1994** Stephen Baxter, *"Timelike Infinity"* (Usenet: rec.arts.sf.written) (Jan. 31): The rest of the book doubleplusungood. "Timelike Infinity" sucks rocks through a flexi-straw.

**2002** D. Margulis *Professional PhotoShop (4th ed.)* 273/1: Previous versions of PhotoShop have no such doubleplusungood feature.

**doublethink** *n.* simultaneously believing that two contradictory ideas are true.

**1949** [G. Orwell] *Nineteen Eighty-Four* 37: His mind slid away into the labyrinthine world of doublethink. To know and not to know, to be conscious of complete truthfulness while telling carefully constructed lies, to hold simultaneously two opinions which cancelled out, knowing them to be contradictory and believing in both of them, to use logic against logic, to repudiate morality while laying claim to it, to believe that democracy was impossible and that the Party was the guardian of democracy.

**1953** *Encounter* (Nov.) 26/1: He will react [...] either with straight abuse or with devious double-think.

**1959** *New York Times Mag.* (July 12) 16/1: New York may very well be a Summer Festival to some millions of visiting outlanders. But to those of us who live here when the asphalt turns gummy underfoot and the subway fans whir feebly, the whole idea takes on monstrous overtones of official doublethink.

**1969** *New Scientist* (Oct. 2) 18/1: This symposium exhibited a form of intellectual doublethink that could pay lip service to global starvation one minute, and assume Britain would always be able to import most of her food the next.

**1998** *New York Times Mag. (letter)* (Nov. 15) 26/1: What a wondrous land of legislative newspeak and doublethink we encounter, as your writer makes the rounds of F.D.A. and E.P.A. offices [...]. The potato developed, raised, marketed, purchased, prepared and eaten as a potato is not a potato.

**downtime** *adv.* in or into the past. Compare UPTIME.

**1973** P. Anderson *There Will Be Time* 51: He would take certain stamps and coins uptime and sell them to dealers; he would go downtime with a few aluminum vessels, which were worth more than gold before the Hall process was invented.

**1978** C. Kilian *Empire of Time* (1985) 6: The Operations Division was interested only in the worlds downtime whose affairs it guided, and in the worlds uptime whose fate it sought to escape.

**1983** J. Varley *Millennium* 21: I fall downtime to the beginning of the universe.

**1993** *Locus* (June) 59/2: A cargo of earthly animal embryos ordered centuries earlier "downtime."

**droid** *n.* [shortening of ANDROID] a robot or android. Also used *fig.*

**1976** G. Lucas *Adventures of Luke Starkiller* (Mar. 15) 42: Information vital to the survival of the Alliance has been placed in this droid.

**1977** *Mountain Democrat-Times (Placerville, Cal.)* (Oct. 12) A10 (caption): Mary Ann Harrison [...] and Terry Huntington construct the armorplate for one of the droids or robots which will appear in the Discovery Players' futuristic Comedy of Errors.

**1982** *Syracuse (New York) Herald-Journal* (Sept. 9) A2/4: Erik Estrada, we now believe, after seeing him once more flashing those pearly whites, is a droid conceived by the American Society of Orthodontists.

**1994** M. M. Smith *Only Forward* 190: Zenda explained that the delivery girls are only pseudo-flesh droids.

**1997** M. Dowd *Syracuse (New York) Herald-Journal* (Dec. 30) A9/1: On one side, a bunch of Chinese terra cotta soldiers at attention in dark suits and red ties: [...] Dick Gephardt (a droid who thinks he's a maverick), Steve Forbes (a droid who is the son of a maverick) and George W. Bush (a droid who is the son of a droid).

**2001** C. Asaro *Ascendant Sun* (2001) 268: The locker door slid open with a quiet hum, revealing a storage room filled with sleeping machines, everything from foot-sized dust sweepers to the lumbering droids that worked the outer hull.

**dropshaft** *n.* a vertical shaft that moves free-floating passengers or freight in a controlled descent or ascent by means of a force field or artificial gravity.

**1952** P. Anderson *Star Plunderer* in *Planet Stories* (Sept.) 58/2: We were herded down the long corridors and by way of wooden ladders (the drop-shafts and elevators weren't working it seemed) to the cells.

**1957** H. Ellison *Deeper Than Darkness* in *Infinity SF* (Apr.) 21/1: The Pyrotic let the drop-shaft lower him, and he found the lifescoot some time later.

**1964** [C. Smith] *Norstrilia* (1994) 123: This dropshaft, moreover, seemed to have more cargo than people in it. Huge boxes [...] floated up and down in the mysterious ever busy traffic of Old Earth.

**1986** C. Sheffield *Nimrod Hunt* 45: It was a race along confused networks of high-speed slideways, a plunge along the vertiginous corkscrews of spiral staircases, and finally a series of long dives through the black depths of vertical drop-shafts.

**1989** G. W. Proctor *Stellar Fist* 71: Containing her mounting rage, Arianne Pillan stepped into a dropshaft and gently descended to the lobby of the Diplomatic Services headquarters.

**Dyson sphere** *n.* [after physicist Freeman J. *Dyson*, who first proposed the idea] an artificial shell, habitable on the inside, that completely surrounds a star.

[**1960** F. J. Dyson *Sci.* (June 3) 1667/2: The mass of Jupiter, if distributed in a spherical shell revolving around the sun as twice the Earth's distance from it, would have a thickness such that the mass is 200 grams per square centimeter of surface area [...]. A shell of this thickness could be made comfortably habitable, and could contain all the machinery required for exploiting the solar radiation falling onto it from the inside.]

**1969** R. Silverberg *Across Billion Years* 218: A Dyson sphere [...] is a concept first put forth by an American physicist, Freeman Dyson, some time in the early years of the Energy Revolution.

**1969** R. Silverberg, *Across Billion Years* 220: A Dyson sphere would not, of course, show up on optical telescopes, since all of the sun's light output is trapped inside the sphere.

**ca 1982** T. M. Disch *Feast of St. Bradbury* in *On SF* (2005) 114: *Battlefield Earth* by L. Ron Hubbard is to other, ordinary dumb books what a Dyson sphere is to an ordinary lampshade—awesomely much bigger, though not much different in kind.

**1993** *SF Age* (Jan.) 20/3: The same episode will also feature breath-taking footage of the Dyson Sphere, an effect meant to replicate a device two

hundred million miles in diameter that was built around the sun of a now vanished alien race.

**1996** L. Schimel & M. A. Garland *To See Stars* in M. Ashley *Random House Book of SF Stories* (1996) 2: All the planets, moons, rocks, dust, and countless comets had been combined to make the Dyson sphere's thin shell of solar panels, like a giant egg with the sun as its yolk.

**dystopia** *n.* **1.** [Gk. *dys-*, "bad" + *topos*, "place," after UTOPIA] an imagined society or state of affairs in which conditions are extremely bad, especially in which these conditions result from the continuation of some current trend to an extreme; the genre of fiction set in such a society. Compare ECOTOPIA, UTOPIA 1.

[**1868** J. S. Mill *Hansard Commons* (Mar. 12) 1517/1: It is, perhaps, too complimentary to call them Utopians, they ought rather to be called dys-topians, or caco-topians. What is commonly called Utopian is something too good to be practicable; but what they appear to favour is too bad to be practicable.]

**1955** C. S. Lewis *George Orwell* in *On Stories* (1982) 104: Again, *1984* belongs to [...] the genre of what may be called "Dystopias," those nightmare visions of the future which began, perhaps, with Wells's *Time Machine* and *The Sleeper Wakes*.

**1991** *Locus* (Nov.) 17/1: "Down and Out in the Year 2000" make us live for a while in their two versions of future dystopia.

**2002** *Dreamwatch* (Sept.) 56/3: But while countless movies have been set in gritty dystopias or fanciful medieval kingdoms, none have paired aspects of those two worlds in such an unusual way.

**2.** a work set in such a society. Compare UTOPIA 2.

**1952** G. R. Negley & J. M. Patrick *Quest for Utopia* 298: The *Mundus Alter et Idem* is [...] the opposite of *eutopia,* the ideal society: it is a *dystopia,* if it is permissible to coin a word.

**1967** *Listener* (Jan. 5) 22: The modern classics—Aldous Huxley's Brave New World and George Orwell's Nineteen Eighty Four—are dystopias.

**1980** D. Brin *Sundiver* 337: Some sort of dystopia, wasn't it?

**2001** *SF Chronicle* (July) 38/3: This novel is described [...] as "A Science Fiction Noir" and it certainly is that, and a dystopia.

**dystopian** *adj.* of or having the qualities of a dystopia.

**1953** D. Knight *SF Adventures* (July) 117: Proteus, like many a dystopian hero before him, becomes increasingly uneasy about the elite to which he belongs and eventually winds up involved in an attempt to overthrow it.

**1968** *New Scientist* (July 11) 96/3: I fear that our real future is more likely to be dystopian.

**1992** *Locus* (Aug.) 17/2: This ecological/spiritual concern pervaded a plot that had wry overtones of fairytale and sudden shocks of dystopian disaster.

**2005** P. Di Filippo *Asimov's SF* (Mar.) 133/2: In its portrayal of a dystopian world, Beckett can stand shoulder to shoulder with Orwell and Burgess.

**dystopic** *adj.* tending to or having the quality of a dystopia.

**1967** W.H.G. Armytage *Disenchanted Mechanophobes in Twentieth Century England* in *Extrapolation* (Dec.) 55: More consistently dystopic, since he was both anti-Wells and anti-Marx, George Orwell kept up a rapid fire of criticism not at the shape of things to come, but at the way they were going.

**1991** *Locus* (May) 19/1: The story is [...] played out in the standing sets of dystopic-cityscape.

**1998** *Futures* (Dec.) 1027: As a reactionary response to the dystopic *X-Files*, *MiB* is an elaborate parody which seeks to recuperate ideological ground lost by the *X-Files'* examination of gender and technology in contemporary culture.

# Earthlings

In science fiction, when beings from different worlds encounter each other, they are generally named by their planet or star of origin; thus Martians are from Mars, and Sirians are from some hypothetical planet orbiting the star Sirius. While there are generally few terms in use for beings from any given planet or solar system, there is much greater variety in the terms for people who are from Earth. Many of these terms have been in use for centuries in other senses. Some, such as **Earthling** and **Terrestrial**, originally designated earthly (as opposed to heavenly or spiritual) beings. **Terrestrian** was once an adjective used to describe animals that lived on land rather than in water. **Earth-man** and **-woman** once referred only to beings that were associated with soil or the ground in some way; once SF writers got hold of them, they added **Earth-folk**, **Earth-girl**, and **Earth-person** as variations. SF writers also coined the fairly common terms **Terran**, **Tellurian** (after *Tellus*, the Roman goddess of the earth), **Earther**, **Earthian**, and **Earthie**, in addition to many more that never quite caught on, including **Earthan**, **Terrene**, and **Terrestial**. However, when faced with creatures from another star system entirely, beings from the Moon or Jupiter may seem slightly less alien, and so the word **Solarian** was coined to refer to any inhabitant of Earth's solar system, human or otherwise—**Earthling**, **Martian**, and **Plutonian** alike.

# e

**Earthborn** *n.* humans who were born on the planet Earth.

**1941** [S. D. Gottesman] *Fire-Power* in *Cosmic S-F* (July) 10/2: Venusian natives were warned off the streets; henceforth none but the Earthborn could show their faces by daylight.

**1959** M. Reynolds *Hunted Ones* in Anon. *Weird Ones* (1962) 96: He stared at it for a long moment, realizing by the nature of its attack that it was probably poisonous—at least to the earth-born.

**1974** N. Spinrad *Riding Torch* in R. Silverberg *Threads of Time* 166: We Earthborn were life's destroyers.

**1988** R. Silverberg *We Are for Dark* in *Collected Stories of Robert Silverberg (Vol. 2: Secret Sharer)* (1993) 357: We have some Earthborn here, still.

**Earthborn** *adj.* from the planet Earth; (of humans) born on the planet Earth.

**1900** G. Griffith *Visit to Moon* in *Pearson's Mag.* (Jan.) 29/2: It is almost exactly at the south pole of the moon, and there [ ... ] is the horizon of the hemisphere which no earthborn eyes but ours and Murgatroyd's have ever seen.

**1942** [P. Edmonds] *Night of Gods* in *Astonishing Stories* (Dec.) 23/2: This is not our world, [ ... ] We are Earth-born, and belong there.

**1953** G. R. Dickson *Bleak & Barren Land* in *Space Stories* (Feb.) 89/1: Letting five hundred Earth-born humans into Modor to settle on the barren land was a fool's trick, and a flat outrage of a sort of unwritten agreement that had existed [ ... ] ever since the first ship had landed.

**1974** R. Silverberg *Schwartz Between Galaxies* in *Feast of St. Dionysus* (1987) 95: Now our own world was once like that starship, a little cosmos, bearing with it all the thousands of Earthborn cultures, Hopi and Eskimo and Aztec and Kwakiutl and Arapesh and Orokolo and all the rest.

**1991** O. S. Card *Xenocide* 22: It's getting into the Earthborn crops that humans need in order to survive on Lusitania.

**Earther** *n.* an EARTHLING. Compare EARTHIAN, EARTHIE, EARTHPERSON, TELLURIAN, TERRAN, TERRESTRIAL, TERRESTRIAN.

**1952** C. M. Kornbluth *Make Mine Mars* in *SF Adventures* (Nov.) 73/2: NEED SOONEST ILLUMINATED SCROLL [ ... ] NOTE MUST BE TERRESTIAL STYLE ART IF NOT ACTUAL WORK EARTHER ACCOUNT ANTIBEM PREJUDICE HERE.

**1966** R. A. Lafferty *Among Hairy Earthmen* in *Galaxy Mag.* (Aug.) 90/2: Even today, the Eretzi or Earthers haven't the details of it right in their histories.

**1967** D. Gerrold *Trouble with Tribbles (Star Trek script)* (Aug. 1) II-20: Klingons are not as luxury-minded as Earthers.

**1991** G. Bear & S. M. Stirling *Man Who Would Be Kzin* in L. Niven, et al. *Man-Kzin Wars IV* 264: Even after a decade, the words *war* and *enemy* still carried a strong flavor of obscenity to most Earthers.

**2003** S. S. Tepper *Companions* (2004) 139: Meantime, he convinced Earthers who owned exempt estates to put their acres in perpetual trust for the growth of earthian flora.

**Earthfall** *n.* [modeled after *landfall*] the arrival (of a spaceship) on the Earth's surface. Compare PLANETFALL.

**1957** T. Sturgeon *Girl Had Guts* in *Venture SF Mag.* (Jan.) 122/1: Status quo, then, far as I knew, from the time we left the planet until we made earthfall.

**1976** S. R. Delany *Trouble on Triton* (1996) 132: We make Earthfall in about an hour.

**1984** W. G. Gray *Qabalistic Concepts* (1997) 65: A modern way of interpreting this is by postulating the "earthfall" of some spacecraft bearing highly advanced beings from a distant galaxy.

**Earthfolk** *pl. n.* EARTHPEOPLE. [1914 quote refers to inhabitants of the Earth's surface.]

[**1914** E. R. Burroughs *At Earth's Core* (1922) 224: And at the first glance there broke upon my horrified vision the most frightful thing I had seen even within Pellucidar. It was a giant dragon such as is pictured in the legends and fairy tales of earth folk.]

**1936** F. B. Long, Jr. *Cones* in *Astounding Stories* (Feb.) 124/1: Intrepid Earthfolk, suicide battalion people, walking slowly in their suits of flexible difrolchrome, [...] and living, from instant to instant, dangerously.

**1949** L. Brackett *Lake of Gone Forever* in *Halfling & Other Stories* (1973) 306: He could not [...] cease to wonder uneasily why the old man had so suddenly left the Earthfolk unwatched.

**1979** P. Anderson *Ways of Love* in *Destinies* (Jan.–Feb.) 14: The Earthfolk, to whom ten is a special number, decided to celebrate the decade with ceremonies.

**2000** D. Pringle *What Is This Thing Called Space Opera* in G. Westfahl *Space & Beyond* 41: Under Thomas Edison's scientific leadership Earthfolk are able to carry the war back to Mars itself.

**2001** C. Stasheff *Wizard in Feud* (2002) 111: Gar realized that a whole planetful of alien plants might well have produced chemicals that could maim or kill Earth folk.

**Earthgirl** *n.* a young woman from the planet Earth; (in more recent usage) a female human child. Compare EARTHMAN, EARTHWOMAN.

**1924** C. K. Michener *Earth Girl* in *Weird Tales* (Dec.) 18/1: Maderna, the Earth Girl, she who had been known in Chicago as Hattie La Salle, arose from the couch on which she awoke, and in the green light of morning looked about her with the puzzled air of one still clouded in the circumstances of interrupted dreams.

**1930** P. Nowlan & R. Calkins *Buck Rogers, 2430 A. D.* in *Oakland (Cal.) Tribune* (Apr. 1) 4M: You'll die for this, Earth girl!

**1936** A. MacFadyen *Time Decelerator* in *Astounding Stories* (July) 39/2: A cloak cut strangely from a cloth of peculiar texture and shade of color, such a thing as no earth girl wore, in 1937 A.D.

**1950** J. D. MacDonald *Shadow on Sand* in *Thrilling Wonder Stories* (Oct.) 40/1: She wanted you for herself and you were paying too much attention to the Earthgirl.

**1955** J. Vance *Meet Miss Universe* in *Fantastic Universe* (Mar.) 6/2: But how in the world could I compare some cute little Earth girl with a Sadal Suud Isobrod? Or one of those Pleiades dragon-women?

**1968** V. Vinge *Conquest by Default* in *Collected Stories of Vernor Vinge* (2001) 161: That idiot Earthgirl was still standing.

**1999** J. Peel *Outer Limits: Alien Invasion from Hollyweird* 100: If I were to marry some nice Earth girl—like you, Melanie—then I could have perfectly normal human babies with her.

**2004** L. J. Singleton *Oh No! UFO!* 72: And Amber looked normal. (Well, as normal as an alien possessing an Earth girl's body can look.)

**Earthian** *n.* an EARTHLING. Compare EARTHER, EARTHIE, EARTHPERSON, TELLURIAN, TERRAN, TERRESTRIAL, TERRESTRIAN.

**1932** R. Gallun *Revolt of Star Men* in *Wonder Stories Quarterly* (Winter) 240/1: A sickening giddiness came over the two Earthians, for there were no devices to produce artificial gravity here.

**1951** G. Conklin *Galaxy SF* (Feb.) 101/1: The tale tells how, from a space station on Pluto, a few Earthians [...] are able to help avert the collision of our universe with another, a crash which would have been "slightly fatal" to both.

**1960** R. E. Banks *Transstar* in D. Drake *Dogs of War* (2002) 187: You are protector to the Earthians.

**2000** S. S. Tepper *Fresco* (2002) 420: While they were waiting, all the Earthians had their pictures taken in front of the window wall of the big ship.

**Earthian** *adj.* of or from the Earth; of an Earthling or Earthlings.

**1934** R. Z. Gallun *Old Faithful* in *Astounding SF* (Dec.) 108/1: Number 774 had constructed a gigantic apparatus and had duplicated the Earthian signals flash for flash.

**1946** R. Bradbury *Million-Year Picnic* in A. Derleth *Strange Ports of Call* (1948) 165: I was looking for Earthian logic, common sense, good government, peace and responsibility.

**1952** W. Kubilius & F. Pratt *Second Chance* in *Fantastic Story Mag.* (Sept.) 93/1: I am to [ ... ] offer the Western Alliance a certain number of our rockets for joint attempts to explore and colonize either Venus or Mars, the pro tempore colonial government to be neither Cominworld nor Western Alliance, but simply Earthian.

**1974** H. Putnam *Mind, Language & Reality* (1997) 224: The typical Earthian speaker of English did not know water consisted of hydrogen and oxygen.

**1999** S. Dedman *Unequal Laws* in *SF Age* (Mar.) 41/1: I don't know much about Earthian politics, but I don't see how they could have stopped them going.

**2003** S. S. Tepper *Companions* (2004) 139: Oloct purchased small, out-of-the-way planets and moons, [ ... ] and adapted them for selected earthian fauna while protecting the indigenous species.

**Earthie** *n.* an EARTHLING. Often *derog.* Compare EARTHER, EARTHIAN, EARTHPERSON, TELLURIAN, TERRAN, TERRESTRIAL, TERRESTRIAN.

**1947** [J. MacCreigh] *Donovan Had Dream* in *Thrilling Wonder Stories* (Oct.) 27/1: "Earthgirl?" the guard repeated. "She didn't look like an Earthie."

**1963** J. Jakes *Underfollow* in *Mag. of Fantasy & SF* (May) 66/1: The blue men of Mica II discriminated against Earthies, considered them inferior since the Micans had conquered the Earthies a hundred years ago.

**1976** S. R. Delany *Trouble on Triton* (1996) 239: You're not an earthie. They don't even do that too much on Mars, now.

**1998** F. Pohl *O Pioneer!* (1999) 151: Only out of some kind of Earthie vanity, some refusal to admit to the rest of the human race that somebody was smarter than they?

**Earthlike** *adj.* resembling the planet Earth (especially in terms of climate, mass, or atmospheric composition) or that which is native to the Earth.

**1928** E. E. Smith & L. H. Garby *Skylark of Space* in *Amazing Stories* (Sept.) 550/1: We found air and Earth-like conditions here.

**1937** O. Stapledon *Star Maker* (1987) 70: On one very small but earthlike planet we discovered a quasi-human race which was probably unique.

**1949** W. L. Bade *Lost Ulysses* in *Astounding SF* (May) 126/1: They found five planets which would support human life, two of them exceptionally earthlike.

**1958** *Gettysburg (Pa.) Times* (Aug. 14) 14/6: Venus—almost earthlike in size—is the next planet on the sun-side of our orbit.

**1983** J. Oberg *Farming Planets* in O. Davies *Omni Book of Space* 15: The earth could serve as a blueprint for the transformation of her sterile sister worlds into earthlike ecologies.

**1993** K. S. Robinson *Red Mars* 90: But it was not Earthlike, that strangely close horizon.

**2004** *San Francisco Chronicle* (Sept. 1) A10/1: These worlds, veiled in atmospheres thousands of miles thick, are so huge and cold that they are presumably inhospitable to Earthlike life.

**Earthling** *n.* [originally used in opposition to heavenly or spiritual beings] an inhabitant of the planet Earth or a person originally from the Earth. Compare EARTHER, EARTHIAN, EARTHIE, EARTHPERSON, TELLURIAN, TERRAN, TERRESTRIAL, TERRESTRIAN.

**1939** [E. Binder] *Impossible World* (1967) 74: The voice of those of our people who do not want a war with the Earthlings.

**1950** P. Anderson *Star Ship* in *Planet Stories* (Oct.) 74/1: There'd been Earthling girls; and not a few Khazaki women had been intrigued by the big Terrestrial.

**1967** *Ampleforth Journal* (Summer) 163: To receive the overspill by immigration [ ... ] the planets might come to the rescue of the Earthlings.

**1984** R. Rucker & B. Sterling *Storming Cosmos* in B. Sterling *Globalhead* (1994) 18: The dog Laika has been shot into the cosmic void. A good dog, a Russian, an Earthling.

**1995** D. W. Smith & K. K. Rusch *Escape* 35: Like Earthlings, though, these people had different-color hair and a finer bone structure.

**Earthman** *n.* [originally referred to beings associated with the ground or soil] a man or human from the planet Earth. Compare EARTHGIRL, EARTHWOMAN.

**1913** R. A. Wetzel *Sci.* (Oct. 3) 469: The fact that the earth-man finds the sun clocks slow, and the sun-man finds the earth clocks slow, in the same ratio is the startling contribution of the theory of relativity.

**1928** E. R. Burroughs *Master Mind of Mars* 2: My eyes always sought out the Red Planet when he was above the horizon and clung there seeking a solution of the seemingly unfathomable riddle he has presented to the Earthman for ages.

**1939** N. S. Bond *Mercurian Menace* in *Dynamic Science Stories* (Feb.) 60/2: Together the Earthman and the creature from Mercury sought the luxury of the spaceship's shower[-]room.

**1950** L. Brackett *Dancing Girl of Ganymede* in *Halfling & Other Stories* (1973) 42: She looked at him, the dark, sinewy Earthman, with a handful of coins, and her look was a curse.

**1960**: see quote in MARTIAN.

**1980** D. Brin *Sundiver* 12: Fagin was also the one extraterrestrial who tried hardest to understand Earthmen.

**2002** M. J. Harrison *Light* (2004) 273: Clusters of barely pressurised vessels like leaky bathtubs, each hosting a failing hydroponic farm and two or three earthmen with lost eyes, bad stubble, radiation ulcers.

**Earthnorm** *n.* EARTH-NORMAL.

**1943** H. F. Parker *Sword of Johnny Damokles* in *Planet Stories* (Mar.) 33/1: He led them down a succession of corridors to a room where temperature and gravity stood at Earth[-]norm, and Callisto constant.

**1957** R. Silverberg *Planet Killers* (1959) 117: Fourth planet of a warm G-type sun, gravity .96 Earthnorm, atmosphere Earthlike to four places.

**1972** L. Carter *Black Legion of Callisto* 16: The heroes of Apollo 11 found an arid desert world [...] with a gravity only a fraction of earth norm.

**2005** J. Whedon *Serenity, Shooting Script* in *Serenity, Official Visual Companion* 125: Gravity's Earthnorm.

**Earthnorm** *adj.* EARTH-NORMAL.

**1951** M. Lesser *"A" as in Android* in *Future* (May) 74/1: Oh, Government had done wonders—and spent fortunes—giving tiny Hyperion a warm breathable atmosphere and earth-norm gravity.

**1969** R. Silverberg *Across Billion Years* 116: Hotchkiss and Ben-Dov were required to put in twelve Earthnorm hours each day.

**1971** R. Silverberg *Something Wild Is Loose* in *World of Thousand Colors* (1984) 6: The regrowth people [...] were under full Earthnorm gravity so that their new hearts would come in with the proper resilience and toughness.

**Earth-normal** *n.* the condition or amount (of something) as it exists on the planet Earth.

**1932** J. W. Campbell, Jr. *Electronic Siege* in *Wonder Stories* (Apr.) 1249/1: The lifeless, defenseless ship careened on through space, her acceleration dropping immediately to Earth normal as automatic machines took up the unconscious pilot's duties.

**1935** R. Z. Gallun *Derelict* in *Astounding Stories* (Oct.) 25/2: Somewhere gravity plates continued to function in this ancient wreck, for he had weight here—perhaps one third Earth-normal.

**1944** F. Brown *Arena* in R. Silverberg *SF Hall of Fame, Vol. I* (1970) 284: Gravity seemed a little more than Earth-normal.

**1998** W. Shatner *Spectre* 132: The exterior atmospheric pressure was 250 torr, about one-third Earth normal.

**Earth-normal** *adj.* similar to a condition or conditions as they exist the planet Earth.

**1942** I. Asimov *Victory Unintentional* in O. Welles *Invasion from Mars* (1949) 147: They had six legs apiece, stumpy and thick, designed to lift tons against two and a half times normal Earth gravity. Their reflexes were that many times Earth-normal speed, to make up for the gravity.

**1952** J. Blish *Bridge* in *Astounding SF* 73/1 (Feb.): None of us have to pretend that our living arrangements would keep us out of jail in Boston, or that they have to involve any Earth[-]normal excuses.

**1972** L. Carter *Black Legion of Callisto* 15: While it is true that Callisto is one of the larger satellites in our solar system, it could not possibly have the earth-normal gravity and atmosphere Captain Dark describes because it is only a fraction of the size of our planet.

**1991** K. Laumer *Judson's Eden* 35: Then *Rocky* settled into her accustomed transit mode as her sensors and autostabilizers recreated Earth-normal conditions aboard.

**1993** V. E. Mitchell *Windows on Lost World* 126: The creature had three triangular teeth that could have [ ... ] broken the carapace of an Earth-normal crab.

**2005** M. Rosenblum *Green Shift* in *Asimov's SF* (Mar.) 109: Ahni levered herself from the padded acceleration recliner, her stomach happy with the 80 percent Earthnormal gravity.

**Earthperson** *n.* a human from or living on the planet Earth. Compare EARTHER, EARTHIAN, EARTHIE, EARTHPERSON, TELLURIAN, TERRAN, TERRESTRIAL, TERRESTRIAN.

**1930** E. E. Smith *Skylark Three* in *Amazing Stories* (Sept.) 559/2: As they walked along the Earth[-]people stared, held by the unearthly beauty of the grounds.

**1951** [I. Seabright] *Mag. of Fantasy & SF* (Apr.) 57: The earth people were impatient with our ritual—they wanted to see us hurting and being hurt.

**1972** M. Z. Bradley *Darkover Landfall* (1987) 9: Earth people had lost their old woodcraft habits and might not be aware any more of what forest fires could do.

**1986** A. C. Clarke *Songs of Distant Earth* 81: It was Tarna's first demonstration of Earthpersons—or rather Earth robots—in action, and the villagers were hugely impressed.

**2002** B. Stableford *Dark Ararat* 66: Living in half-gravity, they had not the same need as Earthpeople for stout, supportive legs.

**Earthside** *adj.* on or from the planet Earth. Compare GROUNDSIDE, PLANETSIDE.

**1951** A. E. van Vogt *This Joe* in *Marvel SF* (Aug.) 73/1: Barron, the only Earthside executive present, stood up and offered me his hand.

**1960** A. E. Nourse *Nine Planets* 68: We can study the Sun from Earth-side laboratories, but what we can see and learn from our observation is enormously limited.

**1969** R. Silverberg *Across Billion Years* 158: Fight fire with fire. Old Earthside proverb.

**1989** G. Benford in G. Dozois *Isaac Asimov's Mars* (1991) 89: Earthside studies showed that a brief Eden might have flourished for a while.

**Earthside** *adv.* to or on the planet Earth. Compare GROUNDSIDE, ON-PLANET, ON-WORLD, PLANETSIDE.

**1948** A. Coppel *Jinx Ship to Rescue* in *Planet Stories* (Winter) 28/1: Cob [ ... ] had been with her a full year [ ... ] which was a record for Execs on the *Aphrodite*. She generally sent them Earthside with nervous breakdowns in half that time.

**1974** G. Benford *Threads of Time* in R. Silverberg *Threads of Time* 84: I want to send it Earthside, to Kardensky, and then the NSF.

**1979** M. Z. Bradley *Bloody Sun* 22: Might as well be back Earthside! Just another spaceport!

**1993** P. Anderson *Harvest of Stars* (1994) 8: She'd paid little attention, for Earthside she mainly associated with company people on company property.

**Earthsider** *n.* someone who lives on the Earth.

**1993** T. Bisson *Shadow Knows* in *Bears Discover Fire & Other Stories* (1993) 206: I had served in and out (or up and down, as earthsiders put it) of Edwards for some twenty years.

**1994** R. Silverberg *Hot Sky at Midnight* 5: Juanito listened to the sound of his breathing, quick and shallow, the way all Earthsiders breathed.

**2005** M. Rosenblum *Green Shift Asimov's SF* (Mar.) 124: I thought maybe on Earthsider could figure it out.

**Earth-type** *adj.* **1.** EARTH-LIKE.

**1941** R. Heinlein *Methuselah's Children* in *Astounding S-F* (Aug.) 98/1: To discover [ ... ] whether it supported an Earth-type planet required a close approach at reasonably low speed.

**1954** A. Norton *Stars Are Ours!* (1955) 96: You expect this sun to produce an earth-type planet because it is a "yellow" one.

**1964** R. Silverberg *To Dark Star* in *World of Thousand Colors* (1984) 137: She came from a world in the Procyon system, where the air was more or less Earth-type.

**1972** M. Z. Bradley *Darkover Landfall* (1987) 6: They all knew that this one was what Earth Expeditionary Forces called a Class M planet— roughly Earth-type and probably habitable.

**1994** *Interzone* (July) 9/1: The search was soon switched to Earthtype planets, and these proved difficult to find.

**1999** L. Frankowski *Boy & His Tank* (2000) 87: Forests of Earth-type trees were rapidly supplanting the native ferns.

**2.** like something manufactured on the Earth.

**1941** E. Hamilton *Son of Two Worlds* in *Thrilling Wonder Stories* 28/2 (Aug.): Most of these Martians wore Earth-type synthesuits of somber hues.

**1957** T. Sturgeon *It Opens Sky* in *Man Who Lost Sea* (2005) 43: We fitted them out with Earth-type controls, but although we know what button to push, we don't know what happens when we push it.

**1969** E. Cooper *Sea-Horse in Sky* (1980) 24: He had switched on the bedside lamp—ordinary earth-type with an ordinary sixty-watt bulb—and had explored further.

**Earthwoman** *n.* [originally referred to beings associated with the ground or soil] a woman from the planet Earth. Compare EARTHGIRL, EARTHMAN.

**1934** F. K. Freas *Famine on Mars* in *Astounding Stories* (Sept.) 77/2: The other remembered all the long years on Earth when I, in common with every other Earthman and Earthwoman, had been flexed and shaped by the insistent pounding of the Combine.

**1943** *New Yorker* (Feb. 13) 39/2: Today the earthmen take their earthwomen with them.

**1972** M. Z. Bradley *Darkover Landfall* (1987) 162: But Judy's alien [ ... ] must be near enough to human to father a child on an Earth-woman.

**1994** D. Spencer *Passing Fancy* 19: Saying her children were with them was like an Earthwoman saying her children were with Jesus.

**ecotopia** *n.* [*eco*logical + u*topia*] an ideal society based on principles designed to minimize the society's negative impact on the environment. Compare DYSTOPIA, UTOPIA.

**1975** E. Callenbach *Ecotopia* 78: For in this as in many areas of life, there is still a strong trend in Ecotopia to abandon the fruits of all modern technology, however innocuous they may be, in favor of a poetic but costly return to what the extremists see as "nature."

**1987** N. Spinrad *Isaac Asimov's SF Mag.* (July) 186/2: Atwood appends a schlocko sci-fi afterword [ ... ] in the form of the proceedings of a congress of supercilious academics picking over the bones of her handmaid's tale in a future fuzzy ecotopia long after wicked Gilead has fallen.

**1996** D. Pepper *Modern Environmentalism* 296: It is tempting to say that there are two "extreme" perspectives among radical ecologists on how ecotopia might be attained and what it might be like.

**2000** I. Stewart & J. Cohen *Wheelers* (2001) 149: The rest of the world collectively renamed itself Ecotopia, made sure its low population *stayed* low, and did its best to find an intelligent way to combine technology and environmentalism.

**edisonade** *n.* [after American inventor Thomas Alva *Edison*, modeled after "Robinsonade," a story similar to Daniel Defoe's novel *Robinson Crusoe*] a story featuring a young (typically American) inventor protagonist who uses his inventions to overcome his or his country's enemies or to explore new territories.

**1993** J. Clute in J. Clute & P. Nicholls *Ency. of SF* 368/2: As used here the term "edisonade" [ ... ] can be understood to describe any story which features a young US male inventor hero who uses his ingenuity to extricate himself from tight spots and who, by so doing, saves himself from defeat and corruption and his friends and nation from foreign oppressors.

**1998** M. Davis *Ecology of Fear* (1999) 295: An irresistible American genre, the "Edisonade." In this popular story type, modeled on Serviss's *Edison's Conquest of Mars*, a brilliant young inventor is initially spurned until his invention [...] proves necessary to save the day.

**1999** *"David Brin's Out of Time" series — what up?* (Usenet: rec.arts.sf.written) (Aug. 17): The Tom Swifts and the edisonade serials were at least marginally sf.

**2004** B. Landon *Less Is More* in N. K. Hayles *Nanoculture* 132: James Kidder [...] creates life, albeit of an extremely miniature form—in the tradition of Victor Frankenstein, although in the clearly American style of the Edisonade.

**eetee** *n.* [pronunciation spelling of E. T.] an EXTRATERRESTRIAL.

**1956** R. A. Heinlein *Double Star* in *Astounding SF* (Apr.) 143/2: I was knocked out the first time when we finally put the eetees—Venusians and Martians and Outer Jovians—into the Grand Assembly.

**1958** H. Ellison *Mealtime Ellison* in *Wonderland* (1962) 97: I hope we don't run up against any eetees. The last batch was enough to turn my stomach for quite a while.

**1988** [C. J. Cherryh] *Cyteen* 196: Eetees with a complex culture and an isolationist sentiment.

**1996** *Interzone* (May) 8/1: She couldn't see any sign of Eetee organisation—no industrial smog, no large structures, no radio or other signals.

**egoboo** *n.* ['igou,bu] [*ego* + *boo*st] the good feeling generated by receiving public recognition or a compliment, especially in the form of a having a letter published or one's name mentioned in a magazine.

[**1947** R. Sneary *Thrilling Wonder Stories* (letter) (June) 100/1: If you must print all these names, why not do it like the old SFL list, just the name and address. In small print. It would ego boo your readers and live [sic] room for the more interesting letters.]

**1948** *Thrilling Wonder Stories (letter)* (Feb.) 98/1: Well after the pile of ego-boo I got in the Oct. issue I just couldn't let it slip by without telling you what I think of this much heralded issue.

**1950** S. Skirvin *Wha' Hoppened?* in *Cinvention Memory Book* 78: So I had to content myself with what ego-boo I got from numerous compliments on the program booklet, all of which warmed the cockles of my heart.

**1969** H. Warner, Jr. *All Our Yesterdays* 34: Evans thought he wasn't getting enough egoboo from angeling Ashley's *Nova*.

**1996** V. Bowen *Model Fan, or Your Ass Is on Net* in *SF Five-Yearly* (Nov.) 14: I had people coming up and telling me that they'd seen my photos, and thought they were magnificent. Not quite the same sort of egoboo as from a fanzine, but still appreciated.

**2005** D. Langford *Ansible* (Internet) (June): Despite its wicked semiprozine claims, *Ansible* won the fanzine category. For this egoboo, much thanks.

**egoscan** *v.* to quickly search for mentions of one's name. Also as *n.* [Originally used with reference to fanzines and letter columns in professional magazines; now primarily used with reference to Internet search engines.]

**1975** E. Weinstein *Fillostrated Fan Dictionary* 43: Egoscan: To check through a fanzine for references [...] concerning oneself.

**1996** *Who Reads Letters Columns?* (Usenet: rec.arts.comics.misc) (Apr. 17): Every now and then I egoscan, as more and more people have been asking my permission to use excerpts from my reviews in their letters column.

**2003** *War On HLA* (Usenet: alt.lang.asm) (Oct. 26): It's no big secret that authors do an "egoscan" with Google (or whatever) from time to time to see what people are saying about their books.

**elsewhen** *n.* an other time; another point in time.

**1943** [A. Boucher] *Elsewhen* in *Astounding S-F* (Jan.) 127/2: The time alibi, the elsewhen that gave the perfect cover up for Partridge's murder—it gives exactly the same ideal alibi to his own murderer.

**1957** A. Bester *Stars My Destination* in *Galaxy* (Jan.) 140/2: He jaunted up the geodesic lines of space-time to an Elsewhere and an Elsewhen.

**1974** J. Brunner *Times without Number* (1981) 69: Father Ramón seemed to come back to the present from a private voyage into the elsewhen.

**1996** D. Pringle, et al. *Ultimate Ency. of SF* 33/2: The simplest of all the templates that are used in science fiction is that in which the normal course of the everyday world [ ... ] is disrupted by intruders from elsewhere or elsewhen.

**elsewhen** *adv.* in or to another point in time.

**1982** R. Silverberg *Far Side of Bell-Shaped Curve* in *Conglomeroid Cocktail Party* (1984) 27: Merely whirling Ilsabet off elsewhen would achieve nothing.

**1989** *Dragon Mag.* 68 (June): You'll travel backward and forward through time, so be advised that some of the folk you meet and places you visit exist only at certain times and not "elsewhen."

**1992** P. David *Imzadi* 3: The man in the greenish yellow shirt, whose mind was elsewhere and elsewhen.

**empath** *n.* a being with the mental ability of empathy.

**1956** [J. T. McIntosh] *Empath* in *New Worlds* (Aug.) 30: "How exactly does the government use empaths?" Tim shrugged. "We can tell the level of a man's loyalty just by meeting him. We can walk around a factory and sense that there's going to be a strike."

**1968** H. Ellison *Try Dull Knife* in *Mag. of Fantasy & SF* (Oct.) 71/1: That was Eddie Burma's problem. He was an empath. He felt. Deep inside himself, on a level most people never even know exists, he felt for the world.

**1973** A. McCaffrey *Bridle for Pegasus* in *Analog SF-Sci. Fact* (July) 24/2: We are both agreed that she is a broadcasting empath?

**1979** M. Z. Bradley *Bloody Sun* 159: Can you think of a better test for an empath?

**1992** S. Stewart *Passion Play* (1993) 66: Nobody feels pain more keenly than an empath.

**2005** M. Rosenblum *Green Shift* in *Asimov's SF* (Mar.) 114: Uh-oh. Another empath. Change tactics. With a mental shrug, in Ahni opened her eyes and gasped, not needing to pretend confusion.

**empathic** *adj.* of empathy; having the ability of empathy. Compare TELEMPATHIC.

**1959** J. White *Visitor at Large* in *New Worlds SF* (June) 8: His new assistant was not a telepath—it could not read thoughts—but it was sensitive to feelings and emotions and would therefore have been aware of Conway's curiosity. Conway felt like kicking himself for forgetting that empathic faculty.

**1972** J. Blish *Star Trek 8* 117: The Argelian empathic contact, sir?

**1993** D. Weber *On Basilisk Station* (1999) 8: Even now, no one had any idea how the empathic links worked, but separating one from its chosen companion caused it intense pain.

**1995** *Extrapolation* 9 (Spring): This woman just happens to be a "female empathic mesomorph."

**2005** M. Rosenblum *Green Shift* in *Asimov's SF* (Mar.) 115: His smile was broader now, which *really* bothered her, because his empathic rating in the personnel file had been 9.

**empathy** *n.* **1.** the psionic ability to feel another's emotions. Hence **empathize**, *v.* [ **1955** P. Anderson *No World of Their Own* in P. Anderson & I. Asimov *No World of Their Own / 1,000-Year Plan* 116: The animal could not only receive the nervous impulses of others, but could at short range induce them. This was the basis of Holatan emotional empathy.]

**1956** [J. T. McIntosh] *Empath New Worlds* (Aug.) 40: The Circle's trying to get Tim without using empathy. They're all blanking out.

**1976** S. Robinson *Telempath* 186: Because of the nature of a Name, Muskies can't *help* empathizing—it's what keeps them together and in contact with the High Muskies.

**1979** M. Z. Bradley *Bloody Sun* 159: Mark him positive for empathy, Kennard.

**2.** the connection between two or more beings created by using such an ability.

**1960** H. Harrison *Deathworld* in *Astounding Sci. Fact & Fiction* (Feb.) 136/2: The talkers must have well-developed psi facilities, that was obvious now. There is no barrier of race or alien form when two creatures share each other's emotions. Empathy first, so there would be no hatred or fear.

**1966** P. Anderson *Ensign Flandry* (1985) 138: In addition, I have developed an empathy with machines. I can be aware, on a level below consciousness, of what they are about to do, and adjust my behavior accordingly.

**1971** J. Blish *Star Trek 4* 39: It appears it learned more from me during our empathy than I did from it.

**1999** L. Norman *Dark Nadir* 88: Try as he might, he could feel no link, no empathy with this alien world—until the visions started. That was the truly frightening part. Now he could feel all that Derwent had been talking about, except it wasn't a maleness he sensed, it was an indisputably female presence.

**energy screen** *n.* a FORCE FIELD.

**1944** A. E. van Vogt *Far Centaurus* in S. Schmidt *Fifty Years of Best SF from Analog* (1980) 118: And they've already spotted us with their spy rays and energy screens.

**1953** P. K. Dick *Variable Man* in *Paycheck* (1990) 202: His gun belt and energy screen were yanked off.

**1960** K. Laumer *Dinochrome* in *Nine by Laumer* (1967) 74: I no longer have my ion-guns, my disruptors, my energy screens; but I have my fighting instinct.

**2001** M. Farren *More Than Mortal* (2002) 246: As they entered, blue flashes flared in concentric circles around each Hummer in turn, like a protective energy screen created from the low-level radiation of the living rock.

**energy weapon** *n.* a weapon that fires a beam or blast of pure energy. Also **energy gun, rifle,** etc.

**1941** A. E. van Vogt *Seesaw* in *Astounding S-F* (July) 60/1: The window display was made up of an assortment of rather curiously shaped guns, rifles as well as small arms; and a glowing sign in the window stated: THE FINEST ENERGY WEAPONS IN THE KNOWN UNIVERSE.

**1952** K. F. Crossen *Caphian Caper* in *Thrilling Wonder Stories* (Dec.) 36/2: As Manning predicted, within twenty four hours one of the Caphian ships appeared and settled to the ground just out of the range of an energy gun.

**1967** K. Laumer *Thunderhead* in *Day Before Forever & Thunderhead* (1968) 157: Stunned

by the direct hit from the energy weapon of the water being, the One-Who-Records fought his way upward through [...] whirling shapes of fire.

**1974** F. Saberhagen *Berserker's Planet* in *Worlds of If* (July–Aug.) 80/1: At close range the energy rifle had opened this crude armor like an egg.

**1981** G. Wolfe *Sword of Lictor* 172: They were not such spears as soldiers have, energy weapons whose heads strike bolts of fire, but simple poles of wood tipped with iron.

**2000** I. M. Banks *Look to Windward* (2002) 70: They ran out into the rain; the building behind them burned and slumped and fell, turned to glowing slag by the energy weapons.

**escape pod** *n.* a small spaceship used for emergency evacuation from a damaged spaceship or space station, frequently possessing only minimal navigational controls. Compare LIFEPOD, LIFEBOAT, LIFESHIP.

**1976** G. Lucas *Adventures of Luke Starkiller* (Apr. 19) 69: Several of the escape pods have been jettisoned.

**1998** E. Moon *Rules of Engagement* 58: A buddy stuffed me in an escape pod, and when old *Cutlass* was blown, I was safely away.

**2001** T. Zahn *Angelmass* 329: There's also a double ring of emergency escape pods set around the tube connecting the catapult and net sections of the station.

**2002** P. McAuley *Making History* 87: Before it took its dive, it travelled most of the way around the planet within the ring system, long enough to drop off its passengers and cargo in escape pods.

**esp** *v.* [< ESP, "extra-sensory perception," the ability to read minds] to read minds, communicate telepathically, or perceive things with one's mind that cannot be seen or heard by the ordinary senses.

**1949** E. F. Russell *Glass Eye* in *Astounding SF* (Mar.) 41/1: Eenif gestured toward the metal wall through which both of them could esp the new world in all its glowing colors.

**1955** R. Sheckley *Lifeboat Mutiny* in *Galaxy SF* (Apr.) 63/2: "I am Lifeboat 324-A," the boat esped again.

**1959** F. Leiber *Green Millennium* (1980) 88: I always trust Sacheverell's notions because he's so good at esping and telepathing that he makes half our living by it.
**1971** M. Z. Bradley *World Wreckers* (1984) 22: We have no legal proof and there's no law against esping a machine to win.

**esper** *n.* a being with the mental ability of extra-sensory perception.
**1950** A. Bester *Devil's Invention* in *Astounding SF* (Aug.) 139/1: "How does he do it?" "I don't know [...] Tell me how Espers does it."
**1952** A. Bester *Demolished Man* in *Galaxy SF* (Jan.) 11/1: A mind-reader...telepath...esper.
**1955** G. O. Smith *Highways in Hiding* in *Imagination* (Mar.) 13/2: Most medicos are highgrade espers, not telepaths. [...] An esper digs the trouble out without having his mind all fogged up by some layman's opinion of what causes the ache and pain.
**1970** A. Norton *Dread Companion* (1980) 24: The matter was only reported to me this morning after the flitter was found. Only a few knew it. But how did she know? Is she esper?
**1978** R. Lupoff *Algol* (Nov.) 48/2: He goes to an institute where espers are trained, and consents to participate in an experiment whereby the personality of a dying person is imprinted on the mind of a telepathic recipient.
**1991** C. Stasheff *Warlock & Son* 31: Rod concentrated on the spell, the compulsion imposed on his son, which [...] made him project his own delusion into other people's minds—with all the titanic strength of the hybrid esper he was.

**ET** *abbr.* Extra-Terrestrial.
**1944** J. B. Speer *Fancyclopedia* 2/1: Lowndes imagines a capitalistic future and offers remedies for horrible new maladies, books on spicy customs of e.t.'s, &c.
**1956** T. Sturgeon *Bulkhead Way Home* 145: Eighteen years each round trip, with [...] a cargo of serums, refractories, machine tools, and food concentrate for the xenologists and e-t mineralogists who were crazy enough to work out there.
**1961** K. Laumer *Hybrid* in *Nine by Laumer* (1967) 5: As soon as he reached home, he would have to enroll in a course in E.T. botany.

**1982** *Nature* (Sept. 23) 377/1: A pop-eyed, stick-figured ET [...] looks out from the cover of *The Biology of Human Conduct.*
**1990** [J. Tiptree, Jr.] *Color of Neanderthal Eyes* 11: What can I tell her convincingly? Of the iron Rule Number One in ET contacts?
**2005** S. H. Elgin *LiveJournal (Internet)* (July 31): The ETs (the Tendu) in Amy Thomson's *The Color of Distance* use a language she calls *skin-speech* that is displayed on the speaker's skin and is under voluntary control.

**everywhen** *n.* all points in time.
**1942** [L. del Rey] *My Name Is Legion* in *Astounding SF* (June) 72/2: The plenum is—well, the composite whole of all that is and was and will be—it is everything and everywhen, all existing together as a unit, in which time does not move, but simply is, like length or thickness.
**1968** H. Ellison *Beast That Shouted Love at Heart of World* in *Galaxy* (June) 20/1: There was a reason the garbage of insanity had ceased to flow through everywhere and everywhen from the drained mind of a seven-headed dragon.

**everywhen** *adv.* in or to all points in time.
**1955** P. Anderson *Time Patrol* in *Time Patrol* (1991) 3: "You're going to be a kind of policeman." "Yeah? Where?" "Everywhere. And everywhen."
**1965** C. D. Simak *All Flesh Is Grass* (1979) 148: So they went everywhere for fun, I thought. And everywhen, perhaps. They were temporal ghouls, feeding on the past.
**2000** D. Eddings & L. Eddings *Redemption of Althalus* 230: You told us that the House is everywhere—all at the same time [...]. It's everywhen then, too, isn't it? What I'm getting at is that there's probably a door to last week somewhere in the House—or one that leads to next year.

**exoskeleton** *n.* an articulated, mechanical framework that surrounds and supports a person's body and increases their effective strength.
**1968** F. Leiber *Specter Is Haunting Texas* in *Galaxy SF* (July) 8/1: I was doubled up like a large bone-and-titanium lazy-tongs, trying to

make the left knee-motor of my exoskeleton behave.

**1986** W. Gibson *Winter Market* in *Burning Chrome* (1986) 145: The exoskeleton carried her across the dusty broadloom with that same walk, like a model down a runway.

**1990** A. Steele *Clarke County, Space* 119: The massive exoskeleton he wore—or, more accurately, piloted—amplified the movements of his arms and legs, transforming him into a juggernaut.

**1993** A. C. Clarke *Hammer of God* 32: He appeared in Stockholm looking like a knight in high-tech armour, wearing one of the powered exoskeletons developed for paraplegics.

**1996** K. S. Robinson *Blue Mars* 403: She wore a rented exoskeleton, made for off-world visitors oppressed by the g.

**1997** W. Shatner *Avenger* 353: Starfleet's greatest doctor was frail, and moved with the aid of exoskeleton braces on his legs.

**expository lump** *n.* an explanation of some element in a story (especially regarding a new technology or piece of world-building) that is overlong or clumsily written and which interrupts the story's narrative flow. Compare INFODUMP.

**1981** V. N. McIntyre *Straining Your Eyes through Viewscreen Blues* in F. Herbert *Nebula Winners Fifteen* 77: If you convey all this necessary information gracelessly, you will end up with an expository lump.

**1987** M. S. Singer *From Out Box* in *Horrorstruck* (Nov./Dec.) 12/1: Each character was introduced with an accompanying block of background information [...]. These expository lumps (sounds like oatmeal, doesn't it?) repeatedly brought the forward motion of the plot to a dead stop.

**1999** H. Turtledove *How I Do What I Do* in *Writer* (Aug.) 11/2: Probably you don't want to put all your research into the story. That way lie the great expository lumps and the "I've done my homework and you're going to suffer for it" syndrome.

**2003** S. M. Stirling *Intro.* in J. J. Astor *Journey in Other Worlds* ix: Apparently the American public of 1894 was prepared to tolerate not merely paragraphs but whole chapters of straightforward expository lump, including

a loving and quite accurate description of how electric plugs would function.

**extra-dimensional** *adj.* from or in another dimension or dimensions.

**1934** E. E. Smith *Skylark of Valeron* in *Astounding Stories* (Aug.) 33/2: Thus DuQuesne, not even dreaming what an incredibly inconceivable distance from the Galaxy Seaton was to attain; nor what depths of extradimensional space Seaton was to traverse before they were again to stand fact to face.

**1949** M. McMahon *Thrilling Wonder Stories (letter)* (Aug.) 147/1: So many of the phenomenal characteristics found here speak of extra-dimensional space.

**1954** J. Highe *What Rough Beast?* in *Galaxy SF* (July) 94/2: "It's extra-dimensional. It's..." He jerked the string with nervous repetition and, suddenly, something was in his hand. Surprised, he dropped it. It disappeared and he felt the tug on the end of the string.

**2001** *SF Chronicle* (July) 44/2: The premise is that extra-dimensional creatures share our Earth, living hidden inside almost every stone, plant, blade of grass, or piece of wood around us.

**extra-planetary** *adj.* from or of other worlds or relating to things from other worlds.

**1931** C. A. Smith *Adventure in Futurity* in *Wonder Stories* (Apr.) 1248/2: Vegetable moulds from Venus, [...] and no one knew what else the morrow would reveal in the way of extra-planetary pests and dangers.

**1946** A. C. Clarke *Loophole* in G. Conklin *Treasury of SF* (1980) 63: To: Chief of Bureau of Extra-Planetary Security. [...] Equip an expedition to the satellite of Earth immediately.

**1956** E. B. Cole *Indirection* in *Astounding SF* (Jan.) 40/1: Can't help but wonder if we actually are babes of the cosmos, and if we haven't been visited and watched by some form of extra-planetary life at one time or another.

**2003** G. Branwyn *Absolute Beginner's Guide to Building Robots* (2004) 340: Because it doesn't look like we "meatbots" are going to be traveling to other worlds any time soon, most of our hope in extra-planetary exploration lies with our metallic brethren.

**extraterrestrial** *n.* [< S.E. *extraterrestrial, adj.*, "coming from outside the Earth"] an ALIEN.

**1941** [S. D. Gottesman] *Cosmic Stories* (July) 15/2: Should a half-breed with the abnormally long hands and black teeth of a Betelgeusian pass the marines, there would be bloodshed and no questions asked. After a few hours of the reign of terror, the extraterrestrials crept into cellars and stayed there for the duration.

**1950** F. Brown *Honeymoon in Hell* in *Galaxy SF* (Nov.) 14/2: Suppose some extra-terrestrials *have* landed somewhere on Earth and have set up a station that broadcasts a ray that is causing the phenomenon.

**1953** R. A. Heinlein *Starman Jones* (1975) 37: He saw the first extra-terrestrial, an eight-foot native of Epsilon Gemini V.

**1966** *New Statesman* (July 8) 58/3: Contact with extra-terrestrials will [ ... ] come suddenly.

**1987** O. Butler *Dawn* (1991) 11: You're one of the few English speakers who never considered that she might be in the hands of extraterrestrials.

**eyetracks** *pl. n.* imaginary marks left on a book by the act of reading it, often said to reduce its value. *Joc.* Also used *fig.*

**1952** A. H. Rapp, L. Hoffman & R. Boggs *Fanspeak* 5/2: When you read a new book you get eyetracks all over it. Then it isn't mint anymore.

**1955** J. Haldeman *Worlds* 150 (2002): "You look good in that, [ ... ]. Especially wet." I'd noticed the difference. "Feel like an ad for a Broadway parlor. I'll be scraping off eyetracks all night."

**1975** E. Weinstein *Fillostrated Fan Dictionary* 45: Eyetracks ruin the mint condition of a book.

**1984** M. Z. Bradley *Inheritor* 180: I tend to get eyetracks all over the books before I sell them.

**1994** *-ish new books?* (Usenet: alt.fan.pratchett) (Jan. 8): That's one reason for wearing reading glasses. It helps prevent the eyetracks.

**2004** *Libary Organization: Literature & Poetry* (Usenet: rec.collecting.books) (Aug. 18): Yeah, how can they have any value if they have "eyetracks"?

# f

**faan** *n.* [fæn] a science fiction fan who is more interested in fandom than in science fiction itself. Often *derog.* Also **faaan.**

**1961** *S-F Five-Yearly* (Nov.) 31: I am a faaan.

**1969** W. Tucker *Intro.* in H. Warner, Jr. *All Our Yesterdays* xii: We were only a couple of faaans (three vowels please, typesetter) staring at one another and privately wondering what-the-hell?

**1969** H. Warner, Jr. *All Our Yesterdays* 242: More evidence of how fans were becoming faaans can be deduced from the activities. The first day consisted of playing records, listening to Liebscher play the piano, playing games, and talking until 4 a.m.

**2005** R. A. Lupoff *Intro.* in P. Lupoff & D. Lupoff *Best of Xero* 13: If you were very, very *fannish*, to the point where you were considered a *faan* rather than merely a fan, you and your publication were *faanish* or even *f-a-a-a-n-i-s-h*.

**faanish** *adj.* [ˈfænɪʃ] interested in or about fandom; typical of a faan or faans. Often *derog.* Hence **faanishness**, *n.*

**1969** H. Warner, Jr. *All Our Yesterdays* 41: "Faanish" originally was pronounced with a bleat indicated by the double vowel, because Tucker invented it to symbolize the sheeplike follow-the-leader habits of lots of fans. Now it usually sounds just like fan and means simply one whose hobby is fandom, not science fiction.

**1969** H. Warner, Jr. *All Our Yesterdays* 97: Pogo as the High Priestess of FooFoo, an early manifestation of pure faanishness.

**1975** E. Weinstein *Fillostrated Fan Dictionary* 4: A few of the copies will be sent to Linguistics departments in a few universities. I realize that this is not a very faanish stunt, but rather more sercon.

**1980** [L. del Rey] *World of SF* 320: A faanish fan is considered lacking in serious interest by some other fans, whom he regards as humorless and stuffy.

**1996** *It is not vital that everything qualify for Hugo* (Usenet: rec.arts.sf.fandom) (May 14): "Faanish" music, by extended usage of "faanish," would refer to music *about* fans.

**fafia** *n.* [ˈfæfiə] [*forced away from it all*, by analogy to GAFIA] the condition of having to quit science fiction fandom because of outside responsibilities or obligations such as school, a job, or family.

**1975** E. Weinstein *Fillostrated Fan Dictionary* 140: WWII was the worst in that a large number of fans were in the Armed forces or other Fafia inducing activities.

**1993** *Tell Old Bill* (Usenet: alt.music.filk) (Jul. 19): Fafia comprised of a trip to Baltimore July 2-11 which at the last minute was...... WITHOUT MY LAPTOP AND MODEM! Gasp! I've survived and am here again.

**2001** *Minicon & further apology (was Re: The False Mirror Analogy)* (Usenet: rec.arts. sf.fandom) (Jan. 23): There's "fafia," when someone is driven away by massive new responsibilities—children, say.

**fafiate** *v.* ['fæfi,eɪt] to quit one's involvement in science fiction fandom because of outside obligations or responsibilities. Compare GAFIATE.

**1989** *gafiated: definition wanted* (Usenet: rec.arts.sf-lovers) (Oct. 13): In a few cases [...], people have been so obnoxious that they were essentially fafiated by fandom itself, the ultimate shame of being outcast by the pariahs...

**1991** L. Niven, J. Pournelle & M. Flynn *Fallen Angels* 19: But why tell me, Bob? I'm fafiated. It's been years since I've dared associate with fen.

**2001** *searching for Maureen O'Brien* (Usenet: rec.music.filk) (Apr. 22): Anybody around Ohio know if she's just covered-up with her day job or had something happen to seriously fafiate her?

**fakefan** *n.* a person with little or no interest in science fiction fandom but who socializes with fans.

[**1939** D. A. Wollheim *"New Fandom" Versus True Fandom* in *MSA Bulletin* (Sept.) 4/1: The culprits responsible for these mags are the former fan and most unrelenting feudist of all times, William S Sykora; the juvenile and semi-illiterate James V Taurasi and the commercially minded fake fan, Sam Moskowitz.]

**1953** R. Bloch *Bloch Denies All* in *S-F Five-Yearly* (1961) (Nov.) 19: I am NOT a fakefan.

**1954** S. Moskowitz *Immortal Storm* 247: Old time fans, sometimes active and interested for decades, when accused by new-comers of being too cynical and lacking interest are wont to make a wry face and retort: "I guess I'm nothing but a fake fan."

**1969** H. Warner, Jr. *All Our Yesterdays* 41: Jack Wiedenbeck was the first "fakefan": one with no basic interest in fandom but with a pleasure in the company of fans. In recent years, it has been diluted often to refer to a person with a mild interest in fandom.

**1998** *Fanzine names on badges at conventions* (Usenet: rec.arts.sf.fandom) (July 28): I consider myself basically a fakefan, in the classical sense of somebody who hangs around fanzine fandom but never actually *does* anything like pub an ish or write a LoC.

**fanac** *n.* [*fan* + *ac*tivity] participation in science fiction fandom, including writing for and publishing fanzines, writing to letter columns, organizing and attending conventions, etc.

[**1950** A. H. Rapp *Timber!* in *Spacewarp* (Apr.) 2: In case anyone wonders, I am as much appalled at the mountains of fanactivity that have piled up on me as you are—or would be.]

**1956** R. Bloch *Some of My Best Fans Are Friends* in *Mag. of Fantasy & SF* (Sept.) 57/1: This, however, is only part of the story—just as fanzines and fan activity (*Fanac*) are only a part of the totality which is fandom.

**1969** H. Warner, Jr. *All Our Yesterdays* 73: Moreover, the more experienced fans arrived at something approaching maturity, and began to acquire some writing and editing ability through their fanac years.

**1971**: see quote in LETTERCOL.

**1984** T. Nielsen Hayden *Over Rough Terrain* in *Making Book* (1994) 89: After Iguanacon my constructive fanac was almost entirely on paper.

**2001** *SF Chronicle* (Mar.) 51/1: Bill was originally a "con fan" and a "club fan"—more interested in the face-to-face socializing offered by fandom than in written fanac.

**faned** *n.* ['fæn,ɛd] [*fan* + *ed*itor] the editor of a fanzine.

[**1945** B. Tucker *Bloomington News Letter* (Dec. 15) 1: Price two-bits [sic], free to faneditors who exchange.]

**1946** B. Tucker *Bloomington News-letter* (Apr.) 1: Sample fanzine advertisement attached; same obtainable free from B.T. for any fan-ed wishing to run them.

**1953** M. Rose & D. MacDonald *Other Worlds* (Jan.) 147/1: We're publishing a fanzine this fall and need illos, stories and articles. [...] Any pointers from other faneds will be appreciated.

**1962** J. Baxter *(letter)* in P. Lupoff & D. Lupoff *Best of Xero* (2005) 145: In short, he's a bloody treasure, and you two are the luckiest faneds in the world for having him on the contents page of *Xero*.

**2000** J. D. Smith [J. Tiptree, Jr.] *Meet Me at Infinity* 187 (2001): Mine were considered "sercon," SF-oriented serious and constructive, as opposed to the lighter tone many faneds adopted.

**fanfic** *n.* FAN FICTION; a work of fan fiction.

**1976** *quoted in American Speech* (1978) (Spring) 55: Granted some of the stories aren't great literature but they do seem to be a reasonably accurate cross section of *short* fan fic.

**1979** D. Schweitzer *Occasionally Mentioning SF* in *SF Rev.* (Jan.) 32/1: Some fanfic zines pay token rates (like a fifth of a cent a word) and pretend to be semi-professional.

**1996** *Baltimore Sun* (Nexis) (Apr. 16) 1F: Many fan-fics can be found on usenet.

**2003** M. Adams *Slayer Slang* (2004) ix: With so many fans writing about the show, and indulging in creative fanfic, together we have extended the language of the Buffyverse.

**fan fiction** *n.* **1.** amateur science fiction and fantasy fiction; fiction that uses characters or a fictional universe originally created by a professional author or for a television show, movie, etc. Also a work of such fiction. Compare FANFIC.

**1939** "B. Tucker" *Le Zombie* (Aug. 19) 2: And Milt is to be congratulated on the story...it is definitly [sic]pro and not fan fiction.

**1965** C. Priest *New Wave—Prozines* in *Zenith Speculation* (Mar.) 10: His first acceptance can be written-off as a trifle; reprinted from Lang's own fanzine *Tensor*; it was little more than good fan-fiction.

**1975** J. Lichtenberg, et al. *Star Trek Lives!* 23: Laura, whose ambition is to become a professional writer, has been writing STAR TREK fiction since her early teens, and was recently nominated for a Hugo Award for fan fiction for her series "Federation and Empire."

**1997** *Entertainment Weekly* (Sept. 26) 84: Chris Carter may bar X-Filers Mulder and Scully forever from consummating their deep bond—but it's a common fantasy in the archives of fan fiction.

**2002**: see quote in SLASH.

**2.** amateur fiction written about science fiction fans or fandom.

**1944** J. B. Speer *Fancyclopedia* 31/1: fan fiction - [...] Properly, the term means fiction about fans, or sometimes about pros, and occasionally bringing in some famous characters from stf stories.

**1969** H. Warner, Jr. *All Our Yesterdays* 51: Fiction about fans, as distinct from fiction written by fans in imitation of prozine stories (both were called fan fiction, indiscriminately) goes back at least to 1934.

**1984** M. Moorcock *Intro.* in *Elric at End of Time* (1985) 11: *Triode* specialized in humorous "fan fiction"—stories written about actual personalities in the SF field.

**fanmag** *n.* a FANZINE.

**1937** B. T. Yerke *Imagination* (Oct.) 5/1: Fan Mag Reviews are out. Or, rather, never were to be "in." There is so little space left over [...] that the chance of a "Fan Mag Review" feature is quite impossible.

**1940** B. Tucker *Le Zombie* (Apr.) 2: LeZ plans, in the future, to print these Cullings regularly, from foreign fanmags, or American mags of small circulation, in the belief that you might otherwise not see the material.

**1952** A. Budrys *Planet Stories* (Nov.) 111/1: The advertising value of fanzines to promags is negligible, for the simple reason that anyone in sufficient contact with STF to read fanmags knows all about the prozines.

**1973** *Oakland (Cal.) Tribune* (Feb. 6) 16/1: Liz [Taylor] and Dick [Burton], as they're chummily called in the fanmags [...] are still avidly tracked and assessed by the print media.

**1999** *LAST G-CON? IS THIS TRUE?* (Usenet: alt.fan.godzilla) (Apr. 11): They publish a fanmag, put up a website for their enterprise and once a year, invite the whole country to G-CON to celebrate giant monsters.

**fanne** *n.* [fæn] *Obs.* a female science fiction fan.

**1944** J. Speer *What Transpired at Michiconference* in *Fancestral Voices* (2004) 98: There are no fannes in the above table, but later someone administered the test to one of the women.

**1947** L. Shaw *Planet Stories (letter)* (Winter) 127/1: I hereby nominate Marion the fanne I'd most like to be marooned on an asteroid with.

**1950** P. Lilly *Thrilling Wonder Stories (letter)* (Oct.) 144/2: My plea is this—is there somewhere in fandom another femme fan who desperately wants to go to the Norwescon [ ... ]? If so, would that femme fan care to share hotel expenses with another fanne in the same situation?

**1966** L. Carter *Handy Phrase-Book in Fannish* in *If* (Oct.) 66/1: A female fan (oh, yes, there are such) is called a *fanne*.

**fanning** *n.* being a fan; participating in science fiction fandom.

**1948** M. Zimmer *Thrilling Wonder Stories (letter)* (Feb.) 102/2: Thanks again for a wonderful story about a character I loved long before my fanning days.

**1961** J. Koning *Withdrawal* in *S-F Five-Yearly* (Nov.) 26: Well, I stayed with the FOCUS group right up to the end, but my heart had gone out of fanning before it was born.

**1969** H. Warner, Jr. *All Our Yesterdays* 124: During his first career in fandom, Tucker had done most of his fanning by mail.

**1983** T. Nielsen Hayden *Hell, 12 Feet* in *Making Book* (1994) 72: It's been a good year for fanning, if nothing else.

**fannish** *adj.* **1.** relating to or characteristic of science fiction fans or fandom. Hence **unfannish,** *adj.*

**1944** J. B. Speer *Fancyclopedia* 1/1: Some of the imaginary incidents reported were of fan interest, fannish names being employed.

**1958** R. M. Holland *Ghu's Lexicon* 9: *Fanzine* [ ... ], a magazine published by and for (?) fans. It is considered unfannish to cater to the whims and desires of readers.

**1961** *National Fantasy Fan* (Feb.) 6: Guy E. Terwilleger has advised me that an unexpectedly heavy load of school duty is forcing him to gafiate from all fannish activity, and to resign as Director of the NFFF.

**1969** H. Warner, Jr. *All Our Yesterdays* 6: Paul Spencer probably wrote the most typical fannish obituary: "Wells' fantasies are the most completely satisfying ever written."

**1977** B. Ash *Visual Ency. of SF* (1978) 275/3: Fannish fanzines deal with fandom itself, often scurrilously.

**1990** *Extrapolation* (Spring) 90: Delany was not exactly a fan at the start of his career, but he knew the evocative power for his readers of a fannish name like Ashton Clark.

**2005** C. Doctorow *Cory Doctorow: Everywhere, All at Same Time* in *Locus* (Jan.) 63/2: No one will cut the binding off a book, scan it one page at a time, and all the rest because they *hated* it. It's totally fannish.

**2.** of or by fans, especially science fiction fans.

**1959**: See quote in BHEER.

**1991** *Locus* (Sept.) 64/2: Also missing are the fannish histories [ ... ] which contain the origins and history of a lot of fannish slang.

**1994** *Interzone* (Dec.) 35/3: The magazine has carried an unexplained millstone of ill-will in the fannish world for many years.

**1997** *Entertainment Weekly* (Sept. 26) 84: Not that Seinfeld inflames the fannish heart.

**fannishness** *n.* the quality or condition of being fannish.

**1959** R. H. Eney *Fancyclopedia II* 164: The active faction insisting that a trufan exhibit his quality by some sort of fanac—crifanac for choice—while others maintained that nomination to or interest in so stefnistic an enterprise as TAFF was sufficient to prove fannishness.

**1969** H. Warner, Jr. *All Our Yesterdays* 3: Any possibility that Scott might achieve a real breakthrough into genuine fannishness was effectively ruined when he was 35 years old.

**1983** T. Nielsen Hayden *Hell, 12 Feet* in *Making Book* (1994) 72: I went to the Worldcon and the fannishness was thick and heady indeed, but what got me through the con was massive and systematic abuse of my medications.

**1997** J. Speer *Phanerofannish Eon* in *Fancestral Voices* (2004) 81: Other advances in technology and affluence have facilitated fannishness; it's frightfully easy now to produce a fanzine.

**fanspeak** *n.* [modeled after NEWSPEAK] the slang or jargon used by science fiction fans.

**1952** A. H. Rapp, L. Hoffman & R. Boggs *Fanspeak* 5/2: *fanspeak.* The language, typography, and cliches of fandom. Term is derived from "newspeak," the language of the future, in George Orwell's *1984.*

**1969** H. Warner, Jr. *All Our Yesterdays* 41: Other manifestations of fanspeak are less confined to newly created words.

**1977** D. Knight *Futurians* 71: In forty years of talking to each other, science fiction fans have evolved a jargon of their own, sometimes called "fanspeak."

**2000** F. Pohl *Chasing Science* 195 (2003): What, you may ask, is a "con"? That is the science fiction fanspeak term for any gathering of people who are interested in science fiction.

**fantascience** *n. Obs.* SCIENCE FANTASY 3A or SCIENCE FICTION 1. Compare FANTASCIENCE, PSEUDO-SCIENCE, SCIENCE FANTASY 2, SCIENTIFIC FANTASY, SCIENTIFIC FICTION, SCIENTIFICTION, SPECULATIVE FICTION 1.

**1934** *Publisher's Preface* in [J. Taine] *Before Dawn* vi: Indeed so decidedly did it appear that this class of book differed from others that an identifying tag seemed useful, if not imperative. Dr. Bell coined the word *fantascience*, which may be roughly defined as literary work having a warp of science and a weft of fantasy.

**1936–37** F. J. Ackerman *Whither Ackermankind?* in *Novae Terrae* (Dec.–Jan.) 7: And publishers of about every one of these periodicals writing me—friendly but fundless—requesting articles on Esperanto or fantascience films or allied subjects.

**1945–46** S. Moskowitz *Immortal Storm* in *Fantasy Commentator* (Winter) 227: The organization adopted the title of the Terrestrial Fantascience Guild.

**1947** J. O. Bailey *Pilgrims through Space & Time* 10: Nearly everybody knows what it is in a general way; everybody has heard the terms "novels of science," "fantascience," "scientifiction," and "science-fiction."

**fantastic** *n.* (of literature or art) that which has the qualities of fantasy.

**1923** S. A. Coblentz *New York Times Book Rev.* (Sept. 9) 2/5: A notable scientific romance by a professional scientist is "Urania," by Camille Flammarion. In this beautiful and impressive tale, wherein the author draws both upon his imagi-

nation and upon his astronomical knowledge to transport the reader not only to the planet Mars but to the remotest depths of interstellar space, there is a philosophic undercurrent that makes the book a delight to the serious reader as well as to the lover of the fantastic.

**1948** J. de Celis *Thrilling Wonder Stories (letter)* (June) 128/1: Lovecraft must have something people like; he is virtually the only legend to survive from the literature of the macabre, or supernatural, or fantastic.

**1981** B. Bova *We Have Met Mainstream...* in F. Herbert *Nebula Winners Fifteen* 175: The literature of the fantastic was the mainstream of world storytelling from the time writing began until the beginning of the Seventeenth Century A.D.

**2002** P. Di Filippo in D. Layne & J. Lake *Polyphony, Vol. 1* (unpag.): SF, Fantasy and Horror—the genres of the ostensibly fantastic—have long ago hit the snooze button and rolled back over for a long lazy hibernation.

**fantastic** *adj.* having the nature of a fantasy.

**1931** O. A. Kline *Writing Fantastic Story* in *Writer* (Jan.) 9/1: One day I was talking to Baird, and he asked me what I had done with my fantastic novel.

**1934** H. Gernsback *Wonder Stories* (Feb.) 793/1: Any one who can enjoy the beautiful tales of Clark Ashton Smith can really appreciate fantastic literature.

**1935** F. J. Ackerman *Wonder Stories (letter)* (Feb.) 1139/1: "The Final Struggle" unfortunately impressed me as being very bad as a science-fictional, fantastic, or any kind of story.

**1971** S. J. Lundwall *SF* 23: Many fantastic stories and novels these days are set upon another world inhabited by people, and if the author of a particular work [ ... ] says, "Here is this world," [ ... ] leaving implications that this is the result of a colonization experiment from Earth of a thousand or two thousand or ten thousand years before, then it would suddenly become a science fiction story.

**fantasy** *n.* **1.** IMAGINATIVE FICTION; a work in this genre. Now chiefly *hist.* Compare

SCIENCE FICTION 3, SCIENTIFANTASY, SPECU-
LATIVE FICTION 2, STFANTASY.

**1932** R. A. Ward *Amazing Stories* (Aug.)
472/1: In *no* "stf" magazine will you find such
marvelous gems of fantasy [sic] as appeared
in the AMAZING STORIES of old.

**1939** *Time* (July 10) 32/2: Scientifiction, which
deals almost exclusively with the world of tomorrow and life on other planets, was inspired by
Jules Verne's and H. G. Wells's fantasies.

**1939** T. Moulton *Unknown (letter)* (July)
128/1: It's hard to find enough words of praise
for the newest [...] of the fantasy magazines.
Yes, even *Astounding* will have to take second
place [...] if *Unknown* maintains, or improves
upon, the standard of its first issue.

**1940** *Thrilling Wonder Stories* (Mar.)
117/2: Raymond Z. Gallun's absorbing sci-
entale, *Renegade from Saturn*, [...] offers
something different in the way of suspense to
fantasy fans. In Gallun's story the hero [...]
has to decide which one of the three transparent cases shown on the cover houses the
menace from Saturn.

**1946** W. S. Baring-Gould *Little Superman,
What Now?* in *Harpers Mag.* (Sept.) 284/1:
But science fiction falls under the general head-
ing of fantasy, not horror.

**1954** F. Brown *Intro.* in *Angels & Spaceships*
1: In its broadest definition as imaginative literature fantasy, of course, includes science fiction.

**1971** T. D. Clareson *Other Side of Realism*
in *SF: Other Side of Realism* 3: Fantasy—the
other side of realism, of which science fiction
is the latest expression—has existed side by
side with what has come to be called the mainstream—the "realistic," the representational—
throughout literature.

**2.** a genre of literature in which magic or
the supernatural is portrayed as being
real; a work in this genre.

**1934** P. Enever *Wonder Stories (letter)* (Feb.)
793/2: Fantasy or pure science, let 'em all
come. But don't attempt to camouflage either
way. Mr. Smith was at his best when he wrote
the "Singing Flame" stories, and they were undoubtedly fantasy. But if he had tried to suggest
that the science contained therein materially
added to the interest he would have been quite
wrong.

**1939** J. W. Campbell, Jr. *Astounding S-F*
(Feb.) 72: Science-fiction readers don't like fantasy. Don't print it.

**1942** R. Rands *Astounding S-F (letter)* (June)
111/2: It had a depth and beauty of setting that
is a little more common to fantasy fiction, perhaps, but the story was really science-fiction.

**1954** F. Brown *Intro.* in *Angels & Spaceships*
1: Fantasy deals with things that are not and that
cannot be.

**1961** G. R. Heap *On Fantasy-Adventure* in
*Ancalagon!* (Mar.) 2: Fantasy-adventure [...],
along with the entire fantasy field, was pushed
into the background by science fiction.

**1978** I. Asimov *Name of Our Field* in *Asimov
on SF* (1981) 26: When we speak of "fantasy"
nowadays, we generally refer to stories that are
not bound by the laws of science, whereas science fiction stories *are* so bound.

**1986** G. K. Wolfe *Critical Terms for SF &
Fantasy* 52: HEROIC FANTASY. Often commercially applied to Sword and Sorcery tales featuring muscular barbarian heroes, but sometimes to
any variety of Epic or Quest fantasy, particularly
those that derive from specific heroic tradition,
such as Arthurian tales.

**1993** *SF Age* (Jan.) 8/2: Yet you're planning to
feature fantasy also. Mistake—S.F. fans don't really want fantasy, or else they'd request it.

**fanzine** *n.* [*fan* + maga*zine*] an amateur periodical published by or for fans,
originally of science fiction, but now of
almost any popular art form or endeavor.
Compare FANMAG.

**1940** L. Chauvenet *Detours* (Oct.) 6: We
hereby protest against the un-euphonious word
"fanag" and announce our intention to plug fanzine as the best short form of "fan-magazine."

**1942** [H. H. Holmes] *Rocket to Morgue* 135:
Infinite numbers of pulp paper scientifiction
magazines and those curious mimeographed
fan bulletins that are known by the portmanteau
name of fanzines.

**1949** *New Republic* (Jan. 17) 16: *Fantasy
Commentator*, perhaps the best of the fanzines,
once ran a history of fan magazines.

**1968** *Time Recorder (Zanesville, Oh.)* (Aug.
25) 3B/1: He decided that there ought to be a
means of exchanging ideas with other fans. To

accomplish that purpose he started publication of a fanzine called "The Zane Grey Collector."

**1980** M. Z. Bradley *Darkover Retrospective* in *Planet Savers/Sword of Aldones* (1982) 310: Immediately I plunged over my head into the world of fanzines and amateur fan publishing.

**1993** *SFRA Rev.* (May–June) 35: Also included is QF's convention schedule and information on filking fanzines which are available from other sources.

**2003** *OT: People needed to help out with Retro Fanzine* (Usenet: uk.games.video.playstation) (June 11): I am looking for people to help me out with a new video games fanzine devoted solely to retro games.

**farside** *n.* the side of something, usually the Moon, that faces away from the Earth. Often *cap.* Compare DARKSIDE 1.

**1961** A. C. Clarke *Fall of Moondust* (1963) 31: When a ship's down on the Moon, it can be spotted very quickly from one of the satellites—either Lagrange II, above Earthside, or Lagrange I, over Farside.

**1974** J. Varley *Picnic on Nearside* in *Mag. of Fantasy & SF* (Aug.) 101/2: All the original settlements had dwindled as people had moved to the comforting empty sky of Farside.

**1984** R. Silverberg *Waiting for Earthquake* in *Conglomeroid Cocktail Party* (1984) 214: His first stop was Meditation Island, the jumping-off point for those who went to visit Virgil Oddum's fantastic and ever-evolving ice sculptures out on Farside.

**1992** A. Steele *Labyrinth of Night* 131: I didn't know myself until about three weeks ago, just before we went around the solar farside.

**faster-than-light** *adj.* exceeding or able to exceed the speed of light.

**1947** [M. Leinster] *Manless Worlds* in *Thrilling Wonder Stories* (Feb.) 32/2: The journeying squadron—every ship wrapped in the utter unapproachability of faster-than-light travel—was oblivious to all that had occurred.

**1952** C. Oliver *First to Stars* in W. F. Nolan *Edge of Forever* (1971) 247: The *Viking* was not, of course, a faster-than-light ship.

**1969** M. Z. Bradley *Brass Dragon* (1980) 50: If they start from Earth, you can't turn on any

faster-than-light drive inside the orbit of Saturn, or you'll crash the asteroids.

**1985** D. Brin *Warm Space Otherness* (1994) 267: Faster-than-light travel was not something anyone gave up on easily, especially a robot with a lifespan of five hundred years.

**1994** R. Silverberg *Hot Sky at Midnight* 190: I speak of our attempts [ … ] to develop a faster-than-light spaceship that will be capable of conducting human colonists to suitable planets outside the solar system.

**faster than light** *adv.* at a speed greater than that of light.

**1912** *Iowa City Daily Press* (Mar. 7) 7/7: Opportunity is the slowest thing in the world when it is approaching you; but when it is going in the other direction it travels faster than light.

**1931** J. W. Campbell, Jr. *Islands of Space* in *Amazing Stories Quarterly* (Spring) 160/1: On the other hand, when we do get out, and get started, we will go faster than light.

**1947** J. Siegel & J. Schuster *Superman* in *Nevada State Journal (Reno) color comics* (Apr. 27) unpag.: Have *you* ever tried to catch a rainbow? It's impossible!—except for *Superman*, who can fly faster than light—therefore making it possible for him to catch up even with an *optical phenomenon!*

**1969** M. Z. Bradley *Brass Dragon* (1980) 149: Very likely their interstellar ships went faster than light.

**2000** R. G. Newton *Thinking about Physics* 131: There certainly are physical phenomena that do travel faster than light.

**feelie, feely** *n.* a movie that also transmits tactile sensations or emotions to the viewer. Usually *pl.*

**1931** A. Huxley *Music at Night* 123: The theatres in which the egalitarians will enjoy the talkies, tasties, smellies, and feelies.

**1932** A. Huxley *Brave New World* 39: Going to the Feelies this evening, Henry? [ … ] The most amazing tactual effects.

**1957** *Daily Independent (Monessen, Pa.)* (Oct. 22) 13/1: "Feelies" are a new kind of movie with an added dimension. You not only hear and see them, you also feel 'em. This is accomplished by beaming messages to the subconscious mind via a process called Precon.

**1963** R. Nelson *Turn Off Sky* in *Mag. of Fantasy & SF* (Aug.) 39/1: They emerged onto the ground floor, a long corridor lined with small shops and feelies screens showing every imaginable kind of show.

**1991** J. Varley *Steel Beach* (1993) 237: If it weren't for the fact that she provided the only costuming role model for the women of the congregation, she might have been dethroned long ago, as the feelies were no longer being made by anyone.

**2001** *Cult Times* (Feb.) 57/5: A swimmer falls for the star of "feelie" films, but he becomes part of the show.

**Feghoot** *n.* [ˈfɛgˌhut] [after Ferdinand *Feghoot*, the title character in a series of short-short stories by Reginal Bretnor, written as by "Grendel Briarton"] a short-short story culminating in an elaborate pun, especially one with a science-fictional setting. Also **Ferdinand Feghoot.** [The term was originally used specifically to describe stories featuring the eponymous character, whether they were written by Briarton or not.]

[**1956** [G. Briarton] (title) *Mag. of Fantasy & SF* (May) 99: Through Time and Space with Ferdinand Feghoot]

[**1960** *Mag. of Fantasy & SF* (Mar.) 4: Some time ago, we received a Ferdinand Feghoot sort of adventure concerning one Fred Flatout who was traveling toward Andromeda on vacation.]

**1961** *Mag. of Fantasy & SF* (Apr.) 74: This is a *Super-Feghoot*. We promise to publish no more than one *Super-Feghoot* a year.—THE KINDLY EDITOR

**1962** *Mag. of Fantasy & SF* (June) 128/1: FEGHOOT BOOK coming in June! The first 45 Feghoots plus 5 never heard of before!

**ca1968** [A. Boucher] *Mag. of Fantasy & SF* (1973) (Apr.) 160/1: A true Feghoot not only culminates in a pun of singular beauty and terror; it is, even before that point, an entertainingly absurd episode of a possible history.

**1986** J. Charlton *Bred Any Good Rooks Lately?* 11: So to call the stories "puns" is to ignore their many dimensions. [ … ] A good case can be made for calling them "feghoots."

**1991** C. Willis *Learning to Write Comedy Writing SF & Fantasy* 82: For awhile in science fiction there were a number of short stories called Ferdinand Feghoots (after the hero of R. Bretnor's versions of this sub-subgenre).

**femfan, femmefan** *n.* (*pl.* **-fans, -fen**) [perh. < slang *fem, femme*, "woman" + *fan*] a female science fiction fan.

**1944** J. B. Speer *Fancyclopedia* 31/2: fannes - Pronounced same as "fans," but used in writing to mean fem fans.

**1948** M. Zimmer *Startling Stories (letter)* (July) 128/1: The next thing I hope will happen will be, that some kind author will write a story with a woman as hero. [ … ] Come on, femme fans, why don't you all write in and ASK the editor to print one!

**1953** *Thrilling Wonder Stories (letter)* (Aug.) 133/2: So, at last, backed by a formidable phalange of femfans, I dare speak up, brave lassie that I am.

**1972** R. Brown *Dear Ted* in *Fantastic SF* (Oct.) 97/2: I was no longer Rich Brown, the fan [ … ], but Rich Brown, the fan-turned-pro who was doing some awfully exciting stuff. Femmefans offered to sit in my lap.

**1991** L. Niven, J. Pournelle & M. Flynn *Fallen Angels* 87: A semicircle of femmefans twisted in their chairs to stare at him.

**fen** *pl. n.* [by analogy to "man", "men"] plural of **fan.** [The term was most likely coined in the summer of 1943 by Art Widner, Louis Russell Chauvenet, and Norm Stanley at the Maine SF convention "Mecon."]

**1944** J. B. Speer *Fancyclopedia* 35/1: *Fen*, alternative plural for "fans," which came into general use after the Mecon solemnly voted its adoption.

**1949** R. F. Nelson *Planet Stories (letter)* (Fall) 104/2: We, the rabid fen, are also a good writer's best press agents with our little fanzines and their free advertising to those people who buy STF mags.

**1952** P. Nowell *Planet Stories (letter)* (Nov.) 112/2: C'mon fen, let's sit down and write to the radio stations about this.

**1965** D. Hoylman *Twilight Zine (letter)* (Apr. 13) 29: I had never been to a con before, didn't know the other fen there [...], and seldom read other conreports.

**1977** S. Wood *Algol* (Summer–Fall) 23/1: All you need are [...] a couple of older fen with experience and enthusiasm (not to mention enough fannish contacts to make up a mailing-list); and a certain amount of mood-enhancers and sheer lunacy.

**1991** L. Niven, J. Pournelle & M. Flynn *Fallen Angels* 87: Very few fen owned homes large enough to house even a small con.

**Ferdinand Feghoot** *n.* see FEGHOOT.

**FIAWOL** *abbr.* ['fiə‚wɔl] [acronym of *fandom is a way of life*] a slogan used by fans for whom participation in science fiction fandom is one of the most important activities in their life. Often *joc.*
[**1952** A. H. Rapp, L. Hoffman & R. Boggs *Fanspeak* 5/2: "*Fandom is a way of life.*" Slogan used apologetically, cynically, resignedly, or scathingly, depending on one's attitude.]

**1969** H. Warner, Jr. *All Our Yesterdays* 10: Moreover, Lovecraft came close to prophesying literally the fiawol philosophy in his talk to the Baltimore Conference of Amateur Journalists in 1921:

**1975** J. Gunn *Alternate Worlds* 182: Why do the fans go to all the trouble? The fans themselves ask the same question. Some of them answer with "fiawol," which is fanese for "fandom is a way of life."

**1981** I. Asimov *Asimov on SF* 241: Many years ago, someone said "Fandom is a way of life" and many fans believe that implicitly. The phrase abbreviated to an acronym, "fiawol," is the rallying cry of the fan movement.

**1997** J. Speer *Phanerofannish Eon* in *Fancestral Voices* (2004) 81: This polarity is represented today in the slogans FIAWOL and FIJAGH, though the fannishest types are likely to be both insurgents and way-of-lifish.

**FIJAGH, FIJAGDH** *abbr.* ['fidʒæg] [acronym of *fandom is just a god(d)amn hobby*] slogan used by science fiction fans for whom their participation in fandom is merely an enjoyable pastime. *Joc.*

**1959** R. H. Eney *Fancyclopedia II* 89: FIJAGH Fandom is Just a Goddamn Hobby

**1976** C. R. McDonough *Preface* in *NESFA Hymnal 1* iii: And remember, F.I.J.A.G.D.H., or is it F.I.A.W.O.L.?

**1991** L. Niven, J. Pournelle & M. Flynn *Fallen Angels* 217: "I see. FIAWOL I know, but what means that other one?" She grinned. "FIJAGH. Fandom Is Just A Goddam Hobby."

**1996** *Paradigm shifts and B5/Trek* (Usenet: rec.arts.sf.tv.babylon5.moderated) (Nov. 27): Some people just need to be beaten with the FIJAGH stick, repeatedly. That's all there is to it.

**filk** *n.* [probably orig. a typographical error for "folk" in an unpublished essay titled "The Influence of Science Fiction on Modern American Filk Music" by Lee Jacobs, submitted for publication to the Spectator Amateur Press Society] a type of music, originally in the folk style but now of any style, with content relating to science fiction, fantasy, science fiction fandom, or other topics of interest to SF fans; a song of this type. Often *attrib.* in **filk song, -singer, -singing,** etc.

**1953** P. Anderson *Zeitschrift für Vollstandigen Unsinn* (Winter) 22: Barbarous Allen: A Filk Song

**1955** [P. A. Kingsley] *Filk Song* in *Zed* (June) 13: The blame/credit (choose one) for the first filk song is a little dubious. Like the man who tried to sit on two stools, it falls in the middle, between Poul Anderson who wrote a filk song called Barbarous Allen and Karen Anderson who egged him on and published it in Zed #774.

**1982** *SF Filk No. 2 of many...* (Usenet: net.sf-lovers) (Oct. 27): In response to the letter that poured in, here is another filksong from the Circle of Janus players

**1991** R. Rogow *Futurespeak* 116: One of Fish's songs has spawned a book of short stories [...], and those stories may well inspire filks in response.

**2006** *San Francisco Chronicle* (Feb. 26) 43/1: A practical definition of today's filk (because filkers won't commit to a standard one) is "lyrical songs of interest to science fiction and fantasy fans."

**filk** *v.* **1.** *intrans.* to write or sing filk songs.
**1978** S. E. Miller *I Could Have Filked All Night* 33/3: I could have filked all night.
**1991** *Fantasy* (Spring) 50/3: I also go to cons occasionally, where I can be found filking late into the night.
**1998** *Buffalo (New York) News* (Nexis) (Aug. 7) 35G: The songwriters had unknowingly been "filking," writing the music of science fiction and fantasy conventions.
**2.** *trans.* to create a filk song using the tune and structure of an existing song.
**1982** *"filk"* (Usenet: net.sf-lovers) (Dec. 29): "Filk" is not used as an abbreviation for "filksong"; it's either a transitive verb (meaning very similar to "parody") or an abbreviation for "filksing."
**1991** R. Rogow *Futurespeak* 116: Many songs are constantly filked; a list of parodies of "The Battle Hymn of the Republic" may run to fifty items or more.
**2006** *Re: More tempests (IAFA-L email list)* (Apr. 18): I just could not resist the temptation to filk "Suwanee River."

**filker** *n.* a person who writes or sings filk songs.
**1982** *To: Arlan Andrews Re: FIlks.* (Usenet: net.sf-lovers) (Nov. 25): When I read the filk you posted a few weeks ago, I passed it along to our filker and editor of the club newsletter, Margret Purdy, and she loved it.
**1997** *Marcon Zone* 49/1: *Tom Smith* is a filker of epic proportions, which he blames on all that Pepsi and pizza. He made his reputation as The World's Fastest Filker here at MarCon.
**2002** *Dot.con Daily* (Fri. Afternoon Aug. 30) 4/2: He was [ ... ] a filker and filksong writer and publisher, and too many other things to mention.

**filking** *n.* the writing or singing of filk songs.

**1981** *SF-LOVERS Digest V3 #140* (Usenet: fa.sf-lovers) (June 5): Phone for those who call during the filking is:
**2000** S. Elgin *Linguistics & SF Newsletter* (Sept.–Oct.): The fact that I'm no longer able to sing distresses me—it seems unspeakably and unsingably unnatural—but it doesn't keep me from being interested in filking and filkmusic.
**2002** *Dot.con Daily* (Fri. Afternoon Aug. 30) 3/1: There will also be [ ... ] Filking at the Fairmont.

**filksing** *n.* a gathering of filkers to perform and listen to filk songs.
**1972** *Boskone 9 Filk-Song Book* Table of contents: Welcome to the Boskone Filksing!
**1995** *There's Filksing Here Saturday Night!* (Usenet: alt.music.filk) (Feb. 8): The last hurrah of the holiday season (Valentine's Day) is almost upon us, so let's get together and massacre some songs. The month's second filksing will be on Saturday, 25 February.
**2006** *San Francisco Chronicle* (Feb. 26) 43/1: These amateur-friendly, interactive filk sings run all day (and all night) during filk conventions and at "house filks" the rest of the year.

**fillo** *n.* [*fill*er + ILLO] a small illustration used to fill up extra space, especially in a fanzine or other fan publication.
**1959** R. H. Eney *Fancyclopedia II* 7: Fragmentary sketches are also used as fillers (hence the byname fillo) or sometimes stuck around on the page to break up the dead-solid type.
**1965** A. Kuhfeld *Twilight Zine* (Aug.–Sept.) 27: Well, I can take a hint as well as the next man, so find enclosed seven fillos, an illo, and a cartoon.
**1974** E. Weinstein (title): Fillostrated Fan Dictionary
**2001** *SF Chronicle* (July) 15/1: In these days of fewer and fewer fan artists, small fillos suitable for use in fanzines are available free from *Randy B. Cleary.*

**first contact** *n.* the first meeting between two intelligent alien species, especially between humans and aliens. Often *cap.*

**1935** [M. Leinster] *Proxima Centauri* in *Astounding Stories* (Mar.) 21/2: He had piloted the Adastra to its first contact with the civilization of another solar system.

**1945** [M. Leinster] *First Contact* in *Astounding SF* (May) 12/1: The first contact of humanity with an alien race was a situation which had been foreseen in many fashions, but never one quite so hopeless of solution as this.

**1964** C. Priest *SF Mag. Survey 1963* in *Zenith SF* (June–July) 19: Stories of first contact with alien races and planets were far too frequent.

**1984** A. Cole & C. Bunch *Wolf Worlds* (1990) 14: Sten itemized: ground packs, weapons, surface suits, survival gear, first-contact pouches.

**1988** [J. Tiptree, Jr.] *Color of Neanderthal Eyes* (1990) 2: Wet has been visited only once before, by a loner named Pforzheimer, who stayed only long enough to claim a First Contact.

**1994** *Interzone* (Aug.) 54/2: We must remember that White Queen was a First Contact novel in which the alien Aleutians came to Earth to trade, and were mistaken for invaders.

**2002** J. E. Czerneda *To Trade Stars* 32: I heard the growing wonder in his voice as he surveyed the being stuffed into his ship. "Rugheran. Sira. Do you realize what this means? First contact."

**fix-up** *n.* a novel composed of previously-written shorter works, frequently with additional material to smooth the transitions between stories. Compare MOSAIC NOVEL.

**1975** A. E. van Vogt *Reflections* 135: Fix-up novel consisting of *Film Library*, *The Search*, *Far Centaurus*, and 50% new material.

**1979** J. Clute in P. Nicholls *Ency. of SF* 627/2: In his autobiographical *Reflections of A. E. van Vogt* (1975), AEVV uses the term "fix-up" in the same sense in which it has been taken over for use in this Encyclopedia—to define a book made up of stories previously published, but altered to fit together, usually with the addition of new cementing material.

**1988** D. Chow *Locus* (Feb.) 28/1: Bantam felt so strongly about his fixup novel, *Life During Wartime*, they did it as a mainstream book.

**1990** M. Bishop *More Than Masterpiece?* in *Quantum* (Spring) 6/1: First, it became a

"novel" by a route often pursued by genre science fiction writers in those days, namely, the route of the "fix-up."

**1997** J. Lethem *Breeding Hybrids in Genre Garden* in *Locus* (Oct.) 72/2: Those first four or so eventually became parts of *Amnesia Moon*, which is a book that is a fix-up, though no one knows it. It's a fix-up of unpublished short stories.

**2002** G. Jones *3SF* (Dec.) 64/1: Ray Bradbury's *From The Dust Returned* is billed as a new novel from the grand master. In reality it's a fix-up of several stories featuring Ray Bradbury's "Addams Family."

**flame pistol** *n.* [perh. modeled after *flame thrower*] a hand weapon that emits flames. Also **flame gun.**

**1932** T. D. Gardner *Last Woman* in *Wonder Stories* (Apr.) 1242/2: "Have you any weapons?" The Last Woman asked the explorer. "Only an automatic and a flame pistol."

**1939** G. Arnold *Sea Things* in *SF* (Mar.) 88/1: His hand jerked swiftly to his belt, and now his own flame gun spat a crackling emanation.

**1946** [R. Rocklynne] *Bottled Men* in *Astounding SF* (June) 84/1: He took up his flame pistol, adjusted the valves. A long smoky flame leaped out. Gull adjusted the valves again and it settled down to an inch-thick sword of flaming, violet-blue energy.

**1951** F. M. Robinson *Untitled Story* in *Astounding SF* (Sept.) 76/2: Lehman had a flame pistol in his hand and Hayssen promptly dropped to the ground. A beam of purple light flared through the air, cutting through the spot where he had been.

**1989** W. Shatner *Tekwar* (1990) 185: The nearer one had a flamegun instead of a left arm.

**flash crowd** *n.* [after Larry Niven's short story, "Flash Crowd" (see 1973 quote); in Niven's story, flash crowds assemble via teleportation] a sudden increase in the number of visitors viewing a website, especially after the site has been mentioned on a more prominent website.

[**1973** L. Niven *Flash Crowd* in R. Silverberg *Three Trips in Time & Space* 63: "He was on the *Tonight Show* and he happened to mention the red tide down at Hermosa Beach. [ ... ] The next thing anyone knows, every man, woman, and child in the country has decided he wants to see the red tide at Hermosa Beach." [ ... ] "Another flash crowd. It figures."]

**1993** *Journal Record (Oklahoma City)* (ProQuest) (Nov. 5): Because informal news about events on the network flows so quickly through electronic word of mouth, what Rosen called "flash crowds" are beginning to appear with increasing frequency to instantly clog computer systems.

**2000** *InternetWeek* (EBSCOhost) (Apr. 3): It's symptomatic of one of the leading causes of site slowdowns: flash crowds. These are the crowds that congregate to a particular site in response to a specific event.

**2005** *Metafilter (Internet)* (Mar. 11): Pro is that no matter how high your traffic, some people will get to see it each hour, unlike if you maxed out your monthly allottment [sic]. Bad is that it can't handle a flash crowd, like a slashdotting (or mefistorm).

**flitter** *n.* a small, usually short-range, aircraft or spaceship.

**1941** E. E. Smith *Vortex Blaster* in *Comet* (July) 10/2: Then all three went out to the flitter. A tiny speedster, really; a torpedo bearing the stubby wings and the ludicrous tail-surfaces, the multifarious driving-, braking-, side-, top-, and under-jets so characteristic of the tricky, cranky, but ultra-maneuverable breed.

**1955** [A. North] *Sargasso of Space* (1957) 53: The small flitters carried by the Queen for exploration work held with comfort a two-man crew—with crowding, three.

**1968** F. Herbert *Heaven Makers* (1977) 158: A file of ten flitters stood ready along the gray ramp, prepared to debark on his orders.

**1982** A. McCaffrey *Crystal Singer* 91: The cost of the flitter craft used by Crystal Singers in the ranges was staggering.

**1994** S. Baxter *Ring* (1996) 43: The flitter tumbled from the shimmering throat of the wormhole transit route from Port Sol to Earthport. Louise Ye Armonk peered out of the cramped cabin, looking for Earth.

**floater** *n.* a vehicle powered by antigravity, especially one that can only fly relatively close to the ground; also, a hovercraft.

**1935** J. W. Campbell, Jr. *Machine* in *Cloak of Aesir* (1952) 75: A dark shadow drifted slowly across the room, and they turned to see a five-passenger floater sinking slowly, gently, to Earth.

**1952** C. Kornbluth *Make Mine Mars* in *SF Adventures* (Nov.) 84/1: After a smooth landing I took an Eastbound chair from the field and whistled as the floater lifted me to the ISN floor.

**1967** C. D. Simak *Werewolf Principle* (1968) 44: Carefully Blake guided the chair-like floater to the ground at one end of the barrier, close to the clump of birch, snapped off the gravity field as it came to rest.

**1979** N. Spinrad *World Between* 33: Carlotta turned on the float unit and the floater rose the standard one meter off the floor. She cranked on a little throttle and the floater moved forward.

**1985** D. Hill *Colsec Rebellion* (1986) 41: Cord then learned that a floater was a vehicle that hovered on a cushion of air.

**1993** G. Wolfe *Nightside Long Sun* 17: The floater had stopped, its roar fading to a plaintive whine as it settled onto the rutted street.

**1999** J. Dalmas *Three-Cornered War* 177: Then he dropped the floater to within a foot of the ground.

**fmz** *abbr.* [fɛmz] [*fan* *m*a*g*a*z*ine] a FANZINE.

**1941** D. Brazier *Frontier* (Feb.) 1: Every *fmz* (pronounced fmz [sic], meaning fan magazine) that I have ever complimented has received the most kind words for its editorial section and any other familiar chit-chat column.

**1941** F. J. Ackerman *FMZ by 4SJ* in *FMZ Digest* (Feb.–Mar.) 1: Then I pickt up the Feb *Frontier*, read Brazier's editorial column therein & found the breve that I've been waiting for. [ ... ] Simple as "stf," it's .fmz.

**1944** J. B. Speer *Fancyclopedia* 13/1: A great deal of the contents of individ fanzines and editorials in other fmz are composed "in the stick," without dummying.

**1959** R. H. Eney *Fancyclopedia II* 71: FMZ [ ... ] Abbreviation for fanzines. Pronounced "femz" but distinguished from "femmes" by accompanying the latter word with a whistle and descriptive gesture.

**1964** J. Linwood *Fanalytic Eye* in *Les Spinge* (Jan.) 27: Under its new editor [ ... ] Rolf Gindorf TBE loses its "Wild abandoned air" and settles down into a fairly typical fmz modelled on US lines.

**1996** *WWW Pages & Ezines (Was Re UseNetiquette)* (Usenet: rec.arts.sf.fandom) (July 29): If someone, other than the reviewer in a fmz, tells me about a review in a printed fmz which I didn't receive it can be a slightly larger problem.

**food pill** *n.* an edible capsule that contains all the nutrition of (at least) a full meal, eliminating the need to prepare and eat food.

[**1915** H. S. Keeler *John Jones's Dollar* in *Black Cat* (Aug.) 50/2: These elements are then synthetically combined into food tablets for those of us who are yet alive.]

**1950** C. Recour *Hydroponic Heaven* in *Amazing Stories* (Nov.) 71/1: Favorite subject of science-fiction satirists from Aldous Huxley to a host of recent writers is the idea of the "food-pill." [ ... ] Imagine receiving all your necessary nourishment in the form of a simple little pill!

**1965** F. Leiber *Mag. of Fantasy & SF* (Dec.) 36/2: This book is for those particularly interested in getting a wider-spectrum view of Russian science fiction, or who have a great nostalgia for food pills, [ ... ] ships that fly through rock by cutting it very fast, and spray-on Omega-ray armor to dissolve bullets.

**1981** W. Gibson *Gernsback Continuum* in *Burning Chrome* (2003) 34: John [ ... ], we've forgotten to take our food pills.

**1996** B. Landon *Ain't No Fiber in Cyberspace* in G. Westfahl, G. Slusser & E. Rabkin *Foods of Gods* 234: Food supplements seem to realize the old SF and comic book ideal of the single food pill that is itself a meal.

**force field** *n.* a barrier of energy, generally used to protect a being, spaceship, planet, etc. from attack or other dangers or to keep someone or something in or

out of a location. Also used *fig.* Also **force screen, force shield.**

**1931** J. W. Campbell, Jr. *Islands of Space* in *Amazing Stories Quarterly* (Spring) 149/1: Arcot had used the force field that produced the directed motion of the molecules as a weapon.

**1939** F. B. Long *Dweller in Outer Darkness* in *Thrilling Wonder Stories* (Aug.) 68/2: The blast tubes in his hands were trained on me, but I knew I'd be safe enough and that Helen Torrey and Miles would remain unscathed. The refracting belts had built up an invisible force-screen about them.

**1944** [G. Vance] *Double-Cross on Mars* in *Amazing Stories* (Sept.) 144/1: Their planet was protected by a force shield whose energy was supplied by a metal peculiar to Venus.

**1949** [R. LaFayette] *Unwilling Hero* in *Startling Stories* (July) 102/2: For ships are frail. Their force shields can sometimes be pierced by a single insentient particle blasting through.

**1963** P. Anderson *After Doomsday* (1968) 24: Not enough radiation to matter. The force screens can block a lot more than that.

**1977** F. Herbert *Dosadi Experiment* 11: Do not intrude any portion of your body beyond the force field.

**1985** O. S. Card *Ender's Game* 115: A second later he smashed into the forcefield of the enemy's door and rebounded with a crazy spin.

**1992** L. Tuttle *Lost Futures* 221: She was aware of projecting a sort of invisible force-field to ward off the weird, the needy.

**1999** M. J. Friedman *My Brother's Keeper* 146: There's a forcefield around it that's playing havoc with our sensors, sir.

**Frankenstein complex** *n.* [after Victor Frankenstein, the main character in Mary Shelley's novel *Frankenstein*, whose creation turns on and eventually destroys him] the fear that a person's or humanity's technological creations (especially robots) will ultimately cause them harm.

**1947** I. Asimov *Little Lost Robot* in *Astounding S-F* (Mar.) 116/1: I'll admit that this Frankenstein Complex you're exhibiting has a certain justification—hence the First Law in the first place.

**1987** L. M. Bujold *Falling Free* in *Analog SF/Sci. Fact* (Dec.) 30/2: You sure you're not harboring just a little of the old Frankenstein complex about all this?

**1990** J. Dewey *In Dark Time* 6: More profound was the revival of the Frankenstein complex, the fear [...] that has haunted Westerners since the age of the machine commenced—that our own technologies can not only dehumanize and enslave us but finally destroy us as well.

**1992** J. C. Segen *Dictionary of Modern Medicine* 234/1: *Frankenstein complex* The fear that machines via artificial intelligence may replace physicians

**2002** D. Langford *Last Robot Story* in *3SF* (Dec.) 13/2: The unknown terrorist cabal is trying to trade on humanity's Frankenstein complex by throwing the blame on to robots.

**free fall** *n.* [orig. the motion of an object under the force of gravity alone] a condition of weightlessness.

**1931** J. W. Campbell, Jr. *Islands of Space* in *Amazing Stories Quarterly* (Spring) 167/1: Since they were to use the space control, though, they would be subject to infinite acceleration, it would be a free fall, and Fuller would remain helplessly weightless.

**1953** *Authentic SF* (Feb. 15) 15: She was weightless at that point, "as I'm in free fall."

**1970** A. McCaffrey *Ship Who Sang* (1991) 108: If you think I'm going to travel free-fall all the way to Regulus, you've another think coming.

**1981** J. Varley *Blue Champagne* in *Blue Champagne* (1986) 37: A disc was better than a wheel for that purpose, since it provided regions of varying gravity, from one gee at the rim to free-fall at the hub.

**1984** W. Gibson *Neuromancer* (1989) 103: Molly and a skinny Zionite called Aerol helped Case negotiate a freefall corridor into the core of a smaller torus.

**1991** *Locus* (Sept.) 29/3: The Robinsons manage to make their characters' introduction to freefall interesting, in the best "Space Cadet" tradition (though Heinlein's teens never got to experiment with freefall sex, that I recall).

**frell** *v.* [coined for use in the television program *Farscape*] used in place of "fuck" in its figurative senses. Compare SMEG.

**2002** *TV Zone* (No. 157) 82/1: If networks want to frell with the fans, then so be it.

**2002** *How to "whack" interactive web site, that has great content* (Usenet: alt.html) (Aug. 13): On the other hand, oh, frell it... there is no other hand.

**2003** *It's official...* (Usenet: aus.tv.buffy) (Feb. 27): Frell me! Is there anything Braga and Berman won't frell over for a few smegging dollars?!?!?!?

**frell** *interj.* used to express anger, dismay, frustration, etc.; in non-*Farscape* use, often a jocular euphemism for "fuck." Compare SMEG.

**2001** D. Bischoff *Ship of Ghosts* (2002) 262: Frell! We're going to have to retreat.

**2003** *Lazy Bastards!* (Usenet: alt.games.tombraider) (July 8): Now, having that hand show up and tell me I can interact or not with an object.., well, frell! No wonder folks are finishing this game so quickly!

**2005** *Adrics Awards Ceremony 2005 (3/8)* (Usenet: alt.drwho.creative) (Oct. 11): Mia groaned. "Oh *frell*..." She managed to scrape together some remaining shreds of composure, and cleared her throat.

**frelling** *adj.* used for emphasis or to express anger, dismay, frustration, etc.; in non-*Farscape* use, often a jocular euphemism for "fucking." Compare SMEGGING.

**1999** *Why Why has it taken this long?* (Usenet: alt.tv.farscape) (Sept. 18): But that's the fluid nature of the television series—as it turned out, it was merely out-frelling-standing...

**2001** K. R. A. DeCandido *Farscape: House of Cards* 187: I want to be away from this frelling planet as soon as possible.

**2003** R. Klaw *Geek Confidential* 43: It looks like a frellin' romance, and not a particularly good one at that.

**2003** *Horn Book Mag.* (July/Aug.) 501: We worked our frelling tails off for a whole year, and it was *much* more intense than BBYA.

**fresher, 'fresher** *n.* [contraction of "re-fresher"] a bathroom or shower.

**1940** R. Heinlein *Coventry* in *Astounding S-F* (July) 78/1: "Where's the 'fresher?" [ . . . ] It was not Dave's idea of a refreshing chamber, but he managed to take a sketchy shower in spite of the slimy floor.

**1968** J. M. Faucette *Crown of Infinity* 38: "You're tired, of course, but you'll feel better after an hour in the 'fresher." [ . . . ] She stepped behind a door and a moment later he heard the soft rush of water in the shower stall.

**1989** L. E. Modesitt, Jr. *Ecolitan Operation* 292: Trying to lift a shuttle on a high gee curve with a full bladder was likely to be uncomfortable, if not fatal. He sighed as he located the fresher and sprinted for it.

**2002** J. E. Czerneda *To Trade Stars* 358: She kept scrubbing. Barac had told her to clean up, and he was waiting for his turn in the fresher.

**fringefan** *n.* (pl. **-fans, -fen**) a science fiction fan whose interests are seen as being peripheral to the main body of science fiction fandom or to a specific subfandom. Hence **fringe fandom,** *n.*

**1969** H. Warner, Jr. *All Our Yesterdays* 263: It got next to no prozine publicity and Los Angeles newspapers ignored it, so the fringefans didn't know about it.

**1977** B. Ash *Visual Ency. of SF* (1978) 273/1: The largest and most recent body of fringe fandom rejoices in a membership of "Trekkies" or "Trekkers"—adherents of the *Star Trek* television series.

**1981** J. Van Hise *SF Rev.* (Summer) 40/1: What fringe-fans on the Trek experience don't realize is that in STAR TREK fan fiction the concept of a character dying is quite common.

**1985** A. Budrys *Benchmarks* 253: Some were undoubtedly fakefans and fringefans, and there was I'm sure a strong surviving increment of Trekkies, as well as a high proportion of what might be called Jedites.

**1991** R. Rogow *Futurespeak* 201: The Trekkers found themselves ostracized from many of the existing cons, where they were stigmatized as fringe fen.

**FTL** *abbr.* faster than light.

**1950** F. Leiber *Enchanted Forest* in *Astounding SF* (Oct.) 111/1: "You fly fast, Elven." [ . . . ] Elven agreed softly without looking around, and added, "FTL"—meaning Faster Than Light.

**1958** D. Berry *Intruder* in *Venture SF Mag.* (Mar.) 81/2: They tell me that I'm not actually traveling FTL, it just *seems* that way. Then why should my clock frequencies be dropping behind?

**1965** L. Niven *Wrong-Way Street* in *Galaxy* (Apr.) 27/1: So if they had time travel to go with it, it adds up to an FTL drive. They can sleep through a hundred-year journey and then move back a hundred years.

**1972** M. Bradley *Darkover Landfall* 66: Infants—or even young children—could not endure interstellar FTL drive.

**1991** A. McCaffrey & E. Moon *Generation Warriors* 153: But there was supposed to be a transfer pod only two light months out, with an FTL pod pre-programmed for the nearest Fleet sector headquarters.

**2001** J. A. Gardner *Ascending* 48: No matter what, keep talking till we're ready to go FTL.

**fugghead** *n.* [alteration of "fuckhead"] a stupid or contemptible person. Hence **fuggheaded.**

**1950** F. T. Laney *Syllabus for Fanzine* in *Spacewarp* (Sept.) 10: Getting constructive for a moment, here is the hap-hazard fuggheaded F. Towner Laney fanzine-throwing-together technique which has worked for 14 issues of ACOLYTE.

**1950** Laney, *Syllabus for Fanzine* 11: If you are a fugghead, you'll have a better magazine if you suppress your fuggheadedness, but this is pretty hard to do.

**1959** D. Knight *Mag. of Fantasy & SF* (Dec.) 91/1: The writing is gassy, with an almost incredible concentration of cliches in places. For contrast, Cooper has had the gall to interpolate this fuggheaded screed with passages from Ecclesiastes and Revelation.

**1961** B. Silverberg *Stars of Slave Giants* in *S-F Five-Yearly* (Nov.) 14: "It's an octopus, you fugghead," the Anemian insisted.

**1986** T. Nielsen Hayden *Over Rough Terrain* in *Making Book* (1994) 82: You *might* guess that someday we'd wind up sitting around together in some hotel room, talking late-model fanpolitics and fuggheads.

**2000** *Right to Bare Legs* (Usenet: alt. sysadmin.recovery) (Aug. 16): He's a fugghead. In fact, he's so much of a fugghead that other fuggheads call him one.

**fuggheadedness** *n.* the act or condition of being a fugghead.

**1949** F. T. Laney *Dust from Bandsaw* in *Fandango* (Fall) 20: I, as a staunch Californian, wish to urge that the convention ALWAYS be held on the East Coast. We have enough fuggheadedness out here without importing more of it.

**1960** J. Speer *Novus Ordo Fandorum* in *Fancestral Voices* (2004) 189: Do thou, O Laney, what traces of fuggheadedness yet remain, graciously cleanse.

**1969** H. Warner, Jr. *All Our Yesterdays* 40: Technically, Laney tried to restrict the use of fugghead to refer to those whose fuggheadedness overshadowed their more useful and reasonable characteristics.

**1980** [L. del Rey] *World of SF* 321: Like entropy, fuggheadedness tends to increase.

**2000** *Kris and Doug* (Usenet: rec.arts. sf.fandom) (Nov. 10): I think that Gary has bursts of fuggheadedness, but they're usually brief, and he usually apologizes for them afterwards.

**future history** *n.* a chronology of the future, as realized in a series of stories set in the same fictional universe; such a series of stories. Hence **future historian,** *n.*

**1941** J. Campbell *Astounding S-F* (Feb.) 67: I'd like to mention something that may or may not have been noticed by the regular readers of Astounding: all Heinlein's science-fiction is laid against a common background of a proposed future history of the world and of the United States.

**1950** R. A. Heinlein *Man Who Sold Moon* 16: The pseudohistory of the immediate future outlined in the chart [...] was worked up [...] as I added new stories [...]. Now I hardly need the chart; the fictional future history embodied in it is at least as real to me as Plymouth Rock.

**1975** L. Niven *Tales of Known Space* xi: Future histories tend to be chaotic. They grow from a common base, from individual stories with common assumptions; but each story must—to be fair to readers—stand by itself. The future history chronicled in the Known Space Series is as chaotic as real history.

**1996** D. Pringle, et al. *Ultimate Ency. of SF* 22/2: Poul Anderson's two series featuring the swashbuckling special agent Dominic Flandry and the cunning trader Nicholas van Rijn combine to form one of sf's most extensive adventures in future history.

**1996** Pringle, et al. *Ultimate Encyc. of SF* 218/1: Harking back to [...] future historians including Asimov and Heinlein, Niven soon showed that he could uncork a potent new brew that synthesized all these elements into something entirely fresh and modern.

**2002** T. Allison *New York Rev. of SF* (Apr.) 1/2: It's popular to liken Barnes to Heinlein for his [...] use of a coherent future history.

**future war** *n.* a genre of science fiction in which the events of wars set in the future, especially those also set on the planet Earth, are described. Compare MILITARY SCIENCE FICTION.

[**1931** *Wonder Stories* (May) 1442/2: Mr. Pratt is a keen student of military affairs. He does not leave reason behind and jump into fantasy, but looking calmly at present trends in warfare he gives us this realistic story of a future war.]

**1942** C. Davis *Astounding S-F (letter)* (June) 110/1: Here's hoping Northrup's point of view will be kept in mind in your accepting and rejecting of the hack future-war stories you are no doubt being deluged with.

**1969** S. Moskowitz in A. H. Norton & S. Moskowitz *Great Untold Stories of Fantasy & Horror* 58: Perhaps his best-known work to fantasy collectors was *The Conquest of America*, a future-war story published by George H. Doran Co. in 1916.

**1975** J. Gunn *Alternate Worlds* 62: The genre might be called the prophetic (or cautionary) novel of future war [...]. Its distinguishing characteristic is a richly detailed description of an imminent war, often fought with future weapons or tactics, which goes badly for the nation attacked.

**1991** *Isaac Asimov's SF Mag.* (mid-Dec.) 115: The author of this gripping future-war tale has had a story published in *Omni,* and is at work on a novel.

**2003** B. Stableford *SF before Genre* in E. James & F. Mendlesohn *Cambridge Companion to SF* 23: The expansion of the future war genre into a much broader speculative genre of "scientific romance" was tentatively begun.

# Expletives & Profanity

The use of swear words in science fiction has a complex history. Until the 1960s, many publishers would not print actual swear words, so writers were required to use their ingenuity if they wanted to use the full range of expression. Perhaps influenced by Norman Mailer's 1948 novel *The Naked and the Dead,* in which the word "fug" was famously substituted for "fuck," Francis Towner Laney coined the fannish slur **fugghead** around 1950. In the late 1960s, Norman Spinrad's novel *Bug Jack Barron* was considered so profane that the bookseller W.H. Smith banned sales of the magazine in which it had been serialized. And no doubt as a commentary on this state of affairs, Larry Niven wrote a series of stories in the 1970s in which the words "censored" and "bleep" had themselves become curses.

Although print standards have relaxed since the 1960s, those in television have been slower to do so, and writers have had to create new, futuristic curses to get past the censors. Some of these terms have even caught on off the air. The BBC's *Red Dwarf* has been by far the most successful—in terms of propagating its made-up invective, anyway—gracing us with the versatile and evocative verb **smeg** (a shortening of "smegma") and its derivatives **smeghead, smegging,** and **smeggy.** The Sci Fi Channel's *Farscape* has also managed to spread the words **frell** and **frelling**, which are used exactly as one would use "fuck" (in its figurative senses). Joss Whedon's *Firefly* is notable both for its coinage **gorram** and for the innovation of having any particularly colorful curses said in Chinese. *Battlestar Galactica* gave us **frak** in the 1970s, but it never caught on; it remains to be seen whether its recent revival will have more success (linguistically speaking, that is).

That these TV profanities have proved so successful in the real world, while curses coined in print have not caught on, is attributable to the fact that TV reaches a much larger audience, including people who may not read SF. But surely the success of these particular terms can also be attributed simply to the fact that they're fun to say, with the added bonus that, since they're not "real" swear words, you (probably) won't get in trouble for it. (And if you don't smegging believe me, just give it a frelling try, gorram it!)

# g

**gadget** *adj.* describing a story or genre in which the plot revolves around an invention, especially where character is secondary to the technology.

**1942** [H. H. Holmes] *Rocket to Morgue* 81: The gadget stories were more interesting. They frequently made honest attempts at forecasting scientific developments. [...] But the writers stopped there. Interest lay in the gadget itself. And science fiction was headed for a blind alley until the realization came that even science fiction must remain fiction, and fiction is basically about people, not subatomic blasters nor time warps.

**1953** I. Asimov *Social SF* in R. Bretnor *Modern SF* 171: Story after story came out in which that stock character, the irascible, eccentric (or even mad) scientist explained his inventions and discoveries in interminable double-talk. We might call this "gadget science fiction."

**1959** R. Heinlein *SF* in B. Davenport, et al. *SF Novel* 20: This indispensable three-fold awareness does not limit the science fiction author to stories about science—he need not write a gadget story; indeed a gadget story would not be science fiction under this definition if the author failed in this three-fold awareness.

**1980** [L. del Rey] *World of SF* 80: On the other hand, such gadget stories as Bob Olson's various "fourth-dimensional" efforts [...] were stories of mere gadgets, based on a misunderstanding of the laws of mechanics and whatever rules could be derived for any physical fourth dimension.

**gafia** *n.* ['gæfiə] **1.** [get(ting) *away from it all*] the condition of participating in science fiction fandom. Now *hist.* Also as *v.*

**1944** J. B. Speer *Fancyclopedia* 41/1: gafia—(Wilson)—Get Away From It All; motto of escapism.

**ca 1944** F. J. Ackerman *Fantasy Flanguage* in [Anon.] *What Is Science Fiction Fandom* 27: So once again there were only 2 Fen, and while one picked up his obliterine and turned toward Mimi, the other, an escapist, picked up a prozine to gafia.

**1969** H. Warner, Jr. *All Our Yesterdays* xx: *Gafia* [...] growing inactive in fandom, and as a verb, to gafiate; originally it meant the opposite, getting away from the mundane world by engaging in fanac.

**1977** D. Knight *Futurians* 71: "Gafia" (getting away from it all) started out being what a fan did when he was fanning.

**2.** the condition of no longer participating in science fiction fandom, often conceived of as a physical location. Compare FAFIA.

**1950** A. H. Rapp *Timber!* in *Spacewarp* (Apr.) 2: GAFIA is an intermittent affliction of fans. The letters stand for Getting Away From It All. Symptoms are sheer boredom while trying to read promags or fanzines, and allowing correspondence to pile up unanswered.

**1961** J. Koning *Withdrawal* in *S-F Five-Yearly* (Nov.) 25: Craig himself lost that ambitious drive about the time he entered college, and then he found that fandom was a game he didn't have the time for anymore, and went gafia.

**1966** T. White *Who Was That Fandom I Saw You With…* in *SF Five-Yearly* (Nov.) 31: It was four years since the last west coast worldcon, and twelve since the last in Southern California, and many fans seem to have been waiting to reappear from the woodwork of gafia.

**1996** A. Hooper *Walking into Midnight* in *SF Five-Yearly* (Nov.) 39: I know what's good for me, and I plan to sink into torpid gafia as soon as the Teamsters are finished pouring the concrete.

**2001** *SF Chronicle* (Mar.) 51/2: He became involved with activities outside fandom and was gafia for more than a decade.

**gafiate** *n.* ['gæfi‚ɪt] a person who is no longer active in science fiction fandom.

**1962** J. Baxter *(letter)* in P. Lupoff & D. Lupoff *Best of Xero* (2005) 146: Westlake's piece is so reminiscent of the old days of fandom, when no gafiate felt he had actually departed until he had alienated everybody on his mailing list.

**1975** E. Weinstein *Fillostrated Fan Dictionary* 145: XX: The familiar double cross signature of a Well-Known Gafiate.

**1996** A. Hooper *Walking into Midnight* in *SF Five-Yearly* (Nov.) 38: He did just run for TAFF and win last year, hardly the act of an over-the-hill gafiate.

**gafiate** *v.* to stop being active in science fiction fandom. Hence **gafiated,** *adj.* Compare FAFIATE.

**1959** R. H. Eney *Fancyclopedia II* 134: *Quandry* [ … ] the famous fanzine published by Lee Hoffman of Savannah Ga. before she gafiated for the first time.

**1969** H. Warner, Jr. *All Our Yesterdays* xviii: Finally, I cling to a hope that today's active and gafiated fans will find pleasure in reviewing the events in which they took part.

**1975** J. Gunn *Alternate Worlds* 182: Why do the fans go to all the trouble? The fans themselves ask the same question. Some of them [ … ] unable to find a satisfactory answer, "gafiate"—get away from it all.

**1992** *Locus* (June) 21/3: Some of the fans gafiated and got real lives; but others became famous writers.

**2004** R. R. Davidson *e-National Fantasy Fan* (Mar.) 18: If I become inundated I'll probably gafiate like others have done in the past.

**gafiation** *n.* [‚gæfi'eɪʃən] a departure or absence from science fiction fandom.

**1959** R. H. Eney *Fancyclopedia II* 61: It was alleged that it folded with the gafiation of Keasler, Vick, and Leeh (especially) and the corresponding lapse of their fanzines.

**1964** J. Speer *Ramac in Sky* in *Fancestral Voices* (2004) 138: After my gafiation, we met again at the Nolecon.

**1977** S. Wood *Algol* (Spring) 43/2: Superfan Hughes recently printed a *new* Willis column presenting the Irish Legend's return to fandom, at the 1976 Eastercon, after an 11-year gafiation.

**1986** J. Gilpatrick *Locus* (Nov.) 33/3: But we did avoid the broken marriages and permanent GAFIAtions that are the traditional progeny of worldcon committees.

**galactic** *n.* **1.** a (usually alien) member of a galaxy-wide civilization. Often *cap.*

**1942** A. E. van Vogt *Asylum* in *Astounding S-F* (May) 9/1: There are no Galactics out here. But there is an Observer. I've been catching the secret *ultra* signals for the last two hours [ … ] warning all ships to stay clear because the system isn't ready for any kind of contact with Galactic planets.

**1954** [R. Dee] *Interlopers* in *Astounding SF* (Sept.) 68/2: The galactics traveled in pursuit of trade, making jumps of a magnitude inconceivable to an Earthman's mind.

**1963** [S. McKettrig] *World by Tale* in *Analog Sci. Fact-SF* (Oct.) 1: As far as the Galactics were concerned, Earth was a little backwater planet that was of no importance.

**1996** D. Pringle, et al. *Ultimate Ency. of SF* 183/1: All extant galactics have been "uplifted" by earlier races, mainly extinct.

**2.** the language spoken in a galaxy-wide civilization. Often *cap.* Compare STANDARD.

**1956** P. Anderson *Peek! I See You!* in *Gods Laughed* (1982) 138: "Okay, buster, you asked for it," said Tombak in English. He returned to Galactic: "The trouble is, these aren't facts you can fit into mass-action equations."

**1957** R. Silverberg *Neutral Planet* in *World of Thousand Colors* (1984) 202: He spoke Galactic with a sharp, crisp accent that Harskin attributed to his ursine ancestry.

**1964** U. K. Le Guin *Semley's Necklace* in T. Shippey *Oxford Book of SF* (1992) 336: "She say, Hail, Lord of Stars," growled one of her squat escorts in Pidgin-Galactic.

**1990** J. Tiptree, Jr. *Color of Neanderthal Eyes* 33: So I will end by having these people transcribe their speech into Galactic!

**galactography** *n.* [*galactic* + *geography*] the science of mapping the positions of stars, planets, and other celestial objects in a galaxy; the relative locations of such objects. Hence **galactographer,** *n.*, **galactographic,** *adj.*

**1950** I. Asimov ... *And Now You Don't* in *Astounding SF* (Jan.) 113/2: Galactography [ ... ] is our greatest enemy. Our admirals make no secret of our almost hopeless, strategic position.

**1950** I. Asimov, ... *And Now You Don't* 115/1: Nor were the galactographic verities of the situation lost upon Stettin.

**1953** R. F. Young *Black Deep Thou Wingest* in *Startling Stories* (June) 109/1: Perimeter planets no longer have names, sir. [ ... ] The Galactography Society considers it more practical to indicate them on the galactic chart simply by a letter appending their star's spectral classification and catalogue number.

**1957** R. A. Heinlein *Citizen of Galaxy* in *Astounding SF* (Sept.) 18/2: "Place" was some estate, or household, or factor's compound, never a particular planet or sun (his notions of astronomy were mostly wrong and he was innocent of galactography).

**1965** E. Hamilton *Return to Stars* in *Amazing Stories* (Apr.) 24/2: Early galactographers had defined it as that part of the galaxy which lay between the eastern and southern kingdoms, and the edge of the island-universe.

**1993** J. Brunner *Muddle Earth* 214: The knowledge pill was good on galactography.

**galaxy-wide** *adj.* extending throughout or across a galaxy. Also as *adv.* Compare PANGALATIC, TRANSGALACTIC.

**1940** I. Asimov *Homo Sol* in *Astounding S-F* (Sept.) 124/1: We have a race of Humanoids of a superlatively technological turn; possessing [ ... ] an incredibly childish predilection toward individuality, singly and in groups, and, worst of all, lack of sufficient vision to embrace a galaxy-wide culture.

**1949** H. Kuttner *Time Axis* in *Startling Stories* (Jan.) 50/1: I immediately assigned an all-out search, Galaxywide.

**1951** L. Brackett *Starmen of Llyrdis* in *Startling Stories* (Mar.) 72/1: All this vast ordered turmoil of routine and activity, all the galaxy-wide trade that centered here, the thousand-year solidity of Vardda commercial monopoly.

**1969** R. Silverberg *Across Billion Years* 3: I guess the proper thing to do tonight is to call you up on the galaxy-wide telepath hookup and wish us a happy birthday.

**1974** J. Gunn *SF & Mainstream* in R. Bretnor *SF, Today & Tomorrow* 190: A new galaxywide government arose to bring mankind back together, wiser and kinder and stronger than before.

**1996** D. Pringle, et al. *Ultimate Ency. of SF* 58/1: Spacefarers in a galaxy-wide civilization stumble across long-isolated worlds where society has developed in an eccentric fashion.

**2002** M. J. Harrison *Light* (2004) 225: Terror dissolved her, because she had so underestimated that fat man, how intelligent he was, how galaxywide.

**gas giant** *n.* a large planet composed mostly of gaseous material thought to surround a solid core.

**1952** J. Blish *Solar Plexus* in J. Merril *Beyond Human Ken* 106: A quick glance over the boards revealed that there was a magnetic field of some strength near by, one that didn't belong to the invisible gas giant revolving half a million miles away.

**1965** *Listener* (Apr. 22) 596/1: This is Uranus, the third of the remote gas-giants, much larger than either Earth or Mars, but so distant that it is never easy to see with the naked eye.

**1983** O. Davies *First Starship* in *Omni Book of Space* 86: Five of the encounter probes would be specially designed to study gas-giant planets similar to Jupiter.

**1983** B. Bova *Winds of Altair* (1988) 19: Riding the earliest gravity field ships, they had explored the dead gas giant worlds of Barnard's Star.

**1995** A. D. Foster *Life Form* 1: The outermost was a gas giant, a lonely but colorful banded sentinel the size of Neptune.

**gate** *n.* a device or portal that transports a being, spaceship, etc. to another point in space or time, or into another dimension. Compare GATEWAY, STARGATE.

**1931** J. Williamson *Through Purple Cloud* in *Wonder Stories* (May) 1408/1: The purple circle that came in front of the plane looked just like that [ ... ]. We have seen the gate to our world opened again—I am sure of it.

**1933**: See quote in DIMENSIONAL.

**1948** J. Blish *Against Stone Beasts* in *Planet Stories* (Fall) 77/2: I discovered in my time a sort of gateway to your time, and to seventeen other nearly synchronous moments, set up by a scientist unknown to me. Each of the gates seems to open upon one single specific instant.

**1955** R. A. Heinlein *Tunnel in Sky* 19: It was extremely expensive in terms of uranium to keep an interstellar gate open.

**1966** P. J. Farmer *Gates of Creation* (1975) 9: Then he would have to find the gate that would give entrance to the pocket universe.

**1982** J. T. Sapienza *Dragon Mag.* (Aug.) 70/3: The cultural setup in FW postulates a system of gates from world to world, and an elite body of specialists that maintains them.

**1995** A. Thomson *Color of Distance* (1999) 453: There's not much to do up here except keep the ship ticking over until the supply ship comes through the gate.

**gateway** *n.* a GATE, especially one between dimensions, planes, parallel universes, etc. Compare STARGATE.

**1933** [H. Vincent] *Wanderer of Infinity* in *Astounding Stories of Super-sci.* (Mar.) 107/1: It is a gateway to your world, a means of contact with your plane of existence for those many vicious hordes that dwell in other planes of the fifth dimension.

**1944** L. Brackett *Veil of Astellar* in *Best of Leigh Brackett* (1977) 96: The angle of tilt and the tuning of the facets against one another made the difference in the result, whether projecting the Veil, or motive power, or hypnosis, or serving as a gateway to another time and space.

**1947** E. Fennel *Black Priestess of Varda* in *Planet Stories* (Winter) 22/1: The progressive civilization of the Superiors had been interrupted by alien creatures, the Luvans, who had opened a Gateway from another world.

**1979** D. Adams *Hitch Hiker's Guide to Galaxy* 148: Magrathea is a gateway back to our own dimension.

**1996** D. Pringle, et al. *Ultimate Ency. of SF* 122/2: An ancient artefact provides a gateway to the far side of the Universe.

**gee** *n.* **1.** [spelling of the letter G, used in physics to represent the acceleration due to Earth's gravity] a measure of gravitation or acceleration.

**1949** M. St. Clair *Sacred Martian Pig* in *Startling Stories* (July) 92/1: I've more muscle than you, and I'm used to greater gee, being from earth.

**1956** R. A. Heinlein *Double Star* in *Astounding SF* (Feb.) 29/2: The *Can Do*—that's this bucket—is about to rendezvous with the *Go For Broke*, which is a high-gee torchship.

**1998** I. McDonald *Days of Solomon Gursky* in G. Dozois *Mammoth Book of Best New SF, 12th Coll.* (1999) 230: Multiple missile racks clipped to high-gee blip-fusion motors, pilots suspended in acceleration gel like flies in amber, hooked by every orifice into the big battle virtualizers.

**2.** a unit of acceleration equal to the acceleration due to Earth's gravity at sea level (~9.8 meters per second per second); a unit of gravitational force equal to the Earth's.

[**1950** A. C. Clarke *Interplanetary Flight* 96: In normal rocket design we are accustomed to accelerations of several gravities, sustained for a period of a minute or so, but a few "milligee" over a period of one or two days would produce the same final result.]

**1953** R. A. Heinlein *Starman Jones* 92: Now we've been gunning at twenty-four gee ever since we left the atmosphere.

**1956** T. L. Thomas *Ceramic Incident* in S. Schmidt *Fifty Years of Best SF from Analog*

(1980) 223: Speed of rotation thirty-two hours. Gravitation—get this, about two gees.

**1965** L. Niven *One Face* in *Galaxy Mag.* (June) 179/2: The drive gives us a good one hundred gee in uncluttered space.

**1974** J. Haldeman *Forever War* (1976) 186: We launched a pre-programmed drone that would decelerate at 300 gees and take a preliminary look around.

**1981**: See quote in FREE FALL.

**1992** V. Vinge *Fire upon Deep* 42: At the Docks' altitude, gravity was still about three-quarters of a gee.

**2000** W. McCarthy *Collapsium* (2002) 321: The gravity was light here—probably no more than half a gee.

**generation** *adj.* describing or designating a vessel designed for travelling distances so great that the passengers will have lived through multiple generations by the time it reaches its destination.

**1977** J. W. Macvey *Interstellar Travel* (1978) 8: These include generation travel (space arks) and the use of cryogenics (suspended animation).

**1979** J. Varley *Titan* (1987) 13: Concur your analysis of Themis as intersteller space vehicle of the generation type.

**1993** P. Nicholls J. Clute & P. Nicholls *Ency. of SF* 480/1: An interesting variation is found in Damien Broderick's idea-packed *The Dreaming Dragons* (1980), in which a generation time machine is uncovered beneath Ayers Rock in the Australian desert.

**generation ship** *n.* a spaceship designed for travelling distances so great that the passengers will have lived through multiple generations by the time it reaches its destination. Also **generation starship.** Compare MULTIGENERATION SHIP, SPACE ARK.

[**1957** *Mag. of Fantasy & SF* (July) 3: There are few more stirringly imaginative themes in science fiction than that of the generations-ship—the spaceship whereby man may cross the light-years separating us from the stars, even at speeds much less than that of light, creating a self-sufficient microcosm in which the great-great-...-great-grandchildren of the original voyagers may at last make planet-fall.]

**1965** S. R. Delany *Ballad of Beta-2* 7: By the time the ten remaining-generation-ships [sic] arrived in the Leffer System, Earth had already established a going-business of trade and cultural exchange.

**1979** J. Varley *Titan* (1987) 100: You've read the stories of generation ships where something went wrong and everybody slipped back to savagery?

**1984** I. Asimov, et al. *Isaac Asimov Presents Best SF Firsts* 95: One of the most interesting concepts is the generation starship, a vehicle which takes centuries and is crewed by generation after generation of persons born, educated, and trained on board.

**1992** A. Steele *Labyrinth of Night* 198: But if they made the journey in a generation-ship or in suspended animation…

**2002** U. K. Le Guin *Foreword* in *Birthday of World* xiii: In this version of it, Earth sends forth ships to the stars at speeds that are, according to our present knowledge, more or less realistic, at least potentially attainable. [...] In other words, this is a generation-ship story.

**genetic engineer** *n.* a scientist who works in the field of genetic engineering.

**1954** P. Anderson *Big Rain* in *Astounding SF* (Oct.) 22/2: Meanwhile [...] the genetic engineers were evolving still other strains of life which could provide a balanced ecology; and the water units were under construction.

**1966** *New Scientist* (June) 762/3: The culture of embryos in the laboratory, destined to develop into adults whose physical and, possibly, intellectual characteristics had been chosen in advance by the genetic engineers.

**1976** J. Keefauver *Short History of U.S. Genetic Engineering Center for Politicians* in *National Review* (July 9) 726/2: The only strange thing was that the human race never again produced a genetic engineer.

**2005** *Engineering Human Personality* (Usenet: rec.games.frp.gurps) (Feb. 15): Suppose you were such a genetic engineer. What personality trait would you try to instill?

**genetic engineering** *n.* the science of manipulating DNA to produce specific characteristics in an organism.

**1951** J. Williamson *Dragon's Island* 180: I was expecting to find that mutation lab filled with some sort of apparatus for genetic engineering.
**1972** *New York Times* (May 1) 39/1: The ethical implications of this and other experiments in "genetic engineering"—including attempts to produce genetically identical copies of individuals—should be thoroughly explored before the work is applied to man.
**1993** *Super Marketing* (Feb.) 23/2: Four American companies are going ahead with genetic engineering in tomatoes aimed at providing longer shelf-life.
**2001** M. Pollan *Botany of Desire* (2001) 188: With genetic engineering, human control of nature is taking a giant step forward.

**genre** *n.* the literary fields of science fiction, fantasy, and horror collectively; imaginative fiction.
**1993** D. Bischoff *Essaying* in *Quantum* (Spring–Summer) 30/1: This professor was ultimately equally contemptuous of [...] SF and mystery magazines in particular. One day he said to me, "David, you seem to have some talent—but why don't you read better literature?" [sic] Actually, I read much fine material outside of my indulgences in genre even then.
**1993** J. Clute *SF Novels of Year* in D. Garnett *New Worlds 3* 210: If there were three best novels of the year, this was one, Swanwick's another and Fowler's a third. All three were hatchlings of genre, all three were mutant.
**1998** L. Shepard *Must Have Been Something I Ate* in J. Dann *Nebula Awards 32* 8: I feel inclined to celebrate the literary traditions of genre if only for a final time, to mention that the two most prominent contributors to the field during the first part of the century, George Orwell and H. G. Wells, were considered literary writers.
**2001** G. Dozois in M. Swanwick *Being Gardner Dozois* 236: Yes, it's quite true that the expectations of genre weight it a bit in one way, toward one interpretation, but my steadfast refusal to admit that they're [i.e., time-travelers] actually real makes it as ambiguous as possible.
**2004** P. Di Filippo *Asimov's SF* (July) 136/2: Deemed in a cover blurb to consist of "interstitial fiction" (the newest synonym for "slipstream"),

this five-story project does indeed navigate the borderland between genre and mainstream.

**genre** *adj.* of or describing fiction that is written, published, or marketed as belonging to a specific category (such as science fiction, mystery, or romance).
**1974** R. Bretnor *SF, Today & Tomorrow* 148: He has sold extensively to both genre and men's magazines as well as to a large number of anthologists.
**1985** N. Spinrad *Isaac Asimov's SF Mag.* (July) 180/1: Not all SF produced by those who may be stereotyped as "genre writers" is necessarily "genre fiction."
**1987** E. Ross *Horrorstruck* (May/June 1987) 32/2: Of all genre writers, the horror writer is criticized more than any other. In addition to fending off all the same charges as Danielle Steel, they must face suggestions that what they write is somehow subversive, dangerous, provocative, even satanic.
**1995** C. de Lint *Mag. of Fantasy & SF* (June) 35/2: So we have a literary tradition (Classic Literature), and one based on entertainment (which includes genre fiction) [...]. Shakespeare and Dickens grip the reader in the same way that a fairy tale does a child, but if they were published today would probably be relegated to genre status.
**2003** R. Klaw *Geek Confidential* 185: Using genre elements, Moorcock created a mainstream novel that captures the essence of London.
**2005** C. Priest *Subterranean Press E-mail List* (Nov. 16): Space operas the size phone books [sic] do not fit nicely onto my tiny nightstand, and [...] I tend to select briefer genre tomes when I need a palate-cleansing piece of someone else's fiction.

**genre science fiction, genre sf** *n.* fiction published under the label "science fiction," especially that which conforms to some notion of what is typical of such fiction.
**1979** P. Nicholls & B. Stableford P. Nicholls *Ency. of SF* 161/2: Publishers apply similar cautionary measures to potential best-sellers; genre sf, when so labelled, usually sells well but seldom enters the best-seller class.

**1985** N. Spinrad *Isaac Asimov's SF Mag.* (July) 184/1: In other words while established literary critics may be prejudiced against "genre SF," it is usually an *ignorant* prejudice.

**1990** V. Hollinger *Cybernetic Deconstructions* in L. McCaffery *Storming Reality Studio* (1991) 216: Cyberpunk helped to generate a great deal of very useful controversy about the role of SF in the 1980s, a decade in which the resurgence of fantastic literature left much genre SF looking rather sheepishly out of date.

**1993** J. Clute *SF Novels of Year* in D. Garnett *New Worlds 3* 200: He was the sound [...] of sf talking to itself, the default voice of American genre sf, which had been born in 1926, had been stricken in 1957 when Sputnik began to asset-strip the playground of space, and had since deceased.

**2004** J. P. Blaylock *Charting Unexamined Territories* in *Postscripts* (Spring) 57: In fact Susan Allison (editor at Ace Books) once told me that if only I wrote genre science fiction or genre fantasy they could probably do something with my career!

**genzine** *n.* [*general* + -ZINE] a fanzine with content of many different types or covering various topics.

**1966** T. White *Who Was That Fandom I Saw You With...* in *SF Five-Yearly* (Nov.) 31: By the time PSY had effectively folded, there were no notable genzines being published at all.

**1986** T. Nielsen Hayden *Over Rough Terrain* in *Making Book* (1994) 80: The first time I put out a genzine [...] it seemed to me that our house had come free of its moorings in time and space.

**2000** J. D. Smith [J. Tiptree, Jr.] *Meet Me at Infinity* (2001) 187: There were two main types of fanzines in the seventies, the large "genzines" (general interest fanzines, with a variety of contents [...]) and the small "personalzines."

**2004** *e-National Fantasy Fan* (Mar.) 13: She blames fmzfen, a Yahoo mailing list, for getting her started in publishing her own genzine Peregrine Nations.

**ghod** *n.* [gɑd] god.
**1952** A. H. Rapp, L. Hoffman & R. Boggs

*Fanspeak* 6/2: Fans usually spell it with an "h" when referring to fannish ghods. This seems to be the only authentic superstitious taboo ever developed in the microcosm.

**1953** D. Clarkson *Thrilling Wonder Stories (letter)* (Aug.) 135/1: It was ghodawful...ghastly...ghruesome.

**1965** A. J. Budrys in D. Eney *Proceedings; Discon* 121: I work for an organization that is represented now in places as far away as Manila [...] to the deepest recesses of the urban male subconscious—where ghod knows what dwells.

**1983** R. Crumb & A. Crumb *Arlene 'n' Bob, That Thing in Back Bedroom* in D. Skinn *Comix Underground Revolution* (2004) 171: No Bob, I'm not...'cause "thank ghod in heaven"...this is only make believe!!

**2000** J. Speer *Missing Issue* in *Fancestral Voices* (2004) 52: About that time, Ghod invented AIDS, and hippies discovered rural communes were hard.

**glassite** *n.* a hard, strong, transparent substance, often used in windows and space helmets.

**1934** F. K. Kelly *Famine on Mars* in *Astounding Stories* (Sept.) 72/1: I was hemmed in on all sides by panels of glassite so perfectly transparent from within as to give the impression that there was nothing, nothing at all, between me and the aching emptiness of the void.

**1940** T. Sturgeon *Artnan Process* in *Microcosmic God* (1995) 252: The Martians squatted in a row against the starboard bulkhead, sipping Earth's legendary cocola through glassite straws.

**1956** M. Lesser *Meet Miss Solar System* in *Fantastic Universe* (Apr.) 61/1: The tank floated with no great haste toward the Jovian section, where two or three of the giants batted it around for a while between them while the tumbling merman began to pound frantically on the inside of his glassite prison.

**1970** R. Zelazny *Nine Princes in Amber* in *Great Book of Amber* (1999) 53: A woman sat upon the throne in the glassite room I almost recalled, and her hair was green, though streaked with silver.

**1984** I. McDonald *Catharine Wheel* in G. Dozois *Worldmakers* (2001) 165: The Lady rumbles over the Raj-Canal into the glassite dome of Pulaski station

**1991** F. M Robinson *Dark beyond Stars* (1998) 162: I kept returning to a large, transparent cylinder in one of the corners. [ ... ] I floated over to it and ran my hands down the glassite walls.

**GOH, GoH, goh** *abbr.* guest of honor; at a science fiction convention, a well-known person (writer, actor, fan, artist, etc.) who usually gives a speech and may also appear on panels, sign autographs, etc., and whose presence is intended to attract people to the convention.

**1967** *Instant Message* (Nov. 14) 2: 23-4 March 1968 - Boskone V at Statler-Hilton in Boston, GoH: - Larry Niven.

**1975** E. Weinstein *Fillostrated Fan Dictionary* 107: It was all in fun, since the owner, Sherry Gottlieb, was the GoH.

**1982** G. Wolfe *Rewards of Authorship* in *Castle of Days* (1995) 283: Boston puts on a good con every year; thousands of people come, no matter who the goh is.

**1994** T. Nielsen Hayden *Over Rough Terrain* in *Making Book* 109: The other Untoward Incident of our convention occurred while Patrick and I were sitting there waiting for the GoH speeches to start.

**2001** [P. Anthony] *How Precious Was That While* (2002) 302: I was invited to be GoH at Sci-Con in Virginia, and declined.

**golden age** *n.* a period at some point in the past perceived as having produced the best or most important works of science fiction. Often *cap.* [Specific dates vary greatly, but the golden age is most often associated with the period in the 1930s and 1940s shortly after John W. Campbell, Jr. began editing *Astounding Stories.*]

**1948** J. W. Patch *Thrilling Wonder Stories (letter)* (June) 137/1: I agree with those who contend that the "golden age" of science-fiction wasn't so golden. [ ... ] The stf that was written in those days made good reading—then. The Model "T" was a good car, too—in those days.

**1953** [A. Boucher] *Publishing of SF* in R. Bretnor *Modern SF* 32: To be completely non-objective, I still think that *Astounding* around say, 1939–1945, represents the high point of the equal stress on both terms in science fiction. [ ... ] There, my children, was the Golden Age....

**1965** A. Budrys *Benchmarks* (1985) 27: There is something rather deeper that the recurrent strain in that "Golden Age" science fiction of the 1940's.

**1976** T. M. Disch *Embarrassments of SF* in *On SF* (2005) 8: He regards the Golden Age of sf as the thirties and forties.

**1999** [H. Clement] *Interview with Hal Clement* in *Extrapolation* (Summer) 132: I'm thinking of the "Golden Age" from about 1926 to 1940, or a little earlier than that.

**2004** D. Broderick *X, Y, Z, T* 132: Its bulk is a gathering of thirteen stories from the true Golden Age of sf, the early and mid-1950s.

**go nova** *v.* (of a star) to become a nova; to explode. Also used *fig.*

**1942** J. W. Campbell *Supernova Centaurus* in *Astounding SF* (Feb.) 6/2: We've considered what might happen if Sol itself went nova. If it should go supernova, no worse could happen; Earth and all life on it would be fused and volatilized in either case.

**1966** R. Sheckley *Mindswap* 56: Let's see... standard stuff about the Company not being responsible for fire, earthquake, atomic warfare, sun going nova, acts of god or gods, and so forth.

**1969** R. Silverberg *Across Billion Years* 212: Nick yielded. He looked like he was ready to go nova, but he yielded.

**1974** T. Sturgeon *SF, Morals, & Religion* in R. Bretnor *SF, Today & Tomorrow* 104: A truly beautiful, powerful, highly cultured alien civilization which is destroyed by its sun's going nova.

**1993** K. S. Robinson *Red Mars* 67: The situation was about to "go nova," as Mission Control put it.

**1997** R. Hatch & C. Golden *Battlestar Galactica: Armageddon* 63: The Lords of the House of Kobol were the first to realize that their system's star was going to go nova.

**goshwow** *adj.* [in imitation of a letter (allegedly published in *Thrilling Wonder*

*Stories*) quoted in an article about SF fans in *Time* that most fans viewed as condescending (see 1939 quote)] (of a science fiction fan) overly enthusiastic, especially pertaining to a childish or uncritical fan; (of a story) catering to such fans. Also *vars.*

[**1939** *Time* (July 10) 32 (caption): Gosh! Wow! Boyohboy! The mosta and the besta!]

**1950** R. Sneary *Spacewarp* (Sept.) 2: As a first issue it was about as sickly a mag as you could ask for, and the fellow that was editing it sounded like the ultimate in "goshwowboyoboy" new fans.

**1961** J. Koning *Withdrawal* in *S-F Five-Yearly* (Nov) 25: Rather than admit that they themselves had gotten rather GoshWowish, most of the now bitter Group blamed Craig Cochran for destroying their hobby, and this, of all the consequences of that one fan's rather Noble ambition, I regard as the most unfortunate.

**1969** A. Widner in H. Warner, Jr. *All Our Yesterdays* 170: Fandom should have some sort of united front to put toward the rest of the world, or it will continue to be regarded as just the juvenile, goshwowboyoboy gang.

**1995** T. M. Disch *Speaker Moonbeam* in *On SF* (2005) 215: Heinlein uses the gosh-wow conventions of pulp-era space opera to advance a political agenda that celebrates America's future as the Rome of the space age.

**1999** U. K. Le Guin *Changing Kingdoms* in M. A. Morrison *Trajectories of Fantastic* (1997) 9: Only the pulpiest goshwow adventure sci-fi ignores the mandates of realism.

**2004** A. Widner *Intro.* in J. Speer *Fancestral Voices* 11: I assume this activity was similar to my own in that same year, writing "goshwowboyoboy" letters to *Amazing, Astounding,* and *Wonder Stories.*

**go supernova** *v.* (of a star) to become a supernova; (generally) to explode.

**1942**: see quote in GO NOVA.

**1964** R. Silverberg *To Dark Star* in *World of Thousand Colors* (1984) 139: When it had converted all its hydrogen to iron-56, it fell into catastrophic collapse and went supernova.

**1974** L. Niven & J. Pournelle *Mote in God's Eye* (1976) 278: They hae been watching yon supergiant for aye their history as it passed across the Coal Sack. 'Twill go supernova and then become a black hole.

**1976** G. Lucas *Adventures of Luke Starkiller* (Apr. 19) 154: Glad you were here to see it… now let's get some distance before that thing goes supernova.

**1995** R. Zelazny *Three Descents of Jeremy Baker* in *Mag. of Fantasy & SF* (July) 127: We were once a race of material beings but we were sufficiently evolved that when we saw our sun was going to go supernova we elected to transform ourselves into this state and study it rather than flee.

**2005** E. Kolbert *Climate of Man—II* in *New Yorker* (May 2) 68/3: If the sun went supernova, there's no question that we could model what would happen.

**graser** *n.* [gamma ray amplification by stimulated emission of radiation, after "laser" or "maser"] a device (in science fiction, usually a weapon) that produces a beam of coherent light in the gamma-ray wavelengths; the beam produced by such a device.

**1974** H. Ellison *Adrift Just off Islets of Langerhans: Latitude 38° 54' N, Longitude 77° 00' 13" W* in *Mag. of Fantasy & SF* (Oct.) 59/1: Not lasers. *Grasers.* Gamma Ray Amplification by Stimulated Emission of Radiation.

**1975** G. C. Baldwin & R. V. Khokhlov *Physics Today* (Feb.) 33/1: The possibility of a nuclear laser, often termed a "graser" (for "gamma-ray laser") or a "gaser," was recognized early in the 1960's.

**1999** D. Weber *On Basilisk Station* 21: "How much broadside armament did it cost us?" she asked after a moment. "All four graser mounts."

**2002** A. Reynolds *Redemption Ark* (2004) 451: The yields were about one hundredth of a crustbuster burst, which was sufficient to power a particle beam or graser with a five-light-second kill range.

**2003** C. Stross *Singularity Sky* (2004) 129: A target selection cursor ghosted briefly across the enemy glyphs, locking grasers onto the distant projected light cones of the enemy flotilla.

**grav** *n.* gravity; apparent gravity due to acceleration.

**1940** N. S. Bond *Castaway* in O. Welles *Invasion from Mars* (1949) 129: There's no doubt about it, things have been going haywire ever since we picked him up. I'll be glad when he lifts gravs off the *Aunty*.

**1957** R. Silverberg *Neutral Planet* in *World of Thousand Colors* (1984) 213: The three men aboard were huddled in their acceleration cradles, groaning in pain as the increasing grav buffeted and bruised them.

**1992** V. Vinge *Fire upon Deep* 337: Pham sank into his restraints under a grav load that wobbled between a tenth gee and an intolerable crush.

**1999** D. Weber *On Basilisk Station* 273: He plummeted downward, the rest of his squad close behind him, and popped his grav canopy.

**gravitic** *adj.* of, caused by, or powered by gravity. Hence **gravitically**, *adv.*

**1939** M. Jameson *Question of Salvage* in *Astounding S-F* (Oct.) 72/2: Some structural damage was suffered by the vessel owing to pounding by gravitic waves, but she returned to base without assistance.

**1944** [W. Long] *Astounding SF* (May) 25/1: Gravitic phenomena propagates at the speed of light raised to the power of 2.71828—That's our limiting velocity.

**1982** I. Asimov *Foundation's Edge* 3: Now it's a colossal mausoleum, but is there a force-field ramp in the place? A slideway? A gravitic lift?—No, just these steps.

**1982** I. Asimov *Foundation's Edge*. 235: This time, we'll be moving gravitically—straight up—as soon as we can be assured the atmosphere above is clear of other ships.

**1990** L. M. Bujold *Vor Game* (1993) 268: The up-and-coming weapon for ship-to-ship fighting in the last couple of years seemed to be the gravitic imploder lance, a modification of tractor-beam technology.

**1998** D. Brin *Heaven's Reach* 72: But right now they are using a supplementary gravitic engine to hasten progress, fleeing unexpected chaos in this stellar system.

**gravitics** *n.* **1.** the science of studying or controlling gravity or anti-gravity.

**1944** M. Jameson *Tricky Tonnage* in *Astounding S-F* (Dec.) 61: Elmer's whole theory of gravitics was pretty involved, and in some spots downright screwy. But on the whole it hung together, and there I was riding along on a stream of moving gravitons to prove it.

**1953** T. Sturgeon *More Than Human* 206: Seems that gravitics is the key to everything. It would lead to the addition of one more item to the Unified Field—what we now call psychic energy, or "psionics."

**1956** I. Asimov *Dead Past* in S. Schmidt *Fifty Years of Best SF from Analog* (1980) 192: By education and inclination, Dr. Potterley, I'm a hyperoptics man with a gravitics minor.

**1967** P. Anderson *Eutopia* (1974) 151: The aircraft was a helicopter—they hadn't discovered gravitics here—piloted by a taciturn young autochthon.

**2003** N. H. Gregersen *From Complexity to Life* 117: These observations hold out hope for a "second law of gravitics" that quantifies the increasing complexity of gravitic systems.

**2.** sensors that use gravity to detect objects in space.

**1982** I. Asimov *Foundation's Edge* 54: I've been trained in space navigation, but not on *these* ships. If something goes wrong with the gravitics, I'm afraid there's nothing I can do about it.

**1997** P. Anderson *Fleet of Stars* (1998) 26: The ship wasn't big, and her mass tanks were nearly empty, but probably optics were registering her, and maybe, by now, gravitics.

**2000** D. Weber *Ashes of Victory* (2004) 353: By using thrusters, she avoided the sensors which most tactical officers tend to rely upon—the Peeps' gravitics—but she was mother naked to everything *else* in their sensor suites.

**gravity drive** *n.* a space drive that uses anti-gravity or some type of gravitic control to propel a spaceship.

**1950** P. Anderson *Star Ship* in *Planet Stories* (Fall) 73/2: None of them had ever built a rocketship, had ever seen one in action even. It was centuries obsolete in Galactic civilization. But gravity drives were out of the question. So—they'd had to design the ship from the ground up.

**1983** B. Bova *Winds of Altair* (1988) 20: Physicists argued bitterly over whether or not the gravity drive actually propelled the ships faster than light.

**1985** O. S. Card *Ender's Game* (1994) 82: Obviously, we can now control gravity. Turn it on and off, change the direction, maybe reflect it—I've thought of lots of neat things you could do with gravity weapons and gravity drives on starships.

**1986** A. McCaffrey *Girl Who Heard Dragons* (1995) 107: I dropped the meteor ruse just in time to switch on the gravity drive and keep us from planting a new crater.

**gravity-free** *adj.* without gravity; without discernable effect from the force of gravity.

**1931** J. W. Campbell, Jr. *Islands of Space* in *Amazing Stories Quarterly* (Spring) 169/1: Arcot floated into the gravity-free room, and struck the wall with a little thump, bouncing back to the floor by a careful manipulation of arms and legs.

**1941** J. Blish *Solar Plexus* in J. Merril *Beyond Human Ken* (1952) 114: Crawling in a gravity-free corridor was a good deal more difficult to manage than walking.

**1961** *Chronicle-Telegram (Elyria, Oh.)* (Oct. 20) 7/1: Once the astronaut is in orbit he is also in gravity-free space.

**1980** J. White *Ambulance Ship* in *Alien Emergencies* (2002) 162: They pulled themselves aft along the ladder of the gravity-free well.

**1990** *Design News* (Feb. 26) 15: The tanks could be converted into laboratories for experiments in pharmaceutical research, crystal growing, and other processes that require a gravity-free environment.

**1997** S. Baxter *Titan* (2001) 551: One carousel spun up, imitating the Earth's gravity, and the other provided a gravity-free environment.

**gravityless** *adj.* GRAVITY-FREE.

**1939** [E. Binder] *Impossible World* in *Startling Stories* (Mar.) 36/1: Shelton was already on his way to the pilot's cupola, pulling himself up the companionway by sheer muscular effort in the gravityless ship.

**1959** *Times Recorder (Zanesville, Oh.)* (June 22) 4/2: In the case of our spaceman, spooning soup in a gravityless environment seems downright dangerous. You could get it in your eye. And if you ever let go of the spoon, you wouldn't know where to look for it.

**1970** P. Anderson *Tau Zero* (1973) 143: It is the fatigue. Pure physical tiredness, from trying to do things in a gravityless environment.

**1991** J. D. Vinge *Summer Queen* (2003) 191: Floating, gravityless, in the night-black void of space, he was surrounded by brilliant flashes of light.

**2004** O. Sacks *Speed* in *New Yorker* (Aug. 23) 68/2: One parkinsonian friend of mine says that [ ... ] being in an accelerated state is like being on ice, frictionless, slipping down an ever-steeper hill, or on a tiny planet, gravityless, with no force to hold or moor him.

**gravity plate** *n. Obs.* a device that creates artificial gravity "above" it, or that nullifies gravity "below" it.

**1933** J. Williamson *Salvage in Space* in *Astounding Stories of Super-sci.* (Mar.) 20/2: The creature's body was so heavy that Thad had to return to the bridge, and shut off the current in the gravity plates along the keel, before he could move it.

**1936** [G. Wilson] *Earth-Venus 12* in *Thrilling Wonder Stories* (Dec.) 104/2: An hour's ascent, with our rocket-tails streaming like a comet behind us; then we shut them off, with the gravity plates set for Earth repulsion and the Moon to pull us on the first leg of the flight.

**1940** T. Sturgeon *Artnan Process* in *Microcosmic God* (1995) 241: The gravity plates under Slimmy's feet went dead and those in the overhead whipped the little man upward.

**1943** F. B. Long *Stellar Vampires SF* (July) 80/1: But there was nothing normal about a gravity plate that had resisted the tug of Mars only to buckle on little Phobos.

**1951** S. A. Peeples, D. A. Kyle & M. Greenberg *Dictionary of SF* in M. Greenberg *Travelers of Space* 23: GRAVITY PLATES [ ... ] Used to permit a person or vehicle to leave a planet's surface or to maintain artificial gravity for passengers on interplanetary trips.

**gravity screen** *n. Obs.* a device that resists or negates the effect of gravity.

**1928** E. Hamilton *Crashing Suns* in *Weird Tales* (Aug.) 200/2: All of his time-honored rules of interplanetary navigation had been upset by this new cruiser, a craft entirely without gravity-screens which was flashing from sun to sun propelled by invisible vibrations only.

**1932** A. G. Stangland *Wonder Stories* (Apr.) 1208/2: Steel tubes [...] sent forth a vast field of gravitation, retarding the motion of the planet. The huge gravity screens of the tubes fed on large vats of silicon dust [...] releasing a powerful negative field of gravity.

**1940** V. Reid *Future's Fair* in *Astonishing Stories* (Oct.) 50/2: Jovian crowds shrieked in terror, then laughed uproariously as they swung suspended in air above the Gravity Screens.

**1947** H. Kuttner *Thrilling Wonder Stories* (Feb.) 113/1: Gravity-screens, to take only one example, make it possible to use android robots of such size that they could exist only in a slight gravity.

**1952** J. Blish *Bridge Astounding SF* (Feb.) 70/2: "*They have antigravity!* Isn't that it?" [...] "How did you know? Of course, it couldn't be a complete gravity screen by any means. But it seems to be a good long step toward it."

**gravity well** *n.* the area of space around a large mass (such as a star or planet) in which the force of gravity from the mass is strong enough that an object will be pulled toward it.

**1963** [W. P. Sanders] *Industrial Revolution* in *Analog SF-Sci. Fact* (Sept.) 22/1: It's actually harder to maintain human-type conditions on so big a mass, with a useless atmosphere around you, than on a lump in space like this. And the gravity wells are so deep.

**1970** A. C. Clarke *Neutron Tide* in *Galaxy Mag.* (May) 84/1: They were still accelerating when a fantastically unlikely accident occurred. *Flatbush* ran straight into the gravity well of a neutron star.

**1987** J. M. Ford *How Much for Just Planet?* 36: They're headed straight for the surface [...]. Any deeper in the gravity well and the tractors won't be reliable.

**1991** E. Arnason *Woman of Iron People, Part I* (1992) 71: No one is ever going to build a ship at the bottom of a gravity well.

**2000** *Interzone* (Aug.) 8/1: The steady push from its network of ion-boosters would give a cumulative effect that would allow Liberty to break out of the Sun's gravity-well.

**gravs** *pl. n.* devices, especially space drives, that control gravity or anti-gravity.

**1940** [G. Danzell] *Castaway* in *Planet Stories* (Winter) 40/1: There's no doubt about it, things have been going haywire ever since we picked him up. I'll be glad when he lifts gravs off the *Aunty.*

**1946** R. S. Shaver *Earth Slaves to Space* in *Amazing Stories* (Sept.) 41/2: There were indeed wonders on this little planet, which had quite a strong gravity, for as we shut off the gravs and all the motors of the *Darkspear*, the load on our feet decreased but little.

**1947** H. Hasse *Trail of Astrogar* in *Amazing Stories* (Oct.) 54/1: Their next stop was the office of Interplanet Passenger Lines, where Curt learned a spacer was hoisting gravs for Earth in two days.

**1950** J. H. Schmitz *Truth About Cushgar* in *Astounding SF* (Nov.) 27/1: Just mess up their gravs! [...] They don't carry prisoners. There'll be some in suits, but we'll handle them.

**grok** *v.* [coined by Robert A. Heinlein] to understand deeply or intuitively; to establish rapport; to enjoy.

**1961** R. A. Heinlein *Stranger in Strange Land* 17: There was so much to grok, so little to grok from.

**1961** R. A. Heinlein *Stranger in Strange Land* 18: Smith had been aware of the doctors but had grokked that their intentions were benign.

**1968** *Playboy* (June) 80: He met her at an acid-rock ball and she grokked him, this ultracool miss loaded with experience and bereft of emotion.

**1969** *New Yorker* (Mar. 15) 35: I was thinking we ought to get together somewhere, Mr. Zzyzbyzynsky, and grok about our problems.

**1971** E. Sanders *Family* 180: Gypsy supposedly at first was extremely hesitant to have affairs with the Satans, but grew to grok it.

**1984** *InfoWorld* (May 21) 32: There isn't any software! Only different internal states of hardware. It's all hardware! It's a shame programmers don't grok that better.
**1987** M. Groening *School Is Hell* unpag.: I'm getting bad vibes from you. The rest of the class groks what is going on—why can't you?
**1994** *TV Guide* (Oct. 29) 52: Today kids "grok" things faster—they're smarter than they were.
**1998** D. Brin *Heaven's Reach* 410: Can you sniff/sense/feel/grok the very thing you covet… and secretly fear?
**2001** J. Lethem *Defending Searchers* in *Disappointment Artist* (2005) 11: In the professor I grokked a fellow obsessive.

**groundcar** *n.* [perh. in opposition to AIR-CAR and AEROCAR] a passenger vehicle that can only travel on the surface of a world; an automobile.
**1937** E. E. Smith *Galactic Patrol* in *Astounding Stories* (Nov.) 136/1: I will return in three hours, as well before sunset the wind makes it impossible to get even a ground car into the port.
**1957** R. A. Heinlein *Citizen of Galaxy* in *Astounding SF* 108/2 (Nov.): To Thorby's surprise Captain Krausa took a slideway outside the Gathering, then whistled down a ground-car.
**1965** M. Z. Bradley *Star of Danger* (1985) 71: He found himself thinking regretfully of the comfortable ground-cars and air-ships of Terran travel.
**1970** F. Herbert *Whipping Star* in *Worlds of If* (Jan.) 16/1: People here on Cordiality are used to seeing me in a groundcar unless I'm on official business and require speed.
**1990** A. McCaffrey & E. Moon *Sassinak* (1991) 149: Trailing a ship through FTL space was, Sassinak thought, like following a groundcar through thick forest at night without using headlights.
**2002** M. McArthur *Time Past* 42: A long groundcar stopped with a hissing of brakes at my frantic waving.

**groundhog** *n.* [perh. < aviation slang *groundhog*, "a nonaviator"] someone who has never been to space, or who prefers to stay on the surface of a planet.

**1942** [A. MacDonald] *Waldo* in *Astounding SF* (Aug.) 18/2: Stevens streaked in after him, displaying a groundhog's harmless pride in handling himself well in space conditions.
**1947** R. A. Heinlein *It's Great to Be Back* in *Saturday Evening Post* 18/1 (July 26): We've both said more than once that we wished we had had sense enough never to have left Earth. We're groundhogs at heart, Jo.
**1976** J. Varley *Bagatelle* in *Galaxy, Incorporating Worlds of If* (Oct.) 10/1: What are you… get your hand off me you…you groundhog.
**1983** M. McCollum *Life Probe* 16: Spacers pick up careful habits…if they live long enough. Where a groundhog would have left the record for later, Brea always checked and double checked everything.
**1999** J. L. Chalker *Priam's Lens* 17: Sharing birth years was an old sport among spacers, although not between them and the groundhogs.

**groundside** *n.* the surface of a planet; a spaceport. Compare PLANETSIDE.
**1958** [C. M. Knox] *Planet of Parasites* in *Super-Sci. Fiction* (Apr.) 2/2: Allenson of groundside speaking. Acknowledge. We'll be waiting for landing. Over and out.
**2001** M. Flynn *Falling Stars* (2002) 187: An' so I departed for groundside again.

**groundside** *adj.* on or from a planet. Compare EARTHSIDE, PLANETSIDE.
**1958** R. Silverberg *Eve & Twenty-Three Adams* in *Venture SF Mag.* (Mar.) 51/2: Captain Bannister turned Eve over to the groundside authorities that first day.
**1992** V. Vinge *Fire upon Deep* (1993) 6: A backdoor into the ship's code, installed when the newborn had subverted the humans' groundside equipment.
**2000** D. Gerrold *Jumping off Planet* (2001) 236: In light of several recent judgments where groundside courts have held the Line authority liable for expenses and damages [ … ] we have become extremely reluctant to expose ourselves to that liability.
**2001** S. Shwartz *Second Chances* (2002) 33: The wardroom was fragrant with [ … ] honest-to-God groundside coffee, not service

brew strong enough to send your eyeballs into Jump.

**groundside** *adv.* PLANETSIDE. Compare EARTHSIDE, ON-PLANET, ON-WORLD.

**1961** F. Leiber *Beat Cluster* in *Galaxy Mag.* (Oct.) 163/1: The new Administrator's planning to ship us all groundside!

**1969** [J. Tiptree, Jr.] *Happiness Is Warm Spaceship* in *Meet Me at Infinity* 41 (2001): Drakes would have lasers, flame-throwers, grenades, and maybe a rocket-launcher or two, groundside.

**1983** W. Gibson *Red Star, Winter Orbit* in *Burning Chrome* (1986) 113: Think what their testimony will be doing to us groundside.

**1995** A. Thomson *Color of Distance* (1999) 89: Rumor had it that Chang landed her present berth because they wanted to get rid of her groundside.

**2000** D. Gerrold *Jumping off Planet* (2001) 236: Up here, attempting to evade authority usually gets you a trip groundside.

**group mind** *n.* a single consciousness or intelligence formed by the union of more than one individual's consciousness or intelligence.

**1930** W. O. Stapledon *Last & First Men* 168: The Martians, it should be noted, had three possible forms, or formations, namely: first, an "open order" of independent and very tenuous cloudlets in "telepathic" communication, and often in strict unity as a group mind; second, a more concentrated and less vulnerable corporate cloud; and third, an extremely concentrated and formidable cloud-jelly.

**1946** A. C. Clarke *Rescue Party* in *Astounding SF* (May) 53/2: Alarkane had written a book trying to prove that eventually all intelligent races would sacrifice individual consciousness and that one day only group-minds would remain in the Universe.

**1977** I. Asimov & B. Bova *Beyond Our Brain* in I. Asimov *Asimov on SF* (1981) 143: A group of five individuals link minds to form a superhuman entity, a group-mind, that is capable of many feats no individual human being can perform.

**1986** T. Nielsen Hayden *Over Rough Terrain* in *Making Book* (1994) 96: I ran into a wandering troupe of millenarian evangelicals who announced that they were all One In The Spirit, and when I figured out they meant they were all a Group Mind they grinned at me with wicked good cheer.

**1990** *Thrust* (Winter) 6/3: When they join together in an eightfold group-mind, a higher consciousness submerges their individual identities.

**2001** W. Spencer *Alien Taste* 303: You saw how they were, human-shaped appendages for Hex, a group mind working as one spread-out body.

# h

**-h-** *infix.* [perh. influenced by *ghost, ghoul,* etc.] (usually following initial "b" or "g") adding -*h*- to a word does not change the word's meaning, but instead indicates that it is being used humorously or in a fannish context. Compare BHEER, GHOD.

**1940** B. Tucker *Le Zombie* (Feb. 10) 4: Recently an influx of new readers cleaned out most of the available back numbers of this ghazette.

**1956** J. White *Not-So-Hot Gospeller White Papers* (1996) 275: Bob Shaw, supreme exponent of the murderous art of Ghoodminton, possessor of the only known fifth-dimensional gut, and late owner—before I bought it—of the Tower Bridge, London.

**1962** B. Kujawa *Cry (letter)* (June) 24: Geo. ain't the shy-Britbhoy he was before the Army days.

**2004** S. Birkhead *Argentus* 31/1: I'm *always* impressed when I see Steve Stiles as a contributor—he's *ghood!*

## hard-core science fiction, hard-core sf
*n.* HARD SCIENCE FICTION.

**1971** A. Budrys *Benchmarks* (1985) 296: Ballantine bills it as "The first major novel from a hard-core science fiction writer."

**1974** T. N. Scortia *SF as Imaginary Experiment* in R. Bretnor *SF, Today & Tomorrow* 139: The closely reasoned technological story has come to be known as a "hard-core science fiction story."

**1980** T. Sturgeon *rubric written for "Slow Sculpture"* in *Perfect Host* (1998) 381: It has nice hardcore s-f content, but the one thing that interests me most is the hulking wordless character on the spaceship, who looks like an ape and thinks like a poet/philosopher.

**1994** B. Bova *Craft of Writing SF That Sells* 9: Hard-core science fiction, the type that is based on the world as we know it, has been my life.

**1999** A. C. Clarke *Aspects of SF* in *Greetings, Carbon-Based Bipeds!* 399: But when *Astounding Stories* printed just such a tale in its March 1944 issue—to the consternation of the FBI—it was hard-core sf, because uranium fission had now been discovered.

## hard science fiction, hard sf
*n.* science fiction in which the technology or science portrayed in the story has been extrapolated from current scientific theories, especially in which the laws of nature (as understood at the time of writing) are not violated.

**1957** P. S. Miller *Astounding SF* (Feb.) 143/1: It is also very characteristic of the best "hard" science fiction of its day.

**1970** [W. Atheling] *More Issues at Hand* 99: Wells used the term originally to cover what we would today call "hard" science fiction, in which a conscientious attempt to be faithful to already known facts (as of the date of writing) was the substrate on which the story was to be built, and if the story was also to contain a miracle, it ought at least not to contain a whole arsenal of them.

**1982** J. Clute *Mag. of Fantasy & SF* (Feb.) 34/1: Like all true hard sf, *Re-entry* is a novel which is what it means to be—glossy, technophilic, ornate, savvy about the frontiers of knowledge, power-obsessed in the name of hardnosed realism: great on carapace; vacuous on the inner depths.

**1987** I. Asimov *Isaac Asimov's SF Mag.* (Sept.) 6/2: In a hard science fiction story, a human being can travel to the nearer stars by using an ion drive once he is out in space, or matter-antimatter interaction, or a laser beam and a solar sail. None of these devices currently exist, but they are all reasonably possible and none violate any laws of nature.

**1990** C. Sheffield *Thrust* (Winter) 18/3: Someone, to help me pass the time, handed me a copy of [...] *Ringworld* [...]. I read it, and I said to myself, "Hey, hard science fiction is not dead."

**1995** *Interzone* (Mar.) 56/1: The basic premise of hard sf is that it takes the spirit of scientific enquiry seriously.

**2001** *Locus* (June) 17/2: It's not a gesture toward transcendence, such as Arthur C. Clarke can get away with without violating his hard SF credentials.

**heat ray** *n.* a weapon that fires a beam of intense heat; the beam fired from such a weapon.

**1898** H. G. Wells *War of Worlds* 39: Only the fact that a hummock of heathery sand intercepted the lower part of the Heat-Ray saved them.

**1930** J. W. Campbell *Black Star Passes* in *Amazing Stories Quarterly* (Fall) 521/2: The heat ray was, even when working at full capacity, quite ineffective against the ten-man ships.

**1952** [L. del Rey] *Pursuit* in *Space SF* (May) 10/2: He couldn't believe that there had been time enough for any group to invent a heat-ray, if such a thing could exist. Yet nothing else would explain the two sudden bursts of flame he had seen.

**1966** S. R. Delany *Babel-17* 170: A Ciribian heat ray [...]. They won't use it unless they're attacked.

**1999** L. Niven *Rainbow Mars* in *Rainbow Mars* 229: Svetz had no idea whether a heat ray would fire through the X-cage's door, or reflect.

**helicab** *n.* [*helicopter* + *cab*] a taxi cab that flies by means of helicopter rotors.

**1950** J. Weston *Heli-cab Hack* in *Amazing Stories* (June) 146/2: I'm a hack, and I'm looking for a new helicab—something in fair condition. What have you got?

**1953** R. A. Heinlein *Starman Jones* (1975) 251: The helicab was parked in front of the house.

**1964** K. Laumer *Plague of Demons* in *If* (Nov.) 7/1: It was ten minutes past high noon when I paid off my helicab, ducked under the air blast from the caged high-speed rotors [...] and looked around.

**1974** A. Nourse *Bladerunner* (1991) 65: One moment he and Billy were stepping from the elevator onto the darkened rooftop of the Merriman's apartment and walking across to board the waiting heli-cab.

**helicar** *n.* [*helicopter* + *car*] a passenger vehicle that flies by means of helicopter rotors.

**1948** E. Fennel *War of Intangibles* in *Astounding SF* (June) 118/1: The helicar's wheels touched and automatic brakes hushed the whirring rotors.

**1955** *New York Times* (Feb. 16) 31/5: It becomes a heli-car with the addition of a second one-cylinder motor that works a set of folding propellers.

**1958** P. Ashwell *Unwillingly to School* in *Astounding SF* (Jan.) 21/2: He says he has a helicar there, if I would care to drive it anywhere I like he will give me the key.

**1959** A. E. van Vogt *War against Rull* in *War against Rull* (1999) 183: It was still pitch-dark as Diddy caught a helicar at Cross 2 and flew to within a block of the hill.

**1995** *Have your players ever \*stunned\* you?* (Usenet: rec.games.frp.misc) (Aug. 1): You mean in your world people \*don't\* live to be 200? And you don't even have \*helicars\*?

**hive mind** *n.* [< the perception of hive insects such as ants and bees as existing as units of a whole, rather than individuals] a GROUP MIND, especially applied to insects or insectoids.

**1950** J. H. Schmitz *Second Night of Summer* in *Galaxy SF* (Dec.) 22/2: The Halpa have the hive-mind class of intelligence, so what goes for the nerve systems of most of the ones they send through to us might be nothing much more than secondary reflex-transmitters.

**1957** A. Norton *Star Born* (1966) 39: All the buildings were the same shape and size [...]. Raf wondered if those who had built them had not been humanoid at all, but perhaps insects with a hive mind.

**1982** J. T. Sapienza *Dragon Mag.* (Aug.) 71/1: Their enemies [...] include a reptilian race and an insectoid hive-mind race.

**1995** *Interzone* (Mar.) 45/2: When it sets about "reassembling" the hive-mind which it assumes to be the natural state of affairs on Earth—bringing an assortment of frightened, suffering, incompetent individuals into a gestalt [...]—it creates an entity far more powerful than the one of which it is a part.

**2006** M. Berry *San Francisco Chronicle* (Feb. 19) M6/2: The phoners, meanwhile, seem to be developing some kind of hive mind.

**holo** *n.* [contraction of *hologram*] a HOLOGRAM.

**1970** L. Niven *Ringworld* 31: You may examine the holo Louis Wu is carrying. That is the only information I can give you at this time.

**1977** G. Bear *Sun-Planet* in *Galaxy, Incorporating Worlds of If* (Apr.) 18/1: It was Green's first good look at the creatures, though he had seen holos.

**1981** J. Varley *Blue Champagne* in *Blue Champagne* (1986) 103: She had flipped on the holo generators, and her bed had vanished in a Mark Twain illusion. They floated down the Mississippi river.

**1984** K. S. Robinson *Icehenge* (1990) 78: Xhosa, give this place a structural check and get holo crews in here. Holos of every room.

**1988** [C. J. Cherryh] *Cyteen* 329: She opened uncle Giraud's present next [...]. It was an awfully nice holo of the whole planet.

**1993** V. Milán *From Depths* 7: Head-up holos sprang into existence between dark jade eyes and the windscreen.

**holo-** *pref.* [*hologram*] **1.** used to indicate that something is used to create or display holograms.

**1968**: see quote in HOLOCAM.

**1974** A. Nourse *Bladerunner* (1991) 99: All the new federal Hospitals built in the last decade, with each patient bed within comfortable view of an outside window, with holo-TV stages with multiple projectors in each room.

**1983** P. Anderson *Ivory, & Apes, & Peacocks* in *Time Patrol* (1991) 157: Having broken out a holocube, he showed Everard what would happen, a year hence.

**1991** J. Varley *Steel Beach* (1993) 76: The drink arrived, in one of the Pig's hologlasses [...]. A chip in the thick glass bottom projects a holo picture just above the surface of the drink.

**1997** W. Shatner *Avenger* 69: The Klingon took a small holoprojector from the pouch.

**2.** used to indicate that something is or uses a hologram.

**1973** [J. Tiptree, Jr.] *Girl Who Was Plugged In* in *Screwtop/Girl Who Was Plugged In* (1989) 11: This is simple: a small exposure in an off-network holoshow.

**1985** J. Shirley *Freezone* in B. Sterling *Mirrorshades* (1986) 143: Rickenharp's holovid and the videos weren't getting airplay.

**1991** G. Wolfe *Seraph from Its Sepulcher* in A. M. Greeley & M. Cassutt *Sacred Visions* 172: They could fly. It's a point upon which all my sources agree, and some holostats show them winged.

**1996** D. Brin *Infinity's Shore* (1997) 485: Lark stared at the holoscene with the same superstitious thrill he felt months ago, encountering Galactic tech for the first time.

**2005** *Onion* (June 23) 2/3: We traced the problem to a malfunctioning holosign over the harbor's low-pressure zone.

**holocam** *n.* [HOLO- + *cam*era] a device for recording three-dimensional images.

**1968** J. Brunner *Stand on Zanzibar* (1971) 33: Strung about with Japanind Holocams with [...] LazeeLaser monochrome lamps.

**1973** [J. Tiptree, Jr.] *Girl Who Was Plugged In* in *Screwtop/Girl Who Was Plugged In* (1989) 2: A holocam bobs above but its shadow never falls on them.

**1991** J. Varley *Steel Beach* (1993) 148: The holocam is a partly mechanical, partly biologic device about the size of a fingernail clipping that is implanted inside the eye.

**2002** K. Baker *Likely Lad* in *Asimov's SF* (Sept.) 67: M. Despres shrugged, hoping his holocam picked up the gesture.

**holocamera** *n.* [HOLO- + *camera*] a HOLO-CAM.

**1980** M. Edwards & R. Holdstock *Tour of Universe* 19: Installing the retinal holo-cameras was less pleasant, and my eyes have been a little sore.

**1984** D. Brin *Practice Effect* 73: The show's host turned to the holo-cameras, smiling devilishly.

**2001** G. Wolfe *Viewpoint* in *Starwater Strains* (2005) 24: Are you going to ask where the holocameras are, sir?

**holodeck** *n.* [HOLO- + *deck* (of a space-ship)] a room-sized chamber that creates a complete holographic environment.

**1987** *Encounter at Farpoint ("Star Trek" script)* (May 22) 65: Lieutenant Commander Data... now located in Holodeck area 4-J.

**1989** D. Dvorkin & D. Dvorkin *Captains' Honor* 252: The turbolift doors opened, and Riker led Gretna down the corridor to the holo-deck entrance. "Now [...] what you'll first see is a completely empty room—but whatever you want to make real in there, you can. Anything is possible in this room. Anything."

**1994** G. A. Matiasz *End Time* (1996) 247: The small holodeck modeled an anatomically correct human brain, a computer generated graphic which rotated for several minutes before detonating.

**1999** N. Spinrad *Greenhouse Summer* (2000) 8: "The Gardens of Allah will fulfill the great dream of your illustrious namesake, [...] at a price you can easily afford," he burbled as Monique booted up the holodeck and loaded the chip.

**2000** *PC World* (Dec.) 180/3: Short of an enormously expensive road trip or a full-fledged holodeck, Microsoft's Links 2001 is as close as you can get to playing golf at St. Andrews.

**hologram** *n.* a typically intangible representation or image that exists in three dimensions, often controlled by an AI and able to interact with its environment. Hence **hologramatic,** *adj.,* **holographic,** *adj.*

**1974** G. Dozois *Strangers* in R. Silverberg *New Dimensions IV* 153: He just sat motionlessly in the center of the office—a gleaming antiseptic cave, [...] filled with oddments, [...] a huge computer terminal, a hologram tank that filled half a wall.

**1978** G. Eklund *Starless World* 86: The events of the past day filled her mind like holograms in a newstape.

**1989** W. Shatner *Tekwar* (1990) 91: He'd located the hologram cartridge he was after and, smiling, held it up toward Jake before inserting it in the base slot. Upon the stage there appeared a life-size, full-dimensional image of Beth Kittridge.

**1989** [G. Naylor] *Red Dwarf* 4: He was just a computer-generated simulation of his former self; he couldn't actually touch anything, except for his own hologramatic body.

**1991** O. S. Card *Xenocide* 257: Ender reached his hand into the display, causing a shadow to fall upward into the hologram.

**1994** *Analog SF & Fact* (Jan.) 211/2: The other three walls were decorated with holographic landscapes and seascapes of Hawaii.

**1995** D. M. Flinn *Fearful Summons* 88: Afterward he went shopping, and watched as a hologram of himself materialized in a number of new tunics.

**holoscreen** *n.* [HOLO- + *screen*] a screen on which holograms are displayed.

**1979** P. K. Dick *Exit Door Leads In* in *We Can Remember It for You Wholesale* (1994) 411: The College terminal [...] showed on its holoscreen a great deal of written information.

**1989** J. Pournelle & S. M. Stirling *Children's Hour* in L. Niven, et al. *Man-Kzin Wars II* (1991) 186: The light from the holo-screen crawled in iridescent streamers across the flared scarlet synthetic of the kzin's helmet and the huge lambent eyes.

**1991** G. Wolfe *Seraph from Its Sepulcher* in A. M. Greeley & M. Cassutt *Sacred Visions* 184: The labyrinthine stone stairs gleamed like new-minted gold in Brook's holoscreen.

**holotank** *n.* [HOLO- + *tank*] a transparent container in which a hologram can be projected.

**1979** J. P. Hogan *Two Faces of Tomorrow* 91: The image in the holo-tank was a miniature

3-D landscape made up of wooded hills, tracts of bare, rolling plain, rivers and forests, complete with towns, roads and bridges.

**1984** D. Brin *Practice Effect* 2: Flaster finished drawing a vague figure in the holo tank at the front of the seminar room.

**1990** A. Steele *Clarke County, Space* 95: Bigthorn stabbed a button on his desk which broke the connection, and Brooks disintegrated in a sparkling haze, leaving behind the blank corner of the holotank.

**1993** D. Beason & K. J. Anderson *Assemblers of Infinity* 14: The transparent holotank took up the center of the hemispherical control center.

**holovision** *n.* [HOLO- + tele*vision*] THREE-V. Compare THREE-D, TRI-D, TRIDEO, TRI-DIM, TRI-V, TRI-VID.

**1968** M. Frayn *Very Private Life* 4: They'll be materializing before them in the special reception chambers, transmitted by way of the wires and beams, and reproduced by the three-dimensional holovision system in all their natural solidity.

**1972** E. Bryant *Poet in Hologram in Middle of Prime Time* in H. Harrison *Nova 2* 97: I would have been regretful, but I would have accepted your resignation. After all, you're one of the top holovision writers in the field.

**1973** [J. Tiptree, Jr.] *Girl who was Plugged In* in *Warm Worlds & Otherwise* (1975) 81: But pass up the sci-fi stuff for now, like for instance the holovision technology that's put TV and radio in museums.

**1987** K. Cramer *Forbidden Knowledge* in R. Rucker *Mathenauts* (1989) 126: As soon as she began to argue with him he refused to discuss [ … ] anything else and turned on the holovision.

**1990** A. McCaffrey & J. L. Nye *Death of Sleep* (1992) 189: Flatscreen pictures don't have enough life in them [ … ]. I prefer holovision every time.

**home galaxy** *n.* the galaxy in which a species originated; the galaxy that an individual being is from.

**1951** J. D. MacDonald *Common Denominator* in *Galaxy SF* (July) 22/1: The Argonauts, as they came to be called, were pleasantly similar to mankind. It was additional proof that only in the rarest instance was the life-apex on any planet in the home Galaxy an abrupt divergence from the "human" form.

**1973** M. L'Engle *Wind in Door* (1993) 127: I find it easier to posit when I am in my home galaxy.

**1993** J. Clute in J. Clute & P. Nicholls *Ency. of SF* (1995) 538/1: The Universe-spanning tale in which an Earthman and his comrades (not necessarily human) discover a cosmic threat to the home Galaxy.

**home planet** *n.* a HOMEWORLD. Compare MOTHERWORLD.

**1930** W. O. Stapledon *Last & First Men* (1931) 198: The Martian colonists, when they observed man's disorganization, prepared, at the instigation of the home planet, a very great offensive.

**1930** J. W. Campbell, Jr. *Black Star Passes* in *Amazing Stories Quarterly* (Fall) 516/1: We may pursue the Nigrians all the way to their home planets, to make sure they stay right there until their star has passed entirely out of our region

**1945** [M. Leinster] *First Contact* in R. Silverberg *SF Hall of Fame, Vol. I* (1970) 316: A solitary Earth-ship and a solitary alien, meeting in a nebula which must be remote from the home planet of each.

**1967** J. Blish *Okie* in D. Knight *Cities of Wonder* 119: Traveling away from Earth for us is very like traveling in time: different distances from the home planet have different year dates.

**1982** M. Z. Bradley *Winds of Darkover* 10: Resigning before a contract was up meant losing your holdback pay and your fee passage back to your home planet—which could strand you on a strange world and wipe out a year's pay.

**2002** G. Wolfe *Shields of Mars* in *Starwater Strains* (2005) 92: My boss here wants me to go off to our home planet.

**home star** *n.* the star around which a being's or species' homeworld orbits.

**1939** C. D. Simak *Cosmic Engineers* in *Astounding S-F* (Apr.) 142: One of the planets of their old home star, fourth out from the Sun.

**1951** P. Anderson *Interloper* in *Mag. of Fantasy & SF* (Apr.) 5: My home star lies clear across the Galaxy, near the periphery; I will not at present be more specific than that.

**1969** R. Silverberg *Across Billion Years* 218: Thereafter, naturally, the home star of the Mirt Korp Ahm ceased to be detectable by conventional optical means.

**1982** [C. J. Cherryh] *Port Eternity* 24: We were in the safe area of our own home star.

**1989** N. Pollotta & P. Foglio *Illegal Aliens* 101: Finding no resistance at first, they established supply lines and built adamantine fortresses in every solar system that surrounded their home star.

**home system** *n.* the solar system in which a species originated.

**1947** [M. Leinster] *Propagandist* in G. Conklin *Possible Worlds of SF* (1951) 212: Everybody knows that their home system was found, and everybody knows that when we tried to open negotiations with them their ships attacked us in a raging ferocity.

**1967** K. Laumer *Thunderhead* in *Day Before Forever & Thunderhead* (1968) 125: We kicked the damned spiders back into their home system ten years ago.

**1992** V. Vinge *Fire upon Deep* 269: The crew watched the death agonies of the home system, and then over the following years [...] died themselves.

**2000** P. F. Hamilton *Confederation Handbook* (2002) 257: Their own homesystem does not have a single homeworld, but rather a ring of planets orbiting their sun.

**homeworld** *n.* the planet on which a species originated or that an individual is from. Compare HOME PLANET, MOTHERWORLD.

**1900** G. Griffith *Visit to Moon* in *Pearson's Mag.* (Jan.) 21: Zaidie stood gazing for nearly an hour at this marvellous vision of the home-world which she had left so far behind her.

**1939** [E. Binder] *Impossible World* (1967) 107: Is Pluto your home world?

**1945** [M. Leinster] *First Contact* in R. Silverberg *SF Hall of Fame, Vol. I* (1970) 315: No one considered the crazy, rank impossibility of a deep-space contact, with neither side knowing the other's home world!

**1957** L. Brackett *All Colors of Rainbow* in *Halfling & Other Stories* (1973) 144: He had

studied weather-control engineering on his home-world at Mintaka.

**1969** R. Silverberg *Across Billion Years* 196: "Do you understand what I mean when I refer to the home world of the Mirt Korp Ahm?" "The world on which their first evolution occurred," said the robot. "The world which is basic to their history."

**1993** D. Carey *Great Starship Race* 3: When we return to the homeworlds, you [...] will be removed from my swarm.

**2000**: see quote in HOME SYSTEM.

**2005** J. Scalzi *Old Man's War* (2005) 45: This will probably be your last chance to see what was your homeworld.

**Homo superior** *n.* the species that will evolve or be developed from *Homo sapiens,* with greater intellect or physical abilities, and often possessing paranormal powers.

**1935** O. Stapledon *Odd John* 271: *Homo Superior* faced the little mob of *Homo Sapiens,* and it was immediately evident that *Homo Superior* was indeed the better man.

**1943** J. W. Campbell, Jr. *Astounding SF* (Aug.) 158/1: How do you decide whether a man is an abnormally brilliant homo sapiens or a low-grade homo superior, anyway?

**1955** [F. Donovan] *Short Life* in *Astounding SF* (Oct.) 48/2: Now you see why I dared not go even farther and release [...] the true Homo superior, the transcendent man.

**1973** J. R. Gregory & R. Price *Visitor* 23: When the three returned to Earth, they had wondered what to call themselves. *Homo superior* sounded [...] well, too superior.

**1996** D. Pringle, et al. *Ultimate Ency. of SF* 51/1: Sf writers [...] have been most interested in the advantageous mutations which might produce the first specimen of *Homo superior.*

**horror** *n.* a genre of fiction, film, etc. in which the object is to instill a feeling of fear in the reader or viewer.

[**1869** *Appleton's Journal* (July 10) 474/1: At an early period in its history, we had the realistic-improper novel, of which Fielding was the sponsor; then the sentimental novel, known as the Minerva; then the mysterious-horror novel of the Radcliffe school.]

# Hugo

**1900** *Bookman* (Dec.) 331/1: Both of these, however, we should rank as tales of horror considerably below "The Man Who Would Be King."

**1917** *New York Times Book Rev.* (Feb. 11) 52/2: Those who enjoy horror, stories overflowing with blood and black mystery, will be grateful to Richard Marsh for writing "The Beetle."

**1934** *New York Times Book Rev.* (Sept. 9) 2/3: "The Fly," as a pure achievement in horror fiction [...] must be ranked as one of the world's masterpieces within that disagreeable genre.

**1939** C. Cottrell *Unknown (letter)* (May) 160/1: I can see where hack writers from the cheap horror, thriller, and terror tale magazines may try to invade Unknown with their bloodcurdling yarns.

**1953** D. Fabun *SF in Motion Pictures, Radio, & Television* in R. Bretnor *Modern SF* 54: Give a science-fiction story the horror elements that have kept poor Frankenstein touring the circuits year after year, throw in a little space and fancy words, and the public will take to it in a big way.

**1972** R. Hodgens *Brief, Tragical History of SF Film* in W. Johnson *Focus on SF Film* 82: The story is regarded as one of the most original and effective science fiction stories, *subspecies* "horror."

**1992** K. K. Rusch *Mag. of Fantasy & SF* (Dec.) 7/1: Science fiction, fantasy and horror are becoming more realistic, with settings closer to home.

**2005** D. G. Hartwell *In Praise of David Drake* in *New York Rev. of SF* (Oct.) 5/2: This military sf is not military pornography, but rather a form of horror fiction.

**Hugo** *n.* [after *Hugo* Gernsback, who published the first magazine devoted solely to science fiction] any of several awards presented annually at the World Science Fiction Convention (beginning in 1953) for excellence in science-fiction or fantasy writing, art, publishing, etc., voted on by the members of the convention. Also **Hugo Award.**

**1950** [B. Tucker] *Big Bloodshot Eye* in *SF News Letter* (July) 4/2: The first annual "Hugo" award will be made for literary merit in the s-f field.

**1953** *Fantasy-Times* (Nov. 2) 3: The *Hugo* was originally presented to Ackerman by the Convention Awards Committee.

**1960** *Analog Sci. Fact-Fiction* (Nov.) 165/1: Here, I suspect, is the Hugo winner as "Best Novel" of 1960, in spite of the five-dollar price.

**1980** *Washington Post Book World* (Sept. 14) 4/1: The 1980 Hugos, given for works published in 1979, contained few surprises.

**2001** *Locus* (June) 12/4: *Kristine Kathryn Rusch* sold [...] a novel version of her Hugo-nominated story.

**humanoid** *n.* [orig. used for hominid apes and proto-humans] an alien or artificial being whose body is similar to a human's in form.

**1940** I. Asimov *Homo Sol* in *Astounding S-F* (Sept.) 118/1: I have here [...] the official report from Alpha Centauri, on whose fifth planet the Humanoids of Sol have landed.

**1958** *Manchester (U. K.) Guardian* (Sept. 26) 4/3: The humanoids who are accidentally brought to earth by these means inevitably turn out to be superior to us.

**1969** R. Silverberg *Across Billion Years* 77: I saw figures moving around, the dome-headed, six-limbed humanoids familiar to us from the plaque designs.

**1983** S. Marshak & M. Culbreath *Triangle* 13: Also one primitive humanoid, about our size—who dies at an early age.

**1999** P. Majer & C. Porter *trans.* K. Čapek *R.U.R.* in K. Čapek *Four Plays* 4: The manufacture of sentient humanoids is highly classified information, of course, Lady Helen.

**humanoid** *adj.* of human shape or form; resembling a human.

**1940** I. Asimov *Homo Sol* in *Astounding S-F* (Sept.) 118/1: Beings of every manlike type and shape were there. [...] There was a delegate with green skin, one with an eight-inch proboscis and one with a vestigial tail. Internally, variation was almost infinite. But all were alike in two things. They were all Humanoid. They all possessed intelligence.

**1952** V. Nabokov *Lance* in *Nabokov's Dozen* (1959) 207: Inhabitants of foreign planets, "intelligent" beings, humanoid or of various mythic makes.

**1954** C. Oliver *Field Expedient* in W. F. Nolan *Edge of Forever* (1971) 141: The ship carried two pilots, a navigator, a doctor, fifty babies, twenty-five special humanoid robots, computers, and supplies.

**1969** E. Hamilton *Return to Stars* 71: Faces humanoid but not human, eyes slitted and saucer-like and pupil-less gleamed in the light.

**1987** O. Butler *Dawn* (1991) 12: What had seemed to be a tall, slender man was still humanoid, but it had no nose—no bulge, no nostrils—just flat, gray skin.

**1994** D. Spencer *Passing Fancy* 161: Figure a humanoid body is, what, ninety percent water, something like that?

**hyperdrive** *n.* a space drive that propels spaceships faster than the speed of light, especially by entering hyperspace. Compare OVERDRIVE, ULTRADRIVE.

**1949** *Startling Stories* (Jan.) 10/2: Construction is still going on and, through a worker's accident, the ship, still incomplete and utterly unarmed, is sent flashing into the "other" space, a universe of complete darkness in which its hyper-drive operates.

**1955** *Forbidden Planet (screenplay)* (Mar. 10) 1: Almost at once there followed the discovery of quanto-gravitetic hyper-drive, through which the speed of light was first attained, and later surpassed.

**1969** M. Z. Bradley *Brass Dragon* (1980) 49: A spaceship traveling at half the speed of light on planetary drive, and three times the speed of light on hyperdrive, expected to call in at three widely separated stars.

**1988** [C. J. Cherryh] *Cyteen* 69: He was scared into hyperdrive.

**1991** J. Varley *Steel Beach* (1993) 332: So I slammed the Blackbird into hyperdrive and listened to the banshee wail as the old ship shuddered and leaped into the fourth dimension.

**1997** R. Hatch & C. Golden *Battlestar Galactica: Armageddon* 237: Both ships slipped out of reality using the Quantum Shift Effect, even as they rocketed into hyperdrive.

**hyperspace** *n.* [orig. used in mathematics to mean space of more than three dimensions] a dimension, continuum, or other theoretical region, coexistent with, but having different physical laws than, the space-time continuum we inhabit, especially one with laws that permit an object entering from one point in our continuum to exit into another point more quickly than it takes light in our continuum to travel between those two points. Compare SUPERSPACE.

**1928** K. Meadowcroft *Invisible Bubble* in *Amazing Stories* (Sept.) 508/2: Are we not justified in supposing, [ ... ] that the boundary lines of space and hyper-space may not be so rigidly drawn as we have supposed?

**1931** J. W. Campbell, Jr. *Islands of Space* in *Amazing Stories Quarterly* (Spring) 161/2: Well, in this hyperspace we are creating, *matter cannot exist at a velocity lower than a certain quantity, and we determine that quantity by using this apparatus.*

**1934** J. Williamson *Legion of Space* in *Astounding Stories* (June) 118/2: Speeds, a mathematician would hasten to add, as measured in the ordinary space that the vessel went *around;* both acceleration and velocity being quite moderate in the hyperspace it really went *through.*

**1951** I. Asimov *Foundation* 12: He had steeled himself just a little for the Jump through hyperspace, a phenomenon one did not experience in simple interplanetary trips.

**1965** S. R. Delany *Ballad of Beta-2* (1977) 8: They'd only been gone sixty years when the hyperspace drive became a large-scale reality.

**1987** D. Brin *Uplift War* 274: Ships kept watch over the five local layers of hyperspace, over nearby transfer points, over the cometary time-drop nexi.

**1990** *Thrust* (Winter) 23/3: Stith has given us hyperspace where lightspeed is a tad over 22 miles per hour.

**1995** A. Thomson *Color of Distance* (1999) 84: Was the mother ship gone as well? Had the *Kotani Maru* made the jump to hyperspace? Could they still come back for her?

**hyperspatial** *adj.* of or in hyperspace.

**1934** [M. Leinster] *Sidewise in Time* in *Astounding Stories* (June) 30/1: We assume in some sense the existence of a hyper-space separating the closed spaces; hyper-spatial coordinates which mark their relative hyper-spatial positions; hyper-spatial—

**1951** T. Sturgeon *Traveling Crag* in *Visions & Ventures* (1978) 278: Now, a cargo ship was travelling between galaxies on hyperspatial drive. In a crazy, billion-to-one odds accident, it emerged into normal space smack in the middle of a planetoid.

**1963** H. B. Piper *Space Viking* (1975) 14: My hyperspatial astrogator, Guatt Kirbey, composes music; he tries to express the mathematics of hyperspatial theory in musical terms.

**1979** D. Adams *Hitchhiker's Guide to Galaxy* (1981) 35: The plans for development of the out-lying regions of the Galaxy require the building of a hyperspatial express route through your star system, and regrettably your planet is one of those scheduled for demolition.

**2006** *Locus Online (Internet)* (Feb. 17): SF novel, sequel to *Geodesica: Ascent* (2005), set in the 24th century, about a "vast hyperspatial labyrinth" called Geodesica.

**hyperspeed** *n.* a speed that is faster than the speed of light.

**1956** P. Anderson *Peek! I See You!* in *Gods Laughed* (1982) 80: The interior maintenance units keep breaking down too. Our top hyper-speed is a hypercrawl. Anything would be better!

**1980** J. White *Ambulance Ship* in *Alien Emergencies* (2002) 110: The safety cutoff on the good generator had failed [ ... ] which meant that a part of the ship had been proceeding at hyperspeed while the rest had been slowed in-stantaneously to sublight velocity.

**1990** J. Lindsey *Warrior's Woman* 133: Before that, our ships could only travel at hy-perspeed. Now we get stellarspeed, which is ten times faster and makes it so much easier to visit neighboring Star Systems.

**1994** M. D. Hahn *Time for Andrew* (1995) 31: The next thing I knew, I was dreaming about a rock-et ship traveling through space at hyperspeed.

**1997** R. Hatch & C. Golden *Battlestar Galactica: Armageddon* 247: The ship seems to have slipped away. It did have hyperspeed ca-pacity, and we can only suppose that the prison-ers somehow managed to wrest control of the vessel.

**hypnopaedia, hypnopedia** *n.* teach-ing by subconscious means (especially by playing sound recordings) while the learner is asleep. Hence **hypnopaedic,** *adj.,* **hypnopaedically,** *adv.*

**1932** A. Huxley *Brave New World* 27: The principle of sleep-teaching, or hypnopædia, had been discovered.

**1932** A. Huxley, *Brave New World* 82: The sort of words that suddenly make you jump [ ... ] they seem so new and exciting even though they're about something hypnopædically obvious.

**1932** A. Huxley, *Brave New World* 173: Listening unconsciously to hypnopædic lessons in hygiene and sociability.

**1947** L. Padgett *Jesting Pilot* in *Astounding SF* (May) 87: It was selective telepathic hyp-nosis, with the so-called Monuments—powerful hypnopedic machines—as the control devices.

**1957** *Astounding SF* (Oct.) 98/1: That night he implanted a very long message in code in the boy's brain by hypnopedia.

**1969** *New Scientist* (Jan. 30) 216/1: Sleep learning or hypnopedia, as its practitioners pre-fer to call it, is now acquiring a new status among Soviet teaching circles.

**1973** A. McCaffrey *Rescued Girls of Refugee* in R. Elwood *Ten Tomorrows* 73: Fight fire with fire. We fought hypnopaedia with hypno-paedia.

# Fanspeak

Science fiction fans, verbally effusive and never at a loss for words, have developed their own distinctive talk over the years, half-slang, half-jargon, and generally known as **fanspeak**. These words have had many different birth methods—everything from bowderlization (**fugghead**), to happy accidents (**filk** was originally a typo), to literary allusions (**slan** refers to a race in a story of the same name), to purest whimsy (**eye tracks**). The most common ways for new fanspeak terms to be made, however, are by abbreviation, acronyming, and affixing.

Simple abbreviations include **ish** for "issue" and **pub** for "publish." Another technique is to combine the first parts of each word of a phrase, so "correction fluid" becomes **corflu**, "ego boost" becomes **egoboo**, and "serious and constructive" becomes **sercon**. Fanspeak acronyms are often based on the first letters of words in a longer phrase, such as **gafia** (Get Away From It All) and **smof** (Secret Master Of Fandom). Words can also be combined by a process sometimes called "scientificombination," in which phrases where the last letter(s) of the first word are the same as the first letter(s) of the second word are combined into a single word. **Scientifiction** is the most successful of these (from "scientific fiction"), but most occurrences are one-off (or "nonce") uses.

Affixes are also very common, and quite productive. **Stf-** and **scienti-** have been added to almost anything to indicate that it is somehow science-fictional: **scientibook, scientifilm, stfield, stfan,** etc. Other common suffixes include **-zine** (see separate sidebar) and **-con**. Fans have also made heavy use of an infix—the letter **h**—which has no precise meaning, but rather makes whatever word it is in somehow more fannish. The -h- is usually used in nonce coinages (**ghood, bhoy**), but the fannish slogan "**bheer** is the one true **ghod**" indicates the most important uses.

Fanspeak, however it is made, emphasizes the playful, creative, efficient, and independent nature of SF fans and fandom.

# i

**illo** *n.* [abbr. of *illustration*] an illustration, especially in a magazine or fanzine.
**1945** *Startling Stories* (Summer) 88/2: And then come the inside illos. It would be nice to see a Finlay every now and then.
**1953** P. Mittelbuscher *Thrilling Wonder Stories (letter)* (Aug.) 137/1: The Lawrence illos for TURNCOAT seemed to be of the hastily done variety.
**1961** G. H. Scithers *Amra* (July) 2: The illo to the immediate left is an experiment—our second try at multicolor work.
**1975** E. Weinstein *Fillostrated Fan Dictionary* 4: This dictionary has a large number of illustrations. At last count, this was near one hundred illos.
**1994** *Interzone* (July) 5/3: The illos are getting better and you are (wisely) not filling up the magazine with inferior illos but letting many of the stories stand alone.
**2002** M. Bishop *New York Rev. of SF* (Dec.) 10/2: The latter—interestingly, at least to me—with photo illos by J. K. Potter.

**imaginative fiction** *n.* literature that is set in a world other than that of the reader, e.g., that is set in an imaginary world, parallel universe, or alternate timeline, or that is set in a world similar to the reader's but in which magic or supernatural creatures are portrayed as real or which features advances in science and technology that have not occurred. Also **imaginative literature, writing,** etc. Compare FANTASY 1, SCIENCE FICTION 3, SCIENTIFANTASY, SPEC-ULATIVE FICTION 2, STFANTASY

**1914** H. P. Lovecraft *To All-Story Weekly* in *Miscellaneous Writings* (1995) 496: Particular professors and sober Scotchmen may denounce as childish the desire for imaginative fiction.
**1923** S. A. Coblentz *New York Times Book Rev.* (Sept. 9) 2/3: But in spite of such perversions science genuinely opens the way not only to a systematic and analytical realism but to imaginative writing of a new and exalted order.
**1936–37** F. J. Ackerman *Whither Ackermankind?* in *Novae Terrae* (Dec.–Jan.) 5: Scientifantasy Field—in my case including imaginative fiction, films, dramas, broadcasts; as applied, as subjects allow, to collecting, reviewing and supplying other fans as salesman.
**1946** W. S. Baring-Gould *Little Superman, What Now?* in *Harpers Mag.* (Sept.) 284/1: In the public mind science fiction is often confused with another branch of imaginative writing: the story of natural, unnatural, supernatural horror.
**1953** L. S. de Camp *Imaginative Fiction & Creative Imagination* in R. Bretnor *Modern SF* 121: In my usage, "imaginative fiction" includes the definite group of stories in the fiction of the modern Western world that are nonrealistic, imaginative, based upon assumptions contrary to everyday experience, often highly fanciful and often laid in settings remote in time and space from those of everyday life.
**1969** A. Budrys *Benchmarks* (1985) 235: In science fiction, or in any other class of imaginative literature, we tend to equate notability and serial complexity.

**1996** D. Pringle, et al. *Ultimate Ency. of SF* 43/1: The elixir of life and the fountain of youth have always been key motifs of imaginative fiction.

**2005** *New Yorker* (Nov. 21) 91/3: Throughout his own imaginative writing, Lewis is always trying to stuff the marvellous back into the allegorical.

**impervium** *n.* a virtually indestructible or impenetrable substance.

**1943** [L. O'Donnell] *Clash by Night* in *Astounding S-F* (Mar.) 9/1: A half mile beneath the shallow Venusian sea the black impervium dome that protects Montana Keep rests frowningly on the bottom.

**1943** H. F. Parker *Sword of Johnny Damokles* in *Planet Stories* (Mar.) 28/2: My impervium hull was supposed to reject light as a mirror would, and so throw itself forward like a beam of light. The thing works too.

**1949** R. Gallun *Mysta of Moon* in *Planet Comics* (Jan.) 43: Don't worry, the impervium plates on the ship will protect us!

**1962** J. Sutton *After Ixmal* in *Amazing Stories* (Oct.) 74/1: Ixmal rapidly evaluated the consequences of such a chain reaction and found he could survive, thanks to the thick impervium-lined walls his makers so thoughtfully had provided.

**1977** P. J. Farmer *Lavalite World* in *World of Tiers: Vol. Two* (1997) 312: Satisfied, Orc had ordered the robots, One and Two, to seal up the control room door with *impervium* flux.

**2001** L. N. Smith *American Zone* (2002) 135: It had a modern Impervium roof, I noticed, and I was willing to bet that if anybody batted a baseball through one of its windows on a sunny summer day, the glass would have healed itself by morning.

**impossible story** *n. Obs.* a work of imaginative fiction.

**1929** Mrs. H. E. Caldwell *Argosy All-Story Weekly (letter)* (Mar.) 141/2: My husband's favorites are Westerns, stories of prize fights, aviators, and other adventure stories, whereas I prefer love stories, detective stories and impossible stories.

**1938** H. Kuttner *Selling Fantasy Story* in *Writer's Digest* (Mar.) 29/1: Impossible stories are the most convincing. They have to be, or editors wouldn't buy them. It's easy to believe in a two-fisted cowboy [...]. But fantasy is a different matter.

**1957** S. Moskowitz *How SF Got Its Name* in *Mag. of Fantasy & SF* (Feb.) 67/1: Another term often found in the readers' departments of Munsey magazines was IMPOSSIBLE STORIES.

**infodump** *n.* a large amount of background information inserted into a story all at once. Hence **infodumping,** *n.* Compare EXPOSITORY LUMP.

**1990** H. Waldrop *Washington Post* (Nexis) (Feb. 25) X8: You find out about Periclean Athens [...]. Writers in my neck of the woods call this stuff "infodump"—putting in your research without bringing the narrative flow to a screeching halt.

**1996** *Interzone* (May) 59/1: Previous authors attempting to broaden out their vision of the future by ladling dollops of the *Encyclopedia Galactica* into their work [...] had generally been thought guilty of the bad practice of "info-dumping."

**1997** G. K. Wolfe *Locus* (Oct.) 18/2: For those impatient with mysteries, the major infodump tale in the collection, "Secret History," is in this latter section.

**1995** *Interzone* (Oct.) 59/2: Most of the first two hundred pages are taken up with long discussions between Moh and Janis about what is going on and what it all means, interspersed with cluttered flashbacks and long infodumps.

**2000** M. Dirda *Bound to Please* (2005) 459: But occasionally some passages sound like mere info-dumps, as in that Gnostic account of creation already quoted.

**2005** P. Di Filippo *Asimov's SF* (Mar.) 133/1: Greenwood inserts canny infodumps that never detour the fluid action, all the while building a believable portrait of a charmingly skewed world.

**inner space** *n.* [after *outer space*] the human psyche, especially the subconscious.

**1953** J. B. Priestley (title) *New Statesman & Nation* (Dec. 5) 712/1: They Come From Inner Space

**1953** [J. B. Priestley, *They Come from Inner Space* 712/3: We have to go somewhere, so we prefer superficially to think of ourselves travelling to the other side of the sun rather than sitting quietly at home and then moving inward, exploring ourselves, the hidden life of the psyche.]

**1959** H. Koch (title) in F. Pohl *Star SF No. 6* 134: Invasion from Inner Space

**1962** J. G. Ballard *Which Way to Inner Space?* in *User's Guide to Millennium* (1997) 197: The biggest developments of the immediate future will take place, not on the Moon or Mars, but on Earth, and it is *inner* space, not outer, that needs to be explored.

**1968** A. Diment *Bang Bang Birds* 143: The Indian and Chinese prophets [...] knew a thing or two about inner space and the turned-on mind. They did it on contemplation though and not mushroom juice.

**1980** [L. del Rey] *World of SF* 261: Certainly no science fiction story explored inner space more effectively than Joyce did with Molly Bloom.

**1989** P. Anderson *Boat of Million Years* (2004) 379: Tremendous things are going on. They simply aren't for us. The creativity, the discovery, has moved to—what? Inner space.

**insectoid** *n.* an insect-like alien.

**1937** O. Stapledon *Star Maker To End of Time* (1953) 340: Of the populations of the sub-galaxy most were descendants of the original Ichthyoids or Arachnoids; but [...] not a few that had sprung from avians, insectoids or plant-men.

**1972** A. D. Foster *Tar-Aiym Krang* (1983) 12: He was only mildly surprised at the insectoid's presence.

**1981** V. N. McIntyre *Straining Your Eyes through Viewscreen Blues* F. Herbert *Nebula Winners Fifteen* 80: This is a slightly less blatant version of the game of space opera, in which one writes a western, then trades earth for Omega Orion XI, [...] and the squinty-eyed bad guys in black hats turn into clones, giant ambulatory carrots, humanoids, virusoids, or insectoids.

**1996** D. Brin *Infinity's Shore* (1997) 242: One by one, the insectoids drifted upslope to the makeshift cavity.

**2002** A. Reynolds *Redemption Ark* (2004) 438: It felt a distant echo of kinship, something that had never troubled it when it was extinguishing ammonia-breathing gasbags or spiny insectoids.

**insectoid** *adj.* insect-like.

**1937** O. Stapledon *Star Maker* in *To End of Time* (1953) 306: The little insectoid units themselves carried on these operations consciously, though without understanding their significance.

**1955** [C. Satterfield] *With Redfern on Capella XII* in *Galaxy SF* (Nov.) 132/1: Miss Garney made sympathetic noises and knelt beside the insectoid creature.

**1972** A. D. Foster *Tar-Aiym Krang* 122: The thranx were as alien as any race man had yet encountered. A hundred-percent insectoid, hard-shelled, open circulatory system, compound eyes, rigid, inflexible joints ... and eight limbs.

**1986** G. Benford *Of Space-Time & River* in *Isaac Asimov's SF Mag.* (Feb.) 26: How a seven-foot insectoid thing with gleaming russet skin can look like an Egyptian I don't know.

**1991** O. S. Card *Xenocide* 118: The insectoid aliens had haunted her nightmares.

**1998** K. W. Jeter *Mandalorian Armor* 168: The short bounty hunter, with the large insectoid eyes and breathing hoses, stood in the doorway.

**in-system** *adj.* designating something or someone that operates only within a solar system. Compare INTRA-SYSTEM.

**1977** G. Zebrowski *Ashes & Stars* 7: A hundred thousand worlds circle their suns here, [...] some cradle pre-space humanoid cultures; still others have in-system space travel; many are dead worlds.

**1982** [C. J. Cherryh] *Merchanter's Luck* 9: In fact, his life had been womanless, except for one very drunk insystem merchanter one night on Mariner.

**1989** Jeff VanderMeer *Sea, Mendeho, & Moonlight* in *Secret Life* (2004) 57: A rare in-system shuttle rumbled into view, a clot of lights soon swallowed by the city's intense glow.

**1995** E. Moon *Winning Colors* 284: By the estimate of the senior engineer aboard the *Paganini*, the other cruiser's insystem drive had lost thirty percent of its power.
**2002** A. Reynolds *Redemption Ark* (2004) 41: The freighter was half the size of *Nightshade*, a typical in-system hauler built one or two centuries ago.

**in-system** *adv.* in or into a solar system; toward the center of a solar system. Compare OUT-SYSTEM.
**1974** F. Saberhagen *Berserker's Planet* in *Worlds of If* (July–Aug.) 101/1: Just punch in a destination, and it'll deliver you in-system, near any civilized world you want.
**1980** D. Brin *Sundiver* 96: I was a junior officer on Calypso. You may recall we got back in system a couple of years ago.
**1989** L. Watt-Evans *Nightside City* 9: Born on Prometheus, came in-system to the nightside at sixteen.
**1997** D. Weber & S. White *In Death Ground* (2000) 7: *Argive* had been in-system for over six days now without detecting anything but lifeless worlds and what *might* be a second warp point just over three light-hours from the star.
**2002** M. J. Harrison *Light* 219 (2004): The *White Cat*, her torch already alight, heading in-system at a shallow angle to the ecliptic on a brutally straight line of fusion product.

**inter-dimensional** *adj.* existing or occuring between two or more dimensions.
**1932** B. Bailey *Amazing Stories* (Aug.) 477/1: I would like to see more interplanetary stories and inter-dimensional tales, and fewer stories of unusual medical operations and the like.
**1965** J. Speer *Fantasy Fiction Decimal Classification* in *Fancestral Voices* (2004) 24: There are not special categories for future war on earth, space war, interdimensional war, or war with intelligent insects.
**1972** K. Laumer *Shape Changer* (1973) 13: This stuff is experimental equipment from a temporal laboratory—where they run experiments in probability, time travel, interdimensional relationships!
**2005** P. Di Filippo *Asimov's SF* (Mar.) 134/1: Genius Hugh has perfected an interdi-

mensional vacuole that exists outside of time and space.

**interplanetary** *n.* a story about travel to other planets. Also as *adj.* in **interplanetary story, tale,** etc.
**1927**: see quote in PLANETEER.
**1931** O. A. Kline *Writing Fantastic Story* in *Writer* (Jan.) 7/1: I wanted to write an interplanetary story, and I believe the reason for this lay in the following incidents.
**1939** C. Hornig *SF* (Oct.) 119/1: Not all interplanetaries—not all laboratory yarns—not all world dooms, but a generous sprinkling of all types.
**1947** [H. Hastings] *Thrilling Wonder Stories* (June) 112/2: The trouble with doing an interplanetary yarn, as far as I'm concerned, is [ … ] the fact that a vessel can travel between planets or stars isn't intrinsically interesting.
**1947** [H. Hastings] in *Thrilling Wonder Stories* 112/2: I hate giant amoebas. I'm going to write an interplanetary.
**1953** L. S. de Camp *S-F Handbook* 69: Some of these had imaginative themes, such as William Wallace Cook's *Adrift in the Unknown,* an interplanetary, in Street and Smith's Adventure Library.
**1979** P. Anderson *SF & Sci.* in *Destinies* (Jan.–Feb.) 256: His various interplanetary tales amount to delighted exploration of the possibilities.

**intersystem** *n.* connecting two or more star systems; traveling from one star system to another.
**1949** [R. LaFayette] *Emperor of Universe* in *Startling Stories* (Nov.) 134/1: His writings [ … ] demonstrate an enormous command of the problems of inter-system government.
**1953** P. K. Dick *Impossible Planet* in B. W. Aldiss *Space Odysseys* (1976) 105: Andrews spun the dial of the intersystem vidsender. Under them the jets throbbed and roared. The lumbering transport had reached deep space.
**1968** S. R. Delany *Nova* (2002) 14: When he finally broke up with the girl, and left Australia, he had his certificate as a cyborg stud for any inter- and intra-system ship.

**interworld** *adj.* **1.** between planets; travelling between planets.

**1942** G. O. Smith *QRM—Interplanetary* in S. Schmidt *Fifty Years of Best SF from Analog* (1980) 92: These reflectors shot the interworld signals across space in tight beams.

**1952** M. Sherman *Matter of Faith* in *Space SF* (Sept.) 66/2: It was easy, too, to enter the planet Grekh; you just boarded an interworld ferry from either of the two sister[-]planets, Pittam or Speewry.

**1955** J. Vance *Meet Miss Universe* in *Fantastic Universe* (Mar.) 6/2: Because it's not just an ordinary beauty-contest—it's more important. An experiment in inter[-]world relations.

**2.** of more than one planet.

**1944** L. Brackett *Veil of Astellar* in *Best of Leigh Brackett* (1977) 73: A message rocket dropped into the receiving chute at the Interworld Space Authority headquarters on Mars.

**1948** N. Loomis *Mr. Zytztz Goes to Mars* in *Thrilling Wonder Stories* (Aug.) 20/2: They delivered the three Zytztes [sic] to the World Council, which during their absence had been renamed the Inter-World Council.

**1959** [C. Smith] *No, No, Not Rogov!* in J. Merril *SF: Best of Best* (1967) 181: Yet all eyes were fixed upon the golden shape which interpreted *"The Glory and Affirmation of Man"* in the Inter-World Dance Festival of what might have been A.D. 13,582.

**3.** existing or operating on more than one planet.

**1979** J. Vance *Face* in *Demon Princes: Vol. Two* (1997) 49: Kotzash evidently maintains an office on Methel; the prospectus lists both Serjeuz and Twanish addresses. Kotzash is, therefore, an interworld corporation and files a yearly report.

**1988** D. W. Jones *Lives of Christopher Chant* (2001) 118: You are too young to be aware of this, but I wish to explain that we are all working full stretch just now in an effort to catch a gang of interworld villains.

**intra-system** *adj.* designating something that operates or exists within a solar system. Compare IN-SYSTEM.

**1968** S. R. Delany *Nova* (2002) 14: When he finally broke up with the girl, and left Australia, he had his certificate as a cyborg stud for any inter- and intra-system ship.

**1994** S. Baxter *Ring* (1996) 222: There must have been research facilities here, built around the nightfighter, as the people of the time tried to pry out the secrets of its intrasystem drive, its hyperdrive, the construction material.

**1996** D. Pringle, et al. *Ultimate Ency. of SF* 232/1: His next novel [ ... ] turned a Stapledonian eye on mankind's intra-system future.

**ion drive** *n.* a space drive that generates thrust by emitting a stream of ions in the direction opposite to that of travel; (especially in modern and scientific use) such a drive that generates a relatively weak but steady acceleration that accumulates over time to produce high sublight velocities.

**1947** J. Williamson *Equalizer* in *Astounding SF* (Mar.) 18/1: It had its own ion drive, a regular crew of six, and plenty of additional space for our party.

**1958** C. C. Adams, et al. *Space Flight* 346: Both rubidium and cesium have been considered as the propellant for the ion drive.

**1962** [C. Smith] *Ballad of Lost C'mell* in T. Shippey *Oxford Book of SF* (1992) 303: They had used chemical rockets to load the interplanetary ion-drive and nuclear-drive vehicles or to assemble the photonic sail-ships for interstellar cruises.

**1979** P. Anderson *Ways of Love* in *Destinies* (Jan.–Feb.) 12: Unforeseen factors, chiefly the enormous magnetic field of the object, wrecked both their ion drives and their transmitter.

**2002** A. Reynolds *Redemption Ark* (2004) 42: The girdle of habitats orbiting Yellowstone had long supported a spectrum of transportation ventures, ranging from prestigious high-burn operations to much slower [ ... ] fusion and ion-drive haulers.

**ish** *n.* an issue of a periodical.

**1939** [B. Tucker] *Le Zombie* (Aug 5) 3: Fantasy Digest says in it's [sic] latest ish.

**1944** J. B. Speer *Fancyclopedia* 9/1: The mazuma paid for such ads went to help get out a big anniversary ish, or defray the cost of some lithoing.

**1950** A. Rapp *Spacewarp* (Jan.) 2: Speaking of editorial policies, what do you think of the third ish of OTHER WORLDS?

**1967** S. Lee *Son of Origins of Marvel Comics* (1975) 66: In order to defeat the Grey Gargoyle last ish, Iron Man was forced to drain his transistorized armor's life-giving energy!

**1977** *Sniffin' Glue* (Mar.) 9/1: We was going to have an article on them in this ish but were waiting till we've got more space for an interview.

**2004** J. Stinson *e-National Fantasy Fan* (Mar.) 5: This ish should benefit from at least at least two sets of eyes having gone over the previous ish.

# j

**jack in** *v.* to connect one's brain directly to a computer or cybernetic device by means of a cybernetically implanted data jack. Also used *fig.* Hence **jacked in,** *adj.*

**1970** R. Silverberg *Tower of Glass* in *Galaxy Mag.* (June) 141/20: Watchman replaced him in the linkup seat. He jacked himself into the computer.

**1986** W. Gibson *Winter Market* in *Burning Chrome* (2003) 129: She couldn't move, not without that extra skeleton, and it was jacked straight into her brain, myoelectric interface.

**1991** L. McCaffery *Intro.* in *Storming Reality Studio* 13: The cyberpunks projected an image of confrontational "reality hacker" artists who were armed, dangerous, and jacked into (but not under the thumb of) the Now and the New.

**1993** *S-F Studies* (Nov.) 450: Buy *Beyond Cyberpunk*, jack in, and learn a lot of the stuff you need to know to get—in Rudy Rucker's brilliant term—"culturally online."

**2004** M. Jarpe & J. A. Sheen *Bad Hamburger* in *Mag. of Fantasy & SF* (Dec.) 63: He tapped his finger on the side of his head, just above his right ear. "I've been jacked in since I spoke to you this morning."

**2005** *Dreamwatch* (Feb.) 73/1: There's so much to digest in this edition that you feel like you're pushing that metal spike into the back of your head and jacking in.

**Jovian** *n.* an inhabitant of Jupiter. Compare JUPITERIAN.

**1871** R. P. Smith *Sci. & Revelation* in *Modern Scepticism* (1871) 155: Let us suppose ourselves philosophers come, we will say, from the planet Jupiter, on a mission intrusted to us by the Jovians, to examine and report upon the nature of the creatures which people the four inferior planets, Terra, Venus, Mercury, and Mars.

**1891** *New-York Times* (May 17) 1/5: The title is "Jack Suehard; or Life on Jupiter." One of its objects is to teach what the people of the earth will be like [ ... ] at the end of the next twenty millions of years. In other words, it is a full description of the Jovians.

**1938** O. J. Friend *Of Jovian Build* in *Thrilling Wonder Stories* (Oct.) 71/1: The Jovian was found in a semi-exhausted condition swimming eastward, bleeding copiously from a bad wound in the shoulder.

**1953** A. C. Clarke *Jupiter Five* in *If* (May) 15/1: We have never found any trace of what might be called a religion among the Jovians.

**1976** *Scientific American* (May) 108/2: They would make for Jovians the same changes of shape that the moon makes for us Terrestrials.

**2000** I. Stewart & J. Cohen *Wheelers* (2001) 495: We and the Jovians—even the plasmoids—are not so dissimilar.

**jump** *n.* a transition from one point in the universe to another that does not pass through the intervening points, often through another continuum or medium such as hyperspace; the transition from normal space into hyperspace. Often *cap.*

**1945** I. Asimov *Dead Hand* in *Astounding S-F* (Apr.) 57/2: In grasshopper jumps of increasing magnitude, the trade ship was spanning the Galaxy in its return to the Foundation.

**1951** I. Asimov *Foundation* 12: He had steeled himself just a little for the Jump through hyper-space, a phenomenon one did not experience in simple interplanetary trips. The Jump remained, and would probably remain forever, the only practical method of travelling between the stars.

**1963** H. B. Piper *Space Viking* (1975) 37: I could have made it a little closer. Need three microjumps, now, and I'll have to cut the last one pretty fine.

**1979** D. Adams *Hitch Hiker's Guide to Galaxy* 49: You'd better be prepared for the jump into hyperspace. It's unpleasantly like being drunk.

**1991** M. Weiss *King's Test* 101: I am making the Jump in exactly one minute.

**1999** A. Thomson *Through Alien Eyes* (2000) 35: I'm looking forward to the jump [ ... ]. It will be good to be moving toward Earth instead of away from Tiangi.

**jump** *v.* to move from one point in the universe to another without passing through the intervening points; to make the transition between normal space and hyperspace. Often *cap.*

**1952** I. Asimov *Currents of Space* in *Astounding SF* (Oct.) 47/2: There are two times when an energy-pattern trace will fail. One, when the ship is not in near space, because it has Jumped through hyperspace and is in another region of the galaxy, and two, when it is not in space at all because it has landed on a planet. I cannot believe that our man has Jumped.

**1974** L. Niven & J. Pournelle *Mote in God's Eye* 103: New Caledonia was a magnificent white point source in the moment before *MacArthur* Jumped. Then Murcheson's Eye was a wide red glare the size of a baseball held at arm's length.

**1979** D. Adams *Hitch Hiker's Guide to Galaxy* 48: Secondly, we are about to jump into hyperspace for the journey to Barnard's Star.

**1992** V. Vinge *Fire upon Deep* (1993) 242: The

ship was doing about ten ultrajumps per second: jump, recompute and jump again.

**1997** P. F. Hamilton *Escape Route* G. Dozois *Good New Stuff* (1999) 399: If we detect any combat wasp launch, then we jump outsystem immediately.

**jump drive** *n.* a spaceship drive that allows a ship to travel from one point in the universe to another without passing through the intervening points.

**1963** H. Harrison *Ethical Engineer* in *Analog SF-Fact* (July) 25/2: "There's nothing wrong with our space drive, so we can make a landing on one of the planets [ ... ]." " Where I will fix the jump drive and continue the voyage to Cassylia."

**1983** N. Spinrad *Void Captain's Tale* (1984) 8: The Pilot [ ... ], cyborged to the Jump Drive by the Harmonizer, [ ... ] navigates the ship through the space-time discontinuity of the Jump and out the other side the requisite number of light-years in the right direction.

**1986** L. M. Bujold *Warrior's Apprentice* (1990) 167: The body of the jump drive, [ ... ] was the pair of Necklin field generator rods that ran from one end of the ship to the other.

**2003** C. Stross *Singularity Sky* 43: The jump drive was, to say the least, more reliable, barring a few quirks. A spaceship equipped with it [ ... ] could then tunnel between the two points without ever actually being between them.

**jump engine** *n.* a JUMP DRIVE.

**1981** *Universe: Roleplaying Game of Future* 74/2: A jump engine does not consume energy.

**1984** [C. J. Cherryh] *Voyager in Night* 69: It knew we were there, knew how small we were. We couldn't support jump engines. It damn well knew.

**2000** J. McDevitt *Infinity Beach* 17: Jump engines [ ... ] moved starships into and out of hyperspace.

**2001** S. Zettel *Kingdom of Cages* 95: Their jump engines are fried. They were trying to make it through normal space.

**jump gate** *n.* a device that transports a spaceship passing through it to another point in the universe in such a way that the ship does not pass through the intervening space. Compare STARGATE.

**1995** L. Tilton *Accusations* 11: We're trying to make it back to the jump gate.

**2000** K. MacLeod *Cosmonaut Keep* (2001) 47: He'd have been absolutely fucking *delighted* with one that could be traversed with some kind of warp-drive or jumpgates or wormholes or similar fanciful mechanism.

**2003** P. Sarath *More to Glory* in S. Lee & S. Miller *Low Port* 188: My favorite part is serving on the bridge. I can't touch anything, but I can watch. I love when we hit the jump gate.

**jump point** *n.* a location in space from which a spaceship is able to make a jump to another location in the universe. Often *cap.*

**1964** C. Anvil *Bill for Delivery* in *Analog Sci. Fact-SF* (Nov.) 76/2: It makes it kind of rough if, through no fault of your own, [ ... ] a jump-point slides out of congruity and hangs the ship up in the middle of nowhere for a month.

**1981** [C. J. Cherryh] *Pride of Chanur* (1991) 24: Beyond Meetpoint in the other direction was stsho space, with a great scarcity of jumppoints to help them along.

**1987** *Analog SF/Sci. Fact* (Dec.) 27/1: The unmanned pod bundle would continue on its slow, cheap way to [...] the anomaly in space that was the Jump point.

**1995** E. Moon *Winning Colours* (1999) 268: Many communication modes for ansible transmission were located near jump points, for ease of maintenance and repair.

**jump ship** *n.* a spaceship equipped with a jump drive. Often *cap.*

**1957** [R. Sharon] *"Lady" Was Tramp* in *Venture SF Mag.* (Mar.) 45/1: A full Lieutenant IBMan would be in charge of SolNav only, with two petty officers under him, both [ ... ] capable of relieving him on duty at the control board during the five or twelve or twenty hours it might take to navigate a jump-ship in or out of the obstacle course of clutter and junk and planets and orbits of any given System.

**1981** [C. J. Cherryh] *Pride of Chanur* (1991) 24: Those masses by which The Pride or any

other jumpship steered; and on the other sides were kif regions.

**1988** L. E. Modesitt, Jr. *In Endless Twilight* 72: A jumpship is certainly an example of diminishing returns for a small system.

**1991** G. Zebrowski *Stranger Suns* 130: The first jump ships needed even more energy, but they gave the alien engineers the capacity to enter otherspace.

**1995** A. Thomson *Color of Distance* (1999) 89: A Jump ship retrieved the crew about ten years ago.

**jump space** *n.* the space a spaceship travels through when it is making a jump. Often *cap.*

**1961** H. Harrison *Sense of Obligation* in *Analog Sci. Fact-Fiction* (Sept.) 26/2: The ship was unchanged, only outside of the port was the red-shot blankness of jump space.

**1977** G. Zebrowski *Ashes & Stars* 27: His skin was growing pale here, as if the few days had really been years. What was time in jumpspace?

**1983** N. Spinrad *Void Captain's Tale* (1984) 91: Jump Space is a mathematical contradiction in terms.

**1994** E. Moon *Sporting Chance* 326: The Benignity has bases on the larger moons of this big lump of gravity we're too close to, and the way we dropped out of jumpspace on their doorstep, they could hardly miss us.

**Jupiterian** *n.* an inhabitant of Jupiter. Compare JOVIAN.

**1941** *Cosmic Stories* (Mar.): Please use literate terminology for the names of planet dwellers. Let's have no Mercutians, Venutians, Plutians, Jupiterians or Terrestrials running around.

**1948** [T. Herrick] *Lost World* in *Planet Comics* (Nov.) 5: Attention fellow Jupiterians! I have just directed the Voltamen, captured in our vivo impulses, to bring in two earthpeople who were observing them.

**1948** H. Guth *Signal Red* in *Planet Stories* (Fall) 70/2: Captain Menthlo, a silver-mustached Jupiterian, broad, huge, yet crushable as a beetle, talked while his hands manipulated a panel of studs in the control room.

# k

**Klingon** *n.* **1.** in the *Star Trek* universe, a member of a species of warlike humanoid aliens. Also in extended use.

**1967** G. Coon *Errand of Mercy ("Star Trek" script)* (Jan. 23) 1: We're to proceed to Organia and take whatever steps necessary to prevent the Klingons from using it as a base.

**1990**: see quote under BEAM ME UP.

**1992** *Tucson (Ariz.) Weekly* (Jan. 15) 28/2: Pappy's dining room is [ ... ] pleasant and almost elegant, but the color scheme must have been selected by Klingons.

**2002** J. Cohen & I. Stewart *Evolving Alien* vii: If we wait for evolution to proceed on such a planet, or look for one that's old enough already, will we find people? Klingons? ET?

**2.** the language of the Klingons. [Created by Marc Okrand for use in the movie *Star Trek III: The Search for Spock* and now studied and spoken by many *Star Trek* fans.]

[**1967** D. Gerrold *Trouble with Tribbles (Star Trek script)* (Aug. 1) II-32: That sagging old rust bucket is designed like a garbage scow! Half the quadrant knows it—that's why they're learning to speak Klingonese!]

**1985** M. Okrand *Klingon Dictionary* 13: The system of writing Klingon [ ... ] in this dictionary has been developed so people who already know how to read English will have a minimum of difficulty.

**1995** *Daily Telegraph (London)* (Nov. 22) 1/6: The Bible is being translated into Klingon.

**2000** S. H. Elgin *Linguistics & SF Newsletter* (Jan.–Feb.) unpag.: While ViA's device cannot translate Klingon to Romulan, it does interpret seven other languages.

**K/S** *abbr.* Kirk/Spock, referring to fan fiction that depicts a (usually erotic) relationship between the *Star Trek* characters Captain Kirk and Mr. Spock. Compare SLASH.

[**1977** S. Bridges *Obsc'zine (letter)* (Aug.) 5/1: I am not trying to attack a Kirk/Spock sexual relationship in general.]

**1978** E. Kobrin *Scuttlebutt* (Apr./May) 12: It's heavy on the K/S relationship, and will delight K/S fans.

**1984** *Not Tonight, Spock!* (Jan.) 1: We hope NTS will become a place for all K/S fans to share thoughts, ideas and opinions concerning our 2 favorite guys as well as a place one can drool over what's available and what's proposed in K/S zines.

**1995** *Extrapolation* (Spring) 45: The primacy of the emotional bond between Kirk and Spock has spawned a genre of fan fiction known as "K/S" or "slash."

**2000** *Out* (Oct.) 36/3: Mizoguchi asserts that *yaoi* and, by extension, K/S and other slash fiction [ ... ] are homophobic.

# Naval Terms

When SF writers want to describe the life of a **spacefaring** society, they frequently use nautical terms. This is so common a practice that I have not been able to include every term that has made the transition from sea to space, and have therefore defined only the most common synonyms for "spaceship" and those that have undergone some change in form.

The analogy between travel in space and travel on the seas is a straightforward one—both entail enclosing people in a self-contained vessel, protected from a hostile environment by only a thin shell, in which they may spend long periods of time between *ports*, whether on islands or planets. This analogy is most directly made by simply using a nautical term in an outer-space setting, so **boat**, **craft**, **ship**, and **vessel**, as well as **cruiser**, *destroyer*, and *dreadnought*, can describe both watercraft and **spacecraft**. Similarly, like a seagoing vessel, a spaceship may be composed of an external *hull*, punctuated with *portholes*, which encases and protects the *decks*, *bulkheads*, *cabins*, and *bridge*, not to mention the *captain* and *crew*. If it is a military vessel, it may belong to a *navy*, in which case the ship's captain probably reports to an *admiral*. Even the familiar science-fictional alien *mother ship* is an appropriation of a naval term. Frequently, SF writers take a nautical word and add "space" or "star" to it, as in **space dock**, **space liner**, **space pirate**, **spaceship**, **starfleet**, **starport**, etc. "Sea" can be replaced in compounds such as **spacefaring**, **space-going**, and **space-sick**, as can "ship," in words like **spaceyard**. Sometimes these appropriations and substitutions can be a matter of expedience, but there is a poetry to it as well; science fiction has often been a literature of exploration and adventure, and drawing on the language of the sea can hearken back to the excitement and romance of the Age of Sail.

**landing cradle** *n.* a mechanism, such as a clamp, that a spaceship docks into when landing on a space station, larger spaceship, etc.

**1942** F. Brown *Star Mouse Planet Stories* (Spring) 34/1: Call the Station. Tell them to train their attracto-repulsors on it and to swing it into a temporary orbit until they prepare a landing-cradle.

**1946** B. I. Kahn *For Public Astounding SF* (Dec.) 88/2: Instead he was in the grand salon of a sumptuous yacht, now resting in the landing cradle of exotic disease control.

**1957** P. Anderson *Among Thieves* H. Turtledove *Best Military SF of Twentieth Century* (2001) 17: He glided into the landing cradle, under the turrets of guns that could pound a moon apart, and let the mechanism suck him down below decks.

**2001** J. Clute *Appleseed* 65: Above him, wrapped into its landing cradle, *Tile Dance* hulked intact, a polished featureless ovoid, an egg unbroken, manifestly not a thing of this planet.

**laser gun** *n.* a weapon that fires a high-powered laser. Also **laser cannon, pistol, rifle,** etc.

**1962** *Family Weekly Post-Crescent (Appleton, Wis.)* (Sept. 16) 2/3: In the event of all-out war, an American artillery sergeant behind a small laser "cannon" conceivably could point a powerful light beam at an enemy missile plunging toward us.

**1964** G. Roddenberry *Cage* in S. E. Whitfield & G. Roddenberry *Making of "Star Trek"* (1968) 49: Mr. Spock and navigator Tyler race there, Laser guns out blasting away at the rock, earth, and strange vegetation which camouflage the entry.

**1972** A. D. Foster *Tar-Aiym Krang* 177: Compact and efficient, the laser pistol could cook a man at five hundred meters or a steak at one.

**1978** B. Shaw *Ship of Strangers* (1979) 22: Apart from Pollen's standard juggling-with-numbers technique, a more empirical approach would be to have Aesop fire a low-powered burst from a laser rifle at each module in turn.

**1979** M. McCollum *Beer Run* in *Analog SF-Sci. Fact* (July) 118/1: I'd attended a couple of lectures on laser weapons.

**1985** O. S. Card *Ender's Game* 41: A laser-gun, it looked like, since the end was solid, clear glass.

**ca1992** R. Grant & D. Naylor *Holoship* in *Son of Soup* (1996) 39: Well, I say let's break out the laser cannons and give 'em both barrels.

**2003** I. M. Banks *Look to Windward* 196: There they had taught him fencing, trained him with a crossbow and with projectile weapons and early laser rifles.

**lay story** *n.* a fan fiction story in which a character from an existing fictional universe (especially *Star Trek*) has sexual intercourse.

**1976** *quoted in American Speech* 55 (1978) (Spring): Many times Mary Sue stories are also lay-someone stories as well.

**1991** R. Rogow *Futurespeak* 178: Lay stories can be effusively romantic or blatantly pornographic.

**1992** C. Bacon-Smith *Enterprising Women* 103: In Jean Lorrah's stories, and those of other lay-Spock writers, however, male emotions are revealed, controlled but available to the partner who manages her husband's more uncontrollable physical urges.

**1999** *On "Mary Sue" and "Lay" stories* (Usenet: alt.startrek.creative.erotica.moderated) (Nov. 25): I am guilty of the "lay" story. Multiple offenses.

**2003** J. M. Verba *Boldly Writing (ed. 2)* 85/2: A "lay-Kirk" story is a story in which the object is to get Kirk sexually involved with another person.

**lettercol** *n.* [*letter* + *col*umn] a section of a magazine that prints readers' letters.

**1958** R. M. Holland *Ghu's Lexicon* 3: LETTERCOL - A letter column. One of the favorite haunts of the actifans. Many fanzines have them, but in prozines they are practically standard equipment. A prozine without a letter column is a fakezine, and no trufan will buy one.

**1964** J. Linwood *Fanalytic Eye* in *Les Spinge* (Jan.) 27: The best part of the 'zine is the controversial letter col which boasts of letters from all over.

**1971** L. Niven *Fourth Profession* in *N-Space* (1991) 205: "What's fanac?" [ … ] I said, "Might be anything. Putting out a zine, writing to the lettercol, helping put on a Con."

**2005** C. S. McNeil *Finder* (Internet) (Oct. 25): Anyone mind if I use their thoughts and insights here on the newsblog, as an on-line lettercol?

**letterhack** *n.* a fan who habitually writes letters to magazine letter columns. Also as *v.*

**1946** T. Jewett *Startling Stories (letter)* (Fall) 102/2: Nowadays a letter-hack says things simply, which is, after all, the best way.

**1947** R. Sneary *Startling Stories (letter)* (Jan.) 98/2: The rest of ther [sic] letter were

pretty good. David Olson is a real promising letter hack.

**1958** R. M. Holland *Ghu's Lexicon* 12: Give the letterhack a ream of paper, stamps, and one or two other letterhacks for him to argue with, and he will keep happy and tractable for months.

**1966** A. Budrys *Benchmarks* (1985) 57: At least, they do if we are to believe such pseudo-documentary novelists as Hank Searls and such reporters as ex-*Planet* letterhack Martin Caidin.

**1969** H. Warner, Jr. *All Our Yesterdays* 10: They corresponded, wrote amateur fiction, articles, and poetry, visited one another, feuded, letter-hacked, collected.

**1980** [L. del Rey] *World of SF* 72: I found, during the period around 1935 when I was what was called a letterhack, that I received quite a few letters from other readers.

**letterzine** *n.* [*letter* + *-zine*] a fanzine in which the contents consist primarily or entirely of letters submitted by the readers.

**1950** A. H. Rapp *Timber!* in *Spacewarp* (Apr.) 4: Unless someone shows up willing to take the letterzine over lock stock and barrel by the end of April, that flourishing enterprise will refund its subs and quietly fold.

**1954** S. Moskowitz *Immortal Storm* 228: The *Voice of the Imagination*, a letter 'zine published by Morojo and Ackerman, usually carried chapter news and announcements.

**1975** E. Weinstein *Fillostrated Fan Dictionary* 78: Letterzine [ … ]: A fanzine consising entirely of letters received from the readers.

**1992** H. Jenkins *Textual Poachers* 151: Letterzines and club newsletters overflowed with pained reactions to the third season as well as equally passionate defenses.

**2003** J. M. Verba *Boldly Writing (ed. 2)* 27/1: This publication was almost entirely composed of letters from fans. Such a newsletter is called a "letterzine."

**levitator** *n.* a device which counteracts gravity.

**1946** E. F. Russell *Metamorphosite* in *Major Ingredients* (2000) 359: Still not looking back, the subject of his speculations turned into an apartment building, took a levitator to the tenth floor.

**1948** J. Blish *Against Stone Beasts* in *Planet Stories* (Fall) 88/1: Atel was not fighting another winged man. He was fighting an Earthman with a levitator.

**1949** M. St. Clair *Sacred Martian Pig* in *Startling Stories* (July) 92/2: Martian buildings, even public ones, rarely had levitators or even lifts. The lesser gee made stair-climbing less onerous than on Terra.

**1988** I. McDonald *Desolation Road* (2001) 10: He had sailed and sailed and sailed [...] gripping wide-eyed with terror to every hand-hold as the wind-board's pro-magnetic levitators fought to hold it aloft.

**lifeboat** *n.* a small spaceship designed for the evacuation of a damaged spaceship. Compare ESCAPE POD, LIFEPOD, LIFESHIP.

**1934** E. E. Smith *Triplanetary* in *Amazing Stories* (Jan.) 17/1: Through the airlock, down through several levels of passengers' quarters they hurried, and into a lifeboat.

**1941** T. Sturgeon *Completely Automatic* in *Astounding S-F* (Feb.) 86/1: They said that spaceships should no more take off without chem supers than they should without lifeboats. The fact that no one within the memory of living man had ever used a lifeboat for anything but joy-riding didn't faze them.

**1946** A. K. Barnes *Siren Satellite* in *Thrilling Wonder Stories* (Winter) 71/1: You and your crew will be packed into a lifeboat and marooned on Triton.

**1963** K. Laumer *End as Hero* in *Nine by Laumer* (1967) 18: I was on the floor next to an unpadded acceleration couch—the kind the Terrestrial Space Arm installs in seldom-used lifeboats.

**1981** M. Bishop & G. W. Page *Murder on Lupozny Station* in M. Bishop *Brighten to Incandescence* (2003) 124: When the interior of the lifeboat was at the same pressure as space itself, I slipped away from the instrument panel and pushed myself aft.

**2004** G. Wolfe *Prize Crew* in *Postscripts* 45/1 (Spring): A light cruiser from the look of her, just drifting way out between suns. She hadn't been hit, so it didn't look like there had been any

reason for the crew to bail out, but [...] the lifeboats were gone.

**lifepod** *n.* an ESCAPE POD. Compare LIFE-BOAT, LIFESHIP.

**1976** G. Lucas *Adventures of Luke Starkiller* (Mar. 15) 5: The safety door snaps shut and with the thunder of exploding latches, the tiny lifepod ejects from the disabled starfighter.

**1992** [L. A. Graf] *Ice Trap* 67: Our idiot company pilot landed the shuttle's life-pod in some sort of Kitka ceremonial ground.

**1993** *Prensa* (ProQuest) (June 25): Passengers and crew members alike race for the life-pods, modest, semi-powered vehicles capable of propelling a small group away from immediate danger but little else.

**1999** A. McCaffrey & E. A. Scarborough *Acorna's People* (2000) 3: Acorna had been jettisoned in a life pod from her parents' ship as an infant to save her from the fatal explosion that claimed the lives of her parents and the attacking Khleevi.

**2002** *Cult Times* (Apr.) 50/4: A group of astrophysicists discover a life-pod containing a man who has been in suspended animation for 15 years.

**lifeship** *n.* a LIFEBOAT. Compare ESCAPE POD, LIFEPOD.

**1940** H. Walton *Moon of Exile* in *Astounding S-F* (Aug.) 125/1: Sharon was still by the control panel when the lifeship whistled down through the upper reaches of Callisto's thin atmosphere.

**1944** [W. Long] *Nomad* in *Astounding S-F* (Dec.) 44/1: But—that was Maynard's sign and he may have survived in some queer manner. We know that the *Mardinex* carried lifeships.

**1957** R. Silverberg *World of Thousand Colors* in *World of Thousand Colors* (1984) 58: The entered a lifeship, a slim gray tube barely thirty meters long, and fastened acceleration cradles.

**1973** J. R. Gregory & R. Price *Visitor* 87: Then we'll tell him that we accept his proposal, and let him take us to the life-ship.

**1991** G. Bear & S. M. Stirling *Man Who Would Be Kzin* in L. Niven, et al. *Man-Kzin Wars IV* 272: They cut loose the kzin lifeship, with Halloran inside, five hours later.

**light** *n.* **1.** a LIGHT-SPEED.

**1934** E. E. Smith *Skylark of Valeron* in *Astounding Stories* (Sept.) 36/1: We're not supposed to know anything about the five-light drive of the Fenachrone, you know.

**1950** P. Anderson *Gypsy* in *Astounding SF* (Jan.) 71/2: Meanwhile, we were limited to pseudovelocities of a couple of hundred lights, and interstellar space mocked us with vastness.

**1954** R. Garrett *Time Fuze* in *If* (Mar.) 68/2: The ship had only been provisioned to go to Alpha Centauri, [ … ] and return. At ten lights, top speed for the ultradrive, it would take better than three months to get back.

**1974** R. Silverberg *Schwartz Between Galaxies* in *Feast of St. Dionysus* (1987) 81: Three boneless Spicans do a twining dance of propitiation to while away the slow hours of nine-light travel.

**2.** a light-year.

**1990** J. Tiptree, Jr. *Color of Neanderthal Eyes* 2: I'd been on a very strenuous year-long tour as Sensitive on an Extended Contact party six lights away.

**1993** V. Vinge *Fire upon Deep* (1992) 297: Sjandra Kei is thirty-nine hundred lights spinward from here, but outside this storm.

**2002** M. J. Harrison *Light* (2004) 12: We have several missions available forty lights down the Beach.

**light sail** *n.* a very large sheet attached to a spaceship that propels the ship by catching the light from the nearest star or from a large laser.

**1963** [C. Smith] *Think Blue, Count Two* in *Galaxy* (Feb.) 48/2: She went by light-sail ship. And she had to cross space—space, where the danger always waits.

**1971** L. Niven *Fourth Profession* in *Quark* (Aug.) 208: With a light-sail you can get push from the solar wind as well as from light pressure.

**1982** W. Gibson *Hinterlands* in *Burning Chrome* (1986) 78: Tsiolkovsky 1 is fixed at the libration point between Earth's gravity and the moon's, but we need a lightsail to hold us here, twenty tons of aluminum spun into a hexagon, ten kilometres from side to side.

**1988** R. Silverberg *We Are for Dark* in *Collected Stories of Robert Silverberg (Vol. 2: Secret Sharer)* (1993) 342: Small unmanned starships, laser-powered robot drones, unfurling great lightsails and gliding starwards on the urgent breath of photonic winds that we ourselves stirred up.

**1998** I. McDonald *Days of Solomon Gursky* in G. Dozois *Mammoth Book of Best New SF, 12th Coll.* (1999) 245: At the end of the centuries—millennia—long flights, the light-sails would brake the packages at their destinations.

**light-speed** *n. Obs.* a unit of speed equal to the speed of light (approximately 300,000 km/s). Compare LIGHT 1.

**1929** E. Hamilton *Star Stealers* in *Weird Tales* (Feb.) 149/1: Turn 30 degrees outward, [ … ] and throttle down to eighty light-speeds until we've passed the star.

**1948** [M. Leinster] *Planet of Sand* in *Famous Fantastic Mysteries* (Feb.) 92/1: At twelve hundred light-speeds, with the Bowdoin-Hall field collapsing forty times per second for velocity control, the stars moved visibly.

**1951** R. Garrett *Waiting Game* in *Analog: Best of SF* (ca1982) 216: However she did it, at top speed she could make nearly a thousand light-speeds, although she wasn't doing that now.

**little green man** *n.* an (often fanciful) intelligent creature from outer space.

**1946** H. Lawlor *Mayaya's Little Green Men* in *Weird Tales* (Nov.) 38/1: She laughed throatily, "Oh, the little green men told me." *The little green men!* Well, we didn't think it so strange at the time. I thought it was just a phrase, a gag, one of those things you say.

**1948** R. Sneary *Startling Stories (letter)* (July) 126/2: Well must run now, the little green men have my dinner, and THEIR [sic] EATING IT!

**1953** *News (Newport, R. I.)* (Dec. 7) 10/2: Maybe a shot of a little green man from Mars leaning out and grinning at the Air Force?

**1967** M. Kenyon *Whole Hog* 42: There was a desert-island cartoon [ … ] and a little-green-men-from-Mars cartoon.

**1998** C. A. Pickover *Sci. of Aliens* 5: Over its several seasons, *The X-Files* TV show has had plenty of little green man–type aliens.

**loc** *abbr.* [letter *of* comment] a letter written to a magazine, especially a fanzine.

**1961** *Fanac* (May 6) 1: The first contributor of an accepted news item (not a COA) is entitled to a free issue, as are all other Good People who send in locs, cartoons, etc.

**1964** *Les Spinge* (Jan.) 2: Available for Trade, LoC, Contribution, goodwill (rarely) or even money.

**1990** *Thrust* (Winter) 30/2: Dealers try to sell me at inflated prices copies of something I happen to have mentioned in a loc.

**2003** J. M. Verba *Boldly Writing (ed. 2)* 27/1: A letter of comment, or loc—pronounced "lock"—may be thought of as a letter to the publication, for publication.

**Luna** *n.* [< L. *luna,* "moon"] the Earth's moon.

**1931** R. Gallun *Lunar Chrysalis* in *Amazing Stories* (Sept.) 528/2: I never regretted my decision to be one of the first men to visit Luna.

**1945** [M. Leinster] *Ethical Equations* in *Astounding SF* (June) 120/2: Freddy Holmes, newly commissioned and assigned to the detector station on Luna which keeps track of asteroids and meteor streams, had discovered a small object coming in over Neptune.

**1969** R. Silverberg *Across Billion Years* 168: I remember the first time I visited Luna, Lorie; I was twelve years old and had never imagined that any place could look so desolate.

**1979** J. Varley *Titan* (1987) 8: They felt the money could be better spent on Earth, on Luna, and at the L5 colonies.

**1999** D. M. Weber *Apocalypse Troll* 92: By the time they got back to Sol, there were colonies on Luna and Mars and large-scale mining operations in the asteroids.

**Luna City** *n.* the principal, first, or only city on the Earth's moon.

**1939** R. Heinlein *Misfit* in *Astounding S-F* (Nov.) 65/2: Then plants, conditioned by thirty-odd generations of low gravity at Luna City, were set out and tenderly cared for.

**1952** F. Pohl & C. M. Kornbluth *Space Merchants* in *Galaxy SF* (July) 156/1: They pooh-poohed that possibility and set me to wait on a bench while queries were sent to the Schocken branch in Luna City.

**1969** R. Silverberg *Across Billion Years* 13: Saul's got the things we just used to day-dream about, the Marsport five-credit with the ultraviolet overprint, the Luna City souvenir sheet perforate and imperforate [...]—everything.

**1986** P. Danziger *This Place Has No Atmosphere* (1987) 69: Once the bus got there, a tube reached out and connected with it, and we walked through the tube into Luna City.

**2001** N. Kress *Probability Sun* (2003) 35: You've never been to Luna City before.

**Lunarian** *n.* an inhabitant of the Earth's moon.

**1708** *British Apollo* (No. 13) 2/2: Be those Lunarians false or true.

**1794** G. Adams *Lectures on Natural & Experimental Philosophy* 23: When it is what we call New Moon, we will appear as a Full Moon to the Lunarians.

**ca 1849** E. A. Poe *Mellonta Tauta* in *Works of Edgar Allen Poe, Vol. IV* (1866) 299: It was amusing to think that creatures so diminutive as the lunarians, and bearing so little resemblance to humanity, yet evinced a mechanical ingenuity so much superior to our own.

**1931** J. Schlossel *Extra-Galactic Invaders* in *Amazing Stories Quarterly* (Spring) 277/2: There, somewhere in the center of that vast host, the Solarians, both men and Lunarians, began to see themselves in their true perspectives.

**1995** P. Anderson *Harvest Fire* (1997) 66: Meanwhile, the existence of Proserpina had been revealed and the migration of disaffected Lunarians began.

# m

**mad scientist** *n.* a scientist or inventor who is insane, especially one whose madness (intentionally or unintentionally) endangers himself, others, or the world; once a stock character in science fiction and horror stories.

**1908** [R. McDonald] (title): Mad Scientist: A Tale of the Future

**1931** M. W. Wellman *Voice from Ether* in *Wonder Stories* (Sept.) 523/1: This was the noted "joy-lamp" invented by a mad scientist to administer a new and unheard-of intoxication to all who came into its light.

**1959** *Lima (Oh.) News* (Feb. 14) Entertainment section 6/5: She is a normal, lovely girl during the day but a mad scientist is experimenting with her by administering potent drugs that turn her nightly into a monster woman.

**1972** B. Turner *Solden's Women* 82: He would have passed for the mad scientist in one of those films which star giant insects.

**1979** I. Asimov *Scientist as Villain* in *Asimov on SF* (1981) 67: The mad scientist is a cliché that went out in the early 1930's.

**1991** *Locus* (May) 31/1: When people say "mad scientist" we never wonder for a moment if perhaps they mean that the fellow is merely angry.

**mag-** *pref.* magnetic.

**1944** [W. Long] *Latent Image* in *Astounding SF* (May) 11/2: In spite of the fact that Dr. Ellson claimed to have discovered a region in the mag-grav spectrum that produced a faint success.

**1948** T. Sturgeon *There Is No Defense* in *Astounding SF* (Feb.) 30/1: Maneuvering was accomplished by variations in field strength by inductance-coupling of the mag-flux coils.

**1992** *Locus* (June) 67/3: He was working on a form of "mag-lev" transportation, the "magnetic flight system," for extremely rapid ground-level train travel.

**1993** W. Gibson *Virtual Light* 135: He showed Rydell how to put the debit-card into a machine that gave him a five-hundred dollar Container City magstrip.

**mainstream** *n.* literature that does not belong to a marketing category (especially science fiction, fantasy, or horror); realistic literature.

**1953** R. Moore (title) in R. Bretnor *Modern SF* 92: Science Fiction and the Main Stream

**1961** J. Blish *Some Comments with Regards to New Maps of Hell* in P. Lupoff & D. Lupoff *Best of Xero* (2005) 62: In general, it is quite plain that Amis had read far more s-f than most of his critics. He is also immensely better read in the mainstream.

**1992** *SFRA Rev.* (July–Aug.–Sept.) 13: Major credit for acceptance of such materials can certainly be attributed to this early [ … ] and influential effort to unite the so-called "mainstream" and science fiction.

**mainstream** *adj.* of or relating to the mainstream. Compare NON-GENRE.

**1953** R. Moore *SF & Main Stream* in R. Bretnor *Modern SF* 95: For the purposes of discussion we shall define mainstream fiction as any fiction which is *not* fantasy or science fiction, an arbitrary distinction made in the interests of clarity.

**1958** [E. Crispin] *Best SF Three* 9: Mainstream fiction [ ... ] has been almost uniformly catatonic in its withdrawal from environment.

**1988** D. Chow *Locus* (Feb.) 28/1: Bantam felt so strongly about his fixup novel, *Life During Wartime*, they did it as a mainstream book.

**1993** J. VanderMeer *Why Should I Cut Your Throat When I Can Just Ask You for Money?* in *Why Should I Cut Your Throat?* (2004) 25: Any non-genre people who attended Georgiacon would realize that most practitioners of genre don't take it any more seriously than mainstream critics.

**2002** N. Gevers *New York Rev. of SF* (Dec.) 10/2: The novella "Blue Kansas Sky" [ ... ] has touches of the fantastic, but is essentially a mainstream coming-of-age story.

**Martian** *n.* **1.** an inhabitant of the planet Mars.

**1874** *The Galaxy* (Jan.) 127/1: The Martians would therefore be in a better position for understanding our attempts at opening up communication than the Venerians.

**1883** W. S. Lach-Szyrma *Aleriel* 109: He [ ... ] brought with him another Martian, differently attired.

**1898** H. G. Wells *War of Worlds* 31: The glimpse I had had of the Martians emerging from the cylinder in which they had come to the earth from their planet.

**1939** F. A. Kummer, Jr. *Stronger* in *Dynamic Science Stories* (Apr.–May) 95/2: The men who lined the bar were for the most part spacehands, tiny red-skinned Martians, squat Jovians, and nondescript waifs from the asteroids.

**1960** P. J. Farmer *Woman Day* 24: The Earthmen on Mars, who thought of themselves as Martians, had secretly introduced a laboratory-bred virus among Earthmen.

**1993** A. C. Clarke *Hammer of God* 64: Olympus Mons was the best example. Martians were fond of saying that it was three times the height of any mountain on Earth.

**2.** the language of the planet Mars' inhabitants.

**1939** F. A. Kummer, Jr. *Stronger* in *Dynamic Science Stories* (Apr.–May) 102/1: Jim's answer, mumbled in halting Martian, brought no response.

**1948** L. Brackett *Beast-Jewel of Mars* in *Planet Stories* (Winter) 16/1: Suddenly she spoke, in sonorous High Martian, a tongue as antique on Mars as Sanskrit is on Earth.

**1959** [C. Smith] *Lady Who Sailed Soul* in *Rediscovery of Man* (1993) 99: By the time she was four years old, she spoke six languages, and was beginning to decipher some of the old Martian texts.

**1969** V. Heinlein *letter* (Aug. 28) in R. A. Heinlein & V. Heinlein *Grumbles from Grave* (1990) 178: I seem to be translating *Giles Goat Boy* into late Martian.

**2003** S. S. Tepper *Companions* (2004) 211: Nonsense. No one ever translated Martian.

**Mary Sue** *n.* [after the main character in a parody of this type of story (see 1973 quote)] a character in a work of fiction (especially fan fiction) who is perceived as carrying out a wish-fulfillment of the author, especially one who has a romantic or sexual relationship with a character from an existing fictional universe; a story featuring this kind of character.

[**1973** P. Smith *Trekkie's Tale* in *Menagerie* (Dec.) 6: "Gee, golly, gosh, gloriosky," thought Mary Sue as she stepped on the bridge of the Enterprise. "Here I am, the youngest lieutenant in the fleet—only fifteen and a half years old."]

**1976** *Menagerie* (Mar.) 2: Too willing are we to smatter down a Mary Sue story and call it high tragedy, or say, "I don't care if it's dumb, if it's about Spock."

**1984** *Ramblings* (Usenet: net.comics) (Aug. 22): This is so Mary Sue it makes me sick. (Mary Sue is a character who is the most beautiful, the most intelligent, the most most...how about the most cardboard.)

**1992** H. Jenkins *Textual Poachers* 171: "Mary Sue" stories, which fit idealized images of the writers as young, pretty, intelligent recruits aboard the Enterprise, the TARDIS, or the Liberator, constitute one of the most disputed subgenres of fan fiction.

**1998** *No Mary Sues for Alex?* (Usenet: alt. tv.x-files.creative) (Sept. 19): A Mary Sue does not have to have sex with a main character, have amazing powers or attractiveness beyond ordinary ken, or become the focus of a story—although they often do.

**matrix** *n.* CYBERSPACE or virtual reality.
**1976** R. Holmes *Dr. Who: Deadly Assassin (BBC TV script)* 50: *Engin.* How can you intercept thought patterns within the matrix itself? *The Doctor:* By going in there. By joining it.
**1984** W. Gibson *Neuromancer* 51: The matrix has its roots in primitive arcade games [...] in early graphics programs and military experimentation in cranial jacks.
**1998** L. Wachowski & A. Wachowski *Matrix* in *Matrix: Shooting Script* (2001) 41: The Matrix is a computer-generated dreamworld built to keep us under control.
**2003** S. Baxter *Real Matrix* in K. Haber *Exploring Matrix* 34: Nick Bostrom, a philosopher at Yale University, has suggested that we may all be living in a Matrix developed by a posthuman society of the future.

**matter transmission** *n.* moving something by means of a matter transmitter; the technology required to create a matter transmitter. Compare TELEPORTATION.
**1945** G. O. Smith *Special Delivery* in *Astounding SF* (Mar.) 74/2: By Franks' matter transmitter to Mojave. Spacecraft to Luna. More matter transmission from Luna to Phobos.
**1953** F. Pratt *Critique of SF* in R. Bretnor *Modern SF* 75: If the author is going to use speed greater than light or matter transmission, he at least owes us a reasonably plausible explanation of how these things work.
**1994** *Analog SF & Fact* (Jan.) 118/1: But that's *matter-transmission*, not time travel.

**matter transmitter** *n.* a device that disassembles a person or object and causes it to be reassembled, unchanged, in a new location. Compare TELEPORT, TELE-PORTER.
**1931** L. F. Stone *Wonder Stories* (Apr.) 1280/1: With me at her side, Geble hastened to the beam station and there in the matter transmitter we dispatched our physical beings to the palace at Tola.

**1946** [M. Leinster] *Disciplinary Circuit* in *Thrilling Wonder Stories* (Winter) 53/2: But in time, more especially after matter-transmitters had made space-craft useless, they were forgotten.
**1961** J. H. Schmitz *Gone Fishing* in G. Conklin *Five-Odd* (1964) 133: Of course it isn't really a matter transmitter. [...] Even an educated layman must realize that one can't simply disassemble a living body at one point, reassemble it at another, and expect life to resume.
**1991** A. D. Foster *Cat.a.lyst* 133: Now somebody's gonna have to explain away that matter transmitter. Or are you going to tell me it was a Kodak moment that brought us all the way across the Andes.
**2005** P. Di Filippo *Asimov's SF* (Mar.) 136/2: Marion Schweda's "Urban Transit," which examines the bureaucratic nonsense that will one day attend regular use of matter transmitters.

**matter transmitting** *adj.* having the quality of a matter transmitter.
**1925** [R. M. Farley] *Radio Beasts* (a1976) 230: The matter-transmitting apparatus was hopelessly wrecked; the radio set partially so.
**1932** J. Williamson *Moon Era* in *Wonder Stories* (Mar.) 1034/1: Any other creature of the moon [...] that might have been brought with her on the matter-transmitting beam.
**1992** *Classic Images* (Dec.) 26 (ad): Men are being mysteriously murdered by a vengeful madman known as "the Telegian," who uses a matter transmitting device to find his intended victims no matter where they hide.

**meat puppet** *n.* [after the musical group "The *Meat Puppets*"] the physical human body, especially as contrasted to virtual reality or an AI; a body controlled by another entity.
**1984** W. Gibson *Neuromancer* (1991) 147: Where's the meat puppet?
**1991** R. Kadrey & L. McCaffery *Cyberpunk 101* in L. McCaffery *Storming Reality Studio* 25: All those amazing chemical reactions going on inside your body right now to protect you aren't going to mean a thing when this lumbering, gas-guzzling pile of metal plows into a Kansas cornfield at 600 MPH with you strapped inside like the meat puppet you are.

**1991** L. McCaffery & W. Gibson *Interview with William Gibson* in *Storming Reality Studio* 267: The meat puppet image in *Neuromancer* [ … ]. I assume you arrived at that metaphor from listening to the cow-punk band Meat Puppets. *WG:* No, I got it from seeing the name in print.

**1996** S. R. Green *Deathstalker Rebellion* 348: A single cybernetic mind running its meat puppets.

**2001** F. P. Wilson *Hosts* 354: Feeling a sob building in his own throat at the thought of Gia and Vicky becoming meat puppets controlled by the Hive.

**2003** J. Clute *SF from 1980 to Present* in E. James & F. Mendlesohn *Cambridge Companion to SF* 76: Humanity as a whole is transfigured into an immense organism, with only a rote modicum of regret for the meat-puppet past.

**2003** C. Stross *Curator Accelerando* (2005) 267: Our friend here's got a problem, no suitable downloadable body. Us meat puppets are all too closely tied to our neural ultrastructure.

**mech** *n.* a robot.
**1938** [L. del Rey] *Helen O'Loy* in R. Silverberg *SF Hall of Fame, Vol. I* (1971) 63: We naturally mulled over the future of the mechs. He was sure that the robots would beat men some day, and I couldn't see it.

**1989** W. Shatner *Tekwar* (1990) 21: "You always preferred to work, back in the days when you were allegedly an honest cop, with human officers rather than androids and robots." "I've worked with plenty of mechs, too."

**1991** *Locus* (Nov.) 21/3: "Manassas, Again" posits a Nineteenth Century that has descended from an ancient world which experienced a Roman Industrial Revolution, and the rebellion of the robotic mechs against their masters.

**megayear** *n.* [*mega-*, "a factor of one million" + *year*] one million years.
**1935** J. W. Campbell, Jr. *Night* in T. Shippey *Oxford Book of SF* (1992) 111: With what we have learned in the uncounted dusty megayears since, we might have been able to save him.

**1961** T. Sturgeon *Tandy's Story* in *Man Who Lost Sea* (2005) 302: It had been made where it was useful to its makers, and one might say it had a life of its own though it had not used it in some millions of megayears.

**1986** V. Vinge *Marooned in Realtime* 19: I was born about ten megayears after the Singularity—the Extinction, Juan calls it.

**1994** S. Baxter *Ring* (1996) 80: Sam wants to go to Tau Ceti and build houses under the light of a new sun; the dark possibilities of five megayears hence couldn't be of less interest to him.

**Mercurian** *n.* an inhabitant of the planet Mercury.
**1698** trans. C. Huygens *Celestial Worlds Discover'd* 106: There's reason to doubt, whether the Mercurians [ … ] are much more airy and ingenious than we.

**1868** W. White *Emanuel Swedenborg (2nd ed.)* 290: When the Mercurians met Swedenborg, they instantly explored his memory in search of all he knew.

**1939** N. S. Bond *Mercurian Menace* in *Dynamic Sci. Stories* (Feb.) 60/1: Buzz took the tiny Mercurian in one hand.

**1946** W. F. Jenkins *From Beyond Stars* in *Thrilling Wonder Stories* (June) 88/1: You old Mercurian! You old Plutonian! You want to blow up Earth!

**1996** K. S. Robinson *Blue Mars* 395: Meetings between the Martian delegation and the Mercurians had been going on in Terminator for weeks.

**microbook** *n.* a book whose text is stored at an extremely small size, requiring a special viewer to read it.
**1943** [A. Boucher] *One-Way Trip* in *Astounding SF* (Aug.) 100/2: There were even microbooks in the rocket, with a small pocket-model viewer; there was hardly space for a projector.

**1944** *College & Research Libraries* (Sept.) 307/1: Why could we not put our micro-books on the (at present entirely unused) backs of their own catalog cards?

**1959** F. Leiber *Green Millennium* (1980) 175: His vest was crammed with enough microbooks to make up a dozen encyclopedias.

**1964** J. Vance *Star King* in *Demon Princes, Vol. One* (1997) 108: Gersen glanced along a row of books: [ ... ] an index to Dasce's micro-book library, a *Star Directory*.

**1971** *British Printer* (Jan.) 80/1: An inventor, who has been working for two years to develop a practicable "micro book," has come up with a solution.

### military science fiction, military sf *n.*

a subgenre of science fiction concerned with future military life and military actions, especially in which the setting is outer space or other worlds. Compare FUTURE WAR.

**1979** J. Pournelle *Intro.* in D. Drake *Hammer's Slammers* (1985) ix: Military science fiction is a highly specialized art form.

**1982** *New York Times Book Rev.* (Nov. 28) 21/2: A few years ago, General Sir John Hackett, [ ... ] wrote a book called "The Third World War: August 1985." He must have thought that more work needed to be done on that scenario of political, or rather military science fiction.

**1993** L. M. Bujold *Touching Reader* in *Quantum* (Spring–Summer) 17/3: When I started off writing Shards of Honor, I really wasn't out to write military SF at all. I was writing a Gothic romance in SF drag [ ... ]. They ended up with this space war more or less to give their characters something to do.

**2001** *SF Chronicle* (July) 42/2: This is military SF by two writers who specialize in that form, so if you're fond of battle scenes and tactical maneuvering, this one should reward you.

**2006** N. Spinrad *Asimov's SF (Internet)* (Apr./May): It does partake of some of the attributes of space opera, and the sub-genre, if you want to call it that, of so-called military science fiction.

### mindlink *n.* a telepathic connection between two or more people. Also used *fig.* Compare MIND-MELD.

**1970** K. Laumer *House in November* 101: But he could have maintained knowledge of his descendants; could have learned of it when you were orphaned, have seen to your care—and established a mind link with you in infancy, before the pattern of acculturation made such contact impossible.

**1982** P. C. Hodgell *God Stalk* (1983) 100: She was still very wet [ ... ] with the cub a shaking

morsel of ice against her right breast. The mind link she had shared with it in that moment of crisis no longer seemed to exist.

**1986** M. M. Snodgrass *Degradation Rites* in G. R. R. Martin *Wild Cards* 145: He reentered the full mindlink. Her mind fluttered beneath his, confused, unable to understand the magnitude of the change that had come over her.

**1989** J. M. Dillard *Lost Years* 226: She would not accept the margin of privacy that other mind-links allowed.

**1994** *Coloradoan (Fort Collins)* (Jan. 1) A1/5: The idea behind the event [ ... ] is to raise peace consciousness by uniting individuals in a "global mind-link."

### mind-meld *n.* in the *Star Trek* universe, a telepathic union between two beings; in general use, a deep understanding. Hence **mind-melding,** *adj.* Compare MINDLINK.

**1968** J. M. Lucas *Elaan of Troyius ("Star Trek" script)* (May 23) 40: Mr. Spock, [ ... ] he refuses to talk. I'll need you for the Vulcan mind-meld.

**1968** S. E. Whitfield in S. E. Whitfield & G. Roddenberry *Making of "Star Trek"* 227: Another unique Vulcan ability exhibited by Spock is a type of ESP that the Vulcans refer to as "mind-melding."

**1978** L. Schlessinger *Sunday Gleaner Mag. (Kingston, Jam.)* (Aug. 4) 5/4: When people are in love, in an intimate relationships, there is not automatic mind[-]meld. People cannot know what is in each other's mind.

**1994** *Inuit Art Quarterly* (Summer) 20/3: When I think of it, all in all, I think we had a pretty good mind-meld. There's this whole other culture, this whole other way of being here, of being on the planet.

**2005** *San Francisco Chronicle* (Jan. 30) F7/5: It was going fine until we noticed that the older couple at the other end was engaged in some sort of unearthly sex—naked, yes, touching, no, just staring at each other in a mind meld.

### mind-meld *v.* to engage (someone) in a mind-meld.

**1976** P. Foglio *And Then...New York* in J. Winston *Startoons* (1979) 170: We're backstage, still waiting for Leonard Nimoy, who has gone thru 3 albums, mind-melded with 4 Trekkies and a Wells Fargo guard, faith healed a sick cat, and is halfway thru his current book.

**1988** S. McCrumb *Bimbos of Death Sun* 20: I'll find him if I have to mind-meld the desk clerk!
**1995** D. M. Flinn *Fearful Summons* 12: No one can mind-meld with a computer.
**1998** W. Shatner *Spectre* 74: I mind-melded with Dr. McCoy.

**mind shield** *n.* a mental barrier that prevents a telepath from reading one's thoughts.
**1940** A. E. van Vogt *Slan* in *Astounding S-F* (Nov.) 132/2: You will lower your mind shield. Of course, I don't expect absolutely free access to your brain.
**1949** J. H. Schmitz *Agent of Vega* in *Agent of Vega* (1962) 15: Why have you been trying to probe through my mind-shields all evening?
**1988** J. McMullen *Wind in Ash Tree* 44: Mrs P has always been a bit psychic. Living with her, I've got used to having my thoughts read and actually put up a kind of mind shield if those thoughts aren't too lovely.
**2000** B. Lumley *Necroscope: Defilers* (2001) 386: A blanket of mental fog, an impenetrable mind-shield. And behind it, someone sleeping.

**monster movie** *n.* a movie that features a monster, often the result of an experiment gone awry, as the principle antagonist or driver of the action. Also **monster film, flick,** etc.
**1932** *Suburban Post (Madison, Wis.)* (Jan. 15) 1/3 (headline): Frankenstein Man Monster Film Coming
**1941** *Mansfield (Oh.) News-Journal* (Mar. 17) 7/1: Karloff, a respected small-town doctor by day and a prowling ape by night, plays a new type of role which is sure to please those who like the "monster" films.
**1956** *New York Times* (May 6) X1/8: It would be a hard man who could find it within his heart to condemn, with an absolute blanket indictment, the so-called monster films.
**1976** R. G. Powers *Intro.* in J. Finney *Body Snatchers* v: Don Siegel turned *The Body Snatchers* unto a B-movie classic, perhaps the best of the 'fifties monster movies.

**1980** *Washington Post Book World* (Dec. 28) 8: It is useful to possess an extensive listing of video sf, including all those really bad invasion and monster flicks of the '50s.
**1999** *New Yorker* (June 2) 91/1: "Jurassic Park" [...] was a kind of all-you-can-eat buffet of monster-movie clichés, one whopping hunk of red meat after another.

**moon base** *n.* a human outpost on the Earth's moon. Often *cap.*
**1948** R. A. Heinlein *Space Cadet* 24: A cabal of high-ranking officers, acting from Moon Base, tried to seize power over the entire world.
**1953** P. K. Dick *Second Variety* in *Space SF* (May) 108/2: The American bloc governments moved to the Moon base the first year.
**1961** *Economist* (Nov. 18) 676/2: Commercial services [...] between New York and Moonbase Alpha in one day.
**1969** *Guardian (London)* (July 15) 6/6: One of the things we shall be doing in those early lunar flights is to find a good place for a moon base.
**1986** W. Strieber & J. Kunetka *Nature's End* (1987) 100: So all we have is the L-5 colony and the moonbases.
**1995** F. Burke & M. Thorn trans. Y. Hoshino *2001 Nights* 29: The moonbase is located at the center of the Sea of Fertility.

**moonsuit** *n.* **1.** a spacesuit designed for use on the Earth's moon. Compare PRESSURE SUIT, SPACE SUIT, SUIT, VAC SUIT, VACUUM SUIT.
**1947** H. M. Sherman *All Aboard for Moon* in *Amazing Stories* (Apr.) 104/1: "Take off your evening clothes, put on these slacks, and I'll help you into your space suit." He crossed over to the store-room alcove where the moon suits were hanging.
**1953** F. Pohl & C. M. Kornbluth *Space Merchants* (1955) 131: Moon suits rented "50 Years Without a Blowout."
**2000** D. W. Jones *Year of Griffin* (2001) 181: He got down to puzzling out articulated joints for his moonsuit.
**2005** M. van Pelt *Space Tourism* 185: A lunar astronaut is restricted from having such a full experience owing to the lack of an atmosphere and the necessary use of a moonsuit.

**2.** any protective suit that resembles a spacesuit.

**1988** N. Stephenson *Zodiac* 49: Riding in one of the Zodiacs was a man dressed up in a moon-suit, one of those dioxinproof numbers with the goggles and the facemasks.

**1992** *New York Times* (May 5) B6/6: Send people in moon suits to spray the entire land-scape with lethal insecticides.

**2001** A. Rosenfeld *Diamond Eye* (2004) 92: I found a bomb squad guy in a moonsuit, drinking a can of soda.

**morph** *n.* an artificial or duplicate body.

**1993** D. Smeds *Suicidal Tendencies* in L. Aronica, et al. *Full Spectrum 4* (1994) 302: Never mind that her body morph presented her as a stylish, if a bit voluptuous, nineteen-year-old blonde. Her carriage betrayed that she was really a prune-faced, four-hundred-year-old gossip.

**1996** W. Gibson *Idoru* 216: That isn't me. It's a morph. If I could prove it was a morph, I could sue you.

**2000** M. Flynn *Lodestar* (2001) 7: Her morph was preprogrammed. An A/S kept the imago smiling and pleasant, and a good thing, too, be-cause there were days when she was not fit company—days when she hated all the stumbling, clumsy, two-legged oafs who did not even dream they possessed what she could never have again.

**morph** *v.* [abbr. of *metamorphosis* or *metamorphose*] to transform a physical body into another shape.

**1982** *Re; Killing Umbers* (Usenet: net.games. rogue) (Sept. 16): A staff of polymorph can help too if you morph him into something "easy."

**1990** J. Cameron & W. Wisher *Terminator 2: Judgement Day* 239: It's changing, morphing, transforming into anything and everything it's ever been so rapidly the eye can barely follow.

**1993** M. Bourne *Being Human* in *Asimov's SF* (Dec.) 100: We're going to morph together into a single bioform and move into one of the hull casings.

**1995** D. Naylor *Last Human* 170: A symbi-otic shape-shifter. Intuitively, they understand your needs and morph into the shape that most pleases you.

**2001** K. A. Applegate *Animorphs: Sacrifice* 5: It is our ability to morph, to transform into other creatures, that makes our species the envy of the galaxy.

**mosaic novel** *n.* a book of short stories that share a common setting or char-acters and which taken together form a larger narrative. Compare FIX-UP.

**1986** G. R. R. Martin (title): *Wild Cards: A Mosaic Novel*

**1997** *Locus* (July) 55/3: SF collection of 21 sto-ries presented in the form of a mosaic novel.

**2003** J. Clute *Intro.* in J. White *General Practice* 8: *Code Blue—Emergency* (1987) is [ ... ] a mosaic novel: a series of stories or episodes, whether or not previously published, joined into a loose narrative.

**2005** R. Bowes *Afterword* in *From Files of Time Rangers* 267: Simple "fix-ups" faded. But because New Wave Speculative Fiction was more open to experimentation with form and subject, the Mosaic Novel flourished.

**motherworld** *n.* the planet on which a species originated. Often *cap.* Compare HOMEWORLD, HOME PLANET.

**1956** A. Norton *Plague Ship Solar Queen* (2003) 338: The descendants of far-flung colo-nists, coming home on visits, found the sparsely populated mother world appealed to some basic instinct so that they remained.

**1970** A. Davidson *Selectra Six-Ten* in *Avram Davidson Treasury* (1999) 270: AGGRESSIVE NONCHERODERMATOID BIPED LANDING YOUR PLANETARY-RAPING PROBE MODULEWS ON THE SACRED CHITIN OF OUR MOTHER[-]WORLD FASCISTICLY TERMED "MOOM"

**1988** I. McDonald *Desolation Road* (2001) 71: There have been people on our world for only seven hundred years, [ ... ] but upon the Motherworld there are civilizations thousands upon thousands of years old.

**1991** G. Wolfe *Seraph from Its Sepulcher* in A. M. Greeley & M. Cassutt *Sacred Visions* 172: I want to find out as much as possible about the Seraphs. I came here from the Motherworld to do that.

**2004** A. Baird *Empire of Stars* (2005) 49: The Emperor's palace was at this time suspended in the skies of Alfaran, the Motherworld.

**multigeneration ship** *n.* a GENERATION SHIP. Also **multigeneration starship.** Compare SPACE ARK.

**1962** J. G. Ballard *Thirteen for Centaurus* in *Best Short Stories of J. G. Ballard* (1995) 158: Without exaggeration, if you did send a dozen people on a multi-generation ship to Alpha Centauri you couldn't do better than duplicate everything that's taken place here, down to the last cough and sneeze.

**1995** P. F. Hamilton *Nano Flower* (1999) 163: There's two ways of traveling between the stars. In a small ship going very fast, say about thirty or fifty percent lightspeed. Or a big multigeneration ship, [ ... ] traveling at one or two percent lightspeed.

**1996** D. Pringle, et al. *Ultimate Ency. of SF* 241/2: Another four-volume work, "The Book of the Long Sun," is set on a run-down, multigeneration starship, now nearing its goal.

**2003** J. C. Wright *Golden Transcendence* 75: Instead, there will be a ship, a ship like no other. Not a spaceship, not a multigeneration ship, but a starship.

**multiversal** *adj.* of or relating to a multiverse.

**1963** M. Moorcock *SF Adventures* (May) 6: The Originators, creators of the multiversal seeding ground for their successors.

**1996** D. Pringle, et al. *Ultimate Ency. of SF* 216/3: New and vigorous multiversal titles [ ... ] emerged to show Moorcock as an Eternal Champion still cruising the aethers.

**1999** *Astronomy* (Sept.) 42: Our universe would then be but one component of the multiverse, which has been growing through a series of Big Bangs for much longer than our little region of the multiversal whole.

**2002** D. Langford *New York Rev. of SF* (Apr.) 8/2: After so much primitive carnage, the multiversal sense-of-wonder jolt comes as a belated infodump rather than developing via a long, effective crescendo.

**multiverse** *n.* a set of many universes. Also used *fig.*

**1963** M. Moorcock *SF Adventures* (May) 3: Within it there were many things, many intelligences who did not realise they dwelt in a multiverse since, within itself, it was comprised of many universes, each one separated from the other by dimensions, like leaves between the layers.

**1987** N. Spinrad *Little Heroes* (1989) 150: How many times had she experienced such a magic moment of reality transformation from on high as the LSD [ ... ] began its rush through her brain, as ordinary earth-bound reality dissolved into the multiverse of the infinite possible, taking her spirit with it?

**1990** *New Scientist* (June 9) 37/2: The wormhole picture changes our view of the "origin" of the Universe in a big bang, which is now seen simply as the event corresponding to our Universe branching off from the greater "multiverse."

**1996** *Interzone* (Mar.) 44/1: I used to be a citizen of the world, but now I'm a citizen of the multiverse.

**2001** *Dreamwatch* (Mar.) 90/4: A battle below threatens the fabric of the multiverse, a battle directed by Gaynor and at the very heart of his family's destiny.

**2005** K. Baker *Rick Bowes: Appreciation* in R. Bowes *From Files of Time Rangers* xii: The Time Rangers themselves are mortals recruited from across a multiverse of war-torn worlds, stationed in decades as other mortals live in neighborhoods.

**mundane** *n.* a person who is not a science fiction fan; by extension, a person who is an outsider to some group.

[**1959** R. H. Eney *Fancyclopedia II* 48: *Dressed-up Mundanes*, hackwork in which fantastic elements could be replaced with non-fantastic ones without changing the plot essentially.]

**1969** H. Warner, Jr. *All Our Yesterdays* 145: He claimed that he was immediately honored by fourteen fans and eight mundanes at a banquet staged for him by the Oak Grove Science Fiction Society.

**1986** A. Thomson *Locus* (Nov.) 29/2: 5500 fans, pros, writers, and a few confused mundanes attended ConFederation.

**1992** G. Wolfe *Aussiecon Two Guest of Honor Speech Castle of Days* (1995) 429: Some have announced with even greater pride that they never read fantastic literature, or that they haven't read a word of it for the past five or ten years—that they are in fact closet mundanes.

**1991** E. Raymond *New Hacker's Dictionary* 1: Not knowing the slang (or using it inappropriately) defines one as an outsider, a mundane.

**2004** S. E. Glasgow *e-National Fantasy Fan* (Mar.) 17: Whenever I felt misunderstood by "mundanes" there was all of you who understood me.

**mundane** *adj.* not relating to science fiction or science fiction fandom, or by extension, to a specific group or subject; (of literature) mainstream.

**1944** J. B. Speer *Fancyclopedia* 3/1: Several former fans have disappeared into the mundane APA's.

**1955** D. Knight *SF Quarterly* (Feb.) 76/1: The other two pass, barely, but are so close to mundane stories that they make me almost equally uncomfortable.

**1959** C. M. Kornbluth *Failure of SF Novel as Social Criticism* in B. Davenport, et al. *SF Novel* 65: Uncle Tom's Cabin: another mundane, contemporary story about real people.

**1978** S. R. Delany *Jewel-Hinged Jaw* 81: I feel the science-fictional-enterprise is richer than the enterprise of mundane fiction.

**1988** J. Clute *Strokes* 42: Arguments about the nature of sf as opposed to "mundane" literature.

**1999** M. J. Pustz *Comic Book Culture* 20: This identification, of course, marks these people as separate from the rest of the "mundane" (non-fan) population.

**2005** R. A. Lupoff *Intro.* in P. Lupoff & D. Lupoff *Best of Xero* 14: The earmarks of fannish writing were [...] a cynical disregard for the mundane or non-fannish world, and a correspondingly high degree of self-concern.

**mundania** *n.* that part of society which is separate from science fiction fandom, or by extension, from a specific endeavor or area of interest.

**1965** R. A. Lupoff *Master of Adventure* (2005) 33: Not quite the experience in "mundania" that was first indicated, but still far from an extravagant romance.

**1969**: see quote in SLAN SHACK.

**1980** [L. del Rey] *World of SF* 323: Mundania is the world of those who haven't discovered science fiction.

**2001** S. M. Pike *Earthly Bodies, Magical Selves* 21: Mundania is cast as the antithesis to festival, a world in which Neopagan values are rarely expressed and Neopagans must hide their identities.

**mutant** *n.* a being who is the result of an extreme genetic mutation, especially one who has extraordinary powers.

**1938** S. Lane *Niedbalski's Mutant* in *Astounding SF* (May) 137/2: And yet I have, even in age, one source of joy. Man no longer calls me the "strange mutant." My card reads simply: "Niedbalski"—the name of the man I love.

**1938** E. Hamilton *He That Hath Wings* in *Weird Tales* (July) 72/1: That accident produced an entirely new gene-pattern in the parents of this child, one which developed their child into a winged human. He's what biologists technically call a mutant.

**1956** J. G. Ballard *Prima Belladonna* in J. Merril *SF: Best of Best* (1967) 72: The gossips at Vermillion Sands soon decided there was a good deal of mutant in her, because she had a rich patina-golden skin and what looked like insects for eyes.

**1961** J. Boardman *Asteroid Light Reprints from SING OUT! Folk Song Mag. Vol. 3* 60: My father was the keeper of the Asteroid Light, He slept with a Martian one fine night. Out of this match came children three. Two were mutants and the other was me.

**1983** *x future issues big screech* (Usenet: net.comics) (Oct. 27): This latter idea is interesting for several reasons—as an example of a mutant who is *very* different from humans and has no interest in living a "normal" life

**2004** D. Broderick *X, Y, Z, T* 65: Candidia is not just a classic Heinlein over-achiever, she is also that marvel of *Astounding*, the mutant superhuman.

**mutation** *n.* a mutant.

**1941** R. A. Heinlein *Universe Astounding S-F* (May) 16/2: Our present wise rule of inspecting each infant for the mark of sin and returning to the Converter any who are found to be mutations was not in force.

**1946** A. E. van Vogt *Hand of Gods* in *Astounding SF* (Dec.) 144/1: It would be impossible for a despised mutation ever to become Lord Leader.

**1989** O. Butler *Imago* (1991) 112: It was well cooked, steaming hot, spicy, and sweet. It had not existed before the Humans had their war. Lilith said it was one of the few good-tasting mutations she had eaten.

**mutie** *n.* a MUTANT. Often *derog.*

**1941** R. A. Heinlein *Universe* in *Astounding S-F* (May) 16/2: There is even some question as to the original meaning of the word "mutie." [...] But they also have in their blood the blood of many of the mutants who were born during the dark age.

**1967** R. Zelazny *He Who Shapes* in D. G. Hartwell *SF Century* (1997) 831: The muties he had seen had all been puppies.

**1978** S. King *Stand* 139: "I'm getting [...] out of here," he said. "You're wise, you'll do the same thing, mutie."

**1993** N. Kress *Beggars* in *Spain* (2004) 52: "Sleepless Mutie Begs for Reversal of Gene Tampering" screamed the headline in the Food Mart.

**2003** J. Ridley *Those Who Walk in Darkness* (2005) 21: That mutie, its hand was so hot it cauterized the wound.

# Robots

**Robot** has an unusual origin for a science fiction word: it is probably the only word in the SF lexicon that was first used in a play, and one of a very few words borrowed from another language. **Robot** comes from *robota*, the Czech word for "forced labor." Karel Čapek used it in his play *R.U.R.* (1920, English translation 1923) to describe an artificial being, although he credited his brother Josef with the idea of using that word. Unlike the mechanical robots we think of today, Čapek's robots were artificial biological creatures, created to do menial labor for humans. Almost immediately after the work appeared in English, writers began using the word figuratively to describe people they perceived to be behaving like automatons. Science fiction writers quickly picked up the word and applied it to mechanical creations, although Čapek's original sense still crops up from time to time.

Science fiction writers also spun off a variety of derivatives. Three of them, **robotic**, **robotics**, and **roboticist**, all came from the pen of Isaac Asimov, who also created (with John W. Campbell, Jr.) the robots' programmed-in code of ethics known as the three laws of robotics. Other SF writers gave us the forms **robotical**, **robotically**, and **roboticized**. In the 1960s, the word was shortened to **'bot** (or sometimes just **bot**). Robot also got shortened into the combining form **robo-**, which can indicate the form or purpose of a robot, as in *roboplane* and *robobar.*

Outside of science fiction, the word **robot** has had an even more varied career. The most common use refers to any of a variety of automated machines, particularly those that are controlled remotely or by computer. Such machines can be known simply as **robots**, or can appear in various compounds such as *robot bomb*. Other senses, not treated elsewhere in this dictionary, include: an automated computer program that interacts with other programs or processes (such as a Web crawler); a traffic signal; a popular dance involving jerky motions; and the suffix *-bot*. The *OED* additionally lists more than a dozen other derivatives, including *roboteer, robothood, robotize, robotomorphic,* and *roboty.*

# n

**nanite** *n.* [probably first used in the *Star Trek: The Next Generation* television episode "Evolution," which first aired in 1989] a nanometer-scale machine that is capable of building other objects.

**1990** *Cinefantastique* (Sept.) 40/1: Evolution [...]. Good character drama, is negated by a silly "sci-fi" premise in which Nannites are accidentally released [...] into the ship's computer system.

**1992** A. Steele *Labyrinth of Night* 315: Raw materials are being fed into the vats, [...] which in turn are being broken down into their basic elements by the nanites and reassembled into solid-state components for the starship.

**1997** J. A. Gardner *Expendable* (1997) 233: There were nanites at work too, microscopically reconstituting any systems that had rotted or corroded since the last time such repairs had been made.

**2003** *Dreamwatch* (Aug.) 12/1: A geeky computer technician is transformed into a superpowerful secret agent for the NSA after he is exposed to nanites.

**Nebula** *n.* any of several awards given annually by the Science Fiction and Fantasy Writers of America for excellence in science fiction and fantasy writing.

**1966** *SFWA Bulletin* (Apr.) 1: "Nebula" Awards for the best science fiction of 1965 were presented on March 11.

**1972** H. Ellison *Intro. to Mathoms from Time Closet* in *Again, Dangerous Visions* 124: Isaac Asimov had been pressed into service at the last moment to read the winners of the Nebulas.

**1987** *Bookseller* (Aug. 28) 913/2: A first novel, William Gibson's Neuromancer, won both the Nebula and the Hugo awards in 1985.

**2001** *SF Chronicle* (July) 36/2: The Nebula is most like the Oscar and is given by professionals, others who are slapping each other on the back.

**needle** *v.* to shoot (someone) with a needle gun or needle ray.

**1943** E. F. Russell *Symbiotica* in *Astounding S-F* (Oct.) 152/2: These things were the remains of the two natives he'd needled, but the needlers had not caused that awful rotting of the flesh.

**1948** H. B. Piper *Police Operation* in *Astounding SF* (July) 18/1: And when I back-slip, after I've been needled, I generate a new timeline? Is that it?

**1957** P. Anderson *Brake* in *Astounding SF* (Aug.) 10/2: Quickly, now, go to my cabin. I shall be behind. If necessary I will needle you and drag you there.

**1979** L. Killough *Doppelganger Gambit* 15: She let go of the gun. No sense needling him now.

**1984** G. R. Dickson *Final Encyclopedia* (1985) 235: Hal [...] went to look at the other two casualties, a woman who had taken a weapon burn in her right shoulder, superficial but painful, and a man who had been needled in the chest.

**needle beam** *n.* a very fine beam or ray fired from an energy weapon. Also **needle ray**.

**1920** [S. Rohmer] *Golden Scorpion* 82: There came a series of dull reports—an uncanny waiting … and the needle ray vanished.

**1934** E. E. Smith *Skylark of Valeron* in *Astounding Stories* (Aug.) 22/2: He spun a couple of wheels briefly, pressed a switch, and from the Violet's heaviest needle-ray projector there flashed out against the prow of the scout patrol a pencil of incredibly condensed destruction.

**1942** [A. MacDonald] *Beyond This Horizon* in *Astounding SF* (Apr.) 12/1: He […] could easily have spent two hours with a man and never notice whether he was wearing a Stokes coagulator or a common needlebeam.

**1946** M. Champion *Unforeseen* in *Astounding SF* (Nov.) 40/1: Randall was […] in possession of a secret or new needle beam gun.

**1970** L. Niven *Ringworld* (1984) 232: Louis clawed the flashlight-laser from his belt, used its green needle beam to free Speaker from his balloons.

**1995**: see quote in NEEDLER.

**needle gun** *n.* a weapon that fires small slivers of metal.

**1941** M. Jameson *Slacker's Paradise* in *Astounding S-F* (Apr.) 87/1: Her armament was so inadequate as never to have given him a qualm. It consisted simply of a 10 mm. needle gun, fit only to detonate a stray mine.

**1949** L. Brackett *Lake of Gone Forever* in *Halfling & Other Stories* (1973) 289: He had hidden a small anaesthetic needle-gun under his coverall in case of need.

**1953** I. Asimov *Sally* in *Fantastic* (May–June) 49/2: And I knew the needle gun was about to fire.

**1965** M. Moorcock *Further Information* in *New Worlds SF* (Dec.) 52: He saw a German looking down at him, sighting along his weapon. Jerry snapped up his needle-gun and shot him full of steel.

**1989** W. Shatner *Tekwar* (1990) 26: He's using one of those new needle guns. You know, it shoots *Bap! BAP! BAP!* and fifty or sixty little steel needles dipped in nerve poison come shooting out.

**needler** *n.* **1.** a weapon that fires needle beams. [1937 quote refers to weapons operators who fire needle beams.]

[**1937** E. E. Smith *Galactic Patrol* in *Astounding Stories* (Sept.) 23/1: "Needlers, fire at will!" […] Keen-eyed needle-ray men, working at spy-ray visiplates, bored hole after hole into the captive.]

**1948** H. B. Piper *Police Operation* in *Astounding SF* (July) 17/2: This chance acquaintance develops into a love affair, and a year later, out of jealousy, she rays you half a dozen times with a needler.

**1953** G. O. Smith *Stop, Look & Dig* in *Space SF* (Mar.) 57/1: I came back with one of his needle-rays and burned the contents of the safe to a black char. I stirred up the ashes with the nose of the needler and then left it in the safe after wiping it clean on my handkerchief.

**1968** R. Silverberg *Fangs of Trees* in *World of Thousand Colors* (1984) 246: He turned the needler aperture to fine and gave the animal a quick burn through the head.

**1995** A. D. Foster *Mid-Flinx* 33: Both men drew compact needlers. "They're set to stun, and I don't think she's faster than a needle beam."

**2.** a NEEDLE GUN.

**1957** T. Sturgeon *It Opens Sky* in *Man Who Lost Sea* (2005) 58: Deeming had Rockhard's specially designed needler out before he moved to the doorway. […] He fired, and the needle disappeared silently into the broad golden chest.

**1961** A. Norton *Star Hunter* 33: Hume went forward, jerked the needler dart from a tree trunk.

**1983** D. Brin *Startide Rising* 386: He checked his weapon. The needler only had a few shots left.

**1993** G. Wolfe *Nightside Long Sun* 320: A silver fountain of needles sprang from the breach of Auk's needler and scattered over the table.

**needle ray** *n.* see NEEDLE BEAM.

**neo** *n.* a NEOFAN.

**1956** R. Bloch *Way of Life* in *Fantastic Universe* (Oct.) 19/2: He taught me, trained me, groomed me for this step by step ever since I was just a neo in the Beanie Brigade.

**1960** *Savoyard* (June) 2: It's a good example of how neos tend to judge better-known fans—in haste, and without being able to see things in the proper perspective.

**1961** J. Koning *Withdrawal* in *S-F Five-Yearly* (Nov.) 23: He was still wide-eyed, a trait left from his neo days, and had an exuberance that was still pure, no one having come along yet to tell him how futile everything was.

**1969** H. Warner, Jr. *All Our Yesterdays* 19: While many fans snubbed Neumann as a neo, Bloch talked with him for hours.

**1984** T. Nielsen Hayden *Over Rough Terrain* in *Making Book* (1994) 89: I was just a neo in those days, running more important folks around in my car and making bricks without straw and covering up for committee members when they had to go off for a spell of hysterics.

**1997** P. Nielsen Hayden M. Resnick & P. Nielsen Hayden *Alternate Skiffy* 110: Goshwow neo he may be, but he understands far too much about editorial *bushido*.

**neofan** *n.* someone who is new to science fiction fandom. Hence **neofannish**, *adj.* Compare NEO.

**1950**: see quote in BNF.

**1953** L. B. Stewart *Thrilling Wonder Stories* *(letter)* (Aug.) 133/2: Ah, well, frustrations gone, I, too, am a genuine *tin carrot* neo-fan.

**1969** H. Warner, Jr. *All Our Yesterdays* 122: He helped out with a fanzine tribute to Ackerman with neofannish enthusiasm late in 1960.

**1977** S. Wood *Algol* (43/1) Spring: I was a neofan, trying hard to be a real published fan, and Ginjer's account of WPSFA's descent on the Baycon made me feel that I'd been there too.

**1992** H. Jenkins *Textual Poachers* 246: Indeed, M.V.D.'s video could introduce a neofan to the particular themes and interests of the fan community.

**2004** R. R. Davidson *National Fantasy Fan* (Jun.) 4: Hopefully we'll get some fans, neo-fans and even fanlings to join us.

**Neptunian** *n.* an inhabitant of Neptune.

**1870** R. A. Proctor *Other Worlds than Ours* 173: The Neptunians would be wholly unable to see Uranus.

**1910** *Westminster Gazette* (Mar. 8) 4/1: Supposing this comet passes anywhere near Neptune [...] and there were inhabitants on Neptune, I wonder how it would appear to those Neptunians?

**1929** C. W. Harris & M. J. Breuer *Baby on Neptune* in *Amazing Stories* (Dec.) 795/1: "Perhaps," suggested Dalton, "the Neptunians live in caverns within their planet."

**2002** J. C. Wright *Golden Age* 34: Neptun-ians experiment with unusual mind forms, but we are not insane.

**neural** *adj.* connected or connecting directly to the brain or nervous system.

**1955** J. H. Schmitz *Grandpa* in *Astounding SF* (Feb.) 127/2: The countless neural extensions that connected it now with the raft came free in a succession of sucking, tearing sounds; and Cord and the yellowhead splashed into the water together.

**1976** M. Bishop *And Strange at Ecbatan Trees* 61: The ones who have roles always require surgical adaptation, electrode implanting, cybernetic neural grafting.

**1986** G. Benford & D. Brin *Heart of Comet* (1987) 10: Tapped into channels through a direct neural link and wrist servos, she scarcely moved.

**1993** *Wired* (Sept.–Oct.) 62/1: The current work in neural prosthesis [...] and mind-driven computers seems almost retro by comparison.

**1996** J. D. Vinge *Dreamfall* (2004) 287: The laws of the Federation made it illegal for a psion to wear implanted bioware, even so much as a neural jack or a commlink.

**2000** M. G. Zey *Future Factor* (2004) 83: He is doing this with a brand new science, *neural implant therapy*, in which computer chips controlled by radio or other signals either interfere with or augment the activity of brain circuitry.

**neuronic** *adj.* (of a weapon) affecting the brain or nervous system.

**1950** I. Asimov *Pebble in Sky* 98: But the sergeant raised his neuronic whip. The contact closed and there was the dim violet flash that reached out and licked at the tall archaeologist. Every muscle in Arvardan's body stiffened in unbearable pain, and he sank slowly to his knees. Then, with total paralysis upon him, he blacked out.

**1968** J. Russ *Picnic on Paradise* 13: "I don't know," he said, rising formally, "just what they are going to fight this war with. [...] For the people every nasty form of explosive of neuronic hand-weapon that's ever been devised."

**1972** A. D. Foster *Tar-Aiym Krang* 28: The other pulled the wicked shape of a neuronic pistol from a shoulder cup and tried to sight on the rapidly moving object.

**1999** K. D. Wentworth *Black on Black* 2: His earliest memories were still the stink of flek slave pens and the throb of the neuronic whip burns across his emaciated ribs.

**2001** D. Kingsbury *Psychohistorical Crisis* (2002) 7: They were armed with neuronic whips; he could go willingly or go paralyzed.

**newspeak** *n.* in George Orwell's *Nineteen Eighty-Four*, the modified form of English created by the government for use in propoganda; in general use, any euphemism or doublespeak, especially as used by a government or for propaganda. Compare OLDSPEAK.

**1949** [G. Orwell] *Nineteen Eighty-Four* 133: Do you know the Newspeak word *goodthinkful*?

**1950** A. A. Roback *Personality in Theory & Practice* 27: I do not think it necessary to resort to "Newspeak" in order to write scientifically.

**1966** *Punch* (July 27) 140/1: Accusing the Prime Minister of "the same old excuses," it labelled "redeployment" as "new-speak," which would be "victimisation of the workers" in any but a Labour Government.

**1972** *Times Literary Supplement* (Aug. 11) 935/2: The new party line, directed this time against "rootless cosmopolitans"—newspeak for Jews.

**1998** *New York Times Mag.* (letter) (Nov. 15) 26/1: What a wondrous land of legislative newspeak and doublethink we encounter, as your writer makes the rounds of F.D.A. and E.P.A. offices [...]. The potato developed, raised, marketed, purchased, prepared and eaten as a potato is not a potato.

**newszine** *n.* a magazine (especially a fanzine) that primarily prints news items.

**1950** [R. Phillips] *Amazing Stories* (Nov.) 151/2: *FANTASY-TIMES*: [...] is still the top newszine in fandom in my opinion.

**1959** R. H. Eney *Fancyclopedia II* 111: Certain usage distinguished the newszine, a fanzine full

of news, from the news[-]letter, often no more than a flier.

**1966** T. White *Who Was That Fandom I Saw You With...* in *SF Five-Yearly* 32 (Nov.): As a newszine, it took the disparate threads of a fragmented fandom and wove them into a whole again. [...] Once again, there was a central clearing house for all the news and quasi-news.

**1988** M. Z. Bradley *Locus (letter)* (Apr.) 36/1: Who would have thought that a little mimeoed newszine would have become a professional trade paper?

**1995** D. Broderick *Reading by Starlight* 170: The Locus Poll is conducted via the semi-professional "newszine" *Locus*.

**2001** *SF Chronicle* (July) 11/3: A complete run of [...] the UK newszine Ansible is available as a PC CD-Rom.

**New Wave** *n.* [< Fr. *nouvelle vague*, "new wave," as applied to a movement in French cinema] a loose movement in science fiction from the mid-1960's to the mid-1970's, characterized by explorations of psychological and social themes rather than the hard sciences and technology, use of experimental writing styles and narrative structures, and explicit portrayals of sex and violence.

[**1961** P. S. Miller *Analog Sci. Fact-Fiction* (Nov.) 167/1: Whatever the answer, there is no question at all about the "new wave": Tubb, Aldiss, and to get to my point, Kenneth Bulmer and John Brunner.]

[**1964** J. Linwood *Fanalytic Eye in Les Spinge* (Jan.) 30: The "New Wave" fanzines have arrived in fandom with the impact of a dud firework.]

**1965** C. Priest *New Wave—Prozines* in *Zenith Speculation* (Mar.) 11: But, more important, the fact that they are experimenting— with favourable results—should ensure that these "new-wave" prozines [i.e. *New Worlds* and *Science Fantasy*] are not only encouraged through loyalty alone.

**1968** A. Budrys *Benchmarks* (1985) 163: This is a pretty good example of why the "New Wave" of SF is evocative, often exciting, always willing, but also illustrative of the fact that, *nevertheless*, it is just as easy as ever to lose control of a story.

**1974** T. N. Scortia *SF as Imaginary Experiment* in R. Bretnor *SF, Today & Tomorrow* 145: The New Wave authors are frequently unschooled in the physical or social sciences and—more—are heirs of the new distrust of the sciences growing in our culture.

**1980** I. Asimov *How SF Came to Be Big Business* in *Asimov on SF* (1981) 125: The New Wave was also much more experimental in style and content; more generous in its use of sex and violence; not as clearly possessing a beginning, a middle, and an end; not as obviously telling a story.

**1990** P. Anderson *Thrust* (Winter) 16/1: To the best of my knowledge, it was first said by Robert Heinlein, whose contributions to science fiction were rather more significant than those of the New Wave.

**2001** *Locus* (June) 21/3: The existential apocalypse of "The Last Train" has an almost New Wave feel to it.

**non-genre** *adj.* **1.** MAINSTREAM.

**1975** G. Jonas *New York Times Book Rev.* (Jan. 12) 32/3: In what the s.f. fan calls "mainstream fiction"—that is, all non-genre writing, including serious literature—the short story does not attract much critical or popular attention today.

**1981** T. M. Disch *Labor Day Group* in *On SF* (2005) 102: Neither Carr nor Dozois cites any stories from non-genre magazines or anthologies.

**1988** V. McIntyre *Isaac Asimov's SF Mag.* (Mar.) 13/2: She never said *Always Coming Home* was not SF. Of course it's SF. Its being nominated for non-genre awards, and ignored by Hugo and Nebula voters, does not change that fact.

**2003** J. VanderMeer *Sudden Hummingbirds, Sudden Dislocations* in *Why Should I Cut Your Throat?* (2004) 47: It removes the ingrained opposition between genre and non-genre to consider the work from a multitude of perspectives.

**2.** describing imaginative literature that is not written or published in a standard marketing label or that does not conform to some notion of what is typical of science fiction or fantasy.

**1997** B. Stableford in J. Clute & J. Grant *Ency. of Fantasy* (1998) 50/1: The secondary worlds of genre fantasy are very often threatened with apocalyptic termination, but the formulaic plots of such works almost invariably require that disaster be averted in the nick of time. [ … ] In non-genre works the urge to wrathful destruction may be given free expression.

**2002** G. K. Wolfe *Malebolge* in *Conjunctions* (39) 418: At the same time that genre materials begin flowing freely into one another, we begin to see evidence of an even more peculiar development: the nongenre genre story.

**2003** D. G. Hartwell & K. Cramer *Intro.* in *Year's Best Fantasy 3* xv: One noticeable trend evident in some of these is toward non-genre, or genre-bending, or slipstream fantastic fiction.

**nonhumanoid** *n.* an alien with a body that does not resemble that of a human.

**1953** [A. Boucher] *Conquest* in F. Pohl *Star SF Stories #2* 124/3: But there were three non-humanoid things about them.

**1954** J. Blish *Beep* in *Galaxy SF* (Feb.) 42/2: And we'll be using non-humanoids there!

**1956** P. Anderson *Live Coward* in *Astounding SF* (June) 119/2: In spite of his claims to ambassadorial rank, Alak found himself ranking low—his only retinue was one ugly nonhumanoid.

**1985** A. Cole & C. Bunch *Court of Thousand Suns* (1990) 20: Prime World humans felt that the nonhumans, the N'Ranya, were underdogs, and preferred to invest their credits accordingly; non-humanoids felt somewhat differently, preferring to back the favorites.

**1993** *SF Age* (Jan.) 20/1: Why can't we have more *non-humanoid aliens*?

**nontelepath** *n.* someone who does not have the mental ability of telepathy. Hence **nontelepathic**, *adj.*

**1937** J. W. Campbell, Jr. *Out of Night* in *New Dawn* (2003) 248: By Aesir, I wish I could follow Drunnel. That he should be one of those rare, complete nontelepaths!

**1945** F. Leiber *Wanted—Enemy* in I. Asimov & M. H. Greenberg *Isaac Asimov Presents Golden Years of SF* (1984) 67: He was speaking vocally at the request of the coleopteroids, because like most nontelepaths he could best organize and clarify his thoughts while talking.

**1952** M. Wolf *Robots of World! Arise!* in *If* (July) 83/1: So I say to all of you nontelepaths, the time is now Strike for your rights.

**1955** E. F. Russell *Legwork* in *Astounding SF* (Apr.) 55/1: So they were mouth-talkers, non-telepathic, routine-minded and natural puppets for any hypno who cared to dangle them around.

**1979** M. Z. Bradley *Bloody Sun* 149: Non-telepaths feel to you like barbarians, or like strange animals, alien, wrong…

**1992** [P. Anthony] & R. E. Margroff *Mouvar's Magic* (1993) 5: Alas, finding another telepath, or even a nontelepath of the right quality, was taking time.

**non-terrestrial** *adj.* not from the planet Earth; extraterrestrial.

**1932** C. A. Smith *Testament of Athammaus* in *Weird Tales* (Oct.) 515/2: My scientific turn of mind [ … ] led me to seek an explanation of the problem in the non-terrestrial side of Knygathin Zhaum's ancestry. I felt sure that the forces of alien biology, the properties of a trans-stellar life-substance, were somehow involved.

**1960** J. Brunner *Atlantic Abomination* 59: You may have heard by now that the biologists assign a nonterrestrial origin to the creature you brought up from Atlantica.

**1964** K. Laumer *Wicker Wonderland* in *Retief!* (2002) 493: Junior Corps officers, ever-mindful of the welfare of emergent non-Terrestrial peoples, labored on in their unending quest to bring the fruits of modern technology to supplement native arts and crafts.

**1970** J. Blish *Spock Must Die!* 97: And your non-terrestrial friend Mr. Spock as well.

**2003** S. S. Tepper *Companions* (2004) 75: If you're interested in seeing some nonterrestrial animals, or visiting some other world.

**normal space** *n.* the type of space that exhibits the physical laws as we know them, as opposed to other spaces such as hyperspace; typically used in reference to space travel.

**1940** *Astonishing Stories* (Oct.) 48: Panic had to be forestalled somehow, when the huge Exposition-World vanished from normal space, so the Publicity Department spread the rumor that they were traveling in time.

**1954** R. Garrett *Time Fuze* in *If* (Mar.) 69/2: What we know about the hyperspace, or super-space, or whatever it is we move through in ul-tradrive is almost nothing. Coming out of it so near to a star might set up some sort of shock wave in normal space.

**1957** T. Sturgeon *It Opens Sky* in *Man Who Lost Sea* (2005) 45: A flickerfield works by mak-ing a ship, in effect, exist and cease to exist in normal space, so that it doesn't exist at any mea-surable time as real mass, and can therefore ex-ceed the velocity C.

**1963** H. B. Piper *Space Viking* (1975) 37: Then, in an instant, the stars, which had literally not been there before, filled the screen with a blaze of splendor against the black velvet back-drop of normal space.

**1978** B. Shaw *Ship of Strangers* (1979) 32: These usually occurred during normal-space planetary approaches or when the ship got into a region that was so congested that the instanta-neous drive could not be used to its full extent.

**1999** D. M. Weber *Apocalypse Troll* 92: Basically, they had used what you'd call the Bussard ram principle to accelerate in normal-space before they translated.

**nova** *v.* to cause a star to become a nova; (of a star) to become a nova.

**1950** J. D. MacDonald *Shadow on Sand* in *Thrilling Wonder Stories* (Oct.) 16/2: We can nova a sun, explode a planet, blast a sea into steam in a tenth of a second.

**1955** G. C. Edmondson *Blessed Are Meek* in *Astounding SF* (Sept.) 126/2: The court as-tronomer had a vision of our planet in flames. I imagine you'd say our sun was about to nova.

**1968** J. Sutton & J. Sutton *Programmed Man* 9: No world is apt to rebel against a power which could nova its sun, Captain.

**1993** L. E. Modesitt, Jr. *Timegod* in *Timegods' World* (2000) 465: Freyda still wanted to sun-tunnel the planet or nova the sun. Odin Thor wanted to send the whole Temporal Guard back with thunderbolts.

**nova bomb** *n.* a weapon armed with an extremely powerful explosive.

**1953** R. A. Heinlein *Gulf* in *Assignment in Eternity* 80: Unless it is switched off any attempt to enter the building in which the arming circuit is housed will also trigger the "Nova" bomb circuit.

**1974** J. Haldeman *Forever War* (2003) 245: All but one of the nova bombs went off below our horizon [ ... ]. The bomb that detonated on our horizon had melted out a semicircular chunk that glowed brilliantly white for several minutes.

**1983** J. Sladek *Tik-Tok* (2002) 71: "Because, though I know I never can be really human, I like to aim for humanity." *With a great big nova bomb*, I thought.

**2004** S. E. McDonald *Waystation* 41: She had no idea what kind of weapon might have caused this particular catastrophe. Nova bombs worked specifically on suns.

**novum** *n.* [L. "new"] the primary element in a work of science fiction by which the work is shown to exist in a different world than that of the reader.

**1972** D. Suvin *On Poetics of SF Genre* in *College English* (Dec.) 373/1: I should like to approach such a discussion [ ... ] by postulating a spectrum or spread of literary subject-matter, running from the ideal extreme of exact recreation of the author's empirical environment to exclusive interest in a strange newness, a *novum*.

**1979** D. Suvin *Metamorphoses of SF* 63: SF is distinguished by the narrative dominance or hegemony of a fictional "novum" (novelty, innovation) validated by cognitive logic.

**1995** D. Broderick *Reading by Starlight* 60: Sf is different, being, as we have seen, at least by vocation a mode grounded in a *novum*.

**2001** M. Dodge & R. Kitchin *Mapping Cyberspace* 183: Cyberpunk's novum was an estranged socio-spatial order rooted in a dystopian framework.

**2002** B. Attebery *Decoding Gender in SF* 189: We favored stories in which the novum is presented playfully and complexly, partly because we were looking for stories that would function out of their original context.

**2003** I. Csicsery-Ronay, Jr. *Marxist Theory & SF* in E. James & F. Mendlesohn *Cambridge Companion to SF* 119: Suvin adopts the concept of the novum from the work of Ernst Bloch, for whom the term refers to those concrete innovations in lived history that awaken human collective consciousness out of a static present to awareness that history can be changed.

**null-g, null-gee** *n.* ZERO-GRAVITY. Compare NULL-GRAV, ZERO-G.

**1956** A. Bester *Stars My Destination* in *Galaxy* (Oct.) 48/1: I cite the Null-G antigravity installations of 2022.

**1974** N. Spinrad *Riding Torch* in R. Silverberg *Threads of Time* 177: D'mahl was aboard a scoutship, playing null-g tennis with an attractive female voidsucker.

**1977** A. D. Foster *End of Matter* 210: The hold was little more than a vast open sphere within which all kinds of cargo could be stored at null g.

**1987** L. M. Bujold *Falling Free* in *Analog SF/ Sci. Fact* (Dec.) 16/1: Leo [ ... ] stretched and relaxed in the pleasurable familiarity of weightlessness. Not for him the unfortunate nauseas of null-*g* that sapped the efficiency of so many employees.

**2003** J. Haldeman *Giza* in *Asimov's SF* (Mar.) 99: Working in null-gee, inside an asteroid, doesn't take as much energy as working on Earth.

**null-grav** *n.* ZERO-GRAVITY. Also **nulgrav**. Compare NULL-G, ZERO-G.

**1956** R. A. Heinlein *Door into Summer* in *Mag. of Fantasy & SF* (Nov.) 26/2: The basic field theory on which NullGrav is based was developed at the University of Edinburgh. But I had been taught in school that gravitation was something that nobody could ever do anything about.

**1968** E. C. Tubb *Winds of Gath* (1981) 95: The rafts had no weight—their nulgrav plates kept them a level three feet from the ground—but they had mass and had to be towed every inch of the way.

**1974** [P. Anthony] *Triple Détente* (1975) 9: Henrys climbed to the null-grav tunnel that passed the full length of the ship.

**1996** D. Carey *Invasion!* 81: I've got him mounted on a null-grav pad.

# O

**off-earth** *adj.* not from or on the planet Earth.

**1958** T. Sturgeon *Comedian's Children* in *Venture SF Mag.* (May) 89: Captain Swope's mission was to accomplish the twelfth off-earth touchdown, and the body on which he touched was Iapetus (sometimes Japetus), the remarkable eighth satellite of Saturn.
**1962** [C. Smith] *Ballad of Lost C'Mell* in *Galaxy Mag.* (Oct.) 19/2: She remembered the off-Earth prince who had rested his head in her lap.
**1979** C. Sheffield *How to Build Beanstalk* in *Destinies* (Aug.–Sept.) 66: The economic impetus to deploy those tools will be provided by a recognition of the value of the off-Earth energy and raw materials.
**2001** A. Steele *SF Chronicle* (July) 30/1: We should pursue [ ... ] opening the space frontier for the purpose of exploiting off-Earth resources.

**off-earth** *adv.* away from the planet Earth.

**1949** [R. LaFayette] *Unwilling Hero* in *Startling Stories* (July) 102/2: At twenty-nine, then, Captain Taylor could truthfully say that he had spent six of his last eight years "off Earth."
**1965** G. R. Dickson *Warrior* in *Analog SF-Sci. Fact* (Dec.) 70/1: So, he went off-Earth and became a professional soldier.
**1987** T. R. McDonough *Architects of Hyperspace* 44: I know you haven't been convicted of anything, but the word's come down that you're under investigation. That means we can't let you go off-Earth.
**2001** B. Bova *Precipice* (2002) 147: I don't think I'd be able to live off-Earth forever.

**off-planet** *n.* OFF-WORLD 1.

**1972** U. K. Le Guin *Word for World Is Forest* in H. Ellison *Again, Dangerous Visions* 37: There were two possibilities. One: an attack from another camp. [ ... ] Two: an attack from off-planet.
**1989** L. Watt-Evans *Nightside City* 40: So who was buying new cabs and bringing them in from off-planet?
**2001** J. A. Gardner *Ascending* 163: No dangerous animals except in zoos [ ... ] and of course, with the League of Peoples, no one has to worry about attacks from off-planet.

**off-planet** *adj.* **1.** in or from the space around a specific planet.

**1945** M. Jameson *Lilies of Life* in *Astounding SF* (Feb.) 31/1: They've trebled the offplanet patrol and tightened up on port inspection
**1963** H. B. Piper *Space Viking* 38: The *Enterprise* carries four pinnaces, the same as the *Nemesis*; in his place, I'd have at least two of them on off-planet patrol. So let's accept it that we'll be detected as soon as we come out of the last jump, and come out with the moon directly between us and the planet.
**1993** J. Pournelle & S. M. Stirling *Prince of Sparta* 17: They've got too much off-planet support.

**2.** to or from someplace other than a specific planet.

**1966** R. A. Heinlein *Moon Is Harsh Mistress* 176: Search of off-planet luggage was tight by then and conducted by bad-tempered Dragoons.

**1979** M. Z. Bradley *Bloody Sun* 24: You're no greenie, still bug-eyed about his first off-planet assignment!

**1982** I. Asimov *Foundation's Edge* 194: Apparently accustomed to off-planet guests, he had smiled paternally as Trevize and Pelorat gingerly scooped at the steaming bits of meat.

**1993** D. A. Smith *In Cube* 203: Private security rods, who lived in the Cube like everyone else, donned breeches, long hose [ ... ] and practiced archaic English, mock-arresting offplanet Tulguts or Adjawi for their podmates' vids.

**off-planet** *adv.* away from a specific planet; in or into space. Also used *fig.*

**1960** *Analog Sci. Fact-Fiction* (Oct.) 136/1: We might have to stick to the old-fashioned rocket to get off-planet.

**1967** K. Laumer *Thunderhead* in *Day Before Forever & Thunderhead* (1968) 154: He could be standing off-planet, looking over the ground.

**1979** M. Z. Bradley *Bloody Sun* 86: If I were you, I'd be on the first ship offplanet.

**1991** O. S. Card *Xenocide* 115: To him, going offplanet meant taking the shuttle to the orbiting station.

**1997** *Sunday Times (London)* (Oct. 26) (Getting Wired Supplement) 11/1 (*ad*): But what really takes this machine off-planet, is the way Mitsubishi combines a superb multimedia configuration with unique connectivity features.

**2005** M. Rosenblum *Green Shift* in *Asimov's SF* (Mar.) 110: She had never before been off-planet.

**off-trail** *adj.* (of a story) fantastic or science-fictional, especially regarding a story that is not easily categorized.

**1938** H. Kuttner *Selling Fantasy Story* in *Writer's Digest* (Mar.) 29/1: Once a few tricks are mastered, the fantasy is one of the easiest stories to write. And there are [ ... ] magazines such as *Argosy, Bluebook, Esquire*, etc., which occasionally run an off-trail yarn of this type.

**1945–46** S. Moskowitz *Immortal Storm* in *Fantasy Commentator* (Winter) 222: They avoid the "off-trail" story because it violates one or another of their editorial taboos, with the result that science-fiction has been sinking into the mire of the commonplace.

**1950** T. Carnell S. Skirvin *Cinvention Memory Book* 42: So, another hope for a British weird, or off-trail fantasy magazine was crushed almost before it started.

**1957** S. Moskowitz *How SF Got Its Name* in *Mag. of Fantasy & SF* (Feb.) 66/2: At first such tales were referred to as OFF-TRAIL STORIES, but this was too all-inclusive and could also mean anything from a story told in the second person to a western yarn with a Christmas setting.

**1975** E. Weinstein *Fillostrated Fan Dictionary* 95: Off Trail[ ... ]: Fantasy that does not fit into any of the usual types.

**off-world** *n.* **1.** someplace other than the planet one is on or referring to. Compare OFF-PLANET.

**1955** A. Norton *Star Guard* (1973) 49: Nature had provided him with a coat of thick curly hair, close in texture to the wool of a sheep, from which came a pungent, oily odor only apparent to those from off world.

**1960** H. Harrison *Deathworld* in *Astounding S-F* (Feb.) 131/2: You are from off-world, that I know. No junkman would have lifted a finger to save my life.

**1974** U. K. Le Guin *Dispossessed* 11: I was given the honor of attending you because of my experience with other visitors from offworld, the ambassadors from Terra and from Hain.

**2000** R. Shelley *Colonel* 13: There was little economic distress due to the almost constant influx of revenue from off-world.

**2.** a planet other than the homeworld.

**1987** *New York Times* (Apr. 5) 24/4: Harrison Ford plays a down-and-dirty police assassin, who has been sent into this underworld to find humanoid robots who have escaped from the offworld and come to earth to find their inventor.

**1995** *Columbian (Vancouver, Wash.)* (ProQuest) (Oct. 30): They centered the action on an offworld called Goblin.

**2000** A. E. Cowdrey *Crux* in *Mag. of Fantasy & SF* (Mar.) 44: But yokels from the offworlds visited Ulanor specifically to gaze upon the grave of this greatest (and bloodiest) Unifier of them all.

**off-world** *adj.* **1.** in space; not on a specific planet.
**1950** B. I. Kahn *Pinch of Culture* in *Astounding SF* (Aug.) 85/2: A ship with a weapon this far out meant an off-world patrol. Planets not expecting trouble would have no reason for watchful expectancy.
**1975** C. Holland *Floating Worlds* (2000) 208: If any of the rAkellaron want off-world markets arranged, we have to do it through you, don't we?
**1992** J. VanderMeer *Detectives & Cadavers* in *Secret Life* (2004) 147: Doomsayers convinced that the city's growing isolation from other Earth enclaves and off-world colonies was directly related to the muttie [sic] expulsion.
**2003** *Dreamwatch* (Aug.) 8/1: The season's 14th and 15th episodes see Fraiser shot and killed while trying to save an SGC member during an off-world fire fight.
**2.** from, of, or characteristic of someplace other than a specific planet.
**1955** A. Norton *Star Guard* (1973) 140: There is a space port near the Venturi holdings at Po'ult [...]. There is no regular schedule of ships, but off-world traders do come.
**1958** T. Sturgeon *Comedian's Children* in *Man Who Lost Sea* (2005) 119: Iapetitis cases underwent some strange undulations, and a hope arose that the off-world virus was losing its strength.
**1977** F. Herbert *Dosadi Experiment* 218: He saw that he would not be allowed to stay, but that he was expected to use his wits, his off-world knowledge.
**1984** S. R. Delany *Stars in My Pocket Like Grains of Sand* (2004) 335: One or two smiled, as if in acknowledgment of my offworld dress. (Save my slippers, I was naked.)
**2002** M. J. Harrison *Light* (2004) 14: He acted as an occasional middleman in what were sometimes called "off-world imports," goods and services inderdicted by Earth Military Contracts.

**off-world** *adv.* away from a specific planet; in or into space.
**1950** A. Coppel *Rebel of Valkyr* in *Planet Stories* (Fall) 8/1: "Where do you go now, Valkyr?" "Off-world."
**1970** A. Norton *Dread Companion* (1970) 16: In any event, I returned to the crèche [...] prepared to cut ties with my old life and lift off-world to a new.
**1982** A. Cole & C. Bunch *Sten* (1990) 16: Below The Eye was the cargo loading area, generally reserved for the Company's own ships. Independent traders docked offworld.
**1985** S. Sucharitkul *Alien Swordmaster* 6: You been off-world as long as me, you won't stand around lecturing people on correct military procedure.
**1992** *World Monitor* (Mar.) 36/1: Earth-dwellers might [...] benefit from the relocation of hazardous industry and materials "off-world."
**1998** K. W. Jeter *Mandalorian Armor* 46: The ship's engines trailed fire as it headed off-world.

**offworlder** *n.* someone from another planet.
**1957** A. Norton *Star Born* 187: It might be easy, now that he had established mental contact with this off-worlder, for the other to pick up a thought as vivid as that.
**1965** M. Z. Bradley *Star of Danger* (1985) 13: I've never spoken to an off-worlder! What is it like to travel in space?
**1978** V. N. McIntyre *Dreamsnake* (1979) 46: It was the place the offworlders sometimes landed.
**1991**: see quote in ON-WORLD, *adj.*
**1999** S. Dedman *Foreign Bodies* (2000) 17: Space travel, unfortunately, was still expensive, and the offworlders accepted only those they needed.

**oldspeak** *n.* in George Orwell's *Nineteen Eighty-Four*, standard English; in general use, plain or straightforward language or language (such as slang or jargon) that has been superseded by newer terminology. Compare NEWSPEAK.
**1949** [G. Orwell] *Nineteen Eighty-Four* 299: It was expected that Newspeak would have finally

superseded Oldspeak (or Standard English, as we should call it) by about the year 2050.

**1960** *Encounter* (Nov.) 10/1: The substitution of "Newspeak" for "Oldspeak" (or present-day English) is designed to effect nothing less than the destruction of human reason by linguistic means.
**1977** *Lincoln (Neb.) Star* (Apr. 18) 16/2: "Mrs. James Jones called police when her husband began breaking up the furniture." That was Oldspeak journalism.
**1990** E. Harth *Dawn of Millennium* 128: There is the art of *maintaining plausible deniability*, which in oldspeak might have been called "covering your tracks and lying through your teeth."
**1998** M. Ivins *Intelligencer Record (Doylestown, Pa.)* (July 23) A14/1: It was a lusty, brawling, wide-open place—a shot-and-a-beer town, and no place for sissies or goo-goos (oldspeak for good government reformers).
**2002** *Northern Times (Austl.)* (Nexis) (Sept. 13): I was using oldspeak, which designated ropes by their circumference. He spoke newspeak, which refers to rope by its diameter.

**on-planet** *adj.* located or occurring on a planet. Compare ON-WORLD, PLANETSIDE.
**1972** U. K. Le Guin *Word for World Is Forest* in H. Ellison *Again, Dangerous Visions* 37: Davidson didn't have a high regard for the Navy, a lot of fancy sunhoppers who left the dirty, muddy, dangerous on-planet work to the Army; but brass was brass, and anyhow it was funny to see Lyubov acting chummy with anybody in uniform.
**1972** J. Tiptree, Jr. *And I Have Come upon This Place by Lost Ways* in *Her Smoke Rose up Forever* (2004) 102: Since this is our last on-planet day, I would like to have it done soonest, sir, if you would.
**1988** [C. J. Cherryh] *Cyteen* 4: There were new on-planet technologies specific to Cyteen.
**1997** J. White *Final Diagnosis* (1998) 198: The arrival of massive medical aid from strangers would have been demeaning to them and might even have been mistaken by the on-planet imperial representative [...] as a hostile invasion from space...
**2003** C. Asaro *Skyfall* 75: Once, after an on-planet battle, Kurj had found a Trader girl huddled in the ruins of an installation.

**on-planet** *adv.* to or on a planet. Compare EARTHSIDE, GROUNDSIDE, ON-WORLD, PLANETSIDE.
**1953** A. Norton *Star Ranger* (1970s) 46: Mutiny! Kartr made himself consider it calmly. In space or on planet Vibor was the Commander of the Starfire.
**1972** U. K. Le Guin *Word for World Is Forest* in H. Ellison *Again, Dangerous Visions* 56: Lepannon and Or had not intended to come on-planet here at all.
**2001** C. Asaro *Spherical Harmonic* (2002) 275: We both knew perfectly well that if the Allieds got me on-planet, they wouldn't let me go.
**2002** M. J. Harrison *Light* (2004) 105: He lived four weeks in a freighter in the Tumblehome parking orbit while Dany Lebre was waiting for the unknown disease she caught on-planet to run its course.

**on-world** *adj.* ON-PLANET. Compare PLANETSIDE.
**1991** J. D. Vinge *Summer Queen* (2003) 383: She had gotten in ahead of all the offworlder entrepreneurs who had been clamoring at the palace gates, and down in Blue Alley, petitioning the onworld and offworld governments.
**2004** [C. J. Cherryh] *Forge of Heaven* 374: No one rebuked the woman, this eternal prisoner of the onworld establishment.
**2004** D. Moles *Third Party* in G. Dozois *Year's Best SF: Twenty-second Annual Coll.* (2005) 53: Cicero tried to remember Solon's face, and found that he couldn't, for all that they, and all the on-world missionaries, had trained together.

**on-world** *adv.* ON-PLANET. Compare EARTHSIDE, GROUNDSIDE, PLANETSIDE.
**1989** S. Perry *97th Step* 24: The Confed didn't think enough of Cibule to have more than a token contingent of administrators onworld.
**1996** D. Christian *Mainline* (1997) 132: She set him up, let him get snagged for a cargo she brought onworld.
**1997** P. Crowther *Killing of Davis-Davis* in B. Linaweaver & E. E. Kramer *Free Space* (1998) 175: His clones exist in every corner...offworld as well as onworld, hidden, waiting to be called to duty should the Davis-Davis on the island be killed.

**2003** C. Doctorow *Down & Out in Magic Kingdom* 8: I couldn't remember the last time I'd heard anyone on-world talk about personal space.

**orbital** *n.* a space station in orbit around a planet or star.

**1986** W. J. Williams *Hardwired* 131: The vast artificial intelligences that keep things moving smoothly for the Orbitals and the governments of the planet.

**2000** I. M. Banks *Look to Windward* (2002) 80: Overhead, the Orbital's far side was just a bright line, the details of its geography lost in that burnished filament.

**2005** M. Rosenblum *Green Shift Asimov's SF* (Mar.) 110: Xai had wanted the Huang Family to invest in the orbitals.

**organlegger** *n.* [*organ* + boot*legger*] someone who illegally removes organs from people or corpses and sells them to hospitals or people who need organ transplants. Hence **organlegging**, *n.*

**1967** L. Niven *Jigsaw Man* in H. Ellison *Dangerous Visions* 220: If the odds broke right, if the right people came down with the right diseases at the right time, the organlegger might save more lives than he had taken.

**1973** L. Niven *Defenseless Dead* in R. Elwood *Ten Tomorrows* 100: But he couldn't be part of an organlegging gang, could he?

**1987** R. Rucker *Wetware* in *Live Robots* (1994) 214: The organleggers took some of their organs right out of newly murdered people; others they purchased from the Moon.

**2003** F. P. Wilson *Sims* 260: Maybe they were stupid organleggers.

**other-dimensional** *adj.* of, in, or from another dimension.

**1934** C. L. Moore *Scarlet Dream* in *Weird Tales* (May) 579/2: When he lifted his eyes to the wall, he knew where he was. Blazoned on the dim stone, burning through the twilight like some other-dimensional fire, the scarlet pattern writhed across the wall.

**1948** *Startling Stories* (July) 127/2: Could be my double in one of those other-dimensional worlds, maybe?????

**1992** *Dragon Mag.* (Feb.) 71/3: The Celtic gods live in an other-dimensional realm known as Avalon.

**2006** G. K. Wolfe *Locus* 63/3 (Mar.): It isn't the sort of thing that can be outlined very coherently in snatches of dialogue from characters who are breathlessly zapping other-dimensional monsters called Jammervochs or fleeing enemy spacecraft.

**outplanet** *n.* an OUTWORLD. Compare RIMWORLD.

**1958** P. Ashwell *Unwillingly to School* in *Astounding SF* (Jan.) 30/2: M'Clare says that is my mistake, Earth had such a rush of sightseers from the Out Planets entrance not permitted any more except on business, only way I can get there is as a student.

**1964** P. K. Dick *Waterspider* in *Minority Report & Other Classic Stories* (2002) 235: To buy a ticket to Mars or the outplanets—routine in our age but utterly out of the question at mid twentieth century.

**1994** D. Doyle & J. D. Macdonald *By Honor Betray'd* 49: So many people in the outplanets thought that all Central Worlders were effete and foolish.

**1997** L. E. Modesitt, Jr. *Ecolitan Enigma* in *Ecolitan Prime* (2003) 344: They suggested, and attempted to carry out, a program which reduced social benefits in order to fund greater infrastructure development on the out[-]planets.

**outplanet** *adj.* on, of, or from another planet or outworld.

**1955** P. K. Dick *Mold of Yancy* in *Minority Report & Other Classic Stories* (2002) 55: There's constant industrial traffic in and out of Callisto; except for the Ganymede syndicate they've got out-planet commerce bottled up.

**1963** P. Anderson *After Doomsday* (1968) 47: So I got an assignment, to study any interesting outplanet mechanical techniques we might happen upon.

**1999** L. E. Modesitt, Jr. *Gravity Dreams* (2000) 176: How could they casually raise the types of questions I had raised and not be sent off to some outplanet station?

**2003** S. S. Tepper *Companions* (2004) 15: Out[-]planet visitors claim to find our separation conventions strange.

**outsystem** *adj.* in, of, or characteristic of another solar system or planets within another solar system; outside a solar system.

**1957** P. K. Dick *Unreconstructed M* in *Minority Report & Other Classic Stories* (2002) 120: Heimie had been mixed up in one of the sprawling slave combines that illegally transported settlers to outsystem fertile planets.

**1989** Jeff VanderMeer *Sea, Mendeho, & Moonlight* in *Secret Life* (2004) 59: A graveyard surrounded him, many of the creatures outsystem forms restructured by the bioneers.

**1993** J. Pournelle & S. M. Stirling *Prince of Sparta* 2: Given the sometimes extremely marginal habitability of the planets concerned [ ... ] and the endemic shortage of capital in the outsystem colonies, casualties among the transportees are often heavy.

**1995** A. D. Foster & E. F. Russell *Design for Great-Day* (1996) 101: We want to know how his ship slipped through the outsystem detection net, how it got past the orbital and atmospheric patrols.

**1997** L. E. Modesitt, Jr. *Ecolitan Enigma* (1998) 49: The probability of some form of armed conflict between the Empire and an outsystem coalition within twelve standard calendar months approaches unity.

**outsystem** *adv.* out of or outside a solar system; toward the edge of a solar system. Compare IN-SYSTEM.

**1957** P. K. Dick *Unreconstructed M* in *Minority Report & Other Classic Stories* (2002) 144: I've been told you can get carried out-system without papers.

**1964** B. Aldiss *Underprivileged* in D. Knight *Cities of Wonder* (1967) 201: I've seen people from out-system amazed at our microfab circuit before.

**1986** [C. J. Cherryh] *Chanur's Homecoming* 169: A destruct mechanism on the station might be set to blow on a signal sent from outsystem.

**1997**: see quote in JUMP GATE.

**1999** D. Simmons *Orphans of Helix* Worlds *Enough & Time* (2002) 86: The thousands of motes of light were headed outsystem, toward the *Helix*.

**outworld** *n.* a planet that is remote from the homeworld or central planets of a civilization. Compare OUTPLANET, RIMWORLD.

**1951** M. Lesser *"A" as in Android* in *Future* (May) 75/2: Orders are beginning to pour in from all over the outworlds.

**1962** [C. Smith] *Ballad of Lost C'Mell* in *Galaxy Mag.* (Oct.) 11/2: His daughter, C'mell, was a girlygirl, earning her living by welcoming human beings and hominids from the outworlds and making them feel at home when they reached Earth.

**1966** J. Brunner *Long Way to Earth* in *If* (Mar.) 10/2: Some of the less scrupulous companies had forcibly colonized outworlds by methods even less polite than the Dictatrix's: luring workers into their net with temptingly high salaries, then abandoning them light-years from any place where they could spend their earnings.

**1988** I. Asimov *Prelude to Foundation* 74: It is important that the officials of the Empire have some common ground [ ... ]. And they can't all be native Trantorians or else the Outworlds would grow restless.

**outworld** *adj.* on or from another planet, especially one remote from the homeworld or central planets of a civilization. Also **outworldish**, **outworldly**.

**1934** H. Bates *Matter of Size* in *Astounding Stories* (Apr.) 71/2: And when [ ... ] the great island that was its home began to sink under the surface of the sea, it was ready, and in thousands of space ships set forth, for some, out-world portions of the solar system, and the rest, to other and more stable parts of Earth.

**1934** H. Bates, *Matter of Size* in *Astounding Stories* 41/2: Who was the outworldly stranger?

**1950** A. Coppel *Rebel of Valkyr* in *Planet Stories* (Fall) 8/2: It was in the next chamber that the out-world warrior paused.

**1967** K. Laumer *Thunderhead* in *Galaxy Mag.* (Apr.) 16/2: Maybe it's some outworld sheep-herder amusing himself.

**1976** S. Engdahl & M. Butler *Timescape* in S. Engdahl *Anywhere, Anywhen* 285: We have learned quite a lot about Earth these past few weeks. It was not as outworld legends have portrayed it; the golden age of innocence is a myth.

**1986** A. C. Clarke *Songs of Distant Earth* 19: It was an awesome responsibility, facing only the second outworld spacecraft in the history of the planet.

**1998** I. Asimov *Prelude to Foundation* 34: The man with the teleprints had [...] looked up at him, more curiously this time—no doubt intrigued by his Outworldish clothing.

**outworlder** *n.* someone from an outworld; an alien.

**1934** H. Bates *Matter of Size* in *Astounding Stories* (Apr.) 41/1: The out-worlder smiled. He sat on a chair and removed one sandal, exposing a foot such as no man on Earth had ever yet possessed.

**1954** R. Sheckley *Milk Run* in *Galaxy* (Sept.) 120/2: Their visitor was an outworlder, to judge by his stocky frame, small head and pale green skin.

**1965** M. Z. Bradley *Star of Danger* (1985) 17: This is your first planet out from Earth? Oh, well, that explains it. After you've seen a couple, you'll realize that there's nothing out there but a lot of barbarians and outworlders.

**1972** A. D. Foster *Tar-Aiym Krang* 31: When the police discovered that the three corpses were outworlders, a search pattern would be put into effect with small delay. Murder was not conducive to increased tourism.

**1990** P. Anderson *Inconstant Star* in L. Niven, et al. *Man-Kzin Wars III* 174: Commercial and cultural as well as political center, it was bound to draw an undue share of outworlders and their influence.

**overdrive** *n.* a space drive that enables spaceships to travel faster than the speed of light. Also used *fig.* Compare HYPERDRIVE, ULTRADRIVE.

**1945** [M. Leinster] *First Contact* in *Astounding SF* (May) 9/2: A nebula is a gas. It is so thin that a comet's tail is solid by comparison, but a ship

traveling on overdrive—above the speed of light—does not want to hit even a merely hard vacuum.

**1953** A. Porges *Ruum* in *Mag. of Fantasy & SF* (Oct.) 25: The cruiser *Ilkor* had just gone into her interstellar overdrive beyond the orbit of Pluto when a worried officer reported to the Commander.

**1964** N. Spinrad *Outward Bound* in *Analog Sci. Fact-SF* (Mar.) 54/2: No, we don't have the secret of Overdrive. It is my opinion that there never will be an Overdrive. Man will never travel faster than light.

**1996** *Times (London)* (Nexis) (Jan. 27): This is an intergalactic adventure story laced with ironies [...]. Hamilton puts British sci-fi back into interstellar overdrive.

**overmind** *n.* a single, non-material consciousness composed of the consciousnesses of a large number of beings, often conceived of as the next or final stage of evolution. Often *cap.*

**1953** A. C. Clarke *Childhood's End* 202: There lay the Overmind, whatever it might be, bearing the same relation to man as man bore to the amoeba. Potentially infinite, beyond mortality, how long had it been absorbing race after race as it spread across the stars?

**1979** J. Varley *Titan* (1987) 286: The satellite brain that held sway over the territory was a tool of the overmind, and had not as yet developed a personality of his own.

**1998** R. J. Sawyer *Factoring Humanity* (2004) 327: For the first time in its existence, the overmind was aware of something else, of some*one* else.

**2003** J. C. Wright *Golden Transcendence* (2004) 68: Your Sophotechs have publicly admitted that their long-term goal is the extinction of all independent life, and the absorption of all thought into one eventual Cosmic Overmind, ruling over a cold universe of dead stars.

# Space Drives

Science fiction writers have, over the years, come up with a wide variety of ways to transport people (aliens, robots, etc.) through space. These are some of the more common ones.

Among the more plausible ones are those that do not allow a spaceship to exceed the speed of light. **Gravity drives** use some type of gravitic control to propel ships, while **torchships** are generally powered by nuclear fusion engines called **torch drives**. Vast electromagnetic "nets," called **ramscoops**, capture interstellar hydrogen for use in a fusion-powered drive. **Ion drives** provide thrust by means of a stream of electrically accelerated ions; this drive was even successfully tested by NASA in the late 1990s. Both ion drives and torch drives are technically varieties of **reaction drives**, which make use of Newton's law that every action has an equal and opposite reaction, and provide thrust by expelling something or other (the possibilities are endless) opposite the direction of travel. Any of these can be used to power a **generation ship**, which takes so long to reach its destination that only the distant descendants of the original crew will be alive when they do get there.

To tell a story about, say, a galactic empire, however, generally requires getting around the limits of slower-than-light travel. A common way around this inconvenient limitation is the **hyperdrive**, which enables starships to enter hyperspace, a region with different physical laws where the speed of light is not a barrier. Others use a **warp drive** that distorts the shape of the space-time continuum. **Jump drives** transport ships instantaneously from one point in space, sometimes called a **jump point**, to another. **Stargates** perform a similar function, much like a teleporter for spaceships. And if you don't feel like wasting time with some kind of theory, however sketchy, there are always the **ultradrive** and the **overdrive**, which at least sound like they should be fast. And sometimes, that may be all that is needed.

# p

**pangalactic** *adj.* GALAXY-WIDE. Compare TRANSGALACTIC.

**1977** J. L. Chalker *Midnight at Well of Souls* (2002) 390: It's interstellar, but not pangalactic. Population a little over one and a quarter trillion.

**1979** D. Adams *Hitchhiker's Guide to Galaxy* (1981) 21: It says the effect of drinking a Pan Galactic Gargle Blaster is like having your brains smashed out by a slice of lemon wrapped round a large gold brick.

**1980** J. Shirley *Final Paranoid Critical Statement* in *Thrust* (Fall) 23/2: A society of beetles part of a huge multi-cultured interstellar pangalactic civilization is going to be impressed by trapeze artists?

**2000** J. D. Vinge *Tangled Up in Blue* (2001) 92: Those legendary geniuses of the Pangalactic Interface's final days had created the sibyl net—a galaxy-spanning artificial intelligence network with living human beings as its ports.

**pantropy** *n.* [< Gk. *pan-*, "all" + Gk. *tropē*, "turning"] the modification of a human's physical body or genetic structure to allow them or their offspring to live on planets that would otherwise be uninhabitable. Hence **pantropic.** Compare TERRAFORMING.

**1952** J. Blish *Surface Tension* in *Galaxy* (Aug.) 6/2: You and I and the rest of us are going to die, Paul. Panatropic techniques don't work on the body, only on the inheritance-carrying factors.

**1952** J. Blish, in *Galaxy* 8/2: There may be just the faintest of residuums—panatropy's given us some data to support the old Jungian notion of ancestral memory.

**1957** M. Lesser *Name Your Tiger* in [Anon.] *Weird Ones* (1962) 56: They had all had pantropic conditioning; now they were Martians.

**1993** P. Nicholls in J. Clute & P. Nicholls *Ency. of SF* 907/2: *Man Plus* (1976) by Frederik Pohl, a novel that tackles several pantropy issues, prepares a man for living on Mars by changing him into a cyborg.

**2001** G. Dozois *Worldmakers* x: Redesigning humans so that they are able to survive on alien planets under alien conditions, has become known as "pantropy."

**parahuman** *n.* a genetically engineered or cyborgized human; a humanoid creature.

**1969** *Christian Century* (May 28) 743/1: A more sinister venture remains; namely the growth in vitro of parahumans, sometimes called cyborgs.

**1981** *Washington Post* (Nexis) (Aug. 21): "Parahumans," evolved from an ancestor common with ours. In other words, a Missing Link.

**1993** A. Toffler & H. Toffler *War & Anti-war* 122: The use of bioengineering or genetic engineering to alter soldiers or to breed "para-humans" to do the fighting.

**2005** R. Bailey *Liberation Biology* 172: Bioethicist Joseph Fletcher once suggested that it would be ethical to create parahumans, that is, human/animal hybrids to do dangerous and demeaning jobs.

**parahuman** *adj.* subhuman or superhuman; (of a being) derived or evolved from ordinary humans. Hence **parahumanity,** *n.*

**1944** O. Stapledon *Sirius* (1972) 198: It was at once human and "para-human," so that she seemed to me not so much cat as fay.

**1960** *Encounter* (May) 79/1: An obscene old woman who runs a gang of sub- or para-human creatures.

**1966** *Daily Gleaner (Kingston, Jam.)* (Nov. 25) 14/6: The production of para-humanity by clonal methods would set enormous problems for our theologians and moralists.

**1991** R. Hardin *Penetrabit: Slime-Temples* in L. McCaffery *Storming Reality Studio* 78: Even a disc galaxy follows this rococo pathology: its tentacles of stars are ragged whorls. A para-human architect is endlessly sketching cochlear temples to its own vacant energies.

**1993** *Orlando Sentinel* (ProQuest) (Jan. 15): X-Men tracks the adventures of a group of young mutants born with parahuman abilities—some physical, some psychic—which have rendered them outcasts from society.

**2003** P. Anderson *For Love & Glory* (2004) 43: Consciousness on Earth—human, parahuman, quantum-net—is not joined in one entity.

**parallel universe** *n.* a universe or space-time continuum that exists alongside ours, and which may possess different physical laws or a different history. Also used *fig.* Compare PARALLEL WORLD.

**1923** H. G. Wells *Men like Gods* 55: We conceive ourselves to be living in a parallel universe to yours, on a planet the very brother of your own.

**1968**: see quote in ALTERNATE WORLD.

**1992** P. David *Imzadi* 25: It's something that has been considered [ ... ] that parallel universes are, in fact, alternative time tracks.

**1994** *Interzone* (Jan.) 10/2: Don't tell me you don't get it! Look, I'm an alternate you from a parallel universe, *capeche*?

**2001** M. Azerrad *Our Band Could Be Your Life* 190: It was definitely a parallel universe, [ ... ] a subculture that had no mainstream intentions at all.

**2002** *Scientific American* (Mar.) 26/2: Another brane—a parallel universe—resides a subsubatomic distance away.

**parallel world** *n.* a PARALLEL UNIVERSE.

**1931** B. Herbert *World Within* in *Wonder Stories* (Aug.) 313/1: The disconcerting change of direction of gravity, catching him unawares while passing along the fourth dimension from that tri-dimensional parallel world so near to ours [ ... ] proved too much for his weakened condition.

**1952** R. A. Heinlein *Letter* (July 16) in R. A. Heinlein & V. Heinlein *Grumbles from Grave* (1990) 224: I do have about three cops-and-robbers jobs which I can do, one a parallel-worlds yarn and the other two conventional space opera.

**1974** *Scientific American* (May) 122/3: He outlines a metatheory in which the universe at every micromicroinstant branches into countless parallel worlds.

**1990** *Thrust* (Winter) 7/3: However, Card's tornado of magic is a far cry from [ ... ] *Unicorn Mountain*, where unicorns suffer from swamp fever and TV programs originate from a parallel world.

**1994** *Analog SF & Fact* (Jan.) 128/1: Our world is just one of an infinite family of "parallel worlds" in which every combination of possibilities occurs.

**2002** A. Reynolds *Redemption Ark* (2004) 115: The idea of parallel worlds had long been at least one conceptual underpinning of quantum theory.

**parking orbit** *n.* a temporary orbit around a planet or other body, taken e.g. by a spaceship prior to landing, in order to send a landing party to the surface, or prior to launching further into space, etc.

**1953** R. A. Heinlein *Starman Jones* 203: They hung in parking orbit while their possible future home was examined from the control room.

**1958** R. Silverberg *Prime Commandment* in *Original SF Stories* (Jan.) 6/1: Even had the strangers come that night, if they had left their ship in a parking orbit and landed on World by dropshaft, it might not have happened.

**1962** *New York Times* (Sept. 13) 16/1: Under this method, a lunar rocket would be formed by a rendezvous of parts orbiting the earth. It would blast off from that parking orbit and land on the moon.

**1967** J. Blish *Star Trek* 79: The planet's effective mass would change, and perhaps even its

center of gravity [ ... ] so that what had been a stable parking orbit for the *Enterprise* at one moment would become unstable and fragment-strewn the next.
**2002**: see quote in ON-PLANET, *adv.*

**passifan** *n.* (pl. **-fans, -fen**) [*passi*ve + *fan*] a science fiction fan who does not actively participate in fan activites, such as publishing a fanzine, organizing conventions, writing letters to magazines, etc. Compare ACTIFAN.
**ca 1944** F. J. Ackerman *Fantasy Flanguage* in [Anon.] *What Is Science Fiction Fandom* 32: *Passifan:* The "unawakened" Fan, interested now only in reading the magazines and books; not yet participating in any activities.
**1948** R. Sneary *Startling Stories (letter)* (Sept.) 124/2: By interesting the pasi[-]fans that write me in ative [sic] fandom, I draw in a little new blood.
**1952** J. Harmon *Thrilling Wonder Stories (letter)* (Dec.) 133/1: I learned that last phrase from a femme passifan Miss Marlene Maples.
**1959** R. H. Eney *Fancyclopedia II* 56: Depending on the extent to which a given fan indulges in anything more than local club activity he may be distinguished as an actifan (as opposed to passifen); stress on crifanac rather than con-going, among actifans, is the chief extensional distinction between trufans and confans.
**1975** E. Weinstein *Fillostrated Fan Dictionary* 98: Passifan[ ... ]: The opposite of Actifan; one not involved with much fanac.

**personalzine** *n.* a fanzine or zine written and published by a single person. Compare PERZINE.
**1975** E. Weinstein *Fillostrated Fan Dictionary* 99: Personalzine[ ... ]: A fanzine written by a single person, generally about his fannish and mundane activities.
**2000** J. D. Smith in [J. Tiptree, Jr.] *Meet Me at Infinity* 188 (2001): There were two main types of fanzines in the seventies, the large "genzines" [ ... ] and the small "personalzines" (which were mostly editor-written, sometimes by fans who proudly stated that they had stopped reading SF when they discovered fandom).
**2004** B. Stableford *Historical Dictionary of SF Literature* 109: By 2000 there were more than 500 sf fanzines, ranging from small "person-alzines" through "reviewzines" and "newszines" to serious critical journals.
**2004** *e-National Fantasy Fan* (Mar.) 13: Peterson [ ... ] has been publishing his personal zine for years.

**perzine** *n.* a PERSONALZINE.
**1975** E. Weinstein *Fillostrated Fan Dictionary* 99: Perzine[ ... ]: A *per*sonal *zine.*
**2002** C. Atton *Alternative Media* 64: Though nominally a fanzine, editor Fred Tomsett's "tour diaries" function in similar fashion to the perzine accounts of Aaron Cometbus.
**2004** S. Glasgow *National Fantasy Fan* (Jun.) 22/1: In fact, I started my second perzine for N'APA the day after I got the first issue.

**phaser** *n.* an energy weapon that fires a beam which can be set to varying degrees of intensity. Also used *fig.* [In SF, primarily associated with the *Star Trek* universe.]
**1966** G. Roddenberry *Memo* (Apr. 26) in S. E. Whitfield & G. Roddenberry *Making of "Star Trek"* (1968) 272: Reference the mating of various components of the phaser weapons [ ... ] when the hand phaser is mated to the pistol, they should appear as *one weapon.*
**1968** S. E. Whitfield in S. E. Whitfield & G. Roddenberry *Making of "Star Trek"* 166: A number of early changes were simply an effort to keep Star Trek's technology ahead of present-day scientific developments. This was the reason Gene [ ... ] discarded the term "Laser," substituting the term "Phaser."
**1968** G. Coon *Arena ("Star Trek" script)* (Nov. 3) 9: We've returned fire with all phaser banks. Negative against his deflector screen.
**1995** *THIS Mag.* (July) 21/2: His oddly reserved nature stands out [ ... ]. Whyte sets his phaser on stun, not kill. In print and in person, he usually gives a nod to his opponents before letting fly.
**1998** M. Flynn *Rogue Star* (1999) 98: "Set phasers on stun," Forrest agreed. Krasnarov raised his head from his eyepiece and gave him an irritated look. Forrest energized the laser.
**2004** *Heritage Signature Auction #811* 185/1: Giolitti's Gold Key art is widely admired, [ ... ] and this is a terrific opportunity to pick up a page—set your phasers on bid.

**plane** *n.* [extended from mystical usage, "a level of spiritual being or existence"] a DIMENSION.

[**1919** R. Cummings *Girl in Golden Atom in* L. Margulies & O. J. Friend *Giant Anthology of SF* (1954) 119: I have thought about it a good deal, and I have reached the conclusion that the inhabitants of any universe in the next smaller or larger plane to ours probably resemble us fairly closely.]

**1927** G. P. Bauer *Below Infra Red* in *Amazing Stories* (Dec.) 883/2: There is much food for thought, or speculation in the thought that there exist sound-waves that no ear can hear, and color-waves that no eye can see. [...] THERE MAY BE BEINGS WHO LIVE IN DIFFERENT PLANES FROM OURSELVES, AND WHO ARE ENDOWED WITH SENSE-ORGANS LIKE OUR OWN, ONLY THEY ARE TUNED TO HEAR AND SEE IN A DIFFERENT SPHERE OF MOTION.

**1930** E. E. Repp *Red Dimension* in *Sci. Wonder Stories* (Jan.) 698/2: Yet I mean just what I say about the planes of existence below and above our senses of vision and hearing.

**1946–47** B. Walton *Princess of Chaos* in *Planet Stories* (Dec.–Feb.) 115/2: Our scientists call them plains [sic] [...]. But they are really worlds coexistent with this one.

**1953** [R. Dee] *Minister Had to Wait* in *Planet Stories Fantastic Universe* (June–July) 142/2: From superspace, the plane of existence immediately above ours [...]. The energy backlash from our generator must have weakened the spatial barrier between dimensions.

**1963** K. Laumer *Long Remembered Thunder* in *Nine by Laumer* (1967) 151: A point of material contact between the Niss world and this plane of space-time.

**2002** U. K. Le Guin *Social Dreaming of Frin* in *Mag. of Fantasy & SF* (Oct./Nov.) 178: On the Frinthian plane dreams are not private property.

**planetary engineering** *n.* the large-scale modification of the environment or geography of a planet. Compare TERRAFORMING.

[**1932** J. Williamson *Electron Flame in Wonder Stories Quarterly* (Fall) 88/2: Bought the satellite for his private estate. Had planetary engineers make all modern improvements.]

**1936** J. Williamson *Cometeers* in *Astounding Stories* (July) 129/1: "Planetary engineering is expensive, Bob," Jay Kalam said. "Especially when the equipment would have to be brought so far. It would have been nearly impossible for any one to develop such a remote asteroid secretly—"

**1951** A. C. Clarke *Exploration of Space* 118: The greatest technical achievements of the next few centuries may well be in the field of what could be called "planetary engineering"—the reshaping of other worlds to suit human needs.

**1964** *Listener* (Oct. 15) 575/1: It will be possible to modify the climates and atmospheres of at least some of the planets, so that we can live on them [...]. This technique of the future has been called "planetary engineering."

**2002** A. Reynolds *Redemption Ark* (2004) 339: Planetary engineering, obviously. They ripped apart three worlds for this, Ana.

**2005** K. S. Robinson *Fifty Degrees Below* 306: A grand exercise in planetary engineering that was exciting worldwide attention, funding, and controversy.

**planetary romance** *n.* a genre of science fiction that describes an adventure taking place on a planet's surface, especially in which the description of the planet is integral to the story; a work in this genre.

**1978** R. Letson *Intro.* in P. J. Farmer *Green Odyssey* v: The major tradition is the subgenre which may be called the planetary romance. This subgenre is distinguished from its close cousins, the space opera and the sword and sorcery fantasy, by its setting (an exotic, technologically primitive planet), although it shares with them the adventure-plot conventions of chases, escapes, and quests.

**1993** J. Clute in J. Clute & P. Nicholls *Ency. of SF* (1995) 934/2: Any sf tale whose primary venue [...] is a planet, and whose plot turns to a significant degree upon the nature of that venue, can be described as a planetary romance.

**1999** M. Dirda *Bound to Please* (2005) 226: He started writing a novel, *A Princess of Mars*, the first in his planetary romances about the swashbuckling adventures of John Carter.

**2000** D. Pringle *What Is This Thing Called Space Opera* in G. Westfahl *Space & Beyond* 45: Sf *is* space opera, or to a lesser extent

planetary romance. [ ... ] To the world at large, science fiction is adventure stories set in outer space or on other planets.
**2002** N. Gevers *Washington Post* (Apr. 7) 5/4: Wolfe weaves intricately together the different strands of his planetary-romance plot, thereby achieving an inclusiveness of texture that [ ... ] has more than a hint of utopian promise.

**planet-bound** *adj.* unable or unwilling to go into space; of someone or something that is unable to go into space. Also as *n.*
**1944** L. Brackett *Veil of Astellar* in *Best of Leigh Brackett* (1977) 77: Things can change. You planet-bound people build your four little walls of thought and roof them in with convention, and you think there's nothing else. But space is big.
**1951** J. H. Schmitz *Space Fear* in *Astounding SF* (Mar.) 13/1: And as Ulphi's entire population was planet-bound by congenital space-fear, the skiff would provide any required amount of transportation.
**1957** T. Sturgeon *It Opens Sky* in *Man Who Lost Sea* (2005) 53: It wouldn't hurt the ship, [ ... ] but the less resilient planet-bound object would not be so fortunate.
**1958** G. H. Smith *Outcasts SF Stories* (Sept.) 101/2: We have a purpose that you planet-bounds seem to lack.
**1960** A. E. Nourse *Nine Planets* 280: Conceivably, the cosmic histories will look upon the First Era of any intelligent race as the planetbound era.
**1987** O. Butler *Dawn* (1991) 36: It would die without us and we would be planetbound without it.
**2003** R. Blackford *New York Rev. of SF* (Jan.) 22/1: By our standards, the gods are inscrutable and amoral, treating planet-bound intelligences such as human beings much as we tend to treat non-human animals.

**planet-buster** *n.* a PLANET-WRECKER. Hence planet-busting, *adj.* Compare PLANET-KILLER, PLANET-SMASHER.
**1950** B. Vanier *Planet Buster!* in *Amazing Stories* (Feb.) 162/2: What will the future be like? No physicists have testified to a limit to bomb size. Does this mean that maybe in ten or twenty years actual "planet-busters" will be made?

**1956** J. J. Ferrat *Testing* in *Fantastic Universe* (Mar.) 115/2: Somebody had slipped when Marshal Wellington Smith selected Rigel IV for his planet-busting test.
**1962** H. B. Piper *Space Viking* in *Analog Sci. Fact-SF* (Nov.) 38/2: I don't see anything to shoot. Five hundred miles; one planetbuster, or four or five thermonuclears.
**1974** R. Bretnor *SF in Age of Space* in R. Bretnor *SF, Today & Tomorrow* 171: We still find World War I aerial dogfights being reintroduced as individual combats between pilots of spaceships armed with planet-busters.
**1986** [J. Tiptree, Jr.] *Collision* in *Isaac Asimov's SF Mag.* (May) 157: We don't have to worry about being shot at; those planet-buster missiles are too big and slow to hit a small mobile target.
**1997** *Interzone* (Dec.) 12/1: You could see it, across a quarter of a million miles, the surface of the Mare Imbrium billowing up into space, as the demonstration planet-buster went off beneath it, a quarter of the Moon's old grey face convulsing in an instant.

**planeteer** *n. Obs.* someone who travels to or explores other planets.
**1927** T. I. Saarela *Amazing Stories (letter)* (Dec.) 908/3: Speaking of reprints, I should like to suggest a few that I should be glad to meet again. "The Planeteer" and its sequel [ ... ] are the best interplanetary stories I have ever read.
**1938** *Thrilling Wonder Stories* (Oct.) 74: Two roving planeteers confront the invisible imps of an empire from beyond the sun and discover that matter is mightier than mind.
**1956** I. Melchior *Vidiot* in *Fantastic Universe* (Mar.) 52/1: "It's like this," he began to explain. [ ... ] "The "Planeteer" has landed and is walking around on the satellite in his space suit. We'll play the whole thing in front of the black drop and put in electronic stars."
**1961** D. Jacobs *Spacey Jones* in *Reprints from SING OUT! Folk Song Mag. Vol. 3* 60: Come all ye spacemen if you want to hear, The story of a great planeteer.
**1961** F. Saberhagen *Planeteer* in *Galaxy Mag.* (Apr.) 11/1: The twenty planeteers who were going down into atmosphere, plus two reserve crews, slouched in their seats and scribbled notes and whispered back and forth about business

**planetfall** *n.* [modeled after *landfall*] the arrival of a spaceship or space-traveler on a planet's surface. Often as *phrasal v.*, **make planetfall.** Compare EARTHFALL.

**1944** G. O. Smith *Off Beam* in *Astounding SF* (Feb.) 6/2: Any message-answering would have to be done thirty hours later, when the ship made planetfall.

**1956** T. Sturgeon *Claustrophile* in *And Now News...* (2003) 102: The ship wasn't designed to make planetfall; it was an orbital, true-space vessel.

**1969** R. Silverberg *Across Billion Years* 212: Some five thousand meters from planetfall he cut the engines and we slipped back into parking orbit.

**1979** M. Z. Bradley *Bloody Sun* 16: The ship was making planetfall for a world called Terra.

**1997** G. K. Wolfe *Locus* 18/1 (Oct.): "I landed and stepped out" is the way a narrator bluntly describes planetfall.

**planet-killer** *n.* a PLANET-WRECKER. Compare PLANET-BUSTER, PLANET-SMASHER. [1959 quote is most likely a reference to people, rather than weapons.]

[**1959** R. Silverberg (title): The Planet Killers.]

**1987** G. Bear *Forge of God* 294: But perhaps it's not a battle at all; just part of the demolition and making of more planet-killer probes.

**1999** M. Reilly *Temple* (2002) 63: A planet killer. A nuclear device so powerful that when detonated, it would completely destroy nearly a third of the Earth's mass.

**2001** M. Flynn *Falling Stars* (2002) 6: The Bean isn't a planet-killer; and most of them don't really believe it will hit us at all.

**planetographer** *n.* someone who studies or maps planets.

**1937** E. E. Smith *Galactic Patrol* in *Astounding Stories* (Nov.) 141/2: Truly, it must be a powerful superstition, indeed, to make that crew of hard-boiled hellions choose certain death rather than face again the imaginary [...] perils of a planet unknown to and unexplored by Boskone's planetographers.

**1961** P. Anderson *Day After Doomsday* in *Galaxy Mag.* (Dec.) 10/2: Kunz the astronomer and Easterling the planetographer were still hunched over their instruments.

**1970** [H. Clement] *Star Light* in *Analog SF-Sci. Fact* (Sept.) 140/1: One of the planetographers remarked that you couldn't blame the eddy on Coriolis force because the lake was only seven degrees from the equator.

**1996** R. Silverberg *Starborne* 113: The ideal exploration party, it seems to me, would include one biologist, one planetographer, and, of course, one man to operate and do necessary maintenance work on the vehicle the party uses.

**planetography** *n.* the study or mapping of planets. Hence **planetographical**, *adj.*

**1955** P. Anderson *Long Way Home* in *Astounding SF* (Apr.) 39/1: Planetography's a sort of hobby with me, which is the only reason I come to your parties, Valti, you kettle-bellied old fraud. Tell me, captain, did you ever touch at Procyon?

**1969** B. Walton *Troubling of Star* in *Venture SF Mag.* (May) 99/2: He dragged out a protractor, heliocentric chart, photometer, astrographical and planetographical references.

**1974** L. Niven & J. Pournelle *Mote in God's Eye* (1975) 244: The physical features of Mote Prime are of some interest, particularly to ecologists concerned with the effects of intelligent life on planetography.

**1997** J. A. Gardner *Expendable* (1997) 68: His programming skills were at least as good as mine, and his planetography intuition was superb.

**planetscape** *n.* [modeled after *landscape*] the surface geography of a planet; a pictorial representation of the surface of a planet.

**1990** A. Steele *Clarke County, Space* 221: It bounced across the planetscape, brown smoke farting from its rear and rivets shaking loose from the seams, before puttering into the sky.

**1991** R. Rogow *Futurespeak* 252: Planetscapes of Mars and Venus have been derived from information received from the Voyager and Venera probes.

**2000** B. Eggleton *Greetings from Earth* 65/2: I started painting a planetscape the way they were supposed to be and upon finishing, or so I thought, I then realized something was missing.

**2004** B. Herbert & K. J. Anderson *Dune: Battle of Corrin* 144: During the javelin's final approach, he stood looking out at the planetscape.

**planetside** *n.* the surface of a planet; a base or other installation on a planet. Compare GROUNDSIDE.

**1959** D. A. Wollheim *Secret of Ninth Planet* 37: Completing the members of the expedition was another trio chosen to act as [ ... ] a trained explorer-fighter unit while on planetside.

**1979** B. Longyear *Dueling Clowns* in *Isaac Asimov's SF Mag.* (Mar.) 138: The rules for visiting planetside are being observed, aren't they?

**2003** S. Westerfeld *Killing of Worlds* 186: When he'd first been assigned to planetside, Private Akman had been glad to escape the *Lynx*.

**planetside** *adj.* on a planet; located or occurring on the surface of a planet. Compare EARTHSIDE, GROUNDSIDE, ON-PLANET, ON-WORLD.

**1955** [A. North] *Sargasso of Space* (1957) 22: The frontier world where they set down at its end was enough like Terra to be unexciting too. Not that Dane got any planet-side leave.

**1963** H. B. Piper *Space Viking* 35: And the ill-feeling on the part of other captains and planetside employers about the men he'd lured away from them.

**1979** M. Z. Bradley *Bloody Sun* 64: The greenest kid, on his first planetside assignment, ought to know better than that!

**1985** S. Sucharitkul *Alien Swordmaster* 11: They were capturing people and salting them away for planetside consumption.

**2005** M. Rosenblum *Green Shift* in *Asimov's SF* (Mar.) 109: She slung her slightly scuffed business brief over her shoulder, looking like your basic mid-level Assist running the boss's errand from the planetside business headquarters.

**planetside** *adv.* to or on a planet. Compare EARTHSIDE, GROUNDSIDE, ON-PLANET, ON-WORLD.

**1955** P. J. Farmer *Father* in *Mag. of Fantasy & SF* (July) 4/1: Though it was well known that he felt a little ridiculous when he wore it planetside, when he was on his ship he walked as a man clad in armor.

**1957** H. Ellison *Run for Stars* in *Touch of Infinity* (1959) 41: Every able-bodied man had been sent planetside to search for the bomb.

**1974** J. Haldeman *Forever War* (1976) 105: We went planetside in two scoutships.

**1990** A. McCaffrey & J. L. Nye *Death of Sleep* (1992) 7: During her remaining days planetside, she had turned over her laboratory work to a co-worker.

**2005** *Subterranean Press Newsletter* (Nov. 21): They include [ ... ] *John Scalzi's* dialogue of a space warrior returning planet-side.

**planet-smasher** *n.* a PLANET-WRECKER. Hence **planet-smashing,** *adj.* Compare PLANET-BUSTER, PLANET-KILLER.

**1947** [M. Leinster] *Propagandist* in *Astounding S-F* (Aug.) 140/1: She was impersonating a barren visitor from the void, spying out the ground for what would be—if she was successful—the monstrous destruction of an entire race by planet-smasher guided missiles and the merciless weapons of an Earth fleet.

**1951** T. Sturgeon *Traveling Crag* in *Baby Is Three* (1999) 160: The ultimate weapon—invented after the planet-smasher, the sun-burster—what incredible thing could it be?

**1952** K. F. Slater *If* (Mar.) 150/2: The same reasoning [ ... ] tends to me to prove the use of the atom-bomb and the planet-smasher improbable in space-war.

**1990** P. Anderson *Beer Mutterings* in *Quantum* (Spring) 14/1: I got to wondering if you really could or should keep the peace with planet-smashing weapons.

**1992** V. Vinge *Fire upon Deep* (1993) 423: "Sjanda Kei never expected the planet-smasher attack. So when the Alliance fleet showed up, ours moved out to meet it—" "—and meantime the KE bombs were coming straight in to the heart of Sjanda Kei."

**planet-wrecker** *n.* an extremely powerful weapon, capable of destroying all of, or large portions of, a planet. Hence **planet-wrecking,** *adj.* Compare PLANET-BUSTER, PLANET-KILLER, PLANET-SMASHER.

**1946** E. F. Russell *Metamorphosite* in *Astounding SF* (Dec.) 12/2: They destroyed both ships with one atomic bomb. Later, a task ship arrived, took the stern action we deemed necessary, and dropped a planet wrecker. The world dissolved into flashing gases.

**1959** J. J. McGuire *To Catch Alien* in F. Pohl *Star SF No. 6* 120: It wasn't a freighter, of course, but a drone ship carrying a planet-wrecker.

**1996** O. S. Card *Children of Mind* (1997) 181: Will we have communicated with these descoladores, these aliens who send out planet-wrecking probes?

**1999** V. Vinge *Deepness in Sky* (2000) 491: Not even planet-wrecker bombs had as dire a reputation for eliminating civilizations.

**plasteel** *n.* [*plas*tic + *steel*] a strong, durable artificial substance that either is a blend of plastic and steel or combines attributes of both plastic and steel.

**1956** H. Ellison *Trojan Hearse* in *Infinity SF* (Aug.) 101/1: There was a momentary silence, then the plasteel-armored guards fired at the spot.

**1977** *Times (London)* (July 19) 6/5 (ad): 80,000 m² of super-stressed multi-panelled flexiglass over a concranium-coated plasteel frame and the architect thinks he could get a design award.

**1984** A. McCaffrey *Survivors: Dinosaur Planet II* (ca 1992) 41: Even a heavyworlder would have had to grunt to bash the sturdy plasteel frame and body skin.

**1985** G. R. R. Martin *Analog SF/Sci. Fact* (mid-Dec.) 32/1: Roggandor's cyborg ambassador was as broad as he was tall, made in equal parts of stainless duralloy, dark plasteel, and mottled red-black flesh.

**1993** H. Harrison *Golden Years of Stainless Steel Rat* in *Stainless Steel Visions* 246: This stripped away the surface plastic that covered the far harder plasteel of the flexible saw inside.

**2002** M. Swanwick *Under's Game* in *SciFi.com* (Internet): Their vectors take them right through the Sun's corona. Their hulls are plasteel—they can take the heat.

**plastiskin** *n.* [*plas*tic + *skin*] artificial skin.

**1953** A. Norton *Star Rangers* 22: Again he wished he could see the expression on the face under that roll upon roll of white plasta-skin.

**1977** G. Wolfe *Marvelous Brass Chessplaying Automaton* in *Storeys from Old Hotel* (1988)

123: Herr Heitzmann, with his appearance considerably altered by a plastiskin mask, left also.

**1987** M. O'Donnell *Nice & Nasty* 17: My plastiskin was added over my exoskeleton.

**1994** S. Barnes *Firedance* (1995) 17: Her plastiskin, the light-conductive plastic on the left side of her body, crackled and arced in time with the music. [ ... ] The artificial flesh was warm, soft, and resilient, porous enough to carry her sweat to the air, or to his tongue.

**1999** M. J. Friedman *My Brother's Keeper* 223: Producing a plastiskin seal, she applied it to the damaged area.

**Plutonian** *n.* an inhabitant of the planet Pluto.

**1931** S. H. Coblentz *Into Plutonian Depths* in *Wonder Stories Quarterly* (Spring) 323/2: Not less than eight or ten distinguished-looking Plutonians had been summoned for the occasion.

**1934** [L. F. Stone] *Rape of Solar System* in D. A. Wollheim *Flight into Space* (1950) 242: From the first, Luna's was a losing battle. Together the Martians and Plutonians drove her back, passed on to earth.

**1947–48** R. A. Bradley *Planet Stories (letter)* (Dec.–Jan.) 121/1: And *don't* expect the Plutonians to send you back. I'm sending you to Sirius!

**1959** D. A. Wollheim *Secret of Ninth Planet* 168: They had found inscriptions on walls [ ... ]. They knew from these what the Plutonians had looked like, and they had a suspicion of what had happened.

**1998** J. Varley *Golden Globe* 78: What a shame no Plutonians actually came out here for a sleigh ride, or to picnic by the little brooks a-gurgling.

**pocket universe** *n.* an artificially created universe that exists within the bounds of another universe. Also used *fig.*

**1946** [M. Leinster] *Pocket Universes* in *Thrilling Wonder Stories* (Fall) 82/2: You used that extensible contrivance, and made a pocket universe that reached from the inside of his baggage to where you were.

**1970** P. J. Farmer *Behind Walls of Terra* 4: Kickaha had been transmitted into an artificial universe, a pocket universe, created by a Lord named Jadawin.

**1980** S. Robinson *Have You Heard One...?* in *Time Travelers Strictly Cash* (2001) 159: No, *compadres*, [...] it is not a hole-o-graph. It is a hyperpocket, a dimensional bridge to a... ahem...pocket universe. *Regardez!*

**1983** G. Gygax *Deities & Demigods of World of Greyhawk* in *Dragon Mag.* (Jan.) 27/1: No one knows where (or when) Istus makes her abode. Some savants postulate that there is a nexus linking the other planes of existence to a pocket universe which only she, and her webs of fate, can enter or exit.

**1996** W. Gibson *Idoru* 163: It was, the Belgian said, as though the city, in its convulsion and grief, had spontaneously and necessarily generated this hidden pocket universe of the soul.

**pod person** *n.* [< *pod*, in Jack Finney's *The Body Snatchers*, and 1956 film adaptation *The Invasion of the Body Snatchers*, an alien, plant-like lifeform capable of relicating a person exactly, killing them in the process (see 1955 quote)] an alien or monster; a stupid person; someone who is not what they seem to be. [1956 quote is from an advertisement for *The Invasion of the Body Snatchers*.]

[**1955** J. Finney *Body Snatchers* (1976) 153: The pods are a parasite on whatever life they encounter. [...] They have the ability to reform and reconstitute themselves into perfect duplication, cell for living cell, of any life form they may encounter.]

**1956** *Post-Standard (Syracuse, New York)* (Mar. 12) 21 (ad): Watch out! The whole world taken over by the pod people!

**1980** *Post-Standard (Syracuse, New York)* (May 12) C3/1: But as a dramatic actress, she can barely utter a sentence properly. She has this vacant-eyed look that sometimes reminds you of the pod-people in "Invasion of the Body Snatchers."

**1986** *Post-Standard (Syracuse, New York)* (Oct. 4) H12/1: But the goo, like a preternatural pod person, tended to swallow the sitter.

**1989** *Chronicle-Telegram (Elyria, Oh.)* (Oct. 29) D10/3: The majority of the sins [...] can be traced upstairs to Tower B, where the pod people sit in suits making decisions guaranteed to tunnel the team under.

**1997** *React* in *Syracuse (New York) Herald-Journal* (Dec. 1–7) 8/2: Is this guy the real McCoy or a pod person?

**2004** *San Francisco Chronicle* (Sept. 7) E10/3: Now put one in the microwave. Will that unleash the power of the space-o-tron pod people? It's worth a shot.

**positronic** *adj.* of, using, or powered by positrons.

**1941** I. Asimov *Reason* in *Astounding S-F* (May) 44/1: By exact count, there are seventy-five thousand, two hundred and thirty-four operations necessary for the manufacture of a single positronic brain.

**1968** *Punch* (Oct. 23) 592/2: Barbarella (Jane Fonda), a respected astronaut in 40,000 AD, is being briefed for her mission to find an important scientist from Earth who has disappeared among the planets with his great invention the positronic ray.

**1995** P. David *Captain's Daughter* 16: Thousands of landing-party assignments had been fed into a vast database, processed through positronic circuitry as perfected in the M9 computer.

**2005** *Onion* (June 23) 4/3: I want these automatons to get it into their intricate positronic brains that some parts of the human body are off limits, no matter how much human women plead.

**post-apocalypse** *adj.* following a large-scale disaster in which civilization has been destroyed or has regressed to a more primitive level; (of a story) having such a setting. Compare POST-APOCALYPTIC, POST-CATASTROPHE, POST-HOLOCAUST.

**1970** J. R. Frakes *Washington Post Book World* (Oct. 18) 2/3: The time is post-apocalypse; the setting, the flats west of the city, a kind of terminal chessboard where every space must be staked out.

**1976** *Times (London)* (Feb. 5) 11/4: Grimly visionary story on the usual post-apocalypse theme, with magic having superseded science as the basis of the last remaining State, and a lone stranger battling it out with malign forces.

**1979** B. Searles, et al. *Reader's Guide to SF* 40: "The Prince in Waiting" series concerns a post-apocalypse future where the culture has returned to the medieval.

**1981** B. N. Malzberg *Engines of Night* in *SF Rev.* (Summer) 40/1: This post-apocalypse story in which the end of the world becomes a metaphor for the shocks and injuries of existence which prefigure and replicate death (and make the state of death their eternal re-enactment) is almost unknown today.

**2004** D. Bailey *End of World as We Know It* in *Mag. of Fantasy & SF* (Oct./Nov.) 83: Some end-of-the-world stories present us with two post-apocalypse survivors, one male and one female.

**post-apocalyptic** *adj.* POST-APOCALYPSE. Compare POST-CATASTROPHE, POST-HOLOCAUST.

**1978** A. Frank *Sci-Fi Now* 33/3: The early scenes as Heston investigated a deserted Los Angeles conveyed the feeling of a post-apocalyptic world although later the movie turned into the sort of action-adventure film more suited to Heston's talents.

**1991** *Callaloo* (Spring) 502: There seems to be a movement in your work from a view of continuance to a view of apocalypse. For example in *Clay's Ark* the civilization has been attacked by a microorganism. But in *Xenogenesis* there is a postapocalyptic scenario.

**1998** R. C. Smith *Nova Express* (Fall–Winter) 35/2: This winter's tale conveys the grim desperation of a post-apocalyptic society. But instead of the usual nuclear holocaust, deadly plague, or environmental calamity, this catastrophe was brought about by [...] a tidal wave of magic which swept away huge chunks of our modern world of science and reason.

**2003** G. K. Wolfe *Locus* (Apr.) 19/2: *Veniss Underground*, a post-apocalyptic far future urban novel with some echoes of Vance and Wolfe, and particularly of the longstanding secret underground city tradition, offers some answers.

**2003** *New York Times Book Rev.* (June 1) 20/2: Atwood returns to a dystopian future in this bleak novel about a man who may be the last human remaining on postapocalyptic earth.

**post-catastrophe** *adj.* POST-APOCALYPSE. Compare POST-APOCALYPTIC, POST-HOLOCAUST.

**1977** T. Robbins *Even Cowgirls Get Blues* (1990) 357: In a postcatastrophe world, your offspring would of necessity intermarry, forming in time a tribe.

**1979** B. Searles, et al. *Reader's Guide to SF* 61: *D&D* [i.e., the novel *Darkness and Dawn*] is still a marvelously exciting example of the post-catastrophe sub-genre of s-f, and the most currently readable of England's work.

**1996** D. Pringle, et al. *Ultimate Ency. of SF* 145/3: The post-catastrophe scenario, in which users of machinery are hounded by witch-hunters, is eventually explained by a device which is more occult than sf.

**1998** M. Davis *Ecology of Fear* (1999) 331: But two very different kinds of postcatastrophe fiction emerged: what might be called the "magical dystopian" and the "armageddonist."

**2003** J. Clute *SF from 1980 to Present* in E. James & F. Mendlesohn *Cambridge Companion to SF* 74: *In the Drift* (1985), was [...] a series of peephole views of a strife-ridden post-catastrophe America.

**post-cyberpunk** *adj.* referring to science fiction that employs many of the themes associated with cyberpunk, especially the effects of highly advanced computer technologies on societies, but generally lacking the alienation and dystopianism characteristic of cyberpunk. Also as *n.*

**1990** *Whole Earth Rev.* (Fall) 61/1: A high quality post-cyberpunk science-fiction magazine. Good writing, great artwork.

**1991** N. Spinrad *Isaac Asimov's SF Mag.* (mid-Dec.) 167/1: *Midas* is right out there on the post-cyberpunk cutting edge and then some, with its unique and gritty extrapolation of the down and dirty Third World realities interfaced with an exploration of the moral and spiritual implications of virtual replicated personalities confronting an all-too-real world.

**2000** G. Dozois *Michael Swanwick: Chameleon Eludes Net* in M. Swanwick *Moon Dogs* 12: Swanwick is now widely accepted as having written one of the two main "Post-Cyberpunk" works with *Stations of the Tide* (the other is Neal Stephenson's *Snow Crash*)—but [...] you can see that he was writing stuff that resembles "post-cyberpunk" *then*, before the Cyberpunk Revolution had even really gotten underway.

**2002** J. VanderMeer *Toxicology* in *Why Should I Cut Your Throat?* (2004) 188: "Tales" being an appropriate word for Aylett's post-cyberpunk technology-invested stylizations.

**2004** B. Stableford *Historical Dictionary of SF Literature* 82: The "punk" elements of the thriller format were carried forward into a "post-cyberpunk" phase that relied even more heavily on the cynical tone of "noirish" crime fiction.

**post-holocaust** *adj.* POST-APOCALYPSE. Compare POST-APOCALYPTIC, POST-CATASTROPHE.

**1977** T. Rogers *Starlog* (Jan.) 19/2: *Genesis II* [ ... ] begins in the year 1979, and quickly moves into the mysterious 22nd century. Like Buck Rogers, the hero [ ... ] wakes up in the post-holocaust world of the future.

**1980** *Thrust* (Fall) inside front cover (*ad*): Harrison's Viriconium Sequence takes place in a post-holocaust dream world of the far, far future: one peopled by feudal fantasy figures, spaceship captains, alchemist dwarves, and resurrected humans known as Reborn Men.

**1982** T. Nielsen Hayden *Apocalypse Now & Then* in *Making Book* (1994) 40: Post-holocaust civilizations saw the wars between the scientists and the religious fanatics, and the rise of mutants with strange powers.

**1986** T. M. Disch *Road to Heaven* in *On SF* (2005) 208: The common practice has been to depict a post-holocaust world as a kind of damaged Eden, where a few survivors scavenge a subsistence living from the wreck of civilization.

**1996** D. Pringle, et al. *Ultimate Ency. of SF* 137/3: A botany professor investigating post-holocaust Britain finds worshippers of Belial indulging in orgiastic rites and offering radiation-damaged babies as human sacrifices.

**2001** G. Dozois in M. Swanwick *Being Gardner Dozois* 144: Obviously the world had been ruined in some sort of catastrophe, and, in fact, the original idea was that this was going to be an After-The-Bomb story, showing how the man and his son survived in a Post-Holocaust world.

**posthuman** *n.* a TRANSHUMAN. Compare CYBORG, PARAHUMAN.

**1985** B. Sterling *Schismatrix* 26: I've met many borderline posthumans in my day, but never one of you.

**1986** D. Moffitt *Second Genesis* 321: Humans and posthumans drew closer together to share an ancient tribal comfort.

**2003** A. M. Steele *Madwoman of Shuttlefield* in *Asimov's SF* (May) 70: A Savant: a posthuman who had once been flesh and blood until he'd relinquished his humanity to have his mind downloaded into cyborg form, becoming an immortal intellect.

**2004** D. Broderick *X, Y, Z, T* 11: These are the exotic places and states humans might enter, even if we begin by paving the earth over and remaking ourselves into posthumans.

**posthuman** *adj.* of posthumans; developing after humans or the human race.

**1936** H. P. Lovecraft *Shadow Out of Time* in I. Asimov, C. G. Waugh & M. H. Greenberg *Great Tales of Classic SF* (1990) 26: What was hinted in the speech of post-human entities of the fate of mankind produced such an effect on me that I will not set it down here.

**1952** P. S. Miller *Astounding SF* (July) 159/2: There are the tendrilless slans [ ... ] with the same distorted organs and magnified physical and mental powers as the true slans, but without the telepathic powers of the post-human race "created" by Samuel Lann at least fifteen hundred years before.

**1971** R. Silverberg *Son of Man* (1979) 189: Now he is caught in a sea of shapes, prehuman and human and posthuman, coming and going, smothering him, demanding comfort from him, seeking redemption, chattering, laughing, weeping—

**1994** *Interzone* (Nov.) 56/3: The strongest and most satisfying sense of strangeness comes from those scenes set in the cold quietus of space, in which the revolt of the freedead and glimpses of an eternal, posthuman future are limned with concise precision.

**2002** L. M. Bujold *Diplomatic Immunity* 191: At the core are the haut lords, who are, in effect, one giant genetics experiment in producing the post-human race.

**2005** C. Doctorow *Cory Doctorow: Everywhere, All at Same Time* in *Locus* (Jan.) 63/3–64/1: We'll upload, we'll transcend, we will be posthuman, *better* than human, multifarious and faster.

**posthumanism** *n.* writing or thought concerning posthumans or the nature of being a posthuman.

**1985** B. Sterling *Schismatrix* 229: Really? Posthumanism! Prigoginic levels of complexity! Fractal scales, bedrock of space-time, precontinuum ur-space! Have I got it right?

**1988** T. Maddox *Wars of Coin's Two Halves* in L. McCaffery *Storming Reality Studio* (1991) 327: With "Cicada Queen," the trope of posthumanism acquires symbolic depth.

**2003** R. Letson *Locus* (Apr.) 25/3: I suspect part of what makes it golden is the way the edges of the old wide-screen space adventure have blurred off into oddly contiguous or harmonious subgenres: the humanism of Jack McDevitt and Nancy Kress; the post-humanism of Greg Egan, Wil McCarthy, Linda Nagata, Karl Schroeder, or John C. Wright.

**posthumanist** *adj.* concerning posthumans or posthumanity.

**1985** B. Sterling *Schismatrix* 208: "Posthumanist," Wellspring insisted.

**1988** T. Maddox *Wars of Coin's Two Halves* in L. McCaffery *Storming Reality Studio* (1991) 325: Shaper and Mechanist name the primary posthumanist modes of being [...]. Technopolitical fusions, they manifest polar strategies of human evolution.

**2004** D. Broderick *X, Y, Z, T* 94: Sterling was in the 1980s a (perhaps *the*) vociferous propagandist for cyberpunk, futurist writing that combined hard-edged, hi-tech gloss with a cynical posthumanist sensibility.

**posthumanity** *n.* the condition of being posthuman; posthumans collectively. Compare TRANSHUMANITY.

**1985** B. Sterling *Schismatrix* 231: Posthumanity's bigger than that.

**1995** I. McDonald *Evolution's Shore* 234: I do not understand these things well. I do not know about Australopithecus and evolution and what you call transhumanity, posthumanity.

**1997** M. Swanwick *Wisdom of Old Earth* in *Asimov's SF* (Dec.) 107: Now consider posthumanity. Our environment is entirely artificial—floating cities, the Martian subsurface, the Venusian and Jovian bubbles. [...] A human

could survive within them, possibly, but she would not thrive.

**precog** *n.* [abbr. of *precognition*] someone who can see the future; someone with the psychic ability of precognition.

**1954** P. K. Dick *World of Talent* in *Galaxy SF* (Oct.) 10/1: He kept on talking to the Norm-class officials grouped around the two Precogs.

**1954** P. K. Dick, *World of Talent* 10/2: His wife's precog span was somewhat greater than his own. She was seeing, at this moment, ahead of his own vision.

**1969** A. McCaffrey *Womanly Talent* in *Analog SF-Sci. Fact* (Feb.) 12/1: Sometimes three and four pre-cogs come up with the same incident, seen from different angles.

**1973** *Daily News (New York)* (Aug. 21) 53/1: Certain precogs prophesy the future with the buckshot approach, generalized predictions.

**1995** P. F. Hamilton *Nano Flower* (1999) 385: Using an empath is routine, it's the least you need. Me, I prefer a precog if I can get me one.

**2000** B. Lumley *Necroscope: Defilers* 43: He turned to the precog. "Ian, how's the future looking?"

**precog** *v.* to see or predict the future.

**1948** H. B. Piper *Police Operation* in *Astounding SF* (July) 23/2: During unconsciousness, the EPC is "time-free"; it may detach, and connect at some other moment, with the ego existing at that time-point. That's how we precog.

**1958** J. W. Campbell *Astounding SF* (Aug.) 106: The editorial chronoscope, whereby we precog the future, developed a fault, somehow, when we were making up the July issue.

**1990** A. McCaffrey *Pegasus in Flight* (1991) 317: Sascha's pre-cogged it. To his intense astonishment.

**pre-space** *adj.* without the technology to achieve space-flight; from a time before the first space-flight. Compare PRESPACEFLIGHT.

**1949** R. Lafayette *Emperor of Universe* in *Startling Stories* (Nov.) 134/1: No one seems to know, although there are many guesses of course, just how pre-space man arrived at the mysterious *A.D.* which he appends on his stone carvings everywhere he first trod.

**1964** [C. Smith] *Boy Who Bought Old Earth* in *Galaxy Mag.* (Apr.) 72/2: That's the oldest song you ever heard, my boy. It's pre-space.

**1977** G. Zebrowski *Ashes & Stars* 7: A hundred thousand worlds circle their suns here, many of them earth-like; [ ... ] some cradle pre-space humanoid cultures.

**1997** D. Weber & S. White *In Death Ground* (2000) 60: Those pre-space denizens of Old Terra who bequeathed Rear Admiral Vanessa Murakuma her married surname would have been shocked.

**prespaceflight** *adj.* PRE-SPACE.

**1972** G. Zebrowski *Omega Point* 16: He is fond of citing vast amounts of earth history, mostly pre-spaceflight and solar system bound.

**1991** J. White *Genocidal Healer* in *General Practice* (2003) 269: To a culture at the pre-spaceflight level of technology, the sudden arrival among them of a vessel of the size and power of *Vespasian*, and the visually monstrous entities it contains, would not be reassuring.

**1993** *Seattle Times* (ProQuest) (Feb. 12): Those of us in leadership roles within education today are products of the '40s, '50s and '60s. Our initial value systems and understandings were shaped by a Cold War, pre-computer, pre-space flight and a Eurocentric world.

**2003** J. Barnes *In Hall of Martian King* 114: The Pertrans car glided through Magnificiti, a pretty little town that looked like a random collection of European architectural ideas from all the prespaceflight centuries.

**pressor** *n.* [perh. alteration of *presser*] a PRESSOR BEAM.

**1931** E. E. Smith *Spacehounds of IPC* in *Amazing Stories* (Sept.) 560/1: Onward and upward flashed the gigantic duplex cone, its entire whirling mass laced and latticed together— into one mammoth unit by green tractor beams and red pressors.

**1973** A. D. Foster *Bloodhype* 48: The idea was that the two shuttles would release their hold at the same moment the main pressor took over.

**1974** J. W. Haldeman *This Best of All Possible Worlds* in *Analog SF-Sci. Fact* (Nov.) 145/2: We both began swimming for an hour or so every

clear day, in the calm, pressor-guarded water off the beach.

**1999** D. Weber *Hard Way Home* (2000) 313: No one could have built an effective wall of pressers all around the resort, but the designers had stationed the generators at strategic points.

**pressor beam** *n.* a beam of force that repells matter; the opposite of a TRACTOR BEAM. Also **presser beam, pressor field.** Compare PRESSOR.

**1931** E. E. Smith *Spacehounds of IPC* in *Amazing Stories* (Sept.) 544/2: We'll have them in three days, and it ought to be fairly simple to dope out the opposite of a tractor, too—a pusher or presser beam.

**1956** P. Anderson *Margin of Profit* in *Astounding SF* (Sept.) 58/1: A pressor beam lashed out, an invisible hammerblow of repulsion, five times the strength of the enemy tractor.

**1960** J. White *O'Mara's Orphan* in *New Worlds SF* (Jan.) 5: Sections [ ... ] often had to be modified to make them join properly, and this necessitated moving the sections together and apart several times with massed tractor and pressor beams.

**1971** R. Silverberg *In Entropy's Jaws* in R. Hoskins *Infinity 2* 182: When you have done this the pressor fields will automatically be activated and you will be fully insulated against injury during the coming period of turbulence.

**1999** D. Weber *Hard Way Home* (2000) 313: Lift towers locked down and threw up barrier panels of their own, and immensely powerful presser beams snarled to life.

**pressure suit** *n.* a protective garment, for use in places with low atmospheric pressure or outer space, that maintains a steady air-pressure around the wearer; a SPACESUIT. Compare MOONSUIT, SUIT, VAC SUIT, VACUUM SUIT.

**1928** E. E. Smith & L. H. Garby *Skylark of Space* in *Amazing Stories* (Sept.) 539/2: Have you fur pressure-suits?

**1934** *Gleaner (Kingston, Jam.)* (Apr. 3) 3/3: I intend to go up in an open basket attached to the balloon. I shall wear an especially designed pressure suit which will withstand the extremes of heat and cold and any amount of atmospheric pressure.

**1949** *Startling Stories* (Sept.) 125/2: The multiple layers of my pressure suit had made movement very difficult.

**1966** *Life* (Jan. 7) 31/2: It may have been a minor thing that no U. S. astronaut ever before had shed his pressure suit in space.

**1976** C. Holland (1977) 461: A man in a pressure suit jogged across the gray dust to the ship.

**1992** B. Bova *Mars* (1993) 3: Through the thick insulation of his pressure suit, Jamie could hear nothing except his own excited breathing.

**prime directive** *n.* the most important rule or law, which must be obeyed above all others. Also in extended use. Often *cap.* [Popularized by the television show *Star Trek*.]

**1947** J. Williamson *With Folded Hands* in *Astounding SF* (July) 18/1: But that is impossible under the Prime Directive [ ... ]. Our function is to serve and obey, and guard men from harm. It is no longer necessary for men to care for themselves, because we exist to insure their safety and happiness.

**1956** P. Anderson *Live Coward* in *Astounding SF* (June) 111/1: The only beautiful concept I have right now is that all of a sudden the Prime Directive was repealed. [ ... ] "Under no circumstances whatever may the Patrol or any unit thereof kill any intelligent being."

**1966** B. Sobelman *Return of Archons ("Star Trek" script)* (Dec. 1) 50: KIRK: Landru must die. SPOCK: Our prime directive of non-interference... KIRK: That refers to a living, growing culture. I'm not convinced that this one is.

**1969** *American Statisical Association Journal* (Mar.) 52: Every competent scientist I've worked with [ ... ] has abided strictly by the prime directive of modern science, the Galilean Rule that "a theory must fit the facts."

**1978** *Daily Intelligencer (Doylestown, Pa.)* (Oct. 7) 6: The last vestiges of a human society struggle to survive the onslaught of giant mechanized Cylon warriors [ ... ], whose prime directive is to destroy all human life.

**1981** C. Harness *Firebird* 74: The Prime Directive: All activity within the Universe is for the benefit of Control.

**1993** *North Hills News Record (Warrendale, Pa.)* (Feb. 19) B7/1: This may be Hollywood's prime directive. Eventually, things work out. The smart girl—the one with poetry in her soul—wins, the others are left with frayed pompons.

**2000** *Syracuse (New York) Herald-Journal* (July 19) D13/3: My prime directive is to be an integral part of a three-man group talking about a football game.

**probability world** *n.* one of many possible universes or timelines.

**1943** A. E. van Vogt *Search* in *Astounding S-F* (Jan.) 53/2: He retired to his farm, and henceforth exerted the very minimum of influence on the larger scene of existence. He lived in his own probability world until his death in 2874.

**1950** C. D. Simak *Time Quarry* in *Galaxy SF* (Dec.) 118/2: You and I may be no more than puppets in some probability world that will pinch out tomorrow.

**1951** P. Anderson *Earthman, Beware!* in *Alight in Void* (1991) 52: Similarly, he supposed, his other centers could control those forces to create or destroy or move matter, to cross space, to scan the past and future probability-worlds, to...

**1990** G. Dozois *Afterword to Playing Game* in G. Dozois, et al. *Slow Dancing through Time* 159: I skewed Jack's idea somewhat, building the story instead around a concept that had long fascinated me—an intuition of how easy it would be to become lost among the billions of probability-worlds that are born and die around us every second of every day.

**prodom** *n.* [modeled after *fandom*] the world of professional writers.

**1953** J. Harmon *Fantasy-Times* (Nov. 2) 4: No large segment of Fandom or Prodom can ever be made to believe the lies, and will know the lies for what they are.

**1969** H. Warner, Jr. *All Our Yesterdays* 229: Louis Garner, who soon got lost to non-science fiction prodom.

**1989** *Nova Express* (Spring) 12/2: You had to make your way past the snarling fanzoids all the way back to the rear bedroom to find the true inner sanctum of prodom.

**2001** [P. Anthony] *How Precious Was That While* (2002) 284: I actually entered prodom and fandom simultaneously.

**promag** *n.* [*pro*fessional *mag*azine] a professionally published magazine, especially one that publishes science fiction or fantasy. Compare PROZINE.

**1939** W. Tucker *Le Zombie* (No. 2) 1: Another new one due any time is to be put out by a fan new to fandom, but old to pro mags.

**1941** J. Fortier *Astounding S-F (letter)* (Apr.) 156/1: I guess that intangible something is closeness to perfection which makes my favorite science-fiction promag so easy to take with nary a word.

**1944** J. Speer *Speer in Los Angeles* in *Fancestral Voices* (2004) 93: Morojo's was a typical fan den, with large shelves of promag files and books.

**1952**: see quote in FANMAG.

**1987** J. White *Exorcists of IF* in *White Papers* (1996) 349: Ranged around the bare plaster walls were the spectral shapes of bookshelves bulging with promags and fanzines.

**proto-cyberpunk** *adj.* prefiguring or having had an influence on cyberpunk, especially in terms of style or subject matter.

**1991** T. Tatsumi *Japanese Reflection of Mirrorshades* in L. McCaffery *Storming Reality Studio* 371: Kazuko Behrens [...] translated Yoshio Aramaki's protocyberpunk tale "Soft Clocks."

**1991** L. Olsen *Shadow of Spirit in William Gibson's Matrix Trilogy* in *Extrapolation* (Fall) 279: The posthuman becomes, to use the title from Anthony Burgess's 1963 protocyberpunk novel, a clockwork orange.

**1994** J. Kessel *Mag. of Fantasy and SF* (Apr.) 24/1: They include hard science stories like [...] Fred Pohl's in-your-face assault "Day Million," a proto-cyberpunk hymn to accelerating social and technological change.

**1996** D. Pringle, et al. *Ultimate Ency. of SF* 184/3: The tale of a plugged-in media figure and his companion AI, who together secretly guide mankind, this novel was in important proto-cyberpunk work.

**proto-science fiction, proto-sf** *n.* literature written before the emergence of science fiction as a distinct genre (usually thought of as being sometime in the late nineteenth or early twentieth century) that contains elements that would later be associated with science fiction, such as futuristic settings, voyages to other planets, fictional inventions, etc.

**1962** D. Knight *Century of SF* 78: But Lucian's narrator got to the moon by magical means; so did Cyrano de Bergerac's, Defoe's and Godwin's; Kepler's got there in a dream. These are proto-science-fiction narratives, if you like.

**1977** G. Dickson *Intro.* in R. Elwood *Futurelove* ix: Science fiction itself owes a particular debt of gratitude to the nineteenth-century storytellers—not only to recognized earlier writers of the genre, such as H. G. Wells and Jules Verne, but to many of the other people then writing in Western literature, who wrote either proto-science fiction or fantasy verging on science fiction.

**1988** B. Stableford *Beginnings* in J. Gunn *New Ency. of SF* 42/2: By 1895 American proto–science fiction was sufficiently distinct and recognizable as a literary subspecies for Edgar Fawcett, in the preface to *The Ghost of Guy Thyrle*, to offer a manifesto on its behalf.

**1989** A. Panshin & C. Panshin *World beyond Hill* 76: There is one Romantic document that is sometimes offered as a proto-SF story with a setting in the Future—Edgar Allan Poe's sketch "Mellonta Tauta" (1849).

**2003** P. Di Filippo *Asimov's SF* (Apr.) 131/2: But there is a sense in which proto-SF was wilder and more outrageous, simply because no borders had yet been established.

**prozine** *n.* [*pro* + -ZINE] a PROMAG.

**1942** G. E. Rennison *Planet Stories (letter)* (Spring) 121/1: In exchange I am willing to send you any British stuff, reprints of two American prozines, Britain's one and only sfn. pro mag., fanzines or whatever you want that I can lay my hands on.

**1944** J. B. Speer *Fancyclopedia* 69/1: Prozines have multiplied from the old days of the Big Three to a peak in 1939.

**1961** D. Thompson *(letter)* in P. Lupoff & D. Lupoff *Best of Xero* (2005) 59: My favorite prozine is *F&SF*. *Amazing* is better than it used to be, but every sf magazine is better than *Amazing* used to be.

**1981** *Dragon Mag.* (June) 23/2: If a reader is willing to deal with the quirks of the editor or some of the writers, one can often get more useful material from a semi-promagazine than from a prozine like White Dwarf, and for a lower price.

**1999** M. J. Pustz *Comic Book Culture* 47: Another important change for fandom in the early 1970s was the growth of "pro-zines," magazines about comics published by industry professionals.

**2004** M. Ashley *How Big's Yours...?* in *Postscripts* (Spring) 119: If we consider first the total number of issues each year, the pro-zines outstripped the semi-prozines until 1990.

**pseudo-grav** *n.* ARTIFICIAL GRAVITY. Compare PSEUDO-GRAVITY.

**1955** I. Asimov *Talking Stone* in *Mag. of Fantasy & SF* (Oct.) 109/1: With ship's pseudo-grav generators shut off, it weighed virtually nothing, but it had its full mass and inertia.

**1960** P. Anderson *Eve Times Four* in *Time & Stars* (1965) 172: Pseudograv could not smooth out all the jerking and buffeting which rocked the boat.

**1963** H. B. Piper *Space Viking* (1975) 33: Abbot lift-and-drive for normal space, Dillingham hyperdrive, power converters, pseudograv, all at the center of the globular ship.

**1999** L. E. Modesitt, Jr. *Gravity Dreams* (2000) 331: Because the pseudograv is too low and because centrifugal force substitutes for gravity?

**pseudo-gravity** *n.* ARTIFICIAL GRAVITY. Also **pseudo-gravitation.** Hence **pseudo-gravitational,** *adj.,* **pseudo-gravitics,** *n.* Compare PSEUDOGRAV.

**1941** R. Heinlein *Common Sense* in *Astounding S-F* (Oct.) 108: Bobo trotted away in the long loping strides permitted by the low pseudo-gravity near the axis of rotation of the Ship.

**1947** J. Williamson *Legion of Space* 111: He knew the fine-spun theories of counterspace, of inverse curvature, of pseudo-gravitation and negative entropy.

**1956** I. Asimov *Dead Past* in S. Schmidt *Fifty Years of Best SF from Analog* (1980) 203: Just as electronics deals with the applications of electron movements and the forces involved, and pseudo-gravitics deals with the applications of artificial gravitational fields.

**1963** P. Anderson *After Doomsday* (1968) 83: Too weak to be felt as such, the pseudogravity of the ship's lunatic spin sent wreckage crawling within the smashed hull.

**1987** T. R. McDonough *Architects of Hyperspace* 191: Where Einstein showed that the bigger the mass, the slower time passes for an object near it, these creatures found some way of creating the same effect through, I suppose, a pseudogravitational field.

**2003** C. Asaro *Moon's Shadow* (2004) 220: But the pseudo-gravity in this region of the rotating Orbiter was only 70 percent human standard.

**pseudo-science** *n. Obs.* SCIENCE FICTION. Compare FANTASCIENCE, PSEUDO-SCIENCE, SCIENCE FANTASY 2, SCIENTIFIC FANTASY, SCIENTIFIC FICTION, SCIENTIFICTION, SPECULATIVE FICTION 1.

**1927** W. K. Jones *Listening in on Editors* in *Author & Journalist* (Aug.) 16/1: When I asked him just what that sort was, he summed up his requirements as "ghost and pseudo-science."

**1944** J. B. Speer *Fancyclopedia* 75/2: Other names for science-fiction are scientifiction, scientific romances, and pseudo-science stories.

**1948** *Growth of S-F & Fantasy Publishing in Book Form* in *Publisher's Weekly* (Dec. 25) 2464/1: The Associated Fantasy Publishers, was formed this summer [ ... ] by nine small publishing houses devoted to fantasy and pseudo-science.

**1948** *Thrilling Wonder Stories* (Feb.) 109/1: After all, the most highly technical pseudo science story is truly nothing but fantasy dressed up with a lot of fantastic, slide rule suppositional gadgets.

**1957** S. Moskowitz *How SF Got Its Name* in *Mag. of Fantasy & SF* (Feb.) 76/2: When a 1949 cover of *The Writer's Monthly* featured a review of "pseudo science" publication requirements, many of the newer writers weren't quite sure what was being referred to, so anachronistic had the term become.

**1966** J. Merril *Mag. of Fantasy & SF* (Mar.) 48/1: Actually, this is a more than adequate adventure yarn—well-told, well-paced, filled with thrills, chills, and spills, and the very model of the modern version of the Pseudoscience Story.

**pseudo-scientific** *adj. Obs.* SCIENCE-FICTIONAL.

**1880** J. B. Matthews *Theatres of Paris* 178: M. Jules Verne had been writing pseudo-scientific tales of adventure for a decade.

**1896** B. W. Wells *Modern French Literature* 394: The modern pseudo-scientific novel is essentially necessitarian, it regards men as the products of birth and environment, while it is a fundamental condition of the drama to show will in action.

**1903** *New York Times* (Apr. 4) 232/2: The name or the nature of the book is not yet known, but it is to be hoped that it will be something like the other books that have gained Mr. Wells such a high place as writer of pseudo-scientific novels.

**1924** *Weird Tales* (Nov.) 45: A fascinating pseudo-scientific story, with a thrill on every page.

**1938** R. Wilson, Jr. *Undersea Kingdom—Criticism & Synopsis* in *Sci. Fantasy Movie Review* (Sept.) 3: Outside of these few discrepancies, "The Undersea Kingdom" is the answer of a scientifilm fan's dream, embodying, as it does, practically every outstanding pseudo-scientific invention that has as yet been thought of.

**1951** H. Kuttner in A. Derleth *Outer Reaches* 133: In a sense, this story attacks irresponsibility, since it devalues a most familiar structure in pseudo-scientific stories: the twin correlates of Now and Utopia.

**1958** *New York Times* (July 15) 18/3: Man's flight to the stars in our age is more a matter of time and waiting than a fantastic dream born in the mind of a science-fiction writer. Or so it appears to several Soviet leaders, who recently charged their own pseudo-scientific writers of showing lack of imagination.

**psionic** *adj.* **1.** [< parapsychological term *psi*] using, affected by, or possessing psychic abilities (such as telepathy, precognition, etc.).

**1951** J. Williamson *Peddler's Nose* in *Astounding SF* (Apr.) 44/1: The bright psionic labels looked blank at first, but they came to shining life under the eyes of the children, responding to the thoughts of each.

**1967** P. K. Dick *Counter-Clock World* (1990) 52: Like Seb he, too, was undoubtedly slightly psionic.

**1994** B. Hambly *Crossroad* 102: I'd get all trusting and tell you [ … ] what he did to break the docilization codes the Consilium keeps on every captain and astrogator and psionic empath in the Fleet.

**2.** of or relating to such abilities.

**1952** *Astounding SF* (Vol. XLIX) 119/2: The psionic translator in his belt would have brought him the sense of every syllable, and enabled even these psionic illiterates to understand him.

**1956** J. H. Schmitz *Sleep No More* in S. Schmidt *Fifty Years of Best SF from Analog* (1980) 294: Before they arrived, she had to be free of their animal—they were making use of its specialized psionic ability to keep in contact with selected prey.

**1979** G.R.R. Martin *Way of Cross & Dragon* in T. Shippey *Oxford Book of SF* (1992) 468: The Church teaches that the psionic powers are one of Satan's traps.

**1986** J. M. Dillard *Mindshadow* 72: As a result of losing the mind rules, his psionic rating has increased.

**psionically** *adv.* by means of psionics.

**1968** J. Russ *Picnic on Paradise* 11: He wears that—that Trivia on his head to give himself twenty-four hours a day of solid nirvana, station NOTHING, turns off all stimuli when you want it to, operates psionically.

**1976** *Psionic Medicine* (Vol. XI) 6: Dr. Wright wondered whether the case histories of patients treated psionically would throw any light on these questions.

**1983** S. Brust *Jhereg* 27: "What's the matter?" I asked him psionically.

**psionics** *n.* psychic powers; the study or science of psychic powers.

**1952** J. Williamson *Man Down* in *Astounding SF* (Mar.) 112/1: Stripped of all those mechanisms that many million minds had helped to make, he couldn't hope to do much with his own small smattering of neutronics and psionics.

**1953** T. Sturgeon *More than Human* 207: Gravitics is the key to everything. It would lead to the addition of one more item to the Unified Field—what we now call psychic energy, or "psionics."

**1960** P. Anderson in E. Crispin *Best SF Five* (1963) 228: Research has taught us just enough about psionics to show we can't imagine its potentialities.

**2005** P. Witcover *Tumbling After* 101: How will you deal with that? By lashing out with your psionics like you're thinking about doing right now?

**pub** *n.* [abbr. of *publish*] to publish. Hence **pubbing**, *n.*

**1951** *Lives & Deaths of Earl Tuckleton* in *S-F Five-Yearly* (Nov.) 5: For a couple of years after that Ear went along in a normal rut, pubbing L'Nethpen pretty regularly and writing for other fanzines.

**1961** R. Ebert *My Last Annish* in P. Lupoff & D. Lupoff *Best of Xero* (2005) 101: Even had you will To crank and pub—which I have not—to get a bill From such a one who says, "This crud I print for you disgusts me."

**1964** J. Linwood *Fanalytic Eye* in *Les Spinge* (Jan.) 30: Presently, when the only publications that have survived from a halcyon period of pubbing are Les Spinge and Skyrack, such an injection is urgently needed.

**1975** E. Weinstein *Fillostrated Fan Dictionary* 138: A column originally in Imagination! that became a fanzine in its own right. Pubbed by Ackerman and Morojo.

**1998**: see quote in FAKEFAN.

**2004** R. R. Davidson *e-National Fantasy Fan* (Mar.) 18: If you never get beyond pubbing for N'APA, that's alright with us.

**pulp science fiction, pulp sf** *n.* science fiction that was published in the pulp magazines; hence, science fiction that is reminiscent of such writing.

**1948** A. H. Rapp *Flaming Fans* in *Chronoscope* (Autumn) 29: How did the superb craftsmanship and delicate enchantment of current pulp science fiction arise from the earlier sagas of stereotyped characters dwindling into atomic-sized universes amid plots packed with improbably lush coincidence?

**1951** [A. Boucher] *Afterword* in *Rocket to Morgue* (1975) 171: Pulp science fiction had, at that time, just reached maturity both in thinking and in writing and was at a fine ripe stage to make converts easily.

**1967** A. Budrys *Benchmarks* (1985) 126: Where, before now, was there a pulp science-fiction writer who wrote a book "primarily during a year of travel in France, Italy, Greece, Turkey and England" who had not steadfastly taken Main Street right along with him?

**1976** T. M. Disch *Embarrassments of SF* in *On SF* (2005) 9: By far the greater part of all pulp science fiction from the time of Wells till now was written to provide a semi-literate audience with compensatory fantasies.

**1996** D. Pringle, et al. *Ultimate Ency. of SF* 26/1: Even in pulp sf, Frank Paul's grandiose images were often juxtaposed with depictions of cities that had been reduced to ruins by all manner of catastrophes.

# r

**raise** *v.* (of a spaceship) to take off from a world's surface. Often in phrase **raise ship.**

**1929** C. W. Harris & M. J. Breuer *Baby on Neptune* in *Amazing Stories* (Dec.) 792/1: They raised their vessel and cruised about, looking for cities, for intelligent beings, and finding nothing but slimy life, settled again.

**1939** R. Heinlein *Misfit* in *Astounding S-F* (Nov.) 54/2: Attention! Man all space details; first section. Raise ship in twelve minutes.

**1958** A. Norton *Star Gate* 56: But there were others of us, Kincar, who [...] had taken Gorth to our hearts. And when we came to think of raising from her, we could not bear it. So we sought another path of flight.

**1979** B. Daley *Han Solo Adventures* 73: If the traitor managed to turn in an alarm, chances were that the Falcon would never raise ship again.

**1987** L. M. Janifer *Knave & Game* (2002) 51: Figure fifteen deaths—maybe ten—and the city slickers raise ship and go looking for an easier job.

**ramscoop** *n.* [infl. by *ramjet*] an electromagnetic field at the front of spaceship that captures interstellar hydrogen to be used as a fuel for a fusion-powered space drive.

**1966** L. Niven *Warriors* in *If* (Feb.) 154/1: It's a light pressure drive powered by incomplete hydrogen fusion. They use an electromagnetic ramscoop to get their own hydrogen from space.

**1979** J. Varley *Titan* (1987) 19: A real big fusion ramscoop. The machinery is in the hub, electromagnetic field generators to funnel the interstellar hydrogen into the center, where it gets burned.

**1989** D. Drake *Space Infantry* 16: It's a light pressure drive powered by incomplete hydrogen fusion. They use an electromagnetic ramscoop to get their own hydrogen from space.

**1991**: see quote in SLOWER THAN LIGHT.

**1999** A. Reynolds *Galactic North* in G. Dozois *Mammoth Book of Best New SF 13* (2000) 92: The ramscoops gasped at interstellar gas, sucking lone atoms of cosmic hydrogen from cubic metres of vacuum.

**ray** *v. Obs.* to shoot with a ray-gun or other energy weapon.

**1930** J. W. Campbell, Jr. *Black Star Passes* in *Amazing Stories Quarterly* (Fall) 509/1: So the ships had been rayed apart, and when Arcot had left, their burning atmosphere had been evolving mighty tongues of flame shooting a mile into the air.

**1934** E. E. Smith *Triplanetary* in *Amazing Stories* (Jan.) 10/2: Anything entering the fourth zone is to be rayed.

**1942** I. Asimov *Black Friar of Flame* in *Planet Stories* (Spring) 18/1: Order the guns placed in readiness and aimed along the avenues. Any Human attempting to pass the cordon is to be rayed mercilessly.

**1957** R. Silverberg *One-Way Journey* in *World of Thousand Colors* (1984) 125: "Ray him again," Warshow said hollowly. "The stunning's wearing off."

**ray gun** *n.* a device that fires a beam of (usually) destructive energy. Also **ray pistol.**

**1916** *Newark (Oh.) Advocate* (Oct. 25) 9/5: The most destructive agent ever evolved is the X-ray gun the height of Yankee ingenuity, in "The Intrigue." [ ... ] This is visibly proven in this remarkable Pallas-Paramount photo[ - ]play.

**1931** *Amazing Stories* (Dec.) 804/1: The ray-guns of the battlecraft, being of superior range, melted down the mortars of the fort at the magazine.

**1941** J. H. Haggard *Derelicts of Uranus Comet* (May) 66/1: "That puts a different light on the entire matter," said Raeburn, getting to his feet and drawing a ray pistol from his pocket.

**1948** A. E. van Vogt *Monster* in T. Shippey *Oxford Book of SF* (1992) 157: The two-legged monster dissolved, writhing, in the beam of a ray gun.

**1957** R. W. Lowndes *SF Stories* (Jan.) 141/1: The first time you vicariously cut down the villain with the ravening energy of a ray pistol, you feel the tremendous surge of power and accomplishment. The fortieth time, it simply seems like an efficient way to get rid of the villain.

**1967** *Autocar* (Dec. 28) 29/3: As the car nears each set of lamps a patrolman [ ... ] points the ray gun at the cell situated between the two lamps. A beamed radio signal from the gun activates the fog warning lamp switch.

**1987** N. Spinrad *Little Heroes* (1989) 262: Like some unseen max metal gunfighter laughing as he fired his rayguns at her feet for the evil pleasure of making her dance.

**1994** *SF Age* (July) 37/2: The Air Force guys never quite figured out the trick of making an effective raygun.

**ray projector** *n.* a device that projects a beam of energy.

**1930** J. W. Campbell, Jr. *Black Star Passes* in *Amazing Stories Quarterly* (Fall) 519/2: Earth and Venus were each equipped with gigantic ray projectors, mighty ray guns that could destroy anything, even a body as large as the moon, at a distance of ten thousand miles.

**1934** E. E. Smith *Triplanetary* in *Amazing Stories* (Jan.) 24/2: Cositgan had seen that there was a third enemy, [ ... ] a pirate who was even then training a ray projector upon him.

**1953** E. F. Russell *Somewhere Voice* in *Other Worlds* (Jan.) 11/2: No face masks. No oxygen cylinders. No portable ray-projectors.

**1961** J. Siegel *Shame of Bizarro Family!* in *Tales of Bizarro World* (2000) 18: Years ago, in Smallville, a scientist accidentally shone an imperfect *duplicator ray* on me, creating an unliving bizarre imitation of me instants before his *ray-projector* exploded.

**reaction drive** *n.* a slower-than-light space drive that generates thrust by ejecting matter in a direction opposite to that of travel.

**1949** T. Sturgeon *Minority Report* in *Astounding SF* (June) 137/1: They fired up the reaction drive and began to move toward the sun.

**1959** R. A. Heinlein *Starship Troopers* (1987) 135: Fifty ships were in our piece of it and they were supposed to come out of Cherenkov drive and into reaction drive.

**1989** P. Anderson *Boat of Million Years* (2004) 381: Those necessities include laser and magnetohydrodynamic systems able to shield against radiation as well as to draw in sufficient interstellar gas for the reaction drive. The drive in turn will consume an amount of antimatter that will deplete our reserves here in the Solar System for years to come.

**1995** P. F. Hamilton *Nano Flower* (1999) 163: What if they didn't use a reaction drive? What if they had some faster than light drive like the science fiction shows on the channels?

**2003** S. Westerfeld *Killing of Worlds* 248: Alexander saw the frigate's reaction drive come alight again, a spark in high orbit above Legis XV.

**redshirt** *n.* [after the red shirts worn by crewmembers in the television show *Star Trek*, who were frequently killed after arriving on a new planet] a character who is not portrayed in any depth; an extra; especially one whose main plot function is to be killed.

**1985** *Major Inconsistancy* (Usenet: net.star-trek) (May 28): You're right, Redshirts are never allowed to survive an episode.

**1994** *Powers... Tim Powers* (Usenet: rec. arts.sf.written) (July 17): I recognize that this particular vice (offhand treatment of "extras" (or "redshirts", if you prefer)) is not unique to Zelazny, but somehow it seems that he disposes of them with unusual relish.

**1994** *SFRA Rev.* (July–Aug.) 43: The weakest part of the book was the use of the dreaded "redshirt syndrome."

**2004** *Ace Double Reviews, 43: Silverberg/ Temple* (Usenet: rec.arts.sf.written) (Apr. 8): The book concerns the first expedition to Venus, led by a lugubrious Captain who believes himself cursed by his first name (Jonah), and crewed by several redshirts.

**relaxacon, relaxicon** *n.* a science fiction convention with little or no organized programming.

**1957** *Mag. of Fantasy & SF* (Aug.) 86: Like so many of the newer s.f. writers, Les Cole comes from science fiction fandom, where he was noted [...] as the inventor of the great concept of the "relaxicon"—a convention with no program whatsoever.

**1984** D. Hartwell *Age of Wonders* 13: Aside from the World Science Fiction Convention, [...] there is [...] an SF film convention, numerous "relaxicons" (at which there is no programming—chronics and omnivores gather to party with like minds for a weekend), and literally dozens of localized conventions.

**1992** *Fantasies* front cover: The Fourth Annual Relax-a-Con.

**2001** C. Low *Minutes of LFS* 9/1: Grossberg invites any LFS members staying over Sunday night to attend a Sunday night "relaxacon" party at his home. Guests of honor Brad Linaweaver and Victor Milan will be there.

**replicant** *n.* in the movie *Blade Runner*, an android that can pass as a human; in extended use, a duplicate or copy.

**1981** *Bladerunner (screenplay)* (Feb. 23) 10: The last census showed a hundred and six million people in the city. Somewhere in the crowd I was supposed to find the four phoney ones [...] the replicants.

**1987** W. Schneider *Atlantic Monthly* (July) 67/1: If the public is dissatisfied with Reagan's performance, why should it vote for a Reagan replicant?

**1994** D. Doyle & J. D. Macdonald *By Honor Betray'd* 251: "What's this I hear about your tame Mageworlder switching a replicant agent for my father's personal aide?" [...] "Her role in replicating Commander Quetaya was limited to the creation of a duplicate body."

**2000** *Chronicle-Telegram (Elyria, Oh.)* (Oct. 15) A8/1: Madame Tussaud's [...] brings a collection of nearly 200 replicant celebrities to a new $50 million Times Square home this week.

**2001** *Syracuse (New York) Herald-Journal* (Mar. 22) C4/5: "First Years" carefully obeys all the rules and commercial calculations and proves to be just another cookie-cutter, formulaic, shamelessly schematic replicant.

**2005** J. Lethem *Disappointment Artist* 72: Omega the Unknown [...] was Gerber's undermining of both Superman and the original Captain Marvel (known to us only as the pathetic replicant Shazam).

**2005** E. Bryant *Fantasy & Horror in Media* in E. Datlow, K. Link & G. J. Grant *Year's Best Fantasy & Horror: Eighteenth Annual Coll.* lxxxvii: Were the rich, powerful, apparently sociopathic men of ideally suburban Stepford using technology to brainwash their independent-minded wives? Or were they replacing their spouses with actual replicants as in the original?

**rim world** *n.* a planet near the edge of the galaxy, generally seen as being remote from the rest of galactic culture. Often *cap.* Also **rim-worlder,** *n.* Compare OUTPLANET, OUTWORLD.

**1957** R. A. Heinlein *Citizen of Galaxy* in *Astounding SF* (Nov.) 121/2: H. G. C. *Hydra* lifted from Hekate, bound for the Rim worlds.

**1959** A. B. Chandler *Astounding SF* (Jan.) 12/1: They don't like Deep Space, these Rim Worlders. They're scared of it. I suppose that it's because for all their lives they've been hanging over the edge of the ultimate pit by their eyebrows.

**1965** J. Brunner *Altar on Asconel* 20: The Empire never embraced the whole of the galaxy, though people generally assume it did. It could be a Rim world, some distance from the hub.

**1982** J. Yolen *Dragon's Blood* xii: Betting syndicates developed, and starship crews on long rim-world voyages began to frequent the planets for illicit gambling.

**2004** D. Stahler, Jr. *Truesight* (2005) 35: Citizenship taught students about the origins of the Foundation, about the settlement of the rim worlds and the founding of their own colony at Harmony Station.

**robo-** *pref.* used to indicate that something is a robot or is controlled robotically.

**1945** A. E. van Vogt *World of Ā* in *Astounding S-F* (Oct.) 83/1: Sensitive detectors must be probing the skies, to make sure no roboplanes or other solar craft were passing overhead.

**1958** R. Silverberg *Passport to Sirius* in *World of Thousand Colors* (1984) 162: The roboteller handed over the cash without comment.

**1963** K. Laumer *Walls* in *Amazing Stories* (Mar.) 83/2: Flora had taken the 1100 car to the roboclinic on the 478th level for her annual check-up.

**1978** B. Shaw *Ship of Strangers* (1979) 216: Mobile robocranes surrounded the *Sarafand.*

**1992** N. Stephenson *Snow Crash* 26: If you surf over a chuckhole, the robo-prongs plumb its asphalty depths.

**1994** H. Harrison *Stainless Steel Rat Sings Blues* 22: The robobar supplied our drinks.

**2005** *San Francisco Chronicle* (Nov. 6) J3/1: Before dawn on Oct. 8, its parking lots bustled with risk-takers of a different sort—the dreamers, academics and defense contractors behind the competing robocars.

**robot** *n.* **1.** [< Czech *robota*, "forced labor"] an intelligent or self-aware artificial being, especially one made of metal. Also used *fig.*

[**1920** K. Čapek *R.U.R. Rossum's Universal Robots* (1923) 17: Tak vidíte, slečno Gloryová. Roboti nelpí na životě. Nemají totiž čím. Nemají požitků. Jsou méně než tráva.]

**1923** P. Selver *trans.* K. Čapek *R.U.R.* 28: You see [...] the Robots have no interest in life. They have no enjoyments.

**1923** *Times (London)* (June 9) 10/5: If Almighty God had populated the world with Robots, legislation of this sort might have been reasonable.

**1925** T. C. Bridges *City of No Escape* 58: "Marse Nick," he demanded, "is dey real men or does dey go by machinery?" [...] "Sort of Robots I'd say."

**1940** E. Hamilton *Calling Captain Future* in *Captain Future* (Spring) 22/1: Grag, the robot, was the first creature created by Roger Newton and the Brain. Their second creation was not of metal but of synthetic plastic flesh.

**1943** J. B. Priestley *Daylight on Saturday* 55: I thought it would be better having a fairly intelligent [...] girl instead of one of these little office robots.

**1944** C. L. Moore *No Woman Born* in *Astounding S-F* (Dec.) 147/2: To Malzer she was pure metal, a robot his own hands and brain had devised, mysteriously animated by the mind of Deirdre, to be sure, but to all outward seeming a thing of metal solely.

**1954** C. Oliver *Field Expedient* in W. F. Nolan *Edge of Forever* (1971) 141: The ship carried two pilots, a navigator, a doctor, fifty babies, twenty-five special humanoid robots, computers, and supplies.

**1968** F. Herbert *Heaven Makers* (1977) 2: The Dispatcher noted Kelexel almost immediately and sent a hovering robot questioner before whose single eye Kelexel bowed.

**1987** N. Spinrad *Little Heroes* (1989) 326: The monotonous, relentless, ancient Bo Diddley riff implied by the lyrics rolling along through percussion, and bassline, and even lead, like a speedfreak rock and roll robot.

**1988** *Locus* (Apr.) 25/2: A young robot and a young genius niece of Jonathan Durant combine to create Hyperdrive.

**2.** a machine that performs a task or action with no or only minimal direct human control.

**1940** *New York Times* (Apr. 11) 28/3: Robots with the ability to outwork dozens of humans are moving into California's specialty crop fields.

**1976** *Scientific American* (Feb.) 77 (caption): Spot-welding robots [...] are used in assembling the under[-]bodies of Chevrolet Novas.

**1980** *Times (London)* (July 1) 19/5: A real robot is programmable; it can be programmed to perform different, and changing tasks. In 1978 Japan put 1,100 playback or programmable robots into its factories.

**1989** *Omni* (Aug.) 64/3: It must have three backup systems for key operations, so that even if two fail, the robot will still be able to function.

**robotic** *adj.* of or relating to a robot; resembling or characteristic of a robot. Hence **robotical,** *adj.,* **robotically,** *adv.,* **roboticized,** *adj.,* **roboticization,** *n.*

**1941** I. Asimov *Liar!* in *Astounding S-F* (May) 50: You'd cut your own nose off before you'd let me get the credit for solving robotic telepathy.

**1946** *American Journal of Psychology* (Vol. LIX) 192: I believe that robotic thinking helps precision of psychological thought.

**1952** E. Wellen *Origins of Galactic Slang* in *Galaxy SF* (Sept.) 43/2: The F. E. G., a roboticized replica of a hated individual, was to be [...] a harmless outlet for emotions repressed because of danger of reprisal.

**1963** *New Worlds SF* (Apr.) 52: Johnston wouldn't have been [...] surprised to find out that more than half of the city's population was robotic, no matter how cleverly they were disguised.

**1976** K. Bonfiglioli *Something Nasty in Woodshed* 53: Sam got up in a robotical sort of way.

**1976** L. Deighton *Twinkle, Twinkle Little Spy* 84: The kind of dispassionate robotic bastard that communism breeds.

**1979** C. Thomas *Snow Falcon* 24: Asked to rehearse once more lines he knew by heart [...]. Robotically, he began.

**1991** M. Weiss *King's Test* 70: A hulking cyborg encased in a protective suit, he twiddled a robotic arm at what was left of the space plane.

**1993** P. Anderson *Harvest of Stars* (1994) 448: Few inhabitants are left in L-5. The roboticization of space operations being well advanced, it has no function except as a tourist resort.

**2000** A. Reynolds *Revelation Space* (2000) 366: The devices moved [...] beyond the hull, becoming, in effect, hugely overcannoned robotic spacecraft.

**roboticist** *n.* someone who makes, works with, or studies robots.

**1940** I. Asimov *Super Sci. Stories* (Sept.) 70/2: Johnson is an expert Roboticist.

**1972** *International Journal of Man-Machine Studies* (Vol. IV) 444: The most obvious computer solution would be to simple search serially through each region to find which was the largest. For a roboticist using a serial computer, that may well be the best approach.

**2004**: see quote in ROBOTICS.

**robotics** *n.* the science of designing, building, or using robots; the study of robots.

**1941** I. Asimov *Astounding S-F* (May) 53: There's irony in three of the greatest experts in robotics in the world falling into the same elementary trap, isn't there?

**1950** I. Asimov *I, Robot* unpag.: THE THREE LAWS OF ROBOTICS 1—A robot may not injure a human being, or, through inaction, allow a human being to come to harm. 2—A robot must obey the orders given it by human beings except where such orders would conflict with the First Law. 3—A robot must protect its own existence as long as such protection does not conflict with the First or Second Law.

**1968** *Times (London)* (Nov. 1) 23/2: Significant technological advances in the field of "robotics"—the use of robots in the field of industrial automation—were announced today.

**2004** M. Predko *123 Robotics Experiments for Evil Genius* 4: Designing a mobile biped robot that can stand up and walk like a human being is considered by many roboticists as the "Holy Grail" of robotics.

**rocketeer** *n.* *Obs.* someone who flies in rocketships. Compare ROCKETMAN.

**1941** N. S. Bond *Day We Celebrate* in G. Conklin *Possible Worlds of SF* (1951) 149: The Rocketeers ain't no diff'rent from any other bunch of conquerors. They do just what England done in India, Holland done in the Pacific, an' the States done in the Philippines.

**1950** K. Bennett *Rocketeers Have Shaggy Ears* in M. Greenberg *Travelers of Space* (1951) 53: Well, Rocketeers, a short life and a merry one. I never did give a damn for riding in these tin cans.

**1950** F. J. Ackerman *Destination Moon* in *Other Worlds* (May) 155/1: I inspected the complex controls of the atomic rocket, saw the hammocks in which the crew are flattened by 6 gravities, visualized how the rocketeers would float in free fall.

**1953** O. Saari *Space Man* in *Mag. of Fantasy & SF* (Apr.) 85: The first moonship was a failure, so you don't hear much about it any more. Jessup was as good a rocketeer as ever lived, but he was tackling a completely new thing. He crash-landed in Imbrium, alive but unable to get back.

**rocketman** *n.* someone, especially a male, who flies in rocketships; a SPACEMAN. Compare ROCKETEER.

**1931** *Puffy* in *Key West (Fla.) Citizen* (Nov. 14) 6: Says Puffy to The Rocket Man: "How fast can that thing go?" The Rocket Man to Puffy says: "It's limit I don't know, But in a test I've gone a thousand miles an hour or so."

**1949** [R. LaFayette] *Unwilling Hero* in *Startling Stories* (July) 102/2: To see Earth and the Moon grow small, to behold the Sun dwindling to an unimpressive star, is an experience which has unnerved many a hardy rocket man.

**1954** R. Bradbury *All Summer in Day* in [A. Boucher] *Best from Fantasy & SF (Fourth Series)* (1955) 100: And this was the way life was forever on the planet Venus, and this was the schoolroom of the children of the rocket men and women who had come to a raining world to set up civilization and live out their lives.

**1959** R. A. Heinlein *Menace from Earth* (1968) 115: Older pilots thought of interplanetary trips with a rocketman's bias in terms of years—trips that a torch ship with steady acceleration covered in days.

**1972** E. John & B. Taupin *Rocketman* in *One Night Only* (2003) 19: And I think it's gonna be a long, long time 'til touchdown brings me round again to find I'm not the man I think am at home. Oh, I'm a rocket man.

**2002** *Post-Standard (Syracuse, New York)* (Dec. 23) A7/3: In my dreams, I was Roy Rogers or one of the various TV cowboys who used to flit across the little home screens. Nowadays, it is monsters, or robots, or futuristic rocketmen that populate the airwaves.

**round robin** *n.* a story written by several authors, each of whom adds a section in turn.

**1944** J. B. Speer *Fancyclopedia* 74/2: round robin—A story each installment of which is by a different author.

**1952** A. H. Rapp, L. Hoffman & R. Boggs *Fanspeak* 10/2: Some of the famouser round robins in fandom were "If I Werewolf" in *Spaceways* and "Stf Broadcasts Again!" in *Spacewarp*.

**1996** *Omni Round-Robin begins* (Usenet: rec.arts.sf.written) (Nov. 21): The First Omni round-robin has begun. James Patrick Kelly has posted the first part of an ongoing (for a month) original sf story on time travel. [...] Next up is Rachel Pollack, then Pat Cadigan, and finally Nancy Kress.

# Star Trek

The television show *Star Trek*, which first aired in 1966, has probably had a greater effect on the English language than any other single science fiction creation, with the possible exception of George Orwell's *Nineteen Eighty-Four*. Words coined for the series and its spin-offs have stuck in the popular imagination, and are used by people in all walks of life. Some, like **mind-meld** and **warp speed**, are mainly used figuratively outside of science fiction. **Starfleet** has found a foothold in science fiction itself, while **cloaking device** and **nanite** straddle both worlds. *Star Trek* also introduced the world to **Klingon**, the language created by linguist Marc Okrand for the movie *Star Trek III: The Search for Spock*, and which has since taken on quite a life of its own.

*Star Trek* also helped popularize some terms that had been around, but for the most part unrecognized, for years: for example, the verb **to beam**, as by a matter transmitter, had appeared occasionally in science fiction since at least the 1950s, but its use on the show popularized it, and "beam me up" (or "beam me up, Scotty," a formulation that was never uttered in the original series) became a catchphrase. The phrase **prime directive** had also appeared previously in science fiction, but was given a boost when the *Star Trek* writers made it the law of the United Federation of Planets. Now, the term is used widely in the world at large, but within science fiction it is almost exclusively associated with *Star Trek*.

The fans of *Star Trek* have also added a number of terms to the language, especially in the realm of fan fiction. **Mary Sue** was originally a character in a *Star Trek* fan fiction parody, and gave her name to any story featuring a transparently idealized version of the author. *Star Trek* fans also named **slash** fiction—fan fiction featuring an erotic relationship between two characters. Early slash fiction often portrayed a relationship between Captain Kirk and Mr. Spock, which became known as **K/S** (for Kirk/Spock) fiction. The slash between the K and the S gave slash fiction its name; it also became the standard nomenclature for fan fiction that focuses on relationships, separating the names or initials of the characters involved. The most familiar fan words, however, are **Trekkie** and **Trekker**, names for the fans themselves (most fans, it should be noted, much prefer the latter term). That these words are so recognizable, even to non-fans, may demonstrate better than anything just how influential the show has been in our popular culture.

# S

**sapience** *n.* [< S.E. *sapience,* "wisdom"] intelligence. Compare SENTIENCE 2.

**1962** H. B. Piper *Little Fuzzy* 44: I think he wants to trick some of our people into supporting his sapience claims.

**1972** M. Z. Bradley *Darkover Landfall* (1987) 111: Not only would it account for the tenacious belief in them against only the sketchiest proof, but it would account for survival where mere sapience would not.

**1993** V. Milán *From Depths* 125: Unless you subscribe to certain fringe theories to the effect that sapience was taught to the ancestors of all present sentient races by some undiscovered agency.

**2003** C. Stross *Singularity Sky* (2004) 370: They milled about downslope, debating the ideological necessity of uplifting non-human species to sapience.

**sapient** *n.* an intelligent being. Compare SENTIENT, SENTIENCE 1, SOPHONT.

**1960** P. J. Farmer *Woman Day* 30: It seemed to him a possibility that the Cold War Corps of March might have contacted hitherto unknown sapients on some just discovered interstellar planet.

**1979** M. Z. Bradley & P. E. Zimmer *Survivors* (1987) 7: There had been a time when Dane thought he would never tire of watching the crowds that thronged these streets, lizard-men, cat-men, bird-men [...] people of every conceivable species of sapient.

**1999** J. May *Orion Arm* 61: If the Earthlings who invaded them were reasonably enlightened— as Rampart was—primitive Indigenous Sapients often prospered.

**2002** J. E. Czerneda *To Trade Stars* 300: They do it so they can get away with eating other sapients?

**sapient** *adj.* [< S.E. *sapient,* "wise"] intelligent. Compare SENTIENT.

**1962** H. B. Piper *Naudsonce* in *Analog Sci. Fact-SF* (Jan.) 9/1: It was inhabited by a sapient humanoid race, and some of them were civilized enough to put it in Class V, and Colonial Office doctrine on Class V planets was rigid.

**1972** M. Z. Bradley *Darkover Landfall* (1989) 88: Arboreal humanoids. [...] Obviously sapient—they're tool-users and makers of artifacts.

**1992** A. Steele *Labyrinth of Night* 275: We passed a rudimentary intelligence test [...] a test designed to prove that we were not only a sapient species, but capable of innovation and creativity as well.

**1998** D. Brin *Heaven's Reach* 189: One of the great mentational dangers of sapient life is egotism—the tendency to see all events in the context of one's own self or species.

**2000** P. Anderson *Genesis* 161: Besides fellow humans he worked closely with sapient machines, and some of them got to be friends too, of an eerie kind.

**Saturnian** *n.* an inhabitant of the planet Saturn.

**1738** *Gentleman's Mag.* (Vol. VIII) 315/2: Some cold Saturnian, when the lifted tube Shows to his wond'ring eye our pensile globe, Pities our thirsty soil, and sultry air.

**1757** T. Smollett & T. Francklin, et al. *trans.* Voltaire *Micromegas* in *Works of M. de Voltaire, Vol. 11* 259: "Alas!" cried the Saturnian, "few, very few on this globe outlive five hundred great revolutions of the sun: (these, according to our way of reckoning, amount to about fifteen thousand years.)"

**1891** O. W. Holmes *Over Teacups* 62: Of course, my companion went on to say, the bodily constitution of the Saturnians is wholly different from that of air-breathing, that is oxygen-breathing, human beings. They are the dullest, slowest, most torpid of mortal creatures.

**1959** H. Koch *Invasion from Inner Space* in F. Pohl *Star SF No. 6* 155: Incidentally, the Saturnians remarked that they had tried for many centuries to communicate with us.

**science fantasy** *n.* **1.** the genres of science fiction and fantasy considered as a whole.

**1935** F. Ackerman *Wonder Stories* (Oct.) 637/2: All the details are contained monthly in FANTASY Magazine, the mirror of the science-fantasy world.

**1955** [A. Boucher] *Intro. Best from Fantasy & SF (Fourth Series)* 7: F&SF has a broader editorial policy than most other science-fantasy publications—a policy which is, in effect, nothing more than to publish originally conceived and well-written imaginative fiction of any and every type.

**1967** J. Merril *SF: Best of Best* 21: Theodore Sturgeon is probably science fantasy's most-reprinted author.

**2.** SCIENCE FICTION 1; a work in this genre. Now chiefly *hist.* Compare FANTASCIENCE, PSEUDO-SCIENCE, SCIENCE FANTASY 2, SCIENTIFIC FANTASY, SCIENTIFIC FICTION, SCIENTIFICTION, SPECULATIVE FICTION 1.

**1939** *New York Times* (Aug. 12) 16/2: Paramount to Film Wells's "Food of the Gods," Science Fantasy.

**1943** P. S. Miller *Fricassee in Four Dimensions* in *Astounding SF* (Dec.) 67/2: "I read a couple of books one time, about the way I am and stuff like that. Fourth-dimension stuff. Tesseracts, and that. You ever seen it?" I had. I've read my share of science fantasies.

**1946** G. Conklin *Intro.* in *Best of SF* xv: Until recently it was remembered only by science-fiction pioneers like H. G. Wells, who has given Stockton credit for helping him along the road which eventually resulted in *The Time Machine, The War of the Worlds*, and his other famous science fantasies.

**1956** J. Merril *S-F: Year's Greatest SF & Fantasy* 345: Science-fantasy has long outgrown both its worship of machines and its fear of emotion. Where emphasis once was on the mechanical sciences, it has shifted now to the psychological.

**1974** F. Pohl *Publishing of SF* in R. Bretnor *SF, Today & Tomorrow* 22: It was almost never labeled science fiction. That term was reserved to the pulp magazines and, in fact, most of them even called it by other names—"science fantasy," or "stories of superscience," or [ ... ] "scientifiction."

**3. a.** a genre of fiction that combines elements or tropes of both science fiction and fantasy; a work in this genre. Compare FANTASCIENCE.

**1948** M. Zimmer *Startling Stories (letter)* (Sept.) 125/2: I may say in conclusion, that Kuttner is noted for his versatility in science-fantasy such as MASK OF CIRCE, in pure fantasy such as CALL HIM DEMON, in humor such as his riotous Hogbens, in science such as LORD OF THE STORM.

**1953** S. Moskowitz *S-F +* (Dec.) 65/1: His [i.e. A. Merritt's] mastery was evidenced most strongly in his tales which may be defined loosely as science-fantasies, stories which have some basis in scientific fact, but which would not qualify under any tight definition of science-fiction.

**1970** T. White *Fantastic Stories* (Dec.) 144/1: Keith Laumer's new serial would have been called "science fantasy" a few years back: a technological gloss laid over basically "magical" situations and events.

**1976** T. M. Disch *Big Ideas & Dead-End Thrills* in *On SF* (2005) 28: Gene Wolfe succeeded at the seemingly impossible task of making literature of the mongrel subgenre of science fantasy.

**1980** G. Wolfe *What Do They Mean, SF?* in *Writer* (Aug.) 13/1: Like fantasy, science fantasy rests upon, and often abounds with, "impossible" creatures and objects—girls asleep for centuries, one-eyed giants, weapons that can speak and may rebel. But it uses the methodology of science fiction to show that these things are not only possible but probable.

**2001** M. Moorcock in R. Klaw *Geek Confidential* (2003) 194: Whereas I grew up reading science fantasy, Leigh Brackett and stuff like that, which, to me, is the perfect combination. You can have magic and science, throw it all in.

**b.** science fiction that includes technologies or abilities that are not generally considered to be scientifically possible; a work of this type. Compare SOFT SCIENCE FICTION 2.

**1958** J. Merril *SF: '58* 11: I decided instead on what you might call an all-purpose science-fantasy: it's got a bit of mutation in it and a spot of *psi*, a few new inventions, much history (past and future) and even, eventually, a whole fleet of space ships.

**1967** R. Silverberg *Voyagers in Time* x: Among some modern science-fiction writers, stories of time-travel are looked upon with faint disdain, because they are not really "scientific." The purists prefer to place such stories in the category of science-*fantasy*, reserved for fiction based on ideas impossible to realize through modern technology.

**1993** *Quality of Next Generation* (Usenet: rec.arts.startrek.current) (Dec. 1): There are some (Arthur C. Clarke among them) who would say Star Trek is not science fiction at all but science fantasy because it involves faster-than-light travel.

**science fiction** *n.* **1.** a genre (of literature, film, etc.) in which the setting differs from our own world (e.g. by the invention of new technology, through contact with aliens, by having a different history, etc.), and in which the difference is based on extrapolations made from one or more changes or suppositions; hence, such a genre in which the difference is explained (explicitly or implicitly) in scientific or rational, as opposed to supernatural, terms. Compare FANTASCIENCE, PSEUDO-SCIENCE, SCIENCE FANTASY 2, SCIENTIFIC FANTASY, SCIENTIFIC FICTION, SCIENTIFICTION, SPECULATIVE FICTION 1.

**1851** W. Wilson *Little Earnest Book upon Great Old Subject* 139: Campbell says that "Fiction in Poetry is not the reverse of truth, but her soft and enchanting resemblance." Now this applies especially to Science-Fiction, in which the revealed truths of Science may be given, interwoven with a pleasing story which may itself be poetical and *true*—thus circulating a knowledge of the Poetry of Science, clothed in a garb of the Poetry of Life.

**1927** *Amazing Stories* (Jan.) 974/2: Remember that Jules Verne was a sort of Shakespeare in science fiction.

**1933** *Astounding Stories* (Dec.) 142/1: The [...] science-fiction fan does not care for stories of the supernatural [...]. Intelligent people, as a rule, will read science fiction.

**1944** J. B. Speer *Fancyclopedia* 75/1: "Science-fiction" has come to include other fiction besides that based upon extrapolation of scientific fact: virtually all tales of the future, the prehistoric past, or of alternate presents or pasts, even tho no connection with our present via time-machine is indicated (example, HGWells's "The Brothers").

**1951** [M. Leinster] *Great Stories of SF* 155: Since it is a story about people in a situation brought about by science, it is a science-fiction story.

**1958** J. Merril *Intro.* in *SF: '58* 9: A few years back, the physical possibility of space flight was still enough in doubt to make space travel a favorite subject for science-fiction, which after all, is *speculative* fiction: meaning a story that answers the question, "What if...?" But in order to be *science*-fiction, the answer must not only be imaginative, but logically reasoned from accepted knowledge of the day.

**1974** R. Bretnor *SF in Age of Space* in R. Bretnor *SF, Today & Tomorrow* 150: *Science fiction:* fiction based on rational speculation regarding the human experience of science and its resultant technologies.

**1974** J. Williamson *SF, Teaching & Criticism* in *SF Today & Tomorrow* 312: Not that the bulk of published science fiction has ever owed any great debt to science.

**1977** *New York Rev. of Books* (Oct. 13) 13/4: The mind produces meaning like a plant branching out in a science-fiction movie.

**ca1982** T. M. Disch *Feast of St. Bradbury* in *On SF* (2005) 125: Usually I would argue that any story set in the future is by its nature science fiction.

**2002** M. Bishop *New York Rev. of SF* (Dec.) 6/1: Sometimes a story casts itself as science fiction because I have been deliberately thinking in sf tropes—aliens, other worlds, time travel, alternate histories.

**2.** a work of science fiction.

**1954** *Herald Press (St. Joseph, Mich.)* (Feb. 27) 2/4: Interest in fiction centers on historical novels and science fictions.

**1961** J. Blish *(letter)* in P. Lupoff & D. Lupoff *Best of Xero* (2005) 117: Can any writer in the audience name a science fiction by Voltaire, or show a single example of its having influenced 20th-century s-f in any way?

**1964** G. Conklin *Five-Odd* 74: This brilliant Scotsman first began writing for American publication in 1950, and has since had a sizable number of first-rate science fictions in our magazines.

**2005** S. Sontag *Report on Journey* in *New York Times Book Rev.* (Feb. 20) 17/1: For instance, both science fictions and philosophical novels need principal characters who are skeptical, recalcitrant, astonished, ready to marvel.

**3.** IMAGINATIVE FICTION. Compare FANTASY 1, SCIENTIFANTASY, SPECULATIVE FICTION 2, STFANTASY.

**1976** T. M. Disch *Mythology & SF* in *On SF* (2005) 22: Myths are everywhere in literature, but especially in science fiction, in which category I would (for present purposes) include all distinctively modern forms of fantasy from Tolkien to Borges.

**1977** P. Nicholls *1975: Year in SF* in U. K. Le Guin *Nebula Award Stories Eleven* 92: *In this very volume you hold in your hand*, containing the Nebula Award winners for the best science fiction of 1975, there are some stories which back in the decaying slums of the center they'd call "fantasy."

**1987** C. Rozeboom *Isaac Asimov's SF Mag. (letter)* (mid-Dec.) 14/1: Now, please understand that my love of science fiction was kindled when, at the ripe age of twelve, I stumbled upon *The Earthsea Trilogy* and was so carried away that I proceeded to devour every Ursula Le Guin book in the public library.

**science-fictional** *adj.* **1.** of, like, relating to, or characteristic of science fiction. Hence **science-fictionalize**, *v.*, **science-fictionalization**, *n.*

**1935** F. J. Ackerman *Wonder Stories (letter)* (Feb.) 1139/1: "The Final Struggle" unfortunately impressed me as being very bad as a science-fictional, fantastic, or any kind of story.

**1949** A. J. Cox *Astounding SF (letter)* (Oct.) 150/1: Grudge is one of the first interesting science-fictional characters to come along in a long while.

**1950** R. Sneary *Planet Stories (letter)* (Fall) 100/2: We will have authors, and fans, auctions and speachs [sic] on science-fictional subjects.

**1965** *Analog SF-Sci. Fact* (Dec.) 149: Next month's feature story will be "Second Seeded," by R. C. FitzPatrick—which has to do with an aspect of a very old problem, but a strictly science-fictional aspect.

**1976** T. M. Disch *Big Ideas & Dead-End Thrills* in *On SF* (2005) 35: The Gaia hypothesis is also a natural for science-fictionalization.

**1980** M. Z. Bradley *Darkover Retrospective* in *Planet Savers/Sword of Aldones* (1982) 310: It never occurred to me to write fantasy until I discovered the science-fictional fantasy style of the novels of Moore and Kuttner.

**1990** *Thrust* (Winter) 9/3: Stableford ingeniously brings vampires over into the science-fictional sphere.

**1991** T. M. Disch *Speaker Moonbeam* in *On SF* (2005) 238: There is never to be any science-fictional accounting for this wonderful journey; the machinery that accomplishes it is transparently aesthetic.

**2003** J. Clute *Intro.* in J. White *General Practice* 8: Other terms for this very science-fictional format include A. E. van Vogt's "fixup," or "suite," which I myself would prefer to use in order to describe the essential sequential nature of White's assembly-work.

**2005** J. Clute *SF Weekly* (Internet) (Sept. 6): In this case the process is science-fictionalized by having the crown prince of the Mid-Galactic Empire 200 centuries hence change consciousnesses with John Gordon, a man bored with civilian life after his experiences in World War II.

**2.** belonging to the genre of science fiction.

**1959** C. M. Kornbluth *Failure of SF Novel as Social Criticism* in B. Davenport, et al. *SF Novel* (1969) 51: This kind of empire-building has resulted in an impressive list of titles allegedly science-fictional going back to classic times or for all I know earlier.

**2003** V. Rosenzweig *New York Rev. of SF* (Jan.) 22/1: This is the most obviously science fictional story in the book: the starship is central to the characters' lives and to the nature of the tale.

**2004** D. Broderick *X, Y, Z, T* 87: Philip Roth's novel *Deception* (1990) is, in effect, a radio drama drawing poignantly upon the death by cancer of his English mistress. By no means science fictional...and yet...

**3.** resembling something that might, or could only, appear in a science fiction story.

**1959** R. A. Heinlein *SF: Its Nature, Faults & Virtues* in B. Davenport, et al. *SF Novel* (1969) 34: The prototype of the space ship... known to mathematical physics since the time of Newton and now being realized on the drawing boards and in the proving grounds of our fabulously science fictional nation.

**1976** I. Murdoch *Henry & Cato* 222: The glossy hexagonal glasses which looked here like the appurtenances of some science fictional spaceman.

**2003** D. Broderick *New Wave & Backwash* in E. James & F. Mendlesohn *Cambridge Companion to SF* 48: By late 1962, the world actually faced just such a science-fictional threat—the Cuban missile crisis, when nuclear war seemed about to erupt.

**2005** D. Langford *Ansible* (Internet) (July): Therefore, stars have been added. Stars which shine straight through that gas-giant planet and its moon. Really science-fictional stars.

**4.** of or relating to science fiction fandom.

**1969** F. Porter in H. Warner, Jr. *All Our Yesterdays* 156: You have made friends here who will forever remember your exceeding kindness to us at a time when we were otherwise simply cut off from the world science-fictional.

**1977** U. K. Le Guin *Nebula Award Stories Eleven* xi: I had three totally science-fictional weeks in Australia around the World Science Fiction Convention.

**science-fictionality** *n.* the quality of being science-fictional; (of a work of fiction) being science-fictional.

**1996** D. Pringle, et al. *Ultimate Ency. of SF* 140/3: Sf purists might not consider it [i.e., the TV show *The Prisoner*] sufficiently wholehearted in its science-fictionality to qualify as the best.

**1997** I. Csicsery-Ronay *S-F Studies* (Mar.) 146: The elements of "science-fictionality" in the everyday life of mass culture are largely ignored.

**2002** M. Bishop *New York Rev. of SF* (Dec.) 7/1: I found her denial of the science-fictionality of *The Sparrow* not only off-putting but as obtuse as the cluelessness of the novel's priest.

**science-fictionally** *adv.* in a manner characteristic of science fiction; from the standpoint of science fiction.

**1936** R. Lowndes *Thrilling Wonder Stories* (letter) (Dec.) 126/2: Science-fictionally speaking, "Blood of the Moon," was enjoyed.

**1969** A. Budrys *Benchmarks* (1985) 234: What some of us appear to have missed is that life has changed fundamentally, and science-fictionally.

**1974** I. Asimov *Before Golden Age* 986: "Who Goes There?" was eventually made into the financially successful but science fictionally contemptible motion picture *The Thing*, for which John was paid a mere few hundred dollars in total.

**2001** *Locus* (June) 69/1: More science-fictionally, the automatic fate [ ... ] will strike down any red-shirted security person.

**science fictioneer** *n.* a SCIENTIFICTIONIST. Now *hist.* Compare SCIENCE FICTIONIST.

**1940** *Super Sci. Stories* (Mar.) 105/1: There is today no real unifying organization to which every fan can belong [ ... ]. To fill that gap, which prevents the fulfillment of many ambitious projects of science fiction readers, we offer *The Science Fictioneers.*

**1941** *Thrilling Wonder Stories* (Jan.) 122: You're not a full-fledged scientifiction fan unless you own a membership card in the *Science Fiction League.* Thousands of science-fictioneers the world over belong to this active, international organization devoted to fantasy fans' fraternization.

**1948** J. W. Campbell, Jr. *Atlantic Monthly* (May) 97/1: The science-fictioneers' prediction of the coming of television at that time was based largely on the proposition that people certainly wanted the gadget—and wanted it badly.

**1964** G. Conklin *Five-Odd* 55: Amis *is* a mainstream writer, who is experienced at creating vividly real characters and situations—something the professional science fictioneers find almost impossible to achieve.

**1966** I. Asimov *TV Guide* (Mar. 5–11) 20/1: However, these television people would have to stay up all night to put one across on an experienced science-fictioneer like myself.

**1977** *Times Literary Supplement* (Jan. 14) 26/1: Put one science-fictioneer on a desert island and he will start a magazine.

**1996** D. Pringle, et al. *Ultimate Ency. of SF* 233/1: The most distinguished science-fictioneers of the late Soviet Union, the Strugatskys were always a subversive pair.

**science fictioner** *n.* a science fiction film or television show. Compare SCIENTIFILM.

**1953** *Tom Corbett, Space Cadet Variety Television Reviews 1951–1953* (Sept. 2) (1988) unpag.: Assuming the flaws will be corrected within the next couple of showings [ ... ] the science fictioner should make good juvenile viewing.

**1968** *News Journal (Mansfield, Oh.)* (Aug. 10) 14/2: *The Unearthly* [ ... ] John Carradine once more reverts to his mad scientist portrayal in this foolish science-fictioner.

**1997** *Megan Ward is babe.* (Usenet: alt. tv.dark-skies) (Mar. 26): I saw her recently in a B-film science-fictioner from the mid-80s (I'm guessing), one of those ubiquitous Mad Max rip-offs.

**science fictionist** *n.* a SCIENTIFICTIONIST. Compare SCIENCE FICTIONEER.

**1936** W. Conover, Jr. *letter* (Feb.) in F. J. Ackerman *Gosh! Wow! (Sense of Wonder) SF* (1982) 211: True, science-fictionists are slightly insane if you call abnormal mentality, insanity.

**1939** J. W. Campbell, Jr. *Astounding S-F* (Jan.) 6: Recently, at the Philadelphia Science-Fiction Convention, a number of fans and other science-fictionists were asked to give their views on the purpose of the subject.

**1945–46** S. Moskowitz *Immortal Storm* in *Fantasy Commentator* (Winter) 229: No one realized at the time that in so doing he had renounced his belief that science-fictionists must be science-hobbyists.

**1950** A. J. Burks *Commentary* in S. Skirvin *Cinvention Memory Book* 84: As a science fictionist, I should be able to elongate time but find I lack the wisdom of many of my own heroes.

**1953** *Eleventh World SF Convention (Program Booklet)* 5/1: This year's guest of honor is Willy Ley, who is that distinctive combination of scientist and science fictionist.

**1991** *Locus* (Sept.) 72/3: Isn't there some way that the international community of science-fictionists can persuade these guys to ask permission before taking stuff?

**science-fictiony** *adj.* like or having the qualities of science fiction, often to a heightened or exaggerated degree.

**1962** *Western Kansas Press (Great Bend, Kan.)* (Oct. 16) 4/1: Too many builders gaze into the future and want to put a heliport on the roof or perhaps build the guest room out of some edible material. [ ... ] But that sort of thing is too science-fictiony. We have to be practical.

**1978** F. Pohl *Way Future Was* 239: The fire-control room was fancier and science-fictiony-er than the bridge of the starship *Enterprise.*

**1982** M. Bishop *Mag. of Fantasy & SF* (Jan.) 54/1: I thought you might say something about these so that if Disch ever discovers my true identity, he won't reduce me to caricature in some future column. Besides, several of his poems are decidedly science-fictiony.

**1993** R. Silverberg *Collected Stories of Robert Silverberg (Vol. 2: Secret Sharer)* 68: A "translation," [...] is an adaptation of a stock format of mundane fiction into s-f by a simple one-for-one substitution of science-fictiony noises for the artefacts of the mundane field.

**2001** *Locus* (June) 15/1: It's the most science-fictiony story you're likely to read in a while; the author explicitly credits Cordwainer Smith and Alfred Bester as inspirations.

**science story** *n. Obs.* a science-fiction story. Also **science tale,** etc.

**1930** *Sci. Wonder Stories* (June) front cover: Science Stories by H. G. WELLS DR. D. H. KELLER STANTON A. COBLENTZ

**1934** C. Jackson *Astounding Stories (letter)* (June) 158/2: I notice some readers criticise science stories saying that they are not true to facts.

**1946** A. V. Bell *Thrilling Wonder Stories (letter)* (Winter) 10/2: After all I was a little starved for my favorite past[-]time [sic], namely science stories such as *Thrilling Wonder Stories* has been in the habit of publishing since I have been reading it.

**1957** S. Moskowitz *How SF Got Its Name* in *Mag. of Fantasy & SF* (Feb.) 68/1: All science tales in Gernsback publications from that time on were referred to as "scientific fiction," with infrequent lapses into SCIENTIFIC STORIES.

**scienti-** *pref. Obs.* used to indicate that something is, or is somehow related to, science fiction. Compare STF-.

**1934**: see quote in SCIENTIFILM.

**1936** *Thrilling Wonder Stories* (Dec.) 121/1: SCIENTIBOOK REVIEW THE REVOLUTION IN PHYSICS. By Ernst Zimmer, translated from the German by H. Stafford Hatfield.

**1944** J. B. Speer *Fancyclopedia* 76/2: scienti- — A prefix which should indicate only "scientific" (as in "scientifiction") but in use may mean "science-fictional" (as in "scientifilm," meaning a fantastic movie), or even stfandomal. In careless hands the rules of scientificombination are often disregarded, as in "Scientiradio."

**scientifantasy** *n.* [SCIENTI- + FANTASY] *Obs.* IMAGINATIVE FICTION. Compare FANTASY 1, SCIENCE FICTION 3, SPECULATIVE FICTION 2, STFANTASY.

**1936–37** F. J. Ackerman *Whither Ackermankind?* in *Novae Terrae* (Dec.–Jan.) 5: Scientifantasy Field—in my case including imaginative fiction, films, dramas, broadcasts; as applied, as subjects allow, to collecting, reviewing and supplying other fans as salesman; and endeavors Esperantic.

**1939** L. Margulies *Le Zombie* 2 (Oct 28): Fellows, CAPTAIN FUTURE is tops in scientifantasy!

**1947** L. Carter *Startling Stories (letter)* (May) 102/1: By sheer poetic beauty, tremendous vocabulary, magnificent characterization and plots, Merritt has outwritten all other modern fantasy authors. He and Stapledon, Lovecraft, Burroughs, Taine and a few others, are generally called the Immortals of Scientifantasy.

**1969** J. Speer in H. Warner, Jr. *All Our Yesterdays* 194: We wish it [i.e., the Fantasy Amateur Press Association] to be a medium in which we consider a great range of subjects, in many of which scientifantasy is not even a flavoring.

**scientific fantasy** *n.* SCIENCE FICTION 1 or PROTO-SCIENCE FICTION; a work of this type. Now chiefly *hist.* Compare FANTASCIENCE, PSEUDO-SCIENCE, SCIENCE FANTASY 2, SCIENTIFIC FANTASY, SCIENTIFIC FICTION, SCIENTIFICTION, SPECULATIVE FICTION 1.

[**1888** *Brooklyn Daily Eagle* (Dec. 2) 7/2: "The Son of a Star," [...] is a story of revolt against Rome and recalls "Ben Hur." Scientific fantasy enters into it, varying the interest of Bulwer with that of Jules Verne.]

**1894** *New-York Times* (Nov. 10) 6/7: His work on "The Day After Death" [...] a sort of scientific fantasy on the transmigration of souls to other planets, was placed in the Roman Index Expurgatorius.

**1914** *Daily News (Frederick, Md.)* (Aug. 12) 3/2: Jules Verne is a name to conjure with. It stands for that school of prophetic scientific fantasy to which the world is indebted for the inspiration that has led to so many modern inventions.

**1949** H. Smith in R. B. Gehman *Imagination Runs Wild New Republic* (Jan. 17) 18/2: The age of invention rapidly became the age of anxiety...and certainly the age of fear.... The scientific fantasy story may, indeed, be explained as a necessary device...as a buffer against known and more conceivable terrors.

**1970** *New York Times* (Jan. 11) D18/3: Directed by Oldrich Lipsky, it is called "Gentlemen, I Have Killed Einstein" and is described as "a scientific fantasy which grapples in a humorous way with the question: would humanity be faced with the threat of atomic annihilation if Einstein had not existed?"

**1978** I. Asimov *Name of Our Field* in *Asimov on SF* (1981) 26: Jules Verne's extraordinary voyages were called "scientific fantasies" in Great Britain and the term "science fantasy" is sometimes used today.

**scientific fiction** *n.* SCIENCE FICTION 1. Now chiefly *hist.* Compare FANTASCIENCE, PSEUDO-SCIENCE, SCIENCE FANTASY 2, SCIENTIFIC FANTASY, SCIENTIFIC FICTION, SCIENTIFICTION, SPECULATIVE FICTION 1.

**1876** W. H. L. Barnes *In Memoriam* in W. H. Rhodes *Caxton's Book* 7: The great master of scientific fiction, Jules Verne would have found the field of his efforts already sown and reaped.

**1892** *Brooklyn Daily Eagle* (Aug. 21) 12/4: Jules Verne was 35 before he turned his attention to scientific fiction in "Five Weeks in a Balloon."

**1929** C. A. Brandt *Amazing Stories* (Dec.) 862/3: This book [i.e., *The Earth Tube* by Gawain Edwards] can safely be recommended to all lovers of scientific fiction.

**1935** J. Crockett *Astounding Stories (letter)* (Oct.) 158/2: You must take into consideration that we are not humorists, but merely scientific-fiction addicts who try to lend originality to our letters.

**1955** *Post-Standard (Syracuse, New York)* (Feb. 4) 20/2: The result is as exciting as any work of scientific fiction you will be able to find. The difference: What Mr. Cohn describes could very well happen.

**1988** G. Benford *Life of H. G. Wells* in H. G. Wells *Invisible Man* (1992) vii: Success brought an invitation to try scientific fiction in 1894.

**scientific romance** *n.* [the term was earlier applied to fanciful or improbable scientific hypotheses (see 1855 quote), and the literary sense may have evolved from that usage] a work of (usually European) SCIENCE FICTION or PROTO-SCIENCE FICTION, written in the late nineteenth or early twentieth centuries; a modern work that emulates or is reminiscent of such writing.

[**1855** F. Bowen *Principles of Metaphysical & Ethical Science Applied to Evidences of Religion* 150: Milton's conception of inorganic matter left to itself, without an indwelling soul, is not merely more poetical, but more philosophical and just, than the scientific romance, now generally repudiated by all rational inquirers, which represents it as necessarily imbued with the seminal principles of organization and life, and waking up by its own force from eternal quietude to eternal motion.]

**1859** *Southern Literary Messenger* (Feb.) 95/2: [Balzac's] *Ursule Mirouet* may be called a scientific romance of mesmerism and exposition of the French law of Inheritance.

**1874** F. Bowen *American Cyclopædia, Vol. 7* 407/2: Jules Verne has written remarkable scientific romances, which have been translated into English and widely read.

**1897** *New York Times Saturday Rev. of Books & Art* (Aug. 21) 6/2: M. Claretie's new book, has the seemingly paradoxical nature of being a scientific romance. [...] In "L'Accusateur," M. Claretie has a man murdered while gazing at the portrait of his friend, and thus the image stamped upon the human retina is that of an innocent man, who is arrested as the assassin.

**1923**: see quote in FANTASTIC, *n.*

**1953** J. B. Priestley *They Come From Inner Space* in *New Statesman & Nation* (Dec. 5) 712/3: The tone and the atmosphere of these new stories are very different from those of the early scientific romances.

**1985** K. S. Robinson (title) (1996): The Memory of Whiteness: A Scientific Romance

**1993** J. Clute *SF Novels of Year* in D. Garnett *New Worlds 3* 203: He [i.e., Arthur C. Clarke] is, it cannot be too often mentioned, a member (Brian Stableford is another) of a different and exceedingly rare species: an author of Scientific Romances.

**2002** M. Bishop *New York Rev. of SF* (Dec.) 7/1: I've always had a backdoor fondness for sf—early on, I read the scientific romances of H. G. Wells.

**scientifiction** *n.* [ˌsaɪəntɪˈfɪkʃən] SCIENCE [*scientific+fiction*] FICTION 1. Now chiefly *hist.* Compare FANTASCIENCE, PSEUDO-SCIENCE, SCIENCE FANTASY 2, SCIENTIFIC FANTASY, SCIENTIFIC FICTION, SCIENTIFICTION, SPECULATIVE FICTION 1.

**1916** H. Gernsback *Electrical Experimenter* (Jan.) 474/1: I am supposed to report Münchhaussen's [sic] doings; am supposed to be writing fiction, *scientifiction*, to be correct.

**1930** *Notes & Queries* (May 10) 339/1: This class of literature is having a tremendous vogue in America just now. Quite a number of popular magazines are devoted to what they have dubbed "Scientifiction."

**1940** [G. Orwell] *Horizon* (Vol. I) 191: H. G. Wells [...] is the father of "Scientifiction."

**1942**: see quote in FANZINE.

**1951** *Marvel Sci. Stories* (May) 120/2: First— Why should scientifiction magazines publish only scientifiction?

**1994** *Interzone* (Sept.) 33/2: It catalyzed the growing awareness of style and technique in science fiction and interrupted the tradition of clumsy formula writing which had persisted, in various guises, ever since the birth of "scientifiction" in the 1920s.

**2002** M. Bishop *New York Rev. of SF* (Dec.) 1/1: I haven't written bona fide beholden-to-Gernsback scientifiction in nine or ten years, when I produced a generation-starship story called "Cri de Coeur."

**scientifictional** *n.* of, relating to, or resembling scientifiction. Hence **scientifictionally,** *adv.*

**1929** *Amazing Stories Quarterly* (Fall) 575: I wish to compliment you on your choice of "scientifictional" stories.

**1939** C. Hornig *Fantasy Fan* in *SF* (Oct.) 116/1: Back in the dim days of the remote past, scientifictionally speaking, Schwartz was the co-founder and co-editor of the very first fan publications in the fantasy field.

**1942** L. V. Engels *Future combined with SF (letter)* (Aug.) 103/1: Perhaps I should write a letter to the editors of the other scientifictional magazines suggesting the same things, but it seems to me, Mr. Editor, that you are in a far better position to do something about making stf writing more "inspirational."

**1966** J. Merril *Mag. of Fantasy & SF* (Feb.) 44/2: Also from Gollancz is a first novel by Leonard Daventry, a book in some ways almost quaintly "scientifictional" in tone—but very new in its examination of the idea of telepathy as a manifestation of the collective unconscious.

**2004** *Backlash against series?* (Usenet: rec. arts.sf.composition) (June 17): It [i.e., *Red Dwarf*] was never afraid to take very left-field scientifictional ideas and run with them.

**2004** J. Lobdell *Scientifiction Novels of C. S. Lewis* 59: Moreover, it seems to me evident that the Othertime is an attempt at "scientifictional" version of the Kingdom of Faerie.

**scientifictionist** *n. Obs.* a fan or writer of science fiction. Compare SCIENCE FICTIONEER, SCIENCE FICTIONIST.

**1933** F. J. Ackerman *Amazing Stories (letter)* (Apr.) 88/1: I correspond with a great number of scientifictionists, and I know they have remarked to me a number of times that AMAZING STORIES ran letters of theirs nine or ten months after they had been submitted.

**1935** R. J. Binder *Wonder Stories (letter)* (Oct.) 634/1: I agree with you in the May issue in regard to Forrie's letter. He is *the* scientifictionist.

**1937** W. Sykora in S. Moskowitz *Immortal Storm Fantasy Commentator* (1946–47) (Winter) 13: It is a challenge to scientifictionists and experimenters alike.

**1944**: see quote in APA.

**1966** C. S. Lewis *On SF* in *On Stories* (1982) 59: Dante takes you there: he describes with all the gusto of the later scientifictionist how surprising it was to see the sun in such a position.

**1967** J. Speer *Resilient Time* in *Fancestral Voices* (2004) 66: A few authors such as Heinlein still think it is possible. However, most scientifictionists eventually became aware that efforts to reconcile the postulate and this theory did not stand close examination.

**scientifilm** *n.* [SCIENTI- + *film*] *Obs.* a science-fiction movie. Compare SCIENCE FICTIONER.

**1934** *Fantasy Mag.* (Sept.) Table of contents: FORREST J. ACKERMAN Scientifilm Editor.

**1935** F. Ackerman *Wonder Stories* (Oct.) 637/2: You will forgive me if the scientifilm-ending to "Mystery of the -/-" seemed obvious to me before completing the story, being a Scientificinemologist by profession.

**1938** R. Wilson, Jr. *Undersea Kingdom—Criticism & Synopsis* in *Sci. Fantasy Movie Rev.* (Sept.) 3: Outside of these few discrepancies, "The Undersea Kingdom" is the answer of a scientifilm fan's dream.

**1939** W. S. Sykora *Astounding S-F (letter)* (Jan.) 157/1: *New Fandom* hopes to obtain the great scientifilm "Metropolis" to be shown at this meeting.

**1957** F. J. Ackerman *Imaginative Tales* (July) 122/1: This is the second scientifilm sale for Fairman, whose "Deadly City" was filmed as *Target—Earth*!

**sci-fi** *abbr.* **1.** ['saɪ'faɪ] [by analogy to *hi-fi*] SCIENCE FICTION. Compare SCI-FIC, SF, SKIFFY. [Although "sci-fi" was coined as a neutral abbreviation, and is still used by some science-fiction fans in this way, its perceived overuse by the media and non–science-fiction readers has caused many fans to disdain its use, and its use may brand the user as an outsider.]

**1949** R. A. Heinlein *letter* (Oct. 1) in R. A. Heinlein & V. Heinlein *Grumbles from Grave* (1990) 94: I have two short stories that I am very hot to do, one a bobby-sox for *Calling All Girls* and one a sci-fi short which will probably sell to slick and is a sure sale for pulp.

**1957** *MD: Medical Newsmag.* (June) 62/1: Modern sci-fi writers follow an honorable tradition.

**1973** [J. Tiptree, Jr.] *Girl Who Was Plugged In* in *Warm Worlds Otherwise* (1975) 81: But pass up the sci-fi stuff for now, like for instance the holovision technology that's put TV and radio in museums.

**1974** *Observer (London)* (Oct. 27) 1/7: The SF fan world abounds in language [ ... ] that can

baffle the novice [ ... ]. Most important of all, you must not say "sci fi"—it's always SF.

**1987** C. Rozeboom *Isaac Asimov's SF (letter)* (mid-Dec.) 14/1: It was only after I had depleted the shelves of unread Le Guin that I ventured to try some of the other names in the scifi racks.

**1994** R. Silverberg *Hot Sky at Midnight* 61: If it does [ ... ] we really *will* end up with a world full of sci-fi monsters instead of human beings.

**2002** P. Di Filippo *Asimov's SF* (Dec.) 134/2: MacLeod's trademark political savvy gets a good workout here, but he never lets his poly-sci get in the way of good ol' sci-fi wonderment.

**2005** *SF Weekly (San Francisco)* (Mar. 16–22) 40/2: Sci-fi readers call this type of thing "steampunk."

**2.** ['saɪ'faɪ;'skɪfi] unoriginal or poor-quality science fiction, especially with regard to movies and television shows.

**1978** I. Asimov *Name of Our Field* in *Asimov on SF* (1981) 28: We can define "sci-fi" as trashy material sometimes confused, by ignorant people, with s.f. Thus, *Star Trek* is s.f. while *Godzilla Meets Mothra* is sci-fi.

**1987** N. Spinrad *Isaac Asimov's SF* (July) 179/1: "Sci-fi"—commercial action-adventure formula plotting, conventionalized image systems, simplistic moral dualism, transparent self-effacing prose, mandatory happy endings, the whole pulp tradition baggage—easily enough characterizes the prevalent literary vices of the SF genre.

**1990** *Thrust* (Winter) 28/3: The result of "sci-fi" being used so heavily by people to whom science fiction meant bad monster movies was that "sci-fi" has come to mean bad monster movies.

**1999**: see quote in GOSHWOW.

**2001** *SF Chronicle* (Mar.) 16/3: All of the media tie-ins are sci fi. They're exploiting the superficial and colorful stuff that science fiction makes possible.

**2004** D. Broderick *X, Y, Z, T* 14: Is the prevalence of *sci fi* necessarily a bad thing? Decades ago, the brilliant sf innovator Alfred Bester remarked with terrifying kindliness: "As for second-rate, commercial writing—ass-licking writing, as it were—what's the harm in that?"

**sci-fic** *abbr.* SCIENCE FICTION. Compare SCI-FI, SF.

**1939** [B. Tucker] *Le Zombie* (Nov. 18) 2: Popular Pubs does not now publish a sci-fic mag.

**1952** J. Merril *Thrilling Wonder Stories* (Dec.) 6/1: Does your science-fiction story taste different lately? Is the flat familiar stale taste disappearing? [...] There's a reason. Its name is Synthesis, and sci-fic is its prophet.

**1979** *Now!* (Sept. 14) 6/4: Arthur C. Clarke is first of five sci-fic writers to talk about their work.

**1987** *Chronicle-Telegram (Elyria, Oh.)* (Feb. 26) E2/5: Weird Tales, Fantasy, Sci-Fic pulp magazines, Walton's Gum Cards.

**seetee** *adj.* [pronunciation spelling of CT, "contraterrene"] *Obs.* CONTRATERRENE. Sometimes as *n.* Compare TERRENE.

**1943** [W. Stewart] *Opposites—React!* in *Astounding S-F* (Jan.) 10/2: He knew that seetee was a key to illimitable power, both physical and political. Because a pebble of it, in contact with any normal matter, reacted with the energy of a ton of detonating tritonite.

**1943** A. E. van Vogt *Storm* in B. W. Aldiss *Space Opera* (1974) 211: The stripped seetee nuclei carried now terrific and unbalanced negative charges and repelled electrons, but tended to attract terrene atom nuclei.

**1954** G. O. Smith *Spacemen Lost* in *Startling Stories* (Fall) 38/1: "They may be contraterrene." "Seetee?"

**1955** G. Gunther *Startling Stories (letter)* (Spring) 8/1: Both parties, the terrene as well as the contra[-]terrene, entertain exactly the same viewpoint of the Universe. But this sameness cannot be communicated across the gulf that separates our form of physical reality from the one of the seetee world.

**Selenite** *n.* [< Gk. *selenites*, "man in the moon" < *selene*, "moon"] a native of the Earth's moon.

**ca1645** Howell *Letter* (1655) 18: The sphear of the Moon is peepled with Selenites or Lunary men.

**1864** T. W. Webb *Intellectual Observer* (Vol. V) 200: Gruithuisen fancied that certain rows of hillocks might contain the habitations of Selenites.

**1901** H. G. Wells *First Men in Moon* 120: Then I perceived it was the slender, pinched body and short and extremely attenuated bandy legs of a Selenite, with his head depressed between his shoulders.

**1999** I. McDonald *Breakfast on Moon, with Georges* in P. Crowther *Moon Shots* 296: Five frail Selenites to one Terrene, the Members of the Anglo-French Expedition to the Moon are borne into the heart of the Temple of Dreams.

**semi-prozine** *n.* [*semi-pro*fessional maga*zine*] a magazine that is between the levels of fanzine and prozine in some category such as circulation, quality of printing, pay scale, etc.

**1975** E. Weinstein *Fillostrated Fan Dictionary* 114: Semi-prozine[...]: Slick, professional [sic] looking fanzines that charge prozine prices.

**1977** S. Wood *Algol* (Summer–Fall) 23/1: You can either pick a really serious stfnal name like, oh, Starship or Science Fiction Essays and go the semi-prozine rout, or you can pick an off-the wall name and be crazy-fannish.

**1987** *Locus* (May) 4/3: These are difficult times for fiction semi-prozines (and their editors).

**2003** D. G. Hartwell & K. Cramer *Intro.* in *Year's Best Fantasy 3* xv: The semi-prozines of our field mirror the "little magazines" of the mainstream in fiction, holding to professional editorial standards and publishing the next generation of writers.

**2004** M. Ashley *How Big's Yours...?* in *Postscripts* (Spring) 118: These semi-professional or small-press magazines were pretty thin on the ground until the 1970s but then, as the professional sf magazines began to fail, and as computer technology allowed for easier and better production, the number of semi-prozines grew like crazy.

**sense of wonder** *n.* a feeling of awakening or awe triggered by an expansion of one's awareness of what is possible or by confrontation with the vastness of space and time, as brought on by reading science fiction.

[**1935** H. P. Lovecraft *Some Notes on Interplanetary Fiction in Miscellaneous Writings* (1995) 119: The important factors being here, as elsewhere, an adequate sense of wonder, adequate emotions in the characters, [ ... ] and a studious avoidance of the hackneyed artificial characters and stupid conventional events.]

**1956** D. Knight *Future SF* (May) 126/2: Science fiction exists to provide what Moskowitz and others call "the sense of wonder": in more precise terms, some widening of the mind's horizons, in no matter what direction—the landscape of another planet, or a corpuscle's-eye view of an artery, or what it feels like to be in rapport with a cat.

**1963** S. Moskowitz *Proceedings; Chicon III* 55: I didn't create the term, "Sense of Wonder," I just used it. And it's been defined by Rollo May in his book, *Man's Search For Himself*, as a sort of opening attitude, a feeling that there is more to the universe than has been yet observed and that of an awakening attitude.

**1965** A. Budrys *Benchmarks* (1985) 7: There is the reader's growing sense of grasping something grand...the sense of wonder, if you will.

**1982** R. Arbur *Leigh Brackett* in T. Staicar *Feminine Eye* (1982) 6: "Sense of wonder" is science fiction's analogue of mainstream literature's "shock of recognition."

**1998** L. Shepard *Must Have Been Something I Ate* in J. Dann *Nebula Awards 32* 7: The field has become glutted with multivolume variations on *Lord of the Rings* and Sense of Wonder bugcrushers written with all the passionate élan of tax-instruction booklets.

**2002**: see quote in MULTIVERSAL.

**sentience** *n.* **1.** an intelligent being. Compare SAPIENT, SENTIENT, SOPHONT.

**1947** G. O. Smith *Kingdom of Blind* in *Startling Stories* (July) 48/1: Secondly, the true schizophrenic paranoid cannot rail against a mechanistic fate. He must find some sentience to fight, some evil mind to combat.

**1991** T. Bisson *They're Made Out of Meat* in *Bears Discover Fire & Other Stories* (1993) 35: First it wants to talk to us. Then I imagine it wants to explore the Universe, contact other sentiences, swap ideas and information. The usual.

**1998** I. MacDonald *Days of Solomon Gursky* in G. Dozois *Mammoth Book of Best New SF, 12th Coll.* (1999) 253: PanLife, that amorphous, multi-faceted cosmic infection of human, transhuman, non-human, PanHuman sentiences, had filled the universe.

**2002** U. K. Le Guin *Social Dreaming of Frin* in *Mag. of Fantasy & SF* (Oct.–Nov.) 185: The duty of the strong-minded person, she holds, is to strengthen dreams, to focus them [ ... ] as a means of understanding the world through a myriad of experiences and sentiences (not only human).

**2.** intelligence. Compare SAPIENCE.

**1954** P. Anderson *Brain Wave* 120: Corinth's memory went back over what he had seen, [ ... ] the life which blossomed in splendor or struggled only to live, and the sentience which had arisen to take blind nature in hand. It had been a fantastic variety of shape and civilization.

**1969** A. McCaffrey *Dramatic Mission* in *Analog SF-Sci. Fact* (June) 64/2: It was a convention among all the sophisticated societies she had encountered that sentience was not permitted to waste itself. Kira Falernova had found it excessively difficult to commit suicide.

**1991** D. Stabenow *Second Star* 180: The Librarian had awakened Archy to sentience, to self-will, to an intelligence unprogrammed, unsupervised, not of human born.

**1994** [L. A. Graf] *Firestorm* 23: Spock, have you started checking out the Johnston observatory's sentience report?

**2001** D. Gerrold *Bouncing off Moon* 307: Intelligence exists as the ability to recognize patterns. Self-awareness is intelligence recognizing the patterns of its own self. Sentience is the ownership of that awareness—the individual begins to function as the source, not the effect of his own perceptions.

**sentient** *n.* an intelligent being. Compare SAPIENT, SENTIENCE 1, SOPHONT.

**1965** P. J. Farmer *Maker of Universes* (1975) 30: The merpeople and the sentients who lived on the beach often hitched rides on these creatures, steering them by pressure on exposed nerve centers.

**1977** F. Herbert *Dosadi Experiment* 30: Dosadi, a planet of thinking creatures—*sentients*.

**1978** J. C. Haldeman *Longshot* in *Another Round at Spaceport Bar* (1992) 85: Those sentients on Dimian really get off on lettuce mold.

**1999** L. Evans *Stray* in D. Weber *Worlds of Honor* (2000) 60: At this juncture, it had been only a couple of T-months since [ ... ] human contact with the native sentients of Sphinx.

**1999** L. Norman *Dark Nadir* 212: It is an offense to read a sentient's thoughts without their permission.

**sentient** *adj.* [< S.E. *sentient,* "capable of perceiving or feeling"] intelligent. Compare SAPIENT.

**1930** *Sci. Wonder Stories* (Jan.) table of contents: ON THE COVER this month is shown the strange sentient visitor from outer space.

**1932** J. B. Harris *Lost Machine* in *Amazing Stories* (Apr.) 42/2: A touch on the lever sent the machine sinking rapidly towards a green rectangle, so regular as to suggest the work of sentient creatures.

**1954** E. F. Russell *Witness* in *Deep Space* (1956) 64: I did not trap it. I knew it was sentient and treated it as such.

**1991** T. Bisson *They're Made Out of Meat* in *Bears Discover Fire & Other Stories* (1993) 34: How can meat make a machine? You're asking me to believe in sentient meat.

**1998** G. Cox *Assignment: Eternity* 23: My superiors [ ... ] are occupied elsewhere in the galaxy, safeguarding the development of sentient races.

**2004** M. Bishop *Angst of God* in *Mag. of Fantasy & SF* (Oct./Nov.) 91: A week later, in a new session, I met a seven-armed, chitin-plated sentient caterpillar from the Tau Ceti system.

**sercon** *n.* a sercon fan or sercon activities.

**1958** R. M. Holland *Ghu's Lexicon* 13: *sercon* (also *sericon*) Originally the business or serious sessions at conventions. Now [ ... ] one who discusses the sordid details of some fan activity instead of following the trufan motto: Let's pretend they aren't there and maybe they'll go away.

**1961** J. Koning *Withdrawal* in *S-F Five-Yearly* (Nov.) 25: The sercons and Socially Conscious types smothered them in significant issues and realistic views.

**1966** L. Carter *Handy Phrase-Book in Fannish* in *If* (Oct.) 66/2: But let's suppose your fan activities are confined to writing scholarly treatises on the Sources Used by H..P. Lovecraft in creating his Cthulhu Mythos, or deadly-serious lit-ry criticism of the latest Ace paperbacks [ ... ]. In this case, you may very well be dismissed as an eggheady old Sercon.

**sercon** *adj.* [*serious* + *constructive*] concerned with serious matters such as criticism or scholarship; (pejoratively) boring or self-important. Hence **serconnishness,** *n.*

[**1952** A. H. Rapp, L. Hoffman & R. Boggs *Fanspeak* 11/1: *serious constructive fan.* One who thinks fan activity is less of a hobby than a means of advancing mankind toward the utopias described in science fiction. Serious constructiveness also extends to advocacy of the N3F as a fan government, and of publishing "high-minded" fanzines in order to impress and recruit outsiders.]

**1959** R. H. Eney *Fancyclopedia II* 4: Anglofandom resembles and has many links with US fandom, but is somewhat more adult in point of age and less plagued with the fuggheaded sorts of serconnishness...the latter, no doubt, being due to the former.

**1959** Eney, *Fancy. II* 162: Isaac Asimov intruded in the normally sercon article pages of Astounding a deadpan exposition of a substance which had, when progressively purified, shorter and shorter solution times.

**1969** H. Warner, Jr. *All Our Yesterdays* 84: Its contents were sercon. There were interviews with Fearn, Eric Frank Russell, and Festus Pragnell, it took great interest in Campbell's future plans for his prozines, and it ran photographs of rocket experiments.

**1969** Warner, *All Our Yesterdays* 247: This seems to have been a sercon, dull group for the first few years.

**1975** E. Weinstein *Fillostrated Fan Dictionary* 4: A few of the copies will be sent to Linguistics departments in a few universities. I realize that this is not a very faanish stunt, but rather more sercon.

**2004** A. Widner *Intro.* in J. Speer *Fancestral Voices* 11: He participated in early fannish tomfoolery [...] but got sercon by becoming a charter member of the Fantasy Amateur Press Association.

**SF, S. F., S-F, sf, s. f., s-f** *abbr.* SCIENCE FICTION; SPECULATIVE FICTION; (occasionally) SCIENCE FANTASY.

**1929** H. M. Reid *Sci. Wonder Stories (letter)* (June) 92/3: The S. F. Magazine. (Science Fiction).

**1939** M. Alger *Thrilling Wonder Stories (letter)* (Oct.) 122/2: "Xandulu," by Jack Williamson, which was printed in the old Wonder [...] still stands out as the very pinnacle of s-f.

**1956** R. A. Heinlein *letter* (Oct. 9) in R. A. Heinlein & V. Heinlein *Grumbles from Grave* (1990) 108: Ginny suggests that I not use it in science fiction [...]. It would not be seriously reviewed in an S-F novel.

**1959** *Times Literary Supplement* (Mar. 20) 166/2: Both are by O.K.-names in the s.f. world.

**1965** P. S. Miller *Analog SF-Sci. Fact* (Dec.) 151/1: Three of the ten stories are not science fiction, though they are "SF" in Judith Merril's broader interpretation.

**1969** S. R. Delany *About Five Thousand One Hundred & Seventy Five Words* in *Extrapolation* (May) 66: To summarize, however: any serious discussion of speculative fiction must get away from the distracting concept of sf content and examine precisely what sort word-beast sits before us.

**1974** R. Bretnor *SF in Age of Space* in *SF, Today & Tomorrow* 150: This is the central fact of science fiction, and if we accept it we can apply it also to *science fantasy* as part of the whole, distinguished from science fiction proper simply by being permitted greater freedom in choosing its bases for extrapolation. (Therefore *sf* is an especially useful term, for it can embrace both without explanation.)

**1979** D. Suvin *Metamorphoses of SF* 68: A look into bookstores will show that a good proportion of what is sold as SF is constituted by tales of more or less supernatural or occult fantasy.

**1990** *Thrust* (Winter) 4/2: Darrell Schweitzer looks once again at recent SF TV and films.

**2001** *Locus* (June) 17/2: In a way the story is saying: SF won't get us our dreams, so maybe fantasy isn't so bad after all.

**2002** M. Bishop *New York Rev. of SF* (Dec.) 6/2: But so much latter-day sf *is* unmitigated crap—*Star Wars* and *Star Trek* novels, role-playing fiction, elf and unicorn franchises, space opera and psychic cat stories.

**2004** D. Broderick *X, Y, Z, T* 13: Sf uses a blend of romantic palette and gritty science, of whimsy and satire, of unchecked *possibility*.

**SF/F/H** *abbr.* science fiction, fantasy, and horror.

**1991** *Locus* (Sept.) 78/3: As a reader (or a writer) of sf/f/h, a writer who writes well enough to make his or her peers jealous is a blessing to readers.

**1993** *SFRA Rev.* (Jan.–Feb.) 10: I will be accepting reviews of science fiction, fantasy *and horror*, well as [sic] supernatural, utopian, dark fantasy, apocalyptic, post-holocaust, and any other kind of word you can put on SF/F/H, both nonfiction and fiction.

**2002** *SF Chronicle* (Apr.) 29/2: They also outsell most other mid-list SF/F/H titles.

**2003** C. Miéville *New Weird* in *Locus* (Dec.) 8/1: There's been some talk and argument about the New Weird, a moment—or is that movement?—in SF/F/H.

**SF-ish** *adj.* SCIENCE-FICTIONAL. Compare SFNAL, STFNAL.

**1976** D. S. Carey *Galaxy SF (letter)* (July) 159/1: It could be used for articles about more sf-ish concepts; space drives, things like Bigger Than Worlds that Niven had in *Analog* some time back.

**1990** J. Russ L. McCaffery *Across Wounded Galaxies* 199: Mainly I was interested in science in a detached, aesthetic way—the SF-ish sense of wonder and marvel that still guides my response to science.

**2001** *Booklist* (July) 1993/1: This is just the world according to Ray Vukcevich, sf-ish enough to get him into the *Magazine of Fantasy and Science Fiction* and *Asimov's* but also resembling the fantastic milieus of Gogol, Kafka, and Looney Toons.

**SFnal** *abbr.* [ˈɛsˈɛfnəl; ˈsɛfnəl] SCIENCE-FICTIONAL. Compare SF-ISH, STFNAL.

**1981** R. Sabella *SF Rev.* (Summer) 58/1: On a more SFnal level, it concerns a fascinating theory about resurrecting ghosts of the past through modern science.

**1986** J. Gilpatrick *Locus* (Nov.) 33/3: *We* thought it was an SFnal hotel.

**1994** K. K. Rusch *Mag. of Fantasy & SF* (Oct.–Nov.) 8/2: Charlie Varon postulates how our reading habits will change when most of us read the *Times* on-line. His fake articles are sfnal and his point is as biting as any science fiction story's can be.

**1998** J. Dann *Nebula Awards Stories 32* 32: "Must and Shall" [...] might be thought of as historical fiction with an SFnal twist: change one thing, extrapolate as rigorously as possible, and see what happens.

**2006** R. Horton *Locus* (Mar.) 63/3: I also liked the SFnal furniture—some interesting sociological speculation and some fascinating technology.

**sharecrop** *n.* a story or novel that is the product of sharecropping.

**1991** J. Clute *SF Novels of Year* in D. Garnett *New Worlds 1* 249: Isaac Asimov and Arthur C. Clarke both "collaborated" in the production of novels both of which—though neither outcome was technically a sharecrop, neither younger partner being sufficiently junior or impoverished to have to work for hire—had all the *seeming* of the sharecrop title.

**1994** *Interzone* (Oct.) 65/3: This planetary romance appears to be a genuine collaboration rather than a sharecrop.

**1996** D. Pringle, et al. *Ultimate Ency. of SF* 222/3: Preuss is a scientist and his "sharecrop" novels in the Arthur C. Clarke's Venus Prime series [...] are technically well-informed and effective of their sort.

**2002** J. Larbalestier *Battle of Sexes in SF* 212: And we talked about Star Wars and other sharecrop franchises.

**2002** M. Resnick *Resnick/Malzberg Dialogues* in *Bulletin of SF & Fantasy Writers of America* (Spring) 19/3: You're a starving writer who has to pay his bills and put food on the table, so you do some TV novelizations, or some sharecrop books.

**sharecrop** *v.* to write a sharecrop. Hence **sharecropped,** *adj.*

**1989** C. N. Brown *Locus* (Feb.) 31/1: 11 Star Trek novels, 11 from other tv series, eight movie novelizations, 14 novels based on games, and 20 sharecropped books—either set in shared universes or based on other authors' franchises.

**1994** *Interzone* (Oct.) 63/1: The sequence looks like a tripleheader, unless Turtledove takes his vengeful humans into space and beards the Kzin-like lizards in their own den, a part of the tale which could easily be sharecropped.

**1994** *Interzone* (Mar.) 69/1: Second of a sharecropped trilogy (mainly by Gentry Lee) based on Clarke's original novel *Rendezvous with Rama.*

**1998** N. Spinrad *Who Is Killing SF?* in J. Dann *Nebula Awards 32* 25: *Star Wars* novels. *Star Trek* novels. *X-Files* novels. Writers sharecropping the universes of other writers, living and dead.

**2002** S. Mohn *New York Rev. of SF* (Apr.) 18/2: With conservative sf readers longing for more of what they love from established writers who have slowed down or died, it is cheaper to sharecrop novels or pursue lucrative media tie-ins.

**sharecropper** *n.* an author who writes sharecrops.

**1987** G. Dozois *Intro.* in *Year's Best SF: Fifth Annual Coll.* xiv: In the case of the "sharecroppers," I also feel, perhaps naively, that young writers ought to be busy developing their own worlds and working out their own ideas and fresh material, rather than reworking ground already broken by older and more successful writers.

**1988** P. Preuss *Locus (letter)* (Nov.) 66/2: Some of us sharecroppers cherish the rich soil we're tilling.

**1991** R. Rogow *Futurespeak* 310: Several people who have accepted sharecropper contracts point out that there is considerable latitude within the guidelines set down by the originators of the various universes.

**1996** G. Slusser *Homeostatic Culture Machine* in G. Westfahl, G. Slusser & E. S. Rabkin *SF & Market Realities* ix:

Commentators look at recent production in economic terms: writers chained to the serial novel become indentured; those working in shared worlds are "sharecroppers" or purchasers of franchises.

**sharecropping** *n.* [< S.E. *sharecropping*, the practice of tenant farmers paying a portion of their crop in rent] the practice of writing fiction set in a universe created by, and usually under license to, another (typically more established) author. [Gardner Dozois, in an email to the OED, says that he did not coin this term.]

**1987** G. Dozois *Intro.* in *Year's Best SF: Fifth Annual Coll.* xiii: This practice of hiring lesser-known authors to create new adventures set "in the world of" some famous SF novel (for instance, a novel set in the world of Robert Heinlein's *Starship Troopers*, or in the world of Robert Silverberg's *Lord Valentine's Castle*) has been referred to as "share-cropping" and strikes me as a very dangerous trend.

**1988** *Locus* (Oct.) 5/2: The newest twist in "sharecropping" or sf franchising started out simply enough a few months ago when Martin H. Greenberg proposed a series of books consisting of famous novellas with modern sequels by new authors.

**1999** M. Swanwick *Z Is for Zothique* in *Puck Aleshire's Abecedary* (2000) 26: So popular did they prove, however, and so great was the public's appetite for more, that other writers were hired to continue the franchise. This early version of sharecropping was so successful that the series has continued to this very day.

**2004** B. Stableford *Historical Dictionary of SF Literature* 15: He lent the selling power of his name to a large number of sharecropping works by other hands, including Foundation novels.

**shared world** *n.* a fictional universe in which multiple authors set their stories, especially one created for this purpose.

**1985** J. C. Bunnell *Dragon Mag.* (Nov.) 32/2: The stories do not truly mesh into a single setting in the distinctive way necessary for Ithkar Fair to qualify as a shared world.

**1988** G. Wolfe *Intro.* in *Storeys from Old Hotel* 8: The idea was to make up a fictional city-state

(Liavek) with its surrounding geography, technology, religions, laws of magic, and so on and so forth, and to persuade a variety of authors to submit stories laid there; compilations of this rather freakish kind are called shared-world anthologies.

**1988** T. Windling *Summation 1987: Fantasy* in E. Datlow & T. Windling *Year's Best Fantasy: First Annual Coll.* xv: One way of getting around that has been the rise of "shared-world" anthologies, where several writers join together to write stories using a single setting and sharing characters.

**1992** *Locus* (Aug.) 28/2: As a rule, shared worlds are to fiction what theme parks are to reality: prefabricated environments.

**1993** J. Clute & P. Nicholls *Ency. of SF* xii/2: We have excluded very few sf authors who have solely written books tied to shared-world endeavours (like *Star Wars* or *Star Trek*).

**shield** *n.* a FORCE FIELD.

**1930** E. E. Smith *Skylark Three* in *Amazing Stories* (Aug.) 408/1: They have already brought knowledge of the metal of power and of the impenetrable shield to the Central System, which is to be our base.

**1962** P. Anderson *Shield* in *Fantastic Stories of Imagination* (June) 62/2: His kinetic energy had been absorbed, taken up by the field itself and shunted to the power pack. As for the noise, none could penetrate the shield.

**1963** F. Herbert *Dune* in *Analog Sci. Fact–SF* (Dec.) 33/2: "One must always remember that the shield turns the fast blow and admits the slow kindjal!" Paul snapped up the rapier, feinted fast and whipped it back in a slow thrust timed precisely to enter a shield's mindless defenses.

**ca1992** R. Grant & D. Naylor *Holoship* in *Son of Soup* (1996) 34: What? Am I the only sane one here? Why don't we lower the defensive shields?

**2004** L. E. Modesitt, Jr. *Ethos Effect* (2004) 418: The Rev tried to flip his shields to bring the heavier forward shields into play, but the strain on drives and shields was too much, and a flare of energy replaced the overstressed corvette.

**ship** *n.* a SPACESHIP. Compare BOAT, CRAFT, CRUISER, SPACE CAN, SPACE CAR, SPACECRAFT,

‍‌‌‍

SPACE CRUISER, SPACE FLYER, SPACER 2, SPACE VEHICLE, SPACE VESSEL, TIN CAN, VESSEL.

**1894** J. J. Astor *Journey in Other Worlds* 97: I think, [...] as that will be the first member of Jupiter's system we pass, and as it will guide us into port, it would be a good name for our ship.

**1925** J. Schlossel *Invaders from Outside* in *Weird Tales* (Jan.) 6/2: The Martians crowded around that ship after the initial shock and roar of its landing was past.

**1946** *Syracuse (New York) Herald-American* (Feb. 10) 10/3: As a means of getting from one side of the earth to the other in a hurry, a space ship will have no rival. A trip from America to Australia will take about half an hour, once the ship gets going.

**1950** L. Brackett *Dancing Girl of Ganymede* in *Halfling & Other Stories* (1973) 42: Lost, strayed or abandoned from the ships that land there out of space, they have thriven in the gutters and the steaming alleys.

**1979** M. Z. Bradley *Bloody Sun* 15: For all you knew, you might have been born on one of the Big Ships; the ships of Terra; the starships that made the long runs between stars doing the business of the Empire.

**2002** A. Reynolds *Redemption Ark* (2004) 579: The ship—it had to be the Triumvir's vessel, *Nostalgia for Infinity*—hovered in interplanetary space.

**shipper** *n.* [abbr. of *relationshipper*] a fan (of a TV show, book series, etc.) who favors a romantic or sexual relationship between two of the characters.

[**1996** *NEW: TITLE 17 [1/1]* (Usenet: alt.tv.x-files.creative) (Apr. 19): I think that everyone, both R'shipper's and Non R'shipper's alike, can enjoy this story.]

**1996** *DD on Frasier* (Usenet: alt.tv.x-files) (May 7): David Duchovny was guest-voice "Tom" on Last [sic] night's Frasier. (courtesy of the 'shippers list).

**1996** *My problem with "anti-relationshippers"* (Usenet: alt.tv.x-files) (May 22): The idea of portraying more of the emotional connection between these two characters, be it romantically or platonically, I would think appeals to all of us. Being a shipper, I of course prefer

the idea that they would be expressing their epic love, but....

**1999** *For all you other D/T fans* (Usenet: alt.fan.brent-spiner) (Aug. 26): Okay, I'm a closet Data/Tasha 'shipper.

**2002** *New York Times (letter)* (June 2) 4/2: One it became generally accepted that Mulder and Scully were romantically involved off screen [...] the shippers lamented not being allowed to witness the transition in the relationship.

**shuttle** *n.* a spaceship designed for short flights, as between an orbiting spaceship and a planet, or that makes regular trips between two destinations. Compare SHUTTLECRAFT, SPACEBOAT.

**1940** N. S. Bond *Legacy* in *Astounding S-F* (Dec.) 39/1: The *Andromeda* has been sold, Bert, [...] to the Ionian freight shuttle. You and the gang are ordered back to Earth.

**1950** T. Sturgeon *Stars Are Styx* in *Galaxy SF* (Oct.) 74/2: I didn't even know he was on that particular shuttle. It's just that, aside from the fact that I happen to be Senior Release Officer on Curbstone, I like to meet the shuttles.

**1951** R. A. Heinlein *Between Planets* 83: A shuttle ship up from the surface could leave any spot on Venus, rendezvous with the ship in orbit, then land on its port of departure or on any other point having expended a theoretical minimum of fuel. As soon as the *Nautilus* had parked such shuttles began to swarm up to her.

**1968** S. R. Delany *Nova* 38 (2002): Around them stood star-freighters. Between them stood the much smaller, hundred-meter shuttles.

**1986** D. Carey *Dreadnought* 21: I was quivering with anticipation as the shuttle arched out over the shimmer of Puget Sound.

**1999** C. Pellegrino & G. Zebrowski *Dyson Sphere* 66: He managed it after two tries, and in a few minutes was ascending through low gravity, into the brightly lit shuttle compartment.

**shuttlecraft** *n.* a SHUTTLE. Compare SPACEBOAT.

**1967** E. Hamilton *Weapon from Beyond* 150: They marched across the blowing sand and into the golden shuttle-craft that would take them to the rescue ship.

**1970** J. Blish *Spock Must Die!* 69: We almost never have any need for a shuttlecraft which can't be filled better and faster by the transporter.

**1981** B. Shaw *Galactic Tours* 13: Our picture shows the practice areas in use by suited and unsuited vacationers, the illusion of actually being in space enhanced by the sight of a shuttle craft approaching one of the station's receiving bays.

**1991** M. Weiss *King's Test* 139: The voice of the captain of the shuttlecraft came over the commlink.

**1998** G. Cox *Assignment: Eternity* 227: We've lost the shuttlecraft hanger doors.

**shuttleport** *n.* a spacefield intended for use by shuttles.

**1973** A. D. Foster *Bloodhype* 21: Instead of making a nice, smooth arrival, you forthwith take off, in full sight of a busy shuttleport crowd, with the most notorious, spoiled young human this backwater capital has to offer.

**1988** R. Frazier *Retrovision* in G. Dozois *Isaac Asimov's Mars* (1991) 56: The bigwigs down at the Sao Paulo shuttleport must have reserved a big transport for the tour this time, judging by the number of visitors.

**1989** J. C. Faust *Desperate Measures* 33: Things did not get any better at the shuttleport. Even at such an early hour of the morning there was still enough of a crowd to make May nervous.

**2005** J. Scalzi *Old Man's War* (2005) 115: Standing (we hoped) more or less at attention on the tarmac of Delta Base's shuttleport.

**singularity** *n.* [< S.E. *singularity,* the massive object at the center of a black hole from which light cannot escape and of which we can therefore have no direct knowledge] a point in the future when a certain level of technological advancement will be achieved, after which no predictions can reasonably be made. Often *cap.*

**1958** S. Ulam *John von Neumann, 1930–1957* in *Bulletin of American Mathematical Society* (May, part 2) 5: One conversation centered on the ever accelerating progress of technology and changes in the mode of human life, which gives the appearance of approaching some essential singularity in the history of the race beyond which human affairs, as we know them, could not continue.

**1983** V. Vinge *Omni* (Jan.) 10/2: We will soon create intelligences greater than our own. When this happens, human history will have reached a kind of singularity, an intellectual transition as impenetrable as the knotted space-time at the center of a black hole, and the world will pass far beyond our understanding.

**1996** K. MacLeod *Stone Canal* (1997) 300: We must work towards being able to control, or at least contain, their development. The same goes for any form of artificial intelligence capable of improving itself. We will do it. The day will come when we control the Singularity.

**1997** D. Broderick *Spike* 2: Around 2050, or maybe even 2030, is when an upheaval unprecedented in human history—a technological singularity, as it's been termed—is expected to erupt.

**2003** F. Mendlesohn *Religion & SF* in E. James & F. Mendlesohn *Cambridge Companion to SF* 270: Those who believe in other forms of transhumanity, need only substitute "apocalypse" for singularity, and "rapture" for "uploading" to become indistinguishable from any fundamentalist Christian in the USA.

**2005** C. Doctorow *Cory Doctorow: Everywhere, All at Same Time* in *Locus* (Jan.) 63/3: The Singularity is a transcendent mystical belief system, not a collection of scientific beliefs, and I think mystical experience has become the combination of some kind of text and some kind of ritual.

**skiffy** *n.* [spelling pronunciation of *sci-fi*] SCIENCE FICTION. Often *joc.*

[ **1982** D. Hartwell *Golden Age of SF Is Twelve* in *Age of Wonders* (1984) 13: The science fiction reader sneers at fake SF, artificially produced film tie-in novels and stories, most SF films, most TV SF. This he calls sci-fi (or "skiffy")—junk no right-thinking omnivore or chronic should read, watch, or support. ]

**1989** B. Sterling *SF Eye* (July) 78/2: "Slipstream" is a parody of "mainstream," and nobody calls mainstream "mainstream" except for us skiffy trolls.

**1994** U. K. Le Guin *Thinking about Cordwainer Smith* in *Wave in Mind* (2004)

60: Dr. Linebarger had to be respectable and responsible and had to guard his tongue. Cordwainer Smith wrote skiffy and babbled whatever he pleased.

**1997** M. Resnick M. in Resnick & P. Nielsen Hayden *Alternate Skiffy* 109: Jack Haldeman is not only a top-notch skiffy author of long standing, but also a BNF (Big Name Fan).

**2004** D. Broderick *X, Y, Z, T* 20: Christopher Priest abandoned accountancy for literature, taking a byway through the skiffy archipelago.

**2005** D. Langford *Ansible* (Internet) (July): Meanwhile someone has decided that the award-nominated cover design, with its striking NASA/JPL Jupiter photograph, was *not skiffy enough.*

**skimmer** *n.* a small aircraft designed for low-altitude flight.

**1949** W. L. Bade *Lost Ulysses Astounding SF* (May) 116/1: Tractors shoved the stuff into piles and skimmers mounting gravity engines carried it away.

**1957** I. Asimov *Profession* in *Astounding SF* (July) 42/2: The skimmer landed at the roof-entry of a hotel.

**1965** R. Zelazny *...And Call Me Conrad* in *Fantasy & SF* (Oct.) 11/1: I stood and drew her to her feet as it buzzed in low—a Radson Skimmer: a twenty-foot cockleshell of reflection and transparency; flat-bottomed, blunt-nosed.

**1981** G. R. R. Martin *Guardians* in *Analog SF/Sci. Fact* (Oct. 12) 21/2: The Guardians had twenty armed skimmers, and there were another hundred-odd skimmers and aircars in private hands.

**1993** J. Brosnan *Opoponax Invasion* (1994) 40: The skimmers are low over the town and obviously carrying out a search.

**2000** *White Dwarf* (May) 29/1: Despite the distinct advantage of all damaging hits only being glancing on fast moving skimmers, they should still seek cover to hide behind.

**skinsuit** *n.* a tight-fitting spacesuit, often intended for short-term or emergency use.

**1971** K. Laumer *Dinosaur Beach* 107: He was dressed in a plain black skin suit with harness and attachments. He looked at an array of miniature meters strapped to his wrist—the underside—and made an adjustment.

**1974** G. Benford *Threads of Time* in R. Silverberg *Threads of Time* 23: The porous elastic mesh of the skinsuit was intact, though, so she probably only had a bad bruise.

**1983** J. Varley *Millennium* 17: I'd been feeling like I'd shrunk inside my skinsuit.

**1992** A. Steele *Labyrinth of Night* 38: They now followed Jessup, all three clad in the lightweight Mylar skinsuits which had recently replaced the more cumbersome hardsuits of first expeditions.

**2002** A. Reynolds *Redemption Ark* (2004) 169: He [...] had been pinned in the rubble for eighteen days with no food or water except the supplies in his skinsuit.

**slan** *n.* [slæn] [after *slan*, a member of a race of super-humans in A. E. van Vogt's story *Slan*] a science fiction fan. Often *joc.* Hence **slanhood**, *n.*, **slannish**, *adj.*

[**1940** A. E. van Vogt *Slan* in *Astounding S-F* (Oct.) 27/1: They [...] accuse Samuel Lann, the human being and biological scientist who first created slans, and after whom slans are named—Samuel Lann: S. Lann: Slan—of fostering in his children the belief that they must rule the world.]

**1944** J. B. Speer *Fancyclopedia* 42/1: The most important thing about a fan gathering is that the slans can get together with their own kind of people [...] and develop their stefnic personalities.

**1944** Speer, *Fancy.* I 30/1: Racial superiority is implied in the claims of star-begottenness and slanhood.

**1955** A. Koestler *Trail of Dinosaur* 143: Fen gather in clubhouses called slanshacks, "slan" meaning a biologically mutated superman.

**1969** H. Warner, Jr. *All Our Yesterdays* 42: "Fans are slans!" became the rallying cry of the Cosmic Circle.

**1995** R. Newsome *Re: Room parties at cons* (Usenet: rec.arts.sf.fandom) (Jul. 29): FTL's keen slannish brain foresaw that if 4E ever found a female of the same strange mutant breed, between them they would rear up a mighty race of drodes, who would someday challenge the slans themselves for the rule of fandom.

**slan shack** *n.* [after *Slan Shack*, the name of one such habitation (see 1969 quote)] a dwelling inhabited by two or more science fiction fans.

**ca1944** F. J. Ackerman *Fantasy Flanguage* in in [Anon.] *What Is Science Fiction Fandom* 33: *Slan Shack; Ivory Tower; Futurian Embassy; The Flat:* Semi-cooperative dwellings inhabited exclusively by Fans.

**1964** J. Linwood *Fanalytic Eye* in *Les Spinge* (Jan.) 26: When Campbell's symbolic psionics-machine was described in ASF, scissors, drawing-pens and screwdrivers in fannish slan-shacks worked overtime in the faint hope that "there might be something in it."

**1969** H. Warner, Jr. *All Our Yesterdays* 33: "Slan Shack," where a batch of active Battle Creek, Michigan, fans lived for nearly two years, was the most famous example of a fannish island in the sea of mundania during the forties.

**1975** E. Weinstein *Fillostrated Fan Dictionary* 44: Epicentre [ ... ]: A slanshack in London inhabited by Clarke and Ken Bulmer.

**1992** *Locus* (June) 21/3: A raggedy bunch of slan-shack fans and would-be writers buried a time capsule on a farm.

**slash** *n.* [< the punctuation mark "/" ("slash") in K/S] fan fiction that depicts a sexual relationship between two characters from television shows, movies, novels, etc.

**1984** *Not Tonight, Spock!* (Jan.) 1: *Recommended Book List...*to include gay books, other slash zines, or media zines with good K/S stories.

**1991** T. Nielsen Hayden *Pastafazool Cycle* in *Making Book* (1994) 156: It's later recycled as a middling-successful and much syndicated TV show, and is used as the background for some quantity of slash fanwriting.

**1993** *SFRA Rev.* (May–June) 64: There is another chapter on slash, or fanzine stories written with the assumption of a homoerotic relationship between male media characters.

**2002** *SF Chronicle* (May) 24/2: We're burning everything [ ... ]. The Wesley/Worf slash fanfiction sent in "just in case we had an interest."

**sleeper ship** *n.* a slower-than-light spaceship that carries a cargo of people in suspended animation, enabling them to arrive at the destination world without dying of old age in transit.

**1968** J. Blish *Space Seed* in *Star Trek: Classic Episodes 1* (1992) 540: I've got it! [ ... ] It's a sleeper ship!

**1988** S. Jackson & W. A. Garton *GURPS Space* (1990) 86/1: *Sleeper ships*, colonists are frozen in suspended animation. This is the most economical method, as more colonists and their supplies can be contained in a ship.

**2002** T. Zahn *Manta's Gift* 131: They didn't arrive by huge colony or sleeper ships or anything else slower-than-light—

**slidewalk** *n.* SLIDEWAY.

**1944** F. Leiber *Sanity* in *Astounding S-F* (Apr.) 168/1: He had stepped on to the corridor slidewalk and had coasted halfway to the elevator before he realized that Phy had followed him and was plucking timidly at his sleeve.

**1947** R. A. Heinlein *It's Great to Be Back* in *Saturday Evening Post* (July 26) 18/2: They went on up to subsurface and took the crosstown slidewalk out to the rocket port.

**1965** H. Ellison *"Repent, Harlequin!" Said Ticktockman* in B. Bova *Best of Nebulas* (1989) 65: As he rounded the cornice of the Time-Motion Study Building, he saw the shift, just boarding the slidewalk.

**1972** M. Z. Bradley *Darkover Landfall* (1987) 9: Certainly the slidewalks and lifts installed to the top of Mount Rainier [ ... ] had made it easier for old women and children to get up there and have a chance to see the scenery.

**1986** L. M. Bujold *Warrior's Apprentice* (1997) 88: "It was my understanding, my lord," said Bothari severely as they left Daum's hotel for the slidewalk, "that Pilot Officer Mayhew here was to transport your cargo."

**2003** T. Harlan *Wasteland of Flint* (2004) 7: There, in cool scented air, slidewalks were conveying parties of rich Imperials through station customs.

**slideway** *n.* a moving sidewalk or walkway.

**1942** R. A. Heinlein *Beyond This Horizon* in *Astounding SF* (Apr.) 9/1: Hamilton Felix let himself off at the thirteenth level of the Department of Finance, mounted a slideway to the left, and stepped off the strip.

**1951** F. Leiber *Poor Superman* in *Galaxy SF* (July) 146/1: As the slideway whisked him gently along the corridor toward his apartment, Jorj was thinking of his spaceship.

**1968** P. Anderson *Satan's World* in *Analog SF-Sci. Fact* (May) 30/2: The slideways were too slow for her. She bounded along them.

**1981** B. Shaw *Galactic Tours* 91/2: The Ultiman's own intricate system of slideways is open to all humans free of charge.

**1991** A. McCaffrey & E. Moon *Generation Warriors* 145: Lunzie presumed that most people used the underground walkways and slideways she and Zebara had used their two previous meetings.

**2002** C. Sheffield *Dark as Day* 175: On the fifteen-minute trip via Ganymede's high-speed elevators and rapid slideways, Magrit wondered if she was about to make a mistake.

**slipstream** *n.* [after MAINSTREAM] literature which makes use of the tropes or techniques of genre science fiction or fantasy, but which is not considered to be genre science fiction or fantasy; the genre of such literature. Hence **slipstreamer**, *n.*, **slipstreamish**, *adj.*, **slipstreamy**, *adj.*

**1989** B. Sterling *SF Eye* (July) 78/2: We could call this kind of fiction Novels of Postmodern Sensibility, but that looks pretty bad on a category rack, and requires an acronym besides; so for the sake of convenience and argument, we will call these books "slipstream."

**1992** *Locus* (Aug.) 11/3: "In Concert" is a slipstream story about an amateur rock musician in Sevastopol trying to gain entry into the stadium.

**1995** *SFRA Rev.* (May–June) 54: A slipstreamy science fiction story about a virus that causes a rather peculiar neurological dysfunction with satisfyingly serendipitous results.

**1995** *Interzone* (Jan.) 61/2: *Territories* issue four is subtitled the *sf and slipstream journal.* In this context, the meaning of "slipstream" is

refreshingly unpretentious, something along the lines of "non-SF things that are likely to interest SF readers."

**2002** *Locus* (Sept.) 15/1: The January issue of *The Silver Web* is their fifteenth, and editor Ann Kennedy chooses a decidedly slipstreamish mix.

**2003** D. G. Hartwell & K. Cramer *Intro.* in *Year's Best Fantasy 3* xv: One noticeable trend evident in some of these is toward non-genre, or genre-bending, or slipstream fantastic fiction.

**2003** P. Di Filippo *Asimov's SF* (Apr.) 132/1: The British fantasist Steve Erikson (not to be confused with US slipstreamer Steve Erickson) extends the vision of his fantasy land of Malazan.

**2003** C. Priest *Guardian (London)* (Internet) (June 14): It includes rather than categorises— while not being magic realism, or fantasy, or science fiction, slipstream literature includes many examples of these.

**slower-than-light** *adj.* (of a spaceship or space drive) unable to exceed the speed of light. Compare SUB-LIGHT 2.

**1953** F. Brown *Lights in Sky Are Stars* (1968) 104: Ellen, we'll reach the stars all right. If we have to, it'll be by slower-than-light ships that take generations for a crossing, or that send colonists in suspended animation for centuries enroute.

**1966** A. Budrys *Galaxy Mag.* (Aug.) 190/1: You would have thought there was no conceivable new switch on the "Universe" story. The slower-than-light interstellar spaceship, pursuing its way through the weary centuries, its crew losing touch with all reality save the interior of their vessel.

**1991** P. McAuley *Eternal Light* (1993) 10: Their ancestors [...] came from the lost nation of the Commonwealth of Soviet Republics, stacked in coldcoffins in the cargo pods of slower-than-light ramscoop ships.

**2005** *Onion* (June 23) 12/1: It [...] is accurate to within three-tenths of a recension for all Sol-neighborhood outer-planetary colonies, ringworlds, and slower-than-light generation ships.

**slugthrower** *n.* a weapon that fires a heavy round of ammunition, such as a bullet.

**1965** G. R. Dickson *Warrior* in *Analog SF-Sci. Fact* (Dec.) 71/2: He had been pulling the trigger of his slugthrower all this time, but now the firing pin clicked at last upon an empty firing chamber.
**1978** P. Anderson *Avatar* (1981) 89: Each had a holstered sidearm: slugthrower, not stunner.
**1990** D. Simmons *Fall of Hyperion* 195: "Are you sure the shots came from Brawne's gun?" The Consul motioned toward the darkness outside. "None of the rest of us carried a slug-thrower."
**1996** J. L. Nye *Ship Errant* (1997) 65: From the confident manner with which she held her long-barreled slugthrower, Mirina guessed that some of the medals were for marksmanship.
**2003** J. Barnes *Princess of Aerie* 283: He had once done some plinking, shooting old bottles and cans with a slug-thrower.

**smeg** *v.* [abbr. of *smegma*] expressing anger, disgust, frustration, or contempt. Usually in phrase **smeg off.** Also as *interj.* In non–*Red Dwarf* use, often a jocular euphemism for "fuck." Compare FRELL.
**ca1988** R. Grant & D. Naylor *Kryten* in *Son of Soup* (1996) 126: Smeg off, dogfood face.
**1988** Grant & Naylor, *Son of Soup* 130: What the smeg is going on?
**1995** *"Survival" REVIEW* (Usenet: rec.arts.drwho) (Mar. 3): Oh smeg…Now you bring this up…Forget what I said in my last paragraph…
**1998** *Question: Tube in Tubeless Tire* (Usenet: rec.motorcycles) (Aug. 16): Oh, shut up and smeg off. You're ridiculous.
**1998** *Wired (Internet)* (May 5): Several times, I tried to get simple information like "Pardon me, but which way is the tailor?" [ … ] and didn't even get "Smeg off, Newbie" in response.
**2000** *Ahh smeg it.* (Usenet: uk.people.support.depression) (Apr. 8): Ah smeg it. I've had enough for today.

**smegging** *adj.* used for emphasis or to express anger, dismay, frustration, etc.; in non–*Red Dwarf* use, often a jocular euphemism for "fucking." Compare FRELLING.

**ca1988** R. Grant & D. Naylor *Me²* in *Son of Soup* (1996) 149: You filthy smegging lying smegging liar.
**1992** P. David *Imzadi* 52: He said it's happened to him on several occasions in the past and suggested that it might be time and I quote, "to learn how to play the smegging thing."
**2003**: see quote in FRELL, *v.*
**2005** *Oakland (Cal.) Tribune* (ProQuest) (Nov. 3): In other words, whenever somebody is upset over the littlest smegging thing, they come to whine and moan about it to me.

**smeggy** *adj.* disgusting. Usually *joc.*
**ca1988** R. Grant & D. Naylor *Kryten* in *Son of Soup* (1996) 120: You're wearing all your least smeggy things.
**2002** S. Howell *Xylophone* in *3:AM Mag.* (Internet): For some reason Ash keeps buying piles of records with unidentifiable substances on them—look. He holds up a particularly smeggy-looking side and says, Linda Ronstadt.
**2003** *Independent (London)* (ProQuest) (May 17): Then you cover the lot in hairspray and it will stay for three or four days. But you have to be prepared to sleep that way. Then in the morning it's horrible and smeggy and you have to force it into position again.

**smeghead** *n.* [after *fuckhead, shithead,* etc.] a fool or contemptible person. Usually *joc.*
**ca1988** R. Grant & D. Naylor *Kryten* in *Son of Soup* (1996) 131: Mr Arnold is not his name. His name is Rimmer. Or smeghead.
**1993** *Comics = Bloody War (Aghh!!)* (Usenet: rec.arts.comics.misc) (Mar. 26): I don't quite know where you're coming from here, Smeghead.
**2002** C. Walter *Punk Rules OK* 181: What a complete and utter bunch of smegheads!
**2004** J. Colgan *Boy I Loved Before* (2005) 96: As well as being trapped in this hellhole with no way out in sight, I had to be a complete smeghead at the same time.

**smof** *v.* to make political deals or discuss the inner workings of fandom with other science fiction fans. *Joc.* Hence **smoffing**, *n.*

**1968** *Proper Boskonian* (Nov.) 1: Smoffing is a Way of Life

**1971** *New York Times* (Sept. 6) 17/1: The fen of science fiction fandom [...] descended on Boston this weekend for their annual worldcon to smof and to buy old fanzines.

**1987** G. Wolfe *Horrorstruck* (Nov.–Dec.) 20/2: From club meetings came meetings between clubs, at which members of the Outsiders might s.m.o.f. (this fan verb is derived from *S*ecret *M*asters *o*f *F*andom and indicates the forging of fannish political deals) with Insiders.

**1997** Minico: *"Still fancy free thanks to BBT" (LONG!)* (Usenet: alt.fandom.cons) (Apr. 11): He and I smoffed in an elevator lobby well after dawn on Monday.

**SMOF** *n.* [secret *m*aster of *f*andom] someone who is influential in the science fiction fan community, especially with regards to running conventions. Often *joc.*

[**1965** [H. Clement] in D. Eney *Proceedings; Discon* 162: He [i.e. Theodore Sturgeon] is also, in case he is willing...no, not in case he is willing; anyway, whether he likes it or not...an Honorary Member of SMOF.]

**1978** [B. Tucker] *Neo-Fan's Guide to SF Fandom* 10: *Secret Masters of Fandom (SMOFs),* people who consider themselves to be the real "rulers" of fandom, making decisions by running fan politics. Actually, these poor fellows are suffering from delusions of grandeur.

**1997** J. C. Haldeman II *History Lesson* in M. Resnick & P. Nielsen Hayden *Alternate Skiffy* 110: Sure, we had our SMOFs and our pros, but everybody just kind of mixed.

**2003** J. M. Verba *Boldly Writing (ed. 2)* 27/2: She appeared in few publications, yet she had such an influence on *Star Trek* fanzines that many considered her a SMOF, or Secret Master of Fandom.

**soft science fiction, soft sf** *n.* **1.** [by analogy to HARD SCIENCE FICTION] science fiction that deals primarily with advancements in, or extrapolations based on, the soft sciences (e.g., anthropology, psychology, sociology, etc.).

**1977** P. Nicholls *1975: Year in SF* in U. K. Le Guin *Nebula Award Stories Eleven* 98: The same list reveals that an already established shift from hard sf (chemistry, physics, astronomy, technology) to soft sf (psychology, biology, anthropology, sociology, and even [...] linguistics) is continuing more strongly than ever.

**1978** G. S. Elrick *SF Handbook* 6: Soft science fiction is basically based on sociology, anthropology, political science, theology, or mythology.

**1984** D. Hartwell *Age of Wonders* 15: Soft science fiction (two alternate types: one in which the character is more important than the SF idea; the other focusing on any science other than physics or chemistry).

**2002** B. Attebery *Decoding Gender in SF* 5: When [...] the format is "soft SF," emphasizing human biology, sociology, or unusual forms of perception, then SF is more likely to challenge than to uphold gender norms.

**2.** science fiction in which the scientific elements are relatively unimportant to the story. Compare SCIENCE FANTASY 3b.

**1982** R. Schlobin *Andre Norton* in T. Staicar *Feminine Eye*: They all write what could be variously labeled as "social," "humanistic," or "soft" science fiction. While all their works contain the extrapolated factual material characteristic of science fiction, they really focus on the future of humanity and its possible future traits and societies.

**1984**: see quote in SOFT SCIENCE FICTION 1.

**1990** D. Fratz *Quantum* (Spring) 19/1: Superbly crafted, no-nuts-and-bolts, soft SF had another good year in 1988.

**1998** P. Anderson *Ideas for SF Writer* (Sept.) 24/2: Two streams run through science fiction. [...] The second derives from H. G. Wells. His own ideas were brilliant, but he didn't care how implausible they might be, an invisible man or a time machine or whatever. He concentrated on the characters, their emotions and interactions. Today, we usually speak of these two streams as "hard" and "soft" science fiction.

**Sol** *n.* [< L. *sol*, "the sun"] the star that the Earth orbits; the sun.

**1929** [L. F. Stone] *Out of Void* in *Amazing Stories* (Aug.) 454/1: Directly behind us lay the

Sun, a great flaming ball that was blinding. A little to the left, appearing as large though not as bright as old Sol, was Mother Earth.

**1939** [E. Binder] *Impossible World* (1967) 116: A dark sun, out in the great gulf between Sol and its surrounding stars.

**1946** E. Hamilton *Forgotton World* in *Thrilling Wonder Stories* (Winter) 16/2: Sol, ahead, was a small and undistinguished yellow sun.

**1952** L. Brackett *Shadows* in *Halfling & Other Stories* (1973) 181: He thought of the honest yellow glare of Sol and wondered what madness it was that sent men out to the ends of the galaxy seeking other suns.

**1968** S. R. Delany *Nova* (2002) 98: They put up rings of remote-control stations as close to the star as Mercury is to Sol.

**1991** G. Wolfe *Seraph from Its Sepulcher* in A. M. Greeley & M. Cassutt *Sacred Visions* 176: A host of blue-white, crimson, and Sol-yellow stars hung above the tableland like innumerable torches suspended from so many balloons.

**2005** M. Rosenblum *Green Shift* in *Asimov's SF* (Mar.) 125: She waited outside, drifting in the fierce flood of energy from Sol.

**Solarian** *n.* **1.** *Obs.* an inhabitant of the Earth's solar system.

**1930** J. W. Campbell *Black Star Passes* in *Amazing Stories Quarterly* (Fall) 521/2: The small ships of the Nigrians were beginning to take a terrific toll in the thin ranks of the Solarians.

**1934** E. E. Smith *Triplanetary* in *Amazing Stories* (Feb.) 78/2: Even to-day there are few Terrestrials—or Solarians for that matter—who can look at a Nevian, eye to eye, without feeling a creeping of the skin.

**1952** P. Anderson *Captive of Centaurianess* in *Planet Stories* (Mar.) 23/1: I thought you vere too, but it seems like you Solarians are more backvard than I supposed.

**1956** C. A. Stearns *Golden Ones* in *SF Quarterly* (Aug.) 30/1: Is it true that all Terrans, and other Solarians are frightfully rich, and go simply everywhere, and do as they please, and that almost nobody works?

**2.** an inhabitant of Sol.

**1942** [H. Clement] *Proof* in *Astounding S-F* (June) 103/1: A record was made, and the Solarian resumed.

**1951** K. Heuer *Men of Other Planets* 59: The idea of solarians, inhabitants of the sun, was based upon theories of the sun's structure, which were developed to explain sunspot phenomena.

**1980** D. Brin *Sundiver* 49: "Only the first and more prosaic species of Solarian was observed. Not the second variety which has caused Dr. Kepler so much concern." Jacob was still confused by the [ ... ] two types of Sun-creatures so far observed.

**Solarian** *adj.* of a Solarian or Solarians; of or from Sol or its solar system.

**1930** J. W. Campbell *Black Star Passes* in *Amazing Stories Quarterly* (Fall) 521/2: The Solarian one-man ships were even smaller than the Nigrian one-man ships, and some of these did a tremendous amount of damage.

**1942** [H. Clement] *Proof Astounding S-F* (June) 104: I had my own cruiser—a special long-period explorer, owned by the Solarian government.

**1956** C. A. Stearns *Golden Ones* in *SF Quarterly* (Aug.) 42/1: Also, if you must know, I dislike the Solarian medic's attitude toward you.

**1999** D. M. Weber *Apocalypse Troll* 92: We'd have had almost eighty years to develop between the time those signals originated and the time they could get back to Solarian space again.

**solido** *n.* [abbr. of SOLIDOGRAPH] a SOLIDOGRAPH.

[**1956** M. Lesser *Chance of Lifetime* in *Super-Sci. Fiction* (Dec.) 82/2: We might as well have stayed on Earth and studied the solidios, for all the good this traveling does you.]

**1958** *Comedian's Children* in T. Sturgeon *Man Who Lost Sea* (2005) 115: After that there's a solido of me sitting way up on the flats in the left rear, oh so whimsically announcing the Player's Pub Players.

**1964** F. Herbert *Analog Sci. Fact–SF* (Jan.) 58/2: A solido tri-D projection appeared on the table surface about a third of the way down from the Duke.

**1970** A. McCaffrey *Ship Who Sang* (1991) 230: It cost a fortune to make even a solido.

**1991** *Omni* (Mar.) 86/2: Unexpectedly a billboard loomed up before them, a glaring six-color solido advertising, of all things, the Imperial Hotel.

**2002** D. Brin *Kiln People* 49: That and a pair of solido-dolls of us hiking together on Denali—her straight brown hair cropped close, almost helmetlike, around a face that Clara always dismissed as too elongated to be pretty.

**solidograph** *n.* [perh. *solid* + phot*ograph*] a solid or three-dimensional reproduction of something.

**1948** H. B. Piper *Police Operation* in *Astounding SF* (July) 17/2: In the middle of this appeared a small solidograph image of the interior of the conveyor, showing the desk, and the control board, and the figure of Verkan Vall seated at it. The little figure of the storm trooper appeared, pistol in hand.

**1950** C. D. Simak *Time Quarry* in *Galaxy SF* (Oct.) 23/1: Thorne would give it the works. He would set it up in solidographs, down to the last shattered piece of glass and plastic.

**1967** G. R. Dickson *Soldier, Ask Not* (1993) 292: I looked down into the face of the young girl in Jamethon's solidograph.

**1983** J. White *Sector General* in *Alien Emergencies* (2002) 218: He broke off as the Colonel pointed slowly to the solidograph on his desk.

**Sol III, Sol Three** *n.* [based on a convention in which a planet is named by its star and its place in the order of the star's planets from nearest in to farthest out] the Earth. Compare TELLUS, TERRA.

**1941** E. E. Smith *Vortex Blaster* in *Comet* (July) 4/1: And even to that individual grain of sand called "Earth"—or, in modern parlance, "Sol Three," or "Tellus of Sol" or simply "Tellus"—the affair was of negligible importance.

**1957** R. Silverberg *Solitary* in *World of Thousand Colors* (1984) 218: Born 21 Dec 2530, New York City, Earth (Sol III).

**1983** M. McCollum *Life Probe* 237: The Scientists and engineers of Sol III will have been drafted into the great effort.

**1997** I. McDonald *After Kerry* in G. R. Dozois *Year's Best SF: Fifteenth Annual Coll.* (1998) 524: "Ya," the ambassador to Sol Three said.

**Sol-type** *n.* similar to the Earth's sun.

**1950** P. Anderson *Star Ship Planet Stories* (Oct.) 74/1: We'd been a few weeks out of Avandar—it was an obscure outpost then, though I imagine it's grown since—when we detected this Sol-type sun.

**1957** R. Silverberg *Godling, Go Home!* in *SF Stories* (Jan.) 69/1: Tranacor was a small, reasonably Earth-type world revolving around a reasonably Sol-type sun, and Cartisser had been happy at the coincidence.

**1960** *Sheboygan (Wis.) Press* (Oct. 17) 19/2: They focused their latest tool, the radiotelescope, at two Sol-type stars some 60 million miles from earth.

**1996** *Interzone* (Sept.) 55/2: A variation on the Dyson Sphere, the Ringworld is a strip of super-strong material in orbit about a Sol-type sun.

**soma** *n.* [< Sk. *soma*, an intoxicating drink used in Vedic rituals] in Aldous Huxley's *Brave New World*, a euphoric, hallucinogenic drug used by the government to control the population; hence, any similar drug.

**1932** A. Huxley *Brave New World* 95: The *soma* had begun to work. Eyes shone, cheeks were flushed, the inner light of universal benevolence broke out on every face in happy, friendly smiles.

**1947** M. St. Clair *Super Whost* in *Startling Stories* (July) 101/2: Would you like a glass of soma? [ ... ] Maybe the excitement's been too much for you. You look sort of pale.

**1968** [J. Le Carré] *Small Town in Germany* 155: If I smoked I'd smoke one of your cigars. I could do with a bit of soma just now.

**somewhen** *adv.* another time; in or to another time.

**1941** [C. Saunders] *Elsewhen* in *Astounding S-F* (Sept.) 114/1: When he "landed" it was not in the world of the future he had visited twice before. He did not know where he was—on earth apparently, somewhere and some*when*.

**1968** A. McCaffrey *Dragonrider* in *Analog SF-Sci. Fact* (Jan.) 150/2: We went somewhere...somewhen, that is, for we are still here now.

**1988** G. A. Landis *Ripples in Dirac Sea* in S. Williams *Hugo & Nebula Award Winners from Asimov's SF* (1995) 297: Trying not to breathe, I punched out a code on the keypad, somewhen, anywhere other than that one instant and I was in the hotel room, five days before.

**2000** D. Eddings & L. Eddings *Redemption of Althalus* 542: I think that might be why nobody can see Emmy's House, since, even though it's always here, Emmy can make it be here somewhen else.

**sophont** *n.* ['soʊfɑnt] [< Gk. *sophos*, "wise" + Gk. *ont-*, "being"] an intelligent being. Compare SAPIENT, SENTIENCE 1, SENTIENT.
**1966** P. Anderson *Trouble Twisters* (1967) 56: Likewise with the psychology of intelligent species. Most sophonts indeed possess basic instincts which diverge more or less from man's.
**1978** P. Anderson *Algol* (Summer–Fall) 17/1: My wife [i.e., Karen Anderson], who is a classical scholar, coined the words "Polesotechnic" and "sophont" for me.
**1980** D. Brin *Sundiver* 46: The other side held that homo sapiens—just as every other known race of sophonts—was part of a chain of genetic and cultural uplifting that stretched back to the fabled early days of the galaxy, the time of the Progenitors.
**1992** V. Vinge *Fire upon Deep* 46: She'd already told Grondr her misgivings about this "selling" of a sophont.
**1992** [E. Bes Shahar] *Darktraders* 15: We went wayaways to a place with "personal and private place for very important sophont" stamped all over it in Intersign glyphs.
**1996** W. Read *Epona* in *Analog SF & Fact* (Nov.) 80/2: One lineage of avians has produced Epona's sophont, the uther. Singularly the most fascinating physiological trait of the species is the interdependence of the parent and neonate.

**space** *v.* **1.** to go into or travel in outer space. Hence **spacing**, *n.*
**1947** B. I. Kahn *Command* in *Astounding SF* (Jan.) 121/2: The sight of a well dressed, impeccably neat commanding officer, no matter how long they had been spacing, maintained the enthusiasm, confidence and morale of the officers and men.
**1956** R. A. Heinlein *Time for Stars* 44: They know we want to space. [...] If we emigrate, we might as well be dead; very few emigrants make enough to afford a trip back to Earth, not while their parents are still alive, at least.

**1963** H. B. Piper *Space Viking* (1975) 35: This ship, the *Enterprise*, spaced out from there several days before I did.
**1972** [J. Tiptree, Jr.] *Milk of Paradise* in H. Ellison *Again, Dangerous Visions* 748: His dear old chum-scout Timor's son, saved from the aliens. Your father and mine spaced together.
**1991** D. Stabenow *Second Star* 128: What I told you about the family firm was true, as far as I went. I've always been more interested in spacing than in building another Terran empire.
**2.** to kill someone by expelling them (from a spaceship or space station) into space without a spacesuit. Hence **spacing**, *n.*
**1952** R. A. Heinlein *Rolling Stones* 244: Sound effect of blow with blunt instrument, groan, and the unmistakable cycling of an air lock—Castor: "Sorry, folks. My assistant has just spaced Mr. Rudolf."
**1972** D. Gerrold *Yesterday's Children* 122: "Hey, does anybody know what the penalty for mutiny is?" "Last I heard, it was death by spacing."
**1975** J. Haldeman *Forever War* in *Analog SF-Sci. Fact* (Jan.) 77: Besides, they'd just space me for desertion. So why bother.
**1990** L. M. Bujold *Vor Game* 171: At last one hand fell open, to point at the guard, who straightened attentively. "Space them," Oser ordered.
**2002** A. Reynolds *Redemption Ark* (2004) 295: I can still space you if you do anything I don't like.

**space alien** *n.* see ALIEN, *n.*

**space ark** *n.* a GENERATION SHIP. Compare MULTIGENERATION SHIP.
**1948** N. B. Wilkinson *Decision Illogical* in *Astounding SF* (July) 38/1: Religious prophets [...] were recruiting funds and followers for huge space arks in which they would journey to a promised planet.
**1973** A. C. Clarke *Rendezvous with Rama* 42: What we have here is undoubtedly a "Space Ark."
**1977**: see quote in GENERATION.
**1998** C. Pellegrino *Afterword* in C. Pellegrino & G. Zebrowski *Dyson Sphere* (1999) 212: By contrast to what has traditionally been known as the large, slow-moving "space ark" approach to

interstellar flight, Valkyrie becomes a low mass speedboat.

**space armor** *n.* a SPACE SUIT. Hence **space-armored,** *adj.*

**1933** J. Williamson *Salvage in Space* in *Astounding Stories of Super-sci.* (Mar.) 6/1: His "planet" was the smallest in the solar system, and the loneliest, Thad Allen was thinking, as he straightened wearily in the huge, bulging, inflated fabric of his Osprey space armor.
**1934** E. E. Smith *Triplanetary* in *Amazing Stories* (Jan.) 13/2: He flipped on the lifeboat's visiphone projector and shot its invisible beam up into the control room, where he saw space-armored figures furiously busy at the panels.
**1939** C. D. Simak *Cosmic Engineers* in *Astounding S-F* (Mar.) 63/1: Gary held her spacesuit for her while she clambered into it, helped her fasten down the helmet. Kingsley was puffing and grunting, hauling the space-armor over his portly body.
**1957** P. Anderson *Light* in *Galaxy SF* (Mar.) 113/2: I looked back once and saw a space-armored shape black against the stars.
**1961** P. Anderson *Hiding Place* in *Analog Sci. Fact-Fiction* (Mar.) 125/2: But at the end of the grace period, when Torrance was issuing space armor, Yamamure reported something new.
**1992** A. McCaffrey & M. Lackey *Ship Who Searched* (2002) 74: It looked like his legs and waist were encased in the bottom half of space armor!

**spaceboat** *n.* a spaceship, especially a small one used for maintenance on, or making short trips from, a larger spaceship. Compare SHUTTLE, SHUTTLECRAFT.

**1934** E. E. Smith *Triplanetary* in *Amazing Stories* (Feb.) 77/2: It is an artificial structure, a small space-boat, and there are three creatures in it.
**1945** [M. Leinster] *Ethical Equations* in G. Conklin *Treasury of SF* (1980) 452: Three minutes later the little spaceboat pulled out from the side of the cruiser. Designed for expeditionary work and tool-carrying rather than as an escape-craft, it was not inclosed.
**1953** W. von Braun *Mars Project* (1991) 2:

The flotilla will coast for months on end along elliptical paths and will require inter[-]ship visiting, necessitating the use of "space boats."
**1969** J. Vance *Dirdir Planet of Adventure* (1991) 353: Elsewhere they noted [...] five or six space-boats in various stages of repair.
**1981** M. Bishop & G. W. Page *Murder on Lupozny Station* in M. Bishop *Brighten to Incandescence* (2003) 122: Five of us [...] had entered the hangar containing Skolit's crusty mining craft and the two oversized spaceboats from the *Baidarka*.
**2001** G. Dozois *Worldmakers* x: It was obvious by the middle of the century that Dejah Thoris wasn't going to be there to greet the boys when they stepped off the spaceboat.

**spaceboot** *n.* footwear designed for use in outer space or on other worlds. Hence **space-booted,** *adj.*

**1945** [M. Leinster] *Incident of Calypso* in O. Welles *Invasion from Mars* (1949) 79: They were footprints. They were narrow, and they were arched, and they had not been made by any space[-]boots that humans ever wore.
**1955** A. Norton *Sargasso of Space* in *Solar Queen* (2003) 164: Then Dane too caught that sound, the ring of boots on stone, space boots with their magnetic sole plates clicking in an irregular rhythm as if the wearer was reeling as he ran.
**1964** *Nevada State Journal (Reno)* (June 19) 11/1: The spacemen returning from the moon are going to cool their space boots in quarantine for at least three weeks.
**1966** F. Saberhagen *Face of Deep* in *Berserker* (1967) 183: Karlsen saw the red light below him through the translucent deck, flaring up between his space-booted feet.
**1971** J. White *Hospital Station* in *Major Operation* (2001) 409: The number of dents and furrows put in the spacecraft's hull by tools and spaceboots had become uncountable.
**2002** *Gleaner (Kingston, Jam.)* (Sept. 18) 10/2: U.S. Astronaut Neil Armstrong walked on the moon wearing space boots with soles made of synthetic material from 3M.

**space-borne** *adj.* in space; traveling or able to travel through space.

**1950** J. D. MacDonald *Shadow on Sand* in *Thrilling Wonder Stories* (Oct.) 26/2: We have statistically determined that even with maximum efficiency, one in ten on the A-list will be space-born [sic] in time but I feel that this is a necessary move.
**1952** M. Shaara *Be Fruitful & Multiply* in *Space SF* (Nov.) 56/1: Three intelligent races had already been discovered. Not yet advanced, but capable of advancing. Eventually there would be found a space-borne civilization on a level with Man. And Man would have to be ready.
**1965** *New Scientist* (Aug. 26) 485/1: One would have thought that the bugs could have been eliminated from the fuel cell system before it ever became space-borne.
**1983** M. Z. Bradley *Thendara House* (1991) 71: One of the Big Ships was there, a ground crew crawling over it, servicing the spaceborne monster which had come here.
**1999** P. Anderson *Operation Luna* 305: Val had blurted an account of herself after she was spaceborne.

**space-burned** *adj.* damaged or darkened by prolonged time spent traveling in space. Hence **space burn**, *n.* Compare SPACE-TANNED.
**1942** [W. Stewart] *Collision Orbit* in *Astounding S-F* (July) 82/1: Drake pushed away his papers, with awkward space-burned hands.
**1944** L. Brackett *Veil of Astellar* in *Best of Leigh Brackett* (1977) 86: His hair was as black as mine used to be, his skin space-burned dark and leathery.
**1946** B. I. Kahn *For Public* in *Astounding SF* (Dec.) 80/2: He couldn't tell the difference between simple acne and malignant space burn.
**1957** A. Norton *Star Born* 208: Though the pilot could see little reason for this he answered as best he could, trying to build first a physical picture of the com-tech and then doing a little guessing as to what lay under the other's space-burned skin.
**1969** B. Walton *Troubling of Star* in *Venture SF Mag.* (May) 98/1: His shaven head and face, in contrast to Rubin's hollow-eyed pallor, was space-burned to dark mahogany.
**1991** K. Laumer *Judson's Eden* 17: As always, the sight of the space-burned tugs and shuttles in their ranked cradles in the ready area gave him a lift of spirits.

**space cadet** *n.* **1.** a juvenile spaceman or spacewoman, or one in training. Now *hist.*
**1948** R. A. Heinlein (title): Space Cadet
**1948** *Thrilling Wonder Stories* (June) 125/1: He is befriended by a young Space Cadet, Healey, and the attachment between these two utterly different forms of life with utterly different origins, becomes ultimately one of the epics of early space travel.
**1952** *Newsweek* (Oct. 13) 39/2 (caption): Test pilot A. M. "Tex" Johnston [...] resembles a space cadet in the new high-altitude helmet and suit designed to protect pilots in the upper air.
**1961** J. Boardman *Asteroid Light* in *Reprints from SING OUT! Folk Song Mag. Vol. 3* 60: When I was but a Space Cadet, They put me in charge of a proton jet.
**1992** G. Slusser & T. Shippey *Fiction 2000* 127: Those "rock-ribbed, competent," stereotypically male space cadets in Heinlein's juvenile hard SF novels nonetheless [...] were wearing makeup during the 1950s.
**2.** someone who appears to be out of touch with reality, as if on drugs.
**1973** C. Eble *Campus Slang* (Nov.) 3: *Space Cadette*—Someone who acts spaced out, i.e., as if he has been on drugs, out of touch with reality. That girl is a space cadette.
**1978** S. Lyle & P. Golenbock *Bronx Zoo* 70: You'd think that he was a space cadet, that he had no damned idea of what anybody is talking about.
**1997** *TV Guide* (Nov. 1) 15: The space-cadet humour will soon wear thin.
**2002** D. Danvers *Watch* 265: He's not *there* anymore. He's *always* someplace else. I mean, he's always been a space cadet, but he'd have his moments, you know? He'd let me in. He paid attention.

**space can** *n. Obs.* a SPACESHIP. Compare BOAT, CRAFT, CRUISER, SHIP, SPACE CAR, SPACECRAFT, SPACE CRUISER, SPACE FLYER, SPACER 2, SPACE VEHICLE, SPACE VESSEL, TIN CAN, VESSEL.

**1948** [M. Leinster] *Space-Can* in *Thrilling Wonder Stories* (June) 124/2: Nothing ever happens on a space-can! Headquarters will hush-hush the story, too. What a life! And those recruiting posters say "Deep Space is Calling! Ride a Comet and See the Worlds!" It's a lie! There ought to be a law!

**1954** G. O. Smith *Spacemen Lost* in *Startling Stories* (Fall) 46/1: And out there in the awful dark Alice was trapped in a space can with a happy-go-lucky hulk of a pilot who lacked the drive and ambition to buck for his own command.

**1957** T. Sturgeon *Pod in Barrier* in *Starshine* (1966) 107: There's no point in putting cute clothes, cute tricks, and heady perfume aboard a space can.

**1965** I. Asimov *Founding Father* in I. Asimov, M. H. Greenberg & C. G. Waugh *Starships* (1983) 314: It had come first while the landing was being scratched out, against all odds, on limping motors and in a battered space can.

**space car** *n.* a SPACESHIP. Compare BOAT, CRAFT, CRUISER, SHIP, SPACE CAN, SPACECRAFT, SPACE CRUISER, SPACE FLYER, SPACER 2, SPACE VEHICLE, SPACE VESSEL, TIN CAN, VESSEL.

**1928** E. E. Smith & L. H. Garby *Skylark of Space* in *Amazing Stories* (Sept.) 538/2: They [...] applied just enough negative acceleration to slow the Skylark down to the speed of the other space-car when they should come up with it.

**1930** B. J. Haines *Air Wonder Stories (letter)* (Mar.) 860: One space car carrying a lot of others; like an ocean liner carrying lifeboats.

**1934** R. Z. Gallun *Old Faithful* in I. Asimov *Before Golden Age: Book 2* (1975) 316: The long fins of the space car were crumpled and broken and covered with the blue-gray ash of oxidation.

**1954** L. S. de Camp *S-F Handbook* 54: In 1894 John Jacob Astor published *A Journey in Other Worlds,* a crude imitation of Greg's story using the same apergy to move Astor's space-car.

**2001** T. K. Harper *Silver Moons, Black Steel* 22: Hands like his would have gripped the controls of a skyhook or guided a spacecar up from the mountains and into the starry void.

**space colony** *n.* a group of beings living in a space station or on a world other than their motherworld; the structure or location in or on which such beings live.

**1949** P. Anderson *Time Heals* in *Astounding SF* (Oct.) 72/1: If dey cannot be adjusted, or will not be [...] dey must eider be sent to space colonies or struggle trough an unhappy life on Eart, witout friends or marriage, witout ewen a group.

**1974** *New York Times* (May 19) IV6/1: The space colonies [...] would provide an alternative to earth if the earth's resources ever reach the point of depletion.

**1979** J. P. Hogan *Two Faces of Tomorrow* (1987) 76: You don't mean the two experimental space colonies they put up before they started building the big ones?

**1997** W. F. Wu *Kwan Tingui* in B. Linaweaver & E. E. Kramer *Free Space* (1998) 70: Beyond the billowing green trees in the distance, he could see the inward surface of the space colony curving upward.

**spacecraft** *n.* a SPACESHIP. Compare BOAT, CRAFT, CRUISER, SHIP, SPACE CAN, SPACE CAR, SPACE CRUISER, SPACE FLYER, SPACER 2, SPACE VEHICLE, SPACE VESSEL, TIN CAN, VESSEL.

**1930** P. Nowlan & R. Calkins *Buck Rogers, 2430 A. D.* in *Oakland (Cal.) Tribune* (May 27) 4M: So great was our speed that it would have killed us to check it completely before reaching the mysterious space craft.

**1930** *Scientific American* (Aug.) 142/1: Valier was the principal proponent of working toward the space craft from the known forms of surface or air craft.

**1946** [M. Leinster] *Disciplinary Circuit* in *Thrilling Wonder Stories* (Winter) 53/2: But in time, more especially after matter-transmitters had made space-craft useless, they were forgotten.

**1962** J. F. Kennedy *New York Times* (Sept. 13) 16/5: The Mariner spacecraft now on its way to Venus is the most intricate instrument in the history of space science.

**1978** B. Shaw *Ship of Strangers* (1979) 144: It was with a disproportionate sense of relief that he saw [...] glimpses of the metal pyramids of the spacecraft themselves.

**1996** *Gettysburg (Pa.) Times* (July 3) A6/1: NASA unveiled the design today for America's first new rocketship in a generation, a futuristic wedge-shaped space[-]craft that will be built by Lockheed Martin Corp. **2003** P. Anderson *For Love & Glory* (2004) 67: Spacecraft shuttled between planet and moon.

**space cruiser** *n.* a SPACESHIP. Compare BOAT, CRAFT, CRUISER, SHIP, SPACE CAN, SPACE CAR, SPACECRAFT, SPACE FLYER, SPACER 2, SPACE VEHICLE, SPACE VESSEL, TIN CAN, VESSEL.
**1930** E. E. Smith *Skylark Three* in *Amazing Stories* (Oct.) 617/1: The mammoth space-cruiser attracted attention even before it landed. **1934** W. K. Sonneman *Amazing Stories* (Sept.) 108/1: A *Venerian* space cruiser, the X-1, raced toward earth. **1958** T. Sturgeon *Comedian's Children* in *Man Who Lost Sea* (2005) 93: The quiet third of the Twenty-First Century came to an end [ ... ] with the return to earth of a modified Fafnir space cruiser under the command of Capt. Avery Swope. **2002** B. Lowry & S. Field *Space Camp* 76: Mandala and I want to meet up when we're eighteen and get work on one of the luxury space cruisers.

**space dock** *n.* a SPACEPORT or space station, especially one where a spaceship can undergo repair or take on supplies.
**1945** H. Walton *Schedule* in M. Greenberg *Men against Stars* (1958) 80: The bustling scene all around him, the hurrying foot traffic of a great space dock, the fussy activity of automatic unloaders, all seemed suddenly as unreal and absurd as the news Matthews had brought him. **1950** E. E. Smith *S-F First: Cinvention on TV* in S. Skirvin *Cinvention Memory Book* 57: I hope to live to see the first trips to the planets by way of a space dock in space, to fuel rockets which will go to the moon. **1962** *Sheboygan (Wis.) Press* (Feb. 24) 20/2: It was President Kennedy who finally cut the red tape, much as the umbilical cords holding Glenn's rocket to its space dock were finally dropped.

**1972** U. K. Le Guin *Word for World Is Forest* in H. Ellison *Again, Dangerous Visions* 37: He saw the golden tower of the space-dock at Central. **1986** D. Carey *Battlestations!* 214: Several weeks in spacedock would realign *Enterprise*'s delicate nacelle balance. **2002** B. Herbert & K. J. Anderson *Dune: Butlerian Jihad* 107 (2003): Vor could not comprehend the lives of the uneducated workers who unloaded heavy crates at the space dock.

**space dog** *n.* a SPACEHOUND.
**1940** N. Bond *Castaway* O. Welles *Invasion from Mars* (1949) 123: He's a good man, Captain McNeally. A seasoned space-dog, canny and wise to the ways of the void, always on deck in moments of emergency. **1946** J. B. Duryea *Astounding SF (letter)* (July) 171/2: Judging from the film, the old space-dog's trick of "balancing her down on the jets" would not be much of a job, provided the gyro-pilot was in good shape. **1980** B. Marszal & F. Simpson *trans.* S. Lem *Return from Stars* 163: How is it, [ ... ] that a customer who could crawl into that stinking hole on Kereneia, an old space dog—an old rhinoceros, rather, a hundred and fifty—now starts to...?

**space drive** *n.* a propulsion system for a spaceship. Compare STAR DRIVE.
**1932**: see quote in ATOMICS 1. **1934** E. E. Smith *Skylark of Valeron* in *Astounding Stories* (Aug.) 31/2: There was the barest perceptible flash of the intolerable brilliance of an exploding universe, succeeded [ ... ] by the utter blackness of the complete absence of all light whatever as the space drive automatically went into action and hurled the great vessel away. **1959** D. A. Wollheim *Secret of Ninth Planet* 36: First, he was introduced to all the other members of the crew, and given a mass of papers to study which outlined the basic means of the new space drive. **1994** R. Silverberg *Hot Sky at Midnight* 52: Its work involves an experimental spacedrive, the first interstellar voyage, faster-than-light travel.

**1998** T. Chiang *Story of Your Life* in *Stories of Your Life & Others* (2002) 174: It didn't exclude the possibility that the heptapods might yet offer us a space drive, or cold fusion, or some other wish-fulfilling miracle.

**space elevator** *n.* a giant cable, the center of gravity of which is in geosynchronous orbit around a planet, connecting a fixed location on the planet's equator to a space station, and along which personnel and materials can be transported without using spacecraft. Compare BEANSTALK.

**1975** A. C. Clarke *Future Space Programs*: Imagine my surprise when I saw that the Russians had come up with the same idea quite independently—the space elevator!

**1979** A. C. Clarke *Fountains of Paradise* 51: At last we can build the Space Elevator—or the Orbital Tower, as I prefer to call it. For in a sense it is a tower, rising clear through the atmosphere, and far, far beyond.

**1988** I. McDonald *Desolation Road* (2001) 206: Just what the hell are they doing out there, building an extra space elevator or something?

**1993** K. S. Robinson *Green Mars* 334: Given the acute population and environmental problems on Earth, and the space elevator currently being constructed there to match the one already on Mars, the gravity wells could be surmounted and mass emigration would certainly follow.

**2002** J. C. Wright *Golden Age* 379 (2003): Approaching in the distance, the size of an ocean liner, ornamental and plush, came the great gold and crystal and ivory car of the space elevator.

**2005** *San Francisco Chronicle* (A198pr. 25) A6: A visionary image of a "Space Elevator" shows it climbing thousands of miles high on an ultra-thin ribbon of carbon nanotubes.

**spacefarer** *n.* a SPACER (sense 1). Compare SPACE FLIER 1, SPACEMAN, SPACE PERSON 2, SPACE TRAVELER, SPACEWOMAN, STARFARER.

**1939** L. Margulies *Le Zombie* (Oct. 28) 2: You'll find Captain Future the most dynamic space-farer the cosmos has ever seen.

**1963** P. Anderson *After Doomsday* (1968) 40: By that time, "civilization" was equated in the minds of space-farers with the ability to travel through space.

**1985** G. Bear *Eon* (1998) 22: They were space-farers, originally assigned to the near-Earth orbit platforms and now working the distances between Earth, Moon and Stone.

**1993** A. C. Clarke & G. Lee *Rama Revealed* 10: The purpose of the Rama series of spacecraft was to acquire and catalogue as much information as possible about spacefarers in the galaxy.

**2002** A. Reynolds *Redemption Ark* (2004) 48: The talk had turned to the various ways in which the remains of spacefarers were dealt with.

**spacefaring** *n.* SPACE-TRAVELING. Compare SPACE FLYING, SPACE TRAVEL.

**1942** N. S. Bond *Ballad of Venus Nell* in *Planet Stories* (Spring) 60: None but the most daring do any space-faring In those lethal, whirl-lagig niches, But spacemen all claim that the Bog is aflame With infinite, fabulous riches.

**1959** P. Anderson *Virgin Planet* (1969) 20: Who had ever begun the idea that spacefaring was one long wild adventure?

**1978** D. R. Mason *Mission to Pactolus R* 11: A long session in a Fingalnan brothel would set them up for another stint of spacefaring.

**spacefaring** *adj.* that travels, or is able to travel, in space. Compare STARFARING.

**1952** A. B. Chandler *Frontier of Dark* in *Astounding SF* (Sept.) 133/1: She's a better ship than any of the spacefaring boudoirs that are turned out by *your* yards!

**1962** J. F. Kennedy *New York Times* (Sept. 13) 16/3: In short our leadership in science and industry, our hopes for peace and security, our obligations to ourselves as well as others all require us to make this effort to solve these mysteries, to solve them for the good of all men and to become the world's leading spacefaring nation.

**1967** A. Budrys *Benchmarks* (1985) 101: The problem is the emergence of a hostile, spacefaring civilization of aliens.

**1987** N. Spinrad *Isaac Asimov's SF* (Oct.) 181/2: If there is one collective value held by the "science fiction community" as a whole, it is a belief in our destiny as a space-faring species.

**2002** K. Schroeder *Permanence* (2003) 109: Consciousness and space-faring toolmaking ability [ ... ] arise by chance.

**space fiction** *n.* science fiction set primarily in space or that involves space travel. Hence **space-fictional,** *adj.*
**1948** W. Sheldon *Perfect Servant* in *Startling Stories* (July) 116/1: In Vienna I make my reputation on musicals. So I come to Hollywood. So what do they give me? An *epic*. About the future, yet. The story they get from a magazine called *Atomic Space Fiction*. I can't even understand it.
**1963** V. Gielgud *Goggle-Box Affair* 191: Space-fictional horrors.
**1974** G. Zebrowski *SF & Visual Media* in R. Bretnor *SF, Today & Tomorrow* 46: They had set [ ... ] the mythopoetic basis of sf film in the rigidly real world of Clarke's space fiction.
**1979** *Daily Telegraph (London)* (Dec. 14) 13/3: Star Trek is the latest in an increasing number of space fiction films which [ ... ] tend to find individuality.
**2000** P. Nicholls *Big Dumb Objects & Cosmic Engines* in G. Westfahl *Space & Beyond* 16: The other great theme of space fiction often, and Big Dumb Objects usually, is transcendence.

**spacefield** *n.* a place on a world where spaceships can take off and land. Compare SPACEPORT, STARPORT.
**1939** C. D. Simak *Cosmic Engineers* in *Astounding S-F* (Mar.) 60/1: The space-suited figures were coming rapidly down the path to the space[-]field.
**1944** C. D. Simak *Huddling Place* in R. Silverberg *SF Hall of Fame, Vol. I* (1970) 268: Webster stood on the broad ramp of the space field and watched the shape that dwindled in the sky with faint flickering points of red lancing through the wintry sunlight.
**1968** S. R. Delany *Nova* (2002) 61: You just pick your crew from people hanging around the spacefield?
**1970** A. McCaffrey *Ship Who Sang* (1991) 31: There is [ ... ] no space field in that vicinity and a meadow has been set aside for your use.
**1993** B. Shaw *Dimensions* (1994) 42: I'm going to set up a checkpoint at the spacefield,

and I'm going to inspect the incoming squelchers' baggage.

**space fleet** *n.* an organized group of spaceships, especially one under military control. Compare STARFLEET.
**1931** P. Nowlan *Buck Rogers 2431 AD* in *Oakland (Cal.) Tribune Comics* (May 3) 1: The *electronographs* and *television* show a *strange space fleet* flashing toward Venus in *battle formation*!!
**1940** J. Williamson *Hindsight* in *Astounding S-F* (May) 104/1: Millions of Earthmen have labored for years to prepare for this rebellion. Earth has built a space fleet.
**1969** E. Hamilton *Return to Stars* 64: They plunged on and now they were passing through the space where, that other time, the space-fleets of the Empire and its allies had fought out their final Armageddon with the League of the Dark Worlds.
**1979** J. Paton *Sea of Rings* 23: William Robert Mahony, ex-Captain, Space Fleet, aged 46.
**1996** D. Pringle, et al. *Ultimate Ency. of SF* 22/2: The hero must do penance for his cavalier destruction of an alien spacefleet.

**space flier** *n.* **1.** *Obs.* a SPACER (sense 1). Compare SPACEFARER, SPACEMAN, SPACE PERSON 2, SPACE TRAVELER, SPACEWOMAN.
**1931** *Wonder Stories* (Feb.) 958: To old and seasoned space[-]fliers like Professor Galloway and myself, there was something ludicrous in all this emotional bustle [ ... ] over a little hop to the Moon.
**1932** *Key West (Fla.) Citizen* (May 19) 1/4 (caption): Dr. Walter S. Adams, astronomer (upper left), says a space flier traveling from the sun with the speed of a light ray would need 300,000,000 years to reach known limits of space.
**1962** *Listener* (Mar. 1) 368/2: All three American space-fliers had had to be landed in the sea.
**2.** see SPACE FLYER.

**space flight** *n.* a journey through outer space; the technology required to undertake such a journey. Compare SPACE FLYING, SPACE TRAVEL.

**1931** *Wonder Stories* (Jan.) 900/1: We know now what conditions are necessary for a space flight.

**1942** [H. Clement] *Proof* in *Astounding S-F* (June) 103/2: Your science, I know, is superior to ours in certain ways, although it was my race which first developed space flight.

**1959** *Scientific American* (Mar.) 47/2: The radiation belts obviously present an obstacle to space flight.

**1980** D. Brin *Sundiver* 238: More males volunteer for spaceflight than females.

**1992** V. Vinge *Fire upon Deep* 45: I'll bet it's an idea older than spaceflight: the "elder races" must be toward the galactic core.

**space flyer** *n. Obs.* a SPACESHIP. Also **space flier.** Compare BOAT, CRAFT, CRUISER, SHIP, SPACE CAN, SPACE CAR, SPACECRAFT, SPACE CRUISER, SPACER 2, SPACE VEHICLE, SPACE VESSEL, TIN CAN, VESSEL.

**1911** H. Gernsback *Ralph 124C 41+* in *Modern Electrics* (Nov.) 516/1: He knew now that Fernand 600 10 had carried off his sweetheart in a space-flyer and that the machine by this time was probably far out from the earth's boundary.

**1929** C. W. Harris & M. J. Breuer *Baby on Neptune* in *Amazing Stories* (Dec.) 794/2: But a geodesic space flier is in no danger from them, because it is not on a world-line.

**1931** J. W. Campbell, Jr. *Islands of Space* in *Amazing Stories Quarterly* (Spring) 221/2: The mere movement of a man was sufficient to deflect the angle of a space-flyer.

**1934** E. E. Smith *Triplanetary* in *Amazing Stories* (Apr.) 54/1: And if these two, who had rebuilt the space-flyer, could hardly control themselves, what of the three in the speedster, who knew nothing whatever of the super-ship's potentialities?

**space flying** *n. Obs.* SPACE TRAVEL. Compare SPACEFARING, SPACE FLIGHT, SPACE TRAVELING.

**1927** H. Gernsback *Space Flying* in *Amazing Stories* (Nov.) 725: Scientifiction writers of note have always taken with avidity to this fascinating subject, while some of the greatest minds have occupied themselves with the problem of space flying.

**1929** H. Noordung *Problems of Space Flying* in *Sci. Wonder Stories* (July) 170/1: It is, we believe, the first serious work of its kind that has appeared in print, where an authority takes the problem of space flying seriously.

**1930** B. J. Haines *Air Wonder Stories (letter)* (Mar.) 860: The stories I refer to are dealing primarily with space flying and inter[-]planetarian flight.

**1939** SF *"There Ain't No Sech Animal"* in *SF* (Mar.) 33: Today, according to this *same* popular belief, space-flying ships for interplanetary travel are ridiculous impossibilities, atomic power can never be achieved, and immortality is but a dreamer's Utopia.

**space force** *n.* the branch of the military that acts in outer space. Often *cap.* or *pl.*

**1940** J. Williamson *Hindsight* in J. W. Campbell, Jr. *Astounding SF Anthology* (1952) 49: Why have you gathered three fourths of your space forces, to crush a handful of plotters?

**1950** A. Bester *Devil's Invention* in *Astounding SF* (Aug.) 144/2: On July 11th he was brevetted to command of the wrecked Space Force [...]. On September 19th he assumed supreme command in the Battle of the Parsec.

**1953** W. von Braun *New York Times* (Oct. 11) 25/2: The tasks of strategic bombing and global reconnaissance will have become a mission of the Space Forces, which by 2003 will have become a separate service on equal status with Army, Navy and Air Force.

**1965** M. Z. Bradley *Star of Danger* (1985) 19: The man who bought this gun from our space-force guard has a collection of rare old weapons.

**1986** W. J. Williams *Hardwired* 321: The two ex-Space Force people, Diego and Maurice, flying second string twenty-five miles behind.

**1994** D. K. Slayton & M. Cassutt *Deke!* 67: The Air Force thought it was the logical service to have some kind of space force.

**2004** M. Bishop *Angst of God* in *Mag. of Fantasy & SF* (Oct./Nov.) 93: Even Counselor Ztang, usually one shut-mouthed bean, let slip that a virulent fungal smut had almost derailed his aspirations to enter the ztun space force.

**space freighter** *n.* a spaceship used to transport materials betweens worlds or space stations.

**1940** A. E. van Vogt *Vault of Beast* in *Astounding S-F* (Aug.) 50/1: It crept along the corridor of the space freighter, fighting the terrible urge of its elements to take the shape of its surroundings.

**1951** I. Asimov *Hostess* in *Galaxy SF* (May) 108/2: Anyone who wants to get away from trouble need only hop the nearest space freighter.

**1955** B. Wells *Ship of Fog Seas* in *Spaceway* (Apr.) 73: In a matter of minutes the battered old space freighter would warp into one of the loading docks and discharge her meager freight of Martian artifacts and uranium.

**2002** J. Williamson *Afterlife* in D. G. Hartwell *Year's Best SF 8* (2003) 419: We settle both great continents, harvested the great forests, loaded fleets of space freighters with precious hardwoods and rare metals.

**2005** *Sci-Tech Today* (Internet) (June 20): A Russian Progress space freighter docked early Sunday at the International Space Station, delivering water, fresh food and spare parts for the two-man crew.

**space-going** *adj.* traveling, or able to travel, in space.

**1946** G. O. Smith *Pattern for Conquest* in *Astounding S-F* (Apr.) 45/1: And bringing up the rear were the myriad upon myriad of supply ships, replacement carriers, machine-shop craft, and even space-going foundries.

**1948** J. Farrell *Hero* in *Astounding SF* (Oct.) 54/2: I'll get into that space-going fuel tank and grin at the newsreel men as if I didn't have a nerve in my body.

**1973** A. D. Foster *Bloodhype* 2: The Vom now tried to attract the ships of another species, but space-going races were scarce in this section of the galaxy.

**1992** A. McCaffrey & M. Lackey *Ship Who Searched* (2002) 2: That had given him a window of opportunity for a little shore leave, in

a base-town that catered to some fairly heavy space-going traffic, and he had taken it.

**2001** *Locus* (June) 15/2: Mada flees space-going assailants by hastily jumping upwhen through time.

**spacehand** *n.* a low-ranking member of a spaceship crew; someone who has experience working in space.

**1938** M. W. Wellman *Men against Stars* in *Astounding S-F* (June) 8/1: Four stubbled faces turned to a common, grinning regard as the pounding roar of the rockets died away at last. The skipper, the rocketman, the navigator, the spacehand.

**1938** F. A. Kummer *Forgiveness of Tenchu Taen* in *Astounding S-F* (Nov.) 120/1: Here in the Olech, squat Jovian spacehands rub shoulders with languid Venusian traders; dark Mercurians drink with the dâk-men of Neptune; and tall Terrestrials swagger contemptuously through the crowds of "reddies," copper-skinned sons of Mars.

**1949** L. Brackett *Lake of Gone Forever* in *Halfling & Other Stories* (1973) 283: They climbed in, six men to a sledge, all burly space[-]hands with the exception of [ ... ] Conway, who had sweated his way up the ranks to Master Pilot.

**1962** M. Z. Bradley *Sword of Aldones* 161: She turned up on Samarra about half an hour after I talked to her here. Times, I'm tempted to throw up this job and turn spacehand.

**1990** P. Anderson *Inconstant Star* in L. Niven, et al. *Man-Kzin Wars III* 287: Maybe, not being a spacehand, she won't obey my order and stay at the boat.

**space helmet** *n.* headgear designed to provide the wearer with a breathable atmosphere in outer space or on other worlds; any headgear resembling such a helmet. Hence **space-helmeted**, *adj.*

**1931** M. W. Wellman *Disc-Men of Jupiter* in *Wonder Stories* (Sept.) 544/1: He took the glass-fronted space helmet and adjusted it on Thiana's head.

**1946** J. Kennedy *Startling Stories* (letter) (Summer) 99/1: Come around sometime in a flimsy space helmet, of the type supposedly worn by women of the future.

**1957** *Time* (July 22) 52/1: From a sealed chamber like the cabin of a rocket ship, and from space-helmeted human guinea pigs who live in it, medical researchers [ ... ] hope to learn answers to some fundamental questions about the body's consumption of fuel and oxygen.

**1973** *Times (London)* (Aug. 29) 3/2: Scientists are developing a "space helmet" respirator to protect miners against dust.

**2001** M. Reilly *Area 7* (2003) 403: Two white briefcase-like life-support systems [ ... ] and a pair of spherical gold-tinted space helmets that clicked onto the neck rings of their pressure suits.

**spacehound** *n. Obs.* an experienced spaceman or spacewoman. Compare SPACE DOG.

**1931** E. E. Smith (title) *Amazing Stories* (July) 294: Spacehounds of IPC

**1931** E. E. Smith *Spacehounds of IPC* in *Amazing Stories* (Sept.) 570/2: Nothing's driving us now, and a fellow's entitled to at least one honeymoon during his life. And what a honeymoon this is going to be, little spacehound of my heart.

**1940** [G. Danzell] *Castaway* in *Planet Stories* (Winter) 37/2: He was a good man, Cap McNeally. A hardened spacehound, canny and wise to the ways of the void, always on deck in moments of emergency.

**1949** A. E. van Vogt *Project Spaceship* in *Thrilling Wonder Stories* (Aug.) 106/1: General [ ... ] you so and so. You're an old spacehound yourself. I repeat, when would you consider the time ripe?

**1951** T. Sturgeon *Special Aptitude* in *Baby Is Three* (1999) 119: I'm just an old space-hound, but I know what I'm talking about.

**space lane** *n.* a route through space between two worlds; outer space. Usually *pl.* Compare SPACEWAYS, STARLANES, STARWAYS.

**1928** E. Hamilton *Crashing Suns* in *Weird Tales* 200/2 (Aug.): He had travelled the space-lanes of the solar system for the greater part of his life, and now all of his time-honored rules of interplanetary navigation had been upset by this new cruiser.

**1938** C. Jacobi *Cosmic Teletype* in *Thrilling Wonder Stories* (Oct.) 38/2: It is believed Tarana arrived secretly on Lirius on a space ship, travelling out of patrolled space-lanes.

**1953** A. Norton *Last Planet* (1955) 186: Maybe there has been a rebellion in this sector. The winner may be systematically mopping up all Patrol bases. That would leave him free to rule the space lanes as he pleases.

**1996** B. Baldwin *Defiance* 124: I hadn't the foggiest notion how to secure a space lane between Atalanta and Gontor.

**2001** J. A. Gardner *Ascending* 109: Since Starbiter was headed for New Earth now, we must be traveling in the same space lane.

**spaceline** *n.* a company that makes passenger space flights between two or more worlds.

**1930** J. W. Campbell, Jr. *Black Star Passes* in *Amazing Stories Quarterly* (Fall) 499/1: The bonds of friendship between the two planets had grown swiftly in those three years, and they were already linked by many regular space lines. These ships made the trips as frequently as the relative positions of the planets permitted.

**1946** G. O. Smith *Impossible Pirate* in *Astounding SF* (Dec.) 64/1: No space line liked to have the job of removing spilled soup from fifty evening gowns, let alone the bad publicity.

**1950** L. S. de Camp *Git Along!* in *Astounding SF* (Aug.) 71/2: For the Osirian space-line did not run ships beyond Sol in that direction, and even the *Viagens Interplanetarias* did not run direct service from the Procyon-Sirius group to the Centaurine group.

**1953** H. B. Fyfe *Fast Passage* in *Other Worlds* (Jan.) 77/2: Was it the reputation of Terra that gave him concern? Or that of the spaceline in which he happened to have a modest investment?

**1998** J. White *Mind Changer* (1999) 182: It is bad in itself and [ ... ] very bad for the future prospects of the small, independent, and, well, economically run spaceline to which *Kreskhallar* belongs.

**spaceliner** *n.* a large, often luxuriously-appointed, spaceship used to transport passengers. Compare STARLINER.

**1931** J. W. Campbell, Jr. *Islands of Space* in *Amazing Stories Quarterly* (Spring) 168/1: S Doradus [...] radiates enough heat from one square inch to run a modern space-liner.

**1934** C. L. Moore *Black Thirst* in *Weird Tales* (Apr.) 425/1: Not even the lowest class of Venusian street-walker dared come along the waterfronts of Ednes on the nights when the space-liners were not in.

**1965** G. R. Dickson *Warrior* in *Analog SF-Sci. Fact* (Dec.) 55/1: The spaceliner coming in from New Earth and Freiland, worlds under the Sirian sun, was delayed in its landing by traffic at the spaceport in Long Island Sound.

**1974** R. Silverberg *Schwartz Between Galaxies* in *Feast of St. Dionysus* (1987) 95: I see a ship voyaging from star to star, a spaceliner of the future, and about that ship is a sampling of many species, many cultures.

**1990** A. Steele *Clarke County, Space* 58: TexSpace SSTO shuttle *Lone Star Clipper* was a few minutes from initiating the OMS burn which would brake the spaceliner for its primary approach to Clarke County.

**spacelock** *n.* an airlock on something (e.g., a spaceship, space station, etc.), the exterior of which is exposed to outer space.

**1930** J. W. Campbell *Black Star Passes* in *Amazing Stories Quarterly* (Fall) 520/2: The others leapt in swift pursuit, rushing swiftly across half a world to the giant space lock that would let them out into the void. Then one at a time they passed out into the mighty sea of space.

**1940** H. Kuttner *Million Years to Conquer* in *Startling Stories* (Nov.) 18/2: At Theron's request, Ardath opened a spacelock. Air surged in with a queerly choking sulphurous odor.

**1948** L. R. Hubbard *240,000 Miles Straight Up* in *Thrilling Wonder Stories* (Dec.) 55/1: Angel put a piece of chocolate into the miniature space lock of his helmet, closed the outer door, opened the inner one with his chin and worried it dog-fashion out of the compartment.

**1953** D. A. Wollheim *Asteroid 745: Mauritia* in M. Ashley *Random House Book of SF Stories* (1996) 43: What we saw was this: The spacelock was open, the air had escaped, and Braun was lying half in and half out, dead from strangulation.

**1996** L. Schimel & M. A. Garland *To See Stars* in M. Ashley *Random House Book of SF Stories* (1996) 4: There was no way to know what it was like to see the stars for real. You would first have to find a way out of the sphere, and everyone knew that all the spacelock exits had been sealed centuries ago.

**spaceman** *n.* someone, especially a male, who works in or travels through outer space. Compare ROCKETMAN, SPACEFARER, SPACE FLIER 1, SPACE PERSON 2, SPACER SPACE TRAVELER, SPACEWOMAN.

**1933** C. L. Moore *Shambleau* in *Weird Tales* (Nov.) 536/1: Smith—as men know from Venus to Jupiter's moons—walks as softly as a cat, even in spaceman's boots.

**1946** D. Calkins & R. Yager *Buck Rogers* in *Oakland (Calif.) Tribune* (Dec. 15) 1st Comic Section unpag.: Then his brother came to th' phone...an' offered t' take Knuckle's place: claims he's a qualified spaceman, too.

**1957** R. Silverberg *En Route to Earth* in *World of Thousand Colors* (1984) 264: Two blueskinned Vegan spacemen lounged against the wall of the Administration Center, chatting with a pilot from Earth.

**1967** *Daily Review (Hayward, Calif.)* (Jan. 28) 3/4: The three spacemen had been in the capsule about five and one-half hours.

**1983** B. Shaw *Orbitsville Departure* (1990) 103: The spaceman, helmet in one hand, was shading his eyes from the sun's vertical rays with his free hand while he scanned the horizon.

**spacemanship** *n.* the skill or practice of piloting a spaceship.

**1932** C. A. Smith *Master of Asteroid* in *Wonder Stories* (Oct.) 438/1: I have passed several more of the asteroids—irregular fragments, little larger than meteoric stones; and all my skill of spacemanship has been taxed severely to avert collision.

**1946** E. Hamilton *Forgotton World* in *Thrilling Wonder Stories* (Winter) 39/1: Harb Land was engaged in the most difficult operation of spacemanship, bringing a ship into exact balanced orbit around a celestial body.

**1952** H. Stine *Greenhorn* in *Fantastic Story Mag.* (Fall) 112/2: Insurance rates on pilots and ships required by Space Code were high, and there was always the human element of error in spacemanship.

**1966** *Life* (Jan. 7) 32 (caption): Down from adventure and spacemanship, Stafford [ ... ] and Schirra pop out for an eye-level look at the sea.

**1996** J. Vance *Night Lamp* (1998) 41: The topic in which he was most interested: namely, the lore of spacemanship, was not considered appropriate and would be discouraged.

## space marine *n.* a warrior who fights in space or on alien worlds.

**1955** E. F. Russell *Waitabits* in *Astounding SF* (July) 68/1: In the last one thousand years the human race has become wholly technological. Even the lowest ranking space-marine is considered a technician, especially by standards of olden times.

**1981** L. Fish *Banned from Argo* in R. Rogow *Futurespeak* (1991) 396: He outranked seven space marines and a demolition crew.

**1990** [I. Douglas] *Luna Marine* (1999) 168: "Flash" had become his nickname, his handle in the platoon, a jeering reference to Flash Gordon and his desire to be a space Marine.

**2000** *White Dwarf* (May) 16/2: Rogue Trader was just as much about a single Space Marine taking on a hive gang, or a few space pirates trying to raid the Imperial armoury.

**2004** *San Francisco Chronicle* (Nov. 23) E5/4: Most of the mayhem involves space marines killing bugs, or bugs killing other bugs.

## space navigator *n.* an ASTROGATOR.

**1930** [G. Edwards] *Rescue from Jupiter* in *Wonder Stories* (Feb.) 778/1: He called the explorers in, the mechanics and engineers, the space-navigators and the rocket-experts.

**1934** E. E. Smith *Triplanetary* in *Amazing Stories* (Feb.) 84/2: Space-navigators both, the two Terrestrial officers soon discovered that it

was even then moving with a velocity far above that of light.

**1951** A. C. Clarke *Exploration of Space* 82: His position is, clearly, only one of the things a space-navigator would want to know.

**1997** A. McCaffrey & M. Ball *Acorna* (2001) 380: That, she considered, was the price she paid for the money that had put her through nav training [ ... ]. She couldn't actually work as a space navigator; that would be beneath her family's status.

## space opera *n.* [by analogy to *soap opera* and *horse opera*] science fiction with an interplanetary or galaxy-wide setting, especially one making use of stock characters and situations; a work of this type.

**1941** [B. Tucker] *Le Zombie* (Jan.) unpag.: In these hectic days of phrase-coining, we offer one. Westerns are called "horse operas," the morning housewife tear-jerkers are called "soap operas." For the hacky, grinding, stinking, outworn space-ship yarn, or world-saving for that matter, we offer "space opera."

**1948** R. A. Heinlein *letter* (Nov. 6) in R. A. Heinlein & V. Heinlein *Grumbles from Grave* (1990) 93: It would be easy enough to cook up another space opera.

**1951** C. Fadiman *Intro.* in [M. Leinster] *Great Stories of SF* x: The trivial but engaging fantasies of the space-opera hack, busily manipulating his androids, his atomic-power inter-galactic ships and his telepathic monsters—are also science fiction.

**1972** D. Suvin *On Poetics of SF Genre College English* (Dec.) 375/2: SF retrogressing into fairy tale (e.g. "space opera" with a hero-princess-monster triangle in astronautic costume) is committing creative suicide.

**1991** *Locus* (Sept.) 15/1: Some of science fiction's greatest and most revered creations are essentially space opera, populated by grandiose archetypes and redolent at once of myth, rocket fuel, and soap.

**1993** *Locus* (June) 5/2: He would go on to produce a number of thoughtful space operas and somewhat more unconventional sf novels in quick succession.

**2005** M. Berry *San Francisco Chronicle* (Jan. 30) C4/5: With "The Family Trade," Stross brings to fantasy the same kind of sly humor and clear-eyed extrapolation that he previously brought to space opera and horror.

**space operatic** *n.* like or of space opera.

**1953** L. S. de Camp *S-F Handbook* 162: His stories are space-operatic with a strong technological bent; little characterization or motivation, but lots of fast action, cosmic gadgetry, and ribald wit.

**2002** D. Langford *New York Rev. of SF* (Apr.) 8/2: Still, it's a rousing space-operatic read.

**2006** P. Di Filippo *Washingtonpost.com (Internet)* (Jan. 15): Hamilton's *The Star Kings* and *Return to the Stars* [ ... ] transport 20th-century Earthman John Gordon to a space-operatic milieu some 200,000 years hence, when golden empires sprawl across the space-lanes of the galaxy and one man can save the universe with daring and courage.

**space patrol** *n.* the police or law enforcement group whose jurisdiction is outer space. Often *cap.* Hence **space patrolman.**

**1936** D. Wandrei *Finality Unlimited* in *Astounding Stories* (Sept.) 31/2: His master, Pilot Venn of the Space Patrol, ruffled the Kotoley's head.

**1942** W. S. Peacock *Thing of Venus* in *Planet Stories* (Spring) 74/2: Never, had he expected again to find himself a welcome friend of a Space Patrolman.

**1945** J. Vance *World-Thinker* in *Thrilling Wonder Stories* (Summer) 39/1: In another day or so she'd be slicing the fringe of the Clantlalan System, where the far-flung space patrol of that dark and inimical empire blasted without warning all approaching vessels.

**1964** K. Laumer *Great Time Machine Hoax* in *Keith Laumer: Lighter Side* (2001) 383: We barely escaped capture by the corrupt Space Patrol, which fears we will reveal what we've learned of their illegal operations.

**1991** J. May *Jack Bodiless* (1993) 379: Officially, the three human space fleets will be only an arm of the Magistratum. A glorified coast guard and space patrol.

**space person** *n.* **1.** an ALIEN. Usually *pl.* Compare STARMAN 1, STAR-PERSON.

**1952** O. Lebeck & A. McWilliams *Twin Earths* in *Post-Standard (Syracuse, New York)* (July 8) 15: Ladies and gentlemen, in a few seconds you will see live specimens of the strange space people who attacked and conquered *Terra*!!

**1959** *Galac-Ticks* (Sept. 1) 3/1: Actually, most human beings are space people, having arrived via birth from otherwheres. Some few carry the memory—most do not.

**1960** *Daily Courier (Connellsville, Pa.)* (July 14) 18 (ad): After all, we DO feature out-of-this-world values in high quality foods, and if space people ever land here, it wouldn't surprise us if they hurried to the MARKET BASKET to stock up with foods and supplies.

**1985** A. Norton *Forerunner: Second Venture* (1986) 9: Violence was not the answer to these spacepeople.

**2002** B. Chepaitis *These Dreams* (2003) 296: He thought she was taking his alimony and paying it to spacepeople who were gonna take over the world.

**2.** a SPACER (sense 1). Usually *pl.* Compare SPACEFARER, SPACE FLIER 1, SPACEMAN, SPACE TRAVELER, SPACEWOMAN.

**1964** J. Vance *Sail 25 Future Tense* 81: On Tuesday morning the cadets took their places in the angel-wagon. Henry Belt presently appeared. "Last chance to play it safe. Anyone decide they're really not space people after all?"

**1996** D. Pringle, et al. *Ultimate Ency. of SF* 226/3: Scott's main series is about the adventures of spaceperson Silence Leigh.

**1988** A. Roberts *Salt* (2000) 66: Trying to swim through the air the way novice spacepeople do in weightless, thrashing pointlessly about our centres of gravity.

**space pirate** *n.* a space-based outlaw who preys on other spaceships or inhabited worlds. Now chiefly *hist.* or *joc.* Hence **space piracy,** *n.*

**1933** H. Vincent *When Comet Returned* in *Amazing Stories* (Apr.) 14/1: He thought of the possibility of a prearranged meeting with space pirates and sat erect with a jerk. But no, that couldn't be it. The days of those fierce outlaws of the space lanes had passed with the advent of the Planetary Patrol.

**1946** G. O. Smith *Impossible Pirate* in *Astounding SF* (Dec.) 60/2: Black Morgan was a space pirate and the place to look for him was in space. That space piracy was impossible for divers reasons seemed to make little difference to Black Morgan. He did it.

**1947** C. Oliver *Startling Stories (letter)* (Jan.) 98/1: Banish the man to Bikini! Make him read space-pirate stories forever! No, wait. I retract that last. It is too horrible.

**1953** A. Norton *Star Rangers* 7: Space pirates raised flags and recruited fleets to gorge on spoil plundered from this wreckage.

**1985** G. R. R. Martin *Portraits of His Children* in S. Williams *Hugo & Nebula Award Winners from Asimov's SF* (1995) 233: When she was a little girl, I used to write stories just for her. Funny animals, space pirates, silly poems.

**2000** [I. Douglas] *Europa Strike* 277: "*Yarr!*" he growled, a mock pirate's battlecry. "I always wanted to be a space pirate!"

**spaceport** *n.* a place where spaceships take off and land; (in non-SF use) a place where spaceships take off only. Compare SPACE FIELD, STARPORT.

**1930** M. J. Breuer & J. Williamson *Birth of New Republic* in *Amazing Stories Quarterly* (Winter) 29/1: The space-ports at the three great cities, were, of course, occupied or blockaded by the Tellurian fleets.

**1946** E. Hamilton *Forgotton World* in *Thrilling Wonder Stories* (Winter) 14/2: Worked since then establishing spaceports for star-ship lines between Rigel, Sharak, Tibor, Algol and other stars.

**1962** *Daily Progress (Charlottesville, Va.)* (Feb. 23) 11: After these few words, Glenn set out for the ride through brilliant sunshine to this space port—where it all began—and his meeting with President Kennedy.

**1976** S. R. Delany *Trouble on Triton* (1996) 138: Bron had the feeling that they had not really left the Earth space-port complex.

**1977** *Daily Telegraph (London)* (July 28) 1/6: The small spaceport at Kagoshima, at the southern tip of Japan, looked more like a station for amateur rocketry than a serious rival to Cape Canaveral.

**1987** D. Brin *Uplift War* 588: Robert blamed the symptoms on the fringing fields of a lifting starship, whose keening engines could be heard all the way from the spaceport.

**2002** M. J. Harrison *Light* 27 (2004): There were spaceports on both its continents, some of them public, others less so.

**spacer** *n.* **1.** someone who works in or travels through outer space. Compare SPACEFARER, SPACE FLIER 1, SPACEMAN, SPACE PERSON 2, SPACE TRAVELER, SPACEWOMAN.

**1940** I. Asimov *Callistan Menace* in *Astonishing Stories* (Apr.) 71/2: I've read books about him. He was the greatest spacer there ever was.

**1955** W. M. Miller, Jr. *Hoofer* in J. Merril *SF: Best of Best* (1967) 9: They all knew he was a spacer because of the white goggle marks on his sun-scorched face.

**1981** C. J. Cherryh *Pride of Chanur* (1991) 105: The papers came back, plasticized and permanent with Tully's face staring back from them, species handwritten, classification general spacer, sex male.

**1987** D. Brin *Uplift War* 306: Sam Tenance was a starship pilot who stopped at Garth every five years or so, one of Megan's three spacer husbands.

**1999**: see quote in GROUNDHOG.

**2.** a SPACESHIP. Compare BOAT, CRAFT, CRUISER, SHIP, SPACE CAN, SPACE CAR, SPACECRAFT, SPACE CRUISER, SPACE FLYER, SPACE VEHICLE, SPACE VESSEL, TIN CAN, VESSEL.

**1942** [C. Corwin] *Crisis* in *SF Quarterly* (Spring) 139/1: First thing after the ultimatum he heard was that Earth had called in all spacers except those related to navigation—fueling stations, etc.

**1947** H. Hasse *Trail of Astrogar* in *Amazing Stories* (Oct.) 46/1: Curt's hopes rose, as they neared the spacer and made out the design.

**1957** P. J. Farmer *Green Odyssey* (1976) 154: I would like to know if you can pilot that spacer and if it's in operating condition.

**1978** D. R. Mason *Mission to Pactolus R* 5: A Fingalnan voice spoke into the quiet command cabin of the hurrying spacer.

**spaceship** *n.* a vehicle designed to be used to travel in outer space. Compare BOAT, CRAFT, CRUISER, SHIP, SPACE CAN, SPACE CAR, SPACECRAFT, SPACE CRUISER, SPACE FLYER, SPACER 2, SPACE VEHICLE, SPACE VESSEL, STARSHIP, TIN CAN, VESSEL.

**1894** J. J. Astor *Journey in Other Worlds* 9: What sort of space-ship do you propose to have?

**1925** *New York Times* (Nov. 22) 4/2: He is now engaged, therefore, in developing his "space-ship" out of the modern airplane.

**1938** C. S. Lewis *Out of Silent Planet* 38: All he ever remembered of his first meal in the space-ship was the tyranny of heat and light.

**1966** S. R. Delany *Babel-17* 27: Managing a spaceship crew takes a special sort of psychology.

**1970** N. Armstrong, et al. *First on Moon* 338: If you're going to run a spaceship you've got to be pretty cautious about how you use your resources.

**1999** A. Thomson *Through Alien Eyes* (2000) 71: The Tendu are suffering from [ ... ] a form of depression caused by their isolation in the artificial setting of this spaceship. The Tendu need a natural environment.

**space-sick** *adj.* afflicted with space-sickness.

**1911** H. Gernsback *Ralph 124C 41+* in *Amazing Stories Quarterly* (Winter, 1929) 52/2: Ralph grew more despondent each day, and his hope of bringing his betrothed back to life grew dimmer and dimmer as the hours rolled on. For the first time since he left the Earth he became *space-sick*.

**1947** R. A. Heinlein *It's Great to Be Back* in *Saturday Evening Post* (July 26) 71/1: Little Gloria Simmons was not space[-]sick. She thought being weightless was fun, and went bouncing off floor plate, overhead and bulkhead like a dimpled balloon.

**1961** *Chronicle-Telegram (Elryia, Oh.)* (Oct. 5) 2/1: The second Soviet spaceman, Gherman S. Titov, was space sick—akin to seasick—during a "considerable" portion of his 25-hour, 17 times around-the-earth space flight in August.

**1976** C. Holland *Floating Worlds* (1977) 92: She was space-sick and she could not eat.

**1999** A. Thomson *Through Alien Eyes* (2000) 102: A sudden wave of queasiness sent her to her seat. She must be more exhausted than she realized; she hadn't been spacesick since she was a small child.

**space-sickness** *n.* an illness or feeling of ill health brought on by the conditions of space travel, especially as caused by weightlessness.

**1911** H. Gernsback *Ralph 124C 41+* in *Amazing Stories Quarterly* (Winter, 1929) 52/2: The effect on the brain results in space-sickness, the first symptoms being violent melancholy and depression followed by a terrible and heart-rending longing for Earth.

**1926** G. C. Wallis & B. Wallis *Star Shell* in *Weird Tales* (Nov.) 605/1: It was an hour after the meal that the space-sickness seized us. Our poor internals, cut off from gravitation, must have been in a terrible muddle.

**1962** *Daily Courier (Connellsville, Pa.)* (Oct. 9) 13/4: Astronaut Walter M. Schirra, when asked if during his six-orbital flight he suffered from the nausea or space sickness experienced by Soviet cosmonaut Gherman Titov:

**1988** A. C. Clarke *2061: Odyssey Three* 76: What the Captain meant, of course, was space-sickness—but that word was, by general agreement, taboo aboard *Universe*.

**2000** W. McCarthy *Collapsium* 147 (2002): The weightlessness—despite the fax filters that had conditioned his body against space sickness—was already making him a bit queasy.

**spacesuit** *n.* a protective garment worn to maintain a safe pressure and atmosphere around the wearer, for use in outer space or on alien worlds. Hence **space-suited,** *adj.* Compare MOONSUIT, PRESSURE SUIT, SUIT, VAC SUIT, VACUUM SUIT.

**1929** *Sci. Wonder Stories* (July) 175/1: Normal communication by speech would be impossible. Of course, this is not true of enclosed, air-filled rooms [ ... ]. But it is true when one is out "in the open" (in the space suit).

**1937** E. E. Smith *Galactic Patrol* in *Astounding Stories* (Sept.) 31/1: Space-suited complete, except for helmets, and with those ready at hand, Kinnison and VanBuskirk sat in the tiny control room of their lifeboat as it drifted through interstellar space.

**1947** M. W. Wellman *Disc-Men of Jupiter* in *Startling Stories* (May) 88/1: The space-suit, designed for use on the outside of just such hulls as these, was furnished with boots that had magnetic soles, and Thiana was thankful for the firm footing they afforded her.

**1958** *Parade* in *Oakland (Cal.) Tribune* (Jan. 5) 6/1: By 1963, only five years from now, a space-suited Columbus may reach the moon.

**1962** J. Glenn, et al. *Into Orbit* 244: G-suits are not to be confused with pressure suits (or, now, spacesuits) which the Astronaut wears during space flight to maintain atmospheric pressure at high altitudes.

**1970** A. McCaffrey *Ship Who Sang* (1991) 20: Jennan broke out spacesuits to the three who would have to remain with him in the airlock.

**1993** K. S. Robinson *Red Mars* 92–93: The walkers were designed for the Martian surface, and were not pressurized like spacesuits.

**space tan** *n.* a darkening or damaging of the skin due to time spent in space.

**1942** [W. Stewart] *Collision Orbit* in *Astounding S-F* (July) 82/1: He saw the excited flush under the space tan on her cheeks.

**1945** H. Walton *Schedule* in M. Greenberg *Men against Stars* (1958) 88: Under his space tan the blood seemed to recede from Matthews' face.

**1956**: see quote in STAR VOYAGING.

**1963** L. J. Stecher, Jr. *When You Giffle…* in *Worlds of Tomorrow* (Dec.) 105/2: In spite of the space tan, I could see him blush.

**1997** W. S. Burroughs *Journal* (Jan. 11) in *Last Words* (2000) 45: L. Ron Hubbard appears in a dream, his face with a deep space tan.

**space-tanned** *adj. Obs.* having a space tan. Compare SPACE-BURNED.

**1942** C. Cartmill *Some Day We'll Find You* in *Astounding S-F* (Dec.) 41/1: Craig's space-tanned face set in lines of puzzlement.

**1950** *Galaxy SF* (Oct.) back cover/1: A tall, lean spaceman stepped out of the tail assembly, proton gun-blaster in a space-tanned hand.

**1951** [W. Stewart] *Seetee Ship* 117: But suddenly he knew he would very much regret it if he had to take this tall, space-tanned girl to the prison on Pallas IV.

**1969** R. Silverberg *Across Billion Years* 151: The captain is straight out of bad movies, a veteran-of-the-spaceways type with seamed space-tanned skin and faded blue eyes; he chews some mildly narcotic weed from a Deneb world and goes around spitting everywhere.

**space travel** *n.* journeying through outer space; the technology required for such travel. Compare SPACEFARING, SPACE FLIGHT, SPACE TRAVEL, SPACE TRAVELING.

[**1929** *Sci. Wonder Stories* (Sept.) 365: The spatial station as a basis for spatial travel.]

**1929** C. W. Harris & M. J. Breuer *Baby on Neptune* in *Amazing Stories* (Dec.) 793/2: Not having ourselves as yet conquered the problems of space-travel, we invite you to visit us on Neptune.

**1939** [E. Binder] *Impossible World* (1967) 6: Yet Earthmen were about to carry their interplanetary exploits to this wayward member of the Solar System, in the year 2050 A.D., less than a hundred years after the advent of space travel.

**1954** *Monessen (Pa.) Daily Independent* (May 6) 13/1: If 50,000,000 Americans would contribute $2 a year each year for 10 years we could have space travel quite soon.

**1956** R. A. Heinlein *letter* (Mar. 9) in R. A. Heinlein & V. Heinlein *Grumbles from Grave* (1990) 77: This is difficult to do in space-travel stories.

**1978** B. Shaw *Ship of Strangers* (1979) 28: No amount of standing on hilltops on dark nights and surveying the heavens could prepare a man for the actuality of space travel.

**1999** C. Pellegrino & G. Zebrowski *Dyson Sphere* 136: "And what was this hope?" [...] "Space travel. It's an ancient dream for them."

**space traveler, space traveller** *n.* a SPACER (sense 1). Compare SPACEFARER, SPACE FLIER 1, SPACEMAN, SPACE PERSON 2, SPACEWOMAN, STAR TRAVELER.

**1929** *Amazing Stories* (Aug.) 478: A space traveler would ultimately reach a zone of no weight or of practically none.

**1930** M. J. Breuer *Fitzgerald Contraction* in *Sci. Wonder Stories* (Jan.) 688/1: The space-travelers closed their door, having motioned us away and warned us by placing their hands across their eyes.

**1965** M. Reynolds *Beehive* in *Analog SF-Sci. Fact* (Dec.) 19/2: Because a few weeks ago, a small exploration task force [ ... ] came upon the three star systems which were the origin of our little dead space traveler.

**1976** *Listener* (July 22) 83/3: A journey of merely five light years would take about 500,000 years [...]. 15,000 generations of men and women [...] would successively replace the original crew of stellar space-travellers en route.

**1991** *New York Times* (Apr. 10) A14/1: The crew also sighted fellow space travelers, two Soviet astronauts, on the space station Mir.

**space-traveling, space-travelling** *n.* journeying through outer space. Compare SPACEFARING, SPACE FLYING, SPACE TRAVEL.

**1931** J. W. Campbell, Jr. *Islands of Space* in *Amazing Stories Quarterly* (Spring) 169/1: The strange, weightless sensation of space-traveling makes it very hard to recognize normally familiar sensations.

**1938** *Times Literary Supplement* (Oct. 1) 625/3: The space-travelling itself forces a more direct comparison with [...] "The First Men in the Moon."

**2002** W. Shatner & C. Walter *I'm Working on That* (2004) 38: Simply by doing some high-speed space traveling, we will have flung ourselves years into the future.

**space-traveling, space-travelling** *adj.* capable of space travel; that travel in space.

**1930** P. Nowlan & R. Calkins *Buck Rogers, 2430 A.D.* in *Oakland (Cal.) Tribune* (June 23) 4M: Following them in our new space-traveling rocket ship, we rescued Tallan.

**1956** T. Sturgeon *Claustrophile* in *And Now News...* (2003) 101: There was a space-traveling

species that achieved space flight in the first place because, of all species, it was most fit.

**1992** O. S. Card *Memory of Earth* (1993) 110: Of course there must be space traveling machines, or how did we get to Harmony from Earth?

**2000** A. McCaffrey & E. A. Scarborough *Acorna's World* (2001) 32: Due to the bravery and innovation Hafiz showed in the rescue of all their important space traveling people.

**space tug** *n.* a small spaceship used for short-range tasks such as maneuvering larger spaceships, construction projects in space, etc.

**1942** E. F. Russell *Describe Circle* in *Astounding SF* (Mar.) 130/2: Martiacast VXV calling *Vanguard*. Can now observe the *Starider*. You've permission to enter the sphere of Mars to make contact with vessel. Are ordering out space tugs.

**1970** *Physics Bulletin* (Apr.) 145/2: A manned moon station is foreseen, as are [ ... ] a "space shuttle" for commuting between the earth and vehicles in low earth orbit, and a "space tug" for transport to Mars in the 1980s.

**1996** K. MacLeod *Stone Canal* (2001) 294: We, here, were [ ... ] in a space construction-site whose workers were for some obscure but accepted reason confined to individual space-tugs.

**2002** D. M. Harland & J. E. Catchpole *Creating International Space Station* 372: The Space Tug was conceived in the mid-1980s as an upper stage intended to collect satellites from a Shuttle in low orbit and deliver them to their operational orbits.

**space vehicle** *n.* a SPACESHIP. Compare BOAT, CRAFT, CRUISER, SHIP, SPACE CAN, SPACE CAR, SPACECRAFT, SPACE CRUISER, SPACE FLYER, SPACER 2, SPACE VESSEL, TIN CAN, VESSEL.

**1930** M. J. Breuer *Fitzgerald Contraction* in *Sci. Wonder Stories* (Jan.) 681/2: Or [ ... ] it might be a space vehicle from a distant planet.

**1946** *New York Times* (July 29) 1/2: They are to serve as pioneers for the long-range guided missiles and "space" vehicles.

**1967** G. Coon *Errand of Mercy ("Star Trek" script)* (Jan. 23) 12: Eight space vehicles are assuming orbit around our planet.

**ca1989** R. Grant & D. Naylor *Backwards* in *Son of Soup* (1996) 89: In your own time, would you like to start the space vehicle, proceed through the cargo bay doors, and off into outer space.

**2005** G. Clément *Fundamentals of Space Medicine* 15: A reusable space vehicle would be developed that would take humans into Earth orbit and return them.

**space vessel** *n.* a SPACESHIP. Compare BOAT, CRAFT, CRUISER, SHIP, SPACE CAN, SPACE CAR, SPACECRAFT, SPACE CRUISER, SPACE FLYER, SPACER 2, SPACE VEHICLE, TIN CAN, VESSEL.

**1929** C. W. Harris & M. J. Breuer *Baby on Neptune* in *Amazing Stories* (Dec.) 798/2: Corrigan moved the space-vessel close to the scene of the tragedy, gradually, with the aid of the infra-red screen.

**1951** A. C. Clarke *Space Travel in Fact & Fiction* in *Greetings, Carbon-Based Bipeds!* (1999) 90: Ignoring the impossibility of its projection, Verne's projectile must be considered the first really scientifically conceived space vessel.

**1960** *Chronicle-Telegram (Elyria, Oh.)* (Jan. 26) 9/6: It will take such a space vessel about two days to reach the moon's velocity.

**1987** J. White *Code Blue—Emergency* in *General Practice* (2003) 27: Useful work can be done in the very restricted conditions found inside a badly damaged space vessel.

**2004** A. McCaffrey & E. A. Scarborough *Acorna's Triumph* 129: They'd picked the Ancestors up in a space vessel and brought them to Vhilinyar.

**spaceward** *adj.* **1.** nearer to outer space.

**1941** C. D. Simak *Masquerade* in *Astounding S-F* (Mar.) 61/2: Let one of those gadgets fail—let one of those spaceward beams sway as much as a fraction of a degree—

**1970** P. Anderson *Tau Zero* (1973) 23: Hands eagerly turned cranks on the spaceward side of the boat, sliding back the plates that covered the glasyl viewports.

**1998** D. Duane *Starrise at Corrivale* 38: They came in real low over Eraklion's spaceward side.

**2.** into or toward outer space.

**1942** [W. Stewart] *Minus Sign* in *Astounding S-F* (Nov.) 73/2: He set up the calculator to find [...] the observed direction and velocity of the rock's inexplicable spaceward flight, taking into account the diminishing gravitational drag of the Sun and the planets, from which it was so swiftly escaping.

**1956** *Lima (Oh.) News* (Oct. 5) 15/1: It will be used as a staging area for preliminary test of the rocket units designed to hurl man's first earth satellite spaceward sometime before January 1957.

**1962** J. G. Ballard *Thirteen to Centaurus* in *Amazing Stories* (Apr.) 40/1: In fifteen years a lot could happen, there might be another spaceward swing of public opinion.

**1970** R. Silverberg *Tower of Glass* in *Galaxy Mag.* (Apr.) 125/2: In one great dynamic sweep the spaceward drive had carried human explorers from Luna to Pluto, to the edge of the solar system and beyond.

**spaceward, spacewards** *adv.* toward, to, or into space.

**1939** C. D. Simak *Cosmic Engineers* in *Astounding S-F* (Mar.) 82/1: He adjusted the screen again and in it they watched the defending ships of the Engineers shooting spaceward, manoeuvered into far-flung battle lines—like little dancing motes against the black of space.

**1949** [R. Lafayette] *Plague* in *Astounding SF* (Apr.) 8/1: At 11:67 [sic] the *Star of Space* lifted from her cradle, hovered and then slowly rose spacewards, doomed.

**1956** J. Sohl *Mars Monopoly* 33: So it was that the eyes of engineers turned spaceward while their brothers frantically sought to wrest further secrets from the atom in laboratories.

**1972** A. D. Foster *Tar-Aiym Krang* 100: A muted growl went audible behind him and he turned to see the bulky shape of a cargo shuttle leap spaceward, trailing its familiar tail of cream and crimson.

**1993** P. Anderson *Harvest of Stars* (1994) 256: Spaceward, stars beswarmed blackness and the Milky Way clove it with ice.

**space warp** *n.* a bend or curvature of space, especially one that facilitates instantaneous or faster-than-light travel from one point to another. Also *fig.* Hence **space-warping,** *adj.* Compare WARP.

**1935** N. Schachner *Son of Redmask* in *Astounding Stories* (Aug.) 101/1: For centuries they had endured [...] wrapped in special defenses which they fondly believed impregnable to the mightiest weapons that human science could bring to bear. Of such were the Space-Warp that flowed in a solid cessation of light around Yorrick [...] and the shimmering Web-Curtain behind which Chico hazed and danced like a mirage.

**1936** J. Williamson *Cometeers* in *Astounding Stories* (May) 22/2: Every atom of ship load and crew was deflected infinitesimally from the space-time continuum of four dimensions, and thus freed of the ordinary limitations of acceleration and velocity, was driven around space, rather than through it, by a direct reaction against the space warp itself.

**1939** [E. Binder] *Impossible World* in *Startling Stories* (Mar.) 36/2: Electricity is fed through the coil matrix and transformed thereby into space-warping energy.

**1941** T. Sturgeon *Artnan Process* in *Astounding S-F* (June) 66/2: As soon as he was out of the planet's effective space warp, he slipped into hyperspace and traveled toward Procyon and its dark companion at many times the speed of light.

**1947** *Journal of British Interplanetary Society* (Vol. VI) 138: Bodies in the region of this artificial "space-warp" therefore acquire a negative weight—what could be simpler?

**1963**: see quote in TIME-HOPPER.

**1975** *News (Port Arthur, Tex.)* (Apr. 24) 6/2: Maybe the ships and planes enter some kind of time or space warp and end up in another dimension.

**1988** N. Stephenson *Zodiac* 3: There was at least an acre back here, tucked away in kind of a space warp caused by Brighton's irrational street pattern.

**spaceways** *pl. n.* routes between worlds through outer space. Compare SPACE LANE, STARLANES, STARWAYS.

**1933** C. L. Moore *Shambleau* in *Weird Tales* (Nov.) 539/2: He heard the gossip of the space-ways, news from a dozen planets of a thousand different events.

**1946** [M. Leinster] *Disciplinary Circuit* in *Thrilling Wonder Stories* (Winter) 53/1: It was a hundred years before the last of the runaway derelicts blundered to destruction or was picked up by other spaceships which then still roved the space-ways.

**1959** S. Palmer *Derelict* in *Fantastic Universe* (Mar.) 83/2: And so it was that the vast Centaurian ship, armed to the teeth with super-weapons that could have brought our world to its knees in a week or less, turned tail and blasted hell-bent back to the safer spaceways of its own system.

**2002** M. J. Harrison *Light* (2004) 220: Seria Mau Genlicher, pilot of the spaceways, dreamed she was ten years old again.

**spacewoman** *n.* a (usually human) female who works in or travels through outer space. Compare SPACEFARER, SPACE FLIER 1, SPACEMAN, SPACE PERSON 2, SPACE TRAVELER.

**1951** [L. del Rey] *Deadliest Female* in *Worlds Beyond* (Feb.) 29: He looked at her insignia, knowing Spacewomen were never promoted higher than lieutenants—his own rank—since they were automatically retired at thirty-five.

**1959** A. B. Chandler *To Run Rim* in *Astounding SF* (Jan.) 22/1: Almost all of them raised their mugs to the spaceman and space-woman in salutation.

**1963** *Valley Independent (Monessen, Pa.)* (May 22) 35/6: Two visiting Soviet technicians said Tuesday Russia hopes soon to put the first spacewoman into orbit.

**1970** A. McCaffrey *Ship Who Sang* (1991) 62: Shoulder-length hair was the common fashion among spacewomen.

**1993** *Chronicle-Telegram (Elyria, Oh.)* (Oct. 29) A8/1: Biochemist Shannon Lucid became the world's most-traveled spacewoman aboard space shuttle Columbia.

**spaceworthiness** *n.* the state or condition of being spaceworthy.

**1934** E. E. Smith *Skylark of Valeron* in *Astounding Stories* (Aug.) 23/1: True, the focal area of the energy was an almost invisibly violet glare of incandescence, [ ... ] but that awful force had had practically no effect upon the spaceworthiness of the stanch little vessel.

**1952** I. Asimov *Space* in *Space SF* (May) 78/2: The Pilot remained at his post to the actual landing, his only thought that of breaking the force of the crash, of maintaining the spaceworthiness of the vessel.

**1960** *New Statesman* (Jan. 30) 146/2: Apparently no other proofs were needed to demonstrate the efficacy of their measures to ensure the space-worthiness of the cosmic vehicle.

**1988** A. C. Clarke *2061: Odyssey Three* 199: It seemed the right thing to do—even though, with any luck, *Galaxy*'s spaceworthiness would soon be of no further concern to anyone.

**spaceworthy** *n.* fit to travel safely in outer space.

**1931** E. E. Smith *Spacehounds of IPC* in *Amazing Stories* (Aug.) 411/1: Slowly but steadily, under Stevens' terrific welding projector, the stubborn steel flowed together, once more to become a seamless, space-worthy structure.

**1958** *Parade* in *Oakland (Cal.) Tribune* (Jan. 5) 6/2: The Russian suit is bulkier than ours, with pleated arms and legs. The helmet is a metal dome with a glass eye-slit. The ensemble is less efficient than ours—but, overall, no less spaceworthy.

**1959** [J. Wyndham] & [L. Parkes] *Outward Urge* 156: She reclaimed the damaged Satellites, and made three of them spaceworthy again.

**1991** M. Weiss *King's Test* 28: Fly off all planes, including those that are damaged if they're at all spaceworthy.

**2002** A. Reynolds *Redemption Ark* (2004) 24: Your ship is outwardly unremarkable, but betrays all the signs of being mechanically sound and spaceworthy.

**space yacht** *n.* a luxurious private spaceship.

**1940** A. E. van Vogt *Vault of Beast* in *Astounding S-F* (Aug.) 60/1: He has commanded his own space yacht; he knows more about the

mathematical end of the work than our whole staff put together; and that is no reflection on our staff.

**1956** R. A. Heinlein *Double Star* (1957) 81: It was just the amount of audience I wanted, enough to tie it down solid that "Mr. Bonforte" had arrived by official car and had left for his space yacht.

**1973** A. D. Foster *Bloodhype* 109: I'm not picky, myself. I wish only a very small space yacht—KK drive equipped, of course—with a platinum head.

**1985** B. Searles *Isaac Asimov's SF Mag.* (Jan.) 183/1: All this takes place in a slightly mad galaxy of space yachts and matter transmission.

**spaceyard** *n.* a place where spaceships are built or repaired.

**1948** [M. Leinster] *Space-Can* in *Thrilling Wonder Stories* (June) 118/1: Such as the story that when the *Winship* was based on Luna, every time she came back to port there were seven girl-dogs and a Venusian vroom-cat waiting at the space[-]yard gate when Rickey sauntered out on his first liberty.

**1958** R. Silverberg *Eve & Twenty-Three Adams* in *Venture SF Mag.* (Mar.) 39/2: The *Donnybrook* and its crew of twenty-three had been in virtual dry-dock for nearly two years: the ship resting on its haunches in the Venusport spaceyards.

**1966** S. R. Delany *Babel-17* 88: He could be a service mechanic on any one of a hundred spaceyards.

**1969** J. Vance *Dirdir* in *Planet of Adventure* (1991) 353: At the opposite end of the spaceyard three ships in commission rested on large black circles.

**2002** J. C. Wright *Golden Age* (2003) 113: Unlike the space yard he had just left, this segment was spun for gravity.

**spec fic** *abbr.* SPECULATIVE FICTION.

**1980** I. Asimov *Speculative Fiction* in *Asimov on SF* (1981) 301: After a few attempts to use it in ordinary conversation, it will be abbreviated to "spec-fic," which sounds like two spits.

**1989** L. Niven *Return of William Proxmire* in *N-Space* (1991) 528: The *New Yorker* ran spec-fic short stories and critical reviews of novels.

**1993** *Locus* (June) 25/3: Okay, fans of the fantastic, here's a pop culture chance to find out just which of you are genuinely liberated sci-fi guys and spec-fic chix.

**2003** M. J. Harrison *No Escape* in *Locus* (Dec.) 69/3: As a result there's already a default description—Speculative Fiction (often rendered "Spec Fic," a very ugly usage indeed).

**2006** *ICFA 27 "Report": Conference Underbelly* (IAFA-L Mailing List) (Mar. 23): Gary K. Wolfe, who shows no signs of aging, is in danger of becoming spec fics's Dick Clark.

**speculative fiction** *n.* **1.** SCIENCE FICTION 1. Compare FANTASCIENCE, PSEUDO-SCIENCE, SCIENCE FANTASY 2, SCIENTIFIC FANTASY, SCIENTIFIC FICTION, SCIENTIFICTION, SPECULATIVE FICTION 1. [Use of "speculative fiction" in this sense may be regarded as pretentious by some science fiction fans.]

**1889** *Lippincott's Monthly Mag.* (Oct.) 597: Edward Bellamy, in "Looking Backward," and George Parsons Lathrop, in a short story, "The New Poverty," have followed the example of Anthony Trollope and Bulwer in speculative fiction put in the future tense.

**1947** R. A. Heinlein *On Writing of Speculative Fiction* in L. A. Eshbach *Of Worlds Beyond* 11: There are at least two principal ways to write speculative fiction—write about people, or write about gadgets.

[**1953** L. S. de Camp *Imaginative Fiction & Creative Imagination* in R. Bretnor *Modern SF* 129: Certainly one danger threatening science fiction is that the progress of science itself answers so many questions raised by science fiction, thereby removing one story idea after another from the domain of the speculative fictioneer.]

**1969** S. R. Delany *About Five Thousand One Hundred & Seventy Five Words* in *Extrapolation* (May) 64: Virtually all the classics of speculative fiction are mystical. In Isaac Asimov's *Foundation* trilogy, one man [...] achieves nothing less than the redemption of mankind.

**1985** B. Hambly *Ishmael* xv: The fathers of speculative fiction. Wells dealt in invasion of the Earth.

**1991** *Locus* (Nov.) 5/3: *Omni* has the opportunity to introduce to a large number of readers the delights and fascination of rigorous speculative fiction and non-fiction.

**2001** B. Stableford *Biotechnology & Utopia* in B. Goodwin *Philosophy of Utopia* 189: Biotechnology played little part in speculative fiction prior to the 1920s.

**2.** IMAGINATIVE FICTION. Compare FANTASY 1, SCIENCE FICTION 3, SCIENTIFANTASY, STFANTASY.

**1952** J. Merril *Preface* in *Beyond Human Ken* xii: The stories included in this collection were written and published over a period of some fifteen years; I think they are the forerunners of the speculative fiction of tomorrow.

**1985** A. Budrys *Benchmarks* xxiv: We had not, during the span of these writings, fully developed the current usage of the term *SF* to mean *speculative fiction,* and we had not yet worked out the clarifying proposition that science fiction and fantasy were equal branches of it.

**2002** K. Cramer *New York Rev. of SF* (Apr.) 23/1: Some critics are intensely interested in how individual works relate to genre, and some others believe that the "field" is all just speculative fiction and that finer definitions don't matter.

**3.** literature that uses tropes or themes of science fiction, but which is not considered to be "science fiction" for one reason or another, often to avoid a perceived stigma associated with the term "science fiction," or because a work is perceived to lack scientific rigor.

**1978** *New York Times* (Mar. 30) C22/3: A 10-part series based on what Mr. Kotlowitz called "speculative fiction," stories that go beyond sci-fi and deal with "ethical and moral demands" made in new worlds to come.

**1979** D. Suvin *Metamorphoses of SF* 67: The so-called speculative fiction (for example, Ballard's) clearly began as and has mostly remained an ideological inversion of "hard" SF.

**2001** *SF Chronicle* (July) 32/1: As to whether or not it's science-fiction, that's one of the questions it asks the audience to answer. Speculative fiction it most certainly is.

**2003** *Dreamwatch* (Aug.) 73/1: Margaret Atwood finds the label of "science fiction" distasteful, and would prefer her work in this area to be known as "speculative fiction."

**2006** M. Cheney *Locus Online (Internet)* (Jan. 23): Though I think Kazuo Ishiguro's *Never Let Me Go* (Knopf) is not so much a novel "about" cloning as it is a novel that utilizes a vague idea of cloning to explore themes of identity, it is nonetheless a novel of speculative fiction, if not a novel of science fiction.

**spinward** *adv.* in or toward the direction that something (a space station, galaxy, etc.) is rotating. Also as *adj.* Compare ANTISPINWARD.

**1970** L. Niven *Ringworld* 310: He knows a few simple skills, and he carries them around the Ringworld as he travels to spinward.

**1985** G. Bear *Eon* (1986) 360: The spinward trip through the forest was pure pleasure for Hoffman.

**1989** S. Perry *97th Step* 48: I just happen to know a man what's looking for a fast exit to points spinward.

**1977** J. Varley *Ophiuchi Hotline* (2003) 23: Further around the curve of the Ring, about sixty degrees to spinward, a dark red arrow appeared.

**1999** A. Thomson *Through Alien Eyes* (2000) 46: We bought another ten hectares just spinward of Toivo's place.

**2003** L. E. Modesitt, Jr. *Ethos Effect* (2004) 475: It was a convenient stop before the *Joyau* headed more spinward along the Arm.

**spy ray** *n.* a device which, by means of a beam of energy, allows the operator to see, hear, or read minds at a distance or through a barrier. Also **spy beam.**

**1934** E. E. Smith *Triplanetary* in *Amazing Stories* (Jan.) 29/2: I'll see if I can locate any of the pirates chasing up. If I do, it'll be by accident; this little spy-ray isn't good for much except close work.

**1941** T. Sturgeon *Artnan Process* in *Astounding S-F* (June) 64/1: We have taken relays on the spy ray; one of us has been watching the ship constantly.

**1944** M. Jameson *Leech* in *Astounding SF* (Jan.) 53/1: We should have tackled telepathics.

What better spy ray would you want than the ability to look into another man's mind?

**1958** R. Silverberg *Stepsons of Terra* 29: I want to know who planted that spy ray in my room, and why I should be warned against dealing with Myreck.

**1980** D. Broderick *Dreaming Dragons* 76: Pink noise. It neutralises bugs, and scrambles maser detection spy-beams bounced off the vehicle.

**1999** P. Di Filippo *Plumage from Pegasus* in *Mag. of Fantasy & SF* (Oct.–Nov.) 196/2: Every word the Pope uttered was picked up by Eddorian spy rays from light-years away.

**Standard** *n.* a language spoken on multiple worlds or by multiple species.

**1965** M. Z. Bradley *Star of Danger* (1985) 4: You could get along all right in Standard, of course—everyone around the Spaceport and the Trade City speaks it.

**1996** J. D. Vinge *Dreamfall* (2004) 153: She spoke Standard, with no real accent.

**2000** M. Thomas *Broken Time* 255: "You're not going to translate for me?" Siggy was frightened again. "They speak Standard," he said.

**2001** D. Weber & J. Ringo *March Upcountry* (2002) 263: As long as they used Standard, no one was going to be able to know what they were talking about.

**starbase** *n.* an outpost in space or on a planet remote from the homeworld, used to facilitate military, governmental, or commercial activities.

**1944** R. M. Williams *Star Base X* in *Amazing Stories* (Sept.) 32/1: Star Base X! The thought thundered in Dawson's mind. Just as Base X, in Labrador, served the needs of the plane communication between the United States and England, this Ahrned base aided them in their communication between the stars.

**1968** S. E. Whitfield in S. E. Whitfield & G. Roddenberry *Making of "Star Trek"* 204: Immediate higher headquarters is Star Base Command. There are seventeen star bases scattered across the small known portion of the galaxy.

**1989** J. C. Faust *Desperate Measures* 64: Well, G. T. C. claims law states that when there are no survivors on a self-contained vessel, all salvaged goods become the property of the nearest planet or starbase.

**1999** J. L. Chalker *Sea Is Full of Stars* 58: The Ghomas likely won't detect you, but if you use the cryogenic settings, you'll reach a Junction or Starbase or a known hospitable Realm world in due time.

**star-cruiser** *n.* a large starship.

**1964** E. Hamilton *Kingdoms of Stars* in *Amazing Stories* (Sept.) 18/2: The royal star-cruiser with the White Sun of Fomalhaut glittering on her bows lifted from the starport, beyond which lay the greatest city of latterday Earth.

**1976** G. Lucas *Adventures of Luke Starkiller* (Mar. 15) 23: Well, my little friend, you've got something jammed in here real good…were you on a star-cruiser or a…

**1987** T. Pratchett *Equal Rites* (1990) 7: Then it comes into view overhead, bigger than the biggest, most unpleasantly-armed starcruiser in the imagination of a three-ring film-maker.

**1995** D. Gerrold *Middle of Nowhere* (2003) 22: Gatineau craned forward eagerly, but abruptly the boat rotated along its own axis, shifting his view of the starcruiser upward and over, completely out of his sight.

**star drive** *n.* a propulsion device which permits a spaceship to travel faster than the speed of light.

**1948** P. Anderson *Genius* in *Astounding SF* (Dec.) 25/1: They'll know the principles of the star drive in a few more generations, and invent a faster-than-light engine almost at once!

**1952** C. Oliver *Blood's Rover* in *Astounding SF* (May) 33/1: Man's horizons exploded to the rims of the universe with the perfection of the star drive—he was no longer living *on* a world but *in* an inhabited universe.

**1969** R. C. Meredith *We All Died at Breakaway Station* in *Amazing Stories* (Jan.) 11/1: The voice of the Organic Computer [ … ] began counting down the seconds until star drive was cut, until the three starships ceased their motionless motion, ceased micro-jumping through universes, returned to normal and real space-time.

**1976** B. Coulson *Reminder* in C. R. McDonough *NESFA Hymnal 1* 2: The Star-Drive was discovered on a planet of Centaurus, By a race which built its cities while the Earth was flaming gas.

**1983** B. Shaw *Orbitsville Departure* (1990) 199: Then came the realisation that he was dealing in physical impossibilities—no star drive yet devised could produce the kind of acceleration which would be compatible with what he was seeing.

**2002** M. J. Harrison *Light* 135 (2004): Every race they met on their way through the Core had a star drive based on a different theory.

**starfarer** *n.* someone who travels between the stars. Compare SPACEFARER, STARMAN 2, STAR TRAVELER.

**1970** A. Norton *Dread Companion* (1984) 140: The skin of his hands and face was very dark, the space tan of a starfarer, but on the less exposed parts of his body it was ivory-white.

**1987** D. Brin *Uplift War* 271: Throughout the Five Galaxies the Thennanin were known as tough fighters and doughty starfarers.

**1996** M. Scott *Night Sky Mine* (1997) 39: You didn't just walk out on a mine platform, especially not that far out on the fringes of a system—hell, the first rule any starfarer learned was to stay with the ship as long as possible.

**1997** D. Weber & S. White *In Death Ground* (2000) 29: Starless warp nexi were as depressing for starfarers as they were frustrating for theorists.

**2000** P. Anderson *Genesis* 43: It transmitted its discoveries and experiences back to the central intelligence and to any humans who cared. Many did, often because the starfarer was not altogether alien.

**starfaring** *n.* STAR VOYAGING. Compare STAR FLIGHT, STAR TRAVEL.

**1973** J. Vance *Trullion: Alastor 2262* 31: If I'm not mistaken it's young Glinnes Hulden, back from starfaring!

**1986** A. C. Clarke *Songs of Distant Earth* 11: "There are no aliens," she said firmly. "At least none intelligent enough to go starfaring."

**1998** P. Anderson *Starfarers* (1999) 162: I didna believe a civilization that went starfaring could die just overnight.

**starfaring** *adj.* that travels, or is able to travel, between stars. Compare SPACEFARING.

**1960** P. Anderson *High Crusade* (1982) 78: Their skirmishes with rival starfaring nations were mostly aerial.

**1986** M. Resnick *Santiago* 119: Virtue stopped to admire a crystal globe of Bokar from the incredibly ancient days when the Bokarites were a seafaring race rather than a planet of starfaring merchants.

**1991** E. Arnason *Woman of Iron People, Part 2* (1992) xiii: We think it's unlikely that you will meet a star-faring species that is aggressive.

**1993** P. J. Thomas *Quantum* (Spring–Summer) 72/3: Vinge posits a wide range of starfaring races, living in harmony on a large number of planets, and united by a loose commercial network.

**2000** P. F. Hamilton *Confederation Handbook* (2002) 257: This system acts as a meeting point for all the sentient starfaring species in their galaxy (and presumably others), where knowledge and ideas can be exchanged.

**starfleet** *n.* an organized group of starships, especially one under military control. Compare SPACE FLEET.

**1968** D. C. Fontana *Enterprise Incident* ("Star Trek" script) (June 13) I-7: Lt. Uhura, code a message to Star Fleet command.

**1972** U. K. Le Guin *Word for World Is Forest* in H. Ellison *Again Dangerous Visions* 64: A Starfleet ship's commander bootlicking two humanoids.

**1982** J. Yolen *Commander Toad & Planet of Grapes* 14: She wipes her nose with a regulation starfleet nose-kerchief and prepares to leap from the skimmer.

**1996** L. E. Modesitt, Jr. *Adiamante* 63: Control had once been the central operations focus for the starfleets of the Rebuilt Hegemony, and had hummed with activity.

**1997** P. L. Pereira *Eagles of New Dawn* 205: The intergalactic starfleet comprises a body of integrated Souls of multisystem origin.

**star flight** *n.* STAR TRAVEL. Compare STARFARING, STAR VOYAGING.

**1944** R. M. Williams *Star Base X* in *Amazing Stories* (Sept.) 32/1: This Ahrned base aided them in their communication between the stars. That was why it was here, hidden away in this northland. It was a base facilitating star flight.

**1951** L. Brackett *Starmen of Llyrdis* in *Startling Stories* (Mar.) 19/1: Star-flight? An alien race coming and going on Earth—and all this in secret, no one knows of it?

**1977** I. Watson *Alien Embassy* 2 (1978): Perhaps to find candidates for starflight, if we're lucky.

**1988** T. Maddox *Wars of Coin's Two Halves* in L. McCaffery *Storming Reality Studio* (1991) 328: It contains the survivors of a group that was nearly annihilated by the Regals for discovering the Investors' technique of star[-]flight.

**2003** C. Asaro *Skyfall* 33: Over the next millennia, the bewildered humans had developed star flight and gone in search of their lost home.

**stargate** *n.* a device that transports something passing through it to another point in the universe (usually another stargate) in a way that bypasses the intervening space. Compare GATE, GATEWAY, JUMP GATE. [1958 quote refers to a dimensional portal.]

[**1958** A. Norton (title): Star Gate]

**1968** A. C. Clarke *2001: Space Odyssey* 222: The Star Gate opened. The Star Gate closed. In a moment of time, too short to be measured, Space turned and twisted upon itself.

**1980** M. Edwards & R. Holdstock *Tour of Universe* 69: Stargates are distortions in space; they are also distortions in time, a fact that is often overlooked.

**ca1992** R. Grant & D. Naylor *Holoship* in *Son of Soup* (1996) 39: Ships of no mass or volume, able to travel as superlight particles—tachyons—through wormholes and stargates.

**1992** R. M. Meluch *Queen's Squadron* 17: Aithar's sun commanded a stargate by which allies of Telegonia, especially Earth, had access to the Empire's homeworld of Eta Cassiopeia A IV.

**starlanes** *pl. n.* STARWAYS. Compare SPACE LANE, SPACEWAYS.

**1949** *Startling Stories* (Sept.) 144/2: You're right about LaFayette. He is already out of planets and has taken to the starlanes as you foresaw.

**1953** G. O. Smith *Troubled Star* in *Startling Stories* (Feb.) 23/2: The three-day variables are used for course markers; [...] the still-longer beacons are used to denote places where various well-travelled starlanes meet, cross or merge.

**1964** [C. Smith] *Planet Buyer* 113: Suggest to all the really rum worlds we know that a good impersonator could put his hands on the McBan money. [...] The starlanes will be full of Rod McBans, complete with phony Norstrilian accents, for the next couple hundred years.

**1984** M. Swanwick *Blind Minotaur* in *Gravity's Angels* (1991) 52: The Wars were less than a year away, but the Lords had no way of knowing that—the cabarets were full, and the starlanes swollen with the fruits of a thousand remarkable harvests.

**1999** D. Feintuch *Patriarch's Hope* (2000) 66: For two hundred years courageous sailors had sailed the starlanes, not to threaten our colonies, but to nurture them.

**starliner** *n.* a large, often luxuriously-appointed, starship used to transport passengers. Compare SPACELINER.

**1965** E. Hamilton *Shores of Infinity* in *Amazing Stories* (Apr.) 16/2: Korkhann sat by the open window looking out at [...] the brilliant lights of Throon City and the distant lights of great star-liners coming down across the star-decked sky.

**1971** R. Silverberg *Something Wild Is Loose* in *World of Thousand Colors* (1984) 6: As always, the hospital was full—people were always coming in sick off starliners.

**1985** M. W. Bonanno *Dwellers in Crucible* 126: Yet she had wept as Gamma Erigena spun out of sight of her port on the starliner going back to Earth.

**starman** *n.* **1.** an ALIEN. Compare SPACE PERSON 1, STAR-PERSON.

**1932** R. Gallun (title) *Wonder Stories Quarterly* (Winter) 222: The Revolt of the Star Men.

**1960** P. Anderson *Longest Voyage* in S. Schmidt *Fifty Years of Best SF from Analog*

(1980) 277: Did you hear what the starman said?

**1972** [D. Bowie] *Starman* in *Best of David Bowie 1969/1974* (1999) 3: There's a starman waiting in the sky He'd like to come and meet us But he thinks he'd blow our minds.

**2.** someone, espeially a male, who travels between the stars or who works on a starship. Compare SPACEMAN, STARFARER, STAR TRAVELER.

**1950** M. Lesser *All Heroes Are Hated!* in *Amazing Stories* (Nov.) 11/1: Kenton often thought of this in self pity, but he had never heard anyone but a starman say it before. Yet this little old man could not be one of them; he was not branded with the black *S.*

**1951** L. Brackett *Starmen of Llyrdis* in *Startling Stories* (Mar.) 37/2: The officers treated him with the affable contempt of the veteran for the amateur, liked him and were patient with his feverish insistence on learning to be a starman.

**1953** N. Arkawy & S. Henig *Operation Switch* in *S-F +* (Dec.) 31/1: He threw his arm over the starman's shoulder and, lifting the bottle to his lips, he took a drink.

**star-person** *n.* an ALIEN. Usually *pl.* Compare SPACE PERSON, STARMAN 1.

**1932** R. Gallun *Revolt of Star Men* in *Wonder Stories Quarterly* (Winter) 240/1: It was the space nausea which had made early interplanetary travel such a nightmare. The Star People, born where gravity is almost unknown, were of course not affected in the least.

**1957** C. M. Kornbluth *Slave* in *Mile beyond Moon* (1958) 107: Before he died he had told Barker in rambling, formless conversations that he had it figured out; the star-people simply knew how to amplify psychokinetic energy.

**1977** I. Watson *Alien Embassy* 25 (1978): And truly we had given up nothing, but rather gained a sane and healthy world; and friendship with star peoples.

**1983** R. Silverberg *Amanda & Alien* in *Collected Stories of Robert Silverberg (Vol. 1: Pluto in Morning Light)* (1993) 132: Now there was the alien, though. A dozen of these star-people had come to Earth last year.

**starport** *n.* a place where starships can take off and land. Compare SPACEPORT, SPACEFIELD.

**1950** E. Hamilton *City at World's End* in *Startling Stories* (July) 60/1: She and Piers Eglin and Gorr Holl were with him in the official car—a sleek machine, very swift and silent, that carried them from the monster starport to the city itself.

**1968** S. R. Delany *Nova* (2002) 64: Cargo shuttles left from here for the big star-port on Triton, Neptune's largest moon.

**1984** M. Swanwick *Blind Minotaur* in *Gravity's Angels* (1991) 49: He smelled [ … ] exhaust fumes from the great shuttles bellowing skyward from the Starport.

**1991** J. D. Vinge *Summer Queen* (2003) 10: Ships at the starport with titanium hulls, if their locks were completely sealed, might even get off the ground.

**2003** C. Asaro *Skyfall* 14: I need a flight out of this starport. As soon as possible. Now, in fact.

**starship** *n.* a vehicle that is capable of traveling to other stars. Compare SPACESHIP.

**1934** *Astounding Stories* (Dec.) 9: To start the year we offer you *Star Ship Invincible*, by Frank K. Kelly.

**1946** E. Hamilton *Forgotton World* in *Thrilling Wonder Stories* (Winter) 14/1: And the old "Larkoom," a second-rate star-ship that couldn't make more than eight light-speeds, was plodding determinedly and monotonously on into it.

**1966** B. Sobelman *Return of Archons ("Star Trek" script)* (Dec. 1) 17: Our mission is to find evidence of the missing Star Ship Archon.

**1979** M. Z. Bradley *Bloody Sun* 15: For all you knew, you might have been born on one of the Big Ships; the ships of Terra; the starships that made the long runs between stars doing the business of the Empire.

**1980** *Daily Telegraph (London)* (Jan. 14) 8/1: Could star ships ever be propelled by the violent mutual annihilation of matter and anti-matter?

**1987** D. Brin *Uplift War* 306: Sam Tenance was a starship pilot who stopped at Garth every five years or so, one of Megan's three spacer husbands.

**1996** L. Shepard *Vermillion* (Oct.) 20: Almost everyone was familiar with the feeling of soul-deep instability that occurred when a starship exited normal space.

**star travel** *n.* journeying between stars or the technology necessary to make such a journey, especially by means of a faster-than-light starship. Compare STARFARING, STAR FLIGHT, STAR VOYAGING.

**1946** E. Hamilton *Forgotten World* in *Thrilling Wonder Stories* (Winter) 16/2: We're a star-traveling race now. But the mind can take only so much of the strain of star-travel.

**1965** M. Z. Bradley *Star of Danger* (1985) 24: Once the Terran Empire comes in to show people what a star-travel civilization *can* be like, people will want progress.

**1969** R. Silverberg *Across Billion Years* 201: Do you have the star travel? The way of going faster than light?

**1977** J. Varley *Ophiuchi Hotline* (2003) 92: Everybody says star travel is impossible, or at least it would take so long it wouldn't be worthwhile.

**1992** C. Sheffield *Cold as Ice* (1993) 162: They say, humans have managed very well without star travel. Why do we need it, they say, when we have problems still to solve right here on Ganymede?

**2000** C. Asaro *Ascendant Sun* (2001) 20: Earth finally developed star travel in her twenty-second century—and had one powerhouse of a shock when she reached the stars.

**star traveler, star traveller** *n.* a STAR-FARER. Compare SPACE TRAVELER, STARMAN 2.

**1957** [H. Clement] *Planetfall* in R. Hoskins *Strange Tomorrows* (1972) 314: The star-traveler already knew, of course, that he was in a valley, partway up one of the sides. The hills bounding it were not particularly high, especially by the standards of this planet. In fact, the Conservationist had a pretty accurate idea of the dimensions of the Himalayas.

**1977** I. Watson *Alien Embassy* 35 (1978): Ask anybody how Bardo made its choice of star travellers, and you would surely get the answer that every child on Earth had a chance.

**1987** M. Bishop *Philip K. Dick Is Dead, Alas* (1994) 334: Similarly, star travelers can better cross vast distances by forsaking the physical plane of the universe than by skating its surface.
**1992** V. Vinge *Fire upon Deep* (1993) 70: Pham Nuwen had already been through two transforming experiences, from pre-tech to star-traveler, and star-traveler to Beyonder.
**2000** J. A. Carver *Eternity's End* (2001) 265: As she passed by the Great Barrier Nebula, the sight caused even the most jaded of star travelers to draw a sharp breath.

**star voyaging** *n.* traveling between stars, especially by means of a faster-than-light starship. Compare STARFARING, STAR FLIGHT, STAR TRAVEL.
**1951** L. Brackett *Starmen of Llyrdis* in *Startling Stories* (Mar.) 28/1: You're mad over this star-voyaging, Trehearne.
**1956** A. Norton *Plague Ship* in *Solar Queen* (2003) 264: Hard muscles moved under his skin, pale where space tan had not burned in the years of his star voyaging.
**2003** J. C. Wright *Golden Transcendence* 363: Eventually, you will return from star voyaging, or human civilization, in ships yet unbuilt, of designs yet undreamed, will overtake you.

**star wars** *n.* [after the movie *Star Wars*] nickname for the Strategic Defense Initiative, a satellite-based defensive weapons system intended to detect and eliminate enemy missiles or aircraft. Often *cap.*
[ **1982** *Space World* (Aug.–Sept.) 10/1: The years from now to the end of the century will be critical in the real "star war" to determine who will exercise control of earth through dominance of space. ]
**1983** *Time* (Apr. 4) 19/2: The first question is one of commitment: whether Ronald Reagan understands what it takes to nudge a doubting, cash-short nation into serious consideration of his star wars defense concept.
**1984** *Nation* (Apr. 7) 405/2: Richard D. DeLauer, Under Secretary of Defense for Research and Engineering, warned that the Star Wars scenario involved a half-dozen unsolved basic problems,

each as formidable and expensive as the entire Manhattan or Apollo project.
**1990** *Intelligencer (Doylestown, Pa.)* (June 26) A9/2: Pentagon designs for initial "star wars" defenses are becoming increasingly reliant on the concept of Brilliant Pebbles—tiny, self-guided missiles parked in space to guard against nuclear attack.
**1999** *Intelligencer (Doylestown, Pa.)* (Feb. 9) A9/5: His successor [ ... ] persuaded the Clinton administration to opt for a more modestly priced "Son of Star Wars."

**starways** *pl. n.* routes between stars. Compare SPACE LANE, SPACEWAYS, STAR-LANES.
[ **1936** [G. Wilson] *Earth-Venus 12* in *Thrilling Wonder Stories* (Dec.) 103/1: I peered down to the landing stage where the arriving passengers were crowding. It was *Inter[-]planetary Starways*, Earth-Venus Voyage Twelve. ]
**1941** *Comet* (July) 82: A tale of the prospectors in the starways—of dangers—
**1942** [R. Rocklynne] *Abyss of Darkness* in *Astonishing Stories* (Dec.) 89/1: You are big enough to have been plunging through the starways for more than a million, perhaps five million years.
**1946** C. Oliver *Thrilling Wonder Stories (letter)* (Winter) 8/2: It may be a sweeping, brilliant epic of the starways. But I don't know.
**1958** S. Mullen *Guppy* in *Astounding SF* (Jan.) 127/2: Together, they roved the starways, trod the dark, soundless emptiness of space.
**1984** R. Silverberg *Symbiont* in *Collected Stories of Robert Silverberg (Vol. 1: Pluto in Morning Light)* (1993) 244: Finding me—finding *anybody* along the starways—wasn't remotely probable.
**2001** D. Bischoff *Ship of Ghosts* (2002) 116: What is coming up, sir, is bits and pieces about a truly ancient race who once plied the galactic starways.

**stasis field** *n.* a field of energy which prevents anything within it from undergoing any changes, including those due to time or aging.
**1942** [A. MacDonald] *Beyond This Horizon*

in *Astounding SF* (Apr.) 31/1: Monroe-Alpha began to understand what they were talking about. It was the so-called Adirondack stasis field.

**1955** R. Sheckley *Ticket to Tranai* in *Galaxy SF* (Oct.) 15/2: Goodman knew that Mrs. Melith had come out of a derrsin stasis field [ ... ]. Sometimes there were good medical reasons for suspending all activity, all growth, all decay.

**1965** L. Niven *World of Ptavvs* in *Worlds of Tomorrow* (Mar.) 12/1: The ship had power, probably, to reach several worlds, but not to slow him down to the speed of any known world. Well, that was all right. In his stasis field Kzanol wouldn't care how hard he hit.

**1980** D. Brin *Sundiver* (1989) 117: Only a computer can adjust the stasis fields fast enough to keep the turbulence from pounding a passenger to jelly.

**1989** [G. Naylor] *Infinity Welcomes Careful Drivers* (1992) 73: Once activated, the booth created a static field of Time; in the same way X-rays can't penetrate lead, Time couldn't penetrate a stasis field.

**1989** D. Dvorkin & D. Dvorkin *Captains' Honor* 222: "Your right forearm"—he looked down, and saw it was held in place by a stasis field—"was broken."

**2002** J. Ringo *When Devil Dances* 121: But the technician's real love was new discoveries, new devices to tinker with, such as the sensor box floating in the stasis field.

**steampunk** *n.* [by analogy to CYBERPUNK] a genre of science fiction with a historical setting in the nineteenth century characterized by technologies extrapolated from the science of that era, but which were not invented at that time. Hence **steampunker, steampunkish.**

[**1987** K. W. Jeter *Locus (letter)* (Apr.) 57/2: Personally, I think Victorian fantasies are going to be the next big thing, as long as we can come up with a fitting collective term for Powers, Blaylock and myself. Something based on the appropriate technology of that era; like "steampunks," perhaps.]

**1987** J. Blaylock *Locus* (May) 57/1: There's railroad trains, a lot of steam-driven stuff, but that's about it. More "steam punk," I suppose.

**1991** *Locus* (May) 66/3: *The Difference Engine* is *not* steampunk, because it is a work of hard sf.

**1995** M. Dirda *Bound to Please* (2005) 124: In a scene that could make a steam-punk short story, the master of nonsense even visits Charles Babbage, the great pioneer of the computer.

**2001** *Interzone* (Sept.) 64/3: Kirkus Reviews said of his previous book: "If Arthur Conan Doyle and H. P. Lovecraft had collaborated on a novel, the result might have been like this"; steampunker Tim Powers also offers some words of praise.

**2004** P. Di Filippo *Asimov's SF* (Apr.–May) 230/2: Now, [ ... ] he's turned his hand to a steampunkish adventure, one that summons up the glory days of television's *The Wild, Wild West.*

**2005** *SF Weekly (San Francisco)* (Mar. 16–22) 40/2: Sci-fi readers call this type of thing "steampunk," a genre characterized by advanced technology powered by old-fashioned methods—usually steam engines—in the style of Jules Verne or H. G. Wells.

**stefnist** *n.* [perh. abbr. of SCIENTI-FICTIONIST combined with a pronunciation spelling of STF] *Obs.* a fan of science fiction.

**1944** J. B. Speer *Fancyclopedia* 22/1: The letter which probably initials the greatest number of fans' calling names: Dale, Dan, Dave, Dick, Doc, Don, Donn, Doug, and others, most of these being used by more than one stefnist.

**1960** J. Speer *Novus Ordo Fandorum* in *Fancestral Voices* (2004) 189: Nevertheless there shall linger some few traces of ancient wrong, the occasion for new and greater wars between the ghodlike stefnists.

**1969** H. Warner, Jr. *All Our Yesterdays* 43: "Stefnist" was proposed as a substitute on several occasions, either as a new term for fan or to represent a former fan with little surviving interest in professional science fiction.

**Stepford** *adj.* [< the title of Ira Levin's novel (1972), and subsequent movie (1975), *The Stepford Wives,* in which suburban wives are murdered and replaced with look-alike subservient robots] possessing a disturbing conformity; subservient or docile; artificial.

**1981** *Washington Post* (July) C6/1: Little Miss Beauty Pagent [ ... ]. Some of the girls in the 4-to-6 division are practicing their modeling on the runway [ ... ]. Walking Barbie Dolls. Stepford Babies.

**1984** *Washington Post* (Nexis) (Feb. 23): The only way the program could be phonier is if all the participants were computer-generated holograms—the Stepford celebrities.

**1994** P. Theroux *Translating LA* 238: The answer was to try to turn everyday life into a theme park, a Stepford City.

**1999** J. VanderMeer *World Fantasy Convention 25: 1999* in *Why Should I Cut Your Throat?* (2004) 110: Everyone was so happy and well-adjusted and outgoing that it couldn't be *real* happiness—it had to be some kind of Stepford happiness.

**2003** *Vanity Fair* (Sept.) 262/1: Will the palace bureaucracy force her to be a Stepford queen, or will she emerge in her own role?

**stf** *abbr.* [stɛf] [scien*ti*fiction] SCIENTI-FICTION or SCIENCE FICTION. Now often *hist.*

**1931** F. J. Ackerman *Wonder Stories (letter)* (May) 1483/1: All those stars of science fiction (or stf., the abbreviation for science fiction adopted by the Boys' Scientifiction Club) in the same issue.

**1932** R. A. Ward *Amazing Stories (letter)* (Aug.) 474/1: In *no* "stf" magazine will you find such marvelous gems of fantansy [sic] as appeared in the AMAZING STORIES of old.

**1946** R. R. Anger *Astounding SF (letter)* (Apr.) 98/1: An stf classic by a great stf author. To say that it is Asimov's best work is to pay it greatest honor.

**1953** L. B. Stewart *Thrilling Wonder Stories (letter)* (Aug.) 133/2: Yes, I listened, shivered, and hastily swallowed back all those witticisms and criticisms that are the birthright of a stf fan.

**1980** [L. del Rey] *World of SF* 139: It now became sf, usually pronounced esseff, and replaced the older stf (from scientifiction) which was pronounced steff, a bit too much like stuff!

**2005** *Sex in SF* (Usenet: rec.arts.sf.written) (Dec. 16): But there's a long tradition of stf about sex: from H. O. Dickinson's "The Sex Serum" [ ... ], to William Tenn's "Venus and the Seven Sexes" (1949, alien biology), to that 1960s novel about an icy planet where people change their sex regularly.

**stf-** *pref.* [scien*ti*fiction] used to indicate that something is, or is related to, scientifiction. Compare SCIENTI-.

**1940**: see cite in STFAN.

**1940** *Thrilling Wonder Stories* (May) 128/2: A Stfilm Committee of five were appointed to meet on Fridays, and plan the whole film project.

**1950** A. H. Rapp *Timber!* in *Spacewarp* (Apr.) 2: Send your manuscripts to SHIVERS or one of the other fanzines specializing in that branch of fantasy. This is a stfanzine.

**1952**: see quote in CON 2.

**1955** J. Speer *1934: Making of Fan* in *Fancestral Voices* (2004) 110: One of the few barbarisms I committed on the body of a stfzine was cutting out this chart to put in my high-school freshman science workbook.

**1997** J. Speer *Phanerofannish Eon* in *Fancestral Voices* (2004) 79: One probably should not say there was a trufan, even *in posse*, until the stfield had been defined by *Amazing Stories*.

**stfan** *n.* ['stɛfæn] (pl. **-fans, -fen**) [STF- + fan] *Obs.* a fan of science fiction, especially one who is not also a fan of fantasy or horror. Hence **stfandom**.

**1940** [Pogo] *Le Zombie* (Jan. 13) 3: Los Angeles Futurians were entertained last nite by Walt Sullivan, visiting stfan [ ... ] from Albuquerque, N. M., at an Italian dinner given in his honor.

**1944** J. B. Speer *Fancyclopedia* 51/2: No important fan words at present being initialed by K, it pleases our whimsy to brush aside one or two that mite [sic] have been stuck in, and leave one letter of the alphabet temporarily unsullied by stfandom.

**1944** J. B. Speer *Fancyclopedia* 7/2: Partly because a silly law in Great Britain hampered rocket fuel experimentation, and partly because more of the leaders are stfans, the BIS, unlike the ARS, has kept its eye set on the conquest of space.

**1952** A. H. Rapp, L. Hoffman & R. Boggs *Fanspeak* 11/2: *stfarr, stefan.* Fan who is primarily interested in science fiction and not in fantasy or weirds.

**1953** R. Ellik *Thrilling Wonder Stories (letter)* (Aug.) 132/2: Sam, it seems to me that you have neglected a very important item to stfen.

**stfantasy** *n.* [stɛˈfæntəsi; -zi] [abbr. of SCIENTIFANTASY or STF- + *fantasy*] *Obs.* IMAGINATIVE FICTION. Compare FANTASY 1, SCIENCE FICTION 3, SCIENTIFANTASY, SPECULATIVE FICTION 2.

**1944** J. B. Speer *Fancyclopedia* 69/1: The average stefnist eats up good stfantasy, has an exaggerated idea of its literary merit, and will leap to defend it against detractors.

**1946** J. Kennedy *Startling Stories (letter)* (Summer) 99/1: I immediately assumed the identity of Kennedy, the mild reporter and stfantasy fan. But by night I don my snazzy costume with the orange stripes and purple spots, and become that dynamic man of mystery—the Blue Bem.

**1947** C. Oliver *Thrilling Wonder Stories (letter)* (Apr.) 98/1: First, many thanks for giving us a de Camp tale. He is, to me, the most literate writer ever produced by stfantasy.

**1953** *Fantastic Universe* (Oct.–Nov.) 189/2: You'll find such stfantasy stand[-]bys here as Edgar Pangborn, H. F. Heard, Theodore Sturgeon, Ray Bradbury, David H. Keller [...], Will Jenkins, Murray Leinster and Harold Lawlor.

**1959** R. H. Eney *Fancyclopedia II* 56: Fan fiction [...]. Properly, it means (2) fiction by fans about fans (or sometimes about pros) having no necessary connection with stfantasy.

**stfdom** *n.* [ˈstɛfdəm] [STF- + -*dom*] *Obs.* the community of science fiction fans and writers.

**1947** *Startling Stories* (July) 110/2: A monumental job by the VAMPIRE man, a 76-page ship of the line, featuring intelligent reviews of all phases of fandom and professional stfdom.

**1952** P. Nowell *Planet Stories (letter)* (Nov.) 112/2: He also said that stfdom should write in about it.

**1959** R. H. Eney *Fancyclopedia II* 129: In practice most of the fan-pro prejudice Tucker re-

marks is turned against those their own sections of stfdom admit to be obnoxious—7th Fandom and the other Beanie Brigadiers, and the less scrupulous or more conceited professionals.

**stfnal** *adj.* [ˈstɛfnəl] [abbr. of SCIENTIFICTIONAL] of or relating to science fiction. Hence **stfnality,** *n.* Compare SF-ISH, SFNAL

**1944** J. B. Speer *Fancyclopedia* 58/1: There have been fantastic movies from the very beginning of motion pictures [...]. Stfnal ones such as Just Imagine have usually been burlesques or anti-scientific.

**1959** R. H. Eney *Fancyclopedia II* 59: Generally comprised of folk [...] whose interests were in collecting stf and scientificomics, and who eagerly hunted down any items with any sort of stfnal significance.

**1966** T. White *Who Was That Fandom I Saw You With...* in *SF Five-Yearly* (Nov.) 30: The peculiar qualities of both fannishness and stfnality—bound up in the irreverence of wit and humor—which characterized Sixth Fandom during QUANDRY's heyhay [sic] did not disappear when Q did.

**1975** E. Weinstein *Fillostrated Fan Dictionary* 78: STFnal closings invented by fans, such as: fannishly, tendrilly yours, or Sciencerely.

**1977**: see quote in SEMI-PROZINE.

**1997** P. M. Cohen *Vermillion (letter)* (Sept.) unpag./1: Matt Howarth is great, and he's at his best when he's stfnal.

**stim, stimm** *n.* a chemical stimulant, which may increase someone's energy, speed, awareness, etc. Often in compounds as **stim-pill, stimtab,** etc.

**1967** J. Blish *Star Trek* 110: Despite the stim-pills McCoy doled out, everyone seemed to be moving very slowly, as if underwater.

**1974** J. Haldeman *Forever War* (1976) 54: We were each allowed one stimtab. Without it, no one could have marched an hour.

**ca1985** [J. Tiptree, Jr.] *Trey of Hearts* in *Meet Me at Infinity* (2001) 97: She wanders out to take a stim-drink under the huge wall of clocks that show the local times all over known space.

**1991** J. D. Vinge *Summer Queen* (2003) 309:

And I've been on stims for three days straight; my body doesn't take it as kindly as it did in my student days.

**2000** *White Dwarf* (May) 108/3: Simultaneously the stimm dispensers grafted into the fleshy stump of his right shoulder activated and shot a cocktail of combat enhancing drugs into his bloodstream.

**2002** K. V. Forrest *Daughters of Amber Noon* 48: Desmond, the stim continuing to sharpen his senses, observed the tall, slender, blond Gruber.

**stun gun** *n.* a weapon that renders its target unconscious. Compare STUNNER.

**1946** M. Champion *Unforeseen* in *Astounding SF* (Nov.) 42/1: Lodner tossed the stun gun on a flange between the stills and the fluxing panels.

**1949** W. L. Bade *Lost Ulysses* in *Astounding SF* (May) 109/2: Sonneman had shot him with a stun-gun. No wonder he felt so miserable!

**1967** *Oshkosh (Wis.) Daily Northwestern* (May 27) 6/6: A Pittsburgh manufacturer has developed a "stun gun." They call it a "chemical mace," or a "chemical baton."

**1981** M. Resnick *Soul Eater* (1992) 8: There'd be the standard hand weapons: the stungun, the screecher, and an old-fashioned laser pistol.

**1991** M. Weiss *King's Test* 179: Four humans, three men and a woman, walked toward her, small stunguns in their hands.

**2005** *San Francisco Chronicle* (Nov. 29) B4/2: Several San Jose community groups are urging the San Jose City Council to adopt written guidelines for officers using stun guns.

**stunner** *n.* a STUN GUN.

**1941** [S. D. Gottesman] *Fire-Power* in *Cosmic S-F* (July) 12/2: Armament, every first-class operative owns a hand-gun and shells. Most of them carry illegal personal electric stunners.

**1957** R. Silverberg *One-Way Journey* in *World of Thousand Colors* (1984) 124: Warshow smiled apologetically, took one step backward, and slid his stunner from its place in his tunic.

**1969** E. Hamilton *Return to Stars* 93: He looked as though he was about to spring at Cyn

Cryver, but the men with the stunners stepped forward.

**1985** M. W. Bonanno *Dwellers in Crucible* 84: They had grappled for the stunner with which he'd hoped to take the old dragon down without pain.

**1992** N. Stephenson *Snow Crash* 292: She's ready with the bundy stunner, which turns their nervous systems into coils of hot barbed wire.

**1997** L. E. Modesitt, Jr. *Ecolitan Enigma* in *Ecolitan Prime* (2003) 393: Perhaps we were mistaken, but we got a message that you'd called. Then one of the staff started firing a stunner at me.

**Sturgeon's Law** *n.* [after Theodore Sturgeon, who first proposed it] a humorous aphorism that holds that ninety percent of any realm of endeavor, or more generally, of everything, is worthless; usually in the form "ninety percent of everything is crap." [In a letter to the OED, Fruma Klass (wife of science fiction writer Phil Klass, a.k.a. William Tenn) writes that Sturgeon first used the phrase "ninety percent of everything is crud" in a lecture he and Tenn gave at New York University in the early 1950s.]

[**1957** T. Sturgeon *Venture SF Mag.* (Sept.) 78: They really do take their horrible examples out of the s f field, a field which is, they inform the world, ninety-percent crud. And on that hangs Sturgeon's revelation. It came to him that s f is indeed ninety-percent crud, but that also—Eureka!—*ninety-percent of* everything *is crud.* All things—cars, books, cheeses, hairstyles, people and pins are, to the expert and discerning eye, crud, except for the acceptable tithe which we each happen to like.]

[**1963** J. Merrill *Proceedings; Chicon III* 35: That was the memorable Sturgeon Law that 90 per cent of everything is crud; including, we regret to say, science fiction.]

**1963** T. R. Cogswell *Proceedings; Chicon* 38: Judy mentioned Sturgeon's Law; she was kind enough not to bring the new revisions which is that 9/10ths of all science fiction is bad enough to be written by Ted Cogswell.

**1974** T. Sturgeon *SF, Morals, & Religion* in R. Bretnor *SF, Today & Tomorrow* 98: Conceded, but then (and this has come to be known as

Sturgeon's Law) ninety percent of *everything* is trash.

**1977** *Washington Post* (Nexis) (Aug. 29): If I may I'd like to quote (sci-fi writer Theodore) Sturgeon's Law: "90 per cent of everything is crap." Television seems to bear that out.

**1979** S. Robinson *Spider vs. Hax of Sol III* in *Destinies* (Jan.–Feb.) 158: If we apply Sturgeon's Law to that five hundred books, there'll be about fifty decent new ones a year.

**1996** *PC World* (Nexis) (Dec.): "Ever heard of Sturgeon's law?" He shook his head. "'Ninety percent of everything is crap.' If that's true of anything, it's true of the Web. Ninety percent of everything on it isn't even worth the time it takes to download."

**2003** R. Klaw *Geek Confidential* 246: The industry was inundated with crap. Sturgeon's Law in overdrive!

**sub-ether** *n.* [< *ether,* a substance formerly believed to permeate all space, and through which light was thought to be transmitted] a substance or medium existing on a smaller scale than the ether, which facilitates faster-than-light communication or travel. Compare HYPERSPACE, SUBSPACE.

**1930** E. E. Smith *Skylark Three* in *Amazing Stories* (Sept.) 562/2: Therefore, if there is anything between the particles of the ether—this matter is being debated hotly among us at the present time—it must be a sub-ether, if I may use that term.

**1936** [E. Binder] *Static* in *Thrilling Wonder Stories* (Dec.) 40/1: It is easy enough [...] to transmit through the ether forms of high frequency energy, but the power loss is tremendous. My approach to the problem was to discover a new medium of transmission—the sub-ether, which—

**1947** J. Shelton *You Are Forbidden!* in *Thrilling Wonder Stories* (June) 94/1: The spacial chit[-]chat, with no time lag since it was sub-ether stuff, was incomprehensible to the layman.

**1954** F. Brown *Answer* in *Angels & Spaceships* 23: The eyes of a dozen television cameras watched him and the sub-ether bore throughout

the universe a dozen pictures of what he was doing.

**1984** D. Duane *My Enemy, My Ally* 82: It mangles the highest and lowest bandwidths and slows down transmission speed. The sub-ether carrier wavicles.

**sub-etheric** *adj.* of, through, or using the sub-ether. Hence **subetherics,** *n.*

**1946–47** [R. Rocklynne] *Distress Signal* in *Planet Stories* (Dec.–Feb.) 36/1: They never tired as the sub-etheric warp hurled them through the dark reaches of infinity at several times light-speed.

**1955** I. Asimov *Talking Stone* in *Mag. of Fantasy & SF* (Oct.) 114/1: They're saving power, hoping they'll get picked up. Right now, they're putting everything they've got into a sub-etheric call, I'll bet.

**1952** I. Asimov *Youth* in *Space SF* (May) 76/2: In a case such as theirs, then, there was little or no chance that another ship would come within range of their subetherics except for the most improbable of coincidences.

**1956** *Claustrophile* T. Sturgeon *And Now News…* (2003) 101: It had an inertialess faster-than-light drive, a suspended animation technology, sub-etheric communications.

**1961** B. Silverberg *Stars of Slave Giants* in *S-F Five-Yearly* (Nov.) 12: A moment later his blaster flashed purple, and the booming laughter of Floyd Scrilch vied with the thunder of the waves as four pirates were converted instantaneously to sub-etheric vibrations.

**subfandom** *n.* a community of people interested in a specific subset of a larger area of interest, especially one within the science fiction and fantasy field.

**1969** H. Warner, Jr. *All Our Yesterdays* 30: Also described elsewhere are such subfandoms as those devoted to dime novels, Shaverism and Lovecraft.

**1975** E. Weinstein *Fillostrated Fan Dictionary* 92: Nostalgia Society: A subfandom that delights in reliving the old.

**1997** J. Speer *Phanerofannish Eon* in *Fancestral Voices* (2004) 81: Its signs are enormous conventions, professional fanzines, the existence of parallel- and sub-fandoms, [...] and a loss of common ground.

**subjunctivity** *n.* [< S.E. *subjunctive,* describing a mood of verbs expressing something that is imagined or that has not happened] the relationship between something portrayed in a text and reality.
**1969** S. R. Delany *About Five Thousand One Hundred & Seventy Five Words* in *Extrapolation* (May) 61: Suppose a series of words is presented to us as a piece of reportage. A blanket indicative tension informs the whole series: *This happened.* [...] The subjunctivity level for a series of words labeled naturalistic fiction is defined by: *Could have happened.*
**1969** S. R. Delany, in *Extrapolation* 62: Fantasy takes the subjunctivity of naturalistic fiction and throws it in reverse [...]: *Could not have happened.*
**1973** J. Russ *Subjunctivity of SF* in *Extrapolation* (Dec.) 56: One does not suspend one's disbelief in reading science fiction—the suspension of disbelief [...] fluctuates constantly. That is, the relation with actuality—what Delany would call the subjunctivity of the story—fluctuates constantly.
**1995** B. Landon *SF after 1900* (2002) 9: It is the notion of subjunctivity that best accounts for the relationship in SF between known science and its necessary deformations, between the reader's world and the world of the SF semblance.
**1999** J. Cortiel *Demand My Writing* 137: From the repetitiveness of everyday life the narrative thus surreptitiously slides towards the subjunctivity of a science fiction story.

**sublight** *n.* a speed slower than that of light.
**1976** J. L. Chalker *Jungle of Stars* 110: The pilot's flagship deployed some of the newcomers along the entire D-line front while keeping the original ships at sub-light.
**1980** D. F. Glut *Empire Strikes Back* 74: At sublight, they may be faster, but we can still outmaneuver them.
**1992** V. Vinge *Fire upon Deep* 50: Nuwen had spent his life crawling at sublight between human-colonized star systems.

**1997** S. Zettel *Fool's War* 44: Navigation past light speed was impossible. To change direction, they would have to drop down to sublight, change the ship's flight angle and jump again.

**sublight** *adj.* **1.** less than, or at a speed less than, the speed of light.
**1950** J. D. MacDonald *Shadow on Sand* in *Thrilling Wonder Stories* (Oct.) 14/1: They were in the eight-minus level, apparently. Later, when he found a reference to the manufacture of radioactives, he quickly revised it to six-minus, knowing that these people were on the verge of Newtonian sub-light space travel.
**1969** R. Meredith *We All Died at Breakaway Station* in *Amazing Stories* (Mar.) 58/2: Port Abell just received an FTL probe saying that he was approaching the system at maximum sub-light speed.
**1980** J. White *Ambulance Ship* in *Alien Emergencies* (2002) 110: The safety cutoff on the good generator had failed [...] which meant that a part of the ship had been proceeding at hyperspeed while the rest had been slowed instantaneously to sublight velocity.
**1993** *SF Age* (Jan.) 42/2: They ambled from star to star at sublight speeds, taking decades for each journey.
**2002** A. Roberts *Stone* (2002) 139: When people from the Wheah made the slow sublight journey through the Tongue they—obviously—chose its narrowest point.
**2.** SLOWER-THAN-LIGHT.
**1960** P. Anderson *High Crusade* (1968) 37: Such dials as those for altitude and speed could readily be mastered. But what did "fuel flow" mean? What was the difference between "sub-light drive" and "super-light drive"?
**1975** G. Bear *Perihesperon* in *Collected Stories of Greg Bear* (2003) 249: She was going to have her body sealed in a sublight ship and shot into a protostar in the Orion nebula.
**1999** C. Asaro *Radiant Seas* (1999) 175: Light speed blocked sublight ships from the superluminal universe the way an infinitely tall tree blocked a road.
**2002** M. J. Harrison *Light* 225 (2004): Some said it originated on the ancient trundling sublight ships of the Icenia Credit.

**sublight** *adv.* in or at a speed slower than that of light.

**1966** P. Anderson *Sun Invisible* in *Analog SF-Sci. Fact* (Apr.) 134/1: They'd also go sublight, and home on the neutrino emission of his power plant.

**1969** R. Meredith *We All Died at Breakaway Station* in *Amazing Stories* (Mar.) 73/2: They'll probably stay sub-light, Bracer thought. Not much point in their going back into star drive now.

**1991** A. McCaffrey & E. Moon *Generation Warriors* 153: That's how emergency calls went out: sublight to the transfer point, which launched the pod.

**1996** D. Weber *Honor Among Enemies* (1997) 152: They'd made the centuries-long voyage sublight, in cryo, only to discover that the original survey had missed a minor point about their new home's ecosystem.

**subspace** *n.* a medium or dimension coexistent with our own, but which is subject to different physical laws that permit faster-than-light communication or travel. Compare HYPERSPACE, SUB-ETHER.

**1940** J. Williamson *Sun Maker* in *Thrilling Wonder Stories* 99/1: Those little coils create a sub-space about the metal bead [ … ]. They warp space itself to form a tiny sphere—in effect, a tiny universe—strong enough to withstand unthinkable pressure and millions of degrees of heat.

**1940** A. E. van Vogt *Vault of Beast* in *Astounding S-F* (Aug.) 56/2: Most Martian histories refer to it as the beast that fell from the sky when Mars was young [ … ] the beast was unconscious when found—said to be the result of its falling out of sub-space.

**1955** P. Anderson & G. R. Dickson *Tiddlywink Warriors* in *Mag. of Fantasy & SF* (Aug.) 106/1: The subspace radio had announced his coming, and preparations consonant with his exalted rank had been made.

**1968** D. C. Fontana *Tomorrow Is Yesterday* in J. Blish *Star Trek 2* (1968) 26: Technically, the bubble of subspace in which the *Enterprise* was enclosed, which would have been moving at 64C had the bubble impossibility been in normal space at all.

**1985** M. W. Bonanno *Dwellers in Crucible* 90: Meanwhile, you do a chatter blitz on the subspace channels, the gossip wavelength.

**1998** D. Brin *Heaven's Reach* 316: And things only got worse as another wave of subspace disruptions hit, causing the planetoid to shake and rattle.

**suit** *n.* a SPACESUIT. Hence **suited,** *adj.* Compare MOONSUIT, PRESSURE SUIT, VAC SUIT, VACUUM SUIT.

**1928** E. E. Smith & L. H. Garby *Skylark of Space* in *Amazing Stories* (Sept. 3) 539/2: These suits were the armor designed by Crane for use in exploring the vacuum and the intense cold of dead worlds.

**1936** [R. Rocklynne] *At Center of Gravity* in *Astounding Stories* (June) 68/1: Both were clad in the tough, insulated, smoothly curving suits that man must wear in space.

**1938** A. K. Barnes *Satellite Five* in *Thrilling Wonder Stories* (Oct.) 28/1: A half-dozen suited figures scurried about the nose of the *Ark*.

**1958**: see quote in SPACEWORTHY.

**1971** *Oakland (Cal.) Tribune* (Feb. 5) 14F/1: The spacemen tried several different switches on their suits and in the spacecraft.

**1972** A. D. Foster *Tar-Aiym Krang* 105: They passed several vessels in parking orbit around the planet [ … ]. Some of the giant craft were in the process of loading or unloading, and men in suits floated about them sparkling like diamond dust.

**1981** B. Shaw *Galactic Tours* 13: Our picture shows the practice areas in use by suited and unsuited vacationers, the illusion of actually being in space enhanced by the sight of a shuttle craft.

**1991** L. Niven, J. Pournelle & M. Flynn *Fallen Angels* 11: Five times his suit had leaked air while they worked to save *Freedom Station*.

**suit radio** *n.* a two-way communication device in the helmet of a spacesuit. Compare COMLINK, COMSET.

**1944** G. O. Smith *Long Way* in *Astounding S-F* (Apr.) 84/2: "But I'll catch up," he promised as he made connection between his suit-radio and the Station communicator system.

**1951** [H. Clement] *Iceworld* in *Astounding SF* (Nov.) 134/2: It had been started automatically by a circuit which ran from a pressure gauge in the torpedo through one of the suit radio jacks as soon as atmospheric pressure had been detectable.
**1960** K. Amis *Hemingway in Space* in J. Merril *6th Annual Edition Year's Best S-F* (1961) 327: Then he was jetting forward at top speed and calling over the suit radio to make for the ship at once.
**1971** *Oakland (Cal.) Tribune* (Feb. 5) 14F/1: Mitchell's suit radio worked well, and the lunar module pilot had to relay messages from Mission Control to his commander.
**2002** A. Reynolds *Redemption Ark* (2004) 23: It had already identified the frequency for her suit radio.

**supernormal** *n.* a being with extraordinary (usually psychic) powers as compared to other members of their race.
**1936** O. Stapledon *Odd John* 214: The three supernormals discussed the situation telepathically, and agreed that drastic action was demanded.
**1950** C. M. Kornbluth *Little Black Bag* in R. Silverberg *SF Hall of Fame, Vol. I* (1970) 413: The handful of supernormals used such devices in order that the vast majority might keep some semblance of a social order going.
**1957** J. T. McIntosh *Unit* in G. Conklin *Five-Odd* (1964) 82: Hence the Unit Fathers—essentially ordinary human beings, in no way processed, cleared or otherwise mentally processed. A brake on the supernormal Uniteers.
**1996** M. Dery *Escape Velocity* 289: Snyder spins out an SF scenario in which "supernormals" enhanced with neural prosthetics "operate computers, typewriters, or turn on a television set just by using their brains."

**super-science** *n.* very highly advanced science.
**1929** *Oakland (Cal.) Tribune* (Feb. 25) 32 (*ad*): It [i.e., "Buck Rogers"] is packed with Love...Passion...Adventure...Thrills and the Super-science of Tomorrow in the Great Narrative Strip.

**1934** *Astounding Stories* (June) 9: We have sought the best in super-science and have given it to you.
**1946** M. St. Clair *Fantastic Adventures* (Nov.) 2/2: I like to write about ordinary people of the future, surrounded by gadgetry of super-science, but who, I feel sure, know no more about how the machinery works than a present day motorist knows of the laws of thermodynamics.
**1971** A. Budrys *Benchmarks* (1985) 285: *Tau Zero* has its biggest problems, in fact, when Anderson tests what I assume to have been his basic assumption—that you can tell a superscience story and a humanistic one at the same time.
**1981** *SF Rev.* (Summer) 36/1: People might be surprised that I list Hogan in the same sentence, considering his old-fashioned super-science plots and cardboard characters.
**2001** *SF Chronicle* (Mar.) 14/1: Some of them [...] are super-science epics which would have done F. Orlin Tremaine proud. Are you now consciously emulating [...] the science fiction you grew up reading?

**super-scientific** *adj.* of or relating to super-science; relating to or generated by the products of super-science.
**1919** C. Fort *Book of Damned* in *Complete Books of Charles Fort* (1974) 260: Then, on the other hand, we may have data of super-scientific attempts to investigate phenomena of this earth from above—perhaps by beings from so far away that they had never even heard that something, somewhere, asserts a legal right to this earth.
**1929** P. Nowlan & R. Calkins *Buck Rogers, 2429 A.D.* in *Syracuse (New York) Herald* (Jan. 14) 16: On the ruins of New York, San Francisco, Detroit, and a dozen others, the Mongols reared cities of superscientific magnificence.
**1947** R. A. Palmer *Observatory* in *Amazing Stories* (Oct.) 6/2: The existence of strange, super-scientific ships in the atmosphere of earth!
**1974** A. Panshin & C. Panshin *SF: New Trends & Old* in R. Bretnor *SF, Today & Tomorrow* 230: Magic has subtleties that super-scientific power or even psi power do not have.
**2003** S. M. Stirling *Intro.* in J. J. Astor *Journey in Other Worlds* ix: Yet amid the superscientific wonders, other interests remain.

**super-scientist** *n.* someone who studies, or creates inventions using, super-science.

**1928** A. C. Doyle *When World Screamed* in *Lost World & Other Stories* (1995) 461: Challenger the super scientist, Challenger the arch pioneer, Challenger the first man of all men whom Mother Earth had been compelled to recognize.

**1934** D. Wandrei *Scientist Divides* in *Astounding Stories* (Sept.) 54/2: Imagine what would happen if a superscientist treated man as such a cell and then, in the laboratory, constructed from one or dozens of men a creature of the year one billion!

**1939** *SF* (Oct.) 105: Kilran, super-scientist of the dim future, finds that the destruction of life on Venus is essential to the continuance of the human race.

**1986**: see quote in SUPER-WEAPON.

**1996** D. Pringle, et al. *Ultimate Ency. of SF* 137/1: Michael Dunn turned frequently in the key role of diminutive superscientist Dr Miguelito Loveless.

**super-weapon** *n.* a weapon, especially an extremely destructive one, based on highly-advanced technology.

**1939** E. E. Smith *Robot Nemesis* in *Thrilling Wonder Stories* (June) 74/1: Neither side dares attack the other; each is waiting for the development of some super-weapon which will give it the overwhelming advantage necessary to insure victory upon a field of action so far from home.

**1953** D. Fabun *SF in Motion Pictures, Radio, & Television* in R. Bretnor *Modern SF* 63: *Captain Video* and his Video Rangers are armed with superweapons, including [ ... ] an atomic rifle that pelts him with atomic energy, [ ... ] an electronic strait jacket which encases the prisoner in invisible restrainers, and an electronic prison cell with invisible walls of force that do the same job.

**1959**: see quote in SPACEWAYS.

**1965** A. Budrys *Benchmarks* (1985) 42: The robot can reel off the specs for all the super-weapons which wasted this world in the first place.

**1986** A. B. Chandler *Don't Knock Rock* in F. Pohl & E. A. Hull *Tales from Planet Earth* 114: If you people are such super-scientists why can't you let me have some super-weapons in exchange for the Monument?

**2004** J. Fforde *Something Rotten* 136: This was the man who had tried to prolong the Crimean War so he could make a fortune out of Goliath's latest superweapon, the Plasma Rifle.

**system-wide** *adj.* extending or existing throughout or across a solar system.

**1943** F. Brown *Daymare* in *Thrilling Wonder Stories* (Fall) 29/1: Under a perfectly democratic government, component part of a stable system-wide organization of planets, there was no need for such activity.

**1950** H. B. Piper *Last Enemy* in *Astounding SF* (Aug.) 12/1: They have a single System-wide government, a single race, and a universal language.

**1963** R. A. Heinlein *Podkayne of Mars* 12: She holds a system-wide license as a Master Engineer, Heavy Construction, Surface or Free Fall.

**1990** R. L. Forward *Rocheworld* 35: Red Vengeance's next call was wending its way through the system-wide comm nets.

**2003** T. Drago *Phobos* (2004) 347: Purificationists take the general System-wide predilection against Martians to the final degree.

# Time Travel

Douglas Adams, in *The Restaurant at the End of the Universe*, wrote that one of the greatest problems facing the time traveler is finding the right grammar. He posited that new verb tenses would be necessary to describe, say, something that was about to happen but which you went forward in time to avoid, and invented tenses such as the "Future Semiconditionally Modified Subinverted Plagal Past Subjunctive Intentional."

Projected humorous verb tenses aside, the greatest change in vocabulary is in the adjectives and adverbs required to describe different "locations" in time. Rather than travelling elsewhere, **chrononauts** travel **elsewhen**. They may also need to refer to **somewhen, anywhen**, and **everywhen** when discussing their adventures. Travelling into the future is going **uptime** (well, usually—it is very rarely used to mean the opposite); consequently, travel into the past is almost always **downtime**.

A specific course of history is known as a **timeline, timepath, time stream,** or **time track**. Changes to one time stream can result in **alternate histories** or **alternate futures** in which events take different courses than they otherwise would have (or did previously). Some such actions appear to be logically impossible (such as doing something in the past to prevent the invention of time travel) and are said to result in **time** (or **temporal**) **paradoxes**.

The most common way to travel in time is via the **time machine**, a technological device that takes or sends you into the past or future. There is also the **time-slip**, a rift in the fabric of time that allows travel from one point in time to another without any technological aid. A **time warp** may act similarly, or it may be created by a time machine, while a **time storm** can indiscriminately send people and things all over the **timescape**. Finally, if all you want is to see what is happening elsewhen, you may be able to peer into the past or future through a **time-viewer** or **chronoscope** from the (relative) safety and comfort of your own home time.

# t

**tanstaafl** *abbr.* ['tɑnstɑfəl] "there ain't no such thing as a free lunch," an aphorism which holds that there is a hidden cost to everything. [The abbreviation was popularized by Robert A. Heinlein, and it subsequently became a catchphrase in science fiction fandom.]

**1949** *Mt. Pleasant (Ia.) News* (Oct. 1) 1/1: Tanstaafl is mnemonic for "there ain't no such thing as a free lunch."

**1966** R. A. Heinlein *Moon Is Harsh Mistress* in *If* (Feb.) 108/2: "Oh, 'tanstaafl.' Means 'There ain't no such thing as a free lunch.' And isn't," I added, pointing to a *Free Lunch* sign across room, [sic] "or these drinks would cost half as much."

**1975** F. P. Wilson *Analog SF-Sci. Fact* (Apr.) 7/2: OK, the government pays for it, but Heinlein's acronym, TANSTAAFL, is never truer than when applied to government action.

**1989** M. Lackey *Burning Water* (1995) 157: TANSTAAFL, my friend. "There ain't no such thing as a free lunch." Magical energy has to come from somewhere.

**1998** E. McCoy S. Chupp, et al. *In Nomine Infernal Player's Guide* 49/1: TANSTAAFL, There Ain't No Such Thing As A Free Lunch— Lilim Motto. There Ain't No Such Thing As A Free Lilim—Mockery of Lilim motto.

**tardis** *n.* **1.** [acronym of *T*ime *A*nd *R*elative *D*imensions *I*n *S*pace; a time machine featured in the television series *Doctor Who* that is much larger on the inside than it is on the outside] something that seems to be larger than its appearance suggests. Often *cap.* Hence **tardis-like,** *adj.* and *adv.*

**1969** *Times (London)* (Mar. 29) 22/3: His best poems are like Doctor Who's Tardis, the solid streetcorner policebox, which actually contains a sidereal spaceship.

**1985** *Christian Sci. Monitor* (Apr. 30) 35: It's [...] a tardis of a poem, unassuming, but renewing, roomy, opportune.

**1986** *Times (London)* (Dec.) 15/6: Tardis-like, the inner dimensions are at odds with the outer.

**1996** *Time Out* (Jan. 17) 41/3: One of the conveniences of having a Tardis for a stomach is that you can order loads of main courses.

**1999** J. Preece *Good Beer Guide* 111/2: A Tardis of a pub—the small frontage conceals a long pub, half serving as a restaurant.

**2001** *Press (Christchurch, N. Z.)* (Nexis) (June 27): Only Mercedes-Benz's Tardis-like A-class comes within cooee of the Echo's space utilisation.

**2.** a time machine or something that appears to be from another time.

**1988** *New Musical Express* (Dec. 24) 33: The shiny streamlined tardis of Kraftwerk.

**1990** *Pink Paper (London)* (Aug. 4) 12/4: This is the perception that comes from the Tardis that seems to be New Scotland Yard, timewarped in the nineteen-sixties.

**2006** *Guardian (London)* (ProQuest) (July 8) headline: You don't need a Tardis to go back to Tudor England. Juliet Rix and her family become time-travellers for the day at Kentwell Hall.

**technothriller** *n.* a work in the mystery or spy genres, the action of which depends on near-future technologies or scientific breakthroughs.

**1986** *Washington Post* (Jan. 20) C16/1: World War III could be [ ... ] waged [ ... ] on cool and bloodless plains of silicon and won by software sabotage of the enemy's crucial computer systems. That is the timely and arresting premise of "Softwar," a French techno-thriller.

**1991** *Locus* (Sept.) 29/3: Toward the end, however, the mood shifts to more of a political techno-thriller, with some major twists in plot. Terrorists seek to stop the Stardancers.

**1996** *SFX* (May) 51/2: Very much a technothriller in nature, *Bugs* is something of a contemporary take on *Mission: Impossible*, with its scenario of three freelance crimebusters using cutting-edge hardware to thwart the bad guys and right wrongs.

**2002** P. Di Filippo *Asimov's SF* (May) 132/1: Ever since Michael Crichton's *The Andromeda Strain* (1969), the type of novel that's come to be known as the "techno-thriller" has assumed the status of science fiction's sexier younger sister, stealing much of the public spotlight away from SF.

**2005** C. Doctorow *Cory Doctorow: Everywhere, All at Same Time* in *Locus* (Jan.) 64/1: Charlie Stross and I have been kicking around an idea of writing a technothriller serial about the first multi-million-dollar heist in a massively multi-player online roleplaying game.

**telempathic** *n.* [< *telepathic* + *empathic*] of or by means of the psionic ability to feel others' emotions. Hence **telempath,** *n.*, **telempathy,** *n.* Compare EMPATHIC.

**1963** V. Simonds *Telempathy* in *Amazing Stories* (June) 63/1–2: I'll do a lot for a dollar, as the girl said to the soldier, but this is ludicrous. Who needs Telempathy? This cat is so phony, any gossoon can peg him.

[**1963** Simonds, *Telempathy* 65/1: Everett and his Telempathetic *Gestalt* have proved to be the equivalent of the world's largest survey sample.]

**1970** J. Blish *Spock Must Die!* 115: The link between the replicate and myself was not telepathy, but something I should call "telempathy"—an emotional rapport, not an intellectual one.

**1976** S. Robinson *Telempath* 213: A telempath is a person who approaches telepathy by way of empathy.

**1976** Robinson, *Telempath* 215: I was still dazed from the shock of telempathic contact with my unborn son.

**1995** I. Carmody *Ashling* (2001) 388: "She is empathizing it," Miky murmured, her face absorbed as she monitored Freya's telempathic emotions.

**1999** J. Lindskold *Queen's Gambit* in D. Weber *Worlds of Honor* 154: They're telempaths, not telepaths. They read vague emotions, not thoughts.

**2004** F. Pohl *Boy Who Would Live Forever* 205: This thing is a version of what you called a dream machine, technically known as a "telempathic psychokinetic transceiver." [ ... ] If the two of you were to get into the two sides of it and it were properly activated, each of you would at once feel everything the other was feeling.

**teleport** *n.* [< parapsychology *teleport,* a person who can make objects or themself disappear from one location and appear in another using only their mind] a MATTER TRANSMITTER. Compare TELEPORTER.

**1944** H. Walton *Boomerang* in *Astounding SF* (June) 119/2: Of course, a teleport paid for itself in a place like this, which most pillars of society would rather not be seen coming to or leaving.

**1945** R. Abernathy *Canal-Builders* in *Astounding SF* (Jan.) 44/1: When we use the teleport, we travel through a sort of interspace between Earth and Mars, in which the distance is insignificant—infinitesimal, so that for practical purposes we have the planets superimposed.

**1980** D. Adams *Restaurant at End of Universe* (1985) 166: He tossed a coin into the teleport and jiggled a switch on the lolling control panel. With a crackle and spit of light, the coin vanished.

**1993** F. M. Busby *Singularity Project* (1994) 24: A teleport? [ ... ] You get in a phone booth in L.A. and dial a number and step out in New York?

**teleport** *v.* [< parapsychology *teleport*, to make objects or oneself disappear from one location and appear in another using only one's mind] to move people or objects by means of a teleport. Hence **teleporting**, *n.*

**1944** I. Asimov *Big & Little* in *Astounding S-F* (Aug.) 19/2: Teleported direct from the capital.

**1948** F. Brown *What Mad Universe?* (1978) 102: Into Mekky also was built the ability to teleport—to transfer himself instantaneously through space without the necessity of having a spaceship to ride in.

**1967**: see quote in TELEPORTER.

**1988** S. McCrumb *Bimbos of Death Sun* 98: Brenda had discovered that reading is as close as you can come to teleporting.

**1997** S. Shinn *Jovah's Angel* 317: "How can I teleport?" This reply, at least, sounded sane. "Type in the word 'teleport' at the prompt, hit Enter, and within twenty seconds move to the inscribed pentagram on the floor in the center of the room."

**teleportation** *n.* [< parapsychology *teleportation*, the act of moving instantaneously from one place to another using only one's mind] MATTER TRANSMISSION.

**1943** T. Sturgeon & J. H. Beard *Bones* in T. Sturgeon *Beyond* (1970) 135: "Are you telling me you *felt* things in those pictures?" Farrel nodded soberly. "Donzey, I was in those pictures." Donzey thought, *What have I got here? Transmigration? Teleportation? Clairvoyance? Why, there's ten billion in it!*

**1984** D. Brin *Practice Effect* 22: Had the ziev effect played another trick on them all and given them teleportation rather than an interstellar drive?

**2001** *Cult Times* (Feb.) 59/5: Martin Brundle [...] is born under the watchful eye of Anton Bartok, an unscrupulous scientific tycoon, determined to discover the secret of the teleportation pods invented by Martin's father.

**teleporter** *n.* a MATTER TRANSMITTER. Compare TELEPORT.

**1967** R. G. Sipes *Of Terrans Bearing Gifts* in *Analog SF-Sci. Fact* (May) 31/2: In a like man-

ner, how could the alleged teleporter work? If one were to "teleport," [...] to a greater or lesser distance from the center of our planet, energy would be gained or lost.

**1973** J. R. Gregory & R. Price *Visitor* 6: Close to him stood the teleporter—the large jaunting-vehicle which could transmit the Tomorrow People and their equipment to any corner of the universe, just as swiftly as Stephen had come here from his own sitting-room.

**1998** E. S. Nylund *Signal to Noise* 203: Wheeler's latest trade. It uses the same cracks in space that the isotope communicates through, only it sends matter, not light. [...] For lack of a better word [...] a teleporter.

**2003** M. Swanwick *Legions in Time* in *Asimov's SF* (Apr.) 76: Something that a day ago she would have sworn couldn't exist. A teleporter, perhaps, or a time machine.

**telescreen** *n.* a VIEWSCREEN. Compare VISION PLATE, VISISCREEN.

**1932** F. Flagg *After Armageddon Wonder Stories* (Sept.) 343/2: It was on the tele-screen that I viewed the mobs coursing through the streets; via the news-dispenser I listened to the latest tidings from all over the country.

**1938** A. J. Burks *Challenge of Atlantis* in *Thrilling Wonder Stories* (Oct.) 52/1: Floods, fires, hold-ups, sports events—nothing escaped the all-seeing powers of the telescreens.

**1949** [G. Orwell] *Nineteen Eighty-Four* 6: The telescreen received and transmitted simultaneously.

**1987** "J. B. Stine" *Spaceballs* 29: Lone Starr looked up at the telescreen.

**1995** J. Lethem *Amnesia Moon* 168: The tel-evangelist shook its head, doubly, the robot moving the telescreen from side to side while video image of the old preacher [...] shook his head sorrowfully.

**Tellurian** *n.* [< L. *Tellus*, the Roman goddess of the earth] an EARTHLING. Compare EARTHER, EARTHIAN, EARTHIE, EARTHPERSON, TERRAN, TERRESTRIAL, TERRESTRIAN.

**1847** T. de Quincey *Joan of Arc* in *Miscellaneous Essays* (1851) 112: If any distant world [...] are so far ahead of us Tellurians in optical resources as to see distinctly through their telescopes all that we do on earth, what is the grandest sight to which we ever treat them?

**1930** M. J. Breuer & J. Williamson *Birth of New Republic* in *Amazing Stories Quarterly* (Winter) 29/1: The Tellurians had learned of such difficulties, to their cost, when they attempted to trap Warrington's army in the crater of Hipparchus.

**1930** [G. Edwards] *Rescue from Jupiter* in *Sci. Wonder Stories* (Feb.) 787/1: Not so very long ago, Tellurians visited us, staying beneath this very roof as guests. Why did the Earth-race die out so quickly?

**1968** E. E. Smith *Skylark Three* 162: DuQuesne, of course—I'll bet a hat no other Tellurian is this far from home.

**1994** J. A. Keel *Complete Guide to Mysterious Beings* (2002) 324: We finally got the idea and now accept dolphins as fellow tellurians (earthlings).

**Tellus** *n. Obs.* the planet Earth. Compare SOL III, TERRA.

**1928** E. E. Smith *Skylark of Space* (1958) 121: Greetings, oh guests from Tellus! I feel more like my self, now that I am again in my trappings and have my weapons at my side.

**1939** [E. Binder] *Impossible World* (1967) 13: Closer, on Long Island itself, lay Tellus Space Port, with its gigantic drome and hangars and its wide-spread landing field.

**1944** C. S. Lewis *Perelandra* (1962) 12: How if my friend were the unwitting bridge, the Trojan Horse, whereby some possible invader were effecting its landing on Tellus?

**1953** R. S. Shaver *Beyond Barrier* in *Other Worlds* (Jan.) 104/1: They swooped down over it, and it was as Tyron said, a very ancient craft, of the indestructible perdurable metal of the ancients who had colonized Tellus so long ago.

**temporal paradox** *n.* a TIME PARADOX.

**1954** R. Sheckley *Thief in Time* in *Galaxy SF* (July) 13/1: He went on to the so-called time paradoxes—killing one's great-great grandfather, meeting oneself, and the like. [ ... ] Alfredex went on to explain that all temporal paradoxes were the inventions of authors with a gift for confusion.

**1969** [K. M. O'Donnell] *July 24, 1970* in *Venture SF Mag.* (May) 92/1: This intimation— that the editor, his magazine and the submission itself might all vanish simultaneously because of temporal paradox is mildly provocative.

**1998** G. Cox *Assignment: Eternity* 24: I can tell you that I'm here to untangle a temporal paradox that threatens both our futures.

**2002** J. F. David *Before Cradle Falls* (2004) 123: Worse yet, if he does change the past and takes away the reason he came back, then there will be a temporal paradox.

**temporal viewer** *n.* see TIME VIEWER.

**Terra** *n.* [< L. *terra*, "earth"] the planet Earth. Compare SOL III, TELLUS.

**1871**: see quote in JOVIAN.

**1900** G. Griffith *Visit to Moon* in *Pearson's Mag.* (Mar.) 248: Well, after all, if you find the United States, or even the planet Terra, too small for you, we've always got the fields of Space open to us.

**1929** C. W. Harris & M. J. Breuer *Baby on Neptune* in *Amazing Stories* (Dec.) 795/1: Once more back in their homes on Terra, the disappointed scientists told the story of their fruitless journey into the depths of interstellar space.

**1942** G. O. Smith *QRM—Interplanetary* in S. Schmidt *Fifty Years of Best SF from Analog* (1980) 67: Talking is not possible, due to the fifteen-minute transmission lag between here and Terra.

**1960** P. Anderson *High Crusade* (1982) 31: Belike, I thought, when Scripture mentioned the four corners of the world, it did not mean our planet Terra at all, but referred to a cubical universe.

**1979** M. Z. Bradley *Bloody Sun* 15: For all you knew, you might have been born on one of the Big Ships; the ships of Terra; the starships that made the long runs between stars doing the business of the Empire.

**1993** K. S. Robinson *Green Mars* 210: Terran stock markets were ballooning hysterically to mark the action, with no end in sight, despite the fact that Mars could only provide Terra with certain metals in certain quantities.

**terraform** *v.* **1.** to modify a world's environment so that it can support Earth life-forms, especially humans. Hence **terraformation,** *n.*

**1942** [W. Stewart] *Collision Orbit* in *Astounding SF* (July) 82/1: Drake was the young spatial engineer he employed to terraform the little rock, only two kilometers through—by sinking a shaft to its heart for the paragravity installation, generating oxygen and water from mineral oxides, releasing absorptive gases to trap the feeble heat of the far-off Sun.

**1974** L. Niven & J. Pournelle *Mote in God's Eye* (1975) 33: The middle two planets are inhabited, both terraformed by First Empire scientists after Jasper Murcheson.

**1986** W. Strieber & J. Kunetka *Nature's End* (1987) 50: The Soviets terraform Mars while we Indians labor here on earth to reconstruct our own ecology.

**1996** K. S. Robinson *Blue Mars* 152: It was precisely the Terrans who showed an intense interest in Mars who were the most troubling to contemplate: certain metanat executives whose corporations had invested heavily in Martian terraformation.

**2003** S. S. Tepper *Companions* (2004) 139: Oloct purchased small, out-of-the-way planets and moons, listed them in star registers as "freight transfer sites," and [...], if the planets were lifeless, terraformed them for earth fauna and flora alone.

**2.** to modify a world's environment so that it can support life that evolved on a planet other than the Earth.

**1969** R. Silverberg *Across Billion Years* 18: What use is this planet to anybody? [...] Why did they bother terraforming it?

**1998** J. Barnes *Earth Made of Glass* (1999) 43: I had been present on Nansen [...] when the first alien ruin had been found and it had been realized that humanity was the *second* intelligent species to terraform Nansen.

**2006** N. Carroll *Film, Emotion, & Genre* in N. Carroll & J. Choi *Philosophy of Film & Motion Pictures* 229/2: Suspense is generated over the question of whether the alien attempt to transform ("terraform") the atmosphere of earth can be unmasked.

**3.** to modify the Earth's environment.

**1997** T. W. Luke *Ecocritique* 109: Seeing Earth as a spaceship is the excuse to terraform Earth to fit the terraforming designs not of creation, but of capital.

**1999** E. S. Nylund *Signal Shattered* (2000) 301: When Wheeler destroyed the Earth, Zero had told Jack he preserved samples of flora and fauna. But what did Zero expect him to do? Terraform the Earth?

**2001** G. Dozois *Preface Worldmakers* xiii: After all, we've already inadvertently "terraformed" *our own Earth*, radically changing our climate and ecosystem, and we didn't even mean to *do* it!

**2005** K. S. Robinson *Fifty Degrees Below* 90: So—we are going to become global biosphere managers. We are going to terraform the Earth!

**terraformed** *adj.* (of a world) having been modified to support life-forms alien to it.

**1942** [W. Stewart] *Minus Sign* in *Astounding S-F* (Nov.) 47/2: Rick omitted breakfast and hurried to the laboratory, just under the crown of the terraformed hill.

**1964** G. R. Dickson *Soldier, Ask Not* in *Galaxy Mag.* (Oct.) 8/1: The great ship behind me which had shifted me free between the stars—from Old Earth to this second smallest of the worlds, this small terraformed planet under the Procyon suns.

**1980** D. Brin *Sundiver* 239: We are challenged by some two-bit species [...] who now own two little terraformed planets that sit right astride our only route to the colony on Omnivarium?

**1991** *Locus* (May) 21/2: Anee, the terraformed moon of a gas giant nearly 200 light-years from Earth.

**1993** K. S. Robinson *Green Mars* 90: All its metals together total about twenty trillion dollars, but the value of a terraformed Mars is more in the neighbourhood of two hundred trillion dollars.

**terraformer** *n.* someone who engages in, or something which is used for, terraforming.

**1942** [W. Stewart] *Minus Sign* in *Astounding SF* (Nov.) 51/2: Beyond a hidden doorway a guarded elevator dropped them to the terraformer room at the center of gravity.

**1988** R. Frazier *Retrovision* in G. Dozois *Isaac Asimov's Mars* (1991) 59: At Geolab, Joaquim studied plugs that had been drilled from the Martian North Pole before it had been melted with an orbiting mirror [ ... ] a strategy that terraformers hoped would chain-react into a greenhouse effect.

**1993** A. C. Clarke *Hammer of God* 74: He *always* had clear skies, and, despite the best efforts of the terraformers, they would remain that way for the next few generations.

**1998** M. Swanwick *Archaic Planets* in *Cigar-Box Faust & Other Miniatures* (2003) 73: During their absence, the terraformers had transformed a hundred and twenty worlds into virtual Edens.

**terraforming** *n.* the modification of the environment of a world, especially to allow it to support life-forms alien to it. Compare PLANETARY ENGINEERING.

**1980** D. Brin *Sundiver* 107: Have only allowed the Pring to colonize class A worlds, devoid of life and requiring terraforming, but free of use restrictions by the Institutes of Tradition and Migration.

**1983** J. Oberg *Farming Planets* in O. Davies *Omni Book of Space* 21: A 1975 NASA study about terraforming coined the word "ecosynthesis" to mean the creation of a stable biological system on a new world.

**1988** G. Slusser *Literary MTV* in L. McCaffery *Storming Reality Studio* (1991) 339: Terraforming has produced the inextricable BAMA (Boston-Atlantic Metropolitan Axis) sprawl.

**1993** I. M. Banks *Against Dark Background* 216: "Pretty thin air." "Getting thinner all the time," she agreed. "Unbreathable in another thousand years; crap terraforming."

**2001** *Locus* (June) 17/2: Recruits [ ... ] work special projects, which in this case is the terraforming of a planet called Downside.

**terraforming** *adj.* relating to or for the purpose of modifying the environment of a world.

**1942** [W. Stewart] *Collision Orbit* in *Astounding SF* (July) 87/2: But the directional

space drive; [ ... ] the peegee terraforming unit, that held man and his precious blanket of air to any tiny rock—those were all unexpected gifts.

**1969** R. Silverberg *Across Billion Years* 18: A terraforming crew was here seventy years back. They planted atmosphere-generators, and by now there's a decent quantity of air, a little thin, but enough to support life.

**1983** J. Oberg *Farming Planets* in O. Davies *Omni Book of Space* 29: A traditional terraforming approach has called for the use of blue-green algae to break down the carbon dioxide.

**1989** [G. Naylor] *Red Dwarf* 294: He'd been smuggling it to the richly paid, insanely bored terraforming engineers of Triton.

**1993** J. Pournelle & S. M. Stirling *Prince of Sparta* 102: The grasses which had claimed this countryside so quickly after the terraforming package made a deep tough sod.

**1998** L. A. Graf & M. J. Friedman *War Dragons* 271: Khan Noonien Sing [ ... ] stole the Genesis Device, a revolutionary terraforming tool.

**Terran** *n.* **1.** an EARTHLING. Compare EARTHER, EARTHIAN, EARTHIE, EARTHPERSON, TELLURIAN, TERRESTRIAL, TERRESTRIAN.

**1946** G. O. Smith *Pattern for Conquest* in *Astounding SF* (May) 132/1: The mission, not entirely understood by the Terrans, consists of destroying a machine sent forth by the Loardvogh, a race that is conquering the Galaxy.

**1955** A. Norton *Star Guard* (1973) 26: Would the Agents' repeated argument have proved true? Would the Terrans, unchecked, have pulled planet after planet into a ruthless struggle for power?

**1969** *New Scientist* (Jan. 23) 191/3: Like our planet, we Terrans tend to be fat and slow or thin and quick.

**1979** M. Z. Bradley *Bloody Sun* 9: I have not been very far abroad, but I have been to Thendara, and I have seen the spaceships of the Terrans there.

**1986** D. Carey *Dreadnought* 21: Meeting more and more Terrans now, here on our ancestral rocks.

**2002** S. L. Viehl *Eternity Row* 335: Joseph, who you will agree was more conservative than most Terrans.

**2.** the language spoken by Terrans.

**1952** K. F. Crossen *Caphian Caper* in *Thrilling Wonder Stories* (Dec.) 18/2: He tried several languages, in addition to Terran, and finally the intergalactic sound code. There was still no answer.

**1958** [E. Rodman] *Slaves of Tree* in *Super-Sci. Fiction* (June) 56/2: Rayner strained to catch the words, but it seemed that they were only partly in Terran, and mainly in some strange and alien language whose words were smooth-flowing and liquid, with many vowels and few harsh consonants.

**1962** K. Laumer *Yllian Way* in *If* (Jan.) 21/2: "I have a surprise for you, Retief," he said in Terran.

**2001** A. McCaffrey & E. A. Scarborough *Acorna's Search* (2002) 180: You speak Terran, I speak Terran, we should be able to come up with some kind of understanding.

**Terran** *adj.* of, from, or relating to the planet Earth; human or of humans. Compare TERRESTRIAN.

[**1881** W. D. Hay *Three Hundred Years Hence* 267: I am speaking of the Terrane Exodus and the Cities of the Sea.]

**1946** G. O. Smith *Pattern for Conquest* in *Astounding SF* (May) 166/1: Seventeen million of the Loard-vogh died in the Battle of Sol, and more than half of them perished because Terran spores crept into chinks in their space armor.

**1958** R. Silverberg *Invaders from Earth* (1987) 113: Twenty minutes after he had left the Terran outpost he saw what could only be the alien village.

**1962** M. Z. Bradley *Planet Savers* in *Planet Savers/Sword of Aldones* (1982) 8: During the last epidemic, a Terran scientist discovered a blood fraction containing antibodies against the fever.

**1971** U. K. Le Guin *Lathe of Heaven* (1973) 69: You believed that overpopulation was a present threat to civilization, to the whole Terran ecosystem.

**1984** D. Brin *Practice Effect* 36: It would be too tempting to interpret what he saw in Terran terms.

**1995** A. Thomson *Color of Distance* (1999) 134: Only eight of them had word-equivalents in any of the Terran languages she knew.

**2002** A. Reynolds *Redemption Ark* (2004) 579: The infra-red signatures of surface flora matched the patterns expected from terran genestock.

**terrene** *adj.* [< S.E. *terrene*, "earthly"] *Obs.* (of matter) consisting of atoms with a positively-charged nucleus surrounded by negatively-charged electrons; not anti-matter. Compare CONTRATERRENE, SEETEE.

**1941**: see quote in CONTRATERRENE.

**1946** F. Brown *Placet Is Crazy Place* in *Astounding SF* (May) 119/2: It boils down to this; Argyle I is terrene matter and Argyle II is contraterrene, or negative matter.

**1946** G. O. Smith *Pattern for Conquest* in *Astounding SF* (May) 155/1: We have the following observations regarding subspace: One is that the matter is unlike Terrene matter.

**1949** A. Coppel, Jr. *Captain Midas* in *Planet Stories* (Fall) 65/2: Contra-terrene matter, perhaps, from some distant island universe where matter reacted differently…drawing energy from somewhere, the energy it needed to find stability in its new environment. Stability as a terrene element—wonderfully, miraculously gold!

**Terrestrial** *n.* [originally used in opposition to heavenly or spiritual beings] *Obs.* an EARTHLING. Compare EARTHER, EARTHIAN, EARTHIE, EARTHPERSON, TELLURIAN, TERRAN, TERRESTRIAN.

**1873** R. A. Proctor *Expanse of Heaven* (1877) 235: Varieties of effect altogether unfamiliar to us terrestrials.

**1911** H. Gernsback *Ralph 124C 41+* (1925) 41: The other was not a Terrestrial, but a visiting Martian.

**1930** E. E. Smith *Skylark Three* in *Amazing Stories* (Oct.) 617/1: The security of the Universe may depend upon the abilities and qualities of you Terrestrials and your vessel.

**1950** P. Anderson *Star Ship* in *Planet Stories* (Oct.) 74/1: There'd been Earthling girls; and not a few Khazaki women had been intrigued by the big Terrestrial.

**1964** P. K. Dick *Little Black Box* in *We Can Remember It for You Wholesale* (1994) 18: Mercer is not on Earth. I would guess that he is not a terrestrial at all.

**Terrestrian** *n. Obs.* an EARTHLING. Compare EARTHER, EARTHIAN, EARTHIE, EARTHPERSON, TELLURIAN, TERRAN, TERRESTRIAL.

**1930** J. W. Campbell, Jr. *Black Star Passes* in *Amazing Stories Quarterly* (Fall) 516/2: This rocket squad was composed almost solely of Terrestrians, for they were used to the greater gravity of Earth, and could stand greater acceleration than could Venerians.

**1932** [H. Vincent] *Faster Than Light* in *Amazing Stories Quarterly* (Fall–Winter) 291/2: He hesitated to plunge his bride of less than a year into a new series of adventures in which she might be subjected to dangers such as those of that memorable first visit of Terrestrians to Venus.

**1939** B. DeVoto *Doom beyond Jupiter* in *Harpers Mag.* (Sept.) 445/1: So, in the Twenty-Eighth Century a terrestrian brings home some of the crystals to earth in his space ship.

**1950** R. F. Jones *Tools of Trade* in *Astounding SF* (Nov.) 55/1: How would it look for the First Administrator to go limping around the galaxies explaining that he was behind schedule because his ship got wrecked on Sol III and the Terrestrians were incapable of matching his drives?

**1953** G. O. Smith *Troubled Star* in *Startling Stories* (Feb.) 48/2: It would show Gant that the mighty Marandanian was no more distant from the lusty chimpanzee than the terrestrian.

**Terrestrian** *adj. Obs.* TERRAN. Usually *cap.*

**1930** J. W. Campbell, Jr. *Black Star Passes* in *Amazing Stories Quarterly* (Fall) 500/1: In the meantime the Terrestrian and Venerian governments were already preparing vigorously for further inroads.

**1933** [H. Vincent] *When Comet Returned* in *Amazing Stories* (Apr.) 10/2: Further information was to be supplied enroute by the terrestrian scientist.

**1946** [H. Clement] *Cold Front* in *Astounding SF* (July) 37/1: Several winged aircraft were parked in the open near each strip, and a single machine, similar in exterior design to the terrestrian lifeboat.

**1949** I. Asimov *Mother Earth* in M. Greenberg *Journey to Infinity* (1951) 160: Field, especially, as a lecturer, scholar and man of modest means quoted chapter and verse from his still uncompleted history of Terrestrian Empire.

**thish** *n.* [*this* + ISH] the current issue of a periodical or the issue under discussion.

**1953** D. Clarkson *Thrilling Wonder Stories (letter)* (Aug.) 135/1: Thish of TWS was really a shock to me, and I'm not pulling any punches!

**1961** L. Hoffman *S-F Five-Yearly* (Nov.) 30: Much thanks to those of you who were going to write for thish, but failed to make the deadline. Deadline nextish is July 1966.

**1962** D. Lupoff *Cry (letter)* (June) 32: I trust, by the way, that you have your copy of Xero 8? Locs have been slow starting thish.

**thoughtcrime** *n.* any thought, especially that which is against the against the government or which is unorthodox, considered as a criminal offense.

**1949** [G. Orwell] *Nineteen Eighty-Four* 22: He had committed—would still have committed, even if he had never set pen to paper—the essential crime that contained all others in itself. Thoughtcrime, they called it.

**1953** *New York Times* (Jan. 25) 15/2: Goaded by Moscow's desire for violent purge, the Communist word-coiners are filling their controlled press with brand new words designed to catch anyone, however innocent, and indict him for "thought crime."

**1968** *Economist* (June 22) 19/1: If it were not the habit of Herr Ulbricht's government to put so many people in prison for thought-crime.

**1989** *New York Times* (Dec. 2) 13/6: Lawyers for the three remaining defendants hailed the jury's rejection of the charges of sedition, calling it "thought crime."

**2002** J. Goodare *Intro.* in *Scottish Witch-Hunt in Context* 5: The authors of the statute intended to punish *acts* of witchcraft [...] rather than the thought-crime of *being* a witch.

**2005** C. Doctorow *RIP: Rip, Mix, Burn* in *Make* (No. 4) 183/1: The entertainment companies have tried to create a new kind of secondary liability—for inducing your users to infringe copyright. This is thoughtcrime.

**three-D, threedee, 3-D** *n.* THREE-V; occasionally, a three-dimensional image. Compare HOLOVISION, TRI-D, TRIDEO, TRI-DIM, TRI-V, TRI-VID.

**1954** T. Godwin *Cold Equations* in R. Silverberg *SF Hall of Fame, Vol. I* (1970) 563: I always thought danger along the frontier was something that was a lot of fun; an exciting adventure, like in the three-D shows.

**1958** P. Anderson & K. Anderson *Innocent at Large* in *Galaxy SF* (July) 135/1: "That is a sexy type of furniture, all right," agreed Doran. He lowered himself into another chair, cocked his feet on the 3-D and waved a cigarette.

**1962** P. Anderson *Shield* in *Fantastic Stories of Imagination* (June) 63/2: The harness included a plastic panel across his chest, with switches, knobs, and three meters. Like some science fiction hero on the 3D.

**1971** G. Benford & G. Eklund *West Wind, Falling* in T. Carr *Universe 1* 16: The mammoth 3D mounted on one wall had been scrounged out of spare parts several years after the Zephyr expedition was launched.

**1986** D. Carey *Dreadnought* 23: That quarter had a few personal items around it: a 3-D of grinning people.

**1989** W. J. Williams *Angel Station* (1991) 251: Maria looked at the empty black threedee screen and wondered how Kit had changed.

**three-v, three-vee, 3V** *n.* [perh. punningly < *T V*] the process of recording and transmitting three-dimensional images, especially as used for entertainment; a device for displaying such images. Compare HOLOVISION, THREE-D, TRI-D, TRIDEO, TRI-DIM, TRI-V, TRI-VID.

**1954** J. Blish *At Death's End* in *Astounding SF* (May) 16/2: Paige supposed that the Believers

had managed to [...] project a 3V tape against the glass crystals with polarized ultraviolet light.

**1964** F. Pohl *Children of Night* in *Galaxy Mag.* (Oct.) 161/1: From the integration room the readout operator could construct a speech, a 3-V commercial, a space ad or anything else [...] and test its appeal on his subjects.

**1965** L. Niven *World of Ptavvs* in *Worlds of Tomorrow* (Mar.) 35/1: She leaned forward and turned on the threevee screen in the seat ahead.

**1967** J. Blish *Star Trek* 121: But, to play the classics, in these times, when most people prefer absurd three-V serials.

**1970** P. Anderson *Rogue Tales of Flying Mountains* (1984) 66: But you were home not so long ago. You talked with people, read the news, watched the ThreeV. Can't you at least give an impression?

**1984** D. Brin *Practice Effect* 72: It was a late-night talk show on the three-vee.

**2002** R. Garcia y Robertson *Ring Rats* in *Asimov's SF* (Apr.) 111: Passengers packed into lounges and staterooms tuned to 3V found themselves staring up from the airless surface of Aetna II.

**tight-beam** *n.* a device that sends communications on a very finely-focused beam of energy (such as a laser); a message sent by such a device.

[ **1930** E. E. Smith *Skylark Three* in *Amazing Stories* (Oct.) 617/2: He's putting it on a tight beam—that's fine, we can chase it up. ]

**1937** E. E. Smith *Galactic Patrol* in *Astounding Stories* (Sept.) 9/1: His command was carried to the very bones of those for whom it was intended—and to no one else—by the tight-beam ultra-communicators strapped upon their chests.

**1943** H. Kuttner & C. L. Moore *Clash by Night* in D. Drake *Dogs of War* (2002) 285: Detectors clamped on a telaudio tight-beam directly overhead.

**1955** [M. Leinster] *Scrimshaw* in *Astounding SF* (Sept.) 131: There was a warning-bell in the shack, and when a rocketship from Lunar City got above the horizon and could send a tight beam, the gong clanged loudly.

**1970** A. McCaffrey *Ship Who Sang* (1991) 32: I need to use your tight beam.

**1989** D. Dvorkin & D. Dvorkin *Captains' Honor* 11: They just sent a tight-beam subspace transmission.

**2002** A. Reynolds *Redemption Ark* (2004) 33: A tight-beam was a needlessly finicky means of communication when two ships were so close. A simple radio broadcast would have worked just as well, removing the need for the zombie ship to point its message laser exactly at the moving target of *Storm Bird*.

**tight-beam** *v.* to send a message by means of a tight-beam. Hence **tight-beamed**, *adj.*

**1994** S. Barnes *Firedance* (1995) 38: There were no notes, no messages, but suddenly he heard a hop-o'-my-thumb whisper in his ear, in some sort of tight-beamed message.

**1999** G. Benford *Martian Race* (2001) 83: We'll have great little portables. On live feed, right back to the hab, tight beamed to us here.

**2002** C. Sheffield *Dark As Day* (2003) 177: This message is being tight-beamed to two and only two locations.

**2002** A. Reynolds *Redemption Ark* (2004) 33: Acknowledge whoever it is [...]. Can we tight-beam them back?

**timecop** *n.* a time-traveler who attempts to prevent the past from being changed, typically as an agent of an organization.

**1953** C. M. Kornbluth *Time Bum* in *Fantastic* (Jan.–Feb.) 143/2: TAIM KOP NABD: PROSKYOOTR ASKS DETH Patrolm'n Oskr Garth 'v thi Taim Polis w'z arest'd toodei at hiz hom.

**1991** J. Clute *SF Novels of Year* in D. Garnett *New Worlds 1* 251: Poul Anderson [...] provided in *The Shield of Time* [...] another meditative time-cops foray into the past, where the gang played pattycake once again with history in order to save some awful new era.

**1996** M. Julius *Action!* 217: And so we have the timecops, guardians of the past who travel back in time to deliver twenty-first century justice to those who dare break the law.

**2004** G. Riley *Sick Notes* in *Tuesday Nights & Wednesday Mornings* 75: "Timecops," I whis-

per to Newton, with one hand cupped around my mouth. "The reason they look like they're from 1965 is that they are from 1965."

**time hopper** *n.* a TIME MACHINE.

**1963** D. Barry *Flash Gordon* in *Newark (Oh.) Advocate* (Aug. 12) 20: I guess we *would* be lying under that mastodon's hooves now, Flash... but for the "space-warp" device in my time-hopper—which moved us *instantly* to another continent.

**1983** P. Anderson *Ivory, & Apes, & Peacocks* in *Time Patrol* (1991) 171: One man on horseback, headed for the Cordillera Oriental that rises beyond the town—one man like ten thousand genuine Creoles—we couldn't go after him on time hoppers.

**2002** V. Terrace *Crime Fighting Heroes of Television* 59: He finds pure satisfaction at home in his private attic lab where he has invented such devices as the Shrink Ray, the Time Hopper (for travel through time) and the Igloo of Health.

**timeline** *n.* a TIME STREAM. Compare TIMEPATH, TIME-TRACK.

**1941** [R. Rocklynne] *Time Wants Skeleton* in *Astounding S-F* (June) 16/2: Gravitons are unable to remain free in three-dimensional space. They escape along the time line, into the past.

**1942** M. Jameson *Anachron, Inc.* in *Astounding S-F* (Oct.) 63/2: At the moment, I was considering a means to cross these lines at right angles, especially since there may be independent time lines parallel to us of which we do not dream.

**1965** H. B. Piper *Lord Kalvan of Otherwhen* in *Analog SF-Fact* (Nov.) 15/2: Well, that's why you're getting those five control-study time-lines.

**1974** T. N. Scortia *SF as Imaginary Experiment* in R. Bretnor *SF, Today & Tomorrow* 138: The hero repeatedly travels through time, altering the future and establishing alternate time lines, in the process having a love affair with his female counterpart and participating in a beach-side homosexual orgy with himself.

**1997** J. Barnes *Patton's Spaceship* 91: "Look, in your timeline, who won the Peloponnesian War, and how long did it last?" Anybody in any branch of history at least knows that.

**2005** L. M. Bujold *Interview with Lois McMaster Bujold* in *Postscripts* (Spring) 39: What's his world going to look like 10,000 years down his timeline, when this human speciation has exploded?

**time machine** *n.* a device which enables the user to travel into the past or future. Compare TIME HOPPER.

**1894** H. G. Wells (title) *National Observer* (Mar. 17) 472/2: The Time Machine
**1894** H. G. Wells *A.D. 12,203 National Observer* (Mar. 31) 499/2: He rose from his easy chair and took the little bronze lamp in his hand, when we reverted to the topic of his Time Machine.
**1943** [A. Boucher] *Elsewhen* in *Astounding S-F* (Jan.) 112: "My dear Agatha," Mr. Partridge announced at the breakfast table, "I have invented the world's first successful time machine."
**1978** I. Watson in C. Priest *Anticipations* 22: The assumption that a time machine should proceed to its destination *instanter* instead of at a snail's pace.
**1993** B. Shaw *Dimensions* (1994) 84–5: Time machines existed in his own age, but it was illegal to use them for forays into the past, so if he really was in Victorian England he was almost certainly stranded.
**2004** S. Utley *Paleozoic Palimpsest* in *Mag. of Fantasy & SF* (Oct./Nov.) 67: I knew I would do excellent and valuable work if I could just scrape together the price of a damn time-machine ticket!

**time paradox** *n.* an event or condition, caused by something a time traveler does while in the past, that is logically impossible based on the state of the universe in their original time. Also **time-travel paradox.** Compare TEMPORAL PARADOX.

[ **1939** *Thrilling Wonder Stories* (Aug.) 128/2 (heading): Paradox in Time ]
**1942** M. Jameson *Anachron, Inc.* in *Astounding SF* (Oct.) 63/1: No reconciliation of the supposed time paradox is necessary, [ ... ] for no paradox exists.

**1949** D. W. Meredith *Next Friday Morning* in *Astounding SF* (Feb.) 137/2: As for applause, I know I'm going to be too busy finding out things about all the time-travel paradoxes that have been plaguing the theory boys.
**1953** D. Knight *SF Adventures* (Dec.) 121: Cyril Kornbluth's *Dominoes* and John Wyndham's *The Chronoclasm* [ ... ] are beautiful jobs of writing, but their time-paradox plots strike me as stale.
**1989** C. S. Gardner *Back to Future II* 67: It creates a time paradox! [ ... ]. A person can't be both alive and dead at the same time! It violates the laws of physics
**2002** M. Dirda *Bound to Please* (2005) 260: Though Pratchett pays homage to many of the elements of time-paradox stories, at its heart *Night Watch* is less about the multiverse and metaphysical matters than about the nature of community.

**timepath** *n. Obs.* a TIME STREAM. Compare TIMELINE, TIME-TRACK.

**1934** M. Leinster *Sidewise in Time* in *Astounding Stories* (June) 22/1: We've traveled sidewise, in a sort of oscillation from one time path to another.
**1939** C. D. Simak *Cosmic Engineers* in *Astounding S-F* (Apr.) 125/1: So you came to me [ ... ]. You came trundling down a crazy timepath to seek me out. So that I could tell you the things you need to know.
**1956** P. K. Dick *Minority Report* in *Fantastic Universe* (Jan.) 19/1: This is explained by the theory of *multiple-futures*. If only one time-path existed, precognitive information would be of no importance, since no possibility would exist, in possessing this information of altering the future.

**timescape** *n.* time conceived of, or perceived as, possessing multiple dimensions.

**1976** S. Engdahl & M. Butler (title) in S. Engdahl *Anywhere, Anywhen* 225: Timescape
**1980** G. Benford *Timescape* 411: Time and space were themselves players, vast lands engulfing the figures, a weave of future and past. There was no riverrun of years. The abiding loops of causality ran both forward and back.

The timescape rippled with waves, roiled and flexed, a great beast in the dark sea.

**1988** R. A. Heinlein *Time Enough for Love* back cover: The capstone and crowning achievement of Heinlein's famous Future History, TIME ENOUGH FOR LOVE follows Lazarus Long through a vast and magnificent timescape of centuries and worlds.

**1991** L. Niven, J. Pournelle & M. Flynn *Fallen Angels* 271: He had the wide, smiling mouth and the perpetually shadowed jaw and the audacity to wander through the timescape of undreamed lands.

**2004** O. Sacks *Speed* in *New Yorker* (Aug. 23) 63/1: A baseball may be approaching at close to a hundred miles an hour, and yet, [ ... ] the ball may seem to be almost immobile in the air, its very seams strikingly visible, and the batter finds himself in a suddenly enlarged and spacious timescape, where he has all the time he needs to hit the ball.

**timeslip** *n.* a rift or flaw in the fabric of time that allows travel between two or more periods of time or timelines. Also as *v.* Hence **timeslipped,** *adj.*
[ **1932** C. A. Brandt *Amazing Stories* (Aug.) 471/1: Of course, this "slipping of the time" system is the easiest way out for the author.]
**1949** [P. Wentworth] *Brading Collection* (1950) 73: Stacy had heard it all before. It brought a horrid feeling that there had been a kind of time-slip—that they had been caught back again, she and Charles, to where they were three years ago.
**1954** [C. H. Liddell] *Where World Is Quiet* in *Fantastic Universe* (May) 152/1: This much I learned: the Other, like Lhar and her robot, had been cast adrift by a time-slip, and thus marooned here. There was no way for it to return to its normal Time-sector.
**1974** *Bookseller* (Aug. 10) 999/2 (ad): Four children, a disused railway line, a time-slip to an Edwardian scene.
**1993** *Locus* (June) 57/2: A timeslip away, in Paradys, most "normal" of the three realities, young Hilde experiences a disastrous doomed passion.
**1996** D. Pringle, et al. *Ultimate Ency. of SF* 33/1: Manly Wade Wellman took the "hunt-

the-celebrity" game a step further when the timeslipped hero of *Twice in Time* (1940) became somebody famous.
**2003** A. Duncan *Alternate History* in E. James & F. Mendlesohn *Cambridge Companion to SF* 214: Characters can purposefully or accidentally travel, or "timeslip," from one timeline to another, like a commuter switching trains.

**time storm** *n.* a disturbance in time which can bring people and things from different times into the same time.
**1942** A. E. van Vogt *Recruiting Station* in *Astounding S-F* (Mar.) 38/1: Your spaceship either by accident or design caught in the eddying current in the resulting time storm—
**1977** G. R. Dickson *Time Storm* 11: He gave us the closest thing to a normal meal that I'd eaten—or the girl had, undoubtedly—since the time storm first hit Earth. [ ... ] The continuity—or discontinuity—lines dividing the time areas usually blocked off radio.
**1994** A. McCaffrey *Girl Who Heard Dragons* (1995) 167: The time storm shifted and that resettlement was enough to rouse Chloe, attuned as she was to the distortion phenomenon.
**2005** P. Di Filippo *Washington Post Book World* (Feb. 20) 13/3: Twenty-two years after the events of *Hubcap King*, America is convulsing under "time storms" and waves of gravity reversal and suffering from a general malaise.

**time stream** *n.* the series of all events from past to future, especially when conceived of as one of many such series. Compare TIMELINE, TIMEPATH, TIME-TRACK.
**1931** C. D. Simak *World of Red Sun* in *Wonder Stories* (Dec.) 879/1: You're traveling in time, my lad [ ... ]. You aren't in space any more. You are in a time stream.
**1931** [J. Taine] *Time Stream* in *Wonder Stories* (Dec.) 837/2: The slightest excess of effort might upset the balance at any point of the time stream, sending them backward into the past or forward into the future independently of my will.
**1942** A. E. van Vogt *Search* in *Destination: Universe* (1953) 150: The Palace of Immortality was built in an eddy of time, the only known Reverse, or Immortality, Drift in the Earth Time Stream.

**1947** R. Dragonette *Eye to Future* in *Astounding SF* (Feb.) 62/2: It seems that something happened to one of their Chronoscopes—those little devices they scattered back in the time stream which would radiate visually, everything that happened within their range.

**1977** R. Scholes & E. S. Rabkin *SF: History, Sci., Vision* 178: Science fiction has provided us not only with visions of time travel and hence of alternate time streams, but of whole alternate universes.

**1990** *Thrust* (Winter) 23/3: "Remaking History" [...] packs much more thought into a similar wordage: having an alternate time-stream relying on a single change necessarily slants things toward the Great Men theory of history.

**2004** J. Fforde *Something Rotten* 30: Unlike my mother, whose husband still returned every so often from the timestream, I had a husband, Landen, who existed only in my dreams and recollections.

**time-track** *n.* a TIME STREAM. Compare TIMELINE, TIMEPATH.

**1942** M. Jameson *Anachron, Inc.* in *Astounding SF* (Oct.) 62/1: They said that the prognosis following a Confederate victory was not good and that we have to assume the moral responsibility for the sort of futures we set up in these branch time-tracks we generate, even if they have no effect on us.

**1947** [M. Leinster] *Time to Die* in *Astounding SF* (Jan.) 145/2: It's branching time tracks [...]. That's the idea! There can be more than one past, and more than one present, and more than one future.

**1963** M. Moorcock *Flux* in *New Worlds SF* (July) 113: We are searching now, trying to pick him up, but outside the Earth's time-track all is chaotic to our instruments—some defect in our understanding of time.

**1977** B. Aldiss *Future & Alternative Histories* in B. Ash *Visual Ency. of SF* 123/3: The *Gate of Time* (1966) sets his pivotal point for the divergence of history in prehistory, and in this timetrack the continent of the Americas does not rise above the surface of the oceans.

**1984** R. Silverberg *Needle in Timestack* in *Conglomeroid Cocktail Party* (1984) 267:

Whatever the symptom, it always meant the same thing: your time-track has been meddled with, your life has been retroactively transformed.

**time travel** *n.* the act of going back in time or skipping forward in time. Compare TIME-TRAVELING.

**1914** *Journal of Philosophy & Scientific Methods* (Sept. 10) 524: But now appears the hardship in time-travel. If real time is the course of natural events, then the tourist who traverses that time traverses history.

**1931** C. D. Simak *World of Red Sun* in *Wonder in Stories* (Dec.) 879/2: They had thought of only one thing, time travel.

**1954** S. Jackson *Bulletin* in *Mag. of Fantasy & SF* (Mar.) 46: Professor Browning's briefcase, set just inside the time travel element, returned, containing the following papers.

**1973** R. A. Heinlein *letter* (Sept. 16) in R. A. Heinlein & V. Heinlein *Grumbles from Grave* (1990) 98: It will be an episodic time-travel fantasy (with a new gimmick for time travel).

**1984** R. Silverberg *Needle in Timestack* in *Conglomeroid Cocktail Party* (1984) 275: Time-travel as tourism held no interest for him [...]. The purpose of Tommy Hambledon's time-travel, it seemed, was to edit his past to make his life more perfect.

**2001** *Locus* (June) 68/1: Minuscule changes caused by time travel to the past result in enormous differences in the present.

**time travel** *v.* to journey to another point in time.

**1941** [R. Rocklynne] *Time Wants Skeleton* in *Astounding S-F* (June) 38/1: One might time-travel and understand at last the unimaginable, utterly baffling process by which the solar system came into being.

**1969** *Punch* (Jan. 1) 35/2: This intelligent and ingenious story [...] has a fascinating climax where people from both sides time-travel back to see the Passion and Crucifixion.

**1986** B. W. Aldiss *Trillion Year Spree* 257: The hero lives in an America where the South won the Battle of Gettysburg; his interference in the battle to which he time-travels, causes the North to win. So matters turn out as we know them today.

**2003** *Cult Times* (May) 59/4: A sorcerer Time-travels to the home of a waitress and casts a spell that makes her age 20 years a day.

**time traveler, time traveller** *n.* someone who travels in time. Compare CHRONO-NAUT.

**1894** H. G. Wells *Sunset of Mankind* in *National Observer* (Apr. 28) 608/1: "There," said the Time Traveller, "I am unable to give you an explanation. All I know is that the climate was very much warmer than it is now, and that the sun seemed brighter."

**1930** *Wonder Stories* (Nov.) 489: We have purposely allowed our time travellers to become known to the people of the eras that they visit, for in this way the great drama of the story becomes apparent.

**1961** F. Leiber *Big Time* (1969) 7: This war is the Change War, a war of time travelers [ ... ]. Our Soldiers fight by going back to change the past, or even ahead to change the future, in ways to help our side win the final victory a billion or more years from now.

**1974** P. K. Dick *Little Something for Us Tempunauts* in *We Can Remember It for You Wholesale* (1994) 336: What in your mind is the greatest terror facing a time traveler? That there will be an implosion due to coincidence on reentry?

**1992** *Locus* (Aug.) 11/3: "The Synthetic Barbarian" concerns time traveler Reggie River's "strangest client," a man determined to go back and hunt dinosaurs.

**2001** *Dreamwatch* (Oct.) 85/1: As any self-respecting time traveller will confirm, going backwards in time to change history is a dodgy business, fraught with the possibility of temporal anomalies, rips in the space/time continuum, etc.

**time-traveling, time-travelling** *n.* TIME TRAVEL.

**1894** H. G. Wells (title) *National Observer* (Mar. 17) 446/2: Time Travelling: Possibility or Paradox

**1895** H. G. Wells *Time Machine* 28: I am afraid I cannot convey the peculiar sensations

of time travelling. They are excessively un-pleasant.

**1933** *Astounding Stories of Super-sci.* (Jan.) 422/1: In the current issue, Mr. Raymond declares time-travelling to be impossible.

**1940** *Thrilling Wonder Stories* (Mar.) 117/2: Who knows—perhaps time traveling is possible!

**1981** P. Craig & M. Cadogan *Lady Investigates* 152: In children's fiction in general [ ... ] magic and time-travelling were acceptable forms of the supernatural; ghosts were not.

**time-traveling, time-travelling** *adj.* able to time travel or for the purpose of traveling in time.

**1937** E. F. Russell & L. T. Johnson in *Astounding Stories* (July) 143/1: "How did you know that I am a time traveler?" I demanded. "Because your time-traveling device materialized out of thin air before the eyes of half a hundred citizens."

**1970** A. Budrys *Benchmarks* (1985) 266: It follows that this is probably a general condition of time-travelling mankind.

**1991** *SF Chronicle* (May) 34/2: This is the third in a series that involves a time travelling alien.

**2004** J. Fforde *Something Rotten* 27: My father was a sort of time-traveling knight errant.

**time-travel paradox** *n.* see TIME PARADOX.

**time viewer** *n.* a CHRONOSCOPE. Also **temporal viewer.** Hence TIME-VIEWING, *adj.*

**1940** J. W. Campbell in *Astounding S-F* (Aug.) 6: Wanted: A Chronoscope. Such a time viewer would be darned handy in many ways, but at the moment [ ... ] one would be useful in devising this page.

**1952** C. D. Simak *Fence* in *Space SF* (Sept.) 37/1: Trace it back, you know, with a temporal viewer. Hour to hour, day to day. Record in detail, and with appropriate comment and deduction, everything that transpired upon the acre.

**1956** I. Asimov *Dead Past* in S. Schmidt *Fifty Years of Best SF from Analog* (1980) 187: I have been trying to obtain permission to do some time viewing—chronoscopy, that is—in connection with my researches on ancient Carthage.

**1956** Asimov, *Dead Past* 211: Do you have a time viewer here, Dr. Foster?

**1957** [R. Burke] *Monday Immortal* in *Fantastic* (May) 49/2: The future was unalterable—Hollister had proved that. No matter what steps you took to change it, it always snapped back to the form the time-viewer revealed, one way or another.

**2001** G. Dozois in M. Swanwick *Being Gardner Dozois* 140: *I* came up with the idea, although of course it's just a variant on the long sub-genre of time-viewer stories.

**time warp** *n.* a distortion in the space-time continuum which allows travel from one time to another, or inside of which time moves at a different speed. Also *fig.* and as *v.*

**1938** R. M. Williams *Flight of Dawn Star* in *Astounding S-F* (Mar.) 36/1: That warp [...]—was a time warp and not a space warp. You went along with the Sun as it moved, and when you came through again, the stars had shifted until you couldn't recognize them. You thought you had been shifted in space.

**1939** C. D. Simak *Cosmic Engineers* in *Astounding S-F* (Apr.) 134/2: They will use a time warp [...]. They will bud out from their universe, but in doing so they will distort the time factor in the walls of their hyperspace.

**1968** D. C. Fontana *Tomorrow Is Yesterday* in J. Blish *Star Trek 2* 31: A time warp landed us back here.

**1971** *Guardian (London)* (June 17) 10/5: The time warp effect was [...] intensified by having David Frost—essentially an early sixties figure.

**1976** N. Thornburg *Cutter & Bone* 13: A sensation that always made him feel as if he had been time-warped back into wet diapers.

**1983** *Listener* (Nov. 3) 32/3: Molly Kean's images are of psychic rather than physical decay, of families able to live beyond their means because they are trapped in a peculiar time-warp.

**1987** N. Spinrad *Little Heroes* (1989) 169: There was [...] God help him, a *sexiness*, that made him wish for a time warp, for certainly there was nothing he would have liked more than to embark upon this adventure with the hot young girl this old lady had so manifestly once been.

**1995** *Parade Mag.* in *Syracuse (New York) Herald-Journal* (July 2) 8: Visiting Cuba is like entering a time warp. It is a country that has been shut down to Americans for more than 30 years, a country where the latest American cars stop at 1959.

**tin can** *n.* a spaceship; (occasionally) a SPACE STATION. Compare BOAT, CRAFT, CRUISER, SHIP, SPACE CAN, SPACE CAR, SPACECRAFT, SPACE CRUISER, SPACE FLYER, SPACER 2, SPACE VEHICLE, SPACE VESSEL, VESSEL.

**1940** [L. Gregor] *Flight to Galileo* in *Astonishing Stories* (Oct.) 101/2: You've asked me that a dozen times, and I still say no. You would make a fine picture going out there in your little tincan, waiting until the attackers came.

**1958** H. Ellison *No Planet Is Safe* in *Super-Sci. Fiction* (June) 110/2: We've been tooling this tin-can through space for five years, and we thank God nightly we're still alive to report back.

**1969** [D. Bowie] *Space Oddity* in *Best of David Bowie 1969/1974* (1999) 18: For here am I floating round my tin can, far above the moon.

**1979** G. Benford *Dark Sanctuary* in *Matter's End* (1996) 147: That happens every time the cylinder boys build a new tin can and need to form an ecosystem inside.

**1987** M. Bishop *Philip K. Dick Is Dead, Alas* (1994) 269: It was hard to deride him as "King Richard" when you were floating along-side him in a fragile tin can one hundred thousand miles from Earth.

**torch** *n.* the fusion reaction that powers a torch drive; the hot material ejected from a reaction drive.

**1953** R. A. Heinlein *Sky Lift* in *Imagination* (Nov.) 14/2: The conversion chamber of a torch was a tiny sun; particles expelled from it approached the speed of light.

**1974** N. Spinrad *Riding Torch* in R. Silverberg *Threads of Time* 176: The first scoutship is launched by the Trek. Crewed by five volunteers, it is powered by a full-sized fusion torch though its mass is only one tenth that of a conventional torchship.

**1979** G. Benford *Dark Sanctuary* in *Matter's End* (1996) 155: The Belt is huge, but the high-burn torch I'd turned loose back there was orders of magnitude more luminous than an ordinary fusion jet.
**1989** W. J. Williams *Angel Station* (1991) 100: Ubu looked at the radar and transponder displays. No ships nearby, no one within range to be cooked by the particle torch. "Ten seconds to torch ignition. Mark."
**1997** S. Zettel *Fool's War* 48: The ship read her fingerprints and sent its signal down to the engine compartment. "Torch lit," she reported, just before a low rumble that echoed all the way up the drop shaft confirmed her call.

**torch** *v.* to fly or accelerate a spaceship, especially by means of a torch drive.
**1956** R. A. Heinlein *Double Star* in *Astounding SF* (Feb.) 29/2: About seventeen seconds and a gnat's wink after we make contact the *Go For Broke* will torch for Mars.
**1974** N. Spinrad *Riding Torch* in R. Silverberg *Threads of Time* 176: D'mahl was a detached observer far out in space watching the scoutship torch ahead of the Trek.
**2000** M. Flynn *Lodestar* (2001) 173: I'll take the parasols with me when I torch for the Moon and drop them off along the way.
**2002** M. J. Harrison *Light* 154 (2004): The *White Cat* torched out in a low fast arc over the South Pole, transmitting ghost signatures, firing off decoys and particle-dogs.

**torch drive** *n.* a fusion-powered, slower-than-light space drive.
**1976** L. Niven *Words in SF* in R. Bretnor *Craft of SF* 182: Torch drive, duplicator, flying belt. Dolphins' hands and telepathically operated tools on tractor treads.
**1989** P. Anderson *Boat of Million Years* (2004) 388: By this time, low boost under the torch drive had built up a considerable speed.
**1999** D. M. Weber *Apocalypse Troll* 93: There they were, ready to smash a bunch of people they expected to find fooling around with atmospheric aircraft, and instead they were being intercepted by ships using a nuclear-powered torch drive!

**torchship** *n.* a spaceship propelled by a torch drive.
**1953** R. A. Heinlein *Sky Lift* in *Imagination* (Nov.) 14/2: Older pilots thought of interplanetary trips with a rocketman's bias, in terms of years—trips that a torchship with steady acceleration covered in days.
**1974**: see quote in TORCH, *n.*
**1986** G. Benford & D. Brin *Heart of Comet* 20: When they arrived the first task awaiting the torch ship's crew was to recover the huge cylinders containing the deep-sleeping majority of the mission crew.
**1990** J. Pournelle & S. M. Stirling *Asteroid Queen* in L. Niven, et al. *Man-Kzin Wars III* 41: The little torchship had not been doing well of late, and the kzin-nominated purchasing combines on the asteroid base of Tiamat had been squeezing harder and harder.
**1992** R. Reed *Remarkables* 5: *Pitcairn* was the last and largest torchship built by Earth, and it's the most famous of the bunch.

**tractor** *n.* a TRACTOR BEAM. Also as *v.*
**1931** E. E. Smith *Spacehounds of IPC* in *Amazing Stories* (July) 308/1: Many of the smaller portions of the wreck, not directly held by the tractors, began to separate from the main mass. As each bit left its place another beam leaped out.
**1949** J. H. Schmitz *Agent of Vega* in *Astounding SF* (July) 34/2: When he does, spear him with a tractor and tell him he's being held for investigation, because there's a General Emergency out!
**1956**: see quote in PRESSOR BEAM.
**1973** G. R. R. Martin *Night Shift* in *Amazing Stories* (Jan.) 46/1: Several light tractor beams *did not* have the power of one heavy-duty one [...]. To be at all effective, paired tractors had to lift at the same time and yank in the same direction.
**1986** L. M. Bujold *Shards of Honor* (1988) 269: The doctor attached a 'scope to his shoulder, and went fishing for the short circuit with a delicate surgical hand tractor.
**1999** C. Pellegrino & G. Zebrowski *Dyson Sphere* 195: Captain Dalen opened the aft hatch and tractored onto the roof of the *Darwin*.

**tractor beam** *n.* a beam of force that pulls matter toward the beam's source, or that is capable of controlling the motion of matter. Also **tractor field, tractor ray,** etc. Compare TRACTOR.

**1931** E. E. Smith *Spacehounds of IPC* in *Amazing Stories* (Sept.) 549/1: Brandon swung mighty tractor beams upon the severed halves of the Jovian vessel, then extended a couple of smaller rays to meet the two little figures racing across the smooth green meadow toward the *Sirius*.

**1939** B. Tucker *Le Zombie* (Sept. 2) 6/2: Search[-]lights find ship, presumably turn to tractor rays, and low [sic] ship to ground.

**1965** R. Zelazny *Furies* in *Amazing Stories* (June) 16/2: As the tractor beams had seized it, as the vibrations penetrated its ebony hull and tore at his flesh, Corgo had called [...] and died just as the words and the tears began.

**1977** A. D. Foster *End of Matter* 210: Gradually Flinx activated the posigravity tractor beams, used for manipulating large cargo.

**1988** *Post-Standard (Syracuse, New York)* (Sept. 8) D3/1: A laser tractor beam is proving to be the first tool that can trap and move structures within a cell without damaging the cell itself.

**1990** A. McCaffrey & E. Moon *Sassinak* (1991) 179: She nodded to Arly, who poured all remaining power to their tractor field.

**1998** W. Shatner *Spectre* 42: Mr. Karo, attach tractor beams to the *Voyager*.

**transdimensional** *adj.* crossing between two or more dimensions.

**1931** C. A. Smith *City of Singing Flame* in *Wonder Stories* (July) 205/2: I had read a number of trans-dimensional stories—in fact, I had written one or two myself; and I had often pondered the possibility of other worlds or material planes which may co-exist in the same space with ours, invisible and impalpable to human senses.

**1990** B. Lumley *House of Doors* 409: *All right,* thought Gill, superimposing his will on the trans-dimensional multinode which was the screen, *now let's see what I can locate here.*

**1995** J. VanderMeer *Pulphouse #18—Jesus Issue* in *Why Should I Cut Your Throat?* (2004) 128: The Reincarnation Board, a transdimensional, multi-world tribunal that will decide if Jesus, who has been judged to have committed hate crimes, will be given a new body.

**2003** C. Doctorow *Nimby & Dimension Hoppers* in D. G. Hartwell & K. Cramer *Year's Best SF 9* (2004) 272: Transdimensional crime fighters hew to no human schedule.

**transgalactic** *adj.* across, crossing, or extending across a galaxy. Compare GALAXY-WIDE, PANGALACTIC.

**1930** W. O. Stapledon *Last & First Men* (1931) 365: Only within the last few years have we succeeded in designing an artificial human dust capable of being carried forward on the sun's radiation, hardy enough to endure the conditions of a trans[-]galactic voyage of many millions of years.

**1953** T. Sturgeon *World Well Lost* in *Saucer of Loneliness* (2000) 63: Of these hindrances, all could be understood but one, and that one was Dirbanu, a transgalactic planet which shrouded itself in impenetrable fields of force whenever an Earth ship approached.

**1957** H. Ellison *Deeper than Darkness* in *Infinity SF* (Apr.) 7/2: While the inverspace ships plied between worlds, while Earth fought its trans[-]galactic wars, in a rural section of the American continents, a strange thing was happening.

**1970** R. Silverberg *Tower of Glass* (2000) 104: They couldn't have reached a technological level that would allow them to send transgalactic messages at all unless they were able to retain the achievements of earlier generations.

**1981** W. Gibson *Hinterlands* in *Burning Chrome* (2003) 65: A constant stream of raw data goes pulsing home to Earth, a flood of rumors, whispers, hints of transgalactic traffic.

**2002** I. Csicsery-Ronay, Jr. *Dis-Imagined Communities* in V. Hollinger & J. Gordon *Edging into Future* 224: Simmons consciously models his transgalactic polity as a dispersed replay of earthly human history. The galaxy is replete with colonies and protectorates linked by several kinds of matter-transmission technology.

**transhuman** *n.* someone whose body or mind has been transformed (e.g. by cyborgization or genetic engineering) so greatly that they are no longer considered human, especially one who now possesses greater abilities than normal humans. Compare CYBORG, PARAHUMAN, POSTHUMAN.

**1978** R. C. W. Ettinger *Intro.: Transhuman Condition* in J. Dann *Immortal* vii: Now that some of us are beginning to take seriously and personally the prospect of life extension and radical improvement of people, we need more. If we are to become practicing immortals and nascent transhumans, we need at least rough outlines and a few details.

**1988** V. Vinge *Blabber* in *Threats ... & Other Promises* 253: I suppose she could be an ego frag. But most of those are brain-damaged transhumans, or obvious constructs.

**1990** E. Regis *Great Mambo Chicken & Transhuman Condition* (1991) 276: People were proposing schemes for [ ... ] *becoming supermen*, making themselves into *transhumans*, and God only knew what other insane blasphemies.

**1999** R. Rucker *Saucer Wisdom* 241: The masters of this saucer rotate themselves into Frank's field of view without even being asked. To Frank's great surprise, they're humans, or rather transhumans: Our descendants from the fifth millennium.

**2001** M. Pesce *True Magic* in J. Frenkel *True Names & Opening of Cyberspace Frontier* 225: We understand nothing of their motivations, only that they serve as the midwives who attend the birth of a trans-human who could—with a wish—destroy the world.

**transhuman** *adj.* of, relating to, or characterized by transhumans. Hence **transhumankind,** *n.*

**1952** *Oakland (Cal.) Tribune* (Sept. 21) 2C/2: Men expand the frontiers of empire as far as the Milky Way, and encounter a hitherto unknown type of enemy in the form of a trans-human mutant.

**1967** R. Silverberg *Those Who Watch* 81: In this time of crisis and doubt, Frederic Storm comes forward to offer himself as a bridge between humankind and transhumankind.

**1979** G. Rix *SF Rev.* (Jan.–Feb.) 50/2: They will resemble their parents except in some not so subtle respects. They will be hermaphrodites and lack human hormonal responses. They will be logical, not emotional. They will move differently; they will think differently. They will be transhuman.

**1990** E. Regis *Great Mambo Chicken & Transhuman Condition* (1991) 147: Time for a major overhaul, one that would take the human animal to a new level, to a more fitting, *transhuman* condition.

**1999**: see quote in SENTIENCE *n.* 1.

**2003** D. Broderick *New Wave & Backwash* in E. James & F. Mendlesohn *Cambridge Companion to SF* 60: John Varley introduced an increasingly detailed and delicious transhuman solar system.

**transhumanity** *n.* the condition of being transhuman; transhumans collectively. Compare POSTHUMANITY.

**1978** R. C. W. Ettinger *Intro.: Transhuman Condition* in J. Dann *Immortal* ix: Moving right along, let's add transhumanity to immortality; now we are in the big time. But it will tax any writer's skill just to convince a human that the way from here is up.

**1991** G. Zebrowski *Stranger Suns* 293: He imagined his colony of ever-changing trans-humanity, each generation reaching deeper into the beast to clear away evolution's stubborn residues.

**1994** I. McDonald *Necroville* (1995) 165: The Isolationists pressed for the immediate expansion of the extant Clades across all the solar system, the establishment and recognition of a dead transhumanity that had severed all ties with planet-bound humanity.

**1995** G. Egan *Wang's Carpets* in G. Bear & M. H. Greenberg *New Legends* (1996) 399: You don't need me to safeguard the future of Carter-Zimmerman on your behalf. Or the future of transhumanity. You can do it in person.

**Trekker** *n.* a fan of the television series *Star Trek* and its sequels and spin-offs. Compare TREKKIE. [See note in TREKKIE.]

**1970** *Deck* (May) 2: I start acting like a bubble-headed trekkie (rather than a sober, dignified—albeit enthusiastic—trekk*er*).

**1978** F. Lynch *Star Trek & Me* in W. Irwin & G. B. Love *Best of Trek* 54: I find that I can label fans only "good-mannered" or "bad-mannered"; the terms Trekker, Trekkie, etc. turn me off.

**1986** D. Carey *Author's Note* in *Dreadnought* 5: As a first-generation Trekker, I am one of the lucky ones who discovered Trek early on.

**1994** *SF Age* (July) 20/3: The biggest concern for loyal Trekkers everywhere is just how both old and new cast members will fare.

**2000** *Interzone* (July) 44/3: And *Galaxy Quest* is nothing if not conscious of its responsibility as a contemporary bigscreen version of what two Generations of Trekkers have always longed for.

**Trekkie** *n.* a fan of the television series *Star Trek* and its sequels and spin-offs, especially an immature or stereotyped fan. Compare TREKKER. [Within *Star Trek* fandom, the use of *Trekkie* is usually depreciatory, with *Trekker* generally being preferred; in non-fan use, *Trekkie* is the more common term.]

**1970**: see quote in TREKKER.

**1972** W. Marsano *TV Guide* (Mar. 25–31) 17/1: The convention started early Friday morning, Jan. 21, when a mob of *Star Trek* fans (known as Trekkies) showed up several hours early, just to be sure they didn't miss anything.

**1973** D. Gerrold *Trouble With Tribbles* 3: They're still writing their *Star Trek* stories even though there's no longer a *Star Trek* to sell them to. But that doesn't stop them, not at all. To a real Trekkie, *Star Trek* goes on forever.

**1978** *Sunday Sun (Brisbane)* (Sept. 17) 45/3: Fans—called Trekkies—still number in their tens of thousands.

**1992** H. Jenkins *Textual Poachers* 21: Fans prefer to describe themselves as "Trekkers" rather than "Trekkies" (a term which has increasingly come to refer only to the media constructed stereotype).

**2004** *San Francisco Chronicle* E10/4 (Aug. 31): He [i.e., James Doohan] blew kisses to a crowd of Trekkie faithful gathered at Sunday's finale of a two-day tribute held at the Renaissance Hollywood Hotel.

**tri-D, tri-dee, tri-di** *n.* THREE-V; occasionally, a three-dimensional image. Compare HOLOVISION, THREE-D, TRIDEO, TRI-DIM, TRI-V, TRI-VID.

**1950** J. Blish *Okie* in *Astounding SF* (Aug.) 90/2: In the meantime, you'll have to see that scientist again. Get a picture of him somewhere, a tri-di if they have them here.

**1954** F. Pohl *Midas Plague* in *Galaxy SF* (Apr.) 9/2: The tri-D was beginning a comedy show; he got up to turn it off, snapping on the tape-player.

**1959** C. Oliver *Transfusion* in S. Schmidt *Fifty Years of Best SF from Analog* (1980) 256: He read the books, saw the tri-di plays.

**1969** [J. Tiptree, Jr.] *Parimutuel Planet* in *Galaxy Mag.* (Jan.) 64/1: He pointed to the tridi where a large ostrich-like fowl was brandishing his pinions and lofting himself easily as he pranced about.

**1970** A. Norton *Dread Companion* (1984) 10: Now—I want a run-through of the Ruhkarv report in comparison with the tridees from Xcothal.

**1973** L. Niven *Flash Crowd* in R. Silverberg *Three Trips in Time & Space* 9: The square brown face looking out of the tridee screen was known throughout the English-speaking world.

**1984** A. D. Foster *Voyage to City of Dead* (1986) 19: What do you suggest I do? Squat here and watch thranx shadowplays on the tridee?

**1990** A. McCaffrey *Pegasus in Flight* (1992) 158: His histrionics defuse a lot of pent-up garbage in a catharsis not generated by passive watching of the Tri-D fare.

**tri-D, tri-di** *adj.* three-dimensional.

**1947** [L. Padgett] *Tomorrow & Tomorrow Astounding SF* (Jan.) 7/2: He opened his eyes slowly, saw the tri-di chessboards in front of him, red and black, and let his lids drop against the light.

**1955** F. Pohl *Galaxy SF* (Apr.) 77/2: Marin was already setting up his co-ordinates [...]. "I have the time now [...]. But the tri-di readings are hard."

**1981** J. May *Many-Colored Land* 78: The screen went from black to living Tri-D color in an orbiter's view of Pliocene Earth, six million years [ ... ] backward in time.

**trideo** *n.* [*tri-* + v*ideo*] THREE-V; also, a show broadcast using such a technology or displayed on such a device. Compare HOLOVISION, THREE-D, TRI-D, TRI-DIM, TRI-V, TRI-VID.

**1953** T. Sturgeon *Mr. Costello, Hero* in *Galaxy SF* (Dec.) 69/2: Actually, I suppose there's really only one—though, of course, there'll be someone else in the studio at the time [ ... ]. But on trideo it looks like four Lucilles, all speaking at once, sort of in chorus.

**1967** M. K. Joseph *Hole in Zero* (1968) 52: Mr. Ironbender had the bland reliable manner appropriate to a conveyancer in the Debatable Lands Development Corporation; but his secret drama was the life of the old-time dragsters in the trideo shows.

**1967** K. Laumer *Star Treasure* (1971) 75: I was allowed to watch trideo, except that certain channels were blacked out from time to time; news broadcasts, I deduced.

**1997** L. E. Modesitt, Jr. *Ecolitan Enigma* 71: Living happily ever after doesn't work as easily as the trideos say.

**tri-di** *n., adj.* see TRI-D.

**tri-dim** *n.* a device that is capable of displaying three-dimensional images; also, a show that is broadcast to such a device or a three-dimensional image. Compare HOLOVISION, THREE-D, THREE-V, TRI-D, TRIDEO, TRI-DIM, TRI-V, TRI-VID.

**1951** R. A. Heinlein *Puppet Masters* 193: The double snout of a tri-dim camera poked out of the overhead.

**1958** R. Silverberg *Four* in *World of Thousand Colors* (1984) 151: Mary had seen the tri-dims projected on the arching screens in General Hall.

**1967** R. Silverberg *Hawksbill Station* in *Galaxy Mag.* (Aug.) 23/2: Fine wine, yes; a tridim of a daughter who would never be embraced again, no.

**1967** W. F. Nolan *Logan's Run* (1995) 22: Logan automatically punched a wall stud and the president was sucked, hissing, back into the Tri-Dim.

**triffid** *n.* in John Wyndham's novel *The Day of the Triffids* and subsequent film adaptation, one of a race of malevolent alien plants which threaten to overrun the world; used mainly *fig.* or allusively. Hence **triffidian,** *adj.,* **triffid-like,** *adj.*

**1951** [J. Wyndham] *Day of Triffids* 46: A catchy little name originating in some newspaper office as a handy label for an oddity—but destined one day to be associated with pain, fear and misery—*triffid.*

**1951** Wyndham, *Day of Triffids* 49: Their characteristic of suddenly losing their immobility and rattling a rapid tattoo against the main stem was some strange form of triffidian amatory exuberance.

**1965** *New Scientist* (Mar. 11) 619/3: Ninety per cent of British households have television [ ... ] and neither bindweed, triffids, nor dragon's teeth grew more rapidly than the angular aerial.

**1971** *Daily Telegraph (London)* (Jan. 16) 10/6: This cactus had run wild and, Triffid-like, had taken over thousands of square miles of good agricultural land.

**1972** S. Hughes in M. Bygrave, et al. *Time Out's Book of London* 90/1: The south is sprouting with tall dark buildings like triffids.

**1991** *Intelligencer (Doylestown, Pa.)* (Oct. 18) A12/3: Although public fears can be characterized as "the triffid syndrome" [ ... ], Crawley nevertheless does acknowledge that "the environmental consequences are potentially very great if anything did go wrong with transgenic plants."

**tri-v, trivee, trivvy** *n.* THREE-V. Compare HOLOVISION, THREE-D, TRI-D, TRIDEO, TRI-DIM, TRI-VID.

**1954** T. Cogswell *Invasion Report* in *Galaxy SF* (Aug.) 89/2: Bill faced the tri-V scanner and held up his hand for attention.

**1964** P. Anderson in *Galaxy Mag.* (June) 23/2: One hears so many arguments and, oh, there are documentaries on TriV and so forth, but all second hand.

**1966** K. Roberts *Synth* in J. Carnell *New Writings in SF 8* 139: The case of Davenport v. Davenport would have raised enough dust to satisfy even the trivvy magnates without the astounding disclosure by Mrs. Ira Amanda Davenport of the nature of the offence allegedly committed by her husband.

**1973** R. E. Peck *Final Solution* 103: Newshawks on all three U-net trivee stations spoke of little else.

**1974** L. Niven & J. Pournelle *Mote in God's Eye* 448: They have given us a tri-v [ ... ] and it is obviously what the humans watch. There were spokesmen for many Masters. You saw.

**1999** A. Thomson *Through Alien Eyes* (2000) 100: Moki and Ukatonen [ ... ] spent most of the day watching the Tri-V or listening to Analin and Eerin talk about them.

**tri-vid** *n.* THREE-V; also, a show broadcast using such a technology or displayed on such a device. Compare HOLOVISION, THREE-D, TRI-D, TRIDEO, TRI-DIM, TRI-V.

**1955** W. Sheldon *Your Time Is Up* in *If* (June) 44/1: But this talk about—about *dial* phones. About *armies*. Why, you sound like one of those historical tri-vids about the twentieth century!

**1964** W. R. Burkett *Sleeping Planet* in *Analog SF-Sci. Fact* (Aug.) 47/2: Shimmering in the thick atmosphere like figures on a faulty tri-vid receiver, they drifted into the charred area.

**1990** J. L. Nye *Volunteers* in B. Fawcett *Far Stars War* 123: Now what are we supposed to do? [ ... ]. I've never been on trivid before.

**1992** *SF Age* (Nov.) 30/1: They [ ... ] took pictures of themselves standing next to it and left already bored and looking forward to the programs on tri-vid that night.

**trufan** *n.* ['tru,fæn] (pl. **-fans, -fen**) [*true* + *fan*] someone who is very active in, and devoted to, science fiction fandom. Hence **trufandom,** *n.,* **trufannishness,** *n.*

**1954** W. Willis & B. Shaw *Enchanted Duplicator* 26: On either side of him were numerous parks and gardens, great and small, and of varying types of beauty, and in them walked shining, godlike figures whom he knew to be Trufans.

**1959** R. H. Eney *Fancyclopedia II* 164: In connection with TAFF a furor arose over the definition of a Trufan, the active faction insisting that a trufan exhibit his quality by some sort of fanac—crifanac for choice—while others maintained that nomination to or interest in so stefnistic an enterprise as TAFF was sufficient to prove fannishness.

**1961** J. Koning *Withdrawal* in *S-F Five-Yearly* (Nov.) 25: There were still the neofans Craig had missed, but they didn't have any BNFs to lead them to "trufannishness."

**1972** R. Nelson *Intro. to Time Travel for Pedestrians* in H. Ellison *Again, Dangerous Visions* 139: You and I were there, and George Young and all those other truefans, and we were all underage and we were all (except you, who don't drink) drinking beer and playing the electric bowling machine.

**1977** S. Wood *Algol* (Spring) 43/1: Trufen reprint Walt Willis columns.

**1993** *Will some REAL fans please move to Chicago?* (Usenet: alt.fandom.cons) (Nov. 6): I'll agree that trufandom isn't pushed much at cons, but whenever I get to a fannish party, SF or fanzines is not as big a topic as other things.

**1997** J. Speer *Phanerofannish Eon* in *Fancestral Voices* (2004) 79: One probably should not say there was a trufan, even *in posse*, until the stffield had been defined by *Amazing Stories*.

**Tuckerism** *n.* [after Wilson "Bob" Tucker who was well-known for the practice] using the names of one's friends or acquaintances as names for fictional characters in a book or story; an instance of this.

**1959** R. H. Eney *Fancyclopedia II* 164: Tuckerism is the practice among professional authors of using their friends' names for characters in stories they are writing, Bob being a leading exponent of this sort of thing.

**1987** N. Spinrad *Isaac Asimov's SF Mag.* (Oct.) 183/2: It was as innocent as the time-honored employment of "Tuckerisms," the injection of names or personas of real SF figures into fictional futures.

**1998** *THE* *Introduce-Yourself Thread* (Usenet: rec.arts.comics.marvel.xbooks) (Sept. 24): The following ramcx'ers, to the best of my recollection, appear in "Thunderbolts: Iconoclasm" [...]. Most of this Tuckerism gone wrong happens in the second half of the story.

**1997** *L. Sprague de Camp* (Usenet: rec.arts.sf.written) (Jan. 28): "Doctor Lyon Sprague decamped with alacrity." Two brownie points for idenitifying this—once famous—tuckerism.

**Tuckerize** *v.* to insert the names of friends or acquaintances into one's fiction. Hence **Tuckerization,** *n.*

**1975** E. Weinstein *Fillostrated Fan Dictionary* 132: Tuckerize [...]: To place the names of ones [sic] friends into a story one is writing.

**1994** *Writing, Publishing & Law* (Usenet: misc.writing) (Apr. 25): I still Tuckerize friends, but not in negative ways, and only friends I feel comfortable won't take it wrong. Anyone else gets heavily modified to avoid potential problems.

**1996** *YAY SIDNE! (Spoiler for L\* #38)* (Usenet: rec.arts.comics.dc.lsh) (May 14): Congratulations to our dear sweet Ms. Ward on her "Tuckerization" in LEGIONNAIRES #38, wherein we discover that Imra's mom's name is "Sydne!"

**2002** P. Di Filippo *Vade Mecum for Third Millennium* in *Bulletin of SF & Fantasy Writers of America* (Summer) 58/3: In these pages you'll learn all the secret tricks to grab editorial attention. Greeting cards on their birthdays; [...] the blatant Tuckerizing of mutual friends.

**Twonk's disease** *n.* a fanciful disease said to afflict science fiction fans; descriptions of symptoms vary, but frequently include the falling of the armpits. *Joc.*

**1944** J. B. Speer *Fancyclopedia* 89/2: Twonk's disease - [...] The ultimate in afflictions of any nature.

**1949** T. Sturgeon *Martian & Moron* in *Perfect Host* (1998) 146: He had Mother call up the office and say he had Twonk's disease, a falling of the armpits.

**1969** H. Warner, Jr. *All Our Yesterdays* 42: Twonk's disease is believed to be spread by germs that live on mimeograph stencils. It is much worse than all other diseases, in that it has no symptoms whatsoever, making it impossible to know when an individual is suffering from it. Fortunately, it is never fatal.

**1975** E. Weinstein *Fillostrated Fan Dictionary* 133: Twonk's disease [...]: The most tragic of all fannish ailments. Not only does it involve the (shudder) falling of the armpits, but it is ALWAYS fatal.

# u

**uchronia** *n.* [< Fr. *uchronie,* < Gk. *ou-,* "not" + Gk. *chronos,* "time"] a work of alternate history. Hence **uchronian,** *adj.,* **uchronic,** *adj.*

[**1876** C. Renouvier (title): Uchronie (L'Utopie dans l'histoire): Esquisse historique apocryphe du développement de la civilisation européenne tel qu'il n'a pas été, tel qu'il aurait pu être]

[**1876** Renouvier, Uchronie i: Le manuscrit latin du curieux ouvrage que nous donnons au public porte ce simple titre: UCHRONIA.]

**1979** F. E. Manuel & F. P. Manuel *Utopian Thought in Western World* 4: The term uchronia, no time, was invented in the late nineteenth century by the French philosopher Charles Renouvier to characterize a fictitious history of the past written on the supposition that a critical turning point had had a different outcome.

**1987** P. K. Alkon *Origins of Futuristic Fiction* 116: This is a complex uchronic history of early Renaissance based upon the premise that Marcus Aurelius had been succeeded as emperor by Avidius Cassius instead of by Commodus.

**1987** J. J. Pierce *Great Themes of SF* 183: Uchronian sf thus developed independently of the tradition of time travel and time paradoxes in Anglo-American sf.

**2002** P. Di Filippo in *Asimov's SF* (Dec.) 134/2: The tale begins as a straightforward uchronia, and there's much pleasure to be had in MacLeod's evocation of the jarring yet mundane touchstones of his alternate history.

**2006** N. Gevers *Locus* (Mar.) 12/1: The continuity of historical fundamentals is emphasized too, and the assumptions of the uchronia are thus interrogated quite rigorously.

**ultradrive** *n.* a space drive that enables spaceships to travel faster than the speed of light. Compare HYPERDRIVE, OVERDRIVE.

**1951** P. Anderson *Tiger by Tail* in *Planet Stories* (Jan.) 38/1: Captain Flandry opened his eyes and saw a metal ceiling. Simultaneously, he grew aware of the thrum and quiver which meant he was aboard a spaceship running on ultra[-]drive.

**1954**: see quote in LIGHT 1.

**1992** V. Vinge *Fire upon Deep* (1993) 62: The wreck had no ultradrive capability; it was truly a Slow Zone design.

**2001** [M. Maloney] *Planet America* 203: He kicked into ultradrive again and was soon passing close to the next moon in line, several million miles away.

**ultraphone** *n.* a device that enables faster-than-light communication. Compare ANSIBLE, ULTRAWAVE.

**1928** P. F. Nowlan *Armageddon—2419 A.D.* in *Amazing Stories* (Aug.) 433/1: In addition we each received an ultrophone, and a light intertron blanket rolled into a cylinder about six inches long by two or three in diameter.

**1934** E. E. Smith *Skylark of Valeron* in *Astounding Stories* (Dec.) 148/1: Radnor's reply to Siblin's message was unheard, for his ultraphones were not upon his person, but were lying disregarded in a corner of the room in which their owner had undergone examination by his captors.

**1952** J. Blish *Surface Tension* in *Galaxy* (Aug.) 6/1: If they had, maybe they'd have left us our ultraphone, so the Colonization Council could hear about our cropper.

**ultraviolence** *n.* extreme violence.

**1962** [A. Burgess] *Clockwork Orange* (1963) 117: You've proved to me that all this dratsing and ultra-violence and killing is wrong wrong and terribly wrong.

**1964** *Chronicle-Telegram (Elyria, Oh.)* (May 23) 34/5: But many Negro leaders who long ago made their reputation as champions of civil rights believe that their policy is paying off. They don't believe ultra[-]violence will pay in the long run.

**1977** *Time* (Jan. 24) 14/2: It was like an orgy of "ultra[-]violence" from Stanley Kubrick's *A Clockwork Orange* [...]. About 200 masked youths rioted last week in the industrial town of Mestre near Venice.

**1999** *Syracuse (New York) Herald-Journal* (Feb. 27) A12/5: Those expecting the bang-bang ultraviolence of gangster dramas like "The Godfather" and "Goodfellas" will be disappointed.

**ultrawave** *n.* a device which enables interplanetary or interstellar communication, especially one which enables faster-than-light communication. Compare ANSIBLE, ULTRAPHONE.

**1934** E. E. Smith *Triplanetary* in *Amazing Stories* (Jan.) 33/2: His ultra-wave observer and sometime clerk was Lyman Cleveland himself, probably the greatest living expert in beam transmission.

**1944** I. Asimov *Big & Little* in I. Asimov, C. G. Waugh & M. Greenberg *SF* (1991) 323: Down in the ultrawave room, a message stormed its way through hyperspace to the Foundation.

**1951** L. Brackett *Starmen of Llyrdis* in *Startling Stories* (Mar.) 60/1: Kerrel's face appeared on the small screen. There was no need now for the ultra-wave and the ordinary visiphone unit had been cut in.

**1954** J. Blish *Beep* in *Galaxy SF* (Feb.) 15/1: If I were to send orders by ultrawave to my Three

Ghosts agent, he'd have to wait three hundred and twenty-four years to get them.

**1970** R. Silverberg *Tower of Glass* in *Galaxy Mag.* (Apr.) 57/1: To the east is the laboratory where the tachyon-beam ultrawave communications equipment is being fabricated—[...] devices with which Krug hopes to send messages to the stars.

**2001** D. Kingsbury *Psychohistorical Crisis* (2002) 143: Ultrawave, because of its probabilistic "speed" of transmission, could deliver packets to Personal Capsules far better than it could modulate a handshaking conversation.

**unhuman** *n.* an intelligent, non-human being (such as an alien, robot, etc.).

**1953** A. Norton *Star Rangers* 192: Even Smitt and Dalgre, for all their inborn suspicion not only of unhumans but also of sensitives, had fallen under the spell of the urbane charm.

**1960** P. Anderson *High Crusade* (1982) 19: We were both cushioned against the frightful vision of our poor folk being harried by unhumans, destroyed or enslaved, because neither of us really believed it.

**1994** C. Novak *trans.* K. Čapek *RUR (Rossum's Universal Robots)* 27: Just tucks its tail between its legs and howls when those unhumans are around, bah!

**2002** M. Moorcock *Lost Sorceress of Silent Citadel* in D. G. Hartwell *Year's Best SF 8* (2003) 479: That vital, sturdy, undiluted stuff will bring us back our power and make Mars know her old fear of the unhumans who ruled her before the Sea Kings ruled.

**universe** *n.* the setting of a work or works of fiction, especially of imaginative fiction.

**1965** P. S. Miller in D. Eney *Proceedings; Discon* 169: I get the feeling that she is also creating herself a universe; in fact that it even may be that races and forces out of her series of books for one publisher are in the background of another series for a different publisher.

**1967** A. Budrys *Benchmarks* (1985) 100: But what we have here is the van Rijn universe, and the van Rijn philosophy all over again.

**1981** P. Matthews in *SF Rev.* (Summer) 60/2: Marvin Kaye's "A Smell of Sulphur" gives the Wicked Witch of the West a moral choice [...]. Kaye has been playing games in well-established universes for some time, and it's fun.
**1996** D. Pringle, et al. *Ultimate Ency. of SF* 215/2: His universes—frequently featuring Kafkaesque situations and ineptly dire aliens—were ones where the ontological deck was stacked against the characters.
**2002** *San Francisco Chronicle Datebook* (Oct. 27) 43: Forty years down the line the Bond universe continues to evolve.

**unperson** *n.* someone who is punished, usually for political reasons, by having all records of their existence erased; hence, anyone whose existence or work is officially denied; someone who is treated as if they are less then human. Also as *v.*, hence **unpersoning,** *adj.*
**1949** [G. Orwell] *Nineteen Eighty-Four* 159: Syme was not only dead, he was abolished, an unperson.
**1954** *Economist* (Sept. 18) 883/2: Beria is already an "unperson," the record of his career "unfacts."
**1961** *Guardian (London)* (Apr. 28) 8/5: The concentration camp was a factory for processing people into un-persons.
**1964** J. Speer *Ramac in Sky* in *Fancestral Voices* (2004) 149: He doesn't just kill the person; he makes him an unperson—wiping out so far as feasible everything he's done.
**1976** *Times Literary Supplement* (Feb. 13) 156/3: The unpersoning process [in Czechoslovakia] had gathered momentum and many of the notables of 1968-69 were being rapidly transmogrified into the nobodies of the 1970s.
**1981** P. Dickinson *Seventh Raven* 151: You've got absolutely nothing to do [...] in hospitals [...]. Places like that tend to turn you into a kind of unperson.
**1983** *Daily Telegraph (London)* (Mar. 12) 14/2: In 1956, Bob [...] brought in Hamilton [...] as editorial director [...]. But in the new edition it looks as if all the work was done by his successor, Harold Harris. "It is no trivial matter to be 'unpersonned'," says Hamilton.

**unsuit** *v.* to take off a spacesuit.
**1964** P. J. Farmer *Tongues of Moon* 93: Without waiting for the man to finish unsuiting, Broward took the scout out of the port and away towards Mars.
**1968** A. Norton *Zero Stone* (ca1969) 61: There was another opening at the end of this space, giving entrance directly to the lock, saving time when one must suit or unsuit in leaving or entering the ship.
**1974** G. Benford *Threads of Time* in R. Silverberg *Threads of Time* 87: They cycled through together and Nikka began unsuiting.
**1987** L. M. Bujold *Falling Free* in *Analog SF/Sci. Fact* (Dec.) 44/1: Later, as his students unsuited in the equipment locker, laughing and joking as they cleaned and stored their work suits, Leo drifted over to the silent and pale Tony.
**2001** C. Bunch *Homefall* 195: "If you and your men want to unsuit, it'll be a lot more comfortable." There was a pause, then the figure reached up, touched seals around its neck, and lifted the helmet clear.

**unsuited** *adj.* not wearing a spacesuit.
**1966** F. Herbert *Destination: Void* 137: *Goodness and mercy?* That was anything which preserved the hope that you could one day walk unsuited beneath an open sky.
**1994** D. Weber *Field of Dishonor* (1997) 126: With pressure in the bay galleries again, we won't have to worry about the integrity of the emergency seals on CIC. That means the yard dogs can work unsuited in the compartment.
**2002** K. Schroeder *Permanence* 126: Michael felt his spirits lift at the prospect of walking unsuited in the air and feeling a real sun on his face.

**uplift** *n.* the making of a sentient species from a non-sentient one. Compare UPLIFTING.
**1980** D. Brin *Sundiver* 11: And from now on the work here at the Center for Uplift would be even more routine.
**1990** S. Jones *GURPS Uplift* 7: Galactic civilization *spreads* life through terraforming, colonization, and (especially) the process of *uplift*, the creation of new sentient species from animal stock.

**2000** D. Freer & E. Flint *Rats, Bats & Vats* 387: The device secretes microfilaments into the brain to obtain raw data, whereafter it acts as an enhancement and logic coprocessor, enabling instant "uplift" of various nonsentient animals.

**2001** J. A. Gardner *Ascending* 235: Ever since their uplift, these species had all grown more decadent, temperamental, and culturally sterile [...] particularly those uplifted for the longest period.

**uplift** *v.* to create a sentient species from a non-sentient one, usually by genetic engineering. Hence **uplifted**, *adj.*

**1980** D. Brin *Sundiver* 22: A young man on the left, wrapped in silver sateen from the throat to toe, held up a placard that said, "Mankind Was Uplifted Too: let our E. T. Cousins Out!"

**1993** *SFRA Rev.* (Jan.–Feb.) 19: Consider [...] Spielberg's child aliens and E. T. fairies, changelings, hobbits [...] Brin's uplifted "child" species.

**1997** J. A. Gardner *Expendable* (1997) 226: That's an AI for you: probably trying to "uplift" me by setting an example of "correct" speech.

**2003** K. MacLeod *Engine City* 84: —genetically uplifted the ancestors of the saurs, and culturally—at least—uplifted the krakens.

**2003** C. Stross *Singularity Sky* (2004) 370: They milled about downslope, debating the ideological necessity of uplifting non-human species to sapience—one of them had taken heated exception to a proposal to giving opposable thumbs and the power of speech to cats.

**uplifting** *n.* UPLIFT.

**1980** D. Brin *Sundiver* 46: The other side held that homo sapiens—just as every other known race of sophonts—was part of a chain of genetic and cultural uplifting that stretched back to the fabled early days of the galaxy, the time of the Progenitors.

**1992** V. Vinge *Fire upon Deep* 221: I know there have been other upliftings.

**2001** K. Davis *Expectations* in *Fantastic Furry Stories* (Oct.) 25: When uplifting became a reality, the scientists went crazy, overgrown kids with the biggest toybox in the world.

**uptime** *adj.* in or from the future.

**1978** C. Kilian *Empire of Time* (1985) 177: And, after Mr. Wordsworth's lawsuit, endochronic artists were entitled to royalties from uptime publication of their works, so I found myself rather well off.

**1983** P. Anderson *Ivory, & Apes, & Peacocks Time Patrol* (1991) 175: However, I've taught our cook several uptime recipes.

**1988** R. Silverberg *House of Bones* in *Collected Stories of Robert Silverberg (Vol. 2: Secret Sharer)* (1993) 157–8: Within a few weeks I realized that something had gone wonky at the uptime end, that the experiment had malfunctioned and that I probably wasn't ever going to get home.

**uptime** *adv.* in, into, or toward the future. Compare DOWNTIME.

**1973**: see quote in DOWNTIME.

**1978** C. Kilian *Empire of Time* (1985) 3: He was Philon Richardson, a Trainable Climber from Los, born 985 BC in Thrace, of Dorian stock. Tested four years ago at age sixteen, and brought uptime [...] for his education.

**1983** J. Varley *Millennium* 25: Uptime, it was already being prepared.

**1984** P. Anderson *Discovery of Past* in *Past Times* 186: Science fiction, of course, generally turns uptime, toward the future.

**1997** J. Kessel *Corrupting Dr. Nice* (1998) 69: Smuggling a dinosaur uptime would be tricky.

**1999** M. Swanwick *Scherzo with Tyrannosaur* in *Tales of Old Earth* (2000) 44: I walked through it all on autopilot, perfunctorily giving orders to have Satan shot, to have the remains sent back uptime, to have the paperwork sent to my office.

**Uranian** *n.* an inhabitant of the planet Uranus or its satellites.

**1870** R. A. Proctor *Other Worlds than Ours* 168: For upwards of 20 years [...] the Uranians—if there are any—never see the small Uranian sun.

**1939** L. A. Eshbach *Mutineers of Space* in *Dynamic Science Stories* (Feb.) 72/1: But it's bound to be something good, for that Uranian knows things—like every other high-born member of his race.

**1996** K. S. Robinson *Blue Mars* 431: At this point, there were no native Uranians, except for a single crèche of young children who had been born to mothers building the settlement. Six moons were now occupied.

**utopia** *n.* **1.** [< Gk. *ou,* "not" + *topos,* "place," after the title of a book by Sir Thomas More (1516, Eng. trans. 1551) depicting such a place] a state, location, or condition which is perfect or ideal with regard to politics, economy, social structure, etc. Often *cap.* Compare DYSTOPIA 1, ECOTOPIA.

**1613** S. Purchase *Pilgrimage* (1614) 708: The reports of this his voyage savour more of an Vtopia, and Plato's Commonwealth, then of true Historie.

**1691** J. Norris *Practical Discourses upon Several Divine Subjects* 177: To contemplate all this not [ ... ] as an uncertain Reversion, or imaginary Vtopia, but as a state that will shortly and certainly be.

**1883** *Manchester (England) Examiner* (Nov. 22) 5/2: Ingenious speculators who hope to reach Utopia by the nationalisation of the land.

**1951** H. Kuttner *Shock in Outer Reaches* 133: In a sense, this story attacks irresponsibility, since it devalues a most familiar structure in pseudo-scientific stories: the twin correlates of Now and Utopia.

**1995** *Interzone* (Nov.) 33/3: It's impossible to read an American survivalist movie in 1995 as anything but an expression of the [ ... ] belief in the possibility of a libertarian utopia without government but with a limitless abundance of guns, gasoline and smokes.

**2.** a work set in such a place. Compare DYSTOPIA 2.

**1947** J. O. Bailey *Pilgrims through Space & Time* 11: The older utopias described imaginary voyages to strange places, but since the principle of evolution was established, utopias have generally described voyages into future times when the race has improved and men have adjusted themselves to the conditions of the future.

**1952** A. Cameron *Fantasy Classification System* 4/1: It should be noted that the so-called "three main divisions of fantasy" do not include everything considered fantastic. In my opinion lost race tales and utopias are a fourth division.

**1979** F. E. Manuel & F. P. Manuel *Utopian Thought in Western World* 432: In many respects the adventure utopias with hackneyed plots of hair-raising captures and rescues are not distinguishable from the flood of escapist literature.

**1993** B. Stableford in J. Clute & P. Nicholls *Ency. of SF* (1995) 1260/2: In many of the classic UK utopias of the 19th century there is a strong vein of antiscientific romanticism. Lord Lytton's *The Coming Race* (*1870*) is more occult romance than progressive utopia.

**2003** B. Attebery *Mag. Era: 1926–1960* in E. James & F. Mendlesohn *Cambridge Companion to SF* 42: Part utopia, part comic variation of the alien-invasion story, *Childhood's End* finishes with a haunting image of the mutated children of Earth destroying their world.

# Weapons

Fighting and warfare have been subjects of science fiction stories from almost the beginning of the genre, and writers have outdone themselves in imagining weapons of the future. The familiar and once ubiquitous **ray gun** is but one of a class of weapons, called **energy** weapons, that fire a beam or ray of various types and lethality. Some of these weapons are described by the type of energy used, such as **heat rays** and **laser guns**. Others describe their effects: **blasters**, **death rays**, **disintegrators**, **disruptors**. **Needle beams** or **rays** (sometimes called **needlers**) are simply very finely focused energy weapons.

Futuristic projectile weapons may also be found. **Needle guns** (which, confusingly, are also called **needlers**) fire tiny slivers of metal at very high velocities. When both energy weapons and modern guns (i.e., ones that merely fire bullets) co-exist, the latter are often known as **slugthrowers**. If you don't have a gun, or find yourself in hand-to-hand combat, a **vibroblade** might come in handy. Vibroblades, knives or swords that vibrate at an extremely high frequency, are frequently able to cut through metal.

With this kind of arsenal available, a being needs to be able to defend itself, and there are a large variety of **energy screens**, **deflector shields**, and **force fields** (not to mention **spy-rays** used to garner intelligence) that can be used to ward off an attack. Non-lethal weapons abound, as well. **Stun-guns** or **stunners** temporarily knock out their victims. **Neuronic** weapons (frequently whips, but other types are used as well) may also simply stun one's enemies, or they may additionally stimulate the pain centers of the brain.

If large-scale havoc is called for (or sometimes even if it's not), **planet-wreckers** (**-busters**, **-killers**, **-smashers**, etc.) are useful for wreaking planetwide mayhem, while **nova bombs** have been used for everything from making a really large hole to destroying a star.

# V

**vac suit** *n.* a SPACESUIT. Hence **vacsuited,** *adj.* Compare MOONSUIT, PRESSURE SUIT, SUIT, VACUUM SUIT.

**1939** [E. Binder] *Impossible World* in *Startling Stories* (Mar.) 19/1: The rest of the men struggled into their vac-suits of neo-rubber. The two pilots helped them clamp the neck fittings of their helmets and clipped oxygen bottles to their belts.

**1942** L. Brackett *Child of Sun* in *Planet Stories* (Spring) 107/2: "Vac suits," he said. "There are two and a spare." They got into them, shuffled through the airlock, and stood still, the first humans on an undiscovered world.

**1967** K. Laumer *Spaceman!* in *If* (June) 100/2: I served my time in vac suits, working outside under the big black sky that wrapped all the way around and seemed to pull at me like a magnet that would suck me away into its deepest blackest depths.

**1981** M. McCollum *Which Way to Ends of Time?* in *Analog SF/Sci. Fact* (Aug. 17) 16/2: Which was why I spent an average of twelve hours every day on the Lunar surface in a smelly vacsuit either being broiled by a too-hot sun or struggling to keep my toes from frostbite.

**1993** D. Weber *On Basilisk Station* 15: Yard mechs swarmed over her in the dock's vacuum, supervised by vacsuited humans.

**vacuum suit** *n.* a SPACESUIT. Hence **vacuum-suited,** *adj.* Compare MOONSUIT, PRESSURE SUIT, SUIT, VAC SUIT.

**1930** E. E. Smith *Skylark Three* in *Amazing Stories* (Sept.) 545/1: As Loring held the steel vessel close to the stranger, DuQuesne donned a vacuum suit and stepped into the airlock.

**1947** R. Abernathy *Failure on Titan* in *Planet Stories* (Winter) 61/1: He removed the helmet, set it carelessly on the desk-top, and, turning, began to unzip his vacuum suit.

**1949** H. Kuttner *Time Axis* in *Startling Stories* (Jan.) 50/1: I passed an Exploratory Station and took a minute to go in and grab a vacuum suit. Carrying it, I headed for a gate in the great dome that covered the city.

**1958** [M. Leinster] *City on Moon* (1958) 20: There should be jeeps carrying burdens, and the chest lights of vacuum-suited figures moving about.

**1988** K. Tyers *Fusion Fire* 64: Polar wandered back toward the star-filled projection tank beside Adiyn's long desk, his black mood enveloping him like a vacuum suit.

**2002** M. J. Harrison *Light* 10 (2004): They had located a single survivor in a vacuum suit, a bulk white figure windmilling its arms.

**Venerian** *n.* [< L. *venerius*, "of Venus"] a VENUSIAN.

**1874** *The Galaxy* (Jan.) 127/1: The Martians would therefore be in a better position for understanding our attempts at opening up communication than the Venerians.

**1930** W. O. Stapledon *Last & First Men* 265: Evidently the marine Venerians resented the steady depletion of their aqueous world, and were determined to stop it.

**1948** R. A. Heinlein *Space Cadet* 181: A triangular head, large as a collie's, broke water about ten feet from them. Tex jumped. The Venerian regarded him with shiny, curious eyes.

**1965** F. Saberhagen *Stone Place* in *If* (Mar.) 13/2: A vertical crease appeared briefly in the High Commander's forehead, and he looked for long thoughtful seconds at the Venerians before resuming his talk.

**1991** J. Womack *Kiss, Wink, Grassy Knoll* in *Omni* (EBSCOHost) (May): Elvis, who in his glory will one day descend from heaven in a shiny silver mother ship, accompanied by a retinue of Venerians, Jovians, and the Lindbergh baby.

**Venusian** *n.* **1.** an inhabitant of the planet Venus. Compare VENERIAN.

**1874** A. Blair *Annals of 29th Century* 56: I suspected from the circumstances the frames of the Venusians were so constituted that sustenance was superfluous.

**1897** J. Munro *Trip to Venus* 173: "The good of it?" rejoined the Venusian; "it is beautiful, and gives us pleasure."

**1943** L. Brackett *Halfling* in *Halfling & Other Stories* (1973) 15: Then the Venusians, human and half-human, let go a yell and the audience came to and tore up the seats.

**1970** A. McCaffrey *Ship Who Sang* (1991) 6: She had [...] enjoyed a music appreciation course that had included [...] the curious rhythmic progressions of the Venusians.

**1995** *Interzone* (Aug.) 19/2: The belief that the Venusians are coming to save us from ourselves is simply an expression of people's deep-rooted worries.

**2.** the language spoken by Venusians.

**1942** R. Wentz *Nose for News* in *Astounding S-F* (June) 58/1: That was Venusian—and God help me if you ever find out what I said.

**1949** L. Brackett *Enchantress of Venus* in *Halfling & Other Stories* (1973) 181: With loud cheerfulness, the lame man said in Venusian, "Come in and drink with me, brother."

**1972** P. Moore *Can You Speak Venusian?* 167: He is fluent in Venusian, Plutonian and Krügerian.

**-verse** *suff.* [< uni*verse*] used in the name of a fictional universe used as the setting of a series, typically appended to a form of the series's title, main character, or creator.

**1985** *Latest issue of ROM (99?) drawn by Ditko!* (Usenet: net.comics) (Jan. 23): It seems to me that Ditko is more of a menace to the marvelverse than the dire wraiths ever were.

**1990** *WHY ALL PROMOTIONS??!!??* (Usenet: rec.arts.startrek) (Jan. 30): If you're not willing to watch the Trek-verse evolve, what's the sense in being a fan?

**1995** *FS: Gaiman Tekno—Instant Collection!* (Usenet: rec.arts.comics.marketplace) (Aug. 10): The Gaimanverse Tekno books are lavishly produced stories set in an imaginary universe created by Neil Gaiman!

**1997** *Entertainment Weekly* (Mar. 7) 41/2: In the Xenaverse—the name given to the show's timeless sense of place by its devotees—history is bunk. Characters spout Shakespearean platitudes one minute, Brooklynese wisecracks the next.

**2002** O. S. Card (title): First Meetings: Three Stories from the Enderverse.

**vessel** *n.* a SPACESHIP. Compare BOAT, CRAFT, CRUISER, SHIP, SPACE CAN, SPACE CAR, SPACECRAFT, SPACE CRUISER, SPACE FLYER, SPACER 2, SPACE VEHICLE, SPACE VESSEL, TIN CAN.

**1900** G. Griffith *Visit to Moon* in *Pearson's Mag.* (Feb.) 146: Another signal went over the wire, the Astronef's propellers slowed down and stopped, and the vessel began to rise swiftly towards the Zenith, which the Sun was now approaching.

**1925** J. Schlossel *Invaders from Outside* in *Weird Tales* (Jan.) 7/1: They next told of the homesickness that had engulfed them and their inability to leave because they were shorthanded. More than half of the crew had died and they could not get their vessel back.

**1938** E. E. Smith *Galactic Patrol* in *Astounding Stories* (Jan.) 131/1: Off he shot, and in due course a fair, green, Earthlike planet lay beneath his vessel's keel.

**1955** *Van Wert (Oh.) Times-Bulletin* (June 18) 4/2: The heat will make steam, which will make electricity, which [...] will atomize one of the rare-earth elements whose particles, spitting through an outlet into space, will move and steer the vessel.

**1968** D. C. Fontana *Enterprise Incident* *("Star Trek" script)* (June 13) I-13: Two of my officers will beam aboard your vessel as exchange hostages while you are here.

**1986** L. M. Bujold *Warrior's Apprentice* (1992) 102: Upon emergence into Tau Verde local space, all vessels will be approached and boarded for inspection.

**2002** A. Reynolds *Redemption Ark* (2004) 579: The ship—it had to be the Triumvir's vessel, *Nostalgia for Infinity*—hovered in interplanetary space.

**vibroblade** *n.* a weapon or tool with a blade that vibrates at very high speeds. Compare VIBROKNIFE.

**1940** R. Heinlein *If This Goes On—* in *Astounding S-F* (Feb.) 18/1: I slipped a vibroblade between his ribs.

**1962** R. Garrett *Unwise Child* (1963) 14: A vibroblade is a nasty weapon. Originally designed as a surgeon's tool, its special steel blade moves in and out of the heavy hilt at speeds from two hundred to two thousand vibrations per second, depending on the size and the use to which it is to be put.

**1979** B. Daley *Han Solo's Revenge* 59: Han identified it as some sort of vibroblade, perhaps a butcher's tool or surgeon's instrument that the weapons scanners would register as an industrial implement.

**1990** A. McCaffrey *Pegasus in Flight* (1992) 178: She got out the vibro-blade […] and sheered [sic] off two screws.

**2002** W. C. Dietz *EarthRise* (2003) 369: Small two-shot .22 Magnum derringers obtained from the humans served as backup weapons— as did the newly released vibro blades.

**vibroknife** *n.* a VIBROBLADE.

**1973** A. D. Foster *Bloodhype* 14: It appears to be a Secun vibraknife, battery powered.

**1985** G. R. R. Martin *Plague Star* in *Analog SF/Sci. Fact* (Jan.) 51/2: Kaj Nevis had produced a vibroknife. The slender, humming blade, which could slice through solid steel,

was a blur of motion less than a centimeter from Tuf's nose.

**1999** L. Evans *Stray* in D. Weber *Worlds of Honor* (2000) 64: Scott fumbled the vibro-knife off his belt clip and switched it on. The blade would cut through virtually anything known.

**2003** L. E. Modesitt, Jr. *Ethos Effect* 85: The first man—blocky and young—had a vibroknife.

**vid** *n.* a video program or recording; a device for playing such programs or recordings. Often *pl.* as **the vids.**

**1985** O. S. Card *Ender's Game* 28: I watched the vids of what he did to the Stilson boy.

**1988** C. J. Cherryh *Cyteen* 124: They're going to put a phone in here. And a vid.

**1992** C. Willis *Doomsday Book* 39: But people didn't simply fall over, except in books or the vids.

**ca1992** R. Grant & D. Naylor *Holoship* in *Son of Soup* (1996) 37: Well, we go for runs…watch gardening programmes on the ship's vid…play blow football…lots of things.

**1993** K. S. Robinson *Green Mars* 207: Mars had been a exotic sideshow, with some good vid, but nothing else to distinguish it from the general morass.

**1994** B. Hambly *Crossroad* 132: The landing party consisted of Kirk..Ensign Lao with a vid pickup, three security yeomen.

**2003** B. Bova *Saturn* (2004) 317: Ruth Morgenthau wanted to sleep, but she had hours and hours of vids to watch and phone taps to listen to.

**videophone** *n.* a communications device capable of transmitting and receiving the voice and image of the users. Also as *v.* Hence **videophonic,** *adj.* Compare VIDPHONE, VIEWPHONE, VISIPHONE.

**1945** A. E. van Vogt *World of Null-A* in *Astounding SF* (Aug.) 9/2: He closed the door, fastened the three plasto-windows and put a tracer on his videophone.

**1949** A. E. van Vogt *Players of Null-A* in *Astounding SF* (Jan.) 120/2: From that near point videophonic communication was established.

**1950** *Oakland (Cal.) Tribune* (Mar. 9) 52D/6: The engineers said the "G-String" also could make possible a videophone system, whereby telephone users could see as well as hear who they are talking to.

**1951** C. L. Moore *No Woman Born* in [M. Leinster] *Great Stories of SF* 186: Maltzer videophoned him on the morning set for her return.

**1966** I. Asimov *Key* in *Mag. of Fantasy & SF* (Oct.) 30/2: Ashley rose. "Where is your videophone?"

**1986** *New York Times* (Apr. 21) D12/1: The plan provides for the wiring of all major French towns and cities by the end of the century with fiber-optic cable, eventually allowing the general use of videophones.

**2004** A. Ries & L. Ries *Origin of Brands* (2005) 80: Despite strenuous efforts by AT&T and others dating back to the 1920s, only 650,000 videophone systems are in worldwide use today, most of them in businesses.

**vidphone** *n.* a VIDEOPHONE. Also as *v.* Compare VIEWPHONE, VISIPHONE.

**1953** P. K. Dick *Variable Man* in *Space SF* (Sept.) 36/1: I called you on the vidphone and they said you weren't available.

**1967** L. Niven *Flatlander* in *If* (Mar.) 82/2: There was an intercom, but it was a flat vidphone, three hundred years old restored at perhaps a hundred times its original cost.

**1969** N. Spinrad *Bug Jack Barron* 11: Wish you could vidphone in color, then I could go to my TV set, screw around with the color controls, and see myself for once as red or green or purple—*colored* folk, y'know?

**1989** W. Shatner *Tekwar* (1990) 23: Should you have any problems, feel free to contact me by vidphone at any hour.

**1997** A. C. Clarke *3001* 234: The room vidphone gave its urgent trio of rising notes [...] and an old friend appeared on the screen.

**vidscreen** *n.* a VISIPLATE. Compare VIEWPLATE 1, VISION SCREEN.

**1969** P. K. Dick *Ubik* (1977) 1: The technician in charge of the night shift at the map room coughed nervously as the massive, sloppy head of Glen Runciter swam up to fill the vidscreen.

**1985** A. Cole & C. Bunch *Court of Thousand Suns* (1990) 98: Marr palmed the switch and the vidscreen went respectfully blank.

**1989** [G. Naylor] *Infinity Welcomes Careful Drivers* (1992) 69: They sat in bed [...] watching, for the third consecutive night, *It's a Wonderful Life* on the sleeping quarters' vid-screen.

**1991** M. Weiss *King's Test* 8: The President pressed a button, turned from the mirror to a vidscreen to see himself as he would look on camera.

**2000** J. A. Gardner *Hunted* 38: While I waited for the Outbreak Team to arrive from some other starbase, I used the captain's vidscreen to watch outside the ship.

**viewphone** *n.* a VIDEOPHONE. Compare VIDPHONE, VISIPHONE.

**1964** F. Pohl *Chilrdren of Night* in *Galaxy Mag.* (Oct.) 187/2: I turned off the viewphone, got up and walked out.

**1966** *New Scientist* (Nov. 24) 440/3: A "viewphone" service (which could enable telephone users, to see each other during a call).

**1978** *Times (London)* (Nov. 3) 27/4: The Post Office itself has listed the main telecommunications services [...] envisaged for the years 1985 and 2000 [...]. By 1985 there will be [...] radiopaging, confravision [...], viewphone.

**2001** G. Dozois in M. Swanwick *Being Gardner Dozois* 140: I had gotten the idea of someone who would call somebody up on a viewphone and expose himself.

**viewplate** *n.* **1.** *Obs.* a VISIPLATE. Compare VIDSCREEN, VISION SCREEN.

**1928** P. F. Nowlan *Armageddon—2419 A. D.* in *Amazing Stories* (Aug.) 448/2: Seen upon the ultroscope viewplate, the battle looked as though it were being fought in daylight, perhaps on a cloudy day, while the explosions of the rockets appeared as flashes of extra brilliance.

**1947** G. O. Smith *Kingdom of Blind* in *Startling Stories* (July) 54/1: Carroll turned his back on them and watched the viewplate on the far wall. It was wavering and distorted but it showed the sky and the sphere of negative mass.

**1947** R. A. Heinlein *"It's Great to Be Back!"* in D. Knight *Cities of Wonder* (1967) 89:

Hello—I *can't* turn on my viewplate; this instrument is a hangover from the dark ages.

**1966** S. R. Delany *Empire Star* (1977) 124: The Geodetic Survey Station faded from the viewplates of the sensory helmet that was lying face-up on the dashboard.

**1969** E. Hamilton *Return to Stars* 141: Gordon peered at the viewplate.

**2.** a window in a spaceship or a transparent visor on a space helmet. Also used *fig.* Compare VIEWPORT.

**1941** *Cosmic Stories* (July): There was even a telescreen whose eyes opened on the forward viewplate, so that the engineer could follow the maneuvering.

**1946** E. Hamilton *Forgotton World* in *Thrilling Wonder Stories* (Winter) 39/2: They crowded around the view-plate in the keel, peering half-blindly down against the glare of the raging Sun-sea below.

**1953** W. Morrison *Divinity* in *Space SF* (Mar.) 100/2: Slowly the moisture evaporated from his viewplates. Slowly he began to see. [ ... ] Some one uttered a hoarse cry and pointed at his helmet. The unclouding of the viewplates must have stricken them with awe.

**1956** T. Sturgeon *Claustrophile* in *And Now News...* (2003) 107: She'll have nothin' in her viewplates from now on but Space Academy blue.

**1957** [R. Burke] *Hot Trip for Venus* in *Imaginative Tales* (July) 92/1: He glanced out the viewplate and saw his relief coming toward him over the field, accompanied by a couple of other men.

**1978** B. Shaw *Ship of Strangers* (1979) 3: The forward view plate, as it had done for days, showed nothing more than ripple patterns of sterile igneous rock unfolding before the vehicle's headlight.

**viewport** *n.* a window in a spaceship. Compare VIEWPLATE 2.

**1935** N. Schachner *Ultimate Metal* in G. Conklin *Best of SF* (1946) 450: Dean moved half consciously to the view-porte [sic] that was tilted at an angle to bring into focus the panorama of the streets.

**1945** [W. Long] *Nomad* in *Astounding SF* (Jan.) 95/1: If we have ten million men that

never see Mephisto from anything but the viewports of the transports, we'll be better off.

**1952** C. Oliver *First to Stars* in W. F. Nolan *Edge of Forever* (1971) 242: But more wonderful still was the soft, steady light from the myriad of stars that were suspended in the black velvet of the viewports.

**1966** *Life* (Apr. 1) 89: The cameras were focused through the viewports of Gemini 8, piloted by astronauts David Scott and Neil Armstrong as it moved alongside the unmanned Agena rocket.

**1984** W. Gibson *Neuromancer* (1989) 173: The bright marbles of its eyes were cut from the synthetic ruby viewport of the ship that brought the first Tessier up the well.

**1991** C. S. Friedman *Black Sun Rising* 400: What rose up [ ... ] betrayed no hint of doorway, viewport, or any structural joining.

**viewscreen** *n.* a screen which displays video images or which facilitates two-way visual and audio communication. Compare TELESCREEN, VISION PLATE, VISISCREEN.

**1939** T. Sturgeon *Ether Breather* in I. Asimov & M. H. Greenberg *Isaac Asimov Presents Golden Years of SF* (1983) 328: The images cleared on the view-screen as the set warmed up.

**1945** V. T. Hamlin *Alley Oop* in *Atchison (Kan.) Daily Globe* (May 9) 9: Chaos reigns in the time-machine laboratory—Wonmug has been seized by a dinosaur he had brought into range on the view-screen of his newly invented area-control unit!

**1958** C. Anvil *Cargo for Colony 6* in *Astounding SF* (Aug.) 68/2: Directly in front of Nevv, the viewscreen flared and lit up, showing a remarkably broad-shouldered individual, with a wide head and wider neck.

**1966** B. Bova *Weathermakers* in *Analog SF-Sci. Fact* (Dec.) 65/2: Finally he said to the viewscreen, "O.K., then we [ ... ] try to make a real storm cell out of it."

**1969** *Sci.* (Oct. 24) 455/2 (*ad*): Telescope for observing infrared emission [ ... ]. Resolves at least 5.5 minutes through focusing eye-piece on viewscreen of its green-emitting image converter.

**1991** M. Pendleton *Professionals* in *Isaac Asimov's SF Mag.* (mid-Dec.) 122: The huge viewscreen looking like a real window into space.

**1999** J. Haldeman *Forever Free* 99: He aimed it at the viewscreen over the keyboard and fired [...]. The result was pretty dramatic. There was more hole than viewscreen.

**virus** *n.* a computer program that is capable of replicating itself and installing these copies onto other computers without the users' knowledge, and which usually also performs damaging or irritating actions on the computers. Compare WORM.

**1972** D. Gerrold *When Harlie Was One* 175: You know what a virus is, don't you? [...]. The VIRUS program does the same thing.

**1975** J. Brunner *Shockwave Rider* 176: I'd have written the worm as an explosive scrambler, probably about half a million bits long, with a backup virus facility and a last-ditch infinitely replicating tail.

**1984** F. Cohen in J. H. Finch & E. G. Dougall *Computer Security* 144: We define a computer "virus" as a program that can "infect" other programs by modifying them to include a possibly evolved copy of itself [...]. Every program that gets infected may also act as a virus and thus the infection grows.

**1985** *Time* (Nov. 4) 94/3: A few years ago, Richard Skrenta Jr. [...] wrote a virus program called Cloner. Every 30th time a disk containing the program is used, the virus harmlessly flashes a few verses across the screen; then the interrupted task resumes where it left off.

**2006** *Seattle Times* (Internet) (Feb. 17): It is believed to be the first such virus aimed specifically at the Mac platform.

**vision plate** *n.* a VIEWSCREEN. Compare TELESCREEN, VISISCREEN.

**1932** J. M. Walsh in *Wonder Stories Quarterly* (Spring) 309/2: "I say, skipper," said the man whose face showed in the vision-plate, "what are you doing there? Someone monkeying with things?"

**1947** [R. Rocklynne] *Distress Signal* in *Planet Stories* (Spring) 40/2: Carl operated

the photo-amplifiers, set the telescopic perilens into position. Space expanded. In the vision plate grew a tiny dot that seemed to rush rapidly into sight though it was still several hundred thousand miles away.

**1955** A. Norton *Sargasso of Space* in *Solar Queen* (2003) 172: Rich was still watching the vision plate. Two new lights appeared on its surface.

**1962** J. White *Hospital Station* in *Beginning Operations* (2001) 38: He said finally, "Well, at least you can see me," and O'Mara's vision plate lit up. It showed a youngish man with close-cropped hair.

**2002** D. Duane *Stealing Elf-King's Roses* 54: Under the spreading Whatsit Tree, in one of the cubicles, a young, short, round, dark-haired, dark-skinned man sat staring at the high-res vision plate set into the cubicle wall.

**vision screen** *n.* a VISIPLATE. Compare VIDSCREEN, VIEWPLATE 1.

**1934** F. K. Kelly *Famine on Mars* in *Astounding Stories* (Sept.) 96/1: I caught him as he fell; then I saw what he had seen on the vision screen. A fleet from Earth. Eight ships, singing through space toward the station.

**1945** [M. Leinster] *First Contact* in G. Conklin *Best of SF* (1946) 575: He had seen the aliens only in the vision screen, and then only in light at least one octave removed from the light they saw by.

**1950** J. Blish *Okie* in D. Knight *Cities of Wonder* (1967) 113: Amalfi watched the vision screens tensely.

**1953** H. B. Piper *Ullr Uprising* in *Space SF* (Mar.) 148/1: The vision-screen lit with the indirect glare of the gun-flash, and the image in it jiggled violently as the ship shook to the recoil.

**1990** [P. Anthony] *And Eternity* (1991) 151: A vision screen came on, showing a fisheye-lens view of the outside.

**visiphone** *n.* a VIDEOPHONE. Also *vars.* and as *v.* Compare VIDPHONE, VIEWPHONE.

**1915** H. S. Keeller *John Jones's Dollar* in *Black Cat* (Aug.) 45/1: The professor of history [...] seated himself in front of the Visaphone and prepared to deliver the daily lecture to his class, the members of which resided in different portions of the earth.

**1930** C. G. Wates *Modern Prometheus* in *Amazing Stories Quarterly* (Fall) 447/1: John Ballantyne was awakened from uneasy slumber by the deep chime of the Visophone bell at his bedside. He reached over to switch on the viewing screen and put the earpiece of the combination telephone to his ear. Simultaneously, the features of a dark-skinned young man appeared upon the screen.

**1934** E. E. Smith *Triplanetary* in *Amazing Stories* (Jan.) 13/2: He flipped on the lifeboat's visiphone projector and shot its invisible beam up into the control room, where he saw space-armored figures furiously busy at the panels.

**1940** [L. del Rey] *Stars Look Down* in *Astounding S-F* (Aug.) 24/1: Stewart had visiphoned that he was coming under a temporary truce, so Erin was not surprised.

**1963** [M. Phillips] *Impossibles* 112: He inclined his head in as courtly a bow as he could manage over a visiphone. "I am deeply honored," he said, "that Your Majesty has called on me. Is there any way in which I might be of service?"

**1983** P. Anderson & G. R. Dickson *Napoleon Crime* in *Analog SF/Sci. Fact* (Mar.) 34/2: In the present case the visiphone was disguised as a Chippendale cabinet.

**1996** M. Coney *Werewolves in Sheep's Clothing* in *Mag. of Fantasy & SF* (Sept.) 140: A lined and elderly face stared out of the visiphone screen trying to look sincere and honest.

**visiplate** *n.* a screen which displays video images. Compare VIDSCREEN, VIEWPLATE 1, VISION SCREEN.

**1930** E. E. Smith *Skylark Three* in *Amazing Stories* (Aug.) 396/2: Crane looked into the visiplate and gasped.

**1944** F. Brown *Arena* in R. Silverberg *SF Hall of Fame, Vol. I* (1970) 283: He worked at the controls to keep that growing dot centered on the crossed spiderwebs of the visiplate.

**1950** R. A. Heinlein *Farmer in Sky* (1975) 83: The rest of the ship was cut in by visiplate.

**1985** R. Chilson *Passing in Night* in *Dragon Mag.* (Oct.) 61/1: That nondescript dot of light in the visiplate represented the enemy.

**2003** M. Swanwick *Legions in Time* in *Asimov's SF* (Apr.) 83: Ellie shrieked, and threw her purse over the visi-plate. "Don't listen to him!" she ordered Nadine. "See if you can find a way of turning this thing off!"

**visiscreen** *n.* a VIEWSCREEN. Compare TELESCREEN, VISION PLATE.

**1938** [J. Beynon] *Sleepers of Mars* in *Tales of Wonder* (No. 2) 23/2: Gordonov went back to his occupation of watching the repair work through the visi-screen.

**1941** T. Sturgeon *Completely Automatic* in *Astounding S-F* (Feb.) 93/1: I went over to what looked to me more like a visiscreen than anything else in the place. There was a switch beside it. I threw it. Nothing happened. "Where's the receiver and transmitter?" I growled.

**1966** J. Decles *Picture Window* in *Mag. of Fantasy & SF* (Oct.) 88/2: Carter went to the visiscreen and called the Public Archives.

**1979** D. Adams *Hitch Hiker's Guide to Galaxy* 79: She sighed and punched up a star map on the visiscreen so she could make it simple for him, whatever his reasons for wanting it to be that way.

**2003** M. Swanwick *Legions in Time* in *Asimov's SF* (Apr.) 86: Then everyone was on his or her feet, all facing the visi-screen, all raising clenched fists in response to the salute, and all chanting as one, "*We are nothing! The Rationality is all!*"

# W

**waldo** *n.* [after the fictional inventor of such a device in a story by Robert A. Heinlein (published as by "Anson MacDonald"); see 1942 quote] a remotely operated body, arm, etc. used variously to extend the user's natural abilities, perform work in an inhospitable environment or at a distance, etc. Hence **waldo-ized,** *adj.* Compare BODY-WALDO.

**1942** [A. MacDonald] *Waldo* in *Astounding SF* (Aug.) 16: Even the [ ... ] humanoid gadgets known universally as "waldoes" [ ... ] passed through several generations of development [ ... ] in Waldo's machine shop before he redesigned them for mass production. The first of them [ ... ] had been designed to enable Waldo to operate a metal lathe.

**1957** R. Silverberg *One-Way Journey* in *World of Thousand Colors* (1984) 131: We make a good team on the waldoes.

**1973** [J. Tiptree, Jr.] *Girl Who Was Plugged In* in *Screwtop/Girl Who Was Plugged In* (1989) 18: But Delphi is no robot. Call her a waldo if you must. The fact is she's just a girl, a real live girl with her brain in an unusual place.

**1978** D. A. Stanwood *Memory of Eva Ryker* 30: The bathyscaphs are both equipped with remote manipulators—the experts call them "Waldos"—for working under the extreme pressure.

**1982** W. Gibson *Burning Chrome* in T. Shippey *Oxford Book of SF* (1992) 500: I was working late in the loft one night, shaving down a chip, my arm off and the little waldo jacked straight into the stump.

**1987** T. Easton *Analog SF/Sci. Fact* (Sept.) 165/1: In Pohl's case, the aliens are using humans as organic waldoes that permit them to meet and bargain for Earth's wealth, and the humans be damned.

**1993** K. S. Robinson *Red Mars* (1993) 373: We're like dwarves in a waldo [ ... ]. One of those really big waldo excavators. We're inside it and supposed to be moving a mountain, and instead of using the waldo capabilities we're leaning out of a window and digging with teaspoons.

**1996** D. Pringle, et al. *Ultimate Ency. of SF* 106/3: The climax comes when Ripley, clad in waldo-ized battle gear, takes on head-to-head the queen of the alien hive in a dazzling set-piece.

**wallscreen** *n.* a video screen that covers all or most of a wall.

**1936** A. L. Zagat *Lanson Screen* in *Thrilling Wonder Stories* (Dec.) 51/2: A panel slides noiselessly sideward, revealing a white screen. A switch clicks, the room dims, the screen glows with an inner light. Rand twirls a knob. The wallscreen becomes half of an oval room, hung with grey draperies, grey-carpeted.

**1956** J. J. Ferrat *Snowstorm on Mars* in *Fantastic Universe* (June) 89/1: At once a wall screen flashed on, revealing a set of file numbers.

**1985** G. Kilworth *Hogfoot Right & Bird-hands* in K. S. Robinson *Future Primitive* (1997) 75: She merely went from one gray day to the next, sleeping, eating, and watching a device called wallscreen, on which she could witness the lives of others, long since dead, over and over again.

**1993** W. Gibson *Virtual Light* 196: She picked up a little remote and turned one of the wallscreens on.

**2004** S. J. Van Scyoc *Virgin Wings* in *Mag. of Fantasy & SF* (Dec.) 39: Lavender shadows shifted across the wallscreen, an abstract suggestion of flowering wisteria.

**warp** *n.* **1.** a SPACE WARP.

**1941** *Cosmic Stories* (May): Oh, he'll be back, I expect, as soon as I release the warp. He's probably wandering around in some impossible world or other.

**1974** J. Blish *Star Trek 10* 13: A peculiar physical warp, Captain, in which none of our established physical laws seem to apply with regularity.

**1983** D. Duane *So You Want to Be Wizard?* 47: "A warp," Nita whispered. "A tunnel through spacetime. Are you a white hole?"

**2.** travel by means of a space warp or warp drive; travel at warp speed.

**1957** R. Silverberg *Solitary* in *World of Thousand Colors* (1984) 223: He emerged from warp uncomfortably close to Bellatrix itself.

**1984** D. Duane *My Enemy, My Ally* 45: She came out of warp and coasted down into 285's feeble little gravity well, settling into a long elliptical orbit around the star.

**1990** A. McCaffrey & J. L. Nye *Death of Sleep* (1992) 300: The ship was capable of running on its own power indefinitely in sublight, or making a single warp jump between short sprints before recharging.

**1994** *SF Age* (July) 36/1: What we do is to check that nobody's doing the type of research that might lead to a magnetic spaceship, inertia-free field, or—worst of all!—an antigravity, warp-capable stardrive.

**1997** J. Vornholt *Mind Meld* 68: It was just the larger scout ship going into warp.

**warp** *v.* to travel by means of a space warp or warp drive.

**1946** F. Brown *Placet Is Crazy Place* in *Astounding SF* (May) 129/1: The Ark [...] would warp through space to a point a safe

distance outside the Argyle I-II system and come in on rocket power.

**1957** T. Sturgeon *Minority Report* in *Astounding SF* (June) 133/1: Earth was ready for him when he warped in.

**1966** B. Sobelman *Return of Archons ("Star Trek" script)* (Nov. 10) 35: If we try to warp out, or even move on impulse engines, we'll lose our shields...and we'll burn up like a cinder!

**1989** J. M. Dillard *Lost Years* 78: If it's excitement you want, we could have you warping all over the galaxy again.

**warp drive** *n.* a star drive that makes use of a space warp in order to exceed the speed of light.

[**1949** F. Brown *Gateway to Darkness* in L. Margulies & O. J. Friend *Giant Anthology of SF* (1954) 94: It's space-warp drive, you know. As I understand it, the last ship you worked on was rocket.]

**1951** M. Gibbs *Marvel Sci. Stories (letter)* (May) 128/1: Let's see yarns about vampires, ghouls, werewolves, and other assorted spooks, as well as ray guns, six-headed Martians, galactic wars, and warp drives.

**1961** R. F. Young *Girl Who Made Time Stop* in *Worlds of Robert F. Young* (1968) 13: Space is warped, just as your own scientists have theorized, and with the new warp drive [...] it's no trick at all, even for an amateur to travel to any place he wants to in the galaxy in a matter of just a few days.

**1970** J. Blish *Spock Must Die!* 1: Though we are not far by warp drive from the Klingon Empire.

**1982** A. Cole & C. Bunch *Sten* (1990) 41: He moved through the exotic crowd—everything from aliens and diplomats to stocky merchantmen and deep-space sailors. Even the talk was strange: star systems and warp drive, antimatter engines and Imperial intrigue.

**1986** D. Carey *Dreadnought* 10: One warp drive nacelle severely damaged, but marginally operable.

**2000**: see quote in JUMP GATE.

**warp speed** *n.* in the *Star Trek* universe, a faster-than-light speed attained by a spaceship using a warp drive; in non–*Star Trek* use, a very fast speed.

[**1968–69** J. L. Arosete *All Our Yesterdays* *("Star Trek" script)*: Beam us up. Maximum warp as soon as we are on board.]

**1977** S. Marshak & M. Culbreath *Price of Phoenix* (1985) 136: I would feel better if we could head out at warp speed.

**1977** *Progress-Review (La Porte City, Ia.)* (Oct. 5) 22/1: Then there was the backfield, who ran plays at Warp speed.

**1987** *Syracuse (New York) Herald American* (July 12) AA7/4: They're often modern men and women chasing careers, going for the gusto and the good life at warp-speed while trying to be super-parents and spouses on the side.

**1998** *Mountain Democrat (El Dorado County, Calif.)* (Dec. 10) A4/3: Even with the windshield wipers on warp-speed, I had horrible visibility.

**1999** M. J. Friedman *My Brother's Keeper* 61: Earth's forces had warp-speed capability, while the Romulans had to rely on mere impulse engines.

**webcast** *n.* a live broadcast transmitted over a computer network, especially the World Wide Web.

**1987** D. K. Moran *Armageddon Blues* 191: He understood that SORCELIS wasn't a secret any longer, if it ever had been—DataWeb News had done an in-depth on it not two weeks ago, and tourists had been trekking up into the New York hills ever since the webcast.

**1995** *NEW SUNDANCE FEST WEBCAST!!* (Usenet: alt.celebrities) (Jan. 18): A FESTIVAL WORLD WIDE WEBCAST: REDFORD'S SUNDANCE FILM FESTIVAL

**1995** *Chicago Tribune* (Nexis) (Aug. 18): WGN-Ch.9 received more than 200 e-mail responses [...] to its Webcast of Tuesday night's Cubs-Dodgers game.

**1999** *New Scientist* (Apr. 10) 17/3: San Francisco's Exploratorium hosts a number of events [...] via webcasts for those who can't make it to the West Coast.

**2003** *Cult Times* (May) 7/1: BBCi's webcast of *Shada*, featuring Paul McGann, Lalla Ward and John Leeson, will commence on 2nd May.

**Whovian** *n.* a fan of the television series *Doctor Who*.

**1982** *Whovian Times* (Sept.) 3/3: Whovians ranging from 2 weeks old to the mid-seventies attended the first annual Doctor Who Fan Club of America's Whovian Festival.

**1984** *TARDIS isomorphism* (Usenet: net.sf-lovers) (July 1): I have a question for avid Whovians.

**1986** *New York Times* 40/1 (Sept. 1): "Dr. Who," carried on most public television stations across the country, is quietly scooping up a growing following of dedicated fans. They are [...] creating a subculture of like-minded folk who call themselves Whovians.

**2001** T. Currie *Radio Times Story* 214: A number of the keenest collectors became regular customers—the inevitable *Dr Who* collectors (known as Whovians) prominent among them.

**widescreen baroque** *n.* a subgenre of science fiction characterized by larger-than-life characters, violence, intrigue, extravagant settings or actions, and fast-paced plotting. Often *cap.*

**1973** B. W. Aldiss *Billion Year Spree* 264: My own preference is for Harness' *The Paradox Men*. [...] In my introduction to the British edition of this novel, I call it Wide Screen Baroque; other novels in the same category are Doc Smith's and A.E.van Vogt's, possibly Alfred Bester's: but Harness' novel has a zing of its own, like whisky and champagne, the drink of the Nepalese sultans.

**1979** B. Aldiss *Afterword: Flight into Tomorrow* in C. L. Harness *Paradox Men* (1984) 201: Most Widescreen Baroque novels are ultimately frivolous.

**1997** M. Kotani *Techno-Gothic Japan* in J. Gordon & V. Hollinger *Blood Read* 194: Since then she has published a wide variety of cyberpunkish and widescreen-baroque novels and short stories.

**1997** *J. Dallman, V. Tenhunen, A. Watson, et al* (Usenet: alt.books.iain-banks) (Aug. 14): It is a very fine example of what Brian Aldis calls Wide Screen Baroque—it's a Culture novel that shows you a lot of the context and goes Boom! quite well.

**1999** *Lem* (Usenet: alt.books.phil-k-dick) (Nov. 4): It was interesting, not quite the "wide-screen baroque," the fast exciting often violent writing of the fifties but almost like that while being quite weird and wonderful.

**wirehead** *n.* someone who directly stimulates the pleasure centers of their brain with electric current, especially someone addicted to this activity.

**1973** L. Niven *Defenseless Dead* in *Playgrounds of Mind* (1992) 386: You can't get a wirehead's attention either, when house current is trickling down a fine wire from the top of his skull into the pleasure center of his brain.

**1979** S. Robinson *God Is Iron* in *Time Travelers Strictly Cash* (2001) 87: But I had never seen a wirehead. It is by definition a solitary vice, and all the public usually gets to see is a sheeted figure being carried out to the wagon.

**1987** N. Spinrad *Little Heroes* (1989) 157: The powers that be couldn't care less if indigents sold to other indigents wirehead devices that would fry their brains beyond employability.

**1996** J. D. Vinge *Dreamfall* (2004) 195: I woke up alone, lying on the floor with the pattern of the carpet pressed into my cheek, like a wirehead sprawled in a gutter after a reality burnout.

**wireheading** *n.* the act of directly stimulating the pleasure centers of one's brain with electric current.

**1973** L. Niven *Flash Crowd* in R. Silverberg *Three Trips in Time & Space* 7: "Legalize direct-current stimulus!" she screamed at him. [ ... ] "*Legalize wireheading!*"

**1979** S. Robinson *God Is Iron* in *Time Travelers Strictly Cash* (2001) 87: I knew about wireheading, of course—I had lost a couple of acquaintances and one friend to the juice.

**1993** *Wired* (Internet) (Sept./Oct.): I heard rumors of brain-power amplification devices, wire-heading (recreational shock therapy), and most disturbing of all, claims that people are actually poking holes in their heads and directly stimulating their brains.

**2001** C. J. Dorsey *Paradigm of Earth* (2002) 74: What about recreational drug use and wire-heading?

**world-building** *n.* the creation of an imaginary world and its geography, biology, cultures, etc., especially for use as a setting in science fiction or fantasy stories, games, etc. Hence **world-builder,** *n.*

**1965** R. A. Lupoff *Master of Adventure* (2005) 244: Certainly Burroughs' world building may seem simplistic compared to much in modern science fiction.

**1979** P. Anderson *SF & Sci.* in *Destinies* 257 (Jan.–Feb.): The enormous world of Mesklin, its weird shape and variable gravity, its [ ... ] physics, chemistry, biology, oceanography, navigation, everything is considered and brought together into a seamless web, as nearly as a mortal may do so. No better job of worldbuilding has ever come forth, nor ever likely will, unless by the author himself.

**1991** R. Rogow *Futurespeak* 219: An important aspect of worldbuilding is the construction of an alien society and its attendant mythos.

**1993** *SF Age* (Jan.) 15/1: Once you step *Inside the Funhouse* [ ... ] you will see that the world-builders are just as weird as the worlds they build.

**1996** D. Pringle, et al. *Ultimate Ency. of SF* 24/1: Such exercises as these have established "world-building" as one of the most important and problematic aspects of modern sf writing.

**2003** P. Drazen *Anime Explosion!* 234: These opening minutes with the Force establish what life on Honneamise is like. It's an elaborate example of "world-building."

**worldlet** *n.* a small, solid celestial body, such as an asteroid or moon; a planetoid.

**1926** *Spectator* (Sept. 11) 375/1: So in turn we visit the asteroids, that belt of tiny worldlets flinging round the sun.

**1937** O. Stapledon *Star Maker* 206: As the aeons advanced, hundreds of thousands of worldlets were constructed.

**1968** S. R. Delany *Nova* (1971) 21: He finally got up a party to land on Deimos and explored the tiny moon as only a worldlet can be explored.

**1985** D. Brin *Warm Space* in *Otherness* (1994) 266: Asteroid-sized arks—artificial worldlets capable of carrying entire ecospheres—remained a dream out of science fiction, economically beyond reach.

**2004** D. Broderick *X, Y, Z, T* 52: An artificial worldlet 50 kilometers long and 16 kilometers across, complete with an internal sea, hurricanes and organic robots, flashes through the solar system, utterly indifferent to human amazement.

**worm** *n.* a piece of computer software capable of replicating itself and transferring copies between computers, which usually performs damaging actions on those computers. Compare VIRUS.

**1975** J. Brunner *Shockwave Rider* 176: I'm just assuming that you have the biggest-ever worm loose in the net, and that it automatically sabotages any attempt to monitor a call to the ten nines.

**1980** *New York Times* (Nov. 13) D2/1: That is essentially what a group of scientists at the Xerox Corporation's Palo Alto, Calif., research center did when they created the Worm, a series of programs that moved through a data network almost at will, replicating, or copying itself, into free machines.

**1988** *PC Mag.* (July) 114/1: The notion of subversive software began back in the 1970s with a program that ran around the US Defense Department's Arpanet messaging system. Dubbed the Creeper, it was one of the first worm programs.

**2006** *Seattle Times (Internet)* (Feb. 17): The worm sends itself to available contacts on the infected users' buddy list in a file called "latestpics.tgz," according to the Sophos Web site.

# Zines

SF fans began writing fanzines in the 1930s and 40s, and the suffix *-zine* has proven very adaptable since then. Most often, the type of contents or subject matter are indicated: *adzine, artzine, filkzine,* **genzine**, **letterzine**, *mediazine*, **newszine**, *reviewzine, Trekzine,* etc. It can be used to indicate a magazine is being published for profit or not, as in **fanzine** and **prozine**. Or it can describe what technology was used to reproduce it *(carbonzine, mimeozine)*; how it is distributed: as part of an Amateur Press Association mailing (**apazine**), from person to person to person *(chainzine)*, or electronically *(ezine)*; or who is producing it (**clubzine**). *Combozines* consist of multiple fanzines bound together in a single issue. And finally, bad fanzines are known as **crudzines**, although not generally by their editors.

# X

xeno- *pref.* [< S.E. *xeno-*, foreign, strange, or foreigner] used to indicate that something is, or relates to something that is, from another world. Sometimes **xen-** before a vowel.

**1949**: see quote in XENOLOGIST.

**1972** M. Bradley *Darkover Landfall* (1987) 21: The first man [...] said, "Marco Zabal, Xenobotanist."

**1980** D. Brin *Sundiver* 22: The former group took their love of aliens to almost a pseudo-religious frenzy. Hysterical Xenophilia?

**1986** *Appendix* in G. R. R. Martin *Wild Cards* 400: Accounts of the incident make it clear that the vessel containing xenovirus Takis-A exploded at an altitude of 30,000 feet.

**1989** J. M. Dillard *Lost Years* 79: She was Nogura's right-hand adviser in current xenoaffairs.

**1994** S. Hawke *Patrian Transgression* 19: She has served as [...] adjunct lecturer in xeno-political studies at Starfleet Academy.

**1996** B. Aldrin & J. Barnes *Encounter with Tiber* 475: Though other linguists, cryptologists, and xenomathematicians were saying that eventually they expected great things, right now matters stood where they had.

**2002** A. Roberts *Stone* 147: Other [sic] still claimed that there *were* no Wheah, that it was part of a larger conspiracy—that the Wheah were alien xenoforms (absurd!).

xenoanthropology *n.* [XENO- + *anthropology*] the study of alien cultures. Also **xenanthropology**. Hence **xenoanthropologist**.

**1966** A. Budrys in *Galaxy* (Oct.) 155/2: Anderson's is about xenathropology, politics and moral courage.

**1987** F. Pohl *Adeste Fidelis* in D. G. Hartwell *Christmas Stars* (2004) 16: He was neither a xenoanthropologist nor a xenobiologist, nor did he have any of the special skills that made the lives of the survivors fairly tolerable.

**1994** S. Hawke *Patrian Transgression* 18: Secretary Wing [...] completed her graduate studies summa cum laude at Princeton, with a doctorate in xenoanthropology.

**2000** N. Kress *Probability Moon* (2002) 57: When he returned to Princeton, he would be an instant star in the small, fierce, fiercely coveted world of xenoanthropology.

xenobiological *adj.* of or relating to xenobiology; alien. Hence **xenobiologically**, *adv.*

**1958** *Mag. of Fantasy & SF* (Feb.) 20: Our xenobiologically-minded authors poured in reports on astonishing alien beings; and readers still cherish the memory of such fascinating creatures as Theodore Sturgeon's often-reprinted *hurkle*.

**1973** A. D. Foster *Bloodhype* 173: And I might suggest a more regulated intake of oxygen. Your present rate of consumption intrigues me only as a xenobiological curiosity.

**1993** A. McCaffrey *Chronicles of Pern: First Fall* 228: How will you ever increase your understanding of xenobiological forms unless you examine closely whatever samples come your way?

**1994** E. Brown *Engineman* 143: Unlike in the outlying districts of the city, where xenobiological specimens flourished without restraint, this garden was designed and tended by a team of the finest off-world horticulturists.
**2001** P. F. Hamilton *Fallen Dragon* (2003) 253: Certainly nobody on Earth knew about them. Which is surprising. From a xenobiological viewpoint I cannot overstate how important they are.
**2002** R. Vajra *Sidehunter* in *Analog SF & Fact* (June) 27/2: I wasn't just another xenobiological troubleshooter. My title was Special Agent Extraordinary. I'd been so good at forensic ecology, the Agency had declared me its premier investigator.

**xenobiologist** *n.* someone who studies or practices xenobiology.
**1954** R. A. Heinlein *Star Lummox* in *Mag. of Fantasy & SF* (May) 60: Once the xenobiologists got their hands on Lummox they would never let him go.
**1971** U. K. Le Guin *Lathe of Heaven* (1973) 160: They're intelligent but Irchevsky, our best xenobiologist, thinks they may not be rational at all.
**1979** F. Pohl *Jem* 138: Professor D. Dalehouse was now a name to conjure with among xenobiologists.
**1991** O. S. Card *Xenocide* 73: Only a few people understood how much was riding on the work that Ela and Novinha, as Lusitania's xenobiologists were doing.
**1996** B. Aldrin & J. Barnes *Encounter with Tiber* 473: Xenobiologists [ ... ] had managed to establish that the tissues of all the dead Tiberians had various kinds of damage brought on by the way their immune systems reacted to long-term exposure to Earth proteins.

**xenobiology** *n.* [XENO- + *biology*] the study of the biology of alien life-forms.
**1954** R. A. Heinlein *Star Lummox* in *Mag. of Fantasy & SF* (July) 90: I have never taken any interest in xenobiology.
**1972** M. Bradley *Darkover Landfall* 64: There have been intelligent life-forms reported from three or four other planets; so far they have reported one simian, one feline, and three unclassifiable—xenobiology isn't my specialty.

**1983** *Nature* (Jan. 13) 106/2: The almost-virgin xeno- prefix should be used to designate extraterrestrial entities [ ... ], concepts and subdisciplines (for example, xeno-biology, xenosociology), and exo- reserved for life outside of but native to Earth.
**1995** A. D. Foster *Life Form* 36: The heretofore grand discoveries of lichen and fungi on Tycho V and Burke had been instantly relegated to the realm of footnotes in the young world of xenobiology.
**1996** W. Shatner *Return* 222: Starfleet's xenobiology records didn't either.

**xenocide** *n.* [XENO- + -*cide* (as in homocide, suicide, etc.)] the killing or attempted killing of an entire alien species; the killing of a single alien. Hence **xenocidal,** *adj.*
**1983** B. A. Freitas, Jr. *Illegal Aliens* in O. Davies *Omni Book of Space* 310: Lawmakers should define the crime of *xenocide*—the slaying of an extraterrestrial person by any other legal person.
**1983** B. A. Freitas, Jr. in *Omni Book of Space* 314: Stiffer sentences might be appropriate for xenocidal acts.
**1986** O. S. Card *Speaker for Dead* 39: Through these Nordic layers of foreignness we can see that Ender was not a true xenocide, for when he destroyed the buggers, we knew them only as varelse.
**1991** M. McArthur *Time Future* (2001) 121: None of the other inhabitants of the station seemed likely candidates for such a flamboyant xenocide.
**1991** J. D. Vinge *Summer Queen* (2003) 272: It's not just about the morality of committing xenocide; it's about enlightened self-interest.
**2002** A. Reynolds *Redemption Ark* (2004) 22: But what she sensed was an aeons-old litany of surgical xenocide; of a dreadful process of cleansing waged upon emergent sentient species.

**xenolinguist** *n.* [XENO- + *linguist*] someone who studies the languages of aliens. Hence **xenolinguistics,** *n.*
**1989** S. Finch *World Waiting* in *Mag. of Fantasy & SF* (Aug.) 36: Outside, someone

was dragging Oona's battered duffel bag with its faded Xenolinguists' Guild insignia across the compound to the guest quarters.

**1995** J. Haldeman *For White Hill* in G. Dozois *Worldmakers* (2001) 275: Then I had it translated by a xenolinguist into a form that she said could be decoded by any creature sufficiently similar to humanity to make any sense of the story.

**1998** J. Barnes *Earth Made of Glass* (1999) 43: If one of the bright fellows in xenolinguistics is deciphering other indicators correctly, the Metallah system may have been a regional capital or administrative post.

**2000** N. Kress *Probability Moon* (2002) 42: From the disaster, xenolinguists had learned the meaning of the alien marking for "disruption."

**2003** R. Nestvold *Looking through Lace* in K. J. Fowler, et al. *James Tiptree Award Anthology 1* (2005) 135: So how did Repnik think he would be able to gather data on the women's language without a female xenolinguist?

**xenological** *n.* of or relating to xenology.
**1950** L. S. de Camp *Hand of Zei* in *Astounding SF* (Oct.) 47/1: Where xenological investigations were concerned, George could take as detached and impersonal an attitude towards Krishnans as if they were microorganisms under his microscope.
**1978** B. Shaw *Ship of Strangers* (1979) 18: What I'm proposing is that we ask Captain Aesop to go through the xenological data stores and estimate the probability of the existence of the Gray Men in the first place.
**1997** J. White *Final Diagnosis* 265: To their data-crammed minds was given the job of original research in xenological medicine and the diagnosis and treatment of new diseases in hitherto unknown lifeforms.
**2001** J. E. Czerneda *In Company of Others* 239: Titan U, in the persona of Secretary Vincente—the voice of power in the Department of Xenological Studies wasn't pleased.
**2006** N. Gevers in *Locus* (Mar.) 12/3: *Constance Cooper* tells a neat xenological parable in "*The King's Tail*," slyly setting out the arrogance of conquerors and their resulting comeuppance.

**xenologist** *n.* someone who studies or practices xenology.
**1949** L. S. de Camp *Animal-Cracker Plot* in *Astounding SF* (July) 69/1: I know more about extraterrestrial life than most professional xenologists.
**1955** T. Sturgeon *Who?* in *Galaxy SF* (Mar.) 116/1: His passengers in coldpacks and a cargo of serums, refractories, machine tools and food concentrate for the xenologists and mineralogists who were crazy enough to work out there.
**1979** P. Anderson *Ways of Love* in *Destinies* (Jan.–Feb.) 9: Perforce, we became a pair of jackleg xenologists.
**1989** A. D. Foster *Quozl* 31: The xenologist would have to be female, since the idea of taking an unbalanced crew was unthinkable.
**2001** *Interzone* (May) 6/2: I'm a xenologist and, since earning my degree, I've focused exclusively on communities descended from humans who were genetically modified to survive in a hostile environment.

**xenology** *n.* [XENO- + *-ology*] the study of aliens, especially of alien biology.
**1954** R. A. Heinlein *Star Lummox* in *Mag. of Fantasy & SF* (May) 27: I mean to major in xenology and exotic biology in college.
**1957** T. Sturgeon *It Opens Sky* in *Man Who Lost Sea* (2005) 45: You have every rotten plague and dangerous plant pest known to xenology, right here in your hand.
**1983** *Nature* (Jan. 13) 106/1: Xenobiology axiomatizes life, hence also fails. The most suitable word must be least limiting, suggesting the rootless forms exology and xenology.
**1998** D. Brin *Heaven's Reach* 160: Lark abruptly recalled something he had read once, in a rare galacto-xenology text, about a type of hydro-life called Zang.
**2002** N. Gevers *New York Rev. of SF* (Dec.) 8/1: Why were you so preoccupied then with the possibilities of xenology and highly speculative anthropology?

**X-Phile** *n.* a fan of the television series *The X-Files.*
[**1994** *TV Guide* (Jan. 15) 20/1: They—the *X*-ophiles, the growing cult audience for *The*

*X-Files*—provided Fox with its best ever ratings for Friday nights.]

**1994** *X-ophiles?* (Usenet: alt.tv.x-files) (Jan. 14): Shouldn't it be X-philes instead?

**1995** C. Carter *Truth Is out There* 83: Haglund was almost entirely unfamiliar with the show, though his role has lured some of the show's die-hard fans, X-Philes, out to see him live.

**1998** *New York Times* (Jan. 11) 41/4: Ms. Fincher, 55, has been a self-described "X-Phile" for the last year and a half.

**1999** M. J. Pustz *Comic Book Culture* 113: There are many more casual viewers watching any given episode of *X-Files* than there are X-Philes who tape every episode [...] and attend *X-Files* conventions.

# Z

**zero-g, zero-gee** *n.* ZERO GRAVITY. Compare NULL-G, NULL-GRAV.

**1952** A. C. Clarke *Islands in Sky* 80: She was escorted by an elderly woman who seemed to be quite at home under zero "g" and gave Linda a helpful push when she showed signs of being stuck.

**1962** F. I. Ordway, J. P. Gardner & M. R. Sharpe *Basic Astronautics* 477: Walking will be impossible in zero G.

**1981** V. N. McIntyre *Entropy Effect* 43: At the crystal growth station in the zero-g section of Aleph Prime.

**1984** W. Gibson *Neuromancer* (1989) 102: Your heartbeat'll speed up in zero-g, and your inner ear'll go nuts for a while.

**1996** *SFX* (May) 16/3: Making *Apollo 13* was an unusual experience for Bill, involving not only zero-G filming but also the chance to meet the character he was playing, Fred Haise.

**1999** A. Thomson *Through Alien Eyes* (2000) 46: We stopped him, but he moved to one of those zero-gee colonies a few months later.

**zero gravity** *n.* a condition in which the effects of gravity are absent or so small as to be unnoticable. Compare NULL-G, NULL-GRAV, ZERO-G.

**1938** J. Binder *If Sci. Reached Earth's Core* in *Thrilling Wonder Stories* (Oct.) 99: Starting at the zero-gravity of earth's core, accumulative acceleration is easily built up in a four-thousand-mile tube.

**1951** A. C. Clarke *Sands of Mars* 5: I'll take you into the zero-gravity section and see how you manage there.

**1968** *Vital Speeches of Day* (Aug. 1) 623/2: These include changes in heart regulation, fluid and electrolyte balance, the energy costs of living and working in zero gravity, mineral and bone metabolism, hormonal shifts, cell development and even the ability to sleep.

**1979** B. Bova *To Be or Not* in *Destinies* (Jan.–Feb.) 145: His heart had started getting cranky, and the zero-gravity they lived in was a necessary precaution for his health.

**1985** O. S. Card *Ender's Game* 24: Day after day, in zero gravity, there are mock battles.

**1994** *Analog SF & Fact* (Jan.) 187/2: About a decade ago, discussion of space-station experiments shifted terminology from "zero-gravity" to "microgravity."

**2001** *Dreamwatch* (Mar.) 82/2: Between having meaningless conversations about the philosophical depths of deep space and zero-gravity sex, they [ ... ] set about trying to rescue a script which is beyond salvation.

**zine** *n.* [abbr. of FANZINE] a FANZINE; any amateur-published periodical. Compare FANMAG.

**1944** J. B. Speer *Fancyclopedia* 34/1: The Check-List also gives variant names of a given zine, summarizes dates by volume and number, and includes information and rumors on proposed magazines that never appeared.

**1950** A. V. Clarke *British Appreciation* in S. Skirvin *Cinvention Memory Book* 65: Sometimes it included one or two page 'zines from other British fans.

**1964** J. Linwood *Fanalytic Eye* in *Les Spinge* (Jan.) 27: The best part of the 'zine is the controversial letter col which boasts of letters from all over.

**1985** *Times (London)* (Jan. 25) 12/2: A zine is what its addicts call a postal games magazine, of which there are about 50 in the country.

**1993** B. Shaw *Dimensions* (1994) 41: For all we know, what you have here are cookery and fashion zines.

**-zine** *suff.* [modeled after FANZINE and PROZINE] used in names of varieties of fanzines or zines, usually with a prefix indicating the type of content, distribution, or method of production. Compare APAZINE, CLUBZINE, CRUDZINE, GENZINE, LETTERZINE, NEWSZINE, PERSONALZINE, PERZINE.

**ca1944**: see quote in APAZINE.

**1952** A. H. Rapp, L. Hoffman & R. Boggs *Fanspeak* 7/1: *individzine*. A one-man fanzine, usually distributed in FAPA or SAPS, in which the contents are mostly by one editor.

**1969** H. Warner, Jr. *All Our Yesterdays* 164: Leslie A. Crouch [...] had begun publishing a carbonzine during the late thirties.

**1975** E. Weinstein *Fillostrated Fan Dictionary* 28: Combozine [...]: A group of fanzines bound together, usually done so for conventions.

**1990** *Thrust* (Winter) 29/2: The letters section is [...] all the more dear to me with the demise of most of the great reviewzines.

**1998** *Interzone* (Aug.) 4/2: Some of these may not be real magazines, but electronic "e-zines" or whatever.

**2004** S. Glasgow *National Fantasy Fan* (June) 21/1: Don't forget everyone, the deadline for the artzine is July 15th.

# Pseudonyms Cited in the Dictionary

Full name is given only when it sheds light on the choice of pseudonym; otherwise only first and last names or working name is given. Writers or configurations of writers who use the same pseudonym are separated by a semicolon; writers who share a joint pseudonym that is sometimes used for stories written by only one or the other writer are indicated by "&/or."

| PSEUDONYM | REAL NAME(S) |
|---|---|
| Anthony, Piers | Piers Anthony Dillingham Jacob |
| Atheling, William | James Blish |
| Bes Shahar, Eluki | Rosemary Edghill |
| Beynon, John | John Wyndham Parkes Lucas Beynon Harris |
| Binder, Eando | Earl Binder & Otto Binder; Otto Binder |
| Boucher, Anthony | William Anthony Parker White |
| Bowie, David | David Jones |
| Briarton, Grendel | Reginald Brentnor |
| Burgess, Anthony | John Anthony Burgess Wilson |
| Burke, Ralph | Robert Silverberg &/or Randall Garrett |
| Cherryh, C. J. | Carolyn Janice Cherry |
| Clement, Hal | Harry Clement Stubbs |
| Corwin, Cecil | C. M. Kornbluth |
| Coupling, J. J. | John R. Pierce |
| Crispin, Edmund | Robert Montgomery |
| Danzell, George | Nelson S. Bond |
| Dee, Roger | Roger D. Aycock |
| del Rey, Lester | Leonard Knapp |
| Donovan, Francis | F. D. Thompson |
| Douglas, Ian | William H. Keith, Jr. |
| Edmonds, Paul | Henry Kuttner &/or C. L. Moore |
| Edwards, Gawain | George Edward Pendray |
| Farley, Ralph Milne | Roger Sherman Hoar |
| Gottesman, S. D. | C. M. Kornbluth; Frederik Pohl & C. M. Kornbluth; Frederik Pohl, C. M. Kornbluth, & R. W. Lowndes |
| Graf, L. A. | Julia Ecklar & Karen Rose Cercone |
| Gregor, Lee | Milton A. Rothman & Frederik Pohl; Milton A. Rothman |
| Hastings, Hudson | Henry Kuttner &/or C. L. Moore |
| Herrick, Thornecliffe | Jerome Bixby; house name for *Planet Comics* |
| Holmes, H. H. | William White |
| Kingsley, P. A. | Poul Anderson & Karen Anderson |
| Knox, Calvin M. | Robert Silverberg |

| | |
|---|---|
| Lafayette, Rene | L(afayette) Ron(ald) Hubbard |
| Le Carré, John | David John M. Cornwell |
| Leinster, Murray | William Jenkins |
| Liddell, C. H. | Henry Kuttner &/or C. L. Moore |
| Long, Wesley | George O. Smith |
| MacCreigh, James | Frederik Pohl |
| MacDonald, Anson | Robert Anson Heinlein |
| Maloney, Mack | Brian Kelleher |
| McDonald, Raymond | Raymond Leger & Edward McDonald |
| McIntosh, J. T. | James MacGregor |
| McKettrig, Seaton | Randall Garrett |
| Naylor, Grant | Rob Grant & Doug Naylor |
| North, Andrew | Andre Norton |
| O'Donnell, K. M. | Barry N. Malzberg |
| O'Donnell, Lawrence | C. L. Moore &/or Henry Kuttner |
| Orwell, George | Eric Blair |
| Padgett, Lewis | C. L. Moore &/or Henry Kuttner |
| Parkes, Lucas | John Wyndham Parkes Lucas Beynon Harris |
| Phillips, Mark | Laurence Mark Janifer & Randall Phillip Garrett |
| Phillips, Rog | Roger P. Graham |
| Pogo | Mary Corrine "Patty" Gray |
| Rocklynne, Ross | Ross L. Rocklin |
| Rodman, Eric | Robert Silverberg |
| Rohmer, Sax | Arthur Ward |
| Rowling, J. K. | Joanne Rowling |
| Sanders, Winston P. | Poul Anderson |
| Satterfield, Charles | Frederik Pohl & Leonard Knapp; Frederik Pohl |
| Saunders, Caleb | Robert A. Heinlein |
| Seabright, Idris | Margaret St. Clair |
| Sharon, Rose | Judith Merril |
| Smith, Cordwainer | Paul Linebarger |
| Stewart, Will | Jack Williamson |
| Stine, Jovial Bob | Robert L. Stine |
| Stuart, Don A. | John W. Campbell, Jr. |
| Taine, John | Eric Temple Bell |
| Tenn, William | Philip Klass |
| Tiptree, James, Jr. | Alice Sheldon |
| Tucker, Bob | Arthur Wilson Tucker |
| Vance, Sgt. Gerald | House name for Ziff-Davis publishers |
| Vincent, Harl | Harold Vincent Schoepflin |
| Wentworth, Patricia | Dora Turnbull |
| Wilson, Gabriel | Ray Cummings & Gabrilla Cummings |
| Wyndham, John | John Wyndham Parkes Lucas Beynon Harris |

# Bibliography of Books Quoted

Because the citations in this dictionary were supplied by a number of different sources, it has not always been possible to determine the publisher of a given edition. In such cases, the publisher is either omitted entirely, or enclosed in brackets if it was possible to make an educated guess.

Abnett, Dan. *Xenos*. Pocket, 2001.

Ackerman, Forrest J., ed. *Gosh! Wow! (Sense of Wonder) Science Fiction*. Bantam, 1982.

Adams, Carsbie Clifton, et al. *Space Flight*. McGraw-Hill, 1958.

Adams, Douglas. *The Hitch-Hiker's Guide to the Galaxy*. Arthur Barker, 1979; *The Hitchhiker's Guide to the Galaxy*. Pocket, 1981.

___. *Mostly Harmless*. Ballantine, 1992.

___. *The Restaurant at the End of the Universe*. Pocket, 1985.

Adams, George. *Lectures on Natural and Experimental Philosophy*. 1794.

Adams, Michael. *Slayer Slang*. Oxford University Press, 2004.

Aldiss, Brian W. *Billion Year Spree: The History of Science Fiction*. Weidenfeld & Nicolson, 1973.

___. *Space Odysseys*. Doubleday, 1976.

___. *Space Opera*. Futura, 1974.

___. *Trillion Year Spree*. Victor Gollancz, 1986.

Aldrin, Buzz, and John Barnes. *Encounter with Tiber*. Hodder and Stoughton, 1996.

Alkon, Paul K. *Origins of Futuristic Fiction*. University of Georgia Press, 1987.

*Analog: The Best of Science Fiction*. Galahad, [ca1982].

Anderson, Poul. *After Doomsday*. Panther, 1968.

___. *Alight in the Void*. Tor, 1991.

___. *Avatar*. Sphere, 1981.

___. *The Boat of a Million Years*. Orb, 2004.

___. *Brain Wave*. Ballantine, 1954.

___. *Ensign Flandry*. Ace, 1985.

___. *Eutopia*. Sphere, 1974.

___. *The Fleet of Stars*. Tor, 1998.

___. *For Love and Glory*. Tor, 2004.

___. *Genesis*. Tor, 2000.

___. *The Gods Laughed*. Tor, 1982.

___. *Harvest of Stars*. Tor, 1994.

___. *Harvest the Fire*. Tor, 1997.

___. *The High Crusade*. Macfadden, 1968; Severn House, 1982.

___. *Operation Luna*. Tor, 1999.

___. *Starfarers*. Tor, 1999.

___. *The Stars Are Also Fire*. Tor, 1994.

___. *Tales of the Flying Mountains*. Tor, 1984.

___. *Tau Zero*. [Coronet], 1973.

___. *There Will Be Time*. Signet, 1973.

___. *Time and Stars*. Macfadden-Bartell, 1965.

___. *The Time Patrol*. Tor, 1991.

___. *The Trouble Twisters*. Berkley Medallion, 1967.

___. *Virgin Planet*. 1969.

Anderson, Poul, and Isaac Asimov. *No World of Their Own / The 1,000-Year Plan*. Ace, 1955.

Anthony, Piers. *And Eternity*. Avon, 1991.

___. *How Precious Was That While*. Tor, 2002.

___. *Triple Détente*. Sphere, 1975.

Anthony, Piers, and Robert E. Margroff. *Mouvar's Magic*. Tor, 1993.

Applegate, Katherine A. *Animorphs: The Sacrifice*. Scholastic, 2001.

Armstrong, Neil, et al. *First on the Moon*. Little, Brown, 1970.

Arnason, Eleanor. *A Woman of the Iron People, Part I*. AvoNova, 1992.

___. *A Woman of the Iron People, Part 2*. AvoNova, 1992.

Aronica, Lou, et al. *Full Spectrum 4*. Bantam, 1994.

Asaro, Catherine. *Ascendant Sun*. Tor, 2001.

___. *The Moon's Shadow*. Tor, 2004.

___. *The Radiant Seas*. Tor, 1999.

___. *Skyfall*. Tor, 2003.

___. *Spherical Harmonic*. Tor, 2002.

Ash, Brian. *The Visual Encyclopedia of Science Fiction*. Harmony, 1977, 1978.

___. *Who's Who in Science Fiction*. Elm Tree, 1976.

Ashley, Mike, ed. *The Random House Book of Science Fiction Stories*. Random House, 1996.

Asimov, Isaac. *Asimov on Science Fiction*. Doubleday, 1981.

___, ed. *Before the Golden Age: A Science Fiction Anthology of the 1930s*. Doubleday, 1974.

___, ed. *Before the Golden Age: Book 2*. Fawcett Crest, 1975.

___. *The Complete Robot*. Voyager, 1995.

___. *End of Eternity*. Doubleday, 1990.

___. *Foundation*. Gnome, 1951.

___. *Foundation's Edge*. Doubleday, 1982.

___. *I, Robot*. Gnome, 1950.

___. *Pebble in the Sky*. Doubleday, 1950.

___. *Prelude to Foundation*. Doubleday, 1988.

Asimov, Isaac, et al., eds. *The Mammoth Book of Short Fantasy Novels*. Robinson, 1986.

Asimov, Isaac, and Martin H. Greenberg, eds. *Isaac Asimov Presents the Golden Years of Science Fiction*. Bonanza, 1983.

Asimov, Isaac, Charles G. Waugh, and Martin Greenberg, eds. *Great Tales of Classic Science Fiction*. Galahad, 1990.

___, eds. *Isaac Asimov Presents Best Science Fiction Firsts*. Beaufort, 1984.

___, eds. *Science Fiction: Classic Stories from the Golden Age of Science Fiction*. Galahad, 1991.

___, eds. *Starships*. Ballantine, 1983.

Astor, John Jacob. *A Journey in Other Worlds*. D. Appleton, 1894; Bison, 2003.

Atheling, William Jr. *More Issues at Hand*. Advent, 1970.

Attebery, Brian. *Decoding Gender in Science Fiction*. Routledge, 2002.

Atton, Chris. *Alternative Media*. SAGE Publications, 2002.

Azzerad, Michael. *Our Band Could Be Your Life: Scenes from the American Indie Underground, 1981–1991*. Little, Brown, 2001.

Bacon-Smith, Camille. *Enterprising Women: Television Fandom and the Creation of Popular Myth*. University of Pennsylvania Press, 1992.

Bailey, J. O. *Pilgrims Through Space and Time: Trends and Patterns in Scientific and Utopian Fiction*. Argus, 1947.

Bailey, Ronald. *Liberation Biology: The Scientific and Moral Case for the Biotech Revolution*. Prometheus, 2005.

Baird, Alison. *The Empire of the Stars*. Aspect, 2005.

Baldwin, Bill. *The Defiance*. Warner, 1996.

Ballard, J. G. *The Best Short Stories of J. G. Ballard*. Picador, 1995.

___. *A User's Guide to the Millennium*. Picador, 1997.

Banks, Iain M. *Against a Dark Background*. [Orbit], 1993.

___. *Look to Windward*. Pocket, 2002.

Barnes, John. *Earth Made of Glass*. Tor, 1999.

___. *In the Hall of the Martian King*. Aspect, 2003.

___. *Kaleidoscope Century*. Phoenix, 1996.

___. *Patton's Spaceship*. Harper Prism, 1997.

___. *A Princess of the Aerie*. Aspect, 2003.

Barnes, Steven. *Firedance*. Tor, 1995.

Baxter, Stephen. *Ring*. HarperCollins, 1996.

___. *Titan*. Eos, 2001.

Bear, Greg. *The Collected Stories of Greg Bear*. Orb, 2003.

___. *Eon*. Tor, 1986.

___. *The Forge of God*. Tor, 1987.

___. *Moving Mars*. Tor, 1993.

___. *Slant*. Legend, 1998.

Bear, Greg, and Martin H. Greenberg, eds. *New Legends*. Legend, 1996.

Beason, Doug, and Kevin J. Anderson. *Assemblers of Infinity*. Bantam Spectra, 1993.

Benford, Gregory. *Matter's End*. Victor Gollancz, 1996.

___. *The Martian Race*. Aspect, 2001.

___. *Timescape*. Simon and Schuster, 1980.

Benford, Gregory, and David Brin. *The Heart of the Comet*. Bantam, 1986.

Bester, Alfred. *The Stars My Destination*. Vintage, 1996.

Binder, Eando. *The Impossible World*. Curtis, 1967.

Bischoff, David. *Ship of Ghosts*. Tor, 2002.

Bishop, Michael. *And Strange at Ecbatan the Trees.* Harper & Row, 1976.

___. *Brighten to Incandescence.* Golden Gryphon, 2003.

___, ed. *Nebula Awards 23.* Harcourt Brace Jovanovich, 1989.

___. *No Enemy But Time.* Science Fiction Book Club, 1982.

___. *Philip K. Dick Is Dead, Alas.* Orb, 1994.

Bisson, Terry. *Bears Discover Fire and Other Stories.* Tor, 1993.

*Bladerunner.* (screenplay), 1981.

Blair, Andrew. *Annals of the 29th Century.* Samuel Tinsley, 1874.

Blish, James. *Spock Must Die!* Bantam, 1970.

___. *Star Trek.* Bantam, 1967.

___. *Star Trek: Classic Episodes 1.* Bantam, 1992.

___. *Star Trek 2.* Bantam, 1968.

___. *Star Trek 4.* Bantam, 1971.

___. *Star Trek 8.* Bantam, 1972.

___. *Star Trek 10.* Bantam, 1974.

Bonanno, Margaret Wander. *Dwellers in the Crucible.* Pocket, 1985.

Bond, Nelson. *No Time Like the Future.* Avon, 1954.

Bonfiglioli, Kyril. *Something Nasty in the Woodshed.* Macmillan, 1976.

*Boskone 9 Filk-Song Book.* NESFA Press, 1972.

Boucher, Anthony, ed. *The Best from Fantasy and Science Fiction (Fourth Series).* Ace, 1955.

___. *Rocket to the Morgue.* Pyramid, 1975.

Bova, Ben, ed. *The Best of the Nebulas.* Tor, 1989.

___. *The Craft of Writing Science Fiction That Sells.* Writers Digest, 1994.

___. *Mars.* NEL, 1993.

___. *The Precipice.* Tor, 2002.

___. *Saturn.* Tor, 2004.

___. *The Winds of Altair.* Tor, 1988.

Bowen, Francis. *The Principles of Metaphysical and Ethical Science Applied to the Evidences of Religion.* Hickling, Swan and Brown, 1855.

Bowes, Richard. *From the Files of the Time Rangers.* Golden Gryphon, 2005.

Bowie, David. *The Best of David Bowie 1969/1974.* Hal Leonard Corporation, [ca1999].

Brackett, Leigh. *The Best of Leigh Brackett.* Nelson Doubleday (bookclub edition), 1977.

___. *The Halfling and Other Stories.* Ace, 1973.

Bradbury, Ray. *The Toynbee Convector.* Bantam Spectra, 1989.

Bradley, Marion. *Darkover Landfall.* Gregg Press, 1972.

Bradley, Marion Zimmer. *The Bloody Sun.* Ace, 1979.

___. *Brass Dragon.* Ace, 1980.

___. *Darkover Landfall.* Arrow, 1987.

___. *The Inheritor.* Tor, 1984.

___. *The Planet Savers / The Sword of Aldones.* Ace, 1982.

___. *Star of Danger.* Ace, 1985.

___. *The Sword of Aldones.* Ace, 1962.

___. *Thendara House.* DAW, 1991.

___. *The Winds of Darkover.* Berkley, 1982.

___. *The World Wreckers.* Berkley, 1984.

Bradley, Marion Zimmer, and Paul Edwin Zimmer. *Survivors.* Arrow Legend, 1989.

Branwyn, Gareth. *Absolute Beginner's Guide to Building Robots.* QUE, 2004.

Bretnor, Reginald. *The Craft of Science Fiction.* Harper & Row, 1976.

___, ed. *Modern Science Fiction: Its Meaning and Its Future.* Coward-McCann, 1953.

___. *Science Fiction, Today and Tomorrow.* Harper & Row, 1974.

Bridges, T. C. *City of No Escape.* George Newnes, 1925.

Brin, David. *Heaven's Reach.* Bantam, 1998.

___. *Infinity's Shore.* Bantam, 1997.

___. *Kiln People.* Tor, 2002.

___. *Otherness.* Orbit, 1994.

___. *The Practice Effect.* Bantam, 1984.

___. *Startide Rising.* Bantam, 1983.

___. *Sundiver.* Bantam, 1980.

___. *Uplift War.* Bantam, 1987.

Broderick, Damien. *The Dreaming Dragons.* Pocket, 1980.

___. *Reading by Starlight.* Routledge, 1995.

___. *The Spike.* Reed, 1997.

___. *X, Y, Z, T: Dimensions of Science Fiction.* Borgo, 2004.

Brosnan, John. *Opoponax Invasion.* Gollancz, 1994.

Brown, Eric. *Engineman.* Pan, 1994.

Brown, Fredric. *Angels and Spaceships.* Dutton, 1954.

___. *The Lights in the Sky Are Stars.* Bantam, 1968.

___. *What Mad Universe?* Bantam, 1978.

Brunner, John. *The Altar on Asconel.* Ace, 1965.

___. *The Atlantic Abomination.* Ace, 1960.

___. *Muddle Earth.* Ballantine, 1993.

___. *The Shockwave Rider.* Harper & Row, 1975.

___. *Stand on Zanzibar.* Arrow, 1971.

___. *Times Without Number.* Elmfield, 1981.

Brust, Steven. *Jhereg.* Ace, 1983.

Budrys, Algis. *Benchmarks.* Southern Illinois University Press, 1985.

___. *Falling Torch.* Baen, 1990.

Bujold, Lois McMaster. *Cordelia's Honor.* Baen, 1999.

___. *Diplomatic Immunity.* Baen, 2002.

___. *Mirror Dance.* Baen, 1994.

___. *Shards of Honor.* Headline, 1988; Baen, 1991.

___. *The Vor Game.* Baen, 1990; Pan, 1993.

___. *The Warrior's Apprentice.* Baen, 1990, 1992, and 1997.

Bunch, Chris. *Homefall.* New American Library, 2001.

Burgess, Anthony. *A Clockwork Orange.* W. W. Norton, 1963.

Burroughs, Edgar Rice. *At the Earth's Core*. Grosset & Dunlap, 1922.

___. *Master Mind of Mars*. Grosset & Dunlap, 1928.

___. *A Princess of Mars*. Grosset & Dunlap, 1917.

Burroughs, William S. *Last Words*. Grove, 2000.

Busby, F. M. *The Singularity Project*. Tor, 1994.

Butler, Octavia. *Dawn*. [Warner], 1991.

___. *Imago*. Warner, 1991.

Bygrave, Mike, et al., eds. *Time Out's Book of London*. Time Out, 1972.

Callenbach, Ernest. *Ecotopia*. Banyan Tree, 1975.

Cameron, Alastair. *Fantasy Classification System*. Canadian Science Fiction Association, 1952.

Cameron, James and William Wisher. *Terminator 2: Judgement Day*. Penguin, 1990.

Campbell, John W., Jr., ed. *The Astounding Science Fiction Anthology*. Simon and Schuster, 1952.

___. *Cloak of Aesir*. Shasta, 1952.

___. *A New Dawn: The Complete Don A. Stuart Stories* NESFA Press, 2003

Capek, Karel. *Four Plays*. Trans. Peter Majer and Cathy Porter. Methuen, 1999.

___. *R.U.R. Rossum's Universal Robots*. Aventinum, 1923.

___. *R.U.R.* Trans. Paul Selver. 1923.

___. *R.U.R. (Rossum's Universal Robots)*. Trans. Claudia Novak. Penguin, 1994.

Card, Orson Scott. *Children of the Mind*. Tor, 1997.

___. *Ender's Game*. Tor, 1994.

___. *First Meetings: Three Stories from the Enderverse*. Subterranean, 2002.

___. *The Memory of Earth*. Tor, 1993.

___. *Speaker for the Dead*. Tor, 1986.

___. *The Worthing Saga*. Tor, 1990.

___. *Xenocide*. Tor, 1991.

Carey, Diane. *Battlestations!*. Pocket, 1986.

___. *Dreadnought*. Pocket, 1986.

___. *Great Starship Race*. Pocket, 1993.

___. *Invasion!*. Pocket, 1996.

Carey, Diane, and James I. Kirkland. *First Frontier*. Simon & Schuster, 1995.

Carlyle, Thomas, and Jane Welsh Carlyle. *The Collected Letters of Thomas Carlyle and Jane Welsh Carlyle Vol. 1*. 1820.

Carmody, Isobelle. *Ashling*. Tor, 2001.

Carnell, John, ed. *New Writings in SF 8*. Corgi, 1966.

Carr, Terry, ed. *Universe 1*. Ace, 1971.

Carré, John Le. *A Small Town in Germany*. Coward-McCann, 1968.

Carroll, Noël, and Jinhee Choi, eds. *Philosophy of Film and Motion Pictures*. Blackwell Publishing, 2006.

Carter, Chris. *The Truth Is out There: The Official Guide to The X-Files*. Harper, 1995.

Carter, Lin. *Black Legion of Callisto*. Dell, 1972.

Carver, Jeffrey A. *Eternity's End*. Tor, 2001.

Casti, John L., and Anders Karlqvist, eds. *Mission to Abisko*. Perseus, 1999.

Chalker, Jack L. *A Jungle of Stars*. Ballantine, 1976.

___. *Midnight at the Well of Souls*. Baen, 2002.

___. *Priam's Lens*. Del Rey, 1999.

___. *The Sea Is Full of Stars*. Ballantine, 1999.

Charlton, James. *Bred Any Good Rooks Lately?* Doubleday, 1986.

Chepaitis, Barbara. *These Dreams*. Washington Square, 2003.

Cherryh, C. J. *Chanur's Homecoming*. Phantasia, 1986.

___. *Cyteen*. Warner, 1988.

___. *Forge of Heaven*. Eos, 2004.

___. *Merchanter's Luck*. DAW, 1982.

___. *Port Eternity*. DAW, 1982.

___. *Pride of Chanur*. DAW, 1991.

___. *Voyager In Night*. DAW, 1984.

Chiang, Ted. *Stories of Your Life and Others*. Tor, 2002.

Christian, Deborah. *Mainline*. Tor, 1997.

Chupp, Sam, et al. *In Nomine Infernal Player's Guide*. Steve Jackson Games, 1998.

Claremont, Chris. *FirstFlight*. Ace, 1987.

Clareson, Thomas D., ed. *SF: The Other Side of Realism*. Bowling Green University Popular Press, 1971.

Clarke, Arthur C. *Childhood's End*. Ballantine, 1953.

___. *The Exploration of Space*. 1951.

___. *Fall of Moondust*. Dell, 1963.

___. *Fountains of Paradise*. Gollancz, 1979.

___. *Future Space Programs*. 1975.

___. *Greetings, Carbon-Based Bipeds!: Collected Essays, 1934–1998*. St. Martin's, 1999.

___. *The Hammer of God*. Gollancz, 1993.

___. *Interplanetary Flight*. 1950.

___. *Islands in the Sky*. John C. Winston Co., 1952.

___. *Profiles of the Future: An Inquiry into the Limits of the Possible*. Victor Gollancz, 1962; trans. into French as *Profil du futur*. Éditions Retz, 1964; Popular Library, 1977.

___. *Rendezvous with Rama*. Victor Gollancz, 1973.

___. *Report on Planet Three and Other Speculations*. Signet, 1972.

___. *3001: Final Odyssey*. HarperCollins, 1997.

___. *The Sands of Mars*. Sidgwick and Jackson, 1951.

___. *The Songs of Distant Earth*. Grafton, 1986.

Clarke, Arthur C., and Gentry Lee. *Rama Revealed*. Victor Gollancz, 1993.

Clément, Gilles. *Fundamentals of Space Medicine*. Springer, 2005.

Clement, Hal. *Half Life*. Tor, 2000.

Clifton, Mark. *Eight Keys to Eden*. Pan, 1965.

Clute, John. *Appleseed*. Tor, 2001.

___. *Strokes*. Serconia, 1988.

Clute, John, and John Grant, eds. *The Encyclopedia of Fantasy*. St. Martin's Griffin, 1998.

Clute, John, and Peter Nicholls, eds. *The Encyclopedia of Science Fiction*. St. Martin's, 1993; St. Martin's Griffin, 1995.

Clute, John, David Pringle, and Simon Ounsley, eds. *Interzone: The 3rd Anthology*. Simon & Schuster, 1988.

Cohen, Jack, and Ian Stewart. *Evolving the Alien*. Ebury, 2002.

Cole, Allen, and Chris Bunch. *The Court of a Thousand Suns*. Ballantine, 1990.

___. *Sten*. Ballantine, 1990.

___. *Wolf Worlds*. Ballantine, 1990.

Colfer, Eoin. *Artemis Fowl*. Viking, 2001.

Colgan, Jenny. *The Boy I Loved Before*. St. Martin's Griffin, 2005.

Conklin, Groff, ed. *The Best of Science Fiction*. Crown, 1946.

___, ed. *Five-Odd*. Pyramid, 1964.

___. *Possible Worlds of Science Fiction*. The Vanguard Press, 1951.

___, ed. *A Treasury of Science Fiction*. Bonanza, 1980.

Coon, Gene. *Errand of Mercy*. (teleplay) Jan. 23, 1967.

Cooper, Edmund. *Sea-Horse in the Sky*. Coronet, 1980.

Cortiel, Jeanne. *Demand My Writing: Joanna Russ/Feminism/Science Fiction*. Liverpool University Press, 1999.

Cox, Greg. *Assignment: Eternity*. Pocket, 1998.

Craig, Patricia, and Mary Cadogan. *The Lady Investigates*. 1981.

Crichton, Michael. *Sphere*. Ballantine, 1987.

Crispin, Edmund. *Best SF Three*. Faber and Faber, 1958.

___. *Best SF Five*. Faber and Faber, 1963.

Crowther, Peter, ed. *Moon Shots*. DAW, 1999.

Currie, Tony. *The Radio Times Story*. Kelly Publications, 2001.

Czerneda, Julie E. *In the Company of Others*. DAW, 2001.

___. *To Trade the Stars*. DAW, 2002.

Daley, Brian. *Han Solo's Revenge*. Ballantine, 1979.

___. *Star Wars: The Han Solo Adventures*. Del Rey, 1979.

Dalmas, John. *The Three-Cornered War*. Baen, 1999.

Dann, Jack, ed. *Immortal: Short Novels of the Transhuman Future*. Harper & Row, 1978.

___, ed. *Nebula Awards 32*. Harcourt Brace, 1998.

Danvers, Dennis. *The Watch*. HarperCollins, 2002.

Danziger, Paula. *This Place Has No Atmosphere*. Dell, 1987.

Datlow, Ellen, Kelly Link, and Gavin J. Grant, eds. *The Year's Best Fantasy and Horror: Eighteenth Annual Collection*. St. Martin's, 2005.

Datlow, Ellen, and Terri Windling. *The Year's Best Fantasy: First Annual Collection*. St. Martin's, 1988.

Davenport, Basil, ed. *The Science Fiction Novel: Imagination and Social Criticism*. Advent, 1959.

David, James F. *Before the Cradle Falls*. Tor, 2004.

David, Peter. *Captain's Daughter*. Pocket, 1995.

___. *Imzadi*. Pocket, 1992.

Davidson, Avram. *The Avram Davidson Treasury*. Tor, 1999.

Davies, Owen, ed. *The Omni Book of Space.* Zebra, 1983.

Davis, Mike. *Ecology of Fear.* Vintage, 1999.

Dawkins, Richard. *Unweaving the Rainbow: Science, Delusion and the Appetite for Wonder.* Mariner, 2000.

de Camp, L. Sprague. *Science-Fiction Handbook.* Hermitage House, 1953.

de Quincey, Thomas. *Miscellaneous Essays.* Ticknor, Reed, and Fields, 1851.

DeCandido, Keith R. A. *Farscape: House of Cards.* Tor, 2001.

Dedman, Stephen. *Foreign Bodies.* Tor, 2000.

Deighton, Len. *Twinkle, Twinkle Little Spy.* Cape, 1976.

del Rey, Lester. *The World of Science Fiction.* Garland Publishing, 1980.

Delany, Samuel R. *Babel-17.* Ace, 1966.

___. *The Ballad of Beta-2.* Ace, 1965; Gregg, 1977.

___. *Empire Star.* Gregg, 1977.

___. *The Jewel-Hinged Jaw.* Berkley Windhover, 1978.

___. *Nova.* Vintage, 2002.

___. *Stars in My Pocket Like Grains of Sand.* Wesleyan University Press, 2004.

___. *Trouble on Triton.* Wesleyan University Press, 1996.

Derleth, August, ed. *The Outer Reaches.* Pellegrini & Cudahy, 1951.

___, ed. *Strange Ports of Call.* Pellegrini & Cudahy, 1948.

Dery, Mark. *Escape Velocity.* Grove, 1996.

Dewey, Joseph. *In a Dark Time.* Purdue Research Foundation, 1990.

Dick, Philip K. *Counter-Clock World.* Grafton, 1990.

___. *Paycheck.* Citadel, 1990.

___. *The Minority Report and Other Classic Stories.* Citadel, 2002.

___. *Ubik.* Bantam, 1977.

___. *We Can Remember It for You Wholesale.* HarperCollins, 1994.

Dickinson, Peter. *The Seventh Raven.* 1981.

Dickson, Gordon R. *The Final Encyclopedia.* Ace, 1985.

___. *Soldier, Ask Not.* Tor, 1993.

___. *Time Storm.* St. Martin's, 1977.

Dietz, William C. *EarthRise.* Ace, 2003.

Dillard, J. M. *The Lost Years.* Pocket, 1989.

___. *Mindshadow.* Pocket, 1986.

Diment, Adam. *The Bang Bang Birds.* 1968.

Dirda, Michael. *Bound to Please.* W. W. Norton, 2005.

Disch, Thomas M. *On SF.* Universtiy of Michigan Press, 2005.

Doctorow, Cory. *Down and Out in the Magic Kingdom.* Tor, 2003.

Dodge, Martin, and Rob Kitchin. *Mapping Cyberspace.* Routledge, 2001.

Dorsey, Candas Jane. *A Paradigm of Earth.* Tor, 2002.

Douglas, Ian. *Europa Strike.* Eos, 2000.

___. *Luna Marine.* Eos, 1999.

Doyle, Arthur Conan. *The Lost World and Other Stories.* Wordsworth Editions Limited, 1995.

Doyle, Debra, and James D. Macdonald. *By Honor Betray'd.* Tor, 1994.

Dozois, Gardner, ed. *The Good New Stuff.* St. Martin's, 1999.

___, ed. *Isaac Asimov's Mars.* Berkley, 1991.

___, ed. *Mammoth Book of Best New SF, 12th Collection.* Robinson, 1999.

___, ed. *Mammoth Book of Best New SF 13.* Robinson, 2000.

___, ed. *Worldmakers.* St. Martin's, 2001.

___, ed. *The Year's Best Science Fiction Fifth Annual Coll.* St. Martin's, 1987.

___, ed. *The Year's Best Science Fiction: Fifteenth Annual Collection.* St. Martin's, 1998.

___, ed. *The Year's Best Science Fiction: Twenty-Second Annual Collection.* St. Martin's, 2005.

Dozois, Gardner, et al. *Slow Dancing through Time.* Ursus, 1990.

Drabble, Margaret, ed. *The Oxford Companion to English Literature (Fifth Edition).* Oxford University Press, 1991.

Drago, Ty. *Phobos.* Tor, 2004.

Drake, David, ed. *Dogs of War.* Aspect, 2002.

___. *Hammer's Slammers.* Arrow, 1985.

___. *Space Infantry.* Berkley, 1989.

Drazen, Patrick. *Anime Explosion!* Stone Bridge, 2003.

Duane, Diane. *My Enemy, My Ally.* Pocket, 1984.

___. *So You Want to Be a Wizard?* Delacorte, 1983.

___. *Starrise at Corrivale.* TSR, 1998.

___. *Stealing the Elf-King's Roses.* Aspect, 2002.

___. *Storm at Eldala.* TSR, 1999.

Dvorkin, Daniel, and David Dvorkin. *Captains' Honor.* Pocket, 1989.

Dyson, George. *Project Orion: The True Story of the Atomic Spaceship.* Henry Holt, 2002.

Eddings, David, and Leigh Eddings. *The Redemption of Althalus.* Voyager, 2000.

Edwards, Malcolm, and Robert Holdstock. *Tour of the Universe.* Pierrot, 1980.

Eggleton, Bob. *Greetings From Earth.* Paper Tiger, 2000.

Eklund, Gordon. *Starless World.* Bantam, 1978.

Elgin, Suzette Haden. *The Judas Rose.* The Feminist Press, 2002.

Ellison, Harlan, ed. *Again, Dangerous Visions.* Doubleday, 1972.

___, ed. *Dangerous Visions.* Doubleday, 1967.

___. *Ellison Wonderland.* Paperback Library, 1962.

___. *A Touch of Infinity.* Ace, 1959.

Elrick, George S. *Science Fiction Handbook.* Chicago Review Press, 1978.

Elwood, Roger, ed. *Futurelove.* Bobbs-Merrill, 1977.

___, ed. *Ten Tomorrows.* Fawcett, 1973.

*Encounter at Farpoint.* (teleplay), May 22, 1987.

Eney, Dick, ed. *The Proceedings; Discon.* Advent, 1965.

Eney, Richard H. *Fancyclopedia II.* 1959; Mirage, 1979.

Engdahl, Sylvia, ed. *Anywhere, Anywhen.* Atheneum, 1976.

Eshbach, Lloyd Arthur. *Of Worlds Beyond.* Fantasy Press, 1947.

Evanovich, Janet. *Visions of Sugar Plums.* St. Martin's, 2002.

Farmer, Philip José. *Behind the Walls of Terra.* Ace, 1970.

___. *Gates of Creation.* Sphere, 1975.

___. *The Green Odyssey.* Sphere, 1976; Gregg, 1978.

___. *The Maker of Universes.* Sphere, 1975.

___. *Tongues of the Moon.* Pyramid, 1964.

___. *A Woman a Day.* Beacon, 1960.

___. *The World of Tiers: Volume 2.* Tor, 1997.

Farren, Mick. *More Than Mortal.* Tor, 2002.

Faucette, John M. *Crown of Infinity.* Ace, 1968.

Faust, Joe Clifford. *Desperate Measures.* Ballantine, 1989.

Fawcett, Bill, ed. *The Far Stars War.* Roc, 1990.

Fawkes, Richard. *Face of the Enemy.* Eos, 2001.

Feintuch, David. *Patriarch's Hope.* Aspect, 2000.

Ferman, Edward L., and Barry N. Malzberg, eds. *Final Stage.* Charterhouse, 1974.

Fforde, Jasper. *The Eyre Affair.* Viking, 2001.

___. *Something Rotten.* Viking, 2004.

Finch, James H., and E. Graham Dougall, eds. *Computer Security: A Global Challenge.* North-Holland, 1984.

Finney, Jack. *The Body Snatchers.* Gregg, 1976.

Flinn, Denny Martin. *The Fearful Summons.* Pocket, 1995.

Flynn, Michael. *Falling Stars.* Tor, 2002.

___. *Lodestar.* Tor, 2001.

___. *Rogue Star.* Tor, 1999.

Fontana, D. C. *The Enterprise Incident.* (teleplay) June 13, 1968.

*Forbidden Planet.* (screenplay), 1955.

Ford, John M. *Heat of Fusion and Other Stories.* Tor, 2004.

___. *How Much for Just the Planet?* Pocket, 1987.

Forrest, Katherine V. *Daughters of an Amber Noon.* Alyson Publications, 2002.

Fort, Charles. *The Complete Books of Charles Fort.* Dover, 1974.

Forward, Robert L. *Rocheworld.* Baen, 1990.

Foster, Alan Dean. *Bloodhype.* Ballantine, 1973.

___. *Cat.a.lyst.* Berkley, 1991.

___. *The End of the Matter.* Ballantine, 1977.

___. *Life Form.* Orbit, 1995.

___. *Mid-Flinx.* Del Rey, 1995.

___. *Quozl.* Ace, 1989.

___. *The Tar-Aiym Krang.* Ballantine, 1972 and 1983.

___. *Voyage to the City of the Dead.* New English Library, 1986.

Foster, Alan Dean, and Eric Frank Russell. *Design for Great-Day.* Tor, 1996.

Fowler, Karen Joy, et al., eds. *The James Tiptree Award Anthology 1.* Tachyon Publications, 2005.

Frank, Alan. *Sci-Fi Now.* Octopus, 1978.

Frankowski, Leo. *A Boy and His Tank.* Baen, 2000.

___. *The Flying Warlord.* Del Rey, 1989.

Frayn, Michael. *A Very Private Life.* The Viking Press, 1968.

Freer, Dave, and Eric Flint. *Rats, Bats and Vats*. Baen, 2000.

Frenkel, James, ed. *True Names and the Opening of the Cyberspace Frontier*. Tor, 2001.

Friedman, C. S. *Black Sun Rising*. DAW, 1991.

Friedman, Michael Jan. *My Brother's Keeper*. Pocket, 1999.

Gardner, Craig Shaw. *Back to the Future II*. Berkley, 1989.

Gardner, James Alan. *Ascending*. Eos, 2001.

___. *Expendable*. Avon, 1997.

___. *Hunted*. Eos, 2000.

Garnett, David, ed. *New Worlds 1*. VGSF, 1991.

___, ed. *New Worlds 3*. Victor Gollancz, 1993.

Garrett, Randall. *Unwise Child*. Mayflower, 1963.

Gernsback, Hugo. *Ralph 124C 41+*. Stratford, 1925; Kemsley Newspapers, 1952.

Gerrold, David. *Bouncing Off the Moon*. Tor, 2001.

___. *Jumping Off the Planet*. Tor, 2001.

___. *The Middle of Nowhere*. BenBella, 2003.

___. *The Trouble With Tribbles*. (teleplay) Desilu Productions, Aug. 1, 1967.

___. *The Trouble With Tribbles*. Ballantine, 1973.

___. *When Harlie Was One*. 1972.

___. *Yesterday's Children*. Dell, 1972.

Gibson, William. *Burning Chrome*. Eos, 2003.

___. *Idoru*. Putnam, 1996.

___. *Neuromancer*. Ace, 1991.

___. *Virtual Light*. Bantam, 1993.

Gielgud, Val. *The Goggle-Box Affair*. Collins, 1963.

Glenn, John, et al. *Into Orbit*. Cassell, 1962.

Glut, Donald. *The Empire Strikes Back*. Sphere, 1980.

Goodare, Julian. *The Scottish Witch-Hunt in Context*. Manchester University Press, 2002.

Goodwin, Barbara, ed. *The Philosophy of Utopia*. Frank Cass & Co., 2001.

Gordon, Joan, and Veronica Hollinger. *Blood Read*. University of Pennsylvania Press, 1997.

Graf, L .A. *Firestorm*. Pocket, 1994.

___. *Ice Trap*. Pocket, 1992.

Graf, L. A., and Michael Jan Friedman. *War Dragons*. Pocket, 1998.

Graff, Gerald. *Literature Against Itself*. The University of Chicago Press, 1979.

Grant, Rob, and Doug Naylor. *Son of Soup*. Penguin, 1996.

Gray, William G. *Qabalistic Concepts*. Red Wheel, 1997.

Greeley, Andrew M., and Michael Cassutt, eds. *Sacred Visions*. Tor, 1991.

Green, Simon R. *Deathstalker Rebellion*. Roc, 1996.

Greenberg, Martin, ed. *Journey to Infinity*. Gnome, 1951.

___, ed. *Men Against the Stars*. Pyramid, 1958.

___, ed. *Travelers of Space*. Gnome, 1951.

Gregersen, Niels Henrik. *From Complexity to Life: On The Emergence of Life and Meaning*. Oxford University Press, 2003.

Gregory, Julian R., and Roger Price. *The Tomorrow People in The Visitor.* Pan, 1973.

Groening, Matt. *School Is Hell.* Pantheon, 1987.

Gunn, James. *Alternate Worlds.* Prentice-Hall, 1975.

___, ed. *The New Encyclopedia of Science Ficton.* Viking Penguin, 1988.

Haber, Karen, ed. *Exploring the Matrix: Visions of the Cyber Present.* St. Martin's, 2003.

Hahn, Mary Downing. *Time For Andrew.* Avon Camelot, 1995.

Haldeman, Jack C. *Another Round at the Spaceport Bar.* New English Library, 1992.

Haldeman, Joe. *Forever Free.* Ace, 1999.

___. *The Forever War.* Eos, 2003.

___. *Worlds.* Gollancz, 2002.

Hambly, Barbara. *Crossroad.* Pocket, 1994.

___. *Ishmael.* Pocket, 1985.

Hamilton, Edmond. *Return to the Stars.* Prestige, 1969.

___. *The Weapon from Beyond.* Ace, 1967.

Hamilton, Peter F. *The Confederation Handbook.* Aspect, 2002.

___. *Fallen Dragon.* Warner, 2003.

___. *The Nano Flower.* Tor, 1999.

Harlan, Thomas. *Wasteland of Flint.* Tor, 2004.

Harland, David M., and John E. Catchpole. *Creating the International Space Station.* Springer, 2002.

Harness, Charles L. *The Paradox Men.* Crown, 1984.

Harness, Charles. *The Firebird.* Pocke, 1981.

Harper, Tara K. *Silver Moons, Black Steel.* Del Rey, 2001.

Harrison, Harry, ed. *Nova 2.* Walker, 1972.

___. *Stainless Steel Rat Sings the Blues.* Bantam, 1994.

___. *Stainless Steel Visions.* Tor, 1993.

Harrison, M. John. *Light.* Bantam, 2004.

Harth, Erich. *Dawn of a Millennium: Beyond Evolution and Culture.* Little, Brown, 1990.

Hartwell, David. *Age of Wonders.* Walker, 1984.

Hartwell, David G., ed. *Christmas Stars.* Tor, 2004.

___, ed. *The Science Fiction Century.* Tor, 1997.

___, ed. *Year's Best SF 8.* Eos, 2003.

Hartwell, David G., and Kathryn Cramer, eds. *Year's Best Fantasy 3.* Eos, 2003.

___, eds. *Year's Best SF 9.* Eos, 2004.

Harvey, Robert C. *The Art of the Comic Book: An Aesthetic History.* University Press of Mississippi, 1996.

Hatch, Richard, and Christopher Golden. *Battlestar Galactica: Armageddon.* Pocket, 1997.

Hawke, Simon. *The Patrian Transgression.* Pocket, 1994.

Hay, William D. *Three Hundred Years Hence.* Newman, 1881.

Hayles, N. Katherine, ed. *Nanoculture.* Intellect, 2004.

Heinlein, Robert A. *Assignment in Eternity.* Fantasy Press, 1953.

___. *Between Planets*. Scribners, 1951.

___. *Double Star*. The New American Library, 1957.

___. *Farmer in the Sky*. Ballantine, 1975.

___. *Friday*. Holt, Rinehart and Winston, 1982.

___. *The Man Who Sold the Moon*. Shasta, 1950.

___. *The Menace from Earth*. Corgi, 1968.

___. *The Moon is a Harsh Mistress*. Putnam, 1966.

___. *Podkayne of Mars*. G. P. Putnam's Sons, 1963.

___. *The Puppet Masters*. Doubleday, 1951.

___. *The Rolling Stones*. Scribners, 1952.

___. *Space Cadet*. Scribners, 1948.

___. *Starman Jones*. Charles Scribner's Sons, 1953.

___. *Starship Troopers*. Ace, 1987.

___. *Stranger in a Strange Land*. Putnam, 1961.

___. *Time Enough For Love*. Ace, 1988.

___. *Time for the Stars*. Scribners, 1956.

___. *Tunnel in the Sky*. Scribners, 1955.

Heinlein, Robert A., and Virginia Heinlein. *Grumbles from the Grave*. Del Rey, 1990.

Herbert, Brian, and Kevin J. Anderson. *Dune: Battle of Corrin*. Tor, 2004.

___. *Dune: The Butlerian Jihad*. Tor, 2003.

Herbert, Frank. *Destination: Void*. Berkley Medallion, 1966.

___. *The Dosadi Experiment*. G. P. Putnam's Sons, 1977.

___. *The Heaven Makers*. Del Rey, 1977.

___, ed. *Nebula Winners Fifteen*. Harper & Row, 1981.

*Heritage Signature Auction #811*. (catalog) Heritage Comics Auctions, 2004.

Heuer, Kenneth. *Men of Other Planets*. Pellegrini & Cudahy, 1951.

Hill, Douglas. *Colsec Rebellion*. Puffin, 1986.

Hodgell, P. C. *God Stalk*. Berkley, 1983.

Hogan, James P. *The Two Faces of Tomorrow*. Del Rey, 1979.

Holland, Cecilia. *Floating Worlds*. Victor Gollancz, 2000.

Holland, Ralph M. *Ghu's Lexicon*. National Fantasy Fan Federation, 1958.

Hollinger, Veronica, and Joan Gordon, eds. *Edging into the Future*. University of Pennsylvania Press, 2002.

Holmes, H. H. *Rocket to the Morgue*. Duell, Sloan and Pearce, 1942

Holmes, Oliver Wendell. *Over the Teacups*. Houghton, Mifflin, 1891.

Holmes, R. *Dr. Who: Deadly Assassin*. (teleplay), 1976.

Hoskins, Robert, ed. *Infinity 2*. Lancer, 1971.

___, ed. *Strange Tomorrows*. Lancer, 1972.

Hunter, I.Q., ed. *British Science Fiction Cinema*. Routledge, 1999.

Huxley, Aldous. *Brave New World*. Chatto & Windus, 1932.

___. *Music at Night*. [Chatto & Windus], 1931.

Irwin, Walter, and G. B. Love, eds. *The Best of Trek*. New American Library, 1978.

Jackson, Steve, and William A. Garton. *GURPS Space*. Steve Jackson Games, 1990.

Janifer, Laurence M. *Knave and the Game*. Doubleday, 2002.

Jenkins, Henry. *Textual Poachers: Television Fans and Participatory Culture.*

Routledge, 1992.

Jeter, K. W. *The Mandalorian Armor.* Bantam, 1998.

John, Elton. *One Night Only: The Greatest Hits.* Warner Bros. Publications, 2003.

Johnson, William. *Focus on Science Fiction Film.* Prentice-Hall, 1972.

Johnson-Smith, Jan. *American Science Fiction TV: Star Trek, Stargate, and Beyond.* Wesleyan University Press, 2005.

Jones, Diana Wynne. *The Lives of Christopher Chant.* HarperTrophy, 2001.

___. *Year of the Griffin.* Greenwillow, 2001.

Jones, Edward, and Farah Mendlesohn, eds. *The Cambridge Companion to Science Fiction.* Cambridge University Press, 2003.

Jones, Stefan. *GURPS Uplift.* Steve Jackson Games, 1990.

Joseph, M. K. *The Hole in the Zero.* Science Fiction Book Club, 1968.

Julius, Marshall. *Action!: The Action Movie A-Z.* Indiana University Press, 1996.

Kapp, Colin. *Chaos Weapon.* Ballantine, 1977.

Keel, John A. *The Complete Guide to Mysterious Beings.* Tor, 2002.

Kessel, John. *Corrupting Dr. Nice.* Tor, 1998.

Keyon, Michael. *The Whole Hog.* Collins, 1967.

Kilian, Crawford. *The Empire of Time.* Ballantine, 1985.

Killough, Lee. *The Doppelganger Gambit.* Ballantine, 1979.

King, Stephen. *The Stand.* Doubleday, 1978.

Kingsbury, Donald. *Psychohistorical Crisis.* Tor, 2002.

Kippax, John R. *The Call of the Stars.* G. P. Putnam's Sons, 1914.

Klaw, Rick. *Geek Confidential: Echoes from the 21st Century.* MonkeyBrain, 2003.

Knight, Damon, ed. *A Century of Science Fiction.* Simon & Schuster, 1962.

___, ed. *Cities of Wonder.* MacFadden-Bartell, 1967.

___. *The Futurians.* John Day, 1977.

___, ed. *Orbit 8.* Berkley Medallion, 1971.

___. *Why Do Birds.* Tor, 1994.

Koestler, Arthur. *The Trail of the Dinosaur and Other Essays* [Macmillan], 1955.

Kornbluth, C. M. *A Mile Beyond the Moon.* Doubleday (Book Club Edition), 1958.

Kress, Nancy. *Beggars in Spain.* Eos, 2004.

___. *Probability Moon.* Tor, 2002.

___. *Probability Sun.* Tor, 2003.

Kyle, David A., ed. *Eleventh World Science Fiction Convention (Program Booklet).* 1953.

Lach-Szyrma, Wladyslaw S. *Aleriel.* Wyman & Sons, 1883.

Lackey, Mercedes. *Burning Water.* Tor, 1995.

Landon, Brooks. *Science Fiction After 1900.* Routledge, 2002.

Larbalestier, Justine. *The Battle of the Sexes in Science Fiction.* Wesleyan University Press, 2002.

Larson, Majliss. *Pawns and Symbols.* Pocket, 1985.

Lasser, David. *Conquest of Space.* Penguin, 1931.

Laumer, Keith. *Assignment in Nowhere.* Berkley Medallion, 1968.

___. *The Day before Forever and Thunderhead.* Doubleday, 1968.

___. *Dinosaur Beach.* Scribner's, 1971.

___. *House in November.* Berkley Medallion, 1970.

___. *Judson's Eden.* Baen, 1991.

___. *Keith Laumer: The Lighter Side.* Baen, 2001.

___. *Nine by Laumer.* Doubleday, 1967.

___. *Retief!* Baen, 2002.

___. *The Shape Changer.* Berkley Medallion, 1973.

___. *The Star Treasure.* Putnam, 1971.

Layne, Deborah, and Jay Lake. *Polyphony, Vol. 1.* Wheatland, 2002.

Le Guin, Ursula K. *The Birthday of the World.* HarperCollins, 2002.

___. *The Dispossessed.* HarperCollins, 1974.

___. *The Lathe of Heaven.* Scribners, 1973.

___, ed. *Nebula Award Stories Eleven.* Bantam, 1977.

___. *Rocannon's World.* Ace, 1966.

___. *The Wave in the Mind: Talks and Essays.* Shambala, 2004.

Lee, Sharon, and Steve Miller. *Low Port.* Meisha Merlin, 2003.

Lee, Stan. *Son of Origins of Marvel Comics.* Simon & Schuster, 1975.

Leiber, Fritz. *The Big Time.* New Enlish Library, 1969.

___. *The Green Millennium.* Gregg, 1980.

Leinster, Murray. *City on the Moon.* Ace, 1958.

___, ed. *Great Stories of Science Fiction.* Random House, 1951.

Lem, Stanislaw. *Return from the Stars.* Trans. Barbara Marszal and Frank Simpson. Harcourt Brace Jovanovich, 1980.

___. *Tales of Pirx the Pilot.* Trans. Louis Iribarne. Harvest, 1990.

L'Engle, Madeleine. *A Wind in the Door.* Farrar Strauss Giroux, 1993.

Lethem, Jonathan. *Amnesia Moon.* Harcourt Brace, 1995.

___. *The Disappointment Artist.* Doubleday, 2005.

Lewis, C. S. *The Dark Tower and Other Stories.* Harcourt Brace, 1977.

___. *On Stories.* Harcourt, 1982.

___. *Out of the Silent Planet.* Bodley Head, 1938.

___. *Perelandra.* Collins, 1962.

Lichtenberg, Jacqueline, et al. *Star Trek Lives!* Bantam, 1975.

Linaweaver, Brad, and Edward E. Kramer, eds. *Free Space.* Tor, 1998.

Lindsey, Johanna. *Warrior's Woman.* Avon, 1990.

Lobdell, Jared. *The Scientifiction Novels of C. S. Lewis.* McFarland & Company, Inc., 2004.

Lovecraft, H. P. *Miscellaneous Writings.* Arkham House, 1995.

Lowachee, Karin. *Burndrive.* Aspect, 2003.

Lowry, Brigid, and Sam Field. *Space Camp.* Allen & Unwin, 2002.

Lucas, George. *The Adventures of Luke Starkiller as taken from the "Journal of the Whills".* (screenplay for *Star Wars*) LucasFilm, Mar. 15, 1976.

Lucas, J. M. *Elaan of Troyius.* (teleplay), 1968.

Luke, Timothy W. *Ecocritique.* University of Minnesota Press, 1997.

Lumley, Brian. *House of Doors.* Tor, 1990.

___. *Necroscope: Defilers.* Tor, 2000 and 2001.

___. *Titus Crow, Volume 1.* Tor, 1997.

Lupoff, Pat, and Dick Lupoff, eds. *The Best of Xero*. Tachyon, 2005.

Lupoff, Richard A. *Master of Adventure*. University of Nebraska Press, 2005.

MacLeod, Ken. *Cosmonaut Keep*. Orbit, 2001.

___. *Engine City*. Orbit, 2003.

___. *The Star Fraction*. Tor, 2001.

___. *The Stone Canal*. Tor, 2001.

Macvey, John W. *Interstellar Travel*. Avon, 1978.

Maloney, Mack. *Planet America*. Ace, 2001.

Manuel, Frank E., and Fritzie P. Manuel. *Utopian Thought in the Western World*. Belknap, 1979.

Margulies, Leo, and Oscar J. Friend, eds. *The Giant Anthology of Science Fiction*. Merlin, 1954.

Margulis, Dan. *Professional Photoshop (4th ed.)*. Wiley, 2002.

Marshak, Sondra, and Myrna Culbreath. *The Price of the Phoenix*. Bantam, 1985.

___. *Triangle*. Timescape, 1983.

Martin, George R. R., ed. *Wild Cards*. Bantam Spectra, 1986.

Mason, Douglas R. *Mission to Pactolus R.* Hale, 1978.

Matiasz, G. A. *End Time*. AK Press, 1996.

Matthews, J. Brander. *The Theatres of Paris*. Charles Scribner's Sons, 1880.

May, Julian. *Jack the Bodiless*. Ballantine, 1993.

___. *The Many-Colored Land*. Houghton Mifflin, 1981.

___. *Orion Arm*. Voyager, 1999.

McArthur, Maxine. *Time Future*. Aspect, 2001.

___. *Time Past*. Aspect, 2002.

McAuley, Paul. *Eternal Light*. Orbit, 1993.

___. *Making History*. Gollancz, 2002.

McCaffery, Larry. *Across the Wounded Galaxies*. University of Illinois Press, 1990.

___, ed. *Storming the Reality Studio: A Casebook of Cyberpunk and Postmodern Science Fiction*. Duke University Press, 1991.

McCaffrey, Anne. *Chronicles of Pern: First Fall*. Easton, 1993.

___. *Crystal Singer*. Ballantine, 1982.

___. *The Girl Who Heard Dragons*. Tor, 1995.

___. *Pegasus in Flight*. Bantam Transworld, 1991; Corgi, 1992.

___. *Survivors: Dinosaur Planet II*. Orbit, [ca1992].

___. *The Ship who Sang*. Ballantine, 1991.

McCaffrey, Anne, and Elizabeth Ann Scarborough. *Acorna's People*. HarperTorch, 2000.

___. *Acorna's Search*. HarperTorch, 2002.

___. *Acorna's Triumph*. HarperTorch, 2004.

___. *Acorna's World*. HarperTorch, 2001.

McCaffrey, Anne, and Elizabeth Moon. *Generation Warriors*. Baen, 1991.

___. *Sassinak*. Orbit, 1991.

McCaffrey, Anne, and Jody Lynn Nye. *Death of Sleep*. Orbit, 1992.

McCaffrey, Anne, and Margaret Ball. *Acorna*. HarperTorch, 2001.

McCaffrey, Anne, and Mercedes Lackey. *Ship Who Searched*. Baen, 2000.

McCarthy, Wil. *The Collapsium*. Bantam, 2002.

___. *Hacking Matter*. Basic, 2003.

McCollum, Michael. *Life Probe*. Ballantine, 1983.

McCrumb, Sharyn. *Bimbos of the Death Sun*. TSR, 1988.

McDevitt, Jack. *Infinity Beach*. HarperCollins, 2000.

McDonald, Ian. *Desolation Road*. Simon & Schuster, 2001.

___. *Evolution's Shore*. Bantam, 1995.

___. *Necroville*. Victor Gollancz, 1995.

McDonald, Raymond. *The Mad Scientist: A Tale of the Future*. Cochrane, 1908.

McDonald, Steven E. *Waystation*. Tor, 2004.

McDonough, Craig R., ed. *The NESFA Hymnal 1*. NESFA Press, 1976.

McDonough, Thomas R. *The Architects of Hyperspace*. Avon, 1987.

McIntyre, Vonda N. *Dreamsnake*. Dell, 1979.

___. *Entropy Effect*. Pocket, 1981.

McIntyre, Vonda N., and James Tiptree Jr. *Screwtop / The Girl Who Was Plugged In*. Tor, 1989.

McMullen, Jeanine. *Wind in the Ash Tree*. W. W. Norton, 1988.

Meluch, R. M. *The Queen's Squadron*. Roc, 1992.

Meredith, Richard C. *At the Narrow Passage*. Berkley, 1975.

Merril, Judith, ed. *Beyond Human Ken*. Random House, 1952.

___, ed. *SF: '58: The Year's Greatest Science Fiction and Fantasy*. Gnome, 1958.

___, ed. *SF: The Best of the Best*. Delacorte, 1967.

___, ed. *S-F: Year's Greatest Science Fiction and Fantasy*. Gnome, 1956.

___, ed. *6th Annual Edition The Year's Best S-F.* Dell, 1961.

Merritt, A. *The Moon Pool*. Easton, 1994.

Meynell, Alice. *Poems*. Burns & Oates, 1913.

Milán, Victor. *From the Depths*. Pocket, 1993.

Miller, S. E. *I Could Have Filked All Night*. 1978.

Mitchell, V. E. *Windows on a Lost World*. Pocket, 1993.

*Modern Scepticism: A Course of Lectures Delivered at the Request of the Christian Evidence Society*. Anson D. F. Randolf and Co., 1871.

Modesitt, L. E., Jr. *Adiamante*. Tor, 1998.

___. *Ecolitan Prime*. Tor, 2003.

___. *The Ecolitan Enigma*. Tor, 1998.

___. *The Ethos Effect*. Tor, 2004.

___. *In Endless Twilight*. Tor, 1988.

___. *The Ecolitan Operation*. Tor, 1989.

___. *Gravity Dreams*. Tor, 2000.

___. *Timegods' World*. Tor, 2000.

Moffitt, Donald. *Second Genesis*. Ballantine, 1986.

Moon, Elizabeth. *Rules of Engagement*. Baen, 1998.

___. *Sporting Chance*. Baen, 1994.

___. *Winning Colors*. Baen, 1995; as *Winning Colours*, Orbit, 1999.

Moorcock, Michael. *Elric at the End of Time*. DAW, 1985

Moore, C. L. *Best of C. L. Moore*. Ed. Lester del Rey. Ballantine, 1978.

Moore, Patrick. *Can You Speak Venusian?: A Guide to the Independent Thinkers*.

David and Charles, 1972.

Moran, Daniel Keyes. *Armageddon Blues.* Bantam, 1987.

Morrison, Michael A., ed. *Trajectories of the Fantastic: Selected Essays from the Four-teenth International Conference on the Fantastic in the Arts.* Greenwood, 1997.

Moskowitz, Sam. *The Immortal Storm.* ASFO Press, 1954.

Munro, John. *A Trip to Venus.* Jarrold & Sons, 1897.

Murdoch, Iris. *Henry and Cato.* Chatto & Windus, 1976.

Nabokov, Vladimir. *Nabokov's Dozen.* Heinemann, 1959.

Naylor, Doug. *Last Human.* Penguin, 1995.

Naylor, Grant. *Infinity Welcomes Careful Drivers.* Roc, 1992.

___. *Red Dwarf.* Penguin, 1989.

Negley, Glenn Robert, and J. Max Patrick. *Quest for Utopia.* 1952.

Newton, Roger P. *Thinking About Physics.* Princeton University Press, 2000.

Nicholls, Peter, ed. *Encyclopedia of Science Fiction.* Doubleday, 1979.

Nielsen Hayden, Theresa. *Making Book.* NESFA Press, 1994.

Niven, Larry. *N-Space.* Tor, 1991.

___. *Playgrounds of the Mind.* Tor, 1992.

___. *Rainbow Mars.* Tor, 2000.

___. *Ringworld.* Ballantine, 1970.

___. *Scatterbrain.* Tor, 2004.

___. *Tales of Known Space.* Ballantine, 1975.

Niven, Larry, et al. *Man-Kzin Wars II.* Orbit, 1991.

___. *Man-Kzin Wars III.* Baen, 1990.

___. *Man-Kzin Wars IV.* Baen, 1991.

___. *Man-Kzin Wars VI.* Baen, 1994.

Niven, Larry, and Jerry Pournelle. *The Mote in God's Eye.* 1975; Pocket, 1993.

Niven, Larry, Jerry Pournelle, and Michael Flynn. *Fallen Angels.* Baen, 1991.

Nolan, William F., ed. *The Edge of Forever.* Sherbourne, 1971.

___. *Logan's Run.* Buccaneer, 1995.

Norman, Lisanne. *Dark Nadir.* DAW, 1999.

Norris, John. *Practical Discourses upon Several Divine Subjects.* 1691.

North, Andrew. *Sargasso of Space.* Ace, 1957.

Norton, Alden H., and Sam Moskowitz, eds. *Great Untold Stories of Fantasy and Horror.* Pyramid, 1969.

Norton, Andre. *Dread Companion.* Ace, 1970; Fawcett Crest, 1980; Ballantine, 1984.

___. *Forerunner: The Second Venture.* Tor, 1986.

___. *Last Planet.* Ace, 1955.

___. *Operation Time Search.* Harcourt, Brace & World, 1967.

___. *The Solar Queen.* Tor, 2003.

___. *Star Born.* The World Publishing Company, 1957.

___. *Star Gate.* Harcourt, Brace, 1958.

___. *Star Guard.* Ace, 1973.

___. *Star Hunter.* Ace, 1961.

___. *Star Rangers.* Fawcett Crest, 1953 and [1970s].

___. *Stars Are Ours!* Ace, 1955.

Nourse, Alan. *The Bladerunner.* David McKay, 1991.

Nourse, Alan E. *Nine Planets.* Harper & Brothers, 1960.

Nye, Jody Lynn. *The Ship Errant.* Baen, 1997.

Nylund, Eric S. *A Signal Shattered.* Eos, 2000.

___. *Signal To Noise.* Avon, 1998.

O'Donnell, Mark. *The Nice and the Nasty.* Dramatists Play Service, 1987.

Ogilvie, John. *The Imperial Dictionary of the English Language (New Edition).* The Century Co., 1883.

Okrand, Marc. *The Klingon Dictionary.* Pocket, 1985.

Oliveira, Tony. *Beyond the Rift.* SSDC, 2005.

Ordway, Frederick Ira, J. P. Gardner, and M. R. Sharpe. *Basic Astronautics.* 1962.

Orwell, George. *Nineteen Eighty-Four,* Harcourt, Brace, 1949.

Panshin, Alexei, and Cory Panshin. *World Beyond the Hill.* Jeremy P. Tarcher, 1989.

Paton, John. *The Sea of Rings.* Hale, 1979.

Peck, Richard E. *Final Solution.* Doubleday, 1973.

Peel, John. *The Outer Limits: Alien Invasion from Hollyweird.* TorKids, 1999.

Pellegrino, Charles, and George Zebrowski. *Dyson Sphere.* Pocket, 1999.

Pepper, David. *Modern Environmentalism.* Routledge, 1996.

Pereira, Patricia L. *Eagles of the New Dawn.* Beyond Words, 1997.

Perry, Steve. *Brother Death.* Ace, 1992.

___. *The 97th Step.* Ace, 1989.

Phillips, Mark. *The Impossibles.* Pyramid, 1963.

Pickover, Clifford A. *The Science of Aliens.* Basic, 1998.

Pierce, John J. *Great Themes of Science Fiction.* Greenwood, 1987.

Pike, Sarah M. *Earthly Bodies, Magical Selves.* University of California Press, 2001.

Piper, H. Beam. *Little Fuzzy.* Avon, 1962.

___. *Space Viking.* Ace, 1963; Garland, 1975.

Poe, Edgar Allen. *The Works of Edgar Allen Poe, Vol. IV.* W.J. Widdleton, 1866.

Pohl, Frederik. *The Age of the Pussyfoot.* Ballantine, 1969.

___. *The Boy Who Would Live Forever.* Tor, 2004.

___. *Chasing Science.* Tor, 2003.

___. *Jem.* St. Martin's, 1979.

___. *O Pioneer!* Tor, 1999.

___, ed. *Star Science Fiction #2.* Ballantine, 1953.

___, ed. *Star Science Fiction No. 6.* Ballantine, 1959.

___. *The Way the Future Was: A Memoir.* Del Rey, 1978.

Pohl, Frederik, and C. M. Kornbluth. *The Space Merchants.* Ballantine, 1955.

Pohl, Frederik, and Elizabeth Anne Hull, eds. *Tales from the Planet Earth.* Tor, 1986.

Pollan, Michael. *The Botany of Desire.* Random House, 2001.

Pollotta, Nick, and Phil Foglio. *Illegal Aliens.* TSR, 1989.

Pournelle, Jerry, and S. M. Stirling. *Prince of Sparta.* Baen, 1993.

Pratchett, Terry. *Equal Rites.* Corgi, 1990.

Predko, Myke. *123 Robotics Experiments for the Evil Genius.* McGraw-Hill, 2004.

Preece, John. *Good Beer Guide.* 1999.

Priest, Christopher, ed. *Anticipations*. Scribners, 1978.

Priestley, J. B. *Daylight on Saturday*. [Harper and Brothers], 1943.

___. *Saturn over the Water*. [Doubleday], 1961.

Pringle, David, ed. *The Ultimate Encyclopedia of Science Fiction*. JG Press, 1996.

*Proceedings; Chicon III*. Advent, 1963.

Proctor, Geo W. *Stellar Fist*. Ace, 1989.

Proctor, Richard A. *The Expanse of Heaven*. 1877.

___. *Other Worlds Than Ours*. 1870.

Prouty, Howard H., ed. *Variety Television Reviews 1951–1953*. 1988.

Purchas, Samuel. *Pilgrimage*. 1614.

Pustz, Mathew J. *Comic Book Culture*. University Press of Mississippi, 1999.

Putnam, Hilary. *Mind, Language and Reality*. Cambridge University Press, 1997.

Quick, W. T. *Dreams of Flesh and Sand*. Futura, 1989.

Rapp, Arthur H. Lee Hoffman, and Redd Boggs. *Fanspeak*. 1952.

Raymond, Eric. *New Hacker's Dictionary*. MIT Press, 1991.

Reed, Robert. *The Hormone Jungle*. Futura, 1989.

___. *The Remarkables*. Bantam, 1992.

Reeve, Philip. *Mortal Engines*. Eos, 2004.

Regis, Edward. *The Great Mambo Chicken and the Transhuman Condition*. Perseus, 1991.

Reilly, Matthew. *Area 7*. St. Martin's, 2003.

___. *Temple*. St. Martin's, 2002.

Renouvier, Charles. *Uchronie (L'Utopie dans L'Histoire)*. Bureau de la Critique Philosophique, 1876.

*Reprints from SING OUT! The Folk Song Magazine Volume Three*. Oak Publications, 1961.

Resnick, Mike, ed. *Alternate Presidents*. Tor, 1992.

___. *Santiago*. Tor, 1986.

___. *Soul Eater*. Warner, 1992.

Resnick, Mike, and Patrick Nielsen Hayden, eds. *Alternate Skiffy*. Wildside, 1997.

Reynolds, Alistair. *Chasm City*. Gollancz, 2001.

___. *Redemption Ark*. Ace, 2004.

___. *Revelation Space*. Gollancz, 2000.

Reynolds, Mack. *The Case of the Little Green Men*. Phoenix, 1951.

Rheingold, Howard. *Virtual Reality: The Revolutionary Technology of Computer-Generated Artificial Worlds—and How It Promises to Transform Society*. Touchstone, 1992.

Rhodes, W. H. *Caxton's Book: A Collection of Essays, Poems, Tales and Sketches*. A. L. Bancroft, 1876.

Richmond, Walt, and Leigh Richmond. *Phoenix Ship / Earthrim*. Ace, 1969.

Ride, Sally, and Susan Okie. *To Space and Back*. HarperCollins, 1986.

Ridley, John. *Those Who Walk in Darkness*. Aspect, 2005.

Ries, Al, and Laura Ries. *The Origin of Brands*. HarperCollins, 2005.

Riley, Gwendoline. *Tuesday Nights and Wednesday Mornings*. Carroll & Graf, 2004.

Ringo, John. *When the Devil Dances*. Baen, 2002.

Ripley, George, and Charles A. Dana, eds. *The American Cyclopædia, Volume 7*. D. Appleton, 1874.

Roback, A. A. *Personality in Theory and Practice*. Sci-art, 1950.

Robbins, Tom. *Even Cowgirls Get the Blues*. Bantam, 1990.

Roberts, Adam. *Salt*. Victor Gollancz, 2000.

\_\_\_. *Stone*. Gollancz, 2002.

Robinson, Frank M. *The Dark beyond the Stars*. Orb, 1998.

Robinson, Kim Stanley. *Blue Mars*. Bantam, 1996.

\_\_\_. *Fifty Degrees Below*. Bantam, 2005.

\_\_\_, ed. *Future Primitive: The New Ecotopias*. Tor, 1997.

\_\_\_. *Green Mars*. HarperCollins, 1993.

\_\_\_. *Icehenge*. Ace, 1984; Tor, 1990.

\_\_\_. *The Memory of Whiteness*. Orb, 1996.

\_\_\_. *Red Mars*. Bantam, 1993.

Robinson, Spider. *Telempath*. Berkley Publishing Corporation, 1976.

\_\_\_. *Time Travelers Strictly Cash*. Tor, 2001.

Rogow, Roberta. *Futurespeak: A Fan's Guide to the Language of Science Fiction*. Paragon House, 1991.

Rohmer, Sax. *The Golden Scorpion*. Robert M. McBride, 1920.

Rosenfeld, Arthur. *Diamond Eye*. Forge, 2004.

Rowling, J. K. *Harry Potter and the Sorcerer's Stone*. Scholastic, 1999.

Rucker, Rudy. *Live Robots*. AvoNova, 1994.

\_\_\_, ed. *Mathenauts*. New English Library, 1989.

\_\_\_. *Saucer Wisdom*. Forge, 1999.

\_\_\_. *Software*. Avon, 1997.

Russ, Joanna. *Picnic on Paradise*. Ace, 1968.

Russell, Eric Frank. *Deep Space*. Eyre and Spottiswoode, 1956.

\_\_\_. *Major Ingredients*. NESFA Press, 2000.

Saberhagen, Fred. *Berserker*. Ballantine, 1967.

Sanders, Ed. *The Family: The Story of Charles Manson's Dune Buggy Attack Battalion*. Dutton, 1971.

Sawyer, Robert J. *Factoring Humanity*. Orb, 2004.

Scalzi, John. *Old Man's War*. Tor, 2005.

Schmidt, Stanley, ed. *Fifty Years of the Best Science Fiction from Analog*. Davis Publications, 1980.

Schmitz, James H. *Agent of Vega*. Permabooks, 1962.

Scholes, Robert, and Eric S. Rabkin. *Science Fiction: History, Science, Vision*. Oxford University Press, 1977.

Schroeder, Karl. *Permanence*. Tor, 2003.

Scott, Melissa. *Night Sky Mine*. Tor, 1997.

Searles, Baird, Martin Last, Beth Meacham, and Michael Franklin. *A Reader's Guide to Science Fiction*. Avon, 1979.

Segen, J. C. *The Dictionary of Modern Medicine*. The Parthenon Publishing Group, 1992.

Shahar, Eluki Bes. *Darktraders*. DAW, 1992.

Shatner, William. *Avenger.* Pocket, 1997.

___. *Return.* Pocket, 1996.

___. *Spectre.* Pocket, 1998.

___. *Tekwar.* Ace, 1990.

Shatner, William, and Chip Walter. *I'm Working on That.* Pocket, 2004.

Shaw, Bob. *Dimensions.* Victor Gollancz, 1994.

___. *Galactic Tours.* Proteus, 1981.

___. *Orbitsville Departure.* [Baen], 1990.

___. *Ship of Strangers.* Ace, 1979.

Sheckley, Robert. *Dramocles.* Holt, Rinehart & Winston, 1984.

___. *Mindswap.* Delacorte, 1966.

Sheffield, Charles. *Cold as Ice.* Tor, 1993.

___. *Dark as Day.* Tor, 2002 and 2003.

___. *Nimrod Hunt.* Baen, 1986.

___. *The Web Between the Worlds.* Ace, 1979.

Shelley, Rick. *Colonel.* Ace, 2000.

Shinn, Sharon. *Jovah's Angel.* Ace, 1997.

Shippey, Tom. *The Oxford Book of Science Fiction.* Oxford University Press, 1992.

Shwatrz, Susan. *Second Chances.* Tor, 2002.

Siegel, Jerry. *Tales of the Bizarro World.* DC Comics, 2000.

Silverberg, Robert. *Across a Billion Years.* The Dial Press, 1969.

___, ed. *Chains of the Sea.* Thomas Nelson, 1973.

___. *The Collected Stories of Robert Silverberg (Vol. 1: Pluto in Morning Light).* Grafton, 1993.

___. *The Collected Stories of Robert Silverberg (Vol. 2: Secret Sharer).* Grafton, 1993.

___. *The Conglomeroid Cocktail Party.* Victor Gollancz, 1984.

___. *The Feast of St. Dionysus.* New English Library, 1987.

___. *Hot Sky at Midnight.* HarperCollins, 1994.

___. *Invaders from Earth.* Tor, 1987.

___, ed. *New Dimensions IV.* Signet, 1974.

___, ed. *The Science Fiction Hall of Fame, Vol. I.* Avon, 1970.

___. *Son of Man.* Panther, 1979.

___. *Starborne.* Spectra, 1996.

___. *Stepsons of Terra.* Ace, 1958.

___. *The Planet Killers.* Ace, 1959.

___. *Those Who Watch.* New American Library, 1967.

___, ed. *Threads of Time.* Thomas Nelson, 1974.

___, ed. *Three Trips in Time and Space.* Hawthorn, 1973.

___. *Tower of Glass.* Victor Gollancz, 2000.

___, ed. *Voyagers in Time.* Meredith, 1967.

___. *World of a Thousand Colors.* Bantam, 1984.

Silverberg, Robert, and Poul Anderson. *The Planet Killers/We Claim These Stars!* Ace, 1959.

Simak, Clifford D. *All Flesh Is Grass.* Magnum, 1979.

___. *Werewolf Principle.* Berkley Medallion, 1968.

Simmons, Dan. *The Fall of Hyperion.* Doubleday, 1990.

___. *Hyperion.* Spectra, 1990.

___. *Worlds Enough and Time.* Eos, 2002.

Singleton, Linda Joy. *Oh No! UFO!* Llewellyn Publications, 2004.

Skinn, Dez. *Comix the Underground Revolution.* Thunder's Mouth, 2004.

Skirvin, Stan, ed. *Cinvention Memory Book.* Don Ford, 1950.

Sladek, John. *Tik-Tok.* Gollancz, 2002.

Slayton, Donald K., and Michael Cassutt. *Deke!* Forge, 1994.

Slusser, George, and Tom Shippey. *Fiction 2000.* University of Georgia Press, 1992.

Smith, Cordwainer. *Norstrilia.* NESFA Press, 1994.

___. *The Planet Buyer.* Pyramid, 1964.

___. *The Rediscovery of Man.* Ed. James A. Mann. NESFA Press, 1993.

Smith, David Alexander. *In the Cube.* Tor, 1993.

Smith, Dean Wesley, and Kristine Kathryn Rusch. *Escape.* Pocket, 1995.

Smith, E. E. *Skylark of Space.* Pyramid, 1958.

___. *Skylark Three.* Pyramid, 1968; Bison, 2003.

___. *Triplanetary.* Fantasy Press, 1948.

Smith, L. Neil. *The American Zone.* Tor, 2002.

Smith, Michael Marshall. *Only Forward.* HarperCollins, 1994.

Sobelman, Boris. *The Return of the Archons.* (teleplay) Nov. 10, 1966.

Sohl, Jerry. *The Mars Monopoly.* Ace, 1956.

Speer, Jack. *Fancestral Voices.* NESFA Press, 2004.

Speer, John Bristol. *Fancyclopedia.* Forrest J Ackerman for NFFF and LASFS, 1944.

Spencer, David. *Passing Fancy.* Pocket, 1994.

Spencer, Wen. *Alien Taste.* Roc, 2001.

Spinrad, Norman. *Bug Jack Barron.* Walker, 1969.

___. *Greenhouse Summer.* Tor, 2000.

___. *Little Heroes.* Grafton, 1989.

___. *The Void Captain's Tale.* Pocket, 1984.

___. *A World Between.* Pocket, 1979.

Stabenow, Dana. *Second Star.* Ace, 1991.

Stableford, Brian. *Dark Ararat.* Tor, 2002.

___. *Fountains of Youth.* Tor, 2000.

___. *Historical Dictionary of Science Fiction Literature.* Scarecrow, 2004.

Stahler, David, Jr. *Truesight.* Eos, 2005.

Staicar, Tom. *The Feminine Eye: Science Fiction and the Women Who Write It.* Ungar, 1982.

Stanwood, Donald A. *The Memory of Eva Ryker.* 1978.

Stapledon, Olaf. *Odd John.* E. P. Dutton & Co., 1936.

___. *Sirius.* Dover, 1972.

___. *Star Maker.* Methuen, 1937; Jeremy P. Tarcher, 1987.

___. *To the End of Time.* Funk & Wagnalls Company, 1953.

Stapledon, W. Olaf. *Last and First Men.* Methuen, 1930; Jonathan Cape and Harrison Smith, 1931.

Stasheff, Christopher. *Warlock and Son*. Ace, 1991.

___. *A Wizard in a Feud*. Tor, 2002.

Steele, Allen. *Chronospace*. Ace, 2001.

___. *Clarke County, Space*. Ace, 1990.

___. *Labyrinth of Night*. 1992.

Stephenson, Neal. *Snow Crash*. Bantam, 1992.

___. *Zodiac*. Bloomsbury, 1988.

Sterling, Bruce. *Globalhead*. Millennium, 1994.

___. *The Hacker Crackdown*. Bantam, 1992.

___, ed. *Mirrorshades*. Ace, 1986.

___. *Schismatrix*. Arbor House, 1985.

Stewart, Ian, and Jack Cohen. *Heaven*. Aspect, 2004.

___. *Wheelers*. Warner, 2001.

Stewart, Sean. *Passion Play*. Ace, 1993.

Stewart, Will. *Seetee Ship*. Gnome, 1951.

Stine, Jovial Bob. *Spaceballs*. Scholastic, 1987.

Stoll, Clifford. *Cuckoo's Egg*. Doubleday, 1989.

Strieber, Whitley, and James Kunetka. *Nature's End*. Warner, 1987.

Stross, Charles. *Accelerando*. Ace, 2005.

___. *Singularity Sky*. Ace, 2003; Orbit, 2004.

Sturgeon, Theodore. *And Now the News...* North Atlantic, 2003.

___. *Baby is Three*. Ed. Paul Williams. North Atlantic, 1999.

___. *Beyond*. Avon, 1970.

___. *The Man Who Lost the Sea*. Ed. Paul Williams. North Atlantic, 2005.

___. *Microcosmic God*. Ed. Paul Williams. North Atlantic, 1995.

___. *More Than Human*. Ballantine, 1953.

___. *The Perfect Host*. Ed. Paul Williams. North Atlantic, 1998.

___. *A Saucer of Loneliness*. Ed. Paul Williams. North Atlantic, 2000.

___. *Starshine*. Pyramid, 1966.

___. *Visions and Ventures*. Dell, 1978.

___. *A Way Home*. Pyramid, 1956.

Sucharitkul, Somtow. *The Alien Swordmaster*. Pinnacle, 1985.

Sutton, Jean, and Jeff Sutton Sutton. *The Programmed Man*. Putnam (Book Club Ed.), 1968.

Suvin, Darko. *Metamorphoses of Science Fiction*. Yale University Press, 1979.

Swanwick, Michael. *Being Gardner Dozois: An Interview by Michael Swanwick*. Old Earth Books, 2001.

___. *Cigar-Box Faust and Other Miniatures*. Tachyon, 2003.

___. *Gravity's Angels*. Arkham House, 1991.

___. *Moon Dogs*. NESFA Press, 2000.

___. *Puck Aleshire's Abecedary*. Dragon Press, 2000.

___. *Tales of Old Earth*. Frog, 2000.

Swift, David W. *Voyager Tales: Personal Views of the Grand Tour*. American Institute of Aeronautics and Astronautics, 1997.

Taine, John. *Before the Dawn*. The Williams & Wilkins Company, 1934.

Tepper, Sheri S. *The Companions*. Eos, 2004.

___. *The Fresco*. Eos, 2002.

___. *Singer from the Sea*. Eos, 2000.

Terrace, Vincent. *Crime Fighting Heroes of Television*. McFarland, 2002.

Theroux, Paul. *Translating LA*. Norton, 1994.

Thomas, Craig. *Snow Falcon*. 1979.

Thomas, Maggy. *Broken Time*. Roc, 2000.

Thomson, Amy. *The Color of Distance*. Ace, 1999.

___. *Through Alien Eyes*. Ace, 2000.

Thornburg, Newton. *Cutter and Bone*. Little, Brown, 1976.

Tilton, Lois. *Accusations*. Dell, 1995.

Tiptree, James Jr. *The Color of Neanderthal Eyes*. Tor, 1990.

___. *Her Smoke Rose Up Forever*. Tachyon Publications, 2004.

___. *Meet Me at Infinity*. Ed. Jeffrey D. Smith. Orb, 2001.

___. *Warm Worlds and Otherwise*. Ballantine, 1975.

Toffler, Alvin, and Heidi Toffler. *War and Anti-War*. Little, Brown, 1993.

Traviss, Karen. *City of Pearl*. Eos, 2004.

*Treasury of Great Science Fiction Stories No. 1*. Popular Library, 1964.

Tubb, E. C. *The Winds of Gath*. Arrow, 1981.

Tucker, Bob. *Neo-Fan's Guide to SF Fandom*. 1978.

Turner, Bill. *Solden's Women*. 1972.

Turtledove, Harry, ed. *The Best Military Science Fiction of the Twentieth Century*. Del Rey, 2001.

Tuttle, Lisa. *Lost Futures*. Dell, 1992.

Tyers, Kathy. *Fusion Fire*. Bantam, 1988.

*Universe: Roleplaying Game of the Future: Gamemasters' Guide*. Simulation Publications, 1981.

van Pelt, Michel. *Space Tourism: Adventures in Earth Orbit and Beyond*. Copernicus, 2005.

van Vogt, A. E. *Destination: Universe!* Signet, 1953.

___. *Reflections*. Fictioneer, 1975.

___. *The War Against the Rull*. Orb, 1999.

Vance, Jack. *The Demon Princes: Volume One*. Orb, 1997.

___. *The Demon Princes: Volume Two*. Tor, 1997.

___. *Future Tense*. Ballantine, 1964.

___. *Night Lamp*. Tor, 1998.

___. *Planet of Adventure*. Orb, 1991.

___. *Trullion: Alastor 2262*. Ballantine, 1973.

VanderMeer, Jeff. *Secret Life*. Golden Gryphon, 2004.

___. *Why Should I Cut Your Throat?: Excursions into the World of Science Fiction, Fantasy and Horror*. MonkeyBrain, 2004.

Varley, John. *Blue Champagne*. Dark Harvest, 1986.

___. *The Golden Globe*. Ace, 1998.

___. *Millennium*. Berkley, 1983.

___. *The Ophiuchi Hotline*. Gollancz, 2003.

___. *Steel Beach.* HarperCollins, 1993.

Verba, Joan Marie. *Boldly Writing 2nd ed.* FTL, 2003.

Viehl, S. L. *Eternity Row.* Roc, 2002.

Vinge, Joan D. *Dreamfall.* Tor, 2004.

___. *Tangled Up in Blue.* Tor, 2001.

___. *The Snow Queen.* Warner, 2001.

___. *The Summer Queen.* Tor, 2003.

Vinge, Vernor. *The Collected Stories of Vernor Vinge.* Tor, 2001.

___. *A Deepness in the Sky.* Tor, 2000.

___. *A Fire upon the Deep.* Tor, 1993.

___. *Marooned in Realtime.* Bluejay, 1986.

___. *Threats...and Other Promises.* Baen, 1988.

Voltaire. *The Works of M. de Voltaire, Volume 11.* Trans. T. Smollett, T. Francklin, et al. 1757.

von Braun, Wernher. *The Mars Project.* Illini, 1991.

Vornholt, John. *Mind Meld.* Pocket, 1997.

Wachowski, Larry, and Andy Wachowski. *The Matrix: The Shooting Script.* Newmarket, 2001.

Wagener, Leon. *One Giant Leap.* Forge, 2004.

Walter, Chris. *Punk Rules OK.* Burn Books, 2002.

Warner, Harry, Jr. *All Our Yesterdays.* Advent, 1969.

___. *A Wealth of Fable.* SCIFI Press, 1992.

Watson, Ian. *Alien Embassy.* Ace, 1978.

Watt-Evans, Lawrence. *Nightside City.* Ballantine, 1989.

Weber, David. *Ashes of Victory.* Baen, 2004.

___. *Field of Dishonor.* Baen, 1997.

___. *Honor Among Enemies.* Baen, 1997.

___. *On Basilisk Station.* Baen, 1993 and 1999.

___. *The Apocalypse Troll.* Baen, 1999.

___. *The Hard Way Home.* Baen, 2000.

___. *Worlds of Honor.* Baen, 2000.

Weber, David, and John Ringo. *March Upcountry.* Baen, 2002.

Weber, David, and Steve White. *In Death Ground.* Baen, 2000.

Weinbaum, Stanley G. *A Martian Odyssey and Others.* Fantasy Press, 1949.

Weinstein, Elliot. *The Fillostrated Fan Dictionary.* "O"Press, 1975.

*Weird Ones.* Belmont, 1962.

Weiss, Margaret. *King's Test.* Bantam, 1991.

Welles, Orson, ed. *Invasion from Mars.* Dell, 1949.

Wells, Benjamin W. *Modern French Literature.* Roberts Brothers, 1896.

Wells, H. G. *The First Men in the Moon.* The Bowen-Merrill Company, 1901.

___. *The Invisible Man.* Tor, 1992.

___. *Men Like Gods.* The MacMillan Company, 1923.

___. *The Time Machine.* W. Heinemann, 1895.

___. *War of the Worlds.* 1898.

Wentworth, K. D. *Black on Black.* Baen, 1999.

Wentworth, Patricia. *The Brading Collection.* J. B. Lippincott Company, 1950.

Westerfeld, Scott. *The Killing of Worlds.* Tor, 2003.

Westfahl, Gary. *Space and Beyond.* Greenwood, 2000.

Westfahl, Gary, George Slusser, and Eric Rabkin, eds. *Foods of the Gods.* University of Georgia Press, 1996.

___, eds. *Science Fiction and Market Realities.* University of Georgia Press, 1996.

Whedon, Joss. *Serenity, the Official Visual Companion.* Titan, 2005.

White, James. *Alien Emergencies.* Orb, 2002.

___. *Beginning Operations.* Orb, 2001.

___. *Final Diagnosis.* Tor, 1998.

___. *General Practice.* Orb, 2003.

___. *Mind Changer.* Tor, 1999.

___. *The White Papers.* NESFA Press, 1996.

White, William. *Emanuel Swedenborg; His Life and Writings.* 2nd ed. Simpkin, Marshall, 1868.

Whitfield, Stephen E., and Gene Roddenberry. *The Making of "Star Trek".* Ballantine, 1968.

Wild, Alan. *Soils, Land and Food.* Cambridge University Press, 2003.

Williams, Sheila, ed. *Hugo and Nebula Award Winners from Asimov's Science Fiction.* Random House, 1995.

Williams, Walter Jon. *Angel Station.* Orbit, 1991.

___. *Hardwired.* Tor, 1986.

___. *Metropolitan.* HarperCollins, 1995.

Williamson, Jack. *Dragon's Island.* 1951.

___. *The Legion of Space.* Fantasy Press, 1947.

Willis, Connie. *Doomsday Book.* Bantam, 1992.

Willis, Walt, and Bob Shaw. *The Enchanted Duplicator.* 1954.

Wilson, F. Paul. *Hosts.* Tor, 2001.

___. *Sims.* Tor, 2003.

Wilson, Robin, ed. *Paragons.* St. Martin's, 1996.

Wilson, William. *A Little Earnest Book upon a Great Old Subject.* 1851.

Winston, Joan. *Startoons.* Playboy Press, 1979.

Witcover, Paul. *Tumbling After.* Eos, 2005.

Wolfe, Gary K. *Critical Terms for Science Fiction and Fantasy: A Glossary and Guide to Scholarship.* Greenwood, 1986.

Wolfe, Gene. *Castle of Days.* Tor, 1995.

___. *Lake of the Long Sun.* Tor, 1994.

___. *Nightside the Long Sun.* Tor, 1993.

___. *Starwater Strains.* Tor, 2005.

___. *Storeys from the Old Hotel.* Kerosina, 1988.

___. *The Sword of the Lictor.* Timescape, 1981.

Wollheim, Donald A., ed. *Flight Into Space.* Frederick Fell, 1950.

___ *Secret of the Ninth Planet.* John C. Winston, 1959.

Wright, John C. *The Golden Age.* Tor, 2002 and 2003.

___. *The Golden Transcendence.* Tor, 2003 and 2004.

*Writing Science Fiction & Fantasy.* St. Martin's, 1991.

Wyndham, John. *The Day of the Triffids.* 1951.

Wyndham, John, and Lucas Parkes. *The Outward Urge.* 1959.

Yolen, Jane. *Commander Toad and the Planet of the Grapes.* Putnam, 1982.

___. *Dragon's Blood.* Dell, 1982.

Young, Robert F. *The Worlds of Robert F. Young.* Panther, 1968.

Zahn, Timothy. *Angelmass.* Tor, 2001.

___. *Manta's Gift.* Tor, 2002.

Zebrowski, George. *Ashes and Stars.* Ace, 1977.

___. *Omega Point.* Ace, 1972.

___. *Stranger Suns.* Easton, 1991.

Zelazny, Roger. *The Great Book of Amber.* Eos, 1999.

Zettel, Sarah. *Fool's War.* Warner, 1997.

___. *Kingdom of Cages.* Warner, 2001.

Zey, Michael G. *The Future Factor: Forces Transforming Human Desiny.* Transaction, 2004.

# Bibliography of Science Fiction Non-Fiction and Reference Books

## General Reference

Ash, Brian. *The Visual Encyclopedia of Science Fiction*. Harmony, 1977.

___. *Who's Who in Science Fiction*. Elm Tree Books, 1976.

Barron, Neil. *Anatomy of Wonder: Science Fiction*. R. R. Bowker Co., 1976. 2nd ed. as *Anatomy of Wonder: A Critical Guide to Science Fiction*. 1981. 5th ed., Libraries Unlimited, 2004.

Cameron, Alastair. *Fantasy Classification System*. Canadian Science Fiction Association, 1952.

Clute, John. *Science Fiction: The Illustrated Encyclopedia*. Dorling Kindersley. 1995.

Gunn, James, ed. *The New Encyclopedia of Science Fiction*. Viking Penguin, 1988.

Holdstock, Robert, ed. *Encyclopedia of Science Fiction*. Octopus Books, 1978.

James, Edward, and Farah Mendlesohn, eds. *The Cambridge Companion to Science Fiction*. Cambridge University Press, 2003.

Kelleghan, Fiona, ed. *Classics of Science Fiction and Fantasy Literature*. Salem, 2002. (Abridgement of *Magill's Guide to Science Fiction and Fantasy Literature*.)

Magill, Frank N., ed. *Survey of Science Fiction Literature*. 5 vols. Salem, 1979. Rev. with *Survey of Modern Fantasy Literature*, 1983 as *Magill's Guide to Science Fiction and Fantasy Literature*. Ed. T. A. Shippey and A. J. Sobczak, 1996.

Mann, George, ed. *The Mammoth Encyclopedia of Science Fiction*. Carroll & Graf Publishers, 2001.

Nicholls, Peter. *The Encyclopedia of Science Fiction: An Illustrated A to Z*. Doubleday, 1979. 2nd ed. coedited with John Clute as *The Encyclopedia of Science Fiction*. Orbit, 1993.

Pringle, David, ed. *The Ultimate Encyclopedia of Science Fiction*. JG Press, 1996.

Robinson, Frank M. *Science Fiction of the 20th Century: An Illustrated History*. Collectors Press, 1999.

Stableford, Brian. *Historical Dictionary of Science Fiction Literature*. Scarecrow Press, 2004.

Tymn, Marshall, and Mike Ashley, eds. *Science Fiction, Fantasy, and Weird Fiction Magazines*. Greenwood, 1985.

Westfahl, Gary. *The Greenwood Encyclopedia of Science Fiction and Fantasy: Themes, Works, and Wonders*. 3 vols. Greenwood Press, 2005.

___. *Science Fiction Quotations: From the Inner Mind to the Outer Limits*. Yale University Press, 2005.

# Dictionaries and Glossaries

Ackerman, Forrest J. "Fantasy Flanguage." *What Is Science Fiction Fandom* National Fantasy Fan Federation, [c. 1944].

Byrd, Patricia. "Star Trek Lives—Trekker Slang." *American Speech* (Spring 1978).

Cameron, Richard Graeme. July 29, 2006. "The Canadian Fancyclopedia." British Columbia Science Fiction Association. <http://members.shaw.ca/rgraeme/home.html>.

Carter, Lin. "A Handy Phrasebook in Fannish." *If* (Oct. 1956).

Costikyan, Greg. "Fanguage." *Verbatim* (Autumn 1980).

Dickson, Paul. "Fantasy, the Future, and Science Fiction." *Slang!: The Topic-by-Topic Dictionary of Contemporary American Lingoes.* Pocket Books, 1990.

Dunn, Jerry. "Science Fiction Fans." *Idiom Savant.* Henry Holt & Company, 1997

Eney, Richard H. *Fancyclopedia II.* 1959.

"FanSpeak Dictionary." Nov. 4, 2003. Ann Arbor Science Fiction Association. <http://stilyagi.org/fanspeak.html>.

Franson, Donald. *A Key to the Terminology of Science-Fiction Fandom.* National Fantasy Fan Federation, 1962.

Holland, Ralph M. *Ghu's Lexicon.* The National Fantasy Fan Federation, 1958.

Jackson, Robert. *Little Dictionary of Terms Used by SF Fans.* BSFA Ltd., 1976.

Peeples, Samuel A., David A. Kyle, and Martin Greenberg, eds. "A Dictionary of Science Fiction." *Travelers of Space* Ed. Martin Greenberg. Gnome Press, 1951.

Rapp, Arthur H. *Fanspeak.* 1950. Rev. ed. by Arthur H. Rapp, Lee Hoffman, and Redd Boggs. 1952.

Raymond, Eric S. May 5, 2006. "Prototype Worlds: A Glossary of SF Jargon." <http://www.catb.org/~esr/sf-words/index.html>.

Rogow, Roberta. *Futurespeak: A Fan's Guide to the Language of Science Fiction.* Paragon House, 1991.

Runté, Robert, ed. 2003. "Fanspeak Glossary." New Canadian Fandom. <http://www.uleth.ca/edu/runte/ncfguide/fangloss.htm>.

Siclari, Joe. Feb. 13, 1997. "Fancyclopedia III (draft copy)." <http://fanac.org/Fannish_Reference_Works/Fancyclopedia/Fancyclopedia_III/>.

Southard, Bruce. "The Language of Science-Fiction Fan Magazines." *American Speech* (Spring 1982).

Speer, John Bristol. *Fancyclopedia.* Forrest J. Ackerman for NFFF and LASFS, 1944.

Tucker, Bob. *The Neo-Fan's Guide to Science Fiction Fandom.* 1955. 8th ed. Kansas City Science Fiction and Fantasy Society, 1997.

*The Turkey City Lexicon.* [c. 1988]. Rev. by Bruce Sterling as "A Workshop Lexicon." *Paragons: Twelve Masters of Science Fiction Ply Their Craft.* Ed. Robin Wilson. St. Martin's Press, 1996.

Warner, Harry, Jr. "Glossary." *All Our Yesterdays* Advent, 1969.

Weinstein, Elliot. *The Fillostrated Fan Dictionary.* "O"Press, 1975.

Wolfe, Gary K. *Critical Terms for Science Fiction and Fantasy: A Glossary and Guide to Scholarship.* Greenwood Press, 1986.

Abbott, Carl. *Frontiers Past and Future: Science Fiction and the American West.* University Press of Kansas, 2006.

Albinski, N. B. *Women's Utopias in British and American Fiction.* Routledge, 1988.

Aldiss, Brian W. *Billion Year Spree,* Weidenfeld & Nicolson. 1973. Rev. with David Wingrove as *Trillion Year Spree.* Gollancz, 1986.

___. *The Detached Retina: Aspects of SF and Fantasy.* Liverpool University Press, 1995.

___. *This World and Nearer Ones: Essays Exploring the Familiar.* Weidenfeld & Nicholson, 1979.

Alkon, Paul K. *Origins of Futuristic Fiction.* University of Georgia Press, 1987.

___. *Science Fiction before 1900: Imagination Discovers Technology.* Twayne, 1994.

Amis, Kingsley. *New Maps of Hell: A Survey of Science Fiction.* Gollancz, 1960.

Anisfield, Nancy, ed. *The Nightmare Considered: Critical Essays on Nuclear War Literature.* Bowling Green University Press, 1991.

Armitt, Lucie, ed. *Where No Man Has Gone Before: Women and Science Fiction.* Routledge, 1991.

Armytage, W. H. G. *Yesterday's Tomorrows: A Historical Survey of Future Societies.* Routledge & Kegan Paul, 1968.

Ashley, Mike. *The History of the Science Fiction Magazines.* 4 vols. New English Library. 1974–78.

___. *The Time Machines: The Story of the Science-Fiction Pulp Magazines from the Beginning to 1950.* Liverpool University Press, 2001.

___. *Transformations: The Story of the Science Fiction Magazines from 1950 to 1970.* Liverpool University Press, 2005.

Asimov, Isaac. *Asimov on Science Fiction.* Doubleday & Company, Inc., 1981.

___. *Asimov's Galaxy: Reflections on Science Fiction.* Doubleday, 1989.

Atheling, William, Jr. [James Blish]. *The Issue at Hand: Studies in Contemporary Magazine Science Fiction.* Advent, 1964.

___. *More Issues at Hand: Critical Studies in Contemporary Science Fiction.* Advent, 1970.

Attebery, Brian. *Decoding Gender in Science Fiction.* Routledge, 2002.

Bailey, J. O. *Pilgrims through Space and Time: Trends and Patterns in Scientific and Utopian Fiction.* Argus, 1947.

Balsamo, Anne. *Technologies of the Gendered Body: Reading Cyborg Women.* Duke University Press, 1996.

Bambridge, William Sims. *Dimensions of Science Fiction.* Harvard University Press, 1986.

Barr, Marleen S. *Alien to Femininity: Speculative Fiction and Feminist Theory.* Greenwood Press, 1987.

Barr, Marleen, and Nicholas Smith. *Feminist Fabulation: Space/Postmodern Fiction.* University of Iowa Press, 1992.

___, eds. *Future Females, the Next Generation: New Voices and Velocities in Feminist Science Fiction Criticism.* Rowman and Littlefield. 2000.

___, eds. *Future Females: A Critical Anthology.* Bowling Green State University Popular Press, 1981.

___. *Lost in Space: Probing Feminist Science Fiction and Beyond.* University of North Carolina Press, 1993.

___, eds. *Women and Utopia: Critical Interpretations.* University Press of America, 1983.

Bartkowski, Frances. *Feminist Utopias.* Lincoln: University of Nebraska Press, 1989.

Bartter, Martha J. *The Way to Ground Zero: The Atomic Bomb in American Science Fiction.* Greenwood, 1988.

Ben-Tov, Sharona. *The Artificial Paradise: Science Fiction and American Reality.* University of Michigan Press, 1995.

Berger, Albert I. *The Magic That Works: John W. Campbell and the American Response to Technology.* Borgo, 1993.

Berger, Harold. *Science Fiction and the New Dark Age.* Bowling Green University Press, 1976.

Bishop, Michael. *A Reverie for Mister Ray.* PS Publishing, 2005.

Blackford, Russell, Van Ikin, and Sean McMullen. *Strange Constellations: A History of Australian Science Fiction.* Greenwood Press, 1999.

Blish, James. *The Tale That Wags the God.* Ed. Cy Chauvin. Advent. 1987.

Bloomfield, P. *Imaginary Worlds or the Evolution of Utopia.* Hamish Hamilton, 1932.

Booker, M. Keith. *Dystopian Literature: A Theory and Research Guide.* Greenwood Press, 1994.

___. *Monsters, Mushroom Clouds, and the Cold War: American Science Fiction and the Roots of Postmodernism, 1946–1964.* Greenwood Press. 2001.

Botting, Fred. *Sex, Machines, and Navels: Fiction, Fantasy, and History in the Future Present.* Manchester University Press, 1999.

Bould, Mark, ed. *Strange Attractors: Papers from the Second Annual AFFN Conference.* AFFN, 1995.

Bretnor, Reginald, ed. *Modern Science Fiction: Its Meaning and Its Future.* Coward-McCann, 1953: Rev. ed. Advent, 1979.

___, ed. *Science Fiction: Today and Tomorrow.* Harper & Row, 1974.

Brians, Paul. *Nuclear Holocausts: Atomic War in Fiction, 1895–1984.* Kent State University Press. 1987.

Brigg, Peter. *The Span of Mainstream and Science Fiction.* McFarland, 2002.

Broderick, Damien, ed. *Earth Is but a Star: Excursions through Science Fiction to the Far Future.* University of Western Australia Press, 2001.

___. *Reading by Starlight: Postmodern Science Fiction.* Routledge, 1995.

___. *Transrealist Fiction: Writing in the Slipstream of Science.* Greenwood Press, 2000.

___. *X, Y, Z, T: Dimensions of Science Fiction.* Borgo Press, 2004.

Brown, E. B. *Brave New World, 1984, and We: Essays on Anti-Utopia.* Ardis, 1976.

Bukatman, Scott. *Terminal Identity: The Virtual Subject in Postmodern Science Fiction.* Duke University Press, 1993.

Butler, Andrew M. *Cyberpunk.* Pocket Essentials, 2000.

Candelaria, James, and Matthew Gunn. *Speculations on Speculation: Theories of Science Fiction.* Scarecrow, 2005.

Carpenter, Charles A. *Dramatists and the Bomb: American and British Playwrights Confront the Nuclear Age, 1945–1964.* Greenwood Press, 1999.

Carter, Paul A. *The Creation of Tomorrow: Fifty Years of Magazine Science Fiction.* Columbia University Press, 1977.

Chalker, Jack L., and Mark Owings. *The Science-Fantasy Publishers: A Critical and Bibliographic History.* Mirage Press, 1991; Rev. ed. 1992.

Chapman, Edgar L., and Carl B. Yoke, eds. *Classic and Iconoclastic Alternate History Science Fiction.* Edwin Mellen, 2003.

Cioffi, Frank. *Formula Fiction? An Anatomy of American Science Fiction, 1930–1940.* Greenwood Press,1982.

Clareson, Thomas, ed. *Many Futures, Many Worlds: Theme and Form in Science Fiction.* Kent State University Press. 1977.

___, ed. *SF: The Other Side of Realism: Essays on Modern Fantasy and Science Fiction.* Bowling Green State University Popular Press, 1971.

___. *Some Kind of Paradise: The Emergence of American Science Fiction.* Greenwood Press, 1985.

___. *Understanding Contemporary American Science Fiction: The Formative Period (1926–1970).* University of South Carolina Press, 1990.

___, ed. *Voices of the Future.* Bowling Green State University Popular Press, 3 vols. (3rd vol. coedited with Thomas L. Wymer), l976–83.

Clark, Stephen R. L. *How to Live Forever: Science Fiction and Philosophy.* Routledge, 1995.

Clarke, I. F. *The Pattern of Expectation: 1644–2001.* Cape, 1979.

___. *Voices Prophesying War: Future Wars 1763–3749.* Oxford University Press, 1966; 2nd ed., 1992.

Clute, John. *Look at the Evidence: Essays and Reviews.* Serconia, 1995.

___. *Scores: Reviews 1993–2003.* Beccon Publications, 2003.

___. *Strokes: Essays and Reviews, 1966–1986.* Serconia, 1988.

Collins, Paul, Steven Paulsen, and Sean McMullen, eds. *The MUP Encyclopedia of Australian Science Fiction and Fantasy.* Melbourne University Press, 1998.

Conklin, Groff. *Possible Worlds of Science Fiction.* The Vanguard Press, 1951.

Cowie, Jonathan, and Tony Chester. *Essential SF: A Concise Guide.* Porcupine Press, 2005.

Davenport, Basil, ed. *The Science Fiction Novel: Imagination and Social Criticism.* Advent, 1959.

Davies, Philip John, ed. *Science Fiction, Social Conflict and War.* Manchester University Press, 1990.

Delany, Samuel R. *The Jewel-Hinged Jaw: Notes on the Language of Science Fiction.* Dragon Press, 1977.

___. *Silent Interviews: On Language, Race, Sex, Science Fiction, and Some Comics.* Wesleyan University Press, 1994.

___. *Starboard Wine: More Notes on the Language of Science Fiction.* Dragon Press, 1984.

del Rey, Lester. *The World of Science Fiction, 1926–1976: The History of a Subculture.* Garland, 1976.

De Vos, Luk, ed. *Just the Other Day: Essays on the Suture of the Future.* Restant, 1985.

Disch, Thomas M. *The Dreams Our Stuff Is Made Of: How Science Fiction Conquered the World.* Free Press, 1998.

___. *On SF.* Universtiy of Michigan Press, 2005.

Donawerth, Jane L. *Frankenstein's Daughters: Women Writing Science Fiction.* Syracuse University Press, 1997.

Donawerth, Jane L., and Carol A. Kolmerten eds. *Utopian and Science Fiction by Women: Worlds of Difference.* Syracuse University Press, 1994.

Dowling, David. *Fictions of Nuclear Disaster.* University of Iowa Press, 1987.

Dunn, Thomas P., and Richard D. Erlich eds. *The Mechanical God: Machines in Science Fiction.* Greenwood Press, 1982.

Elliott, Rohert C. *The Shape of Utopia: Studies in a Literary Genre.* University of Chicago Press, 1970.

Emme, Eugene E., ed. *Science Fiction and Space Futures Past and Present.* American Astronautical Society, 1982.

Erlich, Richard D., and Thomas P. Dunn eds. *Clockwork Worlds: Mechanical Environments in SF.* Greenwood Press, 1983.

Featherstone, Mike, and Roger Burrows. *Cyberspace/Cyberbodies/Cyberpunk: Cultures of Technological Embodiment.* Sage, 1995.

Ferns, Chris. *Narrating Utopia: Ideology, Gender, Form in Utopian Literature.* Liverpool University Press, 1999.

Ferreira, Maria Aline Salgueiro Seabra. *I Am the Other: Literary Negotiations of Human Cloning.* Praeger Publishers, 2005.

Fischer, William B. *The Empire Strikes Out: Kurd Lasswitz, Hans Dominik and the Development of German Science Fiction.* Popular Press, 1984.

Fisher, Peter S. *Fantasy and Politics: Visions of the Future in the Weimar Republic.* University of Wisconsin Press, 1991.

Foote, Bud. *The Connecticut Yankee in the Twentieth Century: Travels to the Past in Science Fiction.* Greenwood Press, 1990.

Fortunati, Vita, and Raymond Trousson eds. *Dictionary of Literary Utopias.* Honoré Champion, 2000.

Franklin, H. Bruce. *War Stars: The Superweapon and the American Imagination.* Oxford University Press, 1988.

Fredericks. Casey. *The Future of Eternity: Mythologies of Science Fiction and Fantasy.* Indiana University Press, 1982.

Freedman, Carl. *Critical Theory and Science Fiction.* Wesleyan University Press, 2000.

Garber, Eric, and Lin Palco. *Uranian Worlds: A Reader's Guide to Alternative Sexuality in Science Fiction and Fantasy.* G. K. Hall, 1983. 2nd ed. 1990.

Gannon, Charles. *Rumors of War and Infernal Machines: Technomilitary Agenda-Setting in American and British Speculative Fiction.* Liverpool University Press, 2003.

Garnett, Rhys, and R. J. Ellis eds. *Science Fiction Roots and Branches: Contemporary Critical Approaches*. St. Martin's Press, 1990.

Gerber, Richard. *Utopian Fantasy: A Study of English Utopian Fiction since the End of the Nineteenth Century*. Routledge. 1955.

Ginway, M. Elizabeth. *Brazilian Science Fiction*. Bucknell University Press, 2004.

Glad, John. *Extrapolations from Dystopia: A Critical Study of Soviiet Science Fiction*. Kingston Press, 1982.

Goswami, Amit, and Maggie Goswami. *The Cosmic Dancers: Exploring the Physics of Science Fiction*. Harper, 1983.

Gottlieb, Erika. *Dystopian Fiction East and West: Universe of Terror and Trial*. McGill-Queens University Press, 2001.

Gove, Philip Babcock. *The Imaginary Voyage in Prose Fiction*. Columbia University Press, 1941.

Green, Roger Lancelyn. *Into Other Worlds: Space Flight in Fiction from Lucian to Lewis*. Ahelard-Schumann, 1958

Greenland, Cohn. *The Entropy Exhibition: Michael Moorcock and the British "New Wave" in Science Fiction*. Routledge, 1983.

Griffiths, John. *Three Tomorrows: American, British, and Soviet Science Fiction*. Barnes and Noble, 1980.

Gunn, James E. *Alternate Worlds: The Illustrated History of Science Fiction*. Prentice-Hall, 1975.

___. *Inside Science Fiction: Essays on Fantastic Literature*. Borgo, 1992. 2nd ed. Scarecrow, 2006.

Guthke, Karl S. *The Last Frontier: Imagining Other Worlds from the Copernican Revolution to Modern Science Fiction*. Cornell University Press, 1990.

Harbottle, Philip, and Steven Holland. *Vultures of the Void: A History of British Science Fiction Publishing, 1946–1956*. Borgo Press, 1993.

Harris-Fain, Darren. *Understanding Contemporary American Science Fiction: The Age Of Maturity, 1970–2000*. University of South Carolina Press, 2005.

Hartwell, David J. *Age of Wonders: Exploring the World of Science Fiction*. Walker, 1984. Rev. ed. Tor, 1996.

Hassler, Donald M. *Comic Tones in Science Fiction: The Art of Compromise with Nature*. Greenwood Press, 1982.

Hayles, N. Katherine. *How We Became Posthuman: Virtual Bodies in Cybernetics, Literature and Informatics*. University of Chicago Press, 1999.

Heuser, Sabine. *Virtual Geographies: Cyberpunk at the Intersection of the Postmodern and Science Fiction*. Rodolpi, 2002.

Hillegas, Mark R. *The Future as Nightmare: H. G. Wells and the Anti-Utopians*. Oxford University Press, 1967.

Hollinger, Veronica, and Joan Gordon eds. *Edging into the Future: Science Fiction and Contemporary Cultural Transformation*. University of Pennsylvania Press, 2002.

James, Edward. *Science Fiction in the Twentieth Century*. Oxford University Press, 1994.

Jameson, Fredric. *Archaeologies of the Future: The Desire Called Utopia and Other Science Fictions*. Verso, 2005.

Jones, Edward, and Farah Mendlesohn eds. *The Cambridge Companion to Science Fiction.* Cambridge University Press, 2003.

Jones, Gwyneth. *Deconstructing the Starships: Science, Fiction and Reality.* Liverpool University Press, 1999.

Joshi, S. T. *Sixty Years of Arkham House.* Arkham House, 1999.

Ketterer, David. *Canadian Science Fiction and Fantasy.* Indiana University Press, 1992.

___. *New Worlds for Old: The Apocalyptic Imagination, Science Fiction, and American Literature.* Indiana University Press, 1974.

Kilgore, De Witt Douglas. *Astrofiturism: Science, Race, and Visions of Utopia in Space.* University of Pennsylvania Press, 2003.

Kincaid, Paul. *A Very British Genre: A Short History of British Fantasy and Science Fiction.* British Science Fiction Association, 1995.

King, Betty. *Women of the Future: The Female Main Character in Science Fiction.* Scarecrow Press, 1984.

Klaic, Dragan. *The Plot of the Future: Utopia and Dystopia in Modern Drama.* University of Michigan Press, 1992.

Klaw, Rick. *Geek Confidential: Echoes from the 21st Century.* MonkeyBrain, 2003.

Knight, Damon. *In Search of Wonder.* Advent, 1956. 2nd. ed. 1967. 3rd ed. 1997.

___. *Turning Points: Essays on the Art of Science Fiction.* Harper and Row, 1977.

Kreuziger, Frederick A. *Apocalypse and Science Fiction: A Dialectic of Religious and Secular Soteriologies.* Scholars Press, 1982.

Kumar, Krishan. *Utopia and Anti-Utopia in Modern Times.* Blackwell, 1987.

Landon, Brooks. *Science Fiction after 1900: From the Steam Man to the Stars.* Twayne, 1997.

Langford, David. *The Complete Critical Assembly: The Collected White Dwarf (and GM and GMI) SF Review Columns.* Cosmos, 2002.

___. *The SEX Column and Other Misprints.* Cosmos, 2005.

___. *Up through an Empty House of Stars: Reviews and Essays 1980–2002.* Cosmos, 2003.

Larbalestier, Justine. *The Battle of the Sexes in Science Fiction.* Wesleyan University Press, 2002.

Lawler, Donald L. *Approaches to Science Fiction.* Houghton Mifflin, 1978.

Lefanu, Sarah. *In the Chinks of the World Machine: Feminism and Science Fiction.* Women's Press, 1988.

Le Guin, Ursula K. *Dancing at the Edge of the World: Thoughts on Words, Women, Places.* Grove. 1989.

___. *The Language of the Night: Essays on Fantasy and Science Fiction.* Putnam, 1979. Rev. ed. HarperCollins, 1992.

___. *The Wave in the Mind: Talks and Essays.* Shambala, 2004.

Lem, Stanislaw. *Microworlds: Writings on Science Fiction and Fantasy.* Ed. Franz Rottensteiner. Harcourt, 1985.

Leonard, Elizabeth Anne, ed. *Into Darkness Peering: Race and Color in the Fantastic.* Greenwood Press. 1997.

Lerner, Frederick Andrew. *A Bookman's Fantasy: How Science Fiction Became Respectable and Other Essays.* NESFA Press, 1995.

___. *Modern Science Fiction and the American Literary Community.* Scarecrow Press, 1985.

Lockhart, Darrell B. *Latin American Science Fiction Writers: An A-to-Z Guide.* Greenwood Press, 2004.

Lofficier, Jean-Marc, and Randy Lofficier. *French Science Fiction, Fantasy, Horror and Pulp Fiction: A Guide to Cinema, Television, Radio, Animation, Comic Books, and Literature from the Middle Ages to the Present.* McFarland, 2000.

Lowndes, Robert A. W. *Three Faces of Science Fiction.* NESFA Press, 1973.

Luckhurst, Roger. *Science Fiction.* Polity Press, 2005.

Lundwall, Sam J. *Science Fiction: What It's All About.* Ace, 1971.

Malmgren, Carl. *Worlds Apart: Narratology of Science Fiction.* Indiana University Press. 1991.

Manuel, Frank E., and Fritzie P. Manuel. *Utopian Thought in the Western World.* Belknap Press, 1979.

Martin, Graham Dunstan. *An Inquiry into the Purposes of Speculative Fiction— Fantasy and Truth.* Edwin Mellen, 2003.

Malik, Rex, ed. *Future Imperfect: Science Fact and Science Fiction.* Francis Pinter, 1980.

Malzberg, Barry N. *The Engines of the Night: Science Fiction in the Eighties.* Doubleday, 1982.

Manlove, Cohn. *Science Fiction: Ten Explorations.* Kent State University Press, 1986.

Matthew, Robert. *Japanese Science Fiction: A View of a Changing Society.* Routledge, 1989.

McCaffery, Larry, ed. *Storming the Reality Studio: A Casebook of Cyberpunk and Postmodern Science Fiction.* Duke University Press, 1991.

McGuire, Patrick L. *Red Stars: Political Aspects of Soviet Science Fiction.* UMI Research Press, 1985.

Merrick, Helen, and Tess Williams, eds. *Women of Other Worlds: Excursions through Science Fiction and Fantasy.* University of Western Australia Press, 1999.

Myers, Robert E., ed. *The Intersection of Science Fiction and Philosophy: Critical Studies.* Greenwood Press, 1983.

Meyers, Walter E. *Aliens and Linguists: Language Study and Science Fiction.* University of Georgia Press, 1980.

Miller, Fred D., Jr., and Nicholas D. Smith eds. *Thought Probes: Philosophy through Science Fiction.* Prentice Hall, 1981.

Mohr, Dunja M. *Worlds Apart: Dualism and Transgression in Contemporary Female Dystopias.* McFarland, 2005.

Moore, Patrick. *Science and Fiction.* Harrap, 1957.

Moskowitz, Sam. *Science Fiction in Old San Francisco.* Vol.1. *History of the Movement from 1854–1890.* Grant, 1980.

___. *Strange Horizons: The Spectrum of Science Fiction.* Scribner, 1976.

___. *Under the Moons of Mars: A History and Anthology of "Scientific Romance" in the Munsey Magazines, 1912–1920.* Holt, 1970.

Mogen, David. *Wilderness Visions: Science Fiction Westerns.* Vol. 1 Borgo Press, 1982;

2nd ed. 1993.

Moylan, Tom, and Raffaella Baccolini eds. *Dark Horizons: Science Fiction and the Utopian Imagination*. Routledge, 2003.

Moylan, Tom. *Demand the Impossible: Science Fiction and the Utopian Imagination*. Methuen, 1986.

___. *Scraps of the Untainted Sky: Science Fiction, Utopia, Dystopia*. Westview Press, 2000.

Myers, Robert E., ed. *The Intersection of Science Fiction and Philosophy: Critical Studies*. Greenwood Press, 1983.

Nahin, Paul J. *Time Machines: Time Travel in Physics, Metaphysics, and Science Fiction*. American Institute of Physics Press, 1999.

Nicholls, Peter, ed. *Science Fiction at Large*. Victor Gollancz, 1976.

Nicholls, Peter, David Langford, and Brian Stableford. *The Science in Science Fiction*. Michael Joseph, 1982.

Nicolson, Marjorie Hope. *Voyages to the Moon*. Macmillan, 1948.

Ordway, Frederick I., and Randy Liebermann eds. *Blueprint for Space: Science Fiction to Science Fact*. Smithsonian Institution, 1992.

Palumbo, Donald, ed. *Erotic Universe: Sexuality and Fantastic Literature*. Greenwood Press, 1986.

Panshin, Alexei, and Cory Panshin. *SF in Dimension: A Book of Explorations*. Advent, 1976. Rev. ed. 1980.

___. *The World beyond the Hill: Science Fiction and the Quest for Transcendence*. Tarcher, 1989.

Parrinder, Patrick., ed. *Learning from Other Worlds: Estrangement, Cognition, and the Politics of Science Fiction and Utopia*. Liverpool University Press, 2000.

___. *Science Fiction: A Critical Guide*. Longmans, 1979.

___. *Science Fiction: Its Criticism and Teaching*. Methuen, 1980.

Pastourmatzi, Domna, ed. *Biotechnological and Medical Themes in Science Fiction*. Aristotle University, 2003.

Phillips, Michael, ed. *Philosophy and Science Fiction*. Prometheus, 1984.

Philmus. Robert M. *Into the Unknown: Science Fiction from Francis Godwin to H. G. Wells*. University of California Press, 1970.

___. *Visions and Re-Visions: (Re-)Constructing Science Fiction*. Liverpool University Press, 2005.

Pierce, Hazel Beasley. *A Literary Symbiosis: Science Fiction/Fantasy Mystery*. Greenwood Press, 1983.

Pierce, John J. *Foundations of Science Fiction: A Study in imagination and Evolution*. Greenwood Press, 1987.

___. *Great Themes of Science Fiction: A Study in Imagination and Evolution*. Greenwood Press, 1987.

___. *Odd Genre: A Study in Imagination and Evolution*. Greenwood Press, 1994.

___. *When World Views Collide: A Study in Imagination and Evolution*. Greenwood Press, 1989.

Polak, Fred. *The Image of the Future*. Elsevier, 1973.

Pordzick, Ralph. *The Quest for Postcolonial Utopia: A Comprehensive Introduction to the Utopian Novel in New English Literature.* Peter Lang, 2001.

Porush, David. *The Soft Machine: Cybernetic Fiction.* Methuen, 1985.

Puschmann-Nalenz, Barbara. *Science Fiction and Postmodern Fiction: A Genre Study.* Peter Lang, 1992.

Riley, Dick, ed. *Critical Encounters: Writers and Themes in Science Fiction.* Ungar, 1978.

Rabkin, Eric S. *Mars: A Tour of the Human Imagination.* Praeger Publishers, 2005.

Rabkin, Eric S., Martin H. Greenberg, and Joseph D. Olander, eds. *No Place Else: Explorations in Utopian and Dystopian Fiction.* Southern Illinois University Press, 1983.

Rabkin, Eric S., Martin H. Greenherg, and Joseph D. Olander, eds. *The End of the World.* Southern Illinois University Press. 1983.

Rassler, Donald M., and Clyde Wilcox, eds. *Political Science Fiction.* University of South Carolina Press, 1997.

Reid, Susan Elizaheth. *Presenting Young Adult Science Fiction.* Twayne, 1998.

Reilly, Robert, ed. *The Transcendent Adventure: Studies of Religion in Science Fiction/ Fantasy.* Greenwood Press, 1984.

Rellekson, Karen. *The Alternate History: Refiguring Historical Time.* Kent State University Press, 2001.

Roberts, Adam. *The History of Science Fiction.* Palgrave Macmillan, 2005.

___. *Science Fiction.* Routledge, 2000.

Roberts, Robin. *A New Species: Gender and Science in Science Fiction.* University of Illinois Press, 1993.

Rose, Mark. *Alien Encounters: Anatomy of Science Fiction.* Harvard University Press, 1981.

___, ed. *Science Fiction: A Collection of Critical Essays.* Prentice Hall, 1976.

Rosenfeld, Gavriel D. *The World Hitler Never Made: Alternate History and the Memory of Nazism.* Cambridge University Press, 2005.

Rosheim, David L. *Galaxy Magazine: The Dark and the Light Years.* Advent: Publishers, 1986.

Rosinsky, Natalie M. *Feminist Futures: Contemporary Women's Speculative Fiction.* UMI Research Press, 1984.

Rottensteiner, Franz, ed. *View From Another Shore: European Science Fiction.* Liverpool University Press, 1999.

Rucker, Rudy. *Seek! Selected Nonfiction.* Four Walls Eight Windows, 1999.

Ruddick, Nicholas. *British Science Fiction: A Chronology, 1478–1990.* Greenwood Press, 1992.

___. *Ultimate Island: On the Nature of British Science Fiction.* Greenwood Press, 1993.

Russ, Joanna. *To Write Like a Woman: Essays in Feminism and Science Fiction.* Indiana University Press, 1995.

Sammons, Martha C. *A Better Country: The Worlds of Religious Fantasy and Science Fiction.* Greenwood Press, 1988.

Samuelson, David. *Visions of Tomorrow: Six Journeys from Outer to Inner Space.* Arno Press, 1975.

Sandison, Alan, and Robert Dingley eds. *Histories of the Future: Studies in Fact, Fantasy, and Science Fiction.* Palgrave, 2001.

Sands, Karen, and Marietta Frank. *Back in the Spaceship Again: Juvenile Science Fiction Series Since 1945*. Greenwood Press, 1999.

Sawyer, Andy, and David Seed, eds. *Speaking Science Fiction: Dialogues and Interpretations*. Liverpool University Press, 2000.

Sayer, Karen, and John Moore, eds. *Science Fiction, Critical Frontiers*. St. Martin's Press, 2000.

___. *The Science Fiction Novel: Imagination and Social Criticism*. Advent, 1959.

Schaer. Roland, Gregory Claes, and Lyman Tower Sargent, eds. *Utopia: The Search for the Ideal Society in the Western World*. Oxford University Press, 2000.

Schenkel, Elmar, and Stefan Welz, eds. *Last Worlds and Mad Elephants: Literature, Science, and Technology, 1700–1900*. Galda + Witch Verlag, 1999.

Scholes, Robert. *The Fabulators*. Oxford University Press, 1967. Rev. as *Fabulation and Metafiction*. University of Illinois Press, 1979.

___. *Structural Fabulation: An Essay on Fiction of the Future*. University of Notre Dame Press, 1975.

Scholes, Robert, and Robert Kellogg. *The Nature of Narrative*. Oxford University Press, 1966.

Scholes, Robert, and Eric Rabkin. *Science Fiction: History/Science/Vision*. Oxford University Press. 1977

Searles, Baird, Martin Last, Beth Meacham, and Michael Franklin. *A Reader's Guide to Science Fiction*. Avon Books, 1979.

Seed, David. *American Science Fiction and the Cold War: Literature and Film*. Fitzroy Dearborn, 1999.

___, ed. *Anticipations: Essays on Early Science Fiction and Its Precursors*. Liverpool University Press, 1995.

___, ed. *A Companion to Science Fiction*. Blackwell Publishing, 2005.

___, ed. *Imagining Apocalypse: Studies in Cultural Crisis*. Macmillan, 2000.

Shaw, Debra Benita. *Women, Science and Fiction: The Frankenstein Inheritance*. Palgrave, 2001.

Shippey, Tom, ed. *Fictional Space: Essays on Contemporary Science Fiction*. Oxford: Blackwell, 1991.

Sisk, David W. *Transformations of Language in Modern Dystopias*. Greenwood Press, 1997.

Slusser, George E., Colin Greenland, and Eric S. Rabkin, eds. *Storm Warnings: Science Fiction Confronts the Future*. Southern Illinois University Press, 1987.

Slusser, George E., George R. Guffey, and Mark Rose, eds. *Bridges to Science Fiction*. Southern Illinois University Press, 1980.

Slusser, George, and Eric S. Rabkin, eds. *Aliens: The Anthropology of Science Fiction*. Southern Illinois University Press, 1987.

___. *Fights of Fancy: Armed Conflict in Science Fiction and Fantasy*. University of Georgia Press, 1993.

___, eds. *Hard Science Fiction*. Southern Illinois University Press, 1986.

___, eds. *Styles of Creation: Aesthetic Technique and the Creation of Fictional Worlds*. University of Georgia Press. 1993.

Slusser, George E., Eric S. Rabkin, and Robert Scholes, eds. *Coordinates: Placing*

*Science Fiction and Fantasy.* Southern Illinois University Press, 1983.

Slusser, George E., and Tom Shippey, eds. *Fiction 2000: Cyberpunk and the Future of Narrative.* University of Georgia Press. 1992.

Smith, Nicholas D., ed. *Philosophers Look at Science Fiction.* Nelson Hall, 1982.

Spinozzi, Paola, ed. *Utopianism/Literary Utopias and National Cultural Identities: A Comparative Perspective.* Cotepra, 2001.

Spinrad, Norman. *Science Fiction in the Real World.* Southern Illinois University Press, 1990.

Stableford, Brian. *Scientific Romance in Britain, 1890–1950.* Fourth Estate, 1985.

___. *The Sociology of Science Fiction.* Borgo Press, 1987.

Staicar, Tom, ed. *The Feminine Eye: Science Fiction and the Women Who Write It.* Ungar, 1982.

Steele, Allen M. *Primary Ignition: Essays 1997–2001.* Wilder Publications, 2003.

Stocker, Jack H., ed. *Chemistry and Science Fiction.* American Chemical Society, 1998.

Stockwell, Peter. *The Poetics of Science Fiction.* Longman, 2000.

Stone, Graham. *Notes on Australian Science Fiction.* Author, 2001.

Stover, Leon. *Science Fiction from Wells to Heinlein.* McFarland, 2002.

Sullivan, C.W., III, ed. *Science Fiction for Young Readers.* Greenwood Press, 1993.

___, ed. *Young Adult Science Fiction.* Greenwood Press, 1999.

Suvin, Darko. *Metamorphoses of Science Fiction: On the Poetics and History of a Literary Genre.* Yale University Press, 1979.

___. *Positions and Presuppositions in Science Fiction.* Kent State University Press, 1988.

___. *Victorian Science Fiction in the U.K.: The Discourses of Knowledge and Power.* G. K. Hall, 1983.

Swanwick, Michael. *The Postmodern Archipelago.* Tachyon Publications, 1997.

Testenko, Tatiana. *Feminist Utopian Novels of the 1970s: Joanna Russ and Dorothy Bryant.* Routledge, 2003.

Thacker, Anthony. *A Closer Look at Science Fiction.* Kingsway Communications, 2001.

Tymn. Marshall B., ed. *The Science Fiction Reference Book.* Starmont House, 1981.

VanderMeer, Jeff. *Why Should I Cut Your Throat?: Excursions into the World of Science Fiction, Fantasy & Horror.* MonkeyBrain Books, 2004.

Wachhorst, Wyn. *The Dream of Spaceflight: Essays on the Near Edge of Infinity.* Basic Books, 2000.

Warrick, Patricia S. *The Cybernetic Imagination in Science Fiction.* MIT Press, 1980.

Weaver, Tom. *Science Fiction Confidential.* McFarland & Company, Inc., 2002.

Webb, Janeen, and Andrew Enstice, eds. *The Fantastic Self: Essays on the Subject of the Self.* Eidolon, 1999.

Weedman, Jane, ed. *Women Worldwalkers: New Dimensions of Science Fiction and Fantasy.* Texas Tech Press, 1985.

Wendland, Albert. *Science, Myth, and the Fictional Creation of Alien Worlds.* UMI Research Press, 1984.

Westfahl, Gary. *Cosmic Engineers: A Study of Hard Science Fiction.* Greenwood Press, 1996.

___. *The Mechanics of Wonder: The Creation of the Idea of Science Fiction.* Liverpool University Press, 1998.

___. *Science Fiction, Children's Literature, and Popular Culture: Coming of Age in Fantasyland.* Greenwood Press, 2000.

___, ed. *Space and Beyond: The Frontier Theme in Science Fiction.* Greenwood Press, 2000.

Westfahl, Gary, and George Slusser, eds. *No Cure for the Future: Disease and Medicine in Science Fiction and Fantasy.* Greenwood Press, 2002.

___, eds. *Science Fiction, Canonization, Marginalization, and the Academy.* Greenwood Press, 2002.

Westfahl, Gary, George Slusser, and David Leiby. *Worlds Enough and Time: Explorations of Time in Science Fiction and Fantasy.* Greenwood Press, 2002.

Westfahl, Gary, George Slusser, and Kathleen Church Plummer, eds. *Unearthly Visions: Approaches to Science Fiction and Fantasy Art.* Greenwood Press, 2002.

Westfahl, Gary, George Slusser, and Eric Rabkin, eds. *Foods of the Gods.* University of Georgia Press, 1996.

___, eds. *Science Fiction and Market Realities.* University of Georgia Press, 1996.

Williamson, Jack, ed. *Teaching Science Fiction: Education for Tomorrow.* Owlswick, 1980.

Willingham, Ralph. *Science Fiction and the Theater.* Greenwood Press, 1993.

Wolfe, Gary K. *The Known and the Unknown: The Iconography of Science Fiction.* Kent State University Press, 1979.

___. *Soundings: Reviews 1992–1996.* Beccon, 2005.

Wollheim, Donald A. *The Universe Makers: Science Fiction Today.* Harper, 1971.

Wolmark, Jenny. *Aliens and Others: Science Fiction, Feminism, and Postmodernism.* University of Iowa Press, 1994.

___, ed. *Cybersexualities: A Reader on Feminist Theory, Cyborgs, and Cyberspace.* Edinburgh University Press, 1999.

Wong Kin Yuen, Gary Westfahl, and Amy Kit Sze Chan, eds. *World Weavers: Globalization, Science Fiction, and the Cybernetic Revolution.* University of Washington Press, 2005.

Wu, Qingyun. *Female Rule in Chinese and English Literary Utopias.* Liverpool University Press, 1995.

Yanarella, Ernest J. *The Cross, the Plow, and the Skyline: Contemporary Science Fiction and the Ecological Imagination.* Brown Walker Press, 2001.

Yoke, Carl B. eds. *Phoenix from the Ashes: The Literature of the Remade World.* Greenwood Press, 1987.

Yoke, Carl B., and Donald M. Hassler, eds. *Death and the Serpent: Immortality in Science Fiction and Fantasy.* Greenwood Press, 1985.

Zaki, Hoda M. *Phoenix Renewed: The Survival and Mutation of Utopian Thought in North American Science Fiction 1965–1982.* Starmont House. 1988. Rev. ed. Borgo Press, 1993.

Zentz, Gregory L. *Jupiter's Ghost: Next Generation Science Fiction*. Praeger Publishers, 1991.

## Science Fiction Fandom

Bacon-Smith, Camille. *Enterprising Women: Television Fandom and the Creation of Popular Myth*. University of Pennsylvania Press, 1992.

___. *Science Fiction Culture*. University of Pennsylvania Press, 2000.

Cogswell, Theodore R., ed. *PITFSC: The Proceedings of the Institute for Twenty-First Century Studies*. Advent, 1992.

Eney, Dick, ed. *The Proceedings; Discon*. Advent, 1965.

Hayden, Theresa Nielsen. *Making Book*. NESFA Press, 1994.

Knight, Damon. *The Futurians: The Story of the Great Science Fiction "Family" of the 30s that Produced Today's Top SF Writers and Editors*. John Day, 1977.

Lupoff, Pat, and Dick Lupoff, eds. *The Best of Xero*. Tachyon Publications, 2005.

Moskowitz, Sam. *The Immortal Storm: A History of Science Fiction Fandom*. Atlanta Science Fiction Organization, 1954.

Sanders, Joe, ed. *Science Fiction Fandom*. Greenwood Press, 1994.

Turek, Leslie, ed. *The Noreascon Proceedings*. NESFA Press, 1976.

Warner, Harry, Jr. *All Our Yesterdays: An Informal History of Science Fiction Fandom in the Forties*. Advent, 1969.

___. *A Wealth of Fable: The History of Science Fiction Fandom in the 1950s*. Fanhistorica, 1976.

Weston, Peter. *With Stars In My Eyes: My Adventures In British Fandom*. NESFA Press, 2004.

## Authors and Editors

WORKS ABOUT MULTIPLE AUTHORS

Aldiss, Brian W., and Harry Harrison eds. *Hell's Cartographers: Some Personal Histories of Science Fiction Writers*. Weidenfeld and Nicolson, 1975.

Blaschke, Jayme Lynn. *Voices of Vision: Creators Of Science Fiction And Fantasy Speak*. Bison Books, 2005.

Bleiler, Everett F., ed. *Science Fiction Writers: Critical Studies of the Major Authors from the Early Nineteenth Century to the Present Day*. Scribner, 1982. 2nd ed. Ed. by Richard Bleiler. 1999.

Cowant, David,and Thomas J. Wymer, eds. *Dictionary of Literary Biography*. Vol. 8, *Twentieth-Century American Science-Fiction Writers*. 2 vols. Gale, 1981.

Davin, Eric Leif. *Pioneers of Wonder: Conversations with the Founders of Science Fiction*. Prometheus, 1999.

Greenberg, Martin H., ed. *Fantastic Lives: Autobiographical Essays by Notable Science Fiction Writers*. Southern Illinois University Press, 1981.

Harris-Fain, Darren, ed. *British Fantasy and Science-Fiction Writers, l918–1960*. Gale. 2003.

___, ed. *British Fantasy and Science-Fiction Writers Before World War I.* Gale, 1997.

___, ed. *British Fantasy and Science-Fiction Writers since 1960.* Gale. 2003.

Jakubowski, Maxim, and Edward James, eds. *The Profession of Science Fiction: Writers on Their Craft and Ideas.* Macmillan. 1991.

Jarvis, Sharon, ed. *Inside Outer Space: Science Fiction Professionals Look at Their Craft.* Ungar, 1985.

McCaffery, Larry, ed. *Across the Wounded Galaxies: Interviews with Contemporary American Science Fiction Writers.* University of Illinois Press, 1990.

Moskowitz, Sam. *Explorers of the Infinite: Shapers of Science Fiction.* World, 1963.

___. *Seekers of Tomorrow: Masters of Modern Science Fiction.* World, 1966.

Platt, Charles. *Dream Makers: The Uncommon People Who Write Science Fiction.* 2 vols. Berkley. 1980–83. Rev. as *Dream Makers: Science Fiction and Fantasy Writers at Work.* Ungar, 1987.

Schweitzer, Darrell. *Speaking of the Fantastic: Interviews with Masters of Science Fiction and Fantasy.* Wildside Press, 2002.

___. *Speaking of the Fantastic II: Interviews with the Masters of Science Fiction and Fantasy.* Wildside Press, 2004.

Schweitzer, Darrell, and Jefrey M. Elliot, eds. *Science Fiction Voices.* 4 vols. Borgo Press, 1979–82.

Stableford, Brian. *Algebraic Fantasies and Realistic Romances: More Masters of Science Fiction.* Borgo Press, 1995.

___. *Outside the Human Aquarium: Masters of Science Fiction.* Borgo Press. 1995.

Tolley, Michael J., and Kirpal Singh, eds. *The Stellar Gauge: Essays on Science Fiction Authors.* Norstilia Press. 1980.

Van Belkom, Edo. *Northern Dreamers: Interviews with Famous Science Fiction, Fantasy and Horror Writers.* Quarry, 1998.

Walker, Paul. *Speaking of Science Fiction.* Luna 1978.

## DOUGLAS ADAMS

Gaiman, Neil. *Don't Panic: The Official Hitch-Hiker's Guide to the Galaxy Companion.* Titan, 1988.

Simpson, M. J. *Hitchhiker: A Biography of Douglas Adams.* Hodder & Stoughton, 2003.

Webb, Nick. *Wish You Were Here: The Official Biography of Douglas Adams.* Ballantine, 2005.

Yeffeth, Glenn, ed. *The Anthology at the End of the Universe: Leading Science Fiction Authors on Douglas Adams' The Hitchhiker's Guide to the Galaxy.* BenBella Books, 2005.

## BRIAN W. ALDISS

Aldiss, Brian W. *Bury My Heart at W. H. Smith's: A Writing Life.* Hodder & Stoughton, 1990.

___. *The Twinkling of an Eye: My Life as an Englishman.* St. Martin's Press, 1999.

Collings, Michael. *Brian W. Aldiss.* Starmont House, 1986.

Griffin, Brian, and David Wingrove. *Apertures: A Study of the Writings of Brian Aldiss.* Greenwood Press, 1984.

Henighan, Tom. *Brian W. Aldiss.* Twayne Publications, 1999.

Mathews, Richard. *Aldiss Unbound: The Science Fiction of Brian W. Aldiss.* Borgo Press, 1977.


POUL ANDERSON

Miesel, Sandra. *Against Time's Arrow: The High Crusade of Poul Anderson.* Borgo Press, 1978.


PIERS ANTHONY

Collings, Michael R. *Piers Anthony.* Starmont House, 1983.


ISAAC ASIMOV

Asimov, Isaac. *I. Asimov: A Memoir.* Doubleday, 1994.

___. *In Joy Still Felt: The Autobiography of Isaac Asimov, 1954–1978.* Doubleday, 1980.

___. *In Memory Yet Green: The Autobiography of Isaac Asimov, 1920–1954.* Doubleday, 1979.

___. *It's Been a Good Life.* Ed. Janet Jeppson Asimov. Prometheus Books, 2002. (Single-volume abridgement of *In Memory Yet Green*, *In Joy Still Felt*, and *I. Asimov*.)

___. *Yours, Isaac Asimov: A Life in Letters.* Main Street Books, 1996.

Fiedler, Jean, and Jim Mele. *Isaac Asimov.* Ungar, 1982.

Freedman, Carl, ed. *Conversations with Isaac Asimov.* University Press of Mississippi, 2005.

Goble, Neil. *Asimov Analyzed.* Mirage Press, 1972.

Gunn, James E. *Isaac Asimov: The Foundations of Science Fiction.* Oxford University Press, 1982. Rev. ed. Scarecrow Press, 2005.

Hassler, Donald M. *Isaac Asimov.* Starmont House, 1991.

Olander, Joseph D., and Martin H. Greenberg, eds. *Isaac Asimov.* Taplinger, 1977.

Palumbo, Donald. *Chaos Theory, Asimov's Foundations and Robots, and Herbert's Dune: The Fractal Aesthetics of Epic Science Fiction.* Greenwood Press, 2002.

Patrouch, Joseph F, Jr. *The Science Fiction of Isaac Asimov.* Doubleday, 1974.

Slusser, George Edgar. *Asimov: The Foundations of His Science Fiction.* Borgo Press, 1980.

Touponce, William F. *Isaac Asimov.* Twayne, 1991.


MARGARET ATWOOD

Cooke, Nathalie. *Margaret Atwood: A Biography.* ECW, 1998.

Thompson, Lee Briscoe. *Scarlet Letters: Margaret Atwood's The Handmaid's Tale.* ECW, 1997.

## J. G. BALLARD

Brigg, Peter. *J. G. Ballard*. Borgo Press, 1985.

Delville, Michael. *J. G. Ballard*. Northcote House, 1998.

Goddard, James, and David Pringle, eds. *J. G. Ballard: The First Twenty Years*. Bran's Head, 1976.

Luckhurst, Roger. *The Angle Between Two Walls: The Fiction of J. G. Ballard*. Liverpool University Press, 1998.

Pringle, David. *Earth Is the Alien Planet: J. G. Ballard's Four-Dimensional Nightmare*. Borgo Press, 1979.

Stephenson, Gregory. *Out of the Night and Into the Dream: A Thematic Study of the Fiction of J. G. Ballard*. Greenwood Press, 1991.

Vale, V., ed. *J.G. Ballard: Conversations*. Re/Search, 2005.

## ALFRED BESTER

Wendell, Carolyn. *Alfred Bester*. Starmont House, 1982.

## JAMES BLISH

Ketterer, David. *Imprisoned in a Tesseract: The Life and Work of James Blish*. Kent State University Press, 1987.

Stableford, Brian. *A Clash of Symbols: The Triumph of James Blish*. Borgo Press, 1979.

## ROBERT BLOCH

Bloch, Robert. *Once around the Bloch: An Unauthorized Autobiography*. Tor, 1993.

Larson, Randall D. *Robert Bloch*. Starmont House, 1986.

___. *The Robert Bloch Companion: Collected Interviews 1969–1989*. Starmont House, 1990.

## LEIGH BRACKETT

Carr, John L. *Leigh Brackett: American Writer*. Drumm, 1986.

## RAY BRADBURY

Aggelis, Steven L., ed. *Conversations With Ray Bradbury*. University Press of Mississippi, 2004.

Bradbury, Ray. *Bradbury Speaks: Too Soon from the Cave, Too Far from the Stars*. William Morrow, 2005.

De Koster, Katie, ed. *Readings on "Fahrenheit 451."* Greenhaven Press, 2000.

Eller, Jonathan R., and William F. Touponce. *Ray Bradbury: The Life of Fiction*. Kent State University Press, 2004.

Johnson, Wayne L. *Ray Bradbury.* Ungar, 1980.

Mogen, David. *Ray Bradbury.* Twayne, 1986.

Olander, Joseph P., and Martin H. Greenberg, eds. *Ray Bradbury.* Taplinger, 1980.

Reid, Robin Anne. *Ray Bradbury: A Critical Companion.* Greenwood Press, 2000.

Slusser, George Edgar. *The Bradbury Chronicles.* Borgo Press, 1977.

Touponce, William E. *Ray Bradbury.* Starmont House, 1989.

___. *Ray Bradbury and the Poetics of Reverie: Fantasy, Science Fiction, and the Reader.* UMI Research Press, 1984.

Weist, Jerry. *Bradbury, an Illustrated Life: A Journey to Far Metaphor.* William Morrow & Company, 2002.

Weller, Sam. *The Bradbury Chronicles: The Life of Ray Bradbury.* William Morrow, 2005.


MARION ZIMMER BRADLEY

Arbur, Rosemarie. *Marion Zimmer Bradley.* Starmont House, 1985.

Breen, Walter. *Darkover Concordance.* Pennyfarthing Press, 1979.


DAVID BRIN

Brin, David, and Kevin Lenagh. *Contacting Aliens: An Illustrated Guide to David Brin's Uplift Universe.* Bantam Spectra, 2002.


JOHN BRUNNER

De Bolt, Joseph W., ed. *The Happening Worlds of John Brunner.* Kennikat Press, 1975.


EDGAR RICE BURROUGHS

Holtsmark, Erling B. *Edgar Rice Burroughs.* Twayne. 1986.

Kudlay, Robert R., and Joan Leiby. *Burroughs' Science Fiction.* School of Library and Information Science, 1973.

Lupoff, Richard A. *Barsoom: Edgar Rice Burroughs and the Martian Vision.* Mirage Press, 1976.

___. *Edgar Rice Burroughs: Master of Adventure.* Canaveral Press, 1965.

McWhorter, George T. *Burroughs Dictionary.* University Press of America, 1987.

Roy, John Hint. *A Guide to Barsoom.* Ballantine, 1976.

Taliaferro, John. *Tarzan Forever: The Life of Edgar Rice Burroughs, Creator of Tarzan.* Scribner, 1999.


OCTAVIA BUTLER

Barr, Marleen S., Richard Law, and Ruth Salvaggio. *Suzy McKee Charnas, Joan Vinge, Octavia Butler.* Starmont House, 1986.

JOHN W. CAMPBELL, JR.

Bangsund, John. *John W. Campbell: An Australian Tribute.* Parergon Books, 1974.
Campbell, John W. *The John W. Campbell Letters, Volume 1.* Ed. Perry A. Chapdelaine, Sr., Tony Chapdelaine, and George Hay. AC Project, 1985.
___. *The John W. Campbell Letters, Volume 2: Isaac Asimov and A. E. van Vogt.* Ed. Perry A. Chapdelaine, Sr., Tony Chapdelaine, and George Hay. AC Project, 1993.

KAREL ČAPEK

Heline, Theodore. *As in the Days of Noah: An Interpretation of Karel Čapek's Drama R.U.R.* New Age Press, 1942.
Klima, Ivan. *Karel Čapek: Life and Work.* Catbird Press, 2002.

ORSON SCOTT CARD

Collings, Michael R. *In the Image of God: Theme, Characterization, and Landscape in the Fiction of Orson Scott Card.* Greenwood Press, 1990.

SUZY MCKEE CHARNAS

Barr, Marleen S., Richard Law, and Ruth Salvaggio. *Suzy McKee Charnas, Joan Vinge, Octavia Butler.* Starmont House, 1986.

C. J. CHERRYH

Carmien, Edward, ed. *The Cherryh Odyssey.* Borgo Press, 2004.

ARTHUR C. CLARKE

Clarke, Arthur C. *Astounding Days: A Science Fictional Autobiography.* Bantam, 1990.
Clarke, Arthur C., and Lord Dunsany. *Arthur C. Clarke and Lord Dunsany: A Correspondence.* Anamnesis Press, 1998.
Clarke, Arthur C., and C. S. Lewis. *From Narnia to a Space Odyssey: The War of Ideas between Arthur C. Clarke and C. S Lewis.* Ed. by Ryder W. Miller. iBooks, 2003.
Hollow, John. *Against the Night, the Stars: The Science Fiction of Arthur C. Clarke.* Harcourt Brace, 1983. Rev. ed. Ohio University Press, 1987.
Olander, Joseph P., and Martin H. Greenberg, eds. *Arthur C. Clarke.* Taplinger, 1977.
Rabkin, Eric S. *Arthur C. Clarke.* Starmont House, 1979. 2nd. ed. 1980.
Reid, Robin Anne. *Arthur C. Clarke: A Critical Companion.* Greenwood Press, 1997.
Slusser, George Edgar. *The Space Odysseys of Arthur C. Clarke.* Borgo Press, 1978.

## HAL CLEMENT

Hassler, Donald M. *Hal Clement.* Starmont House. 1982.

## MICHAEL CRICHTON

Trembley, Elizabeth A. *Michael Crichton: A Critical Companion.* Greenwood Press, 1996.

## JOHN CROWLEY

Turner, Alice K., and Michael Andre-Driussi. *Snake's Hands: The Fiction of John Crowley.* Cosmos Books, 2003.

## SAMUEL R. DELANY

Barbour, Douglas. *Worlds Out of Words: The SF Novels of Samuel R. Delany.* Bran's Head, 1979.
Delany, Samuel R. *1984.* Voyant Publishing, 2000.
McEvoy, Seth. *Samuel R. Delany.* Ungar, 1983.
Slusser, George Edgar. *The Delany Intersection.* Borgo Press, 1977.
Tucker, Jeffrey Allen. *A Sense of Wonder: Samuel R. Delany, Race, Identity, and Difference.* Wesleyan University Press, 2004.
Weedman, Jane Branhan. *Samuel R. Delany.* Starmont House, 1982.

## PHILIP K. DICK

Butler, Andrew. *Philip K. Dick.* Pocket Essentials, 2000.
Carrere, Emmanuel. *I Am Alive and You Are Dead: The Strange Life and Times of Philip K. Dick.* Holt/Metropolitan, 2003.
Gillespie, Bruce, ed. *Philip K. Dick: Electric Shepherd.* Norstrilia Press, 1975.
Greenberg, Martin H., and Joseph P. Olander, eds. *Philip K. Dick.* Taplinger, 1983.
Mackey, Douglas A. *Philip K. Dick.* Twayne, 1988.
Mullen, R. D., Istvan Csisery-Ronay, Jr., and Arthur B. Evans eds. *On Philip K. Dick: 40 Articles from Science-Fiction Studies.* SF-TH, 1992.
Palmer, Christopher. *Philip K. Dick: Exhilaration and Terror of the Postmodern.* Liverpool University Press, 2003.
Pierce, Hazel. *Philip K. Dick.* Starmont House, 1982.
Rickman, Gregg. *To the High Castle: Philip K. Dick, a Life.* Fragments West/Valentine Press, 1989.
Robinson, Kim Stanley. *The Novels of Philip K. Dick.* UMI Research Press, 1984.
Sutin, Lawrence. *Divine Invasions: A Life of Philip K. Dick.* Harmony, 1989.
Taylor, Angus. *Philip K. Dick and the Umbrella of Light.* T-K Graphics, 1975.
Umland, Samuel J., ed. *Philip K. Dick: Contemporary Critical Interpretations.* Greenwood Press, 1995.

Warrick, Patricia S. *Mind in Motion: The Fiction of Philip K. Dick.* Southern Illinois University Press, 1987.

THOMAS M. DISCH

Delany, Samuel R. *The American Shore: Meditations on a Tale of Science Fiction by Thomas M. Disch—Angouleme.* Dragon Press, 1978.

GARDNER DOZOIS

Swanwick, Michael. *Being Gardner Dozois.* Old Earth Books, 2001.

HARLAN ELLISON

Slusser, George Edgar. *Harlan Ellison: Unrepentant Harlequin.* Borgo Press, 1977.
Weil, Ellen, and Gary K. Wolfe. *Harlan Ellison: The Edge of Forever.* Ohio State University Press, 2002.

PHILIP JOSÉ FARMER

Brizzi, Mary T. *Philip José Farmer: A Reader's Guide.* Starmont House, 1980.
Chapman, Edgar L. *The Magic Labyrinth of Philip José Farmer.* Borgo Press, 1985.

JOHN RUSSELL FEARN

Rarbottle, Philip J. *The Multi-Man: A Biographic and Bibliographic Study of John Russell Fearn.* Author, 1968.

JACK FINNEY

Seabrook, Jack. *Stealing Through Time: On the Writings of Jack Finney.* McFarland & Company, 2006.

WILLIAM GIBSON

Cavallaro, Dani. *Cyberpunk and Cyberculture: Science Fiction and the Work of William Gibson.* Athione Press, 2000.
Olsen, Lance. *Reader's Guide to William Gibson.* Starmont House, 1992.

CHARLOTTE PERKINS GILMAN

Gough, Val, and Jill Rudd, eds. *A Very Different Story: Studies on the Fiction of Charlotte Perkins Gilman.* Liverpool University Press, 1998.

JOE HALDEMAN

Gordon, Joan. *Joe Haldeman*. Starmont House, 1980.

HARRY HARRISON

Stover, Leon. *Harry Harrison*. Twayne, 1990.

M. JOHN HARRISON

Bould, Mark, and Michelle Reid, eds. *Parietal Games: Critical Writings by and on M. John Harrison*. Science Fiction Foundation, 2005.

ROBERT A. HEINLEIN

Franklin. H. Bruce. *Robert A. Heinlein: America as Science Fiction*. Oxford University Press, 1980.

Gifford, James. *Robert A. Heinlein: A Reader's Companion*. Nitrosyncretic Press, 2000.

Greenberg, Martin H., and Joseph P. Olander, eds. *Robert A. Heinlein*. Taplinger, 1978.

Heilein, Robert A. *Grumbles from the Grave*. Ed. Virginia Heinlein. Ballantine, 1989.

Panshin, Alexei. *Heinlein in Dimension: A Critical Analysis*. Advent, 1968.

Major, Joseph T. *Heinlein's Children: The Juveniles*. Advent, 2006.

Patterson, William H. Jr., and Andrew Thornton. *The Martian Named Smith: Critical Perspectives on Robert A. Heinlein's Stranger in a Strange Land*. Nitrosyncretic Press, 2001.

Schulman, J. Neil. *The Robert Heinlein Interview and Other Heinleiniana*. Pulpless. com, 1999.

Slusser, George Edgar. *The Classic Years of Robert A. Heinlein*. Borgo Press, 1977.

___. *Robert A. Heinlein: Stranger in His Own Land*. Borgo Press, 1976.

Stover, Leon. *Robert A. Heinlein*. Twayne, 1987.

FRANK HERBERT

Herbert, Brian. *Dreamer of Dune: The Biography of Frank Herbert*. Tor, 2003.
McNelly, Willis E. *The Dune Encyclopaedia*. Berkley, 1984.
Miller, David M. *Frank Herbert*. Starmont House, 1980.
O'Reilly, Timothy. *Frank Herbert*. Ungar, 1981.

ALDOUS HUXLEY

Baker, Robert S. *Brave New World: History, Science, and Dystopia*. Macmillan/Twayne, 1990.

Daiches, Jenni. *Huxley and Orwell, Brave New World and Nineteen Eighty-four.* Edward Arnold, 1976.

De Koster, Katie, ed. *Readings on Brave New World.* Greenhaven, 1999.

Firchow, Peter Edgerly. *The End of Utopia: A Study of Aldous Huxley's Brave New World.* Bucknell University Press, 1984.


DANIEL KEYES

Keyes, Daniel. *Algernon, Charlie and I: A Writer's Journey.* Challcrest Press, 2000.


URSULA K. LE GUIN

Bernardo, Susan M., and Graham J. Murphy. *Ursula K. Le Guin: A Critical Companion.* Greenwood Press, 2006.

Bittner, James. *Approaches to the Fiction of Ursula K. Le Guin.* UMI Research Press, 1984.

Bucknall, Barbara J. *Ursula K. Le Guin.* Ungar, 1981.

Cadden, Mike. *Ursula K. Le Guin Beyond Genre: Fiction for Children and Adults.* Routledge, 2004.

Cummins, Elizabeth. *Understanding Ursula K. Le Guin.* University of South Carolina Press, 1990. Rev. ed. 1993.

DeBolt, Joseph W., ed. *Ursula K. Le Guin: Voyager to Inner Lands and Outer Space.* Kennikat Press, 1979.

Olander, Joseph P., and Martin H. Greenberg. *Ursula K. Le Guin.* Taplinger, 1979.

Rochelle, Warren G. *Communities of the Heart: The Rhetoric of Myth in the Fiction of Ursula K. Le Guin.* Liverpool University Press, 2001.

Selinger, Bernard. *Le Guin and Identity in Contemporary Fiction.* UMI Research Press, 1988.

Slusser, George Edgar. *The Farthest Shores of Ursula K. Le Guin.* Borgo Press, 1976.

Spivack, Charlotte. *Ursula K. Le Guin.* Twayne, 1984.


FRITZ LEIBER

Byfield, Bruce. *Witches of the Mind: A Critical Study of Fritz Leiber.* Necronomicon Press, 1991.

Frane, Jeff. *Fritz Leiber.* Borgo Press, 1980.

Staicar, Tom. *Fritz Leiber.* Ungar, 1983.


STANISLAW LEM

Davis, Marion J. *Stanislaw Lem.* Starmont House, 1990.

Swirski, Peter. *Between Literature and Science: Poe, Lem, and Explorations in Aesthetics, Cognitive Science, and Literary Knowledge.* Liverpool University Press, 2001.

Ziegfeld, Richard E. *Stanislaw Lem.* Ungar, 1985.

DORIS LESSING

Fishburn, Katherine. *The Unexpected Universe of Doris Lessing: A Study in Narrative Technique.* Greenwood Press, 1985.
Perrakis, Phyllis Sternberg, ed. *Spiritual Exploration in the Works of Doris Lessing.* Greenwood Press, 1999.

C. S. LEWIS

Clarke, Arthur C., and C. S. Lewis. *From Narnia to a Space Odyssey: The War of Ideas between Arthur C. Clarke and C. S Lewis.* Ed. by Ryder W. Miller. iBooks, 2003.
Lobdell, Jared. *The Scientifiction Novels of C.S. Lewis: Space and Time in the Ransom Stories.* McFarland & Company, Inc., 2004.
Murphy, Brian. *C. S. Lewis.* Starmont House, 1983.

DAVID LINDSAY

Pick, J. B., E. H. Visiak, and Colin Wilson. *The Strange Genius of David Lindsay.* John Baker, 1970.
Wolfe, Gary K. *David Lindsay.* Starmont House, 1982.

H. P. LOVECRAFT

Burleson, Donald R. *H. P. Lovecraft: A Critical Study.* Greenwood Press, 1983.
Cannon, Peter H. *Lovecraft Remembered.* Arkham House, 1998.
Carter, Lin. *Lovecraft: A Look behind the Cthulhu Mythos.* Ballantine, 1972.
Gatto, John Taylor. *The Major Works of H.P. Lovecraft.* Monarch Press, 1977.
Houellebecq, Michel. *H. P. Lovecraft: Against the World, Against Life.* McSweeney's Books, 2005.
Joshi, S. T. *A Dreamer and a Visionary: H. P. Lovecraft in His Time.* Liverpool University Press, 2001.
___. *H. P. Lovecraft.* Starmont House, 1982.
___. *H. P. Lovecraft: A Life.* Necronomicon Press, 1996.
___. *A Subtler Magick: The Writings and Philosophy of H. P. Lovecraft.* Wildside Press. 1999.
Joshi, S. T., and David E. Schultz. *An H. P. Lovecraft Encyclopedia.* Greenwood Press, 2001.
___, eds. *Lord of a Visible World: Autobiography In Letters.* Ohio University Press, 2000.
Lovecraft, H. P. *H. P. Lovecraft: Letters from New York.* Ed. S. T. Joshi and David E. Schultz. Night Shade Books, 2005.
___. *Selected Letters I (1911–1924).* Ed. August Derleth and Donald Wandrei. Arkham House, 1965.

___. *Selected Letters II (1925–1929)*. Ed. August Derleth and Donald Wandrei. Arkham House, Arkham House, 1968.

___. *Selected Letters III (1929–1931)*. Ed. August Derleth and Donald Wandrei. Arkham House, Arkham House, 1971.

___. *Selected Letters IV (1932–1934)*. Ed. August Derleth and James Turner. Arkham House, 1976.

___. *Selected Letters V (1934–1937)*. Ed. August Derleth and James Turner. Arkham House, 1976.

Lovecraft, H.P., and Donald Wandrei. *Mysteries of Time and Spirit: Letters of H.P. Lovecraft and Donald Wandrei*. Ed. S. T. Joshi and David E. Schultz. Night Shade Books, 2002.

Mitchell, Charles P. *The Complete H. P. Lovecraft Filmography*. Greenwood Press, 2001.

Pearsall, Anthony Brainard. *The Lovecraft Lexicon: A Reader's Guide to Persons, Places and Things in the Tales of H.P. Lovecraft*. New Falcon Publications, 2005.

Schweitzer, Darrell, ed. *Discovering H. P Lovecraft*. Wildside Press, 2001.

___. *The Dream Quest of H. P Lovecraft*. Borgo Press, 1978.

GEORGE LUCAS

Baxter, John. *Mythmaker: The Life and Work of George Lucas*. Spike, 1999.

KEN MACLEOD

Butler, Andrew M., ed. *The True Knowledge of Ken MacLeod*. Science Fiction Foundation, 2003.

ANNE MCCAFFREY

Brizzi, Mary T. *Anne McCaffrey*. Starmont House, 1986.

McCaffrey, Todd. *Dragonholder: The Life and Dreams (So Far) of Anne McCaffrey*. Ballantine Del Rey, 1999.

Roberts, Robin. *Anne McCaffrey: A Critical Companion*. Greenwood Press, 1996.

LOUIS-SEBASTIEN MERCIER

Forsström, Riikka. *Possible Worlds: The Idea of Happiness in the Utopian Vision of Louis-Sébastien Mercier*. Suomalaisen Kirjallisuuden Seura, 2002.

JUDITH MERRIL

Merril, Judith, and Emily Pohl-Weary. *Better to Have Loved: The Life of Judith Merril*. Between the Lines, 2002.

WALTER M. MILLER, JR.

Secrest, Rose. *Glorificemus: A Study of the Fiction of Walter M. Miller, Jr.* University Press of America, 2002.

MICHAEL MOORCOCK

Greenland, Cohn. *Michael Moorcock: Death Is No Obstacle.* Savoy, 1992.

TERRY NATION

Bignell, Jonathan, and Andrew O'Day. *Terry Nation.* Manchester University Press, 2004.

GEORGE ORWELL

Bolton, W. F. *The Language of 1984: Orwell's English and Ours.* Blackwell, 1984.
Burgess, Anthony. *1985.* Little, Brown, 1978.
Carter, Steven. *A Do-It-Yourself Dystopia: The Americanization of Big Brother.* University Press of America, 2000.
Daiches, Jenni. *Huxley and Orwell, Brave New World and Nineteen Eighty-Four.* Edward Arnold, 1976.
Gleason, Abbott, Jack Goldsmith, and Martha Craven Nussbaum, eds. *On Nineteen Eighty-Four: Orwell and Our Future.* Princeton University Press, 2005.
Hynes, Samuel Lynn. *Twentieth Century Interpretations of 1984: A Collection of Critical Essays.* Prentice-Hall, 1971.
Kroes, Rob. *Nineteen Eighty-Four and the Apocalyptic Imagination in America.* Free University Press, 1985.
Plank, Robert. *George Orwell's Guide through Hell: A Psychological Study of Nineteen Eighty-Four.* Borgo, 1986. Rev. ed. 1994.
Reed, Kit. *George Orwell's 1984.* Barron's, 1984.
Reilly, Patrick. *Nineteen Eighty-Four: Past, Present, and Future.* Twayne, 1989.
Steinhoff, William R. *George Orwell and the Origins of 1984.* University of Michigan, 1975.

FREDERIK POHL

Clareson, Thomas D. *Frederik Pohl.* Starmont House, 1987.
Pohl, Frederik. *The Way the Future Was: A Memoir.* Ballantine, 1979.

CHRISTOPHER PRIEST

Butler, Andrew M., ed. *Christopher Priest: The Interaction.* SF Foundation, 2005.
Ruddick, Nicholas. *Chrtstopher Priest.* Starmont House, 1989.

ROBERT REGINALD

Reginald, Robert. *Trilobite Dreams or, The Autodidact's Tale, A Romance of Autobiography.* Ariadne, 2006.

GENE RODDENBERRY

Alexander, David. *Star Trek Creator: The Authorized Biography of Gene Roddenberry.* Roc, 1994.

Engel, Joel. *Gene Roddenberry: The Man and the Myth Behind Star Trek.* Hyperion, 1994.

Fern, Yvonna. *Gene Roddenberry: The Last Conversation.* University of California Press, 1994.

Gross, Edward, and Mark A. Altman. *Great Birds of the Galaxy: Gene Roddenberry & the Creators of Trek.* Image, 1994.

Van Hise, James. *The Man Who Created Star Trek: Gene Roddenberry.* Pioneer, 1992.

KEITH ROBERTS

Roberts. Keith. *Lemady: Episodes of a Writer's Life.* Wildside Press. 1999.

JOANNA RUSS

Cortiel, Jeanne. *Demand My Wnting: Joanna Russ, Feminism, Science Fiction.* Liverpool University Press, 1999.

JULIUS SCHWARTZ

Schwartz, Julius. *Man of Two Worlds: My Life in Science Fiction and Comics.* Harper Paperbacks, 2000.

ROBERT SILVERBERG

Chapman, Edgar L. *The Road to Castle Mount: The Science Fiction of Robert Silverberg.* Greenwood Press, 1999.

Clareson, Thomas D. *Robert Silverberg.* Starmont House, 1983.

Elkins, Charles L., and Martin H. Greenberg, eds. *Robert Silverberg's Many Trapdoors: Critical Essays on His Science Fiction.* Greenwood Press, 1992.

CLARK ASHTON SMITH

Clark Ashton Smith, *Selected Letters of Clark Ashton Smith.* Ed. by David E. Schultz and Scott Connors. Arkham House, 2003.

Behrends, Steve. *Clark Ashton Smith.* Starmont House, 1991.

CORDWAINER SMITH

Hellekson, Karen. *The Science Fiction of Cordwainer Smith*. McFarland, 2001.
Lewis, Anthony R. *Concordance to Cordwainer Smith*. NESFA Press, 1984. 2nd ed., 1994. 3rd ed. 2000.
Porter, Andrew, ed. *Exploring Cordwainer Smith*. Algol Press, 1975.

E. E. SMITH

Ellik, Ron, and Bill Evans. *The Universes of E. E. Smith*. Advent, 1966.
Sanders, Joe. *E. E. "Doc" Smith*. Starmont House. 1986.

OLAF STAPLEDON

Crossley, Robert. *Olaf Stapledon: Speaking for the Future*. Liverpool University Press, 1994.
Fiedler, Leslie A. *Olaf Stapledon: A Man Divided*. Oxford University Press, 1983.
Kinnaird, Jon. *Olaf Stapledon*. Starmont House, 1986.
McCarthy, Patrick A. *Olaf Stapledon*. Twayne, 1982.
McCarthy, Patrick A., Charles Elkins, and Martin Harry Greenberg, eds. *The Legacy of Olaf Stapledon: Critical Essays and an Unpublished Manuscript*. Greenwood Press, 1989.

ARKADY AND BORIS STRUGATSKY

Potts, Stephen W. *The Second Marxian Invasion: The Fiction of the Strugatsky Brothers*. Borgo Press, 1991.

THEODORE STURGEON

Diskin, Lalina E. *Theodore Sturgeon*. Starmont House, 1981.
Menger, Lucy. *Theodore Sturgeon*. Ungar, 1981.

JAMES TIPTREE, JR.

Dozois, Gardner. *The Fiction of James Tiptree, Jr.* Algol Press, 1977.
Phillips, Julie. *James Tiptree, Jr.: The Double Life of Alice B. Sheldon*. St. Martin's Press, 2006.
Siegel, Mark. *James Tiptree, Jr.* Starmont House, 1985.
Van der Spek, Inez. *Alien Plots: Female Subjectivity and the Divine in the Light of James Tiptree's "A Momentary Taste of Being."* Liverpool University Press, 2000.

GEORGE TURNER

Buckrich, Judith Raphael. *George Turner: A Life*. Melbourne University Press, 1999.

JACK VANCE

Cunningham, A. E., ed. *Jack Vance: Critical Appreciations and a Bibliography*. British Library, 2000.
Mead, David G. *An Encyclopedia of Jack Vance, 20th-Century Science Fiction Writer*. 3 vols. Mellen, 2002.
Rawlins, Jack. *Demon Prince: The Dissonant Worlds of Jack Vance*. Borgo Press, 1986.
Temianka, Dan. *The Jack Vance Lexicon: From Ahulph to Zipangote*. Underwood-Miller, 1992.
Tiedman, Richard. *Jack Vance: Science Fiction Stylist*. Coulson, 1965.
Underwood, Tim, and Chuck Miller, eds. *Jack Vance*. Taplinger, 1980.


A. E. VAN VOGT

Drake, H. L. *A. E. van Vogt: Science Fantasy's Icon*. Author, 2001.


JULES VERNE

Butcher, William. *Jules Verne: The Definitive Biography*. Thunder's Mouth Press, 2006.
___. *Verne's Journey to the Centre of the Self: Space and Time in the Voyages Extraordinaires*. Macmillan, 1990.
Chesneaux, Jean. *The Political and Social Ideas of Jules Verne*. Thames and Hudson, 1972.
Costello, Peter. *Jules Verne, Inventor of Science Fiction*. Scribner, 1978.
Evans, Arthur B. *Jules Verne Rediscovered: Didacticism and the Scientific Novel*. Greenwood Press, 1988.
Evans, I. O. *Jules Verne and His Work*. Arco, 1965.
Freedman, Russell. *Jules Verne, Portrait of a Prophet*. Holiday House, 1965
Haining, Peter. *The Jules Verne Companion*. Pictorial Presentations, 1978.
Jules-Verne, Jean. *Jules Verne: A Biography*. Taplinger, 1976.
Lottman, Herbert R. *Jules Verne: An Exploratory Biography*. St. Martin's Press, 1996.
Lynch, Lawrence W. *Jules Verne*. Twayne, 1992.
Martin, Andrew. *The Mask of the Prophet: The Extraordinary Fictions of Jules Verne*. Oxford University Press, 1990.
Smyth, Edmund J., ed. *Jules Verne: Narratives of Modernity*. Liverpool University Press, 2000.
Taves, Brian, and Stephen Michaluk, Jr. *The Jules Verne Encyclopedia*. Scarecrow Press, 1996.
Unwin, Timothy. *Jules Verne: Journeys in Writing*. Liverpool University Press, 2005.


JOAN D. VINGE

Barr, Marleen S., Richard Law, and Ruth Salvaggio. *Suzy McKee Charnas, Joan Vinge, Octavia Butler*. Starmont House, 1986.

Boon, Kevin Alexander, ed. *At Millennium's End: New Essays on the Work of Kurt Vonnegut.* State University of New York Press, 2001.

Goldsmith, David H. *Kurt Vonnegut: Fantasist of Fire and Ice.* Popular Press, 1972.

Klinkowitz, Jerome. *Kurt Vonnegut.* Methuen, 1982.

Klinkowitz, Jerome, and John Somer, eds. *The Vonnegut Statement.* Delacorte, 1973.

Leeds, Marc. *The Vonnegut Encyclopedia: An Authorized Compendium.* Greenwood Press, 1995.

Leeds, Marc, and Peter J. Reed, eds. *Kurt Vonnegut: Images and Representations.* Greenwood Press, 2000.

Lundquist, James. *Kurt Vonnegut.* Ungar, 1977.

Mayo, Clark. *Kurt Vonnegut: The Gospel from Outer Space.* Borgo Press, 1977.

Merrill, Robert, ed. *Critical Essays on Kurt Vonnegut.* G. K. Rail, 1990.

Morse, Donald E. *The Novels of Kurt Vonnegut: Imagining Being an American.* Praeger, 2003.

Mustazza, Leonard. *Forever Pursuing Genesis: The Myth of Eden in the Novels of Kurt Vonnegut.* Bucknell University Press, 1990.

___, ed. *The Critical Response to Kurt Vonnegut.* Greenwood Press, 1994.

Rackstraw, Loree, ed. *Draftings in Vonnegut: The Paradox of Hope.* University of Northern Iowa, 1988.

Reed, Peter J. *Kurt Vonnegut, Jr.* Warner, 1972.

___. *The Short Fiction of Kurt Vonnegut.* Greenwood Press, 1997.

Reed, Peter J., and Marc Leeds, eds. *The Vonnegut Chronicles: Interviews and Essays.* Greenwood Press, 1996.

Schatt, Stanley. *Kurt Vonnegut, Jr.* Twayne, 1976.

DONALD WANDREI

Lovecraft, H.P., and Donald Wandrei. *Mysteries of Time and Spirit: Letters of H.P. Lovecraft and Donald Wandrei.* Ed. S. T. Joshi and David E. Schultz. Night Shade Books, 2002.

H. G. WELLS

Beresford, J. D. *H. G. Wells.* Nisbet, 1915.

Bergonzi, Bernard. *The Early H. G. Wells: A Study of the Scientific Romances.* University of Toronto Press, 1961.

___, ed. *H. G. Wells: A Collection of Critical Essays.* Prentice-Hall, 1976.

Costa, Richard Hauer. *H. G. Wells.* Twayne, 1985.

Crossley, Robert. *H. G. Wells.* Starmont House, 1986.

Gill, Stephen. *The Scientific Romances of H. G. Wells.* Vesta. 1975.

Hammond, John R. *H. G. Wells and the Short Story.* St. Martin's Press, 1992.

___. *H. G. Wells's The Time Machine: A Reference Guide.* Praeger Publishers, 2004.

Haynes, Roslynn D. *H. G. Wells, Discoverer of the Future: The Influence of Science on His Thought.* Macmillan, 1980.

Huntington, John. *The Logic of Fantasy: H. G. Wells and Science Fiction.* Columbia University Press, 1982.

Kemp, Peter. *H. G. Wells and the Culminating Ape: Biological Themes and Imaginative Obsessions.* Macmillan, 1982.

McConnell, Frank. *The Science Fiction of H. G. Wells.* Oxford University Press, 1981.

Niles, P. H. *The Science Fiction of H. G. Wells: A Concise Guide.* Auriga, 1980.

Parrinder, Patrick. *Shadows of the Future: H. G. Wells, Science Fiction and Prophecy.* Liverpool University Press, 1996.

Partington, John. *Building Cosmopolis: The Political Thought of H. G. Wells.* Ashgate, 2003.

Scheick, William J., ed. *The Critical Response to H.G. Wells.* Greenwood Press, 1995.

Slusser, George, Patrick Parrinder, and Daniele Chatelain eds. *H. G. Wells's Perennial Time Machine: Selected Essays from the Centenary Conference: "The Time Machine: Past, Present and Future," Imperial College, London, July 26–29, 1995.* University of Georgia Press, 2001.

Suvin, Darko, and Robert M. Philmus eds. *H. G. Wells and Modern Science Fiction.* Bucknell University Press, 1977

Wagar, W. Warren. *H. G. Wells: Traversing Time.* Wesleyan University Press, 2004.

Williamson, Jack. *H. G. Wells: Critic of Progress.* Mirage Press, 1973.

Yeffeth, Glenn, ed. *The War of the Worlds: Fresh Perspectives on the H. G. Wells Classic.* BenBella Books, 2005.

JACK WILLIAMSON

Williamson, Jack. *Wonder's Child: My Life in Science Fiction.* Bluejay, 1984. Rev. ed. BenBella Books, 2005.

GENE WOLFE

Andre-Driussi, Michael. *Lexicon Urthus: A Dictionary of the Urth Cycle.* Sirius, 1994.

Borski, Robert. *Solar Labyrinth: Exploring Gene Wolfe's BOOK OF THE NEW SUN.* iUniverse, 2004.

Borski, Robert. *The Long and the Short of It.* iUniverse, 2006.

Gordon, Joan. *Gene Wolfe.* Starmont House, 1986.

Wright, Peter. *Attending Daedalus: Gene Wolfe, Artifice and the Reader.* Liverpool University Press, 2003.

IVAN YEFREMOV

Grebens, G. V. *Ivan Yefremov's Theory of Soviet Science Fiction.* Vantage Press, 1978.

ROGER ZELAZNY

Krulik, Theodore. *Roger Zelazny.* Ungar, 1986.

Yoke, Carl B. *Roger Zelazny.* Starmont House, 1979.

# Writing Guides

Bova, Ben. *Notes to a Science Fiction Writer.* Scribner, 1975. Rev. ed. Houghton Mifflin, 1981.

Bova, Ben, and Anthony R. Lewis. *Space Travel: A Writer's Guide to the Science of Interplanetary and Interstellar Travel.* Writer's Digest Books, 1997.

Bretnor, Reginald, ed. *The Craft of Science Fiction.* Harper, 1976.

Budrys, Algis. *Writing Science Fiction and Fantasy.* Pulphouse, 1990.

Card, Orson Scott. *How to Write Science Fiction and Fantasy.* Writer's Digest, 1990.

Costello, Matthew J. *How to Write Science Fiction.* Paragon Houss, 1992.

de Camp, L. Sprague. *Science Fiction Handbook: The Writing of Imaginative Fiction.* Hermitage House, 1953. Rev. ed. with Catherine C. de Camp, as *Science Fiction Handbook-Revised: A Guide to Writing Imaginative Literature.* McGraw-Hill, 1975.

Delany, Samuel R. *About Writing: Seven Essays, Four Letters, and Five Interviews.* Wesleyan University Press, 2005.

Doctorow, Cory, and Karl Schroeder. *Complete Idiot's Guide to Publishing Science Fiction.* Alpha Books, 2000.

Eshbach, Lloyd Arthur, ed. of *Worlds Beyond:* The *Science of Science Fiction Writing.* Fantasy Press, 1947

Evans, Christopher. *Writing Science Fiction.* A & C Black, 1988.

Gillett, Stephen. *World-Building: A Writer's Guide to Constructing Star Systems and Life-supporting Planets.* Writer's Digest Books, 2001.

Gunn, James. *The Science of Science Fiction Writing.* Rowman & Littlefield, 2000.

Kilian, Crawford. *Writing Science Fiction and Fantasy.* Self-Counsel Press, 1998.

Nahin, Paul J. *Time Travel: A Writer's Guide to the Real Science of Plausible Time Travel.* Writer's Digest Books, 1997.

Rusch, Kristine Kathryn, and Dean Wesley Smith. *Science Fiction Writers of America Handbook: The Professional Writer's Guide to Writing Professionally.* Writers Notebook Press, 1990.

Schmidt, Stanley. *Aliens and Alien Societies: A Writer's Guide to Creating Extraterrestrial Life-Forms.* Writer's Digest Books, 1996.

Shaw, Bob. *How to Write Science Fiction.* Allison and Busby, 1993.

Stableford, Brian. *Writing Fantasy & Science Fiction.* Teach Yourself Books, 1997.

Tuttle, Lisa. *Writing Fantasy and Science Fiction.* A & C Black, 2001.

Wilhelm, Kate. *Storyteller: Writing Lessons and More from 27 Years of the Clarion Writers' Workshop.* Small Beer Press, 2005.